CW00375084

**Director, Evidence and Analytics** Matthew Har
Paul Weller **Product Manager, Clinical Decisio**
**Product Manager, Clinical Decision Support** E
Bedford **Editor, BMJ Clinical Evidence** Caroline
Kathleen Dryburgh **Acting Scientific Editor Te**
**Editors** Tannaz Aliabadi-Zadeh, Helena Delgado
O'Brien, Emma Scott, Kam Uppell **Head of Digital Publishing** Alan Thomas **Digital
Content Editors** Cathryn Denney, David Morrison, Vanessa Sibbald, Nils van der
Linden **Digital Production** Yen Chau, Isaac Menso **Content Managers** Lisa Parker,
Laura Stephenson **Contributor Manager** Gemma Spink **Evidence Team Lead**
Samantha Barton **Evidence Services Manager** Lauren Wallis **Evidence Reviewers**
Claire Dickie, Natalie Masento **Senior Evidence Reviewers** Sarah Boyce, Alex
McNeil, Eno Umoh **Information Specialists** Olwen Beaven, Alex McNeil **Head,
Business Management** Amelia Cooke **Administrator** Varsha Mistry **Indexer** Jeremy
Mills Publishing **Chief Technology Officer** Sharon Cooper **Print Production** Catherine
Harding-Wiltshire

# Acknowledgements

BMJ thanks the following people and organisations for their advice and support: Phil Alderson; Gary Belfield; the British National Formulary; Iain Chalmers; The Cochrane Collaboration; Luis Gabriel Cuervo; Paul Garner; Brian Haynes; Carl Heneghan; Alejandro Jadad; Doug Kamerow; Ryuki Kassai; Martindale: The Complete Drug Reference; Ann McKibbon; Dinesh Mehta; the Oxford Centre for Evidence-Based Medicine; Sharon Strauss; and Justin Whatling. We would also like to thank previous staff who have contributed to *BMJ Clinical Evidence*, and the clinicians, epidemiologists, and members of patient groups who have acted as contributors, advisors, and peer reviewers.

BMJ values the ongoing support it has received from the global medical community for *BMJ Clinical Evidence*. We are grateful to the clinicians and patients who have taken part in our user panel and focus groups, which are crucial to the development of *BMJ Clinical Evidence*. Finally, we would like to acknowledge the readers who have taken the time to send us their comments and suggestions.

# BMJ Clinical Evidence

# Handbook | DECEMBER 2015

The international source of the
best available evidence for
effective healthcare

**Editorial office**
BMJ, BMA House, Tavistock Square, London, WC1H 9JR, United Kingdom. Tel: +44 (0)20 7387 4410 ●
Fax: +44 (0)20 7554 6780 ● company.bmj.com

**Rights and permission to reproduce**
For information on translation rights, please contact Julie Halfacre at jhalfacre@bmj.com.
To request permission to reprint all or part of any contribution in *BMJ Clinical Evidence*, please contact
Laura Stephenson at permissions.evidencecentre@bmj.com.

**Copyright**
© BMJ Publishing Group Ltd 2015

All rights reserved. No part of this publication may be reproduced, translated, stored in a retrieval
system, or transmitted, in any form or by any means, electronic, mechanical, photocopying, recording
and/or otherwise, without the permission of the publishers.

British Library Cataloguing in Publication Data. A catalogue record for this book is available from the
British Library. ISSN 1475–9225, ISBN 978-0-7279-1874-1

Produced with assistance from Jeremy Mills Publishing Ltd, Huddersfield, West Yorkshire.

Typeset in the UK by Letterpart Ltd, Caterham on the Hill, Surrey CR3 5XL.

Printed in Italy by Rotolito Lombarda S.p.A.

Designed by Paragraphics Ltd, London, UK.

Welcome to the
*Clinical Evidence Handbook*

How *Clinical Evidence* works

# Contents

# Contents

# Contents

# Contents

## SUPPORTING CLINICAL DECISION MAKING

*BMJ Clinical Evidence* helps healthcare professionals find answers to important clinical questions. We provide systematic overviews of the most important conditions that healthcare workers have to deal with every day. The evidence is supplemented by clinical interpretation, links to validated guidelines, drug safety alerts, and citations of recently published articles, as well as evidence-based medicine tools and resources. In all, we systematically review the research literature on over 2500 interventions, and provide answers to over 600 clinical questions.

## *BMJ CLINICAL EVIDENCE* IS A UNIQUE RESOURCE

**We make it easy to find and use the evidence.**

**We focus on the evidence that matters the most**, concentrating our efforts around the clinical questions that are the highest priority for clinicians and patients, and where an overview of the evidence will have maximum impact on clinical decision making.

**Our expert team of information specialists searches the world's literature** for important new findings, selecting high-quality studies and systematic reviews that report the outcomes that matter most to clinicians, patients, and medical researchers.

**Leading medical experts check and summarise the evidence** and, together with our specialist editors, provide summaries describing what is known about the benefits and harms associated with particular interventions.

**"Clinical Evidence presents the dark as well as the light side of the moon."** This phrase by Jerry Osheroff, who has led much of the research on clinicians' information needs, highlights the fact that one of our main purposes is to identify important research gaps, and help clinicians discern when their uncertainty stems from a lack of evidence rather than their lack of knowledge.

**We place new evidence in the context of what is already known** and regularly completely reappraise each systematic overview.

**We support patient–doctor partnerships** by ensuring that professionals have easy access to the answers to patients' questions, and are best placed to promote realistic expectations of the effects of interventions.

## *BMJ CLINICAL EVIDENCE* SUPPORTS EBM AT THE POINT OF CARE

Evidence-based medicine (EBM) is well into its third decade, and yet worldwide the challenges of bringing EBM into clinical practice are a constant cause for debate. In a systematic review published in *The BMJ*, Kawamoto, Houlihan, Balas, and Lobach identified four features that, where present, improved the likelihood of clinical decision support systems improving patient care:

- automatic provision of decision support as part of clinician workflow
- provision of recommendations rather than just assessments
- provision of decision support at the time and location of decision making
- computer-based decision support.

Of 32 systems possessing all four features, 30 (94%) significantly improved clinical practice.

This review provides a guide to where evidence-based resources should be positioning themselves in the future.

The *BMJ Clinical Evidence Handbook*, which is updated bi-annually, provides an instant overview of the current evidence, easily accessible at the point of care.

The full edition of *BMJ Clinical Evidence* is available online — easily searchable, with up-to-the-minute coverage of the evidence, and structured to help you get straight to the information you need. It also provides a suite of tools to help students and clinicians learn and teach EBM, and apply it to clinical practice.

Using the latest 'responsive design' interface, *BMJ Clinical Evidence* can now adjust its display to different screen sizes, displaying equally well on desktops, tablets, and smartphones, providing access to evidence wherever it's needed.

For more information on other formats of *BMJ Clinical Evidence*, please visit: clinicalevidence.bmj.com.

## FEEDBACK

We encourage and appreciate all feedback via our website. You can contact us at support@bmj.com or use the 'Contact Us' button on every page. Users who do not have access to email or the website can contact the Editor of *BMJ Clinical Evidence*, Dr Caroline Blaine, by post to BMJ. We are particularly interested to know the clinical question that led you to consult *BMJ Clinical Evidence* and the extent to which this was answered. If you have comments on any of our content, think that important evidence might have been missed, or have suggestions for new reviews or questions, please let us know.

Readers who would like to be involved, either as contributors, peer reviewers, or members of our user panel, are invited to review the required profiles and apply online at http://clinicalevidence.bmj.com/x/set/static/cms/contributors-page.html.

The *BMJ Clinical Evidence* website (clinicalevidence.bmj.com) summarises the current state of knowledge and uncertainty about interventions used for prevention and treatment of important clinical conditions. It aims to find answers to key questions health professionals are facing today and to aid clinical decision making in areas where systematic review evidence has either been lacking or will have the most impact. To achieve this, we systematically search and appraise the world literature to provide rigorous systematic reviews of evidence on the benefits and harms of clinical interventions.

Making summaries involves excluding some detail, and users of *BMJ Clinical Evidence* need to be aware of the limitations of the evidence presented. It is not possible to make global statements that are both useful and apply to every patient or clinical context that occurs in practice. For example, when stating that we found evidence that a drug is beneficial, we mean that there is evidence that the drug has been shown to deliver more benefits than harms when assessed in at least one group of people, using at least one outcome at a particular point in time. It does not mean that the drug will be effective in all people given that treatment or that other outcomes will be improved, or even that the same outcome will be improved at a different time after the treatment.

## OUR CATEGORISATION OF INTERVENTIONS

Each systematic overview contains a page that lists key clinical questions and interventions, and describes whether they have been found to be effective or not.

We have developed these efficacy categories from one of the Cochrane Collaboration's first and most popular products, *A guide to effective care in pregnancy and childbirth*.[1] The categories are explained in the table below.

| Intervention | Description |
| --- | --- |
| Beneficial | For which efficacy has been demonstrated by clear evidence from systematic reviews, RCTs, or the best alternative source of information, and for which expectation of harms is small compared with the benefits. |
| Likely to be beneficial | For which efficacy is less well established than for those listed under "beneficial". |
| Trade-off between benefits and harms | For which clinicians and patients should weigh up the beneficial and considerable harmful effects according to individual circumstances and priorities. |
| Unknown effectiveness | For which there are currently insufficient data or data of inadequate quality. |
| Unlikely to be beneficial | For which lack of efficacy is less well established than for those listed under "likely to be ineffective or harmful". |
| Likely to be ineffective or harmful | For which inefficacy or associated harm has been demonstrated by clear evidence. |

Fitting interventions into these categories is not always straightforward. For one thing, the categories represent a mix of several hierarchies: the size of benefit (or harm), the strength of evidence (RCT or observational data), and the degree of certainty around the finding (represented by the confidence interval). Another challenge is that much of the evidence most relevant to clinical decisions relates to comparisons between different interventions rather than versus placebo or no intervention. Where necessary, we have indicated the comparisons. A third consideration is that interventions may have been tested, or found to be effective, in only one group of people, such as those at high risk of an outcome. Again, we have indicated this where possible. But perhaps most difficult of all is trying to maintain consistency across different systematic overviews. We continue to work on refining the criteria for categorising interventions. Interventions that cannot be tested in an RCT for ethical or practical reasons are sometimes included in the interventions table, and identified with an asterisk and footnote.

## HOW MUCH DO WE KNOW?

*BMJ Clinical Evidence* aims to help people make informed decisions about which treatments or preventative interventions to use. It can also show where more research is needed. For clinicians and patients, we wish to highlight treatments that work and for which the benefits outweigh the harms, especially those treatments that may currently be underused. We also wish to highlight treatments that do not work or for which the harms outweigh the benefits. For the research community, our intention is to highlight gaps in the evidence, where there are currently no good RCTs or no RCTs that look at particular groups of people or at important patient outcomes.

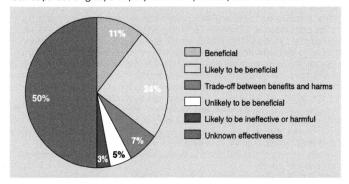

Figure 1.

So, what can *BMJ Clinical Evidence* tell us about the state of our current knowledge? Figure 1 illustrates what percentage of the around 2500 treatments included in *BMJ Clinical Evidence* fall into each efficacy category. Dividing treatments into categories is never easy — hence our reliance on our large team of experienced information specialists, evidence scanners and analysts, editors, peer reviewers, and expert contributors. Categorisation always involves a degree of subjective judgement, and is sometimes controversial. We do it because users tell us that it is helpful, but like all tools it has benefits and limitations. For example, an intervention may have multiple indications and may be categorised as 'Unknown effectiveness' for one condition but 'Beneficial' for another. Included within the category of 'Unknown effectiveness' are many treatments that come under the description of complementary medicine, for example, acupuncture for acute low back pain and echinacea for the common cold, but also many psychological, surgical, and medical interventions, such as interpersonal therapy for depression in children, uterine artery embolisation for fibroids, and increased-dose corticosteroids for chronic wheezing in infants. The categorisation of 'Unknown effectiveness' often reflects difficulties in conducting RCTs of an intervention, and is also applied to treatments for which the evidence base is still evolving. As such, these data reflect how treatments stand up in the light of evidence-based medicine and are not an audit of the extent to which treatments are used in practice.

The National Institute for Health Research Health Technology Assessment (NIHR HTA) Programme regularly reviews clinical uncertainties which have been identified by *BMJ Clinical Evidence* systematic overviews. This way we help to inform commissioning of important new research about the effectiveness of different healthcare treatments for those who use, manage, and provide care in the NHS. Further details of published and ongoing research funded by the NIHR HTA Programme may be found at http://www.nets.nihr.ac.uk/programmes/hta.

### ADDITIONAL FEATURES AVAILABLE ON *BMJ CLINICAL EVIDENCE* ONLINE

#### DATA TABLES, REFERENCES, AND CLINICAL GUIDE

A detailed exploration of the evidence will require looking up the detail on *BMJ Clinical Evidence* online (clinicalevidence.bmj.com). Detailed quantitative results are presented online, where we are able to discuss their interpretation in more detail. Your suggestions on improvements are welcome.

The electronic version of each review on the *BMJ Clinical Evidence* website links, whenever possible, to abstracts of the original research in *PubMed* or published online versions. In this way, *BMJ Clinical Evidence* is also designed to act as a pointer and to aid research dissemination, by connecting clinicians rapidly to relevant original evidence. Our expert contributors enrich the presented data with clinical guidance for the topic as a whole as well as for individual interventions. The new topic landing pages outline the rationale for the topic's coverage of clinical questions, provide general comments about the state of the evidence in this area, and give a brief summary of the search and appraisal results of the most recent update.

## GRADE TABLES

*BMJ Clinical Evidence* performs a GRADE analysis to evaluate the quality of a body of evidence for combinations of specific patient groups, intervention comparisons and clinical outcomes ('PICOs'). The internationally renowned GRADE system takes into account flaws in methods within the component studies, issues about consistency of results across different studies, how generalisable the research results are to all patients who have the condition, and how beneficial or harmful the treatments have been shown to be. All treatment comparisons are given one of four GRADE scores reflecting the quality of the evidence surrounding the effects of the intervention on outcomes that matter to patients and clinicians: high-, moderate-, low-, or very low-quality evidence. When considered in the context of our existing efficacy categorisations, we believe that this will give clinicians a clearer idea about how certain they can be that their patient is likely to benefit from a particular intervention.

- High-quality evidence: further research is very unlikely to change our confidence in the estimate of effect
- Moderate-quality evidence: further research is likely to have an important impact on our confidence in the estimate of effect and may change the estimate
- Low-quality evidence: further research is very likely to have an important impact on our confidence in the estimate of effect and is likely to change the estimate
- Very low-quality evidence: any estimate of effect is very uncertain.

The categorisation of the quality of the evidence (high, moderate, low, or very low) reflects the quality of evidence available for our chosen outcomes in our defined populations of interest. These categorisations are not necessarily a reflection of the overall methodological quality of any individual study, because the *BMJ Clinical Evidence* population and outcome of choice may represent only a small subset of the total outcomes reported, and population included, in any individual trial.

GRADE scores have led to improved summary statements for each intervention in *BMJ Clinical Evidence* systematic overviews, structured around the most clinically important outcomes. The results of all GRADE evaluations for a given topic are summarised in its GRADE table.

## CITATIONS

Citations incorporate the McMaster PLUS email surveillance system to collect and review the best evidence from the medical literature published since the last *BMJ Clinical Evidence* systematic search for a given topic.

## GUIDELINES

To assist clinicians with applying evidence in their daily practice, *BMJ Clinical Evidence* reviews now have links to the full text of major guidelines relevant to the topic's clinical area. All linked guidelines have been produced by national or international government sources, professional medical organisations or medical speciality societies, and have met predetermined quality requirements. New guidelines are added regularly, and old guidelines are replaced by their revised versions as these are published.

## PATIENT INFORMATION LEAFLETS

These are aligned with *BMJ Clinical Evidence* systematic reviews, summarising important condition information in plain English certified by The Information Standard, in an easily downloadable format to be given to patients at the point of care.

## DISCOVER MORE ABOUT EVIDENCE-BASED MEDICINE

*BMJ Clinical Evidence* online also provides a suite of tools to help students and clinicians learn and teach EBM, and apply it to clinical practice.

## REFERENCES

1   Enkin M, Keirse M, Renfrew M, et al. A guide to effective care in pregnancy and childbirth. Oxford: Oxford University Press, 1998.

# Hodgkin's lymphoma

Evangelos Terpos and Amin Rahemtulla

## KEY POINTS

- People with Hodgkin's lymphoma usually present with a lump in the neck or upper chest, but a quarter of people also have fever, sweating, weight loss, fatigue, and itch.

  Almost all people with localised disease can be cured, and, even among people with relapsed advanced disease, almost 80% of them survive event free for 4 years or more.

- In people with localised Hodgkin's lymphoma, consensus is that ABVD plus radiotherapy is the gold standard treatment, with ABVD preferred to MOPP as single-regimen chemotherapy. However, we don't know whether this is the most effective regimen.

  ABVD seems less likely than MOPP to cause infertility and secondary leukaemia. However, ABVD increases the risk of cardiotoxicity and pulmonary adverse effects, especially if given with radiotherapy.

  Adding ABVD to radiotherapy seems to reduce the risk of relapse at 7 years compared with radiotherapy alone. However, ABVD plus radiotherapy seems to be no more effective than ABVD alone at improving overall survival, and is associated with more adverse effects.

  Adding MOPP or VBM regimens to radiotherapy does not improve overall survival compared with radiotherapy alone in people with localised Hodgkin's lymphoma, and increases the risk of adverse effects.

  Adding radiotherapy to CVPP does not improve survival compared with chemotherapy alone.

  We don't know whether adding radiotherapy to MOPP is more effective than chemotherapy alone.

  Compared with MOPP plus radiotherapy, ABVD plus radiotherapy seems to be associated with improved progression-free survival and less gonadal toxicity.

  EBVP plus radiotherapy seems to have similar efficacy to MOPP/ABV plus radiotherapy in increasing overall survival, but it seems to be less effective at improving failure-free survival rates.

- In people with localised Hodgkin's lymphoma, involved-field radiotherapy is as effective as extended-field radiotherapy in increasing overall survival, but it is less likely to cause adverse effects. We don't know which radiotherapy dose regimen is most likely to improve survival.

- In people with advanced Hodgkin's lymphoma, ABVD is as effective as other chemotherapy regimens, such as MOPP, MOPP/ABV, MEC, and Stanford V, at improving long-term survival, with a more favourable adverse effect profile.

  Intensified chemotherapy with ChlVPP/EVA may improve 5-year survival compared with VAPEC-B, and escalating-dose BEACOPP may be more effective, but has greater toxicity, than COPP-ABVD.

- In people with advanced disease, adding radiotherapy to MOPP or to MOPP/ABV does not improve survival compared with the chemotherapy regimen alone. Adding radiotherapy to ABVPP may worsen survival rates compared with ABVPP alone.

  Adding radiotherapy to COPP-ABVD does not seem to improve relapse rates compared with the chemotherapy regimen alone.

ⓘ **Please visit http://clinicalevidence.bmj.com for full text and references**

## What are the effects of single-regimen chemotherapy treatments for first-presentation stage I or II non-bulky Hodgkin's lymphoma?

| Beneficial | • ABVD (may be as effective alone as ABVD plus radiotherapy [current gold standard treatment] and may be associated with fewer adverse effects) |
|---|---|
| Trade-off Between Benefits And Harms | • MOPP (no evidence on effectiveness compared with ABVD alone; increased risk of infertility and secondary leukaemia compared with ABVD) |

## What are the effects of combined chemotherapy and radiotherapy treatments compared with radiotherapy alone for first-presentation stage I or II non-bulky Hodgkin's lymphoma?

| Likely To Be Beneficial | • ABVD plus radiotherapy (improved freedom from treatment failure compared with radiotherapy alone and reduced risk of relapse at 7 years) (combination is international gold standard for early-stage Hodgkin's lymphoma)* |
|---|---|
| Trade-off Between Benefits And Harms | • MOPP plus radiotherapy (reduces treatment failure at 10 years compared with radiotherapy alone, but this combination regimen is associated with increased adverse effects) |
| Unknown Effectiveness | • VBM plus radiotherapy (insufficient evidence to compare versus radiotherapy alone) |

## What are the effects of combined chemotherapy and radiotherapy treatments compared with the same chemotherapy agent alone for first-presentation stage I or II non-bulky Hodgkin's lymphoma?

| Likely To Be Beneficial | • ABVD plus radiotherapy (may be as effective as ABVD alone, but may be associated with increased adverse effects; the combination is international gold standard for early-stage Hodgkin's lymphoma)* |
|---|---|
| Unknown Effectiveness | • CVPP plus radiotherapy (insufficient evidence to compare versus CVPP alone)<br><br>• MOPP plus radiotherapy (no evidence to compare versus MOPP alone) |

## What are the effects of specific combined chemotherapy and radiotherapy treatments versus each other in stage I or II non-bulky Hodgkin's lymphoma?

| | |
|---|---|
| Beneficial | • ABVD plus radiotherapy (improved progression-free survival compared with MOPP plus radiotherapy, and less gonadal toxicity) |
| Unlikely To Be Beneficial | • EBVP plus radiotherapy (reduced failure-free survival compared with MOPP/ABV plus radiotherapy) |

## What are the effects of different radiotherapy treatment strategies in stage I or II non-bulky Hodgkin's lymphoma?

| | |
|---|---|
| Beneficial | • Involved-field radiotherapy (similar rates of overall survival compared with extended-field radiotherapy but associated with fewer adverse effects) |
| Unknown Effectiveness | • Increased dose regimens (insufficient evidence to compare different regimens) |

## What are the effects of single-regimen chemotherapy treatments for first-presentation stage II (bulky), III, or IV Hodgkin's lymphoma?

| | |
|---|---|
| Beneficial | • ABVD |
| Trade-off Between Benefits And Harms | • MOPP |

## What are the effects of dose-intensified chemotherapy treatments for first-presentation stage II (bulky), III, or IV Hodgkin's lymphoma?

| | |
|---|---|
| Trade-off Between Benefits And Harms | • Escalating-dose BEACOPP (more effective than COPP-ABVD, but increased adverse effects) |
| Unknown Effectiveness | • ChlVPP-EVA (seems to improve overall survival compared with VAPEC-B; no evidence for comparisons with other regimens) |

## What are the effects of combined chemotherapy plus radiotherapy treatments compared with chemotherapy alone for first-presentation stage II (bulky), III, or IV Hodgkin's lymphoma?

| | |
|---|---|
| Unlikely To Be Beneficial | • ABVPP plus radiotherapy (lower 5-year survival rates than with ABVPP alone) |
| | • COPP-ABVD plus radiotherapy (no improvement in relapse rates compared with COPP-ABVD alone) |
| | • MOPP plus radiotherapy (similar overall survival at 10 years compared with MOPP alone) |

- MOPP/ABV plus radiotherapy (similar disease-free and overall survival rates at 5 years compared with MOPP/ABV alone)

**Search date September 2008**

*Categorisation based on consensus.

**DEFINITION** Hodgkin's lymphoma, also known as Hodgkin's disease, is a malignancy of the lymph nodes and lymphatic system. Most people present with an enlarged but otherwise asymptomatic lump, most often in the lower neck or supraclavicular region. Mediastinal masses are frequent and are revealed after routine chest X rays. About a quarter of people present systemic symptoms at diagnosis, such as unexplained fever, profuse sweating, fatigue, itchy skin, and unexplained weight loss. Hepatosplenomegaly, anaemia, lymphocyto-penia, and eosinophilia are also non-specific manifestations of the disease. Hodgkin's lymphoma is categorised according to appearance under the microscope (histology) and extent of disease (stage). **Histology:** Diagnosis is based on the recognition of Reed–Stenberg cells and/or Hodgkin cells in an appropriate cellular background in tissue sections from a lymph node or another organ, such as the bone marrow, lung, or bone. Fine needle aspiration biopsy is not adequate for diagnosis of Hodgkin's lymphoma; an open biopsy is always required. Reed–Stenberg cells are typically multinucleated giant cells, which in 98% of cases are thought to be derived from the germinal centre of peripheral B cells. The WHO classification is based on histological subtype. The distribution of histological subtypes varies between age groups, with young adults reportedly showing a greater proportion of nodular sclerosis compared with older adults. Nodular lymphocyte-predominant (LP) Hodgkin's lymphoma is a rare subtype that usually has a more indolent natural history, and is often treated differently. This subtype is not covered by this review. **Stage:** There are several different staging classification systems for Hodgkin's lymphoma. Computerised tomography (CT) scanning is the major method of staging both intra-thoracic and intra-abdominal disease, while bone marrow trephine biopsy is used for the detection of marrow infiltration by malignant cells. MRI scanning and fluorodeoxyglucose positron emission tomography (FDG-PET) scanning may also have a role in Hodgkin's lymphoma staging, mainly by revealing disease in sites that would be difficult to discover by CT imaging. Classification systems include the Ann Arbor classification and the Cotswolds. Staging methods have changed substantially over the past 20 years. Staging laparotomy with splenectomy is no longer routine practice due to a number of possible complications (including post-splenectomy sepsis, small-bowel obstruction, and even mortality), delay to the start of treatment, similar survival rates between people with or without a staging laparotomy, and the introduction of combined modality treatment for all stages. **Population:** For the purposes of this review, we considered adults with a first presentation of Hodgkin's lymphoma. We considered treatments separately in two groups of people: stage I or II non-bulky disease, and II (bulky), III, or IV disease; most studies used the Ann Arbor classification system.

**INCIDENCE/PREVALENCE** The annual incidence of Hodgkin's lymphoma is about 3 in 100,000 in the UK, without any large variations in incidence or in nature between countries or population groups. However, the age distribution of Hodgkin's lymphoma differs across geographical areas, as well as ethnic groups. In resource-rich countries, there is a bimodal age distribution with peaks at 15 to 34 years and over 60 years, with nodular sclerosis being the most common subtype. Early-stage nodular sclerosis Hodgkin's lymphoma is the most common form in children living in resource-rich countries, but advanced mixed cellularity and lymphocyte-rich subtypes are seen most commonly in resource-poor countries. In children in Europe and the US, incidence in males is double that of incidence in females, but in adolescents there is an equal distribution between sexes. The incidence of Hodgkin's lymphoma generally correlates with the level of economic development.

**AETIOLOGY/RISK FACTORS** The exact cause of Hodgkin's lymphoma remains unclear. However, it is accepted that Hodgkin's lymphoma is a heterogeneous condition that probably consists of more than one aetiological entity. The Epstein–Barr virus has been implicated in the development of Hodgkin's lymphoma, but this association varies with age, with positivity being most prominent in children and older people. Epstein–Barr virus positivity is high in childhood Hodgkin's lymphoma worldwide, but low in adolescents in resource-poor countries with nodular sclerosis Hodgkin's lymphoma. Histological subtype, age, sex, socioeconomic status, and ethnic background have all been shown to influence the association between the Epstein–Barr virus and Hodgkin's lymphoma. Although the pathogenesis of Hodgkin's disease is not yet fully understood, the nature of the Hodgkin/Reed–Stenberg (H/RS) cell has been recognised. The H/RS cell is derived from a B lymphocyte with clonal rearrangements in the V, D, and J segments of the IgH chain locus. Regulation of Fas-mediated apoptosis, and the nuclear factor-kappa B pathway, seem to be strongly implicated in the pathogenesis of Hodgkin's lymphoma.

**PROGNOSIS Overall survival:** The outcome in both localised and advanced Hodgkin's lymphoma has improved greatly over the past 20 years. The disease is now considered curable in the majority of cases. Even if first-line treatment fails, the person may be cured later. Therefore, doctors confront the dilemma of whether it is preferable to use more intensive treatment initially to cure the maximum number of people possible, or use less aggressive treatment initially and rely on more intensive salvage treatment in a greater proportion of people. The overall survival differs in terms of disease extent. People with localised disease (stage I/II) have a 6-year overall survival of more than 90% even in poor-risk groups. People with advanced disease (stage III/IV) have a 5-year overall survival of almost 85%. **Relapse:** The event-free survival at 4 years is near 99% for people with localised disease and almost 80% in people with advanced disease. **Prognostic indicators:** Despite an enormous effort to define clinically relevant and generally acceptable prognostic factors, stage and systemic B-cell symptoms are still the two key determinants for stratifying people with Hodgkin's lymphoma. Bulky disease (>10 cm nodal mass) has recently emerged as a third prognostic factor that meets general acceptance. In the US, most centres treat people according to the traditional classifications of early stages (I–IIA or B) and advanced stages (III–IVA or B; I–IIB with bulky disease), which is the classification used for the purposes of this review. The International Prognostic Score (IPS) has been used by several study groups that are currently tailoring treatment strategies at first diagnosis depending on the risk for treatment failure (IPS 0–2 and 3–7), but stratifying people on the basis of the IPS is still an experimental approach. Another group looked at prognostic factors specifically for children and young adults with Hodgkin's disease treated with combined modality treatment. They analysed 328 people aged 2 to 20 years old (48% were aged over 14 years) and multivariate analysis identified five pretreatment factors that correlated with inferior disease-free survival: male sex; stage IIB, IIIB, or IV disease; bulky mediastinal disease; white blood count of more than $13.5 \times 10^9$/L; and haemoglobin less than 11.0 g/dL. In the study, age was not a significant prognostic factor (14 years and under compared with >14 years old). Using this prognostic score, people with Hodgkin's lymphoma could be stratified into four groups with significantly different 5-year disease-free survivals. Response to initial chemotherapy was also shown to be a predictor of outcome. Other paediatric studies found nodular sclerosis histology and B symptoms also correlated with inferior outcome.

# 6 NHL (diffuse large B-cell lymphoma)

Fiona Kyle and Mark Hill

## KEY POINTS

- Non-Hodgkin's lymphoma (NHL) is the sixth most common cancer in the UK, with a 10% increase in incidence between 1993 and 2002.

  Risk factors include immunosuppression, certain viral and bacterial infections, and exposure to drugs and other chemicals.

  Overall 5-year survival is around 55%. The main risk factors for a poor prognosis are older age, elevated serum lactate dehydrogenase levels, and severity of disease.

- CHOP 21 has been shown to be superior or equivalent to all other combination chemotherapy regimens in terms of overall survival or toxicity in adults older or younger than 60 years.

  Adding radiotherapy to a short CHOP 21 schedule (3 cycles) increases 5-year survival, while reducing the risks of congestive heart failure, compared with longer schedules of CHOP 21 alone.

  Adding rituximab to CHOP 21 increases response rates and 5-year survival compared with CHOP 21 alone.

  CHOP 14 may increase 5-year survival compared with CHOP 21 in people aged over 60 years, but effects are less clear in younger adults. Toxicity is similar for the two regimens.

- Consensus is that conventional-dose salvage chemotherapy should be used in people with relapsed NHL. Phase II studies report similar response rates with a number of different chemotherapy regimens.

  Adding rituximab to salvage chemotherapy may improve initial response rates, but no more than 10% of people remain disease-free after 3 to 5 years.

- High-dose salvage chemotherapy plus autologous bone-marrow transplantation may increase 5-year event-free survival and overall survival compared with conventional-dose chemotherapy in people with relapsed chemotherapy-sensitive disease, but it increases the risk of severe adverse effects.

  We don't know whether allogenic bone-marrow transplantation improves survival. Retrospective studies suggest that it increases the risk of graft-versus-host disease and complications of immunosuppression.

(i) **Please visit http://clinicalevidence.bmj.com for full text and references**

| What are the effects of first-line treatments for aggressive NHL (diffuse large B-cell lymphoma)? | |
|---|---|
| Beneficial | • CHOP 21 (alternative regimens: MACOP-B, m-BACOD, ProMACE-CytaBOM, PACEBOM not shown to be superior to CHOP 21) |
| | • CHOP 21 plus radiotherapy (increases disease-free survival compared with CHOP 21 alone) |
| | • CHOP 21 plus rituximab (increases survival compared with CHOP 21 alone) |
| Likely To Be Beneficial | • CHOP 14 |

## What are the effects of treatments for relapsed aggressive NHL (diffuse large B-cell lymphoma)?

| | |
|---|---|
| **Likely To Be Beneficial** | • Conventional-dose salvage chemotherapy (consensus that treatment should be given but relative benefits of different regimens unclear)* <br><br> • High-dose chemotherapy plus autologous transplant stem-cell support (increases survival compared with conventional-dose chemotherapy in people with chemosensitive disease) |
| **Unknown Effectiveness** | • Allogeneic stem-cell support |

**Search date January 2010**

*Based on consensus

**DEFINITION** Non-Hodgkin's lymphoma (NHL) consists of a complex group of cancers arising mainly from B lymphocytes (85% of cases), and occasionally from T lymphocytes. NHL usually develops in lymph nodes (nodal lymphoma), but can arise in other tissues almost anywhere in the body (extranodal lymphoma). NHL is categorised according to its appearance under the microscope (histology) and the extent of the disease (stage). **Histology:** Since 1966, 4 major different methods of classifying NHLs according to their histological appearance have been published. At present, the WHO system is accepted as the gold standard of classification. The WHO system is based on the underlying principles of the REAL classification system. Historically, NHLs have been divided into slow-growing 'low-grade' lymphomas and fast-growing 'aggressive' lymphomas. This review deals only with the most common aggressive NHL — diffuse B-cell lymphoma (WHO classification). Interpretation of older studies is complicated by the fact that histological methods have changed and there is no direct correlation between lymphoma types in the WHO and other classification systems. Attempts to generalise results must therefore be treated with caution. We have, however, included some older studies referring to alternative classification methods, if they included people with the following types of aggressive lymphomas, which overlap substantially with the WHO classification of interest: Working Formulation classification — primarily intermediate grades (grades E–H); Kiel classification — centroblastic, immunoblastic, and anaplastic; and Rappaport classification — diffuse histiocytic, diffuse lymphocytic, poorly differentiated, and diffuse mixed (lymphocytic and histiocytic). **Stage:** NHL has traditionally been staged according to extent of disease spread using the Ann Arbor system. The term 'early disease' is used to describe disease that falls within Ann Arbor stage I or II, whereas 'advanced disease' refers to Ann Arbor stage III or IV. However, all people with bulky disease, usually defined as having a disease site larger than 10 cm in diameter, are treated as having advanced disease, regardless of their Ann Arbor staging. **Relapsed disease:** Relapsed disease refers to the recurrence of active disease in a person who has previously achieved a complete response to initial treatment for NHL. Most studies of treatments in relapsed disease require a minimum duration of complete response of 1 month before relapse.

**INCIDENCE/PREVALENCE** NHL is the sixth most common cancer in the UK; 9443 new cases were diagnosed in the UK in 2002 and it caused 4418 UK deaths in 2003. Incidence rates show distinct geographical variation, with age-standardised incidence rates ranging from 17 per 100,000 in northern America to 4 per 100,000 in south-central Asia. NHL occurs more commonly in males than in females, and the age-standardised UK incidence increased by 10.3% between 1993 and 2002.

**AETIOLOGY/RISK FACTORS** The aetiology of most NHLs is unknown. Incidence is higher in individuals who are immunosuppressed (congenital or acquired). Other risk factors include viral infection (human T-cell leukaemia virus type-1, Epstein–Barr virus, HIV), bacterial infection (e.g., *Helicobacter pylori*), previous treatment with phenytoin or antineoplastic drugs, and exposure to pesticides or organic solvents.

*(continued over)*

*(from previous page)*

**PROGNOSIS Overall survival:** Untreated aggressive NHLs would generally result in death in a matter of months. High-grade lymphomas, particularly diffuse large B-cell lymphomas and Burkitt's lymphomas, have a high cure rate with both initial and salvage chemotherapy. The 5-year relative age-standardised survival for people diagnosed with and treated for NHL between 2000 and 2001 was 55% for men and 56% for women. **Relapse:** About 50% of people with NHL will be cured by initial treatment. Of the rest, about 30% will fail to respond to initial treatment (so called 'chemotherapy refractory disease'), and about 20% to 30% will relapse. Most relapses occur within 2 years of completion of initial treatment. Up to 50% of these have chemotherapy-sensitive disease; the remainder tend to have chemotherapy-resistant disease. **Prognostic indicators:** Prognosis depends on histological type, stage, age, performance status, and lactate dehydrogenase levels. Prognosis varies substantially within each Ann Arbor stage, and further information regarding prognosis can be obtained from applying the International Prognostic Index (IPI). The IPI model stratifies prognosis according to the presence or absence of 5 risk factors: age (under 60 years *v* over 60 years), serum lactate dehydrogenase (normal *v* elevated), performance status (0 or 1 *v* 2–4), Ann Arbor stage (I or II *v* III or IV), and number of extranodal sites involved (0 or 1 *v* 2–4). People with two or more high-risk factors have a less than 50% chance of relapse-free and overall survival at 5 years. IPI staging is currently the most important system used to define disease stage and treatment options. However, most studies identified by our search predate the IPI staging system.

Martin M Meremikwu and Uduak Okomo

## KEY POINTS

- In sub-Saharan Africa, up to a third of adults are carriers of the defective sickle cell gene, and 1% to 2% of babies are born with the disease.

  Sickle cell disease causes chronic haemolytic anaemia, dactylitis, and painful acute crises. It also increases the risk of stroke, organ damage, bacterial infections, and complications of blood transfusion.

- We don't know whether avoidance of cold environments, physical exercise, or rehydration can prevent crises or complications in people with sickle cell disease.

  Blood transfusion (prophylactic) reduces stroke in children at increased risk of stroke, but increases the risks of iron overload, allo-immunisation, hypertensive or circulatory overload, febrile non-haemolytic reactions, allergic reactions, and haemolytic events.

  Penicillin prophylaxis in children <5 years of age reduces invasive pneumococcal infections regardless of pneumococcal vaccination status. We don't know whether penicillin prophylaxis is beneficial in older children.

  Malaria chemoprophylaxis is considered useful in preventing malaria-induced crises, but we found few studies evaluating its benefit.

  Polyvalent polysaccharide pneumococcal vaccine does not reduce the incidence of pneumococcal infections in people with sickle cell disease. Pneumococcal conjugate vaccines have been reported to have protective efficacy in children <2 years of age, but this protective effect has not been shown in infants with sickle cell disease.

- Hydroxyurea may reduce some complications of sickle cell disease, such as painful crises compared with placebo, but long-term effects and safety are unknown.

- Morphine is widely used to treat severe pain, but we found no RCT evidence comparing it with placebo in people with sickle cell crises. Controlled-release oral morphine and patient-controlled analgesia may be as effective as repeated intravenous doses of morphine. Oral morphine increases the risk of acute chest syndrome compared with intravenous administration.

  High-dose corticosteroids may reduce the need for analgesia when added to intravenous morphine in people with a sickle cell crisis, but may increase the risks of adverse effects (such as infections, hypertension, and metabolic problems).

- It is still unclear whether acupuncture, blood transfusion, hydration, oxygen, aspirin, codeine, diflunisal, ibuprofen, ketorolac, or paracetamol reduce pain during sickle cell crisis.

 **Please visit http://clinicalevidence.bmj.com for full text and references**

| What are the effects of non-pharmaceutical interventions to prevent sickle cell crisis and other acute complications in people with sickle cell disease? | |
| --- | --- |
| **Trade-off Between Benefits And Harms** | • Blood transfusion (prophylactic) for sickle cell crisis |
| **Unknown Effectiveness** | • Avoidance of cold environment |
| | • Limiting physical exercise |
| | • Rehydration |

## What are the effects of pharmaceutical interventions to prevent sickle cell crisis and other acute complications in people with sickle cell disease?

| | |
|---|---|
| **Beneficial** | • Penicillin prophylaxis in children <5 years of age |
| **Likely To Be Beneficial** | • Hydroxyurea<br>• Malaria chemoprophylaxis |
| **Unknown Effectiveness** | • Antibiotic prophylaxis in children >5 years of age<br>• Pneumococcal vaccines |

## What are the effects of non-pharmaceutical interventions to treat pain in people with sickle cell crisis?

| | |
|---|---|
| **Unknown Effectiveness** | • Acupuncture<br>• Blood transfusion for sickle cell pain<br>• Hydration<br>• Oxygen |

## What are the effects of pharmaceutical interventions to treat pain in people with sickle cell crisis?

| | |
|---|---|
| **Likely To Be Beneficial** | • Patient-controlled analgesia |
| **Trade-off Between Benefits And Harms** | • Corticosteroid as adjunct to narcotic analgesics<br>• Morphine (oral versus intravenous) |
| **Unknown Effectiveness** | • Aspirin<br>• Codeine<br>• Diflunisal<br>• Ibuprofen<br>• Ketorolac<br>• Paracetamol |

**Search date March 2010**

**DEFINITION** Sickle cell disease refers to a group of disorders caused by inheritance of a pair of abnormal haemoglobin genes, including the sickle cell gene. It is characterised by chronic haemolytic anaemia, dactylitis, and acute episodic clinical events called 'crises'. Vaso-occlusive (painful) crises are the most common, and because of a resistance to nitric oxide, cause tissue ischaemia. Other crises are acute chest syndrome, sequestration crisis, and aplastic crisis. A common variant of sickle cell disease, also characterised by haemolytic anaemia, occurs in people with one sickle and one thalassaemia gene. **Sickle cell trait** occurs in people with one sickle gene and one normal gene. People with sickle cell trait have no clinical manifestation of illness. This review covers people with sickle cell disease with or without thalassaemia.

**INCIDENCE/PREVALENCE** Sickle cell disease is most common in people living in or originating from sub-Saharan Africa. The disorder also affects people of Mediterranean, Caribbean, Middle-Eastern, and Asian origin. The sickle cell gene is most common in areas where malaria is endemic — sickle cell trait affects about 10% to 30% of Africa's tropical populations. Sickle cell disease affects an estimated 1% to 2% (120,000) of infants in Africa annually. About 178 babies (0.28/1000 conceptions) are affected by sickle cell disease in England annually. About 60,000 people in the US and 10,000 in the UK suffer from the disease.

**AETIOLOGY/RISK FACTORS** Sickle cell disease is inherited as an autosomal recessive disorder. For a baby to be affected both parents must have the sickle cell gene. In parents with sickle cell trait the risk of having an affected baby is 1 in 4 for each pregnancy. Painful (vaso-occlusive) crisis is the most common feature of the disease, and these episodes start in infancy and early childhood. Factors that precipitate or modulate the occurrence of sickle cell crisis are not fully understood, but infections, hypoxia, dehydration, acidosis, stress (such as major surgery or childbirth), and cold are believed to play some role. In tropical Africa, malaria is the most common cause of anaemic and vaso-occlusive crisis. High levels of fetal haemoglobin are known to ameliorate the severity and incidence of sickle cell crisis and other complications of the disease.

**PROGNOSIS** People affected by sickle cell disease are predisposed to bacterial infections, especially those caused by encapsulated organisms such as *Pneumococcus*, *Haemophilus influenzae*, *Meningococcus*, and *Salmonella* species. Severe bacterial infections (such as pneumonia, meningitis, and septicaemia) are common causes of morbidity and mortality, especially among young children. About 10% of children with sickle cell anaemia may develop a stroke, and more than 50% of these may suffer recurrent strokes. Abnormal features of cerebral blood vessels, shown by transcranial Doppler scan, predict a high risk of stroke in children with sickle cell disease. Frequent episodes of crisis, infections, and organ damage reduce the quality of life of people with sickle cell disease. A high rate of vaso-occlusive (painful) crisis is an index of clinical severity that correlates with early death. Life expectancy remains low, especially in communities with poor access to health services. In some parts of Africa, about 50% of children with sickle cell disease die before their first birthday. The average life expectancy with sickle cell disease in the US is about 42 years for men and about 48 years for women. Frequent blood transfusions could increase the risk of immune reactions and infections, such as HIV and hepatitis B or C viruses, and Chagas' disease. The need for repeated blood transfusions in people with sickle cell disease predisposes them to the risk of iron overload.

Laurence O'Toole

## KEY POINTS

- Stable angina is a sensation of discomfort or pain in the chest, arm, or jaw brought on predictably by factors that increase myocardial oxygen demand, such as exertion, and relieved by rest or nitroglycerin.

  Stable angina is usually caused by coronary atherosclerosis, and affects up to 16% of men and 10% of women aged 65–74 years in the UK. Risk factors include hypertension, elevated serum cholesterol levels, smoking, physical inactivity, and overweight.

  People with angina are at increased risk of other cardiovascular events and mortality compared with people without angina.

  Among people not thought to need coronary artery revascularisation, annual mortality is 1–2% and annual non-fatal MI rates are 2–3%.

  We found no long-term, adequately powered RCTs of anti-anginal drugs versus placebo or comparing the use of a single anti-anginal drug versus combinations of anti-anginal drug classes. There is a consensus that monotherapy with beta-blockers, calcium channel blockers, nitrates, and potassium channel openers are effective for treating the symptoms of stable angina in the long term, although we found few studies to confirm this. There is also consensus that the concurrent use of two of these classes of drug has an additional beneficial effect on anginal symptoms and quality of life. It has not been established that this approach reduces cardiovascular events.

  Monotherapy with beta-blockers or calcium channel blockers seems equally effective at reducing angina attacks, and they are equally well tolerated in the long term.

  Adding a calcium channel blocker to existing anti-anginal drug treatments slightly reduces the need for coronary artery surgery, but has no effect on other cardiovascular events.

  Monotherapy with nitrates may be as effective as monotherapy with calcium channel blockers at reducing angina attacks and improving quality of life.

  We found no RCTs on the effects of long-term monotherapy with potassium channel openers in people with stable angina, but a large RCT of a potassium channel opener as an adjunct to existing anti-anginal drug treatments found a reduction the number of cardiovascular events compared with placebo.

 **Please visit http://clinicalevidence.bmj.com for full text and references**

| What are effects of long-term single-drug treatment for stable angina? | |
| --- | --- |
| Likely To Be Beneficial | • Beta-blockers as monotherapy* |
| | • Calcium channel blockers as monotherapy* |
| | • Nitrates as monotherapy* |
| | • Potassium channel openers as monotherapy* |

| What are the effects of long-term combination drug treatment for stable angina? | |
| --- | --- |
| Likely To Be Beneficial | • Beta-blockers combined with calcium channel blockers (more effective than beta-blockers alone)* |

- Calcium channel blockers combined with beta-blockers (more effective than calcium channel blockers alone)*
- Nitrates in combination with other anti-anginal drug treatments*
- Potassium channel openers combined with other anti-anginal drug treatments*

| What are the effects of long-term adjunctive drug treatment in people with stable angina who are receiving anti-anginal treatment? | |
|---|---|
| Likely To Be Beneficial | • Calcium channel blockers in addition to existing anti-anginal drug treatment* <br> • Potassium channel openers in addition to existing anti-anginal drug treatment |
| Unknown Effectiveness | • Beta-blockers in addition to existing anti-anginal drug treatment <br> • Nitrates in addition to existing anti-anginal drug treatment |

**Search date June 2007**

*Based on consensus.

**DEFINITION** Angina pectoris, often simply known as angina, is a clinical syndrome characterised by discomfort in the chest, shoulder, back, arm, or jaw. Angina is usually caused by coronary artery atherosclerotic disease. Rarer causes include valvular heart disease, hypertrophic cardiomyopathy, uncontrolled hypertension, or vasospasm or endothelial dysfunction not related to atherosclerosis. The differential diagnosis of angina includes non-cardiac conditions affecting the chest wall, oesophagus, and lungs. Angina may be classified as stable or unstable. **Stable angina** is defined as regular or predictable angina symptoms that have been occurring for over 2 months. Symptoms are transient and typically provoked by exertion, and alleviated by rest or nitroglycerin. Other precipitants include cold weather, eating, or emotional distress. This review deals specifically with stable angina caused by coronary artery atherosclerotic disease. For management of **unstable angina**, see separate review on acute coronary syndromes.

**INCIDENCE/PREVALENCE** The prevalence of stable angina remains unclear. Epidemiological studies in the UK estimate that 6–16% of men and 3–10% of women aged 65–74 years have experienced angina. Annually, about 1% of the population visit their general practitioner with symptoms of angina, and 23,000 people with new anginal symptoms present to their general practitioner each year in the UK. These studies did not distinguish between stable and unstable angina.

**AETIOLOGY/RISK FACTORS** Stable angina resulting from coronary artery disease is characterised by focal atherosclerotic plaques in the intimal layer of the epicardial coronary artery. The plaques encroach on the coronary lumen and may limit blood flow to the myocardium, especially during periods of increased myocardial oxygen demand. The major risk factors that lead to the development of stable angina are similar to those that predispose to CHD. These risk factors include increasing age, male sex, overweight, hypertension, elevated serum cholesterol level, smoking, and relative physical inactivity.

**PROGNOSIS** Stable angina is a marker of underlying CHD, which accounts for 1 in 4 deaths in the UK. People with angina are 2–5 times more likely to develop other manifestations of CHD than people who do not have angina. One population-based study (7100 men aged

*(continued over)*

*(from previous page)*

51–59 years at entry) found that people with angina had higher mortality than people with no history of coronary artery disease at baseline (16-year survival rate: 53% with angina *v* 72% without coronary artery disease *v* 34% with a history of MI). Clinical trials in people with stable angina have tended to recruit participants who were not felt to be in need of coronary revascularisation, and prognosis is better in these people, with an annual mortality of 1–2%, and an annual rate of non-fatal MI of 2–3%. Features that indicate a poorer prognosis include: more-severe symptoms, male sex, abnormal resting ECG (present in about 50% of people with angina), previous MI, left ventricular dysfunction, easily provoked or widespread coronary ischaemia on stress testing (present in about a third of people referred to hospital with stable angina), and significant stenosis of all three major coronary arteries or the left main coronary artery. In addition, the standard coronary risk factors continue to exert a detrimental and additive effect on prognosis in people with stable angina. Control of these risk factors is dealt with in the *Clinical Evidence* review on secondary prevention of ischaemic cardiac events, p 48.

Gregory Y.H. Lip and Stavros Apostolakis

## KEY POINTS

- Acute atrial fibrillation is rapid, irregular, and chaotic atrial activity of less than 48 hours' duration. It resolves spontaneously within 24 to 48 hours in more than 50% of people. In this review, we have included studies on patients with onset up to 7 days previously.

  Risk factors for acute atrial fibrillation include increasing age, CVD, alcohol abuse, diabetes, and lung disease.

  Acute atrial fibrillation increases the risk of stroke and heart failure.

- The consensus is that people with haemodynamically unstable atrial fibrillation should have immediate direct current cardioversion. In people who are haemodynamically stable, direct current cardioversion increases reversion to sinus rhythm compared with intravenous propafenone.

  There is consensus that antithrombotic treatment with heparin should be given before cardioversion of recent-onset atrial fibrillation to reduce the risk of embolism in people who are haemodynamically stable, but we found no studies to show whether this is beneficial.

- Oral or intravenous flecainide, propafenone, or amiodarone increase the likelihood of reversion to sinus rhythm compared with placebo in people with haemodynamically stable acute atrial fibrillation.

- CAUTION: Flecainide and propafenone should not be used in people with ischaemic heart disease as they can cause (life-threatening) arrhythmias.

- We don't know whether sotalol increases reversion to sinus rhythm in people with haemodynamically stable atrial fibrillation, as few adequate trials have been conducted.

  Digoxin does not seem to increase reversion to sinus rhythm compared with placebo. We don't know whether verapamil increases reversion to sinus rhythm compared with placebo.

- No one drug has been shown to be more effective at controlling heart rate. However, there is general consensus that intravenous bolus amiodarone is more effective than digoxin.

- Treatment with digoxin may control heart rate in people with haemodynamically stable atrial fibrillation, despite its being unlikely to restore sinus rhythm.

- We don't know whether diltiazem, timolol, and verapamil are effective at controlling heart rate, but they are unlikely to restore sinus rhythm.

  We don't know whether sotalol, bisoprolol, metoprolol, atenolol, nebivolol, or carvedilol are effective at controlling heart rate in people with acute atrial fibrillation who are haemodynamically stable. However, sotalol may cause arrhythmias at high doses.

(i) **Please visit http://clinicalevidence.bmj.com for full text and references**

### What are the effects of interventions to prevent embolism in people with recent-onset atrial fibrillation who are haemodynamically stable?

| Unknown Effectiveness | • Antithrombotic treatment before cardioversion |
|---|---|

## What are the effects of interventions for conversion to sinus rhythm in people with recent-onset atrial fibrillation who are haemodynamically stable?

| | |
|---|---|
| **Likely To Be Beneficial** | • Direct current cardioversion for rhythm control |
| **Trade-off Between Benefits And Harms** | • Amiodarone for rhythm control<br>• Flecainide for rhythm control<br>• Propafenone for rhythm control |
| **Unknown Effectiveness** | • Sotalol for rhythm control<br>• Verapamil for rhythm control |
| **Unlikely To Be Beneficial** | • Digoxin for rhythm control |

## What are the effects of interventions to control heart rate in people with recent-onset atrial fibrillation who are haemodynamically stable?

| | |
|---|---|
| **Likely To Be Beneficial** | • Amiodarone for rate control*<br>• Digoxin for rate control<br>• Diltiazem for rate control<br>• Timolol for rate control<br>• Verapamil for rate control |
| **Unknown Effectiveness** | • Atenolol for rate control<br>• Bisoprolol for rate control<br>• Carvedilol for rate control<br>• Metoprolol for rate control<br>• Nebivolol for rate control<br>• Sotalol for rate control |

**Search date April 2014**

---

*Categorisation based on consensus.

**DEFINITION** Acute atrial fibrillation is rapid, irregular, and chaotic atrial activity of recent onset. Various definitions of acute atrial fibrillation have been used in the literature, but for the purposes of this review we have included studies where atrial fibrillation may have occurred up to 7 days previously. Acute atrial fibrillation includes both the first symptomatic onset of chronic or persistent atrial fibrillation and episodes of paroxysmal atrial fibrillation. It is sometimes difficult to distinguish new-onset atrial fibrillation from previously undiagnosed long-standing atrial fibrillation. By contrast, chronic atrial fibrillation is more sustained and can be described as paroxysmal (with spontaneous termination and sinus rhythm between recurrences), persistent, or permanent atrial fibrillation. This review deals with people with acute and recent-onset atrial fibrillation who are haemodynamically stable. The consensus is that people who are not haemodynamically stable should be treated with immediate direct current cardioversion. We have excluded studies in people with atrial fibrillation arising during or soon after cardiac surgery. **Diagnosis:** Acute atrial fibrillation should be suspected in people presenting with dizziness, syncope, dyspnoea, or palpitations. Moreover, atrial fibrillation can contribute to a large number of other non-specific symptoms. Palpation of an irregular pulse is generally only considered sufficient to raise suspicion of atrial fibrillation; diagnosis requires confirmation with ECG. However, in those with paroxysmal atrial fibrillation, ambulatory monitoring may be required.

**INCIDENCE/PREVALENCE** We found limited evidence on the incidence or prevalence of acute atrial fibrillation. Extrapolation from the Framingham study suggests an incidence in men of 3 per 1000 person-years at age 55 years, rising to 38 per 1000 person-years at age 94 years. In women, the incidence was 2 per 1000 person-years at age 55 years and 32.5 per 1000 person-years at age 94 years. The prevalence of atrial fibrillation ranged from 0.5% for people aged 50 to 59 years to 9% in people aged 80 to 89 years. Among acute emergency medical admissions in the UK, 3% to 6% had atrial fibrillation, and about 40% of these were newly diagnosed. Among acute hospital admissions in New Zealand, 10% (95% CI 9% to 12%) had documented atrial fibrillation.

**AETIOLOGY/RISK FACTORS** Common precipitants of acute atrial fibrillation are acute MI and the acute effects of alcohol. Age increases the risk of developing acute atrial fibrillation. Men are more likely than women to develop atrial fibrillation (38 years' follow-up from the Framingham Study; RR, after adjustment for age and known predisposing conditions, 1.5). Atrial fibrillation can occur in association with underlying disease (both cardiac and non-cardiac) or can arise in the absence of any other condition. Epidemiological surveys found that risk factors for the development of acute atrial fibrillation include ischaemic heart disease, hypertension, heart failure, valve disease, diabetes, alcohol abuse, thyroid disorders, and disorders of the lung and pleura. In a British survey of acute hospital admissions of people with atrial fibrillation, a history of ischaemic heart disease was present in 33%, heart failure in 24%, hypertension in 26%, and rheumatic heart disease in 7%. In some populations, the acute effects of alcohol explain a large proportion of the incidence of acute atrial fibrillation. Paroxysms of atrial fibrillation are more common in athletes.

**PROGNOSIS Spontaneous reversion:** Observational studies and placebo arms of RCTs found that more than 50% of people with acute atrial fibrillation revert spontaneously within 24 to 48 hours, especially if atrial fibrillation is associated with an identifiable precipitant such as alcohol or MI. **Progression to chronic atrial fibrillation:** We found no evidence about the proportion of people with acute atrial fibrillation who develop more chronic forms of atrial fibrillation (e.g., paroxysmal, persistent, or permanent atrial fibrillation). **Mortality:** We found little evidence about the effects on mortality of acute atrial fibrillation where no underlying cause is found. Acute atrial fibrillation during MI is an independent predictor of both short- and long-term mortality. **Heart failure:** Onset of atrial fibrillation reduces cardiac output by 10% to 20%, irrespective of the underlying ventricular rate, and can contribute to heart failure. People with acute atrial fibrillation who present with heart failure have worse prognoses. **Stroke:** Acute atrial fibrillation is associated with a risk of imminent stroke. One case series using transoesophageal echocardiography in people who had developed acute atrial fibrillation within the preceding 48 hours found that 15% had atrial thrombi. An ischaemic stroke associated with atrial fibrillation is more likely to be fatal, have a recurrence, or leave a serious functional deficit among survivors than a stroke not associated with atrial fibrillation.

## 18 | Atrial fibrillation (chronic)

Deirdre A. Lane, Christopher J. Boos, and Gregory Y.H. Lip

### KEY POINTS

- Atrial fibrillation is a supraventricular tachyarrhythmia characterised by the presence of uncoordinated atrial activation and deteriorating atrial mechanical function. Risk factors for atrial fibrillation are increasing age, male sex, co-existing cardiac disease, thyroid disease, pyrexial illness, electrolyte imbalance, cancer, and acute infections.

- This review examines the effects of different oral medical treatments to control heart rate in people with chronic (longer than 1 week) non-valvular atrial fibrillation. We have focused on medical treatments and have not included other types of interventions.

- Overall, we found a lack of good-quality large RCTs on which to base robust conclusions.

- Consensus is that beta-blockers are more effective than digoxin for controlling symptoms of chronic atrial fibrillation, but very few trials have been found. When a beta-blocker alone is ineffective, current consensus supports the addition of digoxin.

- Current consensus is that calcium channel blockers are more effective than digoxin for controlling heart rate, but very few RCTs have been found. When a calcium channel blocker alone is ineffective, the addition of digoxin is effective in improving exercise tolerance and reducing heart rate.

- The choice between using a beta-blocker or a calcium channel blocker is dependent on individual risk factors and co-existing morbidities.

(i) **Please visit http://clinicalevidence.bmj.com for full text and references**

| What are the effects of oral medical treatments to control heart rate in people with chronic (>1 week) non-valvular atrial fibrillation? | |
|---|---|
| Likely To Be Beneficial | • Beta-blockers plus digoxin versus beta-blockers alone (beta-blockers plus digoxin more effective than beta-blockers alone)* |
| | • Beta-blockers versus digoxin (beta-blockers more effective than digoxin in controlling symptoms)* |
| | • Calcium channel blockers (rate-limiting) plus digoxin versus calcium channel blockers (rate-limiting) alone (calcium channel blockers plus digoxin more effective than calcium channel blockers alone) |
| | • Calcium channel blockers (rate-limiting) versus digoxin (calcium channel blockers more effective than digoxin for controlling heart rate)* |
| Trade-off Between Benefits And Harms | • Beta-blockers versus rate-limiting calcium channel blockers (selection is dependent on individual risk factors and co-existing morbidities) |

**Search date May 2014**

*Categorisation based on consensus.

**DEFINITION** Atrial fibrillation is the most frequently encountered and sustained cardiac arrhythmia in clinical practice. It is a supraventricular tachyarrhythmia characterised by the presence of uncoordinated atrial activation and deteriorating atrial mechanical function. On the surface ECG, P waves are absent and are replaced by rapid fibrillatory waves that vary in size, shape, and timing, leading to an irregular ventricular response when atrioventricular conduction is intact. **Classification:** Chronic atrial fibrillation is most commonly classified according to its temporal pattern. Faced with a first detected episode of atrial fibrillation, four recognised patterns of chronic disease may develop: (1) 'paroxysmal atrial fibrillation' refers to self-terminating episodes of atrial fibrillation, usually lasting <48 hours (both paroxysmal and persistent atrial fibrillation may be recurrent); (2) 'persistent atrial fibrillation' describes an episode of sustained atrial fibrillation (usually >7 days) that does not convert to sinus rhythm without medical intervention, with the achievement of sinus rhythm by either pharmacological or electrical cardioversion; (3) 'long-standing persistent atrial fibrillation' pertains to atrial fibrillation with a duration of 1 year or longer where a decision has been taken to implement a rhythm-control strategy; (4) 'permanent atrial fibrillation' describes episodes of persistent (usually >1 year) atrial fibrillation, in which cardioversion is not attempted or is unsuccessful, with atrial fibrillation accepted as the long-term rhythm for that person. 'Lone atrial fibrillation' is largely a diagnosis of exclusion and refers to atrial fibrillation occurring in the absence of concomitant CVD (e.g., hypertension) or structural heart disease (normal echocardiogram), with an otherwise normal ECG (with the exception of atrial fibrillation) and chest x-ray. This review covers only chronic atrial fibrillation (persistent and permanent). Acute atrial fibrillation is covered in a separate review (see atrial fibrillation [acute onset], p 15). **Diagnosis:** In most cases of suspected atrial fibrillation, a 12-lead ECG is sufficient for diagnosis confirmation. However, where diagnostic uncertainty remains, such as in chronic permanent atrial fibrillation, the use of 24-hour (or even 7-day) Holter monitoring or event recorder (e.g., Cardiomemo®) may also be required. The most common presenting symptoms of chronic atrial fibrillation are palpitations, shortness of breath, fatigue, chest pain, dizziness, and stroke.

**INCIDENCE/PREVALENCE** In the developed world, the prevalence of atrial fibrillation is currently estimated to be around 1.5% to 2% of the general population. The prevalence of atrial fibrillation is highly age-dependent, and increases markedly with each advancing decade of age, from 0.5% at age 50 to 59 years to almost 9% at age 80 to 90 years. Data from the Framingham Heart Study suggest that the lifetime risk for development of atrial fibrillation for men and women aged 40 years and older is approximately 1 in 4. This risk is similar to that reported by the Rotterdam Study investigators, who found that the lifetime risk associated with developing atrial fibrillation in men and women aged 55 years and above was 24% and 22%, respectively. The Screening for Atrial Fibrillation in the Elderly (SAFE) project reported that the baseline prevalence of atrial fibrillation in people aged over 65 years was 7.2%, with a higher prevalence in men (7.8%) and in people aged 75 years or more, with an incidence of 0.69% to 1.64% per year, depending on screening method. The US Census Bureau reports that the number of people with atrial fibrillation is projected to be 12.1 million by 2050, assuming that there are no further increases in age-adjusted incidence of atrial fibrillation. These incidence data refer to cross-sectional study data, whereby most people would have atrial fibrillation of over 7 days' duration (persistent, paroxysmal, or permanent atrial fibrillation), and do not refer to acute atrial fibrillation.

**AETIOLOGY/RISK FACTORS** Atrial fibrillation is linked to a variety of risk factors such as increasing age, hypertension, and to all types of cardiac conditions, including heart failure (where a reciprocal relationship exists) and cardiothoracic surgery. It is also linked to a large number of non-cardiac conditions, such as thyroid disease, any pyrexial illness, electrolyte imbalance, cancer, and acute infections.

**PROGNOSIS** Chronic atrial fibrillation confers an enormous and significant clinical burden. It is an independent predictor of mortality, and is associated with an odds ratio for death of 1.5 for men and 1.9 in women, independent of other risk factors. It increases the risk of ischaemic stroke and thromboembolism an average of fivefold. Furthermore, the presence of chronic atrial fibrillation is linked to more severe strokes, with greater disability and lower discharge rate to patients' homes. Chronic atrial fibrillation is a frequent (3%–6%) cause of all medical admissions and results in longer hospital stays. In addition, chronic atrial fibrillation increases the risk of developing heart failure and adversely affects quality of life, including cognitive function.

# 20 | Cardiovascular medication: improving adherence

Liam Glynn and Tom Fahey

## KEY POINTS

- Adherence to medication is generally defined as the extent to which people take medications as prescribed by their healthcare providers.

  It can be assessed in many ways (e.g., by self-reporting, pill counting, direct observation, electronic monitoring, or through pharmacy records). In this review, we have reported adherence to cardiovascular medications however it has been measured.

- The RCTs we found used a variety of different interventions in different populations, measured adherence differently, and expressed and analysed results differently.

  The diversity and complexity of interventions employed in RCTs makes it difficult to separate out any individual components that might be of benefit.

- We found evidence that simplified dosing regimens may increase adherence compared with more complex regimens.

  While simplifying the frequency of dosage may increase adherence, it is not known whether simplified regimens may increase adherence when someone is taking multiple drugs, as may be the case with cardio-vascular medicines.

  In altering a drug regimen simply to increase adherence, any changes could potentially affect the effectiveness of the treatment, and could also potentially increase adverse effects.

- Prompting mechanisms may also increase adherence to medication.

  Some prompting mechanisms may be simple and inexpensive (e.g., mailed reminders), while others (e.g., daily telephone calls, installing videophones) seem impracticable for use in routine practice.

- Patient health education may also increase adherence to medication but more data are needed to draw conclusions.

  Adherence behaviour is complex. Traditional education methods may fail to address this. However, more patient-centred approaches, particularly those that are nurse- or pharmacist-led, using video or telephone strategies, may be beneficial and require further investigation.

  We found some evidence that a combination of strategies, such as education plus prompting, may be more successful than a single educa-tional strategy.

- We found no evidence from one RCT that reminder packaging (a calendar blister pack) was effective, and found insufficient evidence on other types of reminder packaging such as multi-dose pill boxes.

- We found one RCT of prescriber education in a developing country, which showed that a 1-day intensive training session of general practitioners on hypertension improved medication adherence compared with usual care but these data are not generalisable to the range of people taking cardio-vascular medication so we cannot draw firm conclusions about this intervention.

(i) **Please visit http://clinicalevidence.bmj.com for full text and references**

| What are the effects of interventions to improve adherence to long-term medication for CVD in adults? | |
|---|---|
| **Likely To Be Beneficial** | • Prompting mechanisms<br>• Simplified dosing |
| **Unknown Effectiveness** | • Patient health education<br>• Prescriber education<br>• Reminder packaging |

**Search date April 2010**

**DEFINITION** **Definition of adherence:** Adherence to a medication regimen is generally defined as the extent to which people take medications as prescribed by their healthcare providers. Adherence, compliance, and concordance are often used interchangeably when studying health behaviour, but their meanings are in fact different, particularly in the context of RCTs examining interventions aimed at improving adherence. Adherence takes into account that people choose to take their medicines, have control over their use, and develop an agreement with healthcare professionals about their management. The main difference between the terms 'adherence' and 'compliance' is on a motivational level, with the latter suggesting that the patient is passively following the physician's orders, and that the treatment plan is not based on a therapeutic alliance or contract established between the patient and the physician. Unfortunately, the term 'concordance' has occasionally, and not always appropriately, replaced the terms 'compliance' or 'adherence'. 'Concordance' aims to describe an agreement between patient and healthcare professional about the whole process of medication-taking as part of a wider consultation, rather than describing the specific extent to which medication is taken. For the purposes of this review, 'adherence' will be defined as the extent to which people take medications as prescribed by their healthcare providers. The reporting of adherence varies, with some studies reporting adherence as a dichotomous outcome, and using an artificial cut-off point (e.g., 80% 'adherent'), whereas other studies compare study arms using continuous outcomes (e.g., a count of pills taken of 75% v 91%). **Measurement of adherence:** The ideal measurement of adherence should: be usable over a prolonged period; be unobtrusive; be non-invasive; be practicable and cheap; yield immediate results; and not be open to manipulation. Based on these stringent criteria, the objective measurement of adherence is difficult, and poses a challenge for researchers and clinicians. Measurement of adherence can be divided into 'direct' (which demonstrate drug ingestion) and 'indirect' (which do not demonstrate drug ingestion) methods. Direct methods include observing people taking medication, or the measurement of medicine, metabolites, or biological markers in the blood. Although objective and accurate, direct adherence measures are often impractical or too expensive for the RCT setting. A variety of indirect adherence measures are commonly employed in RCTs, and each one has strengths and weaknesses. These include self-reporting by patients, prescribing data, pill counting, measurement of physiological markers, and electronic monitoring. Patient self-reporting of adherence is simple, inexpensive, and probably the most practical and useful in the clinical setting. It is, however, subject to considerable bias, as the person may wish to please the investigator, be worried about admitting to not taking medication, or simply not accurately remember. Prescribing data, such as the rate of prescription refills or cessation of refills (discontinuation rate), are easy to obtain through pharmacies, but require a closed-pharmacy system to be accurate, and cannot be regarded as equivalent to ingestion of medication. However, this information affords a useful proxy, and may be easier to measure over long follow-up periods. Pill counts provide a direct measure of adherence. However, they may be manipulated by people if they are aware that the pills are being counted (e.g., pill dumping), and it does not necessarily mean that medication has been taken at the correct time. Measurement of physiological markers (e.g., measuring heart rate in patients taking beta-blockers) is easy to perform, but is greatly limited by its assumption of a cause-and-effect relationship, which is rarely applicable. Electronic monitoring methods have greatly

*(continued over)*

*(from previous page)*

advanced recently and allow recordings of the timing and frequency of drug ingestion, which make them the only method to provide data on drug-taking patterns. However, they are expensive, and there is no guarantee that opening of the medication container is followed by ingestion of the correct dose. It could also be argued that placing an electronic cap to measure compliance is an intervention in itself as people are aware that they are being monitored (Hawthorne effect). This effect may or may not persist in the longer term when people become used to the electronic cap. Although electronic monitoring is closest to a 'gold standard' in measuring adherence, it has so far been used mainly as a research tool owing to its relatively high cost.

**INCIDENCE/PREVALENCE** Not applicable for this review.

**AETIOLOGY/RISK FACTORS** The reasons for not adhering to prescribed cardiovascular medication are complex, and non-adherence may lead to various sequelae. For example, the prescribing clinician may alter or discontinue a regimen believing it not to be working when, in fact, it may have been taken only inconsistently or not at all. Failure to adhere to a prescribed regimen may increase adverse effects from the regimen, in that medication is taken incorrectly, and may fail to improve symptoms from the underlying condition for which it was prescribed. **Interventions to improve adherence:** Interventions to improve adherence can potentially be divided into a variety of different categories or groupings. In this review we have grouped RCTs under the categories of: prescriber education; prompting mechanisms; patient health education; simplified dosing; and reminder packaging (blister packs and pill boxes), and have explained what we have included under each category where necessary. However, interventions to improve adherence are complex by nature and will often be combined in a multi-factorial or 'complex intervention' approach. This approach is necessary as there are many factors that contribute to poor adherence, although this does make it difficult to tease out the individual components of many adherence interventions. Educational interventions can be directed at prescribers, patients, and their family members using written material, videotapes, or individual or group training. Prompting mechanisms are intended to stimulate medication-taking through mailed or telephoned reminders or through the use of electronic medication-reminder caps. Simplified dosing is intended to improve adherence through the reduction of dosing frequency (e.g., once-daily regimens *v* twice-daily regimens, or twice-daily regimens *v* 3-times-daily regimens). Reminder packaging falls into two distinct categories: those that are packaged in pill boxes (multi-compartment compliance aid, dose administration aid) or those that are pre-packaged into blister packs (calendar blister, unit dose, monitored dosage system).

**PROGNOSIS Patterns of medication-taking behaviour and adherence:** Patterns of medication-taking behaviour have been accurately described using electronic monitoring devices. Six general patterns of taking medication emerge among people treated for chronic illnesses who continue to take their medications: approximately one sixth come close to perfect adherence to a regimen; one sixth take nearly all doses, but with some timing irregularity; one sixth miss an occasional single day's dose and have some timing inconsistency; one sixth take drug holidays three to four times a year, with occasional omissions of doses; one sixth have a drug holiday monthly or more often, with frequent omissions of doses; and one sixth take few or no doses while giving the impression of good adherence. Most deviations in taking medication occur as omissions of doses (rather than additions) or delays in the timing of doses. Levels of adherence are poorly described, with those studies of higher quality limited by smaller numbers, and those studies of larger populations limited by crude measures of adherence. However, in terms of adherence to cardiovascular medication, most studies have examined adherence in relation to lipid-lowering drugs. It is evident that target cholesterol concentrations are only achieved in less than 50% of people receiving lipid-lowering drugs, and that only one in four people continue taking cholesterol-lowering drugs long term. In adherence studies of people without CHD taking lipid-lowering drugs for the purposes of primary prevention, discontinuation rates are higher compared with people taking lipid-lowering drugs for the purpose of secondary prevention, indicating a possible relationship between adherence and awareness of illness.

Robert S McKelvie

## KEY POINTS

- Heart failure occurs in 3% to 4% of adults aged over 65 years, usually as a consequence of coronary artery disease or hypertension, and causes breathlessness, effort intolerance, fluid retention, and increased mortality.

  The 5-year mortality in people with systolic heart failure ranges from 25% to 75%, often owing to sudden death following ventricular arrhythmia. Risks of cardiovascular events are increased in people with left ventricular systolic dysfunction (LVSD) or heart failure.

- Multidisciplinary interventions may reduce admissions to hospital and mortality in people with heart failure compared with usual care. Exercise may reduce admissions to hospital due to heart failure compared with usual care. However, long-term benefits of these interventions remain unclear.

- ACE inhibitors, angiotensin II receptor blockers, and beta-blockers reduce mortality and hospital admissions from heart failure compared with placebo, with greater absolute benefits seen in people with more severe heart failure.

  Combined treatment with angiotensin II receptor blockers and ACE inhibitors may lead to a greater reduction in hospital admission for heart failure compared with ACE inhibitor treatment alone.

- Aldosterone receptor antagonists (spironolactone, eplerenone, and canrenoate) may reduce all-cause mortality in people with heart failure, but increase the risk of hyperkalaemia.

- Digoxin slows the progression of heart failure compared with placebo, but may not reduce mortality.

- Hydralazine plus isosorbide dinitrate may improve survival and quality-of-life scores compared with placebo in people with chronic congestive heart failure.

- We don't know whether amiodarone, anticoagulants, or antiplatelets are effective at reducing mortality or hospital re-admission rates.

- CAUTION: Positive inotropic agents (other than digoxin), calcium channel blockers, and antiarrhythmic drugs (other than amiodarone and beta-blockers) may all increase mortality and should be used with caution, if at all, in people with systolic heart failure.

- Implantable cardiac defibrillators and cardiac resynchronisation therapy can reduce mortality in people with heart failure who are at high risk of ventricular arrhythmias. However, studies evaluating cardiac resynchronisation therapy were performed in centres with considerable experience, which may have overestimated the benefits.

- We don't know how coronary revascularisation and drug treatment compare for reducing mortality in people with heart failure and left ventricular dysfunction because all the trials assessing this comparison were conducted before ACE inhibitors, aspirin, beta-blockers, and statins were in routine use, thus limiting their applicability to current clinical practice.

- ACE inhibitors delay the onset of symptomatic heart failure, reduce cardiovascular events, and improve long-term survival in people with asymptomatic LVSD compared with placebo.

  Angiotensin II receptor blockers and ACE inhibitors seem equally effective at reducing all-cause mortality and cardiovascular mortality in people at high risk of heart failure.

  The combination of angiotensin II receptor blockers and ACE inhibitors seems no more effective than ACE inhibitors alone and causes more adverse effects.

- ACE inhibitors or angiotensin II receptor blockers seem no more effective at reducing mortality or rate of hospital admissions for cardiovascular events in people with diastolic heart failure compared with placebo.

   We don't know whether treatments other than angiotensin II receptor blockers are beneficial in reducing mortality in people with diastolic heart failure as we found only one trial.

 **Please visit http://clinicalevidence.bmj.com for full text and references**

## What are the effects of multidisciplinary interventions for heart failure?

| Beneficial | • Multidisciplinary interventions |
|---|---|

## What are the effects of exercise in people with heart failure?

| Likely To Be Beneficial | • Exercise |
|---|---|

## What are the effects of drug treatments for heart failure?

| Beneficial | • ACE inhibitors for treating heart failure |
|---|---|
| | • Angiotensin II receptor blockers for treating heart failure |
| | • Beta-blockers |
| | • Digoxin (improves morbidity in people already receiving diuretics and ACE inhibitors) |
| Likely To Be Beneficial | • Aldosterone receptor antagonists |
| | • Hydralazine plus isosorbide dinitrate |
| Unknown Effectiveness | • Amiodarone |
| | • Anticoagulation |
| | • Antiplatelet agents |
| Likely To Be Ineffective Or Harmful | • Antiarrhythmics other than amiodarone |
| | • Calcium channel blockers |
| | • Positive inotropes other than digoxin |

## What are the effects of devices for treatment of heart failure?

| Beneficial | • Implantable cardiac defibrillators in people at high risk of arrhythmia |
|---|---|
| Likely To Be Beneficial | • Cardiac resynchronisation therapy |

## What are the effects of coronary revascularisation for treatment of heart failure?

| Unknown Effectiveness | • Coronary revascularisation |
|---|---|

## What are the effects of drug treatments in people at high risk of heart failure?

| Beneficial | • ACE inhibitors in people with asymptomatic left ventricular dysfunction or other risk factors |
|---|---|
| Likely To Be Beneficial | • Angiotensin II receptor blockers in people at high risk of heart failure |

## What are the effects of treatments for diastolic heart failure?

| Unknown Effectiveness | • Treatments other than angiotensin II receptor blockers for diastolic heart failure |
|---|---|
| Unlikely To Be Beneficial | • ACE inhibitors or angiotensin II receptor blockers |

**Search date August 2010**

**DEFINITION** Heart failure occurs when abnormal cardiac function causes failure of the heart to pump blood at a rate sufficient for metabolic requirements under normal filling pressure. It is characterised clinically by breathlessness, effort intolerance, fluid retention, and poor survival. Fluid retention and the congestion related to this can often be relieved with diuretic therapy. However, diuretic therapy should generally not be used alone and, if required, should be combined with the pharmacological treatments outlined in this review. Heart failure can be caused by systolic or diastolic dysfunction, and is associated with neurohormonal changes. Left ventricular systolic dysfunction (LVSD) is defined as a left ventricular ejection fraction (LVEF) <0.40. It may be symptomatic or asymptomatic. Defining and diagnosing diastolic heart failure can be difficult. Proposed criteria include: (1) clinical evidence of heart failure; (2) normal or mildly abnormal left ventricular systolic function; (3) evidence of abnormal left ventricular relaxation, filling, diastolic distensibility, or diastolic stiffness; and (4) evidence of elevated N-terminal-probrain natriuretic peptide. However, assessment of some of these criteria is not standardised.

**INCIDENCE/PREVALENCE** Both incidence and prevalence of heart failure increase with age. Studies of heart failure in the US and UK found annual incidence in people 45 years or over to be between 29 and 32 cases/1000 people/year and, in those over 85 years of age, incidence was considerably higher, at 45 to 90 cases/1000 people/year. The study carried out in the US reported a decline in incidence of heart failure (all age groups) over a 10-year period, with incidence falling from 32.2 cases/1000 people/year in 1994 to 29.1 cases/1000 people/year in 2003. However, analysis of those aged 65 years or over indicated an increase in prevalence of heart failure (from 89.9 cases/1000 people in 1994 to 121 cases/1000 people in 2003). Prevalence of heart failure was higher in men (130 cases/1000 men) compared with women (115 cases/1000 women). In older people (65 years or over), incidence of heart failure after a myocardial infarction (MI) is on the rise, with one study finding an increase of 25.1% in in-hospital heart failure from 1994 through to 2000 (from 31.4% to 39.3%, P = 0.001). Furthermore, the study noted that 76% of people who survived MI had developed heart failure at 5 years' follow-up. Prevalence of asymptomatic LVSD is 3% in the general population, and the mean age of people with asymptomatic

*(continued over)*

*(from previous page)*

LVSD is lower than that of symptomatic individuals. Both heart failure and asymptomatic LVSD are more common in men. Prevalence of diastolic heart failure in the community is unknown. Prevalence of heart failure with preserved systolic function in people in hospital with clinical heart failure varies from 13% to 74%. Less than 15% of people with heart failure under 65 years of age have normal systolic function, whereas prevalence is about 40% in people over 65 years of age.

**AETIOLOGY/RISK FACTORS** Coronary artery disease is the most common cause of heart failure. Other common causes include hypertension and idiopathic dilated congestive cardiomyopathy. After adjustment for hypertension, the presence of left ventricular hypertrophy remains a risk factor for the development of heart failure. Other risk factors include cigarette smoking, hyperlipidaemia, and diabetes mellitus. The common causes of left ventricular diastolic dysfunction are coronary artery disease and systemic hypertension. Other causes are hypertrophic cardiomyopathy, restrictive or infiltrative cardiomyopathies, and valvular heart disease.

**PROGNOSIS** The prognosis of heart failure is poor, with 5-year mortality ranging from 26% to 75%. Up to 16% of people are re-admitted with heart failure within 6 months of first admission. In the US, heart failure is the leading cause of hospital admission among people over 65 years of age. In people with heart failure, a new MI increases the risk of death (RR 7.8, 95% CI 6.9 to 8.8). About one third of all deaths in people with heart failure are preceded by a major ischaemic event. Sudden death, mainly caused by ventricular arrhythmia, is responsible for 25% to 50% of all deaths, and is the most common cause of death in people with heart failure. Women with heart failure have a 15% to 20% lower risk of total and cardiovascular mortality compared with men with heart failure (risk after adjustment for demographic and social economic characteristics, comorbidities, cardiovascular treatments, and LVEF). The presence of asymptomatic LVSD increases an individual's risk of having a cardiovascular event. One large prevention trial found that the risk of heart failure, admission for heart failure, and death increased linearly as ejection fraction fell (for each 5% reduction in ejection fraction: RR for mortality 1.20, 95% CI 1.13 to 1.29; RR for hospital admission 1.28, 95% CI 1.18 to 1.38; RR for heart failure 1.20, 95% CI 1.13 to 1.26). The annual mortality for people with diastolic heart failure varies in observational studies (1–18%). Reasons for this variation include age, presence of coronary artery disease, and variation in the partition value used to define abnormal ventricular systolic function. The annual mortality for left ventricular diastolic dysfunction is lower than that found in people with systolic dysfunction.

Abel P Wakai

## KEY POINTS

- About one quarter of people who have a myocardial infarction (MI) in the USA will die from it, half of them within 1 hour of the onset of symptoms.

  Cardiogenic shock develops in over 5% of people who survive the first hour after an MI, with a mortality of 50% to 80% in the first 48 hours.

- Aspirin reduces mortality, reinfarction, and stroke at 1 month compared with placebo in people with an acute MI.

  Thrombolysis within 6 hours reduces mortality but increases the risk of stroke or major bleeding in people with acute MI, with different agents seeming to have similar efficacy.

  Adding low molecular weight heparin to thrombolytics may reduce the risk of further cardiovascular events, but the combination has not been shown to improve survival.

- Beta-blockers reduce reinfarction in people with acute MI, but have no effect on mortality in the short term, and increase cardiogenic shock.

- ACE inhibitors reduce mortality in people with acute MI compared with placebo.

  Nitrates reduce mortality and improve symptoms in people not receiving thrombolysis, but may not be beneficial in people after thrombolysis.

  Calcium channel blockers have not been shown to reduce mortality after an acute MI, and early treatment with nifedipine may increase mortality.

- Primary PTCA within 12 hours of onset of chest pain reduces the risk of death, reinfarction, and stroke compared with thrombolysis.

- In people with cardiogenic shock, invasive cardiac revascularisation within 48 hours of acute MI reduces mortality at 12 months compared with medical treatment alone, but people aged over 75 years may not benefit.

  We don't know whether thrombolysis, vasodilators, intra-aortic balloon counterpulsation, ventricular assistance devices and cardiac transplantation, or early cardiac surgery improve survival in people with cardiogenic shock.

  There is a consensus that positive inotropes and pulmonary artery catheterisation are beneficial, but we found no trials that confirmed this.

(i) **Please visit http://clinicalevidence.bmj.com for full text and references**

| Which treatments improve outcomes in people with myocardial infarction (ST-elevation)? | |
| --- | --- |
| Beneficial | • ACE inhibitors |
| | • Aspirin |
| | • Primary PTCA versus thrombolysis (performed in specialist centres) |
| | • Thrombolysis |
| Likely To Be Beneficial | • Adding low molecular weight heparin (enoxaparin) to thrombolytics (reduces reinfarction) |
| | • Nitrates (without thrombolysis) |
| Trade-off Between Benefits And Harms | • Beta-blockers |

| | |
|---|---|
| | • Glycoprotein IIb/IIIa inhibitors (in people having PTCA only) |
| Unlikely To Be Beneficial | • Adding unfractionated heparin to thrombolytics<br>• Nitrates (in addition to thrombolysis; for reducing mortality and reinfarction) |
| Likely To Be Ineffective Or Harmful | • Calcium channel blockers |

## Which treatments improve outcomes in people with cardiogenic shock after acute MI?

| | |
|---|---|
| Beneficial | • Early invasive cardiac revascularisation |
| Unknown Effectiveness | • Early cardiac surgery<br>• Intra-aortic balloon counterpulsation<br>• Positive inotropes<br>• Pulmonary artery catheterisation<br>• Thrombolysis<br>• Vasodilators<br>• Ventricular assistance devices and cardiac transplantation |

**Search date October 2009**

**DEFINITION Acute MI:** Acute MI is myocardial cell death caused by prolonged ischaemia due to sudden occlusion of a coronary artery. There are two types of acute MI: ST-segment elevation MI (STEMI; clinically appropriate symptoms with ST-segment elevation on ECG) and non-ST-segment elevation MI (NSTEMI; clinically appropriate symptoms with ST-segment depression or T-wave abnormalities on ECG). **Cardiogenic shock:** Defined clinically as a poor cardiac output plus evidence of tissue hypoxia that is not improved by correcting reduced intravascular volume. When a pulmonary artery catheter is used, cardiogenic shock may be defined as a cardiac index below 2.2 L/minute/m$^2$ despite an elevated pulmonary capillary wedge pressure (at least 15 mmHg).

**INCIDENCE/PREVALENCE Acute MI:** Acute MI is one of the most common causes of mortality worldwide. In 1990, ischaemic heart disease was the world's leading cause of death, accounting for about 6.3 million deaths. The age-standardised incidence varies among and within countries. Each year, about 900,000 people in the US experience acute MI, about 225,000 of whom die. About half of these people die within 1 hour of the onset of symptoms and before reaching a hospital. Event rates increase with age for both sexes and are higher in men than in women and in poorer than in richer people at all ages. The incidence of death from acute MI has fallen in many Western countries over the past 20 years. **Cardiogenic shock:** Cardiogenic shock occurs in about 7% of people admitted to hospital with acute MI. Of these, about half have established cardiogenic shock at the time of admission to hospital, and most of the others develop it during the first 24 to 48 hours after admission.

**AETIOLOGY/RISK FACTORS Acute MI:** Identified major risk factors for CVD include increasing age, male sex, raised low-density lipoprotein cholesterol, reduced high-density lipoprotein cholesterol, raised blood pressure, smoking, diabetes, family history of CVD, obesity, and sedentary lifestyle. For many of these risk factors, observational studies show a continuous gradient of increasing risk of CVD with increasing levels of the risk factor, with no obvious threshold level. The immediate mechanism of acute MI is rupture or erosion of an atheromatous plaque causing thrombosis and occlusion of coronary arteries and myocardial cell death. Factors that may convert a stable plaque into an unstable plaque (the 'active plaque') have yet to be fully elucidated. Shear stresses, inflammation, and autoimmunity have been proposed. The changing rates of CHD in different populations are only partly explained by changes in the standard risk factors for ischaemic heart disease (particularly a fall in blood pressure and smoking). **Cardiogenic shock:** Cardiogenic shock after acute MI usually follows a reduction in functional ventricular myocardium, and is caused by left ventricular infarction (79% of people) more often than by right ventricular infarction (3% of people). Cardiogenic shock after acute MI may also be caused by cardiac structural defects, such as mitral valve regurgitation due to papillary muscle dysfunction (7% of people), ventricular septal rupture (4% of people), or cardiac tamponade after free cardiac wall rupture (1% of people). Major risk factors for cardiogenic shock after acute MI are previous MI, diabetes mellitus, advanced age, hypotension, tachycardia or bradycardia, congestive heart failure with Killip class II–III, and low left ventricular ejection fraction (ejection fraction under 35%).

**PROGNOSIS Acute MI:** May lead to a host of mechanical and cardiac electrical complications, including death, ventricular dysfunction, congestive heart failure, fatal and non-fatal arrhythmias, valvular dysfunction, myocardial rupture, and cardiogenic shock. **Cardiogenic shock:** Mortality for people in hospital with cardiogenic shock after acute MI vary between 50% to 80%. Most deaths occur within 48 hours of the onset of shock. People surviving until discharge from hospital have a reasonable long-term prognosis (88% survival at 1 year).

Michael L Sarkees and Anthony A Bavry

## KEY POINTS

- Non ST-elevation acute coronary syndrome (NSTE-ACS, here defined as unstable angina and non ST-elevation MI) is characterised by episodes of chest pain at rest or with minimal exertion, which increase in frequency or severity, often with dynamic ECG changes.

- Aspirin reduces the risk of death, MI, and stroke compared with placebo in people with NSTE-ACS at doses up to 325 mg daily; higher doses of aspirin are no more effective, and increase the risk of bleeding complications.

   Adding clopidogrel to aspirin may reduce the combined outcome of mortality, stroke, or MI, but may increase the risk of bleeding.

- Intravenous glycoprotein IIb/IIIa platelet receptor inhibitors may reduce the combined end point of death and MI in NSTE-ACS, but increase the risk of bleeding.

- Unfractionated or low molecular weight heparin plus aspirin may reduce death or MI at 1 week, but longer-term benefits are unclear.

   Low molecular weight heparin may reduce MI compared with unfractionated heparin.

- Fondaparinux (a factor Xa inhibitor) seems to be as effective as low molecular weight heparin at reducing death or MI, and cause less major bleeding.

- Compared with unfractionated heparin, direct thrombin inhibitors (hirudin and bivalirudin) may result in similar frequency of mortality or MI and may reduce the risk of bleeding.

- Warfarin has not been shown to be beneficial and increases the risk of major bleeding.

- We don't know whether intravenous nitrates, beta-blockers, or calcium channel blockers reduce the risk of MI or death, although they may reduce the frequency and severity of chest pain.

- We found insufficient RCT evidence to assess statins in people with NSTE-ACS but observational data suggest that intensive lipid therapy is beneficial if initiated within 12 days of NSTE-ACS presentation and that statins improve clinical outcomes in the long term.

- CAUTION: Short-acting dihydropyridine calcium channel blockers may increase mortality in people with CHD.

- Early routine cardiac catheterisation and revascularisation may reduce death and non-fatal MI compared with conservative strategies (medical treatment with or without later cardiac catheterisation and revascularisation).

(i) **Please visit http://clinicalevidence.bmj.com for full text and references**

| **What are the effects of antiplatelet treatments in people with non ST-elevation acute coronary syndrome?** | |
| --- | --- |
| Beneficial | • Aspirin<br>• Clopidogrel |
| Trade-off Between Benefits And Harms | • Intravenous glycoprotein IIb/IIIa inhibitors |

| **What are the effects of antithrombin treatments in people with non ST-elevation acute coronary syndrome?** | |
| --- | --- |
| Likely To Be Beneficial | • Direct thrombin inhibitors |

| | |
|---|---|
| | • Fondaparinux (as effective as enoxaparin at reducing mortality and MI and associated with similar risk of major bleeding) |
| | • Low molecular weight heparin |
| | • Unfractionated heparin |
| **Unlikely To Be Beneficial** | • Warfarin |

### What are the effects of anti-ischaemic treatments in people with non ST-elevation acute coronary syndrome?

| **Unknown Effectiveness** | • Beta-blockers (for MI or death) |
|---|---|
| | • Calcium channel blockers (for MI or death) |
| | • Nitrates (for MI or death) |

### What are the effects of lipid-lowering treatments in people with non ST-elevation acute coronary syndrome?

| **Likely To Be Beneficial** | • Statins |
|---|---|

### What are the effects of invasive treatments in people with non ST-elevation acute coronary syndrome?

| **Likely To Be Beneficial** | • Routine early cardiac catheterisation and revascularisation |
|---|---|

**Search date December 2009**

---

**DEFINITION** Acute coronary syndrome (ACS) is a term that encompasses unstable angina, non ST-elevation MI (alternatively described as non Q-wave MI, often referred to as non-STEMI), and ST-elevation MI (alternatively described as Q-wave MI, often referred to as STEMI). Unstable angina and non-STEMI are overlapping entities and will be discussed together in this review as non ST-elevation ACS (NSTE-ACS). STEMI is discussed elsewhere (see review on acute myocardial infarction, p 27). Unstable angina and non-STEMI is a spectrum of disease that involves an imbalance of supply and demand of oxygen available to the myocardium. This balance is sometimes disrupted, causing symptoms such as new-onset exertional angina, pre-existing angina that is refractory to nitroglycerin, or angina at rest. The pathophysiology governing anginal symptoms is usually due to atherosclerotic plaque that nearly obstructs coronary vessels. The distinguishing feature between unstable angina and non-STEMI is the presence of elevated cardiac markers such as troponin, which imply myocardial damage. Patient history alone is insufficient to make a diagnosis of ACS. The clinical dilemma of distinguishing between cardiac and non-cardiac pain requires a combination of patient history, ECG, and biomarkers. Overlapping clinical entities in the ACS spectrum of disease allows for similar treatment strategies, and many trials include people with either unstable angina or non-STEMI. We have included systematic reviews and RCTs in a mixed population of people with unstable angina, non-STEMI, or both, which we refer to here as NSTE-ACS.

**INCIDENCE/PREVALENCE** In the USA, NSTE-ACS accounts for more than 1.4 million hospital admissions a year. In industrialised countries, the annual incidence of unstable angina is about 6/10,000 people in the general population.

*(continued over)*

---

*(from previous page)*

**AETIOLOGY/RISK FACTORS** Risk factors are the same as for other manifestations of ischaemic heart disease — older age, previous atheromatous CVD, diabetes mellitus, smoking, hypertension, hypercholesterolaemia, male sex, and a family history of premature ischaemic heart disease. NSTE-ACS can also occur in association with other disorders of the circulation, including valvular disease, arrhythmias, and cardiomyopathies.

**PROGNOSIS** Between 9% and 19% of people with NSTE-ACS die in the first 6 months after diagnosis, with about half of these deaths occurring within 30 days of diagnosis. Several risk factors may indicate poor prognosis and include severity of presentation (e.g., duration of pain, speed of progression, evidence of heart failure), medical history (e.g., previous ACS, acute MI, left ventricular dysfunction), other clinical parameters (e.g., age, diabetes), ECG changes (e.g., severity of ST-segment depression and deep T-wave inversion), biomarkers (e.g., presence of troponin concentration elevation), and change in clinical status (e.g., recurrent chest pain, silent ischaemia, haemodynamic instability). However, several key prognostic indicators associated with adverse outcomes may be used to aid clinical decision making. Variables including age 65 years or over, at least three risk factors for coronary artery disease, known significant coronary stenosis, degree of ST-segment deviation, recurrent anginal symptoms in 24 hours, use of aspirin in last 7 days, and elevated cardiac biomarkers can be used to generate a scoring system to predict high-risk patients who may experience true ischaemic cardiac events and death (TIMI [thrombolysis in MI] risk score). The more of these factors that are present, the greater the likelihood of adverse ischaemic events. This helps in stratifying patients according to risk, and in identifying high-risk patients.

Kevin Cassar

## KEY POINTS

- Up to 20% of adults aged over 55 years have detectable peripheral arterial disease of the legs, but this may cause symptoms of intermittent claudication in only a small proportion of affected people.

   The main risk factors are smoking and diabetes mellitus, but other risk factors for CVD are also associated with peripheral arterial disease.

   Overall mortality after the diagnosis of peripheral arterial disease is about 30% after 5 years and 70% after 15 years.

- Antiplatelet agents reduce major cardiovascular events, arterial occlusion, and revascularisation compared with placebo, with the overall balance of benefits and harms supporting treatment of people with peripheral arterial disease.

- Regular exercise increases maximal walking distance compared with no exercise.

   Stopping smoking and taking vitamin E may also increase walking distance when combined with exercise.

- Statins have been shown to reduce cardiovascular events in large trials including people with PVD, and they may increase walking distance and time to claudication compared with placebo.

   Cilostazol may improve walking distance compared with placebo.

   Cilostazol may reduce the incidence of cerebrovascular events compared with placebo but may be no more effective at reducing cardiac events.

   Cilostazol may be more effective than pentoxifylline at improving claudication distance.

   We don't know whether pentoxifylline improves symptoms compared with placebo, and it may be less effective than cilostazol.

- Percutaneous transluminal angioplasty (PTA) may improve walking distance compared with no intervention, but the benefit may not last beyond 6 months. Adding a stent to PTA may confer additional benefit over PTA alone.

- Bypass surgery may improve arterial patency at 12 months compared with PTA, but there seems to be no long-term benefit. Bypass surgery may be associated with improved survival in severe limb ischaemia in the longer term (3–7 years) compared with angioplasty.

- Prostaglandins may improve amputation-free survival in critical ischaemia at 6 months when surgical revascularisation is not an option.

   Prostaglandins may not be of benefit in intermittent claudication.

   Prostaglandins are associated with higher rates of adverse effects, including headache, vasodilation, diarrhoea, tachycardia, and vasodilation compared with placebo.

(i) **Please visit http://clinicalevidence.bmj.com for full text and references**

| What are the effects of treatments for people with chronic peripheral arterial disease? | |
|---|---|
| Beneficial | • Antiplatelet agents |
| | • Exercise |
| Likely To Be Beneficial | • Bypass surgery (compared with percutaneous transluminal angioplasty [PTA]) |
| | • Cilostazol |

| | |
|---|---|
| | • Percutaneous transluminal angioplasty (PTA; transient benefit only)<br>• Smoking cessation*<br>• Statins (HMG-CoA reductase inhibitors) |
| **Trade-off Between Benefits And Harms** | • Prostaglandins |
| **Unknown Effectiveness** | • Pentoxifylline |

**Search date May 2010**

*Based on observational evidence and consensus.

**DEFINITION** Peripheral arterial disease arises when there is significant narrowing of arteries distal to the arch of the aorta. Narrowing can arise from atheroma, arteritis, local thrombus formation, or embolisation from the heart, or more central arteries. This review includes treatment options for people with symptoms of reduced blood flow to the leg that are likely to arise from atheroma. These symptoms range from calf pain on exercise (intermittent claudication) to rest pain, skin ulceration, or symptoms of ischaemic necrosis (gangrene) in people with critical limb ischaemia.

**INCIDENCE/PREVALENCE** Peripheral arterial disease is more common in people aged over 50 years than in younger people, and is more common in men than in women. The prevalence of peripheral arterial disease of the legs (assessed by non-invasive tests) is about 14% to 17% in men and 11% to 21% in women over 55 years of age. The overall annual incidence of intermittent claudication is 4.1 to 12.9 per 1000 men and 3.3 to 8.2 per 1000 women.

**AETIOLOGY/RISK FACTORS** Factors associated with the development of peripheral arterial disease include age, sex, cigarette smoking, diabetes mellitus, hypertension, hyperlipidaemia, obesity, and physical inactivity. The strongest associations are with smoking (RR 2.0–4.0) and diabetes mellitus (RR 2.0–3.0).

**PROGNOSIS** The symptoms of intermittent claudication can resolve spontaneously, remain stable over many years, or progress rapidly to critical limb ischaemia. About 15% of people with intermittent claudication eventually develop critical limb ischaemia, which endangers the viability of the limb. The annual incidence of critical limb ischaemia in Denmark and Italy in 1990 was 0.25 to 0.45 per 1000 people. CHD is the major cause of death in people with peripheral arterial disease of the legs. Over 5 years, about 20% of people with intermittent claudication have a non-fatal cardiovascular event (MI or stroke). The mortality rate of people with peripheral arterial disease is two to three times higher than that of age- and sex-matched controls. Overall mortality after the diagnosis of peripheral arterial disease is about 30% after 5 years and 70% after 15 years.

Hermione Clare Price and Adam Nicholls

## KEY POINTS

- Diet is an important cause of many chronic diseases.

    Individual change in behaviour has the potential to decrease the burden of chronic disease, particularly cardiovascular disease (CVD).

- This review examines evidence solely from RCTs and systematic reviews of RCTs.

- To reduce confounding, this review has examined the effects of separate elements of dietary advice alone in improving cardiovascular outcomes in healthy people without existing CVD or elevated risk factors.

    We have excluded non-clinical outcomes such as behavioural change (e.g., change in the proportion of saturated fats in the diet, or change in the number of servings of vegetables per week).

- Intensive advice to reduce sodium intake alone may reduce blood pressure compared with no advice in healthy people without hypertension.

    Intensive advice seems to reduce sodium intake as measured by sodium excretion.

    However, it is unclear whether advice to reduce sodium intake reduces mortality or cardiovascular events as we found insufficient evidence.

    The intensive advice interventions used in some studies may not be practicable in routine clinical practice.

- We found insufficient evidence from RCTs on the effects of advice to reduce and/or modify fat intake alone on cardiovascular outcomes.

- Some RCTs have found that advice to increase fruit and vegetable intake alone may improve systolic blood pressure at 6 to 12 months compared with no advice; we found insufficient evidence from RCTs on the effects of advice to increase fruit and vegetable intake alone on CVD events or death. However, we also found no harm from advice to increase fruit and vegetables.

- We found insufficient evidence from RCTs on the effects of advice to increase fibre intake alone on risk factors for CVD, CVD events, or death.

- RCTs may only provide limited evidence on longer-term outcomes such as mortality or cardiovascular events due to the restricted numbers included in most trials and the length of follow-up needed to identify any differences between groups.

- Large observational studies may provide important evidence on these longer-term outcomes.

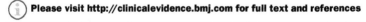 **Please visit http://clinicalevidence.bmj.com for full text and references**

| What are the effects of dietary advice in generally healthy adults without existing CVD or increased CVD risk factors to improve cardiovascular outcomes (mortality, cardiovascular events, and cardiovascular risk factors)? | |
|---|---|
| Likely To Be Beneficial | • Advice to reduce sodium intake alone (intensive advice may be more effective than no advice at marginally reducing blood pressure; no evidence of a reduction in mortality) |
| Unknown Effectiveness | • Advice to increase fibre intake alone |

- Advice to increase fruit and vegetable intake alone

- Advice to reduce and/or modify fat intake alone

**Search date March 2014**

**DEFINITION** Diet is important in the cause of many chronic diseases. Individual change in dietary behaviour has the potential to decrease the burden of chronic disease, particularly cardiovascular disease (CVD). This review focuses on the evidence that specific interventions to modify and improve diet may reduce CVD risk. Clinically overt ischaemic vascular disease includes acute myocardial infarction (MI), angina, stroke, and peripheral vascular disease. Many adults have no symptoms or obvious signs of vascular disease, even though they have atheroma and are at increased risk of ischaemic vascular events because of one or more risk factors. In this review, we have taken primary prevention to apply to people who have not had clinically overt CVD. **Population:** In this review, we have included studies in free living healthy adults (aged 18 years or older) with no evidence of clinically overt CVD, and with less than 10% of the population with existing cardiovascular risk factors (hypertension, dyslipidaemia, or diabetes), but have included studies in people with impaired glucose tolerance. We have included dietary advice given by healthcare professionals such as nurses, doctors, and dietitians, which may have been supplemented by paper-based self-help resources. We have excluded Web-based or electronic advice and public-health measures. Primary prevention of CVD in people with hypertension, p 41 or dyslipidaemia, p 38 is covered in separate *Clinical Evidence* reviews, as is secondary prevention of CVD in people with existing CVD (see reviews on Secondary prevention of ischaemic cardiac events, p 48 and Angina [chronic stable], p 12).

**INCIDENCE/PREVALENCE** CVD was responsible for 32% of UK deaths in men, and 21% of UK deaths in women in 2010. Half of these were from coronary heart disease (CHD), and one quarter were from stroke. CVD is also a major cause of death before 75 years of age, causing 28% of early deaths in men and 19% of deaths before 75 years of age in women. CHD deaths rose dramatically in the UK during the 20th century, peaked in the 1970s, and have fallen since then. Numbers of people living with CVD are not falling, and the British Heart Foundation estimates that there are about 1.5 million men and 1.2 million women who have or have had an MI or angina. Worldwide, it is estimated that 17 million people die of CVDs every year. More than 60% of the global burden of CHD is found in resource-poor countries. The US has a similar burden of heart disease to the UK; in 2002, 18% of deaths in the US were from heart disease, compared with 20% in the UK. The US lost 8 disability-adjusted life years (DALYs) per 1000 population to heart disease and a further 4 DALYs per 1000 population to stroke, and the UK lost 7 DALYs per 1000 population to heart disease and 4 DALYs per 1000 population to stroke. Afghanistan has the highest rate of DALYs lost to heart disease (36 DALYs per 1000 population), and France, Andorra, Monaco, Japan, Korea, Dominica, and Kiribati have the lowest (1–3 DALYs per 1000 population). Mongolia has the highest rate for stroke (25 DALYs per 1000 population lost) and Switzerland the lowest (2 DALYs per 1000 population lost).

**AETIOLOGY/RISK FACTORS** Deaths from CHD are not evenly distributed across the population. They are more common in men than in women; 67% more common in men from Scotland and the north of England than in the south of England; 58% more common in male manual workers; twice as common in female manual workers than in female non-manual workers; and about 50% higher in South Asian people living in the UK than in the average UK population. In the UK, there are 18% more CHD deaths in men, and 21% in women over the winter months compared with the rest of the year. CVD in the UK generally results from the slow build-up of atherosclerosis over many decades, with or without thrombosis. The long development time of atherosclerosis means that small changes in lifestyle may have profound effects on risk of CVD over decades. However, while there is strong evidence from epidemiological studies for the importance of lifestyle factors (such as smoking, physical activity, and diet) in the process of development of CVD, adjusting for confounding can be difficult, and the long timescales involved make proving the effectiveness of preventive interventions in trials difficult. In practice, risk factors — rather than disease outcomes —

are often the only practical outcomes for intervention studies in low-risk people. Such risk factors include blood pressure, body mass index (BMI), serum lipids, and development of diabetes.

**PROGNOSIS** Improvements in diet may lower the risk of cardiovascular disease by exerting favourable changes on CVD risk factors (obesity, high blood pressure, elevated serum lipids, diabetes).

George Fodor

## KEY POINTS

- Dyslipidaemia, defined as elevated total or low-density lipoprotein (LDL) cholesterol levels, or low levels of high-density lipoprotein (HDL) cholesterol, is an important risk factor for coronary heart disease (CHD) and stroke.

  The incidence of dyslipidaemia is high: in 2000, approximately 25% of adults in the US had total cholesterol greater than 6.2 mmol/L, or were taking lipid-lowering medication.

  There is a continuous, graded relationship between the total plasma cholesterol concentration and ischaemic heart disease (IHD) morbidity and mortality. IHD is the leading single cause of death in high-income countries and the second in low- and middle-income countries.

  Primary prevention in this context is defined as long-term management of people at increased risk, but with no clinically overt evidence of CVD, such as MI, angina, stroke, and peripheral vascular disease, and who have not undergone revascularisation.

- Statins have been shown to be highly effective, particularly in treating people at high risk of CHD (at least 1.5% annual risk of CHD). Although effective in people in all risk categories (low risk, medium risk), it seems that the magnitude of benefit is related to the individual's baseline risk of CHD events.

- In people at medium risk of CHD (0.6–1.4% annual risk of CHD), fibrates have been shown to reduce the rate of CHD, but not of overall mortality, compared with placebo.

  We don't know whether resins are beneficial in reducing non-fatal MI and CHD death in people at medium risk of CHD. We found no evidence relating to the effects of niacin (nicotinic acid) in people at medium risk of CHD.

  We found no evidence that examined the efficacy of niacin, fibrates, or resins in people either at low or high risk of CHD.

  We found no evidence on the effects of ezetimibe in people at low, medium, or high risk of CHD events.

- A reduced- or modified-fat diet may be beneficial in reducing cardiovascular events in people at risk of CHD events.

 **Please visit http://clinicalevidence.bmj.com for full text and references**

| What are the effects of pharmacological cholesterol-lowering interventions in people at low risk (<0.6% annual risk) of CHD? | |
|---|---|
| **Likely To Be Beneficial** | • Statins in people at low risk |
| **Unknown Effectiveness** | • Ezetimibe in people at low risk |
| | • Fibrates in people at low risk |
| | • Niacin in people at low risk |
| | • Resins in people at low risk |

## What are the effects of pharmacological cholesterol-lowering interventions in people at medium risk (0.6–1.4% annual risk) of CHD?

| | |
|---|---|
| Beneficial | • Fibrates in people at medium risk |
| Likely To Be Beneficial | • Statins in people at medium risk |
| Unknown Effectiveness | • Ezetimibe in people at medium risk<br>• Niacin in people at medium risk<br>• Resins in people at medium risk |

## What are the effects of pharmacological cholesterol-lowering interventions in people at high risk (1.5% or more annual risk) of CHD?

| | |
|---|---|
| Beneficial | • Statins in people at high risk |
| Unknown Effectiveness | • Ezetimibe in people at high risk<br>• Fibrates in people at high risk<br>• Niacin in people at high risk<br>• Resins in people at high risk |

## What are the effects of reduced- or modified-fat diet in people at low, medium, or high risk of CHD?

| | |
|---|---|
| Likely To Be Beneficial | • Reduced- or modified-fat diet in people at low, medium, or high risk |

**Search date December 2009**

**DEFINITION** Dyslipidaemia, defined as elevated total or low-density lipoprotein (LDL) cholesterol levels, or low levels of high-density lipoprotein (HDL) cholesterol, is an important risk factor for CHD and stroke (cerebrovascular disease). This review examines the evidence for treatment of dyslipidaemia for primary prevention of CHD. Primary prevention in this context is defined as long-term management of people at increased risk, but with no clinically overt evidence of CVD, such as acute MI, angina, stroke, and PVD, and who have not undergone revascularisation. Most adults at increased risk of CVD have no symptoms or obvious signs, but they may be identified by assessment of their risk factors (see aetiology/risk factors below). We have divided people with no known CVD into 3 groups: low risk (<0.6% annual CHD risk), medium risk (0.6–1.4% annual CHD risk), and high risk (1.5% or more annual CHD risk). Prevention of cerebrovascular events is discussed in detail elsewhere in *Clinical Evidence* (see review on stroke prevention, p 54). In the US, the preferred method to calculate CVD risk would be to use the Framingham risk equations, the best validated method from a US population.

**INCIDENCE/PREVALENCE** Dyslipidaemia, defined as elevated total or LDL cholesterol, or low HDL cholesterol, is common. Data from the US National Health and Nutrition Examination Survey (NHANES) survey conducted in 1999–2000 found that 25% of adults had total cholesterol >6.2 mmol/L, or were taking a lipid-lowering medication. According to the World Health Report 1999, ischaemic heart disease was the leading single cause of death in the world, the leading single cause of death in high-income countries, and second

*(continued over)*

*(from previous page)*

only to lower respiratory tract infections in low- and middle-income countries. In 1998, it was the leading cause of death, with nearly 7.4 million estimated deaths a year in member states of the WHO, and causing the eighth highest burden of disease in the low- and middle-income countries (30.7 million disability-adjusted life years).

**AETIOLOGY/RISK FACTORS** Major risk factors for ischaemic vascular disease include increased age, male sex, raised LDL cholesterol, reduced HDL cholesterol, raised blood pressure, smoking, diabetes, family history of CVD, obesity, and sedentary lifestyle. For many of these risk factors, including elevated LDL cholesterol, observational studies show a continuous gradient of increasing risk of CVD with increasing levels of the risk factor, with no obvious threshold level. Although, by definition, event rates are higher in high-risk people, most ischaemic vascular events that occur in the population are in people with intermediate levels of absolute risk, because there are many more of them than there are people at high risk.

**PROGNOSIS** One Scottish study found that about half of people who have an acute MI die within 28 days, and two-thirds of acute MI occur before the person reaches hospital. People with known CVD are at high risk for future ischaemic heart disease events (see review on secondary prevention of ischaemic cardiac events, p 48), as are people with diabetes. For people without known CVD, the absolute risk of ischaemic vascular events is generally lower, but varies widely. Estimates of absolute risk can be based on simple risk equations or tables. Such information may be helpful in making treatment decisions.

Joseph Cheriyan, Kevin M. O'Shaughnessy, and Morris J. Brown

## KEY POINTS

- Hypertension (persistent diastolic blood pressure of 90 mmHg or greater and systolic blood pressure 140 mmHg or greater) affects 20% of the world's adult population, and increases the risk of cardiovascular disease, end-stage renal disease, and retinopathy.

  Risk factors for hypertension include age, sex, race/ethnicity, genetic predisposition, diet, physical inactivity, obesity, and psychological and social characteristics.

- No antihypertensive drug has been found to be more effective than the others at reducing all-cause mortality, cardiovascular mortality, or MI.

  Apparent differences in outcomes with different antihypertensive drugs may be due to different levels of blood pressure reduction.

  Diuretics may be more effective than ACE inhibitors, calcium channel blockers, and alpha-blockers at reducing heart failure.

  Beta-blockers may be as effective as diuretics at reducing stroke, but calcium channel blockers may be even more effective than beta-blockers or diuretics.

  ACE inhibitors may be more effective than calcium channel blockers for prevention of coronary heart disease.

  Choice of second-line antihypertensive agent should be based on other co-morbidities and likely adverse effects as we don't know which is the most likely to reduce cardiovascular events.

- We found no RCT evidence assessing whether dietary modification reduces morbidity or mortality from hypertension compared with a normal diet.

  Advice to reduce dietary intake of salt to below 50 mmoles daily and fish oil supplementation may reduce systolic blood pressure by approximately 1 to 5 mmHg and reduce diastolic blood pressure by 1 to 3 mmHg in people with hypertension.

  We do not know whether supplementation with potassium, magnesium, or calcium is effective in reducing blood pressure.

  Potassium supplementation should not be used in people with kidney failure, or in people taking drugs that can increase potassium levels.

  Combinations of potassium plus calcium, potassium plus magnesium, and calcium plus magnesium may be no more effective than no supplementation in reducing blood pressure.

 **Please visit http://clinicalevidence.bmj.com for full text and references**

| What are the effects of different antihypertensive drugs for people with hypertension? | |
|---|---|
| Unknown Effectiveness | • Antihypertensive drugs (unclear which antihypertensive drug is more effective) |

| What are the effects of dietary modification in people with hypertension? | |
|---|---|
| Likely To Be Beneficial | • Fish oil supplementation<br>• Low-salt diet |
| Unknown Effectiveness | • Calcium supplementation<br>• Magnesium supplementation |

- Potassium supplementation

**Search date December 2007**

---

**DEFINITION** Hypertension, a clinically important elevation in blood pressure, is usually defined in adults as a diastolic blood pressure of 90 mmHg or greater, or a systolic blood pressure of 140 mm Hg or greater. The WHO defines grade 1 hypertension as surgery blood pressures ranging from 140 to 159 mmHg systolic or 99 to 99 mmHg diastolic, grade 2 hypertension as pressures of 160 to 179 mmHg systolic or 100 to 109 mmHg diastolic, and grade 3 hypertension as pressures 180 mmHg or greater systolic and 110 mmHg diastolic. Systematic reviews have consistently shown that treating essential hypertension (namely the elevation of systolic and diastolic blood pressures, in isolation or combination, with no secondary underlying cause) with antihypertensive drugs, reduces fatal and non-fatal stroke, cardiac events, and total mortality compared with placebo in those with severe hypertension or high cardiovascular risk owing to age or other co-morbid risk factors. This review therefore focuses on the effects of treating essential hypertension with different pharmacological agents and also examines the effect of treating hypertension with non-pharmacological agents compared with placebo. **Diagnosis:** It is usually recommended that clinicians diagnose hypertension only after obtaining at least two elevated blood pressure readings at each of at least two separate visits over a period of at least 1 week. This recommendation follows the pattern of blood pressure measurement in the RCTs of antihypertensive treatment, and represents a compromise between reliable detection of elevated blood pressure and clinical practicality.

**INCIDENCE/PREVALENCE** Coronary heart disease is a major cause of morbidity and mortality throughout the world. It is a leading cause of disability and rising healthcare costs, and it is responsible for 13% of deaths worldwide. Most of this burden of heart disease can be linked to several 'traditional' risk factors, including age, sex, increasing blood pressure, increasing cholesterol, smoking, diabetes, and left ventricular hypertrophy. Of these, hypertension is most common, affecting 20% of the world adult population. The relative risk of adverse events associated with hypertension is continuous and graded. The absolute risk of adverse outcomes from hypertension depends on the presence of other cardiovascular risk factors, including smoking, diabetes, and abnormal blood lipid levels, as well as the degree of blood pressure elevation. Even modest elevations in blood pressure in young adulthood are associated with increased risk of cardiovascular events in middle age.

**AETIOLOGY/RISK FACTORS** Identified risk factors for hypertension include age, sex, genetic predisposition, diet, physical inactivity, obesity, and psychological and social characteristics. In addition, certain ethnic groups, such as non-Hispanic black people, are at higher risk of hypertension.

**PROGNOSIS** People with hypertension have a two to four times increased risk of stroke, MI, heart failure, and peripheral vascular disease than those without hypertension. Additionally, they have an increased risk of end-stage renal disease, retinopathy, and aortic aneurysm. The absolute risk of adverse outcomes from hypertension depends on other cardiovascular risk factors and on the degree of blood pressure elevation (see incidence/prevalence section).

David Stensel

**KEY POINTS**

- Increasing physical activity has been associated with reduced risk of mortality and CVD.

    The proportion of people doing no physical activity in a week varies between countries, but can reach nearly 25% in Europe and the Americas.

- In this review, we have looked at healthy people older than 18 years who have no evidence of existing CVD.

- Counselling people to increase physical activity may increase people's activity levels over 3 to 12 months, particularly if accompanied by written materials and telephone follow-up.

- However, the nature of the counselling interventions varied widely among RCTs, and results varied by the exact counselling intervention employed.

    Counselling people to do higher-intensity exercise may increase activity levels more than counselling people to do lower-intensity exercise.

    People counselled to perform a higher-intensity exercise programme were also found to adhere to it better than those given a more moderate-intensity programme.

- We don't know whether counselling people to increase physical activity compared with no counselling reduces CVD, or whether counselling people to do higher-intensity exercise compared with counselling them to perform lower-intensity exercise reduces CVD, as we found insufficient evidence.

(i) **Please visit http://clinicalevidence.bmj.com for full text and references**

| **Does counselling people to increase physical activity lead to increased physical activity in healthy people without existing CVD?** | |
|---|---|
| Likely To Be Beneficial | • Counselling people to increase physical activity versus no advice |
| | • Counselling people to perform higher- versus lower-intensity exercise programmes |

| **What are the health benefits of increasing physical activity in relation to cardiovascular outcomes in healthy people without existing CVD?** | |
|---|---|
| Unknown Effectiveness | • Counselling people to increase physical activity versus no advice |
| | • Counselling people to perform higher- versus lower-intensity exercise programmes |

**Search date September 2008**

**DEFINITION** There are no internationally agreed definitions of physical activity. It has been defined as "any bodily movement produced by contraction of skeletal muscle that substantially increases energy expenditure". Activities include formal exercise programmes as well as walking, hiking, gardening, sport, and dance. The common element is that these activities result in substantial energy expenditure, although the intensity and duration can vary considerably. Exercise is considered a subcategory of physical activity and may be defined

*(continued over)*

*(from previous page)*

as planned, structured, and repetitive bodily movements performed to improve or maintain one or more components of physical fitness. Level of physical activity is important in the causes of many chronic diseases. Individual change in behaviour has the potential to decrease the burden of chronic disease, particularly CVD. This review focuses on the evidence that specific interventions may lead to increases in physical activity, and that these changes may prevent CVD. The relationship between physical activity and physical fitness is complex. There is consensus that increasing levels of both activity and fitness may reduce CVD. However, it is unclear whether activity or fitness is more important for health. There are many types of physical fitness — cardiovascular fitness, muscular strength, muscular endurance, flexibility, coordination, speed, and power. The most common descriptor of physical fitness is cardiovascular fitness, which is usually determined using either prediction or direct measurement of maximum oxygen uptake. It is important to note that moderate-intensity physical activity may not necessarily lead to an increase in physical fitness (as defined by maximum oxygen uptake), but studies suggest that there will still be benefits from such activity in terms of lowering disease risk. We have therefore, in this review, assessed outcomes of both increases in intensity, frequency, and duration of physical activity, and increases in physical fitness. Primary prevention in this context is the long-term management of people at increased risk of CVD, but with no evidence of overt ischaemic CVD. We have only included studies in adults aged over 18 years who are free-living and healthy, and excluded studies if more than 10% of participants had a reported diagnosis such as obesity, diabetes, or hypertension. Prevention of cerebrovascular events is discussed in detail elsewhere in *Clinical Evidence* (see review on stroke prevention, p 54). In this review, we have included interventions involving counselling or advising people to increase physical activity however given (e.g., from a physician, exercise therapist, whether administered directly, by telephone, or through media [e.g., videos, television programmes]), but have excluded interventions where counselling did not form the major part of the intervention, involved intensive monitoring, or where incentives to change behaviour were a major focus of the intervention.

**INCIDENCE/PREVALENCE** For general health benefits, it is recommended in government guidelines that adults achieve a minimum of 30 minutes a day of at least moderate-intensity aerobic (endurance) physical activity on 5 or more days of the week, or vigorous-intensity aerobic physical activity for a minimum of 20 minutes on 3 days each week. Combinations of moderate- and vigorous-intensity activity can be performed to meet this recommendation. The recommended levels of activity can be achieved either by doing all the daily activity in one session, or through several shorter bouts of 10 minutes or more. The activity can be lifestyle activity, or structured exercise or sport, or a combination of these. In addition, all adults are advised to perform activities that maintain or increase muscular strength and endurance a minimum of 2 days each week. Activity levels in England are low. About 60% of men and 70% of women report less than 30 minutes of moderate-intensity physical activity a day on at least 5 days per week. Levels of physical activity in the UK fall just below the EU average. In a survey of 15 EU countries, the percentage of adults reporting no moderate physical activity (e.g., "carrying light loads, cycling at a normal pace, doubles tennis") ranged from 8% to 53%. International comparisons of physical activity/inactivity are difficult, because there are no internationally agreed definitions. Some data are available from the WHO, however, and these indicate that the prevalence of complete inactivity ("doing no or very little physical activity at work, home, for transport or in discretionary [leisure] time") is: 11% to 12% in Africa; 20% to 23% in the Americas; 18% to 19% in the Eastern Mediterranean; 17% to 24% in Europe; 15% to 17% in South East Asia; and 16% to 17% in the Western Pacific region.

**AETIOLOGY/RISK FACTORS** Low levels of physical activity and lack of physical fitness are strong risk factors for CHD. Both confer an increased risk similar to that associated with smoking, hypertension, and high blood cholesterol. The most frequently cited reasons for inactivity in the general population are increased urbanisation and mechanisation. Most occupations now involve little physical activity, while television viewing and computer use compete with more active pursuits in leisure time. Greater use of cars along with an increase in the use of labour-saving devices has also reduced the need for physical activity. There has been a decline in walking and cycling as modes of transport — a 2001 survey in the UK reported that the number of miles travelled by each person a year on foot and on bicycle declined by about a quarter between 1975–1976 and 1999–2001. One proposed reason for the decline in walking is increased fears over personal safety. Barriers to physical activity include physical barriers such as an injury, emotional barriers such as embarrassment, motivational barriers such as a perceived lack of energy, time barriers, and availability barriers such as lack of facilities.

**PROGNOSIS** Increases in physical activity may lower the risk of CVD by exerting favourable changes on CVD risk factors (lowering blood pressure, triglyceride concentrations, and blood cholesterol concentrations, and raising high-density lipoprotein cholesterol concentrations) and by exerting direct effects on the heart (reduced heart rate, increased stroke volume) and on blood vessels (improved endothelial function which increases the ability of blood vessels to vasodilate and enhance blood supply when necessary). In the Harvard Alumni Health study (10,269 men aged 45–84 years), men who reported changing their lifestyles after baseline to include moderately vigorous activity (4 METs or more) had a 23% lower risk of all-cause mortality at follow-up after about 20 years compared with men who continued not to engage in such activity (RR 0.77, 95% CI 0.58 to 0.96; P <0.02). The main cause of death was CVD. In the Aerobics Centre Longitudinal Study (9777 men aged 20–82 years), men classified as unfit on their first examination but fit on their second (mean of 4.9 years between examinations) had a 52% lower risk of CVD mortality during follow-up (RR 0.48, 95% CI 0.31 to 0.74) than men classified as unfit on both examinations. Fitness was assessed by a treadmill test, and the 20% of people with lowest treadmill times were classed as "unfit". The Nurses' Health Study (72,488 female nurses aged 40–65 years) assessed physical activity using a questionnaire. It found that women reporting higher levels of energy expenditure had lower rates of coronary events over 6 years. Women who walked the equivalent of 3 hours or more a week at a brisk pace (5 km an hour or more [3 miles an hour]) had significantly lower rates of coronary events compared with women who walked infrequently (RR 0.65, 95% CI 0.47 to 0.91). Similar results were found in the Women's Health Initiative prospective cohort study of 73,743 postmenopausal women.

## 46 | Raynaud's phenomenon (primary)

Janet Pope

### KEY POINTS

- Raynaud's phenomenon is an episodic, reversible vasospasm of the peripheral arteries (usually digital). It causes pallor, followed by cyanosis and/or redness, often with pain and, at times, paraesthesia. On rare occasions, it can lead to ulceration of the fingers and toes (and, in some cases, of the ears or nose). This review focuses on primary (idiopathic) Raynaud's phenomenon occurring in the absence of an underlying disease.

    Prevalence, which varies by sex and country, is around 3% to 5% in most population studies, 80% to 90% of which is primary Raynaud's phenomenon; it is slightly higher in women than in men.

    Attacks may last from several minutes to a few hours, and long-term sufferers of initially idiopathic Raynaud's phenomenon can later go on to display features of underlying disorders such as systemic sclerosis.

- Nifedipine seems to reduce the frequency and severity of Raynaud's attacks, although it is associated with high rates of adverse effects such as tachycardia, headache, and flushing.

- We found no evidence of sufficient quality to judge the effectiveness of amlodipine or diltiazem in treating primary Raynaud's phenomenon.

- Nicardipine may successfully treat primary Raynaud's phenomenon, but we found no studies large enough to enable us to draw firm conclusions.

 **Please visit http://clinicalevidence.bmj.com for full text and references**

| What are the effects of drug treatments for primary Raynaud's phenomenon? | |
|---|---|
| Trade-off Between Benefits And Harms | • Nifedipine |
| Unknown Effectiveness | • Amlodipine<br>• Diltiazem<br>• Nicardipine |

**Search date August 2013**

**DEFINITION** Raynaud's phenomenon is an episodic, reversible vasospasm of the peripheral arteries (usually digital). It causes pallor, followed by cyanosis and/or erythema, which can cause pain and, at times, paraesthesia. On rare occasions, it can lead to ulceration of the fingers and toes (and, in some cases, of the ears or nose). Primary or idiopathic Raynaud's phenomenon (Raynaud's disease) occurs without an underlying disease. Secondary Raynaud's phenomenon (Raynaud's syndrome) occurs in association with an underlying disease — usually connective tissue disorders, such as systemic sclerosis (SSc; scleroderma), systemic lupus erythematosus, rheumatoid arthritis, Sjogren's syndrome, or polymyositis. This review excludes secondary Raynaud's phenomenon. **Diagnosis:** The diagnosis of Raynaud's phenomenon is by a history of clearly demarcated pallor of digit(s), followed by at least one other colour change (cyanosis, erythema), which is usually precipitated by cold. A good history, physical examination, and laboratory results can help rule out secondary Raynaud's phenomenon. Review of symptoms or signs for connective tissue disease should be done. Laboratory testing may include full blood count (FBC), ESR, and ANA with pattern if connective tissue diseases are suspected. Magnification of the nail-beds to observe abnormal capillaries is also important in order to rule out Raynaud's phenomenon associated with connective tissue diseases.

**INCIDENCE/PREVALENCE** The prevalence of primary Raynaud's phenomenon varies by sex, country, and workplace exposure to vibration. One large US cohort study (4182 people) found symptoms in 9.6% of women and 8.1% of men, of whom 81% had primary Raynaud's phenomenon. Smaller cohort studies in Spain have estimated the prevalence of Raynaud's phenomenon to be 3.7% to 4.0%, of which 90% is primary Raynaud's phenomenon. One study in Japan (332 men, 731 women) found symptoms of primary Raynaud's phenomenon in 3.4% of women and 3.0% of men. A study of 12,907 people in the UK reported that 4.6% of people had demarcated finger blanching with cold exposure.

**AETIOLOGY/RISK FACTORS** The cause of primary Raynaud's phenomenon is unknown. There is evidence for genetic predisposition, usually in those with early-onset Raynaud's phenomenon (aged <40 years). One prospective observational study (424 people with Raynaud's phenomenon) found that 73% of sufferers first developed symptoms before the age of 40 years. Women are at higher risk than men (OR 3.0, 95% CI 1.2 to 7.8, in one US case control study of 235 people). The other known risk factor is occupational exposure to vibration from tools (symptoms developed in about 8% with exposure *v* 2.7% with no exposure in two cohorts from Japan). People who are obese may be at lower risk. Exposure to cold or heightened emotion can worsen symptoms.

**PROGNOSIS** Attacks may last from several minutes to a few hours. One systematic review (search date 1996, 10 prospective observational studies, 639 people with primary Raynaud's phenomenon) found that 13% of long-term sufferers later manifested an underlying disorder, such as systemic sclerosis. In a large cohort of patients diagnosed with Raynaud's phenomenon without a known connective tissue disease who were seen in a specialist rheumatology clinic, 13% developed systemic sclerosis over time. Those who progressed to systemic sclerosis had both abnormal dilated capillaries at the nail folds and systemic-sclerosis-specific antibodies. Complications of Raynaud's phenomenon, such as digital ulceration or severe ischaemia, may indicate a secondary cause. In general, complications of primary Raynaud's phenomenon do not occur. However, some patients without a known underlying cause have complications. They may over time manifest as secondary Raynaud's phenomenon but are not yet able to be diagnosed. For instance, a small proportion (1% to 2%) of people with primary Raynaud's phenomenon may transition to secondary Raynaud's phenomenon annually. The latter are likely the patients who have complications of Raynaud's phenomenon.

Jane S Skinner and Angela Cooper

## KEY POINTS

- Coronary artery disease is the leading cause of mortality in resource-rich countries, and is becoming a major cause of morbidity and mortality in resource-poor countries.

  Secondary prevention in this context is long-term treatment to prevent recurrent cardiac morbidity and mortality in people who have had either a prior MI or acute coronary syndrome, or who are at high risk due to severe coronary artery stenoses or prior coronary surgical procedures.

- Of the antithrombotic treatments, there is good evidence that aspirin (especially combined with clopidogrel in people with acute coronary syndromes or MI), clopidogrel (more effective than aspirin), and anticoagulants all effectively reduce the risk of cardiovascular events.

  Oral anticoagulants substantially increase the risk of haemorrhage. These risks may outweigh the benefits when combined with antiplatelet treatments.

  Adding oral glycoprotein IIb/IIIa receptor inhibitors to aspirin seems to increase the risk of mortality compared with aspirin alone.

- Other drug treatments that reduce mortality include beta-blockers (after MI and in people with left ventricular dysfunction), ACE inhibitors (in people at high risk, after MI, or with left ventricular dysfunction), and amiodarone (in people with MI and high risk of death from cardiac arrhythmia).

  There is conflicting evidence on the effect of calcium channel blockers. Some types may be effective at reducing mortality in the absence of heart failure, whereas others may be harmful.

  Contrary to decades of large observational studies, multiple RCTs show no cardiac benefit from HRT in postmenopausal women.

- Lipid-lowering treatments effectively reduce the risk of cardiovascular mortality and non-fatal cardiovascular events in people with CHD.

- There is good evidence that statins reduce the risk of mortality and cardiac events in people at high risk, but the evidence is less clear for fibrates.

- The magnitude of cardiovascular risk reduction in people with coronary artery disease correlates directly with the magnitude of blood pressure reduction.

- Cardiac rehabilitation (including exercise) and smoking cessation reduce the risk of cardiac events in people with CHD.

  Antioxidant vitamins (such as vitamin E, beta-carotene, or vitamin C) have no effect on cardiovascular events in high-risk people, and in some cases may actually increase risk of cardiac mortality.

  We don't know whether changing diet alters the risk of cardiac episodes, although a Mediterranean diet may have some survival benefit over a Western diet.

  Advice to increase fish oil consumption or fish oil consumption may be beneficial in some population groups. However, evidence was weak.

  Some psychological interventions may be more effective than usual care at improving some cardiovascular outcomes. However, evidence was inconsistent.

- In selected people, such as those with more-extensive coronary disease and impaired left ventricular function, CABG may improve survival compared with an initial strategy of medical treatment. We don't know how PTCA compares with medical treatment.

- We found no consistent difference in mortality or recurrent MI between CABG and PTCA with or without stenting, because of varied results among subgroups and insufficient evidence on stenting when comparing the interventions. CABG may be more effective than PTCA with or without stenting at reducing some composite outcomes, particularly those including repeat revascularisation rates.

PTCA with stenting may be more effective than PTCA alone.

(i) **Please visit http://clinicalevidence.bmj.com for full text and references**

## What are the effects of antithrombotic treatment for secondary prevention of ischaemic cardiac events?

| Beneficial | • Aspirin |
| --- | --- |
| | • Combinations of antiplatelets (clopidogrel plus aspirin more effective than aspirin alone in people with ischaemia undergoing PCI) |
| Likely To Be Beneficial | • Thienopyridines |
| Trade-off Between Benefits And Harms | • Anticoagulants in addition to antiplatelet treatment |
| | • Anticoagulants in the absence of antiplatelet treatment |
| Likely To Be Ineffective Or Harmful | • Glycoprotein IIb/IIIa receptor inhibitors (oral) |

## What are the effects of other drug treatments for secondary prevention of ischaemic cardiac events?

| Beneficial | • ACE inhibitors (in people with and without left ventricular dysfunction) |
| --- | --- |
| | • Amiodarone |
| | • Angiotensin II receptor blockers |
| | • Beta-blockers |
| Unknown Effectiveness | • Angiotensin II receptor blockers plus ACE inhibitors |
| Likely To Be Ineffective Or Harmful | • Calcium channel blockers |
| | • Class I antiarrhythmic agents (quinidine, procainamide, disopyramide, encainide, flecainide, and moracizine) |
| | • HRT |

| What are the effects of cholesterol reduction for secondary prevention of ischaemic cardiac events? | |
|---|---|
| Beneficial | • Non-specific cholesterol reduction<br>• Statins |
| Likely To Be Beneficial | • Fibrates |

| What are the effects of blood pressure reduction for secondary prevention of ischaemic cardiac events? | |
|---|---|
| Beneficial | • Blood pressure reduction |

| What are the effects of non-drug treatments for secondary prevention of ischaemic cardiac events? | |
|---|---|
| Beneficial | • Cardiac rehabilitation (including exercise) |
| Likely To Be Beneficial | • Advice to eat a Mediterranean diet<br>• Advice to increase fish oil consumption (from oily fish or capsules)<br>• Psychological and stress management<br>• Smoking cessation |
| Unknown Effectiveness | • Advice to eat less fat<br>• Advice to eat more fibre |
| Unlikely To Be Beneficial | • Antioxidant vitamin combinations<br>• Multivitamins<br>• Vitamin C |
| Likely To Be Ineffective Or Harmful | • Beta-carotene<br>• Vitamin E |

| What are the effects of revascularisation procedures for secondary prevention of ischaemic cardiac events? | |
|---|---|
| Beneficial | • CABG versus medical treatment alone<br>• PTCA with intracoronary stents (more effective than PTCA alone) |
| Likely To Be Beneficial | • CABG (conventional, MIDCAB, or OPCAB) versus PTCA (with or without stenting) |
| Unknown Effectiveness | • PTCA with or without stenting versus medical treatment |

**Search date May 2010**

**DEFINITION** Secondary prevention in this context is the long-term treatment to prevent recurrent cardiac morbidity and mortality, and to improve quality of life in people who had either a prior MI or acute coronary syndrome, or who are at high risk of ischaemic cardiac events for other reasons, such as severe coronary artery stenoses or prior coronary surgical procedures.

**INCIDENCE/PREVALENCE** Coronary artery disease is the leading cause of mortality in resource-rich countries, and is becoming a major cause of morbidity and mortality in resource-poor countries. There are international, regional, and temporal differences in incidence, prevalence, and death rates. In the USA, the prevalence of coronary artery disease is over 6%, and the annual incidence is over 0.33%.

**AETIOLOGY/RISK FACTORS** Most ischaemic cardiac events are associated with atheromatous plaques, which may rupture or erode and lead to acute thrombosis and obstruction of coronary arteries. Many of these are preventable. Coronary artery disease is more likely in people who are older, male, or who have risk factors, such as smoking, hypertension, high cholesterol, and diabetes mellitus.

**PROGNOSIS** Within 1 year of having a first MI, 25% of men and 38% of women will die. Within 6 years of having a first MI, 18% of men and 35% of women will have another MI, 22% of men and 46% of women will have heart failure, and 7% of men and 6% of women will die suddenly.

| 52 | # Stroke management: decompressive hemicraniectomy |

Josef A. Alawneh, Peter A.J. Hutchinson, and Elizabeth Warburton

## KEY POINTS

- Stroke is characterised by rapidly developing clinical symptoms and signs of focal, and at times global, loss of cerebral function lasting over 24 hours or leading to death, with no apparent cause other than that of vascular origin.

  Ischaemic stroke accounts for about 80% of all acute strokes. It is caused by vascular insufficiency (such as cerebrovascular thromboembolism) rather than haemorrhage.

  Stroke is the third most common cause of death in most developing countries, with about 4.5 million people worldwide dying from stroke each year.

- Space-occupying ischaemic stroke, also termed malignant middle cerebral artery (MCA) infarct, is a rare complication of ischaemic infarct that occurs, usually in young people with very large infarcts.

  Oedema develops in the first few days, which leads to enlargement of the infarct, pressure on the surrounding brain tissue, and increased intracranial pressure.

  This may lead to death due to severe cerebral hypoperfusion and/or brain herniation.

- We found six RCTs, all of which included a highly selected and precisely defined population with malignant MCA infarct. Three trials included people aged up to 60 years, while the other three trials included people up to 80 years of age. All the trials excluded people with a pre-stroke modified Rankin Scale score (mRS) of 3 or less.

  People in the surgical arms were operated on within 30 hours (2 RCTs), 48 hours (2 RCTs), or 96 hours (2 RCTs) of the onset of symptoms.

- Most trials found consistent evidence that decompressive hemicraniectomy reduced mortality compared with standard/best medical treatment.

- Decompressive hemicraniectomy may be more effective than standard/best medical treatment at reducing the composite outcome of death or disability, defined as an mRS score above 4 (unable to walk and attend to own bodily needs without assistance).

  However, it may be no more effective than standard/best medical treatment at reducing the composite outcome of death or disability, defined as an mRS score of above 3 (requiring some help, but able to walk without assistance).

  One analysis found a higher proportion of survivors with an mRS score of 4 or 5 with decompressive hemicraniectomy compared with standard/best medical care, but differences between groups did not reach significance.

  It should be noted that the mRS scale is not specifically designed for this circumstance as there is no mention of the expected disability that is upper limb loss of function.

- These results may only apply to the highly selected populations of people with malignant MCA infarct included in the trials, and relative or absolute benefits may vary depending on individual circumstances.

- Acceptable or unacceptable levels of residual disability may vary among survivors or carers, as might their overall views and values. The mRS cut-off for favourable outcome is, therefore, very subjective. The patient's condition will change over the subsequent month of rehabilitation, and all those factors require addressing with the family and patient when deciding about the procedure.

- We don't know whether decompressive hemicraniectomy is more effective than standard/best medical treatment at improving quality of life scores. This would be the challenge for future research as the procedure unequivocally saves lives, and studies similar to the above will be considered unethical in the future.

Other requirements of future research include: a) whether an mRS score of 4 can be considered a favourable outcome following decompressive craniectomy or whether the dichotomy should be 3, or even 2, or less; b) whether the mRS is indeed the most appropriate measure of outcome and is a good enough proxy for future quality of life; c) if there is an absolute age limit for decompressive craniectomy following MCA stroke; and d) if a treatment window of 48 hours should apply to all patients with malignant MCA infarction, given that some deteriorate later.

 **Please visit http://clinicalevidence.bmj.com for full text and references**

## What are the effects of decompressive hemicraniectomy in acute ischaemic stroke on mortality and subsequent disability and quality of life?

| Likely To Be Beneficial | • Decompressive hemicraniectomy |
|---|---|

**Search date April 2014**

**DEFINITION** Stroke is characterised by rapidly developing clinical symptoms and signs of focal, and at times global, loss of cerebral function lasting more than 24 hours or leading to death, with no apparent cause other than that of vascular origin. Ischaemic stroke is stroke caused by vascular insufficiency (such as cerebrovascular thromboembolism) rather than by haemorrhage. Space-occupying ischaemic stroke, also termed malignant MCA infarct, is a rare complication of ischaemic infarct that occurs usually in young people with very large infarcts. Oedema develops in the first few days, and this leads to enlargement of the infarct, pressure on the surrounding brain tissue, and increased intracranial pressure. The process continues with severe swelling and death due to brain herniation and hypoperfusion that can occur up to 1 week after onset. Hemicraniectomy is a surgical procedure where a large flap of the skull is removed and the dura is opened; this gives space for the swollen brain to bulge and reduces the intracranial pressure.

**INCIDENCE/PREVALENCE** Stroke is the third most common cause of death in most developed countries. It is a worldwide problem; about 4.5 million people die from stroke each year. Stroke can occur at any age, but half of all strokes occur in people aged over 70 years. Malignant MCA infarction is not common but often seen in young people who have large infarcts; this has been estimated to be 2% to 8% of all hospitalised ischaemic strokes.

**AETIOLOGY/RISK FACTORS** About 80% of all acute strokes are ischaemic, usually resulting from thrombotic or embolic occlusion of a cerebral artery. Young people with large infarct from proximal MCA or internal carotid artery occlusion are at increased risk of developing malignant MCA syndrome with oedema.

**PROGNOSIS** About 10% of people with acute ischaemic stroke will die within 30 days of stroke onset. Of those who survive the acute event, about 50% will still experience some level of disability after 6 months. In malignant MCA infarction, conservative medical treatment is associated with around 80% mortality.

Gregory YH Lip and Lalit Kalra

### KEY POINTS

- Prevention in this context is the long-term management of people with previous stroke or TIA, and of people at high risk of stroke for other reasons, such as atrial fibrillation.

  Risk factors for stroke include: previous stroke or TIA; increasing age; hypertension; diabetes; cigarette smoking; and emboli associated with atrial fibrillation, artificial heart valves, or MI.

- Antiplatelet treatment effectively reduces the risk of stroke in people with previous stroke or TIA.

  High-dose aspirin (500–1500 mg/day) seems as equally effective as low-dose aspirin (75–150mg/day), although it may increase GI adverse effects.

  Adding dipyridamole to aspirin is beneficial in reducing composite vascular end points and stroke compared with aspirin alone. Risk reduction appears greater with extended-release compared with immediate-release dipyridamole.

  The net risk of recurrent stroke or major haemorrhagic event is similar with clopidogrel and aspirin plus dipyridamole.

- Treatments to reduce blood pressure are effective for reducing the risk of serious vascular events in people with previous stroke or TIA.

  Blood pressure reduction seems beneficial irrespective of the type of qualifying cerebrovascular event (ischaemic or haemorrhagic), or even whether people are hypertensive.

  Aggressive blood pressure lowering should not be considered in people with acute stenosis of the carotid or vertebral arteries, because of the risk of precipitating a stroke.

- Carotid endarterectomy effectively reduces the risk of stroke in people with greater than 50% carotid stenosis, is not effective in people with 30% to 49% carotid stenosis, and increases the risk of stroke in people with less than 30% stenosis. However, it does not seem beneficial in people with near occlusion.

- Cholesterol reduction using statins seems to reduce the risk of stroke irrespective of baseline cholesterol or coronary artery disease (CAD).

  Non-statin cholesterol reduction does not seem to reduce the risk of stroke.

- We found insufficient evidence to judge the efficacy of carotid percutaneous transluminal angioplasty, carotid percutaneous transluminal angioplasty plus stenting, or vertebral percutaneous transluminal angioplasty in people with recent carotid or vertebral TIA or stenosis.

- Vitamin B supplements (including folate) do not seem beneficial in reducing mortality or the risk of stroke.

- Anticoagulation does not seem beneficial in reducing stroke in people with previous ischaemic stroke and normal sinus rhythm, but does increase the risk of intra- and extracranial haemorrhage. This is especially true for patients with TIAs or minor ischaemic stroke as the qualifying event.

- In people with atrial fibrillation, oral anticoagulants reduce the risk of stroke in people with previous stroke or TIA, and in people with no previous stroke or TIA who are at high risk of stroke or TIA, but we don't know whether they are effective in people with no previous stroke or TIA who are at low risk of stroke or TIA.

  In people with atrial fibrillation, we don't know whether aspirin reduces the risk of stroke in people with previous stroke or TIA, or in people without previous stroke or TIA who are at low risk of stroke or TIA, but they may be unlikely to be effective in people without previous stroke or TIA who are at high risk of stroke or TIA.

 **Please visit http://clinicalevidence.bmj.com for full text and references**

## What are the effects of preventive non-surgical interventions in people with previous stroke or TIA?

| | |
|---|---|
| Beneficial | • Alternative antiplatelet regimens to aspirin (adding dipyridamole to aspirin shows benefit in reducing composite vascular end points and stroke compared with aspirin alone; no evidence that any other regimen alone has any major advantages over aspirin alone) |
| | • Antiplatelet treatment (better than no antiplatelet treatment) |
| | • Blood pressure reduction (better than placebo or no treatment) |
| | • Cholesterol reduction (better than placebo or no treatment) |
| Unknown Effectiveness | • Different treatments to reduce blood pressure (no evidence that any regimen is more or less effective than any other) |
| Unlikely To Be Beneficial | • High-dose versus low-dose aspirin (no additional benefit but may increase harms) |
| | • Vitamin B supplements (including folate) |
| Likely To Be Ineffective Or Harmful | • Anticoagulation in people in sinus rhythm (may be no more effective than placebo or no treatment) |

## What are the effects of preventive surgical interventions in people with previous stroke or TIA?

| | |
|---|---|
| Beneficial | • Carotid endarterectomy in people with moderately severe (50%–69%) symptomatic carotid artery stenosis |
| | • Carotid endarterectomy in people with severe (>70%) symptomatic carotid artery stenosis |
| Likely To Be Beneficial | • Carotid endarterectomy in people with asymptomatic but severe carotid artery stenosis |
| Unknown Effectiveness | • Carotid percutaneous transluminal angioplasty |
| | • Carotid percutaneous transluminal angioplasty plus stenting (no evidence that one intervention is more or less effective than the other) |
| | • Eversion carotid endarterectomy (no more effective than conventional carotid endarterectomy) |

| | • Vertebral percutaneous transluminal angioplasty |
|---|---|
| Unlikely To Be Beneficial | • Carotid endarterectomy in people with moderate (30%–49%) symptomatic carotid artery stenosis<br><br>• Carotid endarterectomy in people with symptomatic near occlusion of the carotid artery |
| Likely To Be Ineffective Or Harmful | • Carotid endarterectomy in people with symptomatic carotid artery stenosis (<30%) |

### What are the effects of preventive anticoagulant and antiplatelet treatments in people with atrial fibrillation and previous stroke or TIA?

| Beneficial | • Oral anticoagulants |
|---|---|
| Unknown Effectiveness | • Aspirin |

### What are the effects of preventive anticoagulant and antiplatelet treatment in people with atrial fibrillation and without previous stroke or TIA and with high risk of stroke or TIA?

| Beneficial | • Oral anticoagulant treatment (adjusted-dose warfarin may be more effective than placebo, low-intensity fixed-dose warfarin, and antiplatelet treatments) |
|---|---|
| Unlikely To Be Beneficial | • Antiplatelet treatment (aspirin in people with contraindications to anticoagulants) |

### What are the effects of preventive anticoagulant and antiplatelet treatment in people with atrial fibrillation and without previous stroke or TIA and with low to moderate risk of stroke or TIA?

| Unknown Effectiveness | • Antiplatelet treatment (aspirin in people with contraindications to anticoagulants)<br><br>• Oral anticoagulation |
|---|---|

**Search date February 2009**

**DEFINITION** Prevention in this context is the long-term management of people with previous stroke or transient ischaemic attack (TIA), and of people at high risk of stroke for other reasons such as atrial fibrillation. **Stroke:** Stroke is characterised by rapidly developing clinical symptoms and signs of focal, and at times global, loss of cerebral function lasting more than 24 hours or leading to death, with no apparent cause other than that of vascular origin. Ischaemic stroke is stroke caused by vascular insufficiency (such as cerebrovascular thromboembolism) rather than by haemorrhage. **TIA:** This is similar to a mild ischaemic stroke, except that symptoms last for less than 24 hours. For management of stroke in the acute phase, see review on stroke management, p 52.

**INCIDENCE/PREVALENCE**    See    incidence/prevalence    under    review    on    stroke management, p 52.

**AETIOLOGY/RISK FACTORS** See aetiology under review on stroke management, p 52. Risk factors for stroke include: previous stroke or TIA; increasing age; hypertension; diabetes; cigarette smoking; and emboli associated with atrial fibrillation, artificial heart valves, or MI. The relationship with cholesterol is less clear. Overviews of prospective studies of healthy middle-aged people found no association between total cholesterol and overall stroke risk. However, two of the overviews found that higher cholesterol increased the risk of ischaemic stroke, but reduced the risk of haemorrhagic stroke.

**PROGNOSIS** People with a history of stroke or TIA are at high risk of all vascular events, such as MI, but are at particular risk of subsequent stroke (about 10% in the first year and about 5% each year thereafter. This risk of stroke after a TIA is greatest in the first 2 weeks, especially in people who are older, have diabetes or hypertension, and have unilateral weakness that lasts for more than 1 hour. People with intermittent atrial fibrillation treated with aspirin should be considered at similar risk of stroke compared with people with sustained atrial fibrillation treated with aspirin (rate of ischaemic stroke/year: 3.2% with intermittent v 3.3% with sustained).

| 58 | **Thromboembolism** |
|---|---|

Richard J McManus, David A Fitzmaurice, Ellen Murray, and Clare Taylor

## KEY POINTS

- Deep venous thrombosis (DVT) or pulmonary embolism may occur in almost 2 in 1000 people each year, with up to 25% of those having a recurrence.

    About 5% to 15% of people with untreated DVT may die from pulmonary embolism.

    The risk of recurrence of thromboembolism falls over time, but the risk of bleeding from anticoagulation remains constant.

- Oral anticoagulants are considered effective in people with proximal DVT compared with no treatment, although we found few trials.

    In people with proximal DVT or pulmonary embolism, long-term anticoagulation reduces the risk of recurrence, but high-intensity treatment has shown no benefit. Both approaches increase the risk of major bleeding.

    Low molecular weight heparin (LMWH) is more effective than unfractionated heparin, and may be as effective as oral anticoagulants, although all are associated with some adverse effects.

    We don't know how effective tapering off of oral anticoagulant agents is compared with stopping abruptly.

    We don't know whether once-daily LMWH is as effective as twice-daily administration at preventing recurrence.

    Home treatment may be more effective than hospital-based treatment at preventing recurrence, and equally effective in reducing mortality.

    Vena cava filters reduce the short-term rate of pulmonary embolism, but they may increase the long-term risk of recurrent DVT.

    Elastic compression stockings reduce the incidence of post-thrombotic syndrome after a DVT compared with placebo or no treatment.

- In people with isolated calf DVT, anticoagulation with warfarin may reduce the risk of proximal extension, although prolonged treatment seems no more beneficial than short-term treatment.

- Anticoagulation may reduce mortality compared with no anticoagulation in people with a pulmonary embolus, but it increases the risk of bleeding. We found few studies that evaluated treatments for pulmonary embolism.

    LMWH may be as effective and safe as unfractionated heparin.

    Thrombolysis seems as effective as heparin in treating people with major pulmonary embolism, but it is also associated with adverse effects.

    The use of computerised decision support may increase the time spent adequately anticoagulated, and reduce thromboembolic events or major haemorrhage, compared with manual dosage calculation.

(i) **Please visit http://clinicalevidence.bmj.com for full text and references**

| What are the effects of treatments for proximal DVT? | |
|---|---|
| **Beneficial** | • Compression stockings for proximal DVT |
| | • Low molecular weight heparin for proximal DVT (reduced mortality, recurrence, and risk of major haemorrhage compared with unfractionated heparin) |
| **Likely To Be Beneficial** | • Home treatment with short-term low molecular weight heparin for proximal DVT |

| | |
|---|---|
| | • Oral anticoagulants for proximal DVT* |
| **Trade-off Between Benefits And Harms** | • Long-term low molecular weight heparin versus long-term oral anticoagulation for proximal DVT (both showed similar levels of benefits but with important adverse effects)<br>• Long-term oral anticoagulation versus short-term oral anticoagulation for proximal DVT<br>• Vena cava filters for proximal DVT (reduce short-term rate of pulmonary embolism, but may increase the long-term risk of recurrent DVT) |
| **Unknown Effectiveness** | • Abrupt discontinuation of oral anticoagulation for proximal DVT<br>• Once-daily versus twice-daily low molecular weight heparin for proximal DVT |
| **Unlikely To Be Beneficial** | • High-intensity oral anticoagulation for proximal DVT |

### What are the effects of treatments for isolated calf DVT?

| | |
|---|---|
| **Likely To Be Beneficial** | • Warfarin for calf DVT (reduced rate of proximal extension compared with no further treatment in people who had received initial heparin and wore compression stockings) |
| **Unlikely To Be Beneficial** | • Prolonged duration of anticoagulation for calf DVT |

### What are the effects of treatments for pulmonary embolism?

| | |
|---|---|
| **Likely To Be Beneficial** | • Anticoagulants (warfarin and heparin) for pulmonary embolism*<br>• Thrombolysis for pulmonary embolism |
| **Trade-off Between Benefits And Harms** | • Prolonged duration of anticoagulation for pulmonary embolism |
| **Unknown Effectiveness** | • Low molecular weight heparin for pulmonary embolism (no clear evidence of a difference in mortality or new episodes of thromboembolism or a difference in risk of major haemorrhage compared with unfractionated heparin) |
| **Unlikely To Be Beneficial** | • High-intensity anticoagulation (based on extrapolated data from people with proximal DVT) |

### What are the effects of interventions on oral anticoagulation management in people with thromboembolism?

| | |
|---|---|
| **Unknown Effectiveness** | • Computerised decision support in oral anticoagulation for thromboembolism (increased time spent in target international normalised range) |

| | • Self-testing and self-management of oral anticoagulation for thromboembolism |
|---|---|

**Search date June 2010**

*Clinical consensus based on observational data.

**DEFINITION** Venous thromboembolism is any thromboembolic event occurring within the venous system, including deep venous thrombosis (DVT) and pulmonary embolism. **DVT** is a radiologically confirmed partial or total thrombotic occlusion of the deep venous system of the legs sufficient to produce symptoms of pain or swelling. **Proximal DVT** affects the veins above the knee (popliteal, superficial femoral, common femoral, and iliac veins). **Isolated calf DVT** is confined to the deep veins of the calf and does not affect the veins above the knee. **Pulmonary embolism** is radiologically confirmed partial or total thromboembolic occlusion of pulmonary arteries, sufficient to cause symptoms of breathlessness, chest pain, or both. **Post-thrombotic syndrome** is oedema, ulceration, and impaired viability of the subcutaneous tissues of the leg occurring after DVT. **Recurrence** refers to symptomatic deterioration due to a further (radiologically confirmed) thrombosis, after a previously confirmed thromboembolic event, where there had been an initial partial or total symptomatic improvement. **Extension** refers to a radiologically confirmed, new, constant, symptomatic intraluminal filling defect extending from an existing thrombosis. **Self-testing** is where the patient is responsible for testing their international normalised ratio (INR) at home using capillary sampling and a point-of-care (POC) device. Dosing of warfarin and frequency of testing is advised by a health professional clinically responsible for their management. **Self-management** is where the patient is responsible for testing their INR at home using capillary sampling and a POC device. Dosing of warfarin and frequency of testing is also managed by the patient with support from the health professional clinically responsible according to an agreed contract.

**INCIDENCE/PREVALENCE** We found no reliable study of the incidence or prevalence of DVT or pulmonary embolism in the UK. A prospective Scandinavian study found an annual incidence of 1.6 to 1.8 per 1000 people in the general population. A more recently published retrospective study from Norway found the incidence of DVT between 1995 and 2001 to be 0.93 per 1000 person-years (95% CI 0.85 per 1000 person-years to 1.02 per 1000 person-years), and of pulmonary embolism to be 0.50 per 1000 person-years (95% CI 0.44 per 1000 person-years to 0.56 per 1000 person-years). A further Australian study found a standardised annual incidence per 1000 residents of 0.57 (95% CI 0.47 to 0.67) for all venous thromboembolism, 0.35 (95% CI 0.26 to 0.44) for DVT, and 0.21 (95% CI 0.14 to 0.28) for pulmonary embolism. Ethnic origin may affect incidence, with one study reporting increased incidence in African-Americans. One postmortem study estimated that 600,000 people develop pulmonary embolism each year in the USA, of whom 60,000 die as a result.

**AETIOLOGY/RISK FACTORS** Risk factors for DVT include immobility, surgery (particularly orthopaedic), malignancy, pregnancy, older age, and inherited or acquired prothrombotic clotting disorders. The oral contraceptive pill is associated with increased risk of death from venous thromboembolism (absolute risk increase [ARI] with any combined oral contraception: 1–3 deaths/million women/year). The principal cause of pulmonary embolism is a DVT.

**PROGNOSIS** The annual recurrence rate of symptomatic calf DVT in people without recent surgery is over 25%. The rate of fatal recurrent venous thromboembolism after anticoagulation has been estimated at 0.3 per 100 patient-years. Proximal extension develops in 40% to 50% of people with symptomatic calf DVT. Proximal DVT may cause fatal or non-fatal pulmonary embolism, recurrent venous thrombosis, and post-thrombotic syndrome. One case series (462 people) published in 1946 found 5.8% mortality from pulmonary emboli in people in a maternity hospital with untreated DVT. More recent cohorts of treated people have reported mortality of 4.4% at 15 days and 10% at 30 days. One non-systematic review of observational studies found that, in people after recent surgery who have an asymptomatic deep calf vein thrombosis, the rate of fatal pulmonary embolism was 13% to 15%. The incidence of other complications without treatment is not known. The risk of recurrent venous thrombosis and complications is increased by thrombotic risk factors and is more common in men.

Paul V Tisi

## KEY POINTS

- Varicose veins are considered to be enlarged tortuous superficial veins of the leg.

    Varicose veins are caused by poorly functioning valves in the veins, and decreased elasticity of the vein wall, allowing pooling of blood within the veins, and their subsequent enlargement.

    Varicose veins affect up to 40% of adults and are more common in obese people, and in women who have had more than two pregnancies.

- Compression stockings are often used as first-line treatment for varicose veins, but we don't know whether they reduce symptoms compared with no treatment.

- Injection sclerotherapy may be more effective than compression stockings, but less effective than surgery, at improving symptoms and cosmetic appearance.

    We don't know which sclerotherapy agent is the best to use.

- Surgery (saphenofemoral ligation, stripping of the great saphenous vein, or avulsion) is likely to be beneficial in reducing recurrence, and improving cosmetic appearance, compared with sclerotherapy alone.

    We don't know whether stripping the great saphenous vein after saphenofemoral ligation improves outcomes compared with avulsion alone after ligation, or what the best method is for vein stripping.

    We found insufficient evidence on the effects of powered phlebectomy, radiofrequency ablation, endovenous laser, or self-help.

    However, endovenous procedures (radiofrequency ablation and endovenous laser) are increasingly used in mainstream clinical practice, and further evidence comparing them to other active treatments is emerging.

(i) **Please visit http://clinicalevidence.bmj.com for full text and references**

| What are the effects of treatments in adults with varicose veins? | |
|---|---|
| Likely To Be Beneficial | • Sclerotherapy (injection, foam: better than conservative treatment or compression stockings, less effective than surgery)<br><br>• Surgery (avulsion)*<br><br>• Surgery (stripping)* |
| Unknown Effectiveness | • Compression stockings<br><br>• Endovenous laser<br><br>• Radiofrequency ablation<br><br>• Self-help (exercise, diet, elevation of legs, avoidance of tight clothing, advice)<br><br>• Surgery (powered phlebectomy) |

**Search date January 2010**

*Categorisation based on consensus.

**DEFINITION** Although we found no consistent definition of varicose veins, it is commonly taken to mean enlarged tortuous subcutaneous veins. Any vein may become varicose, but the term "varicose veins" conventionally applies to the superficial veins of the leg, which may appear green, dark blue, or purple in colour. The condition is caused by poorly functioning (incompetent) valves within the veins and decreased elasticity of the vein walls, which allow deoxygenated blood to be pumped back to the heart, and to flow backward and pool in the superficial veins, causing them to enlarge and become varicose. This often occurs in the saphenofemoral and saphenopopliteal junctions, and in the perforating veins that connect the deep and superficial venous systems along the length of the leg. The presence or absence of reflux caused by venous incompetence can be determined by clinical examination, handheld Doppler, or duplex ultrasound. Symptoms of varicose veins include pain, itching, limb heaviness, cramps, and distress about cosmetic appearance, although most lower limb symptoms may have a non-venous cause. This review focuses on uncomplicated, symptomatic varicose veins. We have excluded treatments for chronic venous ulceration and other complications. We have also excluded studies that solely examine treatments for small, dilated veins in the skin of the leg, known as thread veins, spider veins, or superficial telangiectasia.

**INCIDENCE/PREVALENCE** One large US cohort study found the biannual incidence of varicose veins was 3% in women and 2% in men. The prevalence of varicose veins in Western populations was estimated in one study to be about 25% to 30% in women and 10% to 20% in men. However, a Scottish cohort study has found a higher prevalence of varices of the saphenous trunks and their main branches in men than in women (40% men v 32% women). Other epidemiological studies have shown prevalence rates ranging from 1% to 40% in men, and 1% to 73% in women.

**AETIOLOGY/RISK FACTORS** One cohort study found that parity with 3 or more births was an independent risk factor for development of varicose veins. A further large case-control study found that women with two or more pregnancies were at increased risk of varicose veins, compared with women with one or no pregnancies (RR about 1.2–1.3 after adjustment for age, height, and weight). It found that obesity was also a risk factor, although only in women (RR about 1.3). One narrative systematic review found insufficient evidence on the effects of other suggested risk factors, including genetic predisposition, prolonged sitting or standing, tight undergarments, low fibre diet, constipation, deep vein thrombosis, and smoking. However, a large Danish population study found that prolonged standing or walking at work was an independent predictor of the need for varicose vein treatment.

**PROGNOSIS** We found no reliable data on prognosis, or on the frequency of complications, which include chronic inflammation of affected veins (phlebitis), venous ulceration, and bleeding rupture of varices.

Eddy S Lang and Kim Browning

## KEY POINTS

- Pulseless ventricular tachycardia and ventricular fibrillation are the main causes of sudden cardiac death, but other ventricular tachyarrhythmias can occur without haemodynamic compromise.

  Ventricular arrhythmias occur mainly as a result of myocardial ischaemia or cardiomyopathies, so risk factors are those of CVD.

- Cardiac arrest associated with ventricular tachyarrhythmias is managed with cardiopulmonary resuscitation and electrical defibrillation, where available.

  Adrenaline is given once intravenous access is obtained or endotracheal intubation has been performed.

  Delivering electrical shocks to the heart (defibrillation) in an effort to terminate the fatal arrhythmias of ventricular tachycardia, and ventricular fibrillation in an effort to restore sinus, together form a mainstay of treatment in cardiac arrest. Biphasic shock is more effective than monophasic shock in restoring people to organised rhythm and spontaneous circulation but it is unclear how different waveforms compare for reducing mortality and increasing neurological recovery.

- Amiodarone may increase the likelihood of arriving alive at hospital in people with ventricular tachyarrhythmia that has developed outside hospital, compared with placebo or with lidocaine, but has not been shown to increase longer-term survival.

  Amiodarone is associated with hypotension and bradycardia.

- We don't know whether lidocaine or procainamide improve survival in people with ventricular tachyarrhythmias in out-of-hospital settings, as we found few studies.

  Procainamide is given by slow infusion, which may limit its usefulness to people with recurrent ventricular tachyarrhythmias.

- We don't know whether bretylium improves survival compared with placebo or lidocaine, and it may cause hypotension and bradycardia. It is no longer recommended for use in ventricular fibrillation or pulseless ventricular tachycardia.

- Controlled induction of moderate hypothermia after cardiac arrest has been shown to improve both survival and neurological outcomes in a population that typically carries a very poor prognosis.

 **Please visit http://clinicalevidence.bmj.com for full text and references**

| What are the effects of electrical therapies for out-of-hospital cardiac arrest associated with ventricular tachycardia or ventricular fibrillation? | |
|---|---|
| Likely To Be Beneficial | • Defibrillation (biphasic more effective than monophasic shock) |

| What are the effects of antiarrhythmic drug treatments for use in out-of-hospital cardiac arrest associated with shock-resistant ventricular tachycardia or ventricular fibrillation? | |
|---|---|
| Unknown Effectiveness | • Amiodarone |
| | • Lidocaine |

| | • Procainamide |
| **Unlikely To Be Beneficial** | • Bretylium |

## What are the effects of treatments for comatose survivors of out-of-hospital cardiac arrest associated with ventricular tachycardia or ventricular fibrillation?

| **Likely To Be Beneficial** | • Therapeutic hypothermia with or without antiarrhythmics |

**Search date February 2010**

---

**DEFINITION** Ventricular tachyarrhythmias are defined as abnormal patterns of electrical activity originating within ventricular tissue. The most commonly encountered ventricular tachyarrhythmias of greatest clinical importance to clinicians, and those that will be the focus of this review, are ventricular tachycardia and ventricular fibrillation. **Ventricular tachycardia** is further classified as monomorphic when occurring at a consistent rate and amplitude, and polymorphic when waveforms are more variable and chaotic. **Torsades de pointes** is a specific kind of polymorphic ventricular tachycardia associated with a prolonged QT interval and a characteristic twisting pattern to the wave signal. It is often associated with drug toxicity and electrolyte disturbances, and is commonly treated with intravenous magnesium. Torsades de pointes will not be specifically covered in this review. **Pulseless ventricular tachycardia** results in similar clinical manifestations, but is diagnosed by a QRS width complex of greater than 120 milliseconds and electrical rhythm of 150 to 200 beats a minute. Waveforms in ventricular fibrillation are characterised by an irregular rate, usually exceeding 300 beats a minute as well as amplitudes generally exceeding 0.2 mV. Ventricular fibrillation usually fades to asystole (flat line) within 15 minutes. Ventricular fibrillation and ventricular tachycardia associated with cardiac arrest and sudden cardiac death (SCD) are abrupt pulseless arrhythmias. **Non-pulseless (stable) ventricular tachycardia** has the same electrical characteristics as ventricular tachycardia, but without haemodynamic compromise. The treatment of stable ventricular tachycardia is not covered in this review. **Ventricular fibrillation** is characterised by irregular and chaotic electrical activity and ventricular contraction in which the heart immediately loses its ability to function as a pump. Pulseless ventricular tachycardia and ventricular fibrillation are the primary causes of SCD. **Population:** In this review we focus on drug treatments and defibrillation, given generally by paramedics, for ventricular tachycardia and ventricular fibrillation associated with cardiac arrest in an out-of-hospital setting.

**INCIDENCE/PREVALENCE** The annual incidence of SCD is believed to approach 2/1000 population, but can vary depending on the prevalence of CVD in the population. It is estimated that 400,000 to 450,000 SCDs are recorded annually in the US, representing 60% of all cardiovascular mortality in that country. Data from Holter monitor studies suggest that about 85% of SCDs are the result of ventricular tachycardia/ventricular fibrillation.

**AETIOLOGY/RISK FACTORS** Ventricular arrhythmias occur as a result of structural heart disease arising primarily from myocardial ischaemia or cardiomyopathies. In resource-rich countries, ventricular tachycardia- or ventricular fibrillation-associated cardiac arrest is believed to occur most typically in the context of myocardial ischaemia. As a result, major risk factors for SCD reflect those that lead to progressive coronary artery disease. Specific additional risk factors attributed to SCD include dilated cardiomyopathy (especially with ejection fractions of <30%), age (peak incidence 45–75 years), and male sex.

**PROGNOSIS** Ventricular fibrillation and ventricular tachycardia associated with cardiac arrest result in lack of oxygen delivery and major ischaemic injury to vital organs. If untreated this condition is uniformly fatal within minutes.

---

Ewa Posner

## KEY POINTS

- Absence seizures are characterised by sudden, brief, frequent periods of unconsciousness, which may be accompanied by automatic movements. They may occur alone, or may coexist with other types of seizures in a child with other epileptic syndromes.

    Absence seizures have a typical spike and wave pattern on the EEG. Atypical absence seizures have different EEG changes and clinical manifestations, and have a different natural history and response to treatment.

    Absence seizures can be differentiated from complex partial seizures by their abrupt ending and lack of a postictal phase.

    About 10% of seizures in children with epilepsy are typical absence seizures, with genetic factors considered to be the main cause. Where they are the only manifestation of epilepsy, they generally resolve spontaneously by the age of 12 years.

- Lamotrigine increases the likelihood of being seizure-free compared with placebo, but it seems to be less effective than valproate and ethosuximide at reducing seizures in children with absence seizures of new onset, and can cause serious skin reactions and aseptic meningitis.

- Ethosuximide seems to be more effective than lamotrigine at reducing seizure frequency in childhood absence seizures of new onset.

    Ethosuximide is rarely associated with aplastic anaemia, skin reactions, and renal and hepatic impairment.

- There is consensus that valproate is beneficial in childhood absence seizures, although we don't know this for sure. We don't know how effective valproate and ethosuximide are, compared with each other, at reducing seizure rate in children with absence seizures.

    Valproate is rarely associated with behavioural and cognitive abnormalities, liver necrosis, and pancreatitis.

- We don't know whether clonazepam or gabapentin reduces the frequency of absence seizures.

 **Please visit http://clinicalevidence.bmj.com for full text and references**

## What are the effects of treatments for typical absence seizures in children?

| Trade-off Between Benefits And Harms | • Ethosuximide |
| --- | --- |
| | • Lamotrigine |
| | • Valproate |
| Unknown Effectiveness | • Clonazepam |
| | • Gabapentin |

**Search date July 2013**

---

**DEFINITION** Absence seizures are sudden, frequent episodes of unconsciousness lasting a few seconds, and are often accompanied by simple automatisms or clonic, atonic, or autonomic components. The differentiation into typical versus atypical seizures is important, as the natural history and response to treatment vary between the two groups. Interventions for atypical absence seizures or for absence seizures secondary to structural lesions are not

*(continued over)*

*(from previous page)*

included in this review. Typical absence seizures display a characteristic EEG showing regular symmetrical generalised spike and wave complexes with a frequency of 3 Hz, and usually occur in children with normal development and intelligence. Typical absence seizures are often confused with complex partial seizures, especially in cases of prolonged seizure with automatisms. However, the abrupt ending of typical absence seizures, without a postictal phase, is the most useful clinical feature in distinguishing the two types. Typical absence seizures should not be confused with atypical absence seizures, which differ markedly in EEG findings and ictal behaviour, and are usually present with other seizure types in a child with a background of learning disability and severe epilepsy.

**INCIDENCE/PREVALENCE** About 10% of seizures in children with epilepsy are typical absence seizures. Annual incidence has been estimated at 0.7 to 4.6 per 100,000 people in the general population, and 6 to 8 per 100,000 in children aged 0 to 15 years. Prevalence is 5 to 50 per 100,000 people in the general population. Similar figures were found in the US (Connecticut) and in Europe-based (Scandinavia, France) population studies. Age of onset ranges from 3 to 13 years, with a peak at 6 to 7 years.

**AETIOLOGY/RISK FACTORS** The cause of childhood absence epilepsy is presumed to be genetic. Seizures can be triggered by hyperventilation in susceptible children. Some anticonvulsants, such as phenytoin, carbamazepine, and vigabatrin, are associated with an increased risk of absence seizures.

**PROGNOSIS** In childhood absence epilepsy, in which typical absence seizures are the only type of seizures suffered by the child, seizures generally cease spontaneously by 12 years of age or sooner. Less than 10% of children develop infrequent generalised tonic clonic seizures, and it is rare for them to continue having absence seizures. In other epileptic syndromes (in which absence seizures may coexist with other types of seizure) prognosis is varied, depending on the syndrome. Absence seizures have a significant impact on quality of life. The episode of unconsciousness may occur at any time, and usually without warning. Affected children need to take precautions to prevent injury during absences, and should refrain from activities that would put them at risk if seizures occurred (e.g., climbing heights, swimming unsupervised, or cycling on busy roads). Often, school staff members are the first to notice the recurrent episodes of absence seizures, and treatment is generally initiated because of the adverse impact on learning.

Roderick P. Venekamp, Roger A.M.J. Damoiseaux, and Anne G.M. Schilder

## KEY POINTS

- Acute otitis media (AOM) is characterised by the presence of middle-ear effusion together with an acute onset of signs and symptoms caused by middle-ear inflammation.

  Middle-ear effusion without signs of an acute infection indicates otitis media with effusion (OME or 'glue ear'), while chronic suppurative otitis media (CSOM) is characterised by continuing (>3 months) middle-ear inflammation and ear discharge through tympanic membrane perforation or ventilation tubes (grommets). Interventions for these conditions are assessed in separate reviews in *Clinical Evidence*.

  The most common pathogens in AOM are *Streptococcus pneumoniae*, non-typeable *Haemophilus influenzae*, and *Moraxella catarrhalis*. Local resistance patterns are important when choosing the type of antibiotic.

  In the UK, antibiotics are prescribed for about 87% of AOM episodes in children's primary care visits.

  Without antibiotics, the clinical symptoms of AOM resolve in about 80% of children within 3 days.

- Analgesics (paracetamol, non-steroidal anti-inflammatory drugs [NSAIDs], and topical anaesthetic drops) may reduce earache compared with placebo.

- Antibiotics seem to reduce pain at 2 to 7 days compared with placebo, but they increase the risks of vomiting, diarrhoea, or rash.

- We do not know whether any one antibiotic regimen should be used in preference to another, although amoxicillin may be more effective than macrolides and cephalosporin.

- Immediate antibiotic use seems most beneficial in children aged under 2 years with bilateral AOM and in children with AOM presenting with ear discharge.

  Immediate antibiotic treatment may provide short-term reduction for some symptoms of AOM, but it increases the risk of rash and diarrhoea compared with delayed treatment.

- Longer courses of antibiotics reduce short-term treatment failure but have no benefit in the longer term compared with shorter regimens (7 days or less).

- Myringotomy may be less effective than antibiotics at reducing symptoms, and we found no evidence that it was superior to no myringotomy.

(i) **Please visit http://clinicalevidence.bmj.com for full text and references**

| What are the effects of treatments (analgesics, antibiotics, and myringotomy) in children with AOM? | |
|---|---|
| Likely To Be Beneficial | • Analgesics (paracetamol, NSAIDs, topical anaesthetic ear drops) |
| Trade-off Between Benefits And Harms | • Antibiotics (reduce symptoms more quickly than placebo but increase adverse effects) |
| | • Choice of antibiotic regimen |
| | • Immediate compared with delayed antibiotic treatment |

|  | • Longer versus shorter courses of antibiotics (reduce treatment failure in the short term but not the long term) |
| --- | --- |
| **Likely To Be Ineffective Or Harmful** | • Myringotomy |

**Search date October 2013**

**DEFINITION** Otitis media, including acute otitis media (AOM) and otitis media with effusion (OME, also known as 'glue ear'), is one of the most common childhood conditions. While closely related, AOM and OME are two different, distinct conditions. AOM is characterised by the presence of middle-ear effusion (MEE) together with an acute onset of signs and symptoms caused by middle-ear inflammation. Symptoms of AOM include earache in older children; or pulling, tugging, or rubbing of the ear or non-specific symptoms such as fever, irritability, or poor feeding in younger children. AOM signs include a distinctly red, yellow, or cloudy tympanic membrane. AOM diagnosis is strengthened by the presence of a bulging tympanic membrane, an air-fluid level behind the tympanic membrane, tympanic membrane perforation, and/or discharge in the ear canal. Pneumatic otoscopy and/or tympanometry can be used to assess the presence (or absence) of middle-ear effusion. In children with ventilation tubes (grommets) in place, ear discharge is a symptom of AOM whereby fluid that has built up in the middle ear drains through the tube into the child's ear canal. Interventions for ear discharge associated with ventilation tubes are beyond the scope of this review. While most children have occasional AOM episodes, an important subset suffer from recurrent AOM, defined as three or more episodes in 6 months or four episodes in 1 year. Middle-ear effusion without signs of an acute infection indicates OME (see review on Otitis media with effusion, p 118), which can arise as a result of AOM, but can also occur independently. Chronic suppurative otitis media (CSOM, see review on CSOM, p 181) is characterised by continuing (>3 months) middle-ear inflammation and ear discharge through the tympanic membrane (perforation or ventilation tubes). Interventions for these conditions are assessed in separate reviews in *Clinical Evidence* (see review page numbers above). For the purposes of this review, the age range used to define children is from birth to 15 years of age.

**INCIDENCE/PREVALENCE** AOM is one of the most common childhood infections and an important reason for primary care visits in the UK. In the UK, antibiotics are prescribed for 87% of these episodes.

**AETIOLOGY/RISK FACTORS** The most common bacterial causes of AOM are *Streptococcus pneumoniae*, non-typeable *Haemophilus influenzae*, and *Moraxella catarrhalis*. There is increasing evidence that the predominant causative pathogen in AOM is changing from *Streptococcus pneumoniae* to non-typeable *Haemophilus influenzae* since the introduction of pneumococcal conjugate vaccines. Group childcare outside the home and passive smoking are thought to be the most important risk factors for AOM. Other risk factors include pacifier use and positive family history of AOM. Breastfeeding for 3 months or longer has a protective effect.

**PROGNOSIS** Without antibiotic treatment, AOM symptoms improve in 24 hours in 60% of children, and symptoms settle spontaneously within 3 days in 80% of children. Serious complications of AOM include acute mastoiditis, meningitis, and, rarely, intracranial complications. If antibiotics are withheld, acute mastoiditis occurs in about 1 to 2 per 10,000 children.

Daphne Keen and Irene Hadjikoumi

## KEY POINTS

- Core symptoms of attention deficit hyperactivity disorder (ADHD) are inattention, hyperactivity, and impulsiveness, although other conditions frequently co-exist with ADHD, including developmental disorders (especially motor, language, autism spectrum disorder, and specific learning disabilities) and psychiatric disorders (especially oppositional defiant and conduct disorder, anxiety, and depressive disorders).

    DSM-5 criteria state that symptoms must be present for at least 6 months, are generally observed in children before the age of 12 years, and cause clinically important impairment in social, academic, or occupational functioning that must be evident in more than one setting.

    Formal diagnostic criteria are most applicable to boys aged 6 to 12 years, and most research data relate to this group. Pre-school children, adolescents, adults, and females may present less typical features, but similar levels of impairment.

    The global prevalence estimates of ADHD are 5.3% for children and adolescents and 4.4% in adulthood, although there is significant variability in the prevalence estimates worldwide, largely explained by methodological procedures.

- We searched for evidence from RCTs and systematic reviews of RCTs on the effectiveness of nutritional supplements (omega-3, iron, or zinc) in children and adolescents with ADHD.

    We found few RCTs that met our inclusion criteria.

    Overall, trials were small and of limited quality.

    Trials were generally short-term; we found no trials that reported outcomes beyond 4 months.

- We don't know whether omega-3 polyunsaturated fatty acid compounds (fish oils) are more effective than placebo at improving symptoms.

- We found no RCTs on the effects of iron supplements.

- We found insufficient evidence on the effects of zinc supplements compared with placebo from one small RCT.

- There is a need for further large high-quality trials in this field.

 Please visit http://clinicalevidence.bmj.com for full text and references

### What are the effects of nutritional supplements in children and adolescents with attention deficit hyperactivity disorder (ADHD)?

| Unknown Effectiveness | • Iron supplements |
| --- | --- |
| | • Omega-3 polyunsaturated fatty acid compounds (fish oils) |
| | • Zinc supplements |

**Search date June 2014**

---

**DEFINITION** Attention deficit hyperactivity disorder (ADHD) is characterised by a pattern of behaviour, present in multiple settings (e.g., school and home) that can result in performance issues in social, educational, or work settings. Symptoms are divided into two categories: inattention; and hyperactivity and impulsivity, which include behaviours such as

*(continued over)*

*(from previous page)*

failure to pay close attention to details, difficulty organising tasks and activities, excessive talking, fidgeting, or an inability to remain seated in appropriate situations. Children must have at least six symptoms from either (or both) the inattention group of criteria and the hyperactivity and impulsivity criteria, while older adolescents and adults (aged >17 years) must present with five. The definition of ADHD has been updated in the fifth edition of the Diagnostic and Statistical Manual of Mental Disorders (DSM-5) to more accurately characterise the experience of affected adults. Using DSM-5, several of the individual's ADHD symptoms must be present prior to age 12 years, compared with 7 years as the age of onset in DSM-IV. DSM-5 includes no exclusion criteria for people with autism spectrum disorder, because symptoms of both disorders co-occur. However, ADHD symptoms must not occur exclusively during the course of schizophrenia or another psychotic disorder and must not be better explained by another mental disorder, such as a depressive or bipolar disorder, anxiety disorder, dissociative disorder, personality disorder, or substance intoxication or withdrawal. The ICD-10 uses the term 'hyperkinetic disorder' for a more restricted diagnosis. It differs from the DSM-5 classification in that: all three problems of attention, hyperactivity, and impulsiveness must be present; more stringent criteria for 'pervasiveness' across situations must be met; and the presence of another disorder is an exclusion criterion. However, in clinical practice, the co-existence of anxiety and mood and autistic spectrum disorders is generally recognised. Formal diagnostic criteria are most applicable to boys aged 6 to 12 years, and most research data relate to this group. Pre-school children, adolescents, and females may present with less typical features but similar levels of impairment. The evidence presented in this overview largely relates to children and adolescents aged 3 to 18 years. There is no distinct boundary between the upper ranges of childhood, adolescence, and adulthood in terms of symptomatology and response to treatment. The research relating to adults is growing. For pre-school children, there is still a paucity of evidence of efficacy and safety of medical treatments and role of behavioural interventions.

**INCIDENCE/PREVALENCE** Prevalence estimates of ADHD vary according to the diagnostic criteria used and the population sampled. The global prevalence estimates of ADHD is 5.3% for children and adolescents and 4.4% in adulthood, although there is significant variability in the prevalence estimates worldwide (largely explained by methodological procedures). As with all mental health disorders, no objective test exists to confirm the diagnosis of ADHD, which remains a diagnosis based on clinical assessment of the nature of the behavioural disorder and functional impairment of cognitive processes. ADHD generally co-exists with other developmental and mental health disorders. Oppositional defiant disorder is present in 35% (95% CI 27% to 44%) of children with ADHD, conduct disorder in 26% (95% CI 13% to 41%), anxiety disorder in 26% (95% CI 18% to 35%), and depressive disorder in 18% (95% CI 11% to 27%). Of the developmental disorders, developmental coordination disorder has been diagnosed in just under 50% of children with ADHD, specific learning disabilities in around 40%, tics in 33%, and Asperger's syndrome in 7%.

**AETIOLOGY/RISK FACTORS** The underlying causes of ADHD are not known. There is some evidence that there is a genetic component: twin studies suggest an average heritability of 76%. However, a high heritability does not exclude the important role of environment acting through gene-environment interactions. The uneven distribution of ADHD in the population, which mirrors that of other mental health and behavioural disorders, also suggests that psychosocial factors are involved. Boys are at a greater risk of developing ADHD compared with girls, with a ratio of about 4:1. Although the link between ADHD and dietary and nutritional factors (such as artificial food colours) is yet to be satisfactorily researched, studies suggest a correlation between artificial food colours and symptoms of hyperactivity in some young children.

**PROGNOSIS** More than 70% of hyperactive children may continue to meet criteria for ADHD in adolescence and up to 65% of adolescents have continuing significant functional impairment in adulthood, although not necessarily meeting formal diagnostic criteria. Changes in diagnostic criteria cause difficulty with interpretation of the few outcome studies that exist. ADHD is also a risk factor for psychiatric diagnosis, persistent hyperactivity, violence, and antisocial behaviours. Follow-up studies of children with ADHD into adulthood indicate an increased risk of antisocial, depressive, and anxiety disorders, and of antisocial personality disorder.

Augusta Okpapi, Amanda J Friend, and Stephen W Turner

## KEY POINTS

- Not all acute wheeze is due to asthma/bronchospasm, particularly in children aged <2 years. If bronchodilators do not improve symptoms, alternative diagnoses (e.g., infection, foreign body) should be considered.

- Although no evidence exists to support the use of oxygen in acute asthma, it is known to be effective and should be administered when oxygen saturations fall below 94% in all cases of acute asthma.

- Although there is little evidence to support the use of inhaled bronchodilators, they remain one of the first-line treatment choices for acute asthma.

  In mild to moderate acute asthma, beta$_2$ agonists may be equally as effective from a metered-dose inhaler/spacer combination compared with nebuliser for control of acute symptoms and may be associated with a shorter duration of stay in the emergency department and reduced side effects.

  In severe acute asthma, we don't know whether there is a difference between continuous and intermittent nebulised beta$_2$ agonists.

  CAUTION: Inhaled salbutamol has been associated with hypokalaemia and tremor.

- The only indication for ipratropium bromide for acute childhood asthma is in combination with salbutamol for acute severe wheeze.

- Although there is little evidence to support the use of oral corticosteroids, they remain one of the first-line treatment choices for acute asthma.

  In mild to moderate asthma, oral corticosteroids are known to be more effective than placebo. We don't know whether high-dose inhaled corticosteroids and oral corticosteroids differ in effectiveness as we found insufficient evidence.

- For severe asthma, addition of intravenous salbutamol, aminophylline, or magnesium sulphate are all effective compared with the addition of placebo.

  In severe acute asthma, we don't know whether intravenous aminophylline and salbutamol differ in effectiveness as we found insufficient evidence from one small RCT.

  CAUTION: Intravenous salbutamol and aminophylline have been associated with cardiac arrhythmias. Salbutamol has been associated with hypokalaemia and aminophylline has been associated with nausea. Intravenous theophylline can cause cardiac arrhythmias and convulsions if therapeutic blood concentrations are exceeded.

 Please visit http://clinicalevidence.bmj.com for full text and references

| What are the effects of treatments for acute asthma in children? | |
|---|---|
| Beneficial | • Beta$_2$ agonists (high-dose inhaled)* |
| | • Corticosteroids (high-dose inhaled) |
| | • Corticosteroids (systemic) |
| | • Ipratropium bromide (inhaled) added to beta$_2$ agonists |
| | • Magnesium sulphate (intravenous) |
| | • Oxygen* |

| | • Salbutamol (intravenous) |
|---|---|
| **Likely To Be Beneficial** | • Theophylline or aminophylline (intravenous) |

**Search date June 2010**

*In the absence of RCT evidence, categorisation based on observational evidence and strong consensus.

**DEFINITION** Asthma is a chronic inflammatory disease of the airways characterised by episodic wheeze and reversible airway obstruction. Acute exacerbations of asthma are characterised by tachypnoea, increased work of breathing (chest wall recession in young children and use of accessory muscles in older children), tachycardia, and reduced oxygen saturations. Acute childhood asthma is a common clinical emergency presenting across a range of ages and with a range of severities. This review was designed to assess the current evidence for best management of acute childhood asthma. Acute asthma may be classified into the following categories: **severe acute asthma:** oxygen saturations <92%, pulse >125 beats/minute (>5 years) or >140 beats/minute (2–5 years), respiratory rate >30 breaths/minute (>5 years) or >40 breaths/minute (2–5 years), obvious use of accessory muscles (>5 years) or obvious chest wall recession (2–5 years), unable to complete sentences in one breath (talks in 1–2 words), too breathless to feed; **moderate acute asthma:** oxygen saturation 92–95%, pulse 100–125 beats/minute (>5 years) or 120–140 beats/minute (2–5 years), respiratory rate 20–30 breaths/minute (>5 years) or 30–40 breaths/minute (2–5 years), some use of accessory muscles (>5 years) or some chest wall recession (2–5 years), talks in short phrases.

**INCIDENCE/PREVALENCE** Acute asthma remains a common and sometimes serious presentation to hospital. The proportion of children with acute asthma presenting to primary care in England and Wales fell between 1993 and 1998. The proportion of all children admitted to hospital in England and Wales who had acute asthma fell slightly between 1998 and 2004 from around 19/1000 to 17/1000 admissions (results presented graphically). Fortunately, deaths from acute asthma are uncommon in children and are also falling. Asthma mortality fell by approximately 70% between 1968 and 2000 but remains highest in children aged 11 to 16 years. Between 1968 and 2000, asthma mortality (per 100,000 children/year) fell from 0.6 to 0.1 in 1–5-year-olds, from 0.5 to 0.2 in 6–10-year-olds and from 1.4 to 0.4 in 11–16-year-olds.

**AETIOLOGY/RISK FACTORS** The predominant precipitant for acute asthma symptoms is viral infection, detected in 80% to 85% of cases. Other causes include exercise, allergen exposure (inhaled and/or ingested), cold weather, and poor air quality. Children aged <5 years with lower respiratory tract infection or foreign body aspiration can present with asthma-like symptoms. Some young children with acute wheeze have a diagnosis of asthma and others a diagnosis or viral induced wheeze but in the acute setting both should be treated in the same manner. Risk factors for asthma admissions include not having or not adhering to a written 'crisis management plan', taking inappropriate preventive treatment or poor compliance, delay of >24 hours in seeking advice.

**PROGNOSIS** A UK longitudinal study of children born in 1970 found that 29% of 5-year-olds wheezing in the past year were still wheezing at the age of 10 years. Another study followed a group of children in Melbourne, Australia, from the age of 7 years (in 1964) into adulthood. The study found that a large proportion (73%) of 14-year-olds with infrequent symptoms had few or no symptoms by the age of 28 years, whereas two-thirds of those 14-year-olds with frequent wheezing still had recurrent attacks at the age of 28 years.

Stephen W Turner, Amanda J Friend, and Augusta Okpapi

## KEY POINTS

- Childhood asthma can be difficult to distinguish from viral wheeze and can affect up to 20% of children.

- Regular monotherapy with inhaled corticosteroids improves symptoms, reduces exacerbations, and improves physiological outcomes in children with asthma symptoms requiring regular short-acting beta$_2$ agonist treatment. Their effect on final adult height is minimal and when prescribed within recommended doses have an excellent safety record. Regular monotherapy with other treatments is not superior to low-dose inhaled corticosteroids.

- Leukotriene receptor antagonists may have a role as first-line prophylaxis in very young children.

- There is consensus that long-acting beta$_2$ agonists should not be used for first-line prophylaxis.

  CAUTION: Monotherapy with long-acting beta$_2$ agonists does not reduce asthma exacerbations but may increase the chance of severe asthma episodes.

- Theophylline was used as first-line prevention before the introduction of inhaled corticosteroids. Although there is weak evidence that theophylline is superior to placebo, theophylline should no longer be used as first-line prophylaxis in childhood asthma because of clear evidence of the efficacy and safety of inhaled corticosteroids.

  Theophylline has serious adverse effects (cardiac arrhythmia, convulsions) if therapeutic blood concentrations are exceeded.

- When low-dose inhaled corticosteroids fail to control asthma, most older children will respond to one of the add-on options available, which include addition of long-acting beta$_2$ agonists, addition of leukotriene receptor antagonists, addition of theophylline, or increased dose of inhaled corticosteroid. However, we don't know for certain how effective these additional treatments are because we found no/limited RCT evidence of benefit compared with adding placebo/no additional treatments.

  Addition of long-acting beta$_2$ agonists may reduce symptoms and improve physiological measures compared with increased dose of corticosteroids in older children. Long-acting beta$_2$ agonists are not currently licensed for use in children under 5 years of age.

  Consensus suggests that younger children are likely to benefit from addition of leukotriene receptor antagonists.

  Although there is weak evidence that addition of theophylline to inhaled corticosteroids does improve symptom control and reduce exacerbations, theophylline should only be added to inhaled corticosteroids in children aged over 5 years when the addition of long-acting beta$_2$ agonists and leukotriene receptor antagonists have both been unsuccessful.

- Omalizumab may be indicated in the secondary care setting for older children (aged over 5 years) with poorly controlled allergic asthma despite use of intermediate- and high-dose inhaled corticosteroids once the diagnosis is confirmed and compliance and psychological issues are addressed. However, we need more data to draw firm conclusions.

(i) **Please visit http://clinicalevidence.bmj.com for full text and references**

## What are the effects of single-agent prophylaxis in children taking as-needed inhaled beta$_2$ agonists for asthma?

| | |
|---|---|
| **Beneficial** | • Corticosteroids (inhaled) |
| **Likely To Be Beneficial** | • Leukotriene receptor antagonists (oral montelukast) |
| **Likely To Be Ineffective Or Harmful** | • Long-acting beta$_2$ agonists (inhaled salmeterol or formoterol)<br><br>• Theophylline (oral) |

## What are the effects of additional prophylactic treatments in childhood asthma inadequately controlled by standard-dose inhaled corticosteroids?

| | |
|---|---|
| **Likely To Be Beneficial** | • Adding leukotriene receptor antagonists (montelukast)*<br><br>• Adding long-acting beta$_2$ agonist (in older children) |
| **Unknown Effectiveness** | • Adding omalizumab<br><br>• Adding oral theophylline<br><br>• Increased dose of inhaled corticosteroid |

**Search date June 2010**

*Categorisation based on consensus.

**DEFINITION** Asthma is characterised by episodic wheeze, cough, and shortness of breath in association with exposure to multiple factors including rhinovirus, exercise, and allergens. The diagnosis remains entirely based on the history coupled with a positive response to treatment. Childhood asthma can affect up to 20% of children and can be difficult to diagnose in preschool children, where many individuals have acute episodic wheeze/viral-induced wheeze. Examination of the child with asthma is invariably normal and although physiological testing will characteristically find reversible airway obstruction and atopy, these tests lack precision for asthma and have no benefit in the majority of children. The absence of a widely accepted definition for asthma, a diagnostic test, and lack of a biomarker with which to objectively monitor the condition can make childhood asthma a clinical challenge, especially in young children. In cases of clinical uncertainty or where symptoms persist despite adequate treatment, referral for specialist opinion should be sought. This review deals with pharmacological management of chronic asthma in children only.

**INCIDENCE/PREVALENCE** Asthma prevalence rose in the UK and other Western countries during the 1980s and 1990s, but recent evidence suggests that asthma prevalence is falling; however, lifetime asthma prevalence is still reported as 24% in children aged 9 to 12 years in the UK. Genetic factors are thought to account for 60% of asthma causation, but genetic change cannot explain the rise in asthma prevalence from 4% in 1964 to present day values. The reasons for the rise and early fall in asthma prevalence are not understood but are likely to involve epigenetics and interactions between genetic predispositions and environmental exposures, including tobacco smoke.

**AETIOLOGY/RISK FACTORS** Asthma is a typical complex condition where genetic and environmental factors interact, often at critical stages of development. Genetic factors explain approximately 60% of asthma causation, but there is no single 'asthma gene' — rather there are approximately 10 genes, each of which confer a modest increased risk for asthma. Environmental factors implicated in asthma causation include exposure to tobacco smoke, diet (including non-breast feeding), early respiratory infection, and indoor and outdoor air quality. Other non-modifiable risk factors include sex (asthma is more common in boys than girls but more common in women than men) and age (many children apparently 'grow out of' their asthma).

**PROGNOSIS** A UK longitudinal study of children born in 1970 found that 29% of 5-year-olds wheezing in the past year were still wheezing at the age of 10 years. Another study followed a group of children in Melbourne, Australia, from the age of 7 years (in 1964) into adulthood. The study found that a large proportion (73%) of 14-year-olds with infrequent symptoms had few or no symptoms by the age of 28 years, whereas two-thirds of those 14-year-olds with frequent wheezing still had recurrent attacks at the age of 28 years.

Jeremy Parr

## KEY POINTS

- Autism is one of a group of pervasive developmental disorders, and is characterised by qualitative impairments in communication and social interaction, and by repetitive and stereotyped behaviours and interests.

  Abnormal development is present before the age of 3 years. A quarter of affected children show developmental regression, with loss of previously acquired skills.

  One third of children with autism have epilepsy, and three quarters have mental retardation. Only 15% of adults with autism will lead independent lives.

  Twin and family studies suggest that most cases of autism occur because of a combination of genetic factors. Autism is not caused by perinatal factors or by the MMR vaccine.

- It may be difficult to apply the results of research in practice, as improvements in outcomes assessed in RCTs using standardised assessment tools may not correlate with improvements in function in a particular child with autism.

- Some interventions are administered by (or in conjunction with) parents, and may be carried out in the home. Consideration of the direct financial costs, indirect costs (through possible lost earnings), and the impact on relationships within the family (to siblings or spouse) must be balanced against likely and possible improvements in outcome for the child with autism.

- There is a lack of good-quality evidence on the effectiveness of early multidisciplinary intervention programmes, or for other treatments for children with autism.

  There is consensus, supported by a systematic review, that early intensive behavioural interventions are likely to be beneficial in children with autism.

  Attendance at a "More Than Words" training course for parents may improve communication between parents and children, as may participation in Child's Talk.

  There is consensus that the Autism Preschool Programme and TEACCH may be effective, although no RCTs or cohort studies evaluating these interventions have been found.

  We don't know whether early intervention using the EarlyBird programme, the Portage scheme, Relationship-Development Intervention, Social stories, music therapy, CBT, facilitated communication or Son-Rise are beneficial in children with autism.

- Methylphenidate may reduce hyperactivity in children with autism.

  Methylphenidate may increase social withdrawal and irritability. Growth and blood pressure monitoring are required.

- Risperidone may improve behaviour in children with autism compared with placebo, but its use is limited by adverse effects such as weight gain, drowsiness, prolactinaemia, and tremors.

- There is consensus that selective serotonin reuptake inhibitors (SSRIs) improve symptoms in children with autism, although no RCTs have been found. The adverse effects of SSRIs, including possible increases in agitation, hostility, and suicidal ideation, are well documented.

- We don't know whether auditory integration training, sensory integration training, chelation, a gluten- and casein-free diet, digestive enzymes, omega-3 fish oil, secretin, vitamin A, vitamin B6 plus magnesium, melatonin, olanzapine, or vitamin C are beneficial for treating children with autism, as few studies have been found.

 **Please visit http://clinicalevidence.bmj.com for full text and references**

## What are the effects of early intensive multidisciplinary intervention programmes in children with autism?

| Likely To Be Beneficial | • Autism Preschool Programme*<br>• Child's Talk*<br>• Early intensive behavioural interventions*<br>• More Than Words*<br>• Picture exchange communication system*<br>• TEACCH* |
|---|---|
| Unknown Effectiveness | • Cognitive behavioural therapy<br>• EarlyBird programme<br>• Facilitated communication<br>• Floortime<br>• Music therapy<br>• Portage scheme<br>• Relationship-development intervention<br>• Social skills training<br>• Social stories<br>• Son-Rise |

## What are the effects of dietary interventions in children with autism?

| Unknown Effectiveness | • Gluten- and casein-free diet<br>• Digestive enzymes<br>• Melatonin<br>• Omega-3 fish oil<br>• Probiotics<br>• Vitamin A<br>• Vitamin B6 (pyridoxine) plus magnesium<br>• Vitamin C |
|---|---|

## What are the effects of drug treatments in children with autism?

| Likely To Be Beneficial | • Methylphenidate (for hyperactivity only) |
|---|---|
| Trade-off Between Benefits And Harms | • Risperidone<br>• SSRIs* |
| Unknown Effectiveness | • Immunoglobulins<br>• Memantine |

| | • Olanzapine |
|---|---|
| **Unlikely To Be Beneficial** | • Secretin |

| **What are the effects of non-drug treatments in children with autism?** | |
|---|---|
| **Unknown Effectiveness** | • Auditory integration training |
| | • Chelation |
| | • Sensory integration training |

**Search date May 2009**

*In the absence of robust RCT evidence in children with autism, categorisation is based on observational evidence and strong consensus belief that these interventions are likely to be beneficial.

**DEFINITION** Autism is one of the pervasive developmental disorders (PDD), a group of conditions that also includes Asperger syndrome, pervasive developmental disorder not otherwise specified (PDD-NOS), Rett syndrome, and childhood disintegrative disorder. Collectively, autism, Asperger syndrome, and PDD-NOS are often referred to as "autistic spectrum disorders" (ASDs). However, Rett syndrome and childhood disintegrative disorder fall outside the autistic spectrum. Autism is characterised by qualitative impairments in communication and social interaction, and by restricted, repetitive, and stereotyped patterns of behaviours and interests. Abnormal development is present before the age of 3 years. The clinical features required for a diagnosis of autism to be made are set out in *International classification of diseases* (ICD-10) and *Diagnostic and statistical manual of mental disorders 4th ed* (DSM-IV). For ICD-10 criteria see table 1. Individuals with autism have a history of language delay (single word or phrase speech delay), and a quarter lose previously acquired skills (regression), most commonly in the second year of life. A third of individuals develop epilepsy, and three quarters have mental retardation. Males are affected more commonly than females (3.5–4.0:1). The findings of this review apply to children and adolescents with autism, and results may not be generalisable to children with other ASDs. **Diagnosis:** The generally accepted "gold standard" assessment tools for autism are the Autism Diagnostic Interview-Revised (ADI-R), a semistructured, interviewer-based schedule administered to the primary caregiver, and the Autism Diagnostic Observational Schedule, a semistructured assessment carried out with the individuals themselves. Although these schedules are informative for the clinician, autism remains a clinical diagnosis.

**INCIDENCE/PREVALENCE** The detected prevalence of autism has increased in recent years, and a recent high-quality UK study found 40/10,000 children to have childhood autism. The prevalence of autism for studies published between 1977 and 1991 was 4.4/10,000, whereas that for the studies published during the period 1992 to 2001 was 12.7/10,000. When considering all autism spectrum disorders, findings suggest the prevalence rises to 120/10,000; many of these people have PDD-NOS.

**AETIOLOGY/RISK FACTORS** Evidence from twin and family studies suggests that most cases of autism arise because of a combination of genetic factors. Family studies indicate that the rate of autism in siblings of autistic individuals is about 2.2%, and the sibling recurrence rate for all PDDs is 5% to 6% — significantly greater than that of the general population. Monozygotic twin studies show 60% to 91% concordance for autism, and therefore it is likely that most cases arise on the basis of multiple susceptibility genes, with influence from environmental or other factors. A minority of cases of autism can be attributed to genetic disorders, including chromosomal abnormalities, fragile X syndrome, tuberose sclerosis, neurofibromatosis type 1, and a variety of other medical conditions. Although perinatal factors have been implicated, it is unlikely that they have a causal role. Research evidence suggests that autism is not caused by the MMR vaccine, or by thimerosal (mercury) in vaccines. There is strong evidence supporting a neurobiological basis of autism.

Ongoing research into the relationship between neurophysiology, neuroanatomy, neurochemistry, and genetic factors is likely to increase our understanding, and represents the best chance of unravelling the complex aetiology of ASD. The presence of phenotypic and genetic heterogeneity may have significant implications for studies of interventions/treatments for autism, as efficacy may vary with phenotype.

**PROGNOSIS** Autism is a lifelong condition with a highly variable clinical course throughout childhood and adolescence. Many adults with autism require lifelong full-time care. About 15% of adults with autism will live independent lives, whereas 15% to 20% will live alone with community support. Verbal and overall cognitive capacity seem the most important predictors of ability to live independently as an adult.

Olga Kapellou

## KEY POINTS

- Blood samples are usually taken from infants via heel punctures or venepuncture.

    Both procedures are likely to be painful, especially in younger infants, but analgesia is rarely given.

    Infants who have already experienced pain during heel punctures seem more likely to show signs of pain during later blood sampling than infants not experiencing such pain initially.

- High concentrations of oral sugar solutions are likely to reduce pain, either given together with a pacifier, or directly into the mouth before blood sampling.

    Oral 24% to 30% sucrose and 25% to 30% glucose solutions reduce signs of pain, especially crying, compared with water or no treatment in term and preterm infants. Oral 30% dextrose solution may also be effective.

    Lower concentrations of sugar solutions (10–12%) do not seem to be effective at reducing pain.

    Long-term use of oral sugar solutions has theoretical risks of hyperglycaemia and necrotising enterocolitis.

- Pacifiers without sugar solutions may also reduce pain responses compared with no treatment.

    Transient choking and oxygen desaturation may occur with the use of pacifiers, or after giving oral sugar solutions directly into the mouth.

- Topical anaesthetics may reduce pain responses to blood sampling compared with placebo.

    Topical lidocaine–prilocaine cream and tetracaine gel or patches reduced signs of pain in most trials of term and preterm infants.

    Adverse effects tend to be minor and transient, but systemic absorption may occur in young infants, which increases the risk of methaemoglobinaemia.

    We do not know whether oral sugars are more or less effective than topical anaesthetics in reducing pain from blood sampling.

 **Please visit http://clinicalevidence.bmj.com for full text and references**

### What are the effects of interventions to reduce pain-related distress and morbidity during venepuncture in preterm or term babies aged under 12 months in a neonatal unit?

| Likely To Be Beneficial | • Oral sweet solutions |
| --- | --- |
| | • Pacifiers |
| | • Topical anaesthetics (lidocaine–prilocaine cream, tetracaine) |

**Search date June 2010**

**DEFINITION** Methods of sampling blood in infants include heel puncture, venepuncture, and arterial puncture. **Venepuncture** involves aspirating blood through a needle from a peripheral vein. Heel puncture involves lancing the lateral aspect of the infant's heel, squeezing the heel, and collecting the pooled capillary blood. Heel puncture and arterial blood sampling are not discussed in this review. For this review, we included premature and term infants aged up to 12 months in a hospital setting.

**INCIDENCE/PREVALENCE** Preterm or ill neonates may undergo from 1 to 21 heel punctures or venepunctures a day. These punctures are likely to be painful. Heel punctures comprise 61% to 87% and venepunctures comprise 8% to 13% of the invasive procedures performed on ill infants. Analgesics are rarely given specifically for blood sampling procedures, but 5% to 19% of infants receive analgesia for other indications. In one study, comfort measures were provided during 63% of venepunctures and 75% of heel punctures.

**AETIOLOGY/RISK FACTORS** Blood sampling in infants can be difficult to perform, particularly in preterm or ill infants. Young infants may have increased sensitivity and prolonged response to pain compared with older age groups. Factors that may affect the infant's pain responses include corrected gestational age, previous pain experience, and procedural technique.

**PROGNOSIS** Pain caused by blood sampling is associated with acute behavioural and physiological deterioration. Experience of pain during heel puncture seems to heighten pain responses during subsequent blood sampling. Other adverse effects of blood sampling include bleeding, bruising, haematoma, and infection.

Thomas Bourke and Michael Shields

**KEY POINTS**

- Bronchiolitis is a virally induced acute bronchiolar inflammation that is associated with signs and symptoms of airway obstruction.

  It is the most common lower respiratory tract infection in infants. It is a common reason for attendance in the emergency department and for admission to hospital.

  Bronchiolitis is associated with increased morbidity and mortality in high-risk children (those with congenital heart disease, chronic lung disease, history of premature birth, hypoxia, immune deficiency, and age <6 weeks).

- In high-risk children, prophylaxis with either respiratory syncytial virus immunoglobulin or the monoclonal antibody palivizumab reduces hospital admissions compared with placebo.

- It seems that nursing interventions, such as cohort segregation, hand washing, and wearing gowns, masks, gloves, and goggles, successfully prevent spreading of the disease in hospital.

- We don't know how effective most current interventions are at treating bronchiolitis.

  Although we do not know whether inhaled bronchodilators such as inhaled adrenaline or inhaled salbutamol are effective at treating bronchiolitis, they may improve overall clinical scores in the short term.

  We don't know whether ribavirin, respiratory syncytial virus immunoglobulin, pooled immunoglobulins or palivizumab, chest physiotherapy, montelukast, surfactants, CPAP, or heliox work better than placebo or no treatment in reducing mortality, duration of hospital stay, or respiratory deterioration. Most of the trials we found may have been too small to detect any clinically important differences between groups in these outcomes.

- Corticosteroids, antibiotics, and oral bronchodilators do not seem to be a useful treatment for bronchiolitis.

- We don't know how effective oxygen is at improving symptoms of bronchiolitis, although discharge on home oxygen therapy may reduce length of stay in hospital without risking readmission.

- We found no trials assessing fluid management or nasal decongestants.

(i) **Please visit http://clinicalevidence.bmj.com for full text and references**

| **What are the effects of prophylactic interventions for bronchiolitis in high-risk children?** | |
|---|---|
| Beneficial | • Respiratory syncytial virus immunoglobulin or palivizumab (monoclonal antibody) in children at high risk |

| **What are the effects of measures to prevent transmission of bronchiolitis in hospital?** | |
|---|---|
| Likely To Be Beneficial | • Nursing interventions (cohort segregation, hand washing, gowns, masks, gloves, and goggles) in children admitted to hospital |

## What are the effects of treatment for children with bronchiolitis?

| | |
|---|---|
| **Unknown Effectiveness** | • Bronchodilators (inhaled salbutamol, inhaled adrenaline [epinephrine])<br><br>• Chest physiotherapy<br><br>• Continuous positive airway pressure<br><br>• Fluid management<br><br>• Heliox<br><br>• Montelukast<br><br>• Nasal decongestants<br><br>• Oxygen<br><br>• Respiratory syncytial virus immunoglobulins, pooled immunoglobulins, or palivizumab (monoclonal antibody) for treating bronchiolitis<br><br>• Ribavirin<br><br>• Surfactants |
| **Unlikely To Be Beneficial** | • Antibiotics<br><br>• Bronchodilators (oral)<br><br>• Corticosteroids |

Search date July 2010

**DEFINITION** Bronchiolitis is a virally induced acute bronchiolar inflammation that is associated with signs and symptoms of airway obstruction. **Diagnosis:** The diagnosis of bronchiolitis, as well as the assessment of its severity, is based on clinical findings (history and physical examination). Bronchiolitis is characterised by a cluster of clinical manifestations in children <2 years of age, beginning with an upper respiratory prodrome, followed by increased respiratory effort and wheezing. Suggestive findings include rhinorrhoea, cough, wheezing, tachypnoea, and increased respiratory distress manifested as grunting, nasal flaring, and chest indrawing. There is no good evidence supporting the value of diagnostic tests (chest radiographs, acute-phase reactants, viral tests) in infants with suspected bronchiolitis. Respiratory syncytial virus (RSV)-test results rarely influence management decisions. Virological tests, however, may be useful when cohorting of infants is feasible. Given these issues, it is not surprising to find wide variation in how bronchiolitis is diagnosed and treated in different settings.

**INCIDENCE/PREVALENCE** Bronchiolitis is the most common lower respiratory tract infection in infants, occurring in a seasonal pattern, with highest incidence in the winter in temperate climates and in the rainy season in warmer countries. Bronchiolitis is a common reason for attendance and admission to hospital. It accounted for around 3% (1.9 million) of emergency department visits in children below 2 years of age between 1992 and 2000 in the US. The RSV-bronchiolitis rate of hospital admission in the US infant population in 2000–2001 was 24.2 per 1000 births. In a retrospective cohort study carried out in the US in 1989–1993, one third of RSV-associated hospital admissions were in infants <3 months old. Admission rates are even higher among infants and young children with bronchopulmonary dysplasia (BPD), congenital heart disease (CHD), prematurity, and other conditions such as chronic pulmonary diseases and immunodeficiency.

*(continued over)*

*(from previous page)*

**AETIOLOGY/RISK FACTORS** Respiratory syncytial virus is responsible for bronchiolitis in 70% of cases. This figure reaches 80% to 100% in the winter months. Reinfections are common and can occur throughout life. Other causal agents include human metapneumovirus, influenza, parainfluenza, and adenovirus.

**PROGNOSIS** Morbidity and mortality: Disease severity is related to the size of the infant, and to the proximity and frequency of contact with infective infants. It is estimated that 66 to 127 bronchiolitis-associated deaths occurred annually between 1979 and 1997 among US children aged under 5 years. Estimated annual RSV-attributed deaths in the UK between 1989 and 2000 were 8.4 per 100,000 in infants aged 1 to 12 months, and 0.9 per 100,000 population per year for children aged 1 to 4 years. Children at increased risk of morbidity and mortality include those with congenital heart disease, chronic lung disease, history of premature birth, hypoxia, immune deficiency, and age <6 weeks. Rates of admission to ICUs are higher in those with one risk factor (17.7%) compared with those with no risk factors (3.2%). Rates of needing mechanical ventilation are also higher in those with one risk factor (13.1%) compared with those with no risk factor (1.5%). The risk of death within 2 weeks is higher for children with congenital heart disease (3.4%) or chronic lung disease (3.5%) compared with other groups combined (0.1%). The percentage of these children needing oxygen supplementation is also high (range 63–80%). **Long-term prognosis:** Studies on the long-term prognosis of bronchiolitis — in particular regarding its association with asthma, allergic sensitisation, and atopy — have not produced clear answers. Possible confounding factors include variation in illness severity, smoke exposure, and being in overcrowded environments.

Hilary Writer

## KEY POINTS

- Cardiorespiratory arrest outside hospital occurs in approximately 1/10,000 children a year in resource-rich countries, with two-thirds of arrests occurring in children under 18 months of age.

    Approximately 45% of cases have undetermined causes, including sudden infant death syndrome. Of the rest, 20% are caused by trauma, 10% by chronic disease, and 6% by pneumonia.

- Overall survival for out-of-hospital cardiorespiratory arrest in children is poor.

    Overall survival for children who sustain cardiorespiratory arrest outside hospital not caused by submersion in water is about 4%.

    Of those who survive, between half and three-quarters will have moderate to severe neurological sequelae.

- There is very poor evidence for any intervention in cardiorespiratory arrest in children. Placebo-controlled trials would be unethical, and few observational studies have been performed.

- Immediate airway management, ventilation, and high-quality chest compressions with minimal interruption are widely accepted to be key interventions.

    Ventilation with a bag and mask seems as effective as intubation. The most suitable method for the situation should be used.

- Direct current cardiac shock is likely to be beneficial in children with ventricular fibrillation or pulseless ventricular tachycardia.

    Ventricular fibrillation or pulseless ventricular tachycardia are the underlying rhythms in 10% of cardiorespiratory arrests in children, and are associated with a better prognosis than asystole or pulseless electrical activity.

    Defibrillation within 10 minutes of the arrest may improve the outcome.

- Intravenous adrenaline is widely accepted to be the initial medication of choice in an arrest.

    The standard dose of intravenous adrenaline is 0.01 mg/kg.

    Weak evidence suggests that higher dose adrenaline (0.1 mg/kg) is no more effective in improving survival.

    The effects of cooling a child after arrest are unknown.

(i) **Please visit http://clinicalevidence.bmj.com for full text and references**

## What are the effects of treatments for non-submersion out-of-hospital cardiorespiratory arrest in children?

| Likely To Be Beneficial | • Airway management and ventilation (including bag–mask ventilation and intubation)*<br><br>• Bystander cardiopulmonary resuscitation*<br><br>• Direct current cardiac shock (for ventricular fibrillation or pulseless ventricular tachycardia)*<br><br>• Intravenous adrenaline (epinephrine) at standard dose* |
|---|---|
| Unknown Effectiveness | • Hypothermia (induced in child after out-of-hospital arrest)<br><br>• Intravenous adrenaline at high dose (compared with standard dose) |

- Intravenous sodium bicarbonate

- Intubation versus bag–mask ventilation (relative benefits unclear)

- Training parents to perform cardiopulmonary resuscitation

**Search date December 2009**

*Although we found no direct evidence to support their use, widespread consensus holds that, on the basis of indirect evidence and extrapolation from adult data, these interventions should be universally applied to children who have arrested. Placebo-controlled trials would be considered unethical.

**DEFINITION** This review covers non-submersion, out-of-hospital cardiorespiratory arrest in children. The paediatric Utstein style definition is cessation of cardiac mechanical activity, determined by the inability to palpate a central pulse, unresponsiveness, and apnoea occurring outside of a medical facility and not caused by submersion in water.

**INCIDENCE/PREVALENCE** We found 19 observational studies (8 prospective, 11 retrospective) reporting the incidence of non-submersion out-of-hospital cardiorespiratory arrest in children. Five studies reported the incidence in both adults and children, and 14 reported the incidence in children alone. The incidence in the general population ranged from 1.3 to 5.7/100,000 people a year (mean 2.9, 95% CI 0.18 to 5.5). The incidence in children ranged from 6.3 to 18.0/100,000 children a year (mean 9.5, 95% CI 2.28 to 16.72). Two prospective studies (761 children in total) found that 40% to 50% of cardiorespiratory arrests in children aged under 12 months occur out of hospital. Two prospective studies identified that children are aged under 18 months in approximately 50% (range 45% to 65%) of out-of-hospital cardiorespiratory arrests.

**AETIOLOGY/RISK FACTORS** We found 33 observational studies reporting the causes of non-submersion pulseless arrests in a total of 2109 children. The most common causes were undetermined (as in sudden infant death syndrome, 47%), trauma (17%), chronic disease (7%), and pneumonia (5%).

**PROGNOSIS** We found no observational studies that investigated non-submersion arrests alone in a complete paediatric population. We found one systematic review (search date 2004) of 41 case series and cohort studies (9 prospective, 32 retrospective; total of 5363 children), which reported outcomes for out-of-hospital cardiopulmonary arrest of any cause, including submersion, in children up to 18 years. Studies were excluded if survival, with survival to hospital discharge as a minimum, was not reported as an outcome. The overall survival rate (to hospital discharge) for the children meeting the paediatric Utstein style definition for out-of-hospital non-submersion arrest was 5% (190/3475 children). Of the 190 surviving children, 43/190 (23%) had no or mild neurological disability, and 147/190 (77%) had moderate or severe neurological disability. Three subsequent prospective cohort studies of a total of 1133 children, including 72 children who sustained submersion events, reported a range of survival to hospital discharge between 0% and 6% (mean 2.8%). One subsequent retrospective cohort study of 84 children with non-submersion out-of-hospital cardiac arrest reported a 4.7% survival rate to hospital discharge, with 50% of the survivors sustaining severe neurological deficits. One prospective cohort of 14 high school athletes who experienced cardiac arrest in school reported a survival in this population of 64%. All members of this cohort had a cardiac aetiology for the sudden cardiac arrest. One cohort of 96 children with known hypertrophic cardiomyopathy recorded a 3% incidence of sudden cardiac death. We found one systematic review (search date 1997), which reported outcomes after cardiopulmonary resuscitation for both in-hospital and out-of-hospital arrests in children of any cause, including submersion. Studies were excluded if they did not report on survival. The review found evidence from prospective and retrospective observational studies that out-of-hospital arrest of any cause in children has a poorer prognosis than within-hospital arrest (132/1568 [8%] children survived to hospital discharge after out-of-hospital arrest v 129/544 [24%] children after in-hospital arrests). About half of the survivors were involved in studies that reported neurological outcome. Of these, survival with 'good neurological outcome' (i.e., normal or mild neurological deficit) was higher in children who arrested in hospital compared with those who arrested elsewhere (60/77 [78%] surviving children in hospital v 28/68 [41%] elsewhere).

# Colic in infants

Peter Lucassen

## KEY POINTS

- Colic in infants is defined as excessive crying in an otherwise healthy and thriving baby. The crying typically starts in the first few weeks of life and usually resolves within 6 months.

  It leads one in six families with children to consult a health professional.

- We found insufficient RCT evidence to judge whether replacing cow's milk or breast milk with casein hydrolysate milk, low-lactose milk, soya-based infant feeds, or whey hydrolysate formula is effective in reducing crying time.

  Breastfeeding mothers should generally be encouraged to continue breast-feeding.

  Soya milk is associated with possible long-term harmful effects on reproductive health.

- We found no direct evidence from RCTs about the effects of cranial osteopathy in infants with colic.

- Spinal manipulation does not appear to reduce the duration of crying associated with infantile colic, nor does it appear to facilitate recovery.

- We found insufficient evidence from high-quality RCTs to determine whether *Lactobacillus reuteri* (probiotic) is effective at reducing crying time in infants with colic.

 **Please visit http://clinicalevidence.bmj.com for full text and references**

## What are the effects of treatments for colic in infants?

| Unknown Effectiveness | • Casein hydrolysate milk (including hypoallergenic diet for breastfeeding mothers) |
|---|---|
| | • Cranial osteopathy |
| | • *Lactobacillus reuteri* (probiotic) |
| | • Low-lactose milk (compared with cow's milk formula or breast milk) |
| | • Soya-based infant feeds (compared with cow's milk formula) |
| | • Spinal manipulation |
| | • Whey hydrolysate milk |

**Search date February 2014**

---

**DEFINITION** Colic in infants is defined as excessive crying in an otherwise healthy and thriving baby. The crying typically starts in the first few weeks of life and usually resolves within 6 months. Excessive crying is defined as crying that lasts at least 3 hours a day, for 3 days a week, for at least 3 weeks. Because of the natural course of infant colic, it can be difficult to interpret trials that do not include a placebo or have no treatment group for comparison.

**INCIDENCE/PREVALENCE** Infant colic leads one in six families (17%) with children to consult a health professional. One systematic review of 15 community-based studies found a wide variation in prevalence, which depended on study design and method of recording. Two prospective studies identified by the review yielded prevalence rates of 5% and 19%. One prospective study (89 breast- and formula-fed infants) found that, at 2 weeks of age, the prevalence of crying over 3 hours a day was 43% among formula-fed infants and 16% among breastfed infants. The prevalence at 6 weeks was 12% among formula-fed infants and 31% among breastfed infants.

**AETIOLOGY/RISK FACTORS** The cause is unclear and, despite its name, infant colic may not have an abdominal cause. It may reflect part of the normal distribution of infantile crying. Other possible explanations are painful intestinal contractions, or parental misinterpretation of normal crying.

**PROGNOSIS** Infant colic improves with time. For most infants, crying and irritability begin to decrease by 4 months of age.

Merit M. Tabbers and Marc A. Benninga

## KEY POINTS

- Although the use of Rome III criteria is recommended for the definition of functional constipation, diagnostic criteria for functional constipation in children still vary across studies. However, they often involve infrequent and possibly painful passing of large, hard stools, with or without faecal incontinence.

    Prevalence of chronic constipation has been estimated at 1% to 5% of children in the UK and US, most of whom have no obvious aetiological factors.

    Half of children with chronic faecal impaction and faecal incontinence have experienced an episode of painful defecation, and many children with chronic constipation exhibit withholding behaviour.

    Disimpaction may be needed if spontaneous expulsion of the faecal mass is unlikely, or if it is causing discomfort or affecting normal feeding.

- The use of polyethylene glycol (PEG) with or without electrolytes is recommended in clinical guidelines as first-line maintenance pharmacological treatment. However, this review has focused on fibre and probiotics as non-pharmacological interventions for constipation in children.

- Low fibre intake is associated with constipation. We found insufficient evidence from RCTs showing that extra fibre intake reduces constipation compared with placebo. We found insufficient evidence on the effects of increased fibre intake compared with lactulose.

- We found insufficient evidence from RCTs on the effects of probiotics versus placebo or versus osmotic laxatives at improving symptoms of constipation.

- Overall, many of the studies we found used different definitions and outcome measures, and the quality of evidence was low. There is a need for further large high-quality RCTs in this condition.

(i) **Please visit http://clinicalevidence.bmj.com for full text and references**

| What are the effects of fibre for children with chronic constipation? | |
|---|---|
| Unknown Effectiveness | • Fibre |

| What are the effects of probiotics for children with chronic constipation? | |
|---|---|
| Unknown Effectiveness | • Probiotics |

Search date May 2014

**DEFINITION** Initially, the Rome II paediatric consortium (1999) defined functional childhood constipation as at least 2 weeks of: scybalous, pebble-like, hard stools for most of the stools; or firm stools two or fewer times per week and no evidence of structural endocrine or metabolic disease. These criteria were not necessarily comprehensive and were found to be restrictive by some researchers. In 2004, the Paris Consensus on Childhood Constipation Terminology (PACCT) group defined childhood constipation as the occurrence of two or more of the following six criteria in the previous 8 weeks: frequency of movements fewer than three per week; more than one episode of faecal incontinence per week; large stools in the rectum or palpable on abdominal examination; passing of stools so large that they may obstruct the toilet; retentive posturing and withholding behaviour; and painful defecation. These criteria were integrated into Rome III criteria (2006). Functional constipation is now defined as the occurrence of two or more of the following six criteria in the previous 2 months in a child with a developmental age of at least 4 years, who has insufficient criteria for the diagnosis of irritable bowel syndrome (including no evidence of an inflammatory, anatomical, metabolic, or neoplastic process): two or fewer defecations in the toilet per week; at least one episode of faecal incontinence per week; history of retentive posturing or excessive volitional stool retention; history of painful or hard bowel movements; presence of a large faecal mass in the rectum; and a history of large diameter stools that may obstruct the toilet. Infants up to 4 years of age have to fulfil two or more criteria for at least 1 month. Many other terms are used in performed studies. Soiling is defined as the involuntary passage of small amounts of stools, resulting in staining of the underwear. The quantity of faecal loss is the main difference between encopresis and soiling. In practice, parents are often unable to accurately estimate the amount of faeces lost in the underwear and, thus, cannot differentiate between encopresis and soiling. Therefore, according to Rome III, the more neutral term of faecal incontinence was adopted, rather than the terms encopresis and soiling. Furthermore, paediatric faecal incontinence is divided into either organic faecal incontinence (e.g., resulting from anorectal malformations or neurological damage) or functional faecal incontinence. Functional faecal incontinence can be subdivided into constipation-associated faecal incontinence and non-retentive faecal incontinence. For this review, we focused on constipation-associated faecal incontinence. In selecting studies for this review, we did not use a singular definition owing to no clear agreement over the definitions. We used the original wording of the authors. Although the use of Rome III criteria are recommended for the definition of functional constipation, diagnostic criteria for functional constipation in children still vary across studies. However, they often involve infrequent and possibly painful passing of large, hard stools with or without faecal incontinence.

**INCIDENCE/PREVALENCE** One systematic review showed a worldwide prevalence of childhood constipation in the general population worldwide ranging from 1% to 30%. Similar prevalence rates were reported for boys and girls.

**AETIOLOGY/RISK FACTORS** Aetiological factors are not found in most children. Hirschsprung's disease, cystic fibrosis, anorectal abnormalities, and metabolic conditions such as hypothyroidism are rare organic causes of childhood constipation. An episode of painful defecation was noted in more than 50% of people who were suffering from faecal soiling or chronic faecal impaction. **Risk factors:** Low fibre intake may be associated with childhood constipation. Prognostic factors could not be identified with one exception; there is strong evidence that the factors of sex or a positive family history have no prognostic value. We found no evidence for a difference between bottle-fed and breastfed babies, although it is generally accepted that bottle-fed babies are more at risk of relative water deficiency and breastfed babies frequently have delays of many days between passing normal stools. Only more recently, was a significant association found between functional constipation and physical, sexual, and emotional abuse.

**PROGNOSIS** On average, 50% of the children referred to a paediatric gastroenterologist will recover and will be without laxatives after 6 to 12 months, 10% will be well while taking laxatives, and 40% will still be symptomatic despite use of laxatives. After 5 and 10 years, 50% and 80% of the children, respectively, will be recovered, with the vast majority no longer taking laxatives. One follow-up study found that symptom duration of 3 months or less before referral was significantly correlated with better outcome. **Faecal impaction:** Disimpaction is necessary if the amount and character of faeces in the colon is of such magnitude that spontaneous expulsion is unlikely, or if it is causing discomfort and affecting normal feeding. Some children with a large rectosigmoid faecaloma may have difficulty passing urine.

David Johnson

## KEY POINTS

- Croup leads to signs of upper airway obstruction, and must be differentiated from acute epiglottitis, bacterial tracheitis, or an inhaled foreign body.

  Croup affects about 3% of children per year, usually between the ages of 6 months and 3 years, and 75% of infections are caused by parainfluenza virus.

  Symptoms usually resolve within 48 hours, but severe upper airway obstruction can, rarely, lead to respiratory failure and arrest.

  Oxygen is standard treatment in children with respiratory distress.

- A single oral dose of dexamethasone improves symptoms in children with mild croup, compared with placebo.

  Although humidification is often used in children with mild to moderate croup, we found no RCT evidence to support its use in clinical practice.

- In children with moderate to severe croup, intramuscular or oral dexamethasone, nebulised adrenaline (epinephrine), and nebulised budesonide reduce symptoms compared with placebo.

  Oral dexamethasone is as effective as nebulised budesonide at reducing symptoms, and is less distressing for the child.

  A dexamethasone dose of 0.15 mg/kg may be as effective as a dose of 0.6 mg/kg. Adding nebulised budesonide to oral dexamethasone does not seem to improve efficacy compared with either drug alone.

  We don't know whether heliox (helium-oxygen mixture) or humidification are beneficial in children with moderate to severe croup.

(i) **Please visit http://clinicalevidence.bmj.com for full text and references**

| What are the effects of treatments (dexamethasone or humidification) in children with mild croup? | |
|---|---|
| Beneficial | • Dexamethasone (oral single dose; reduced need for further medical attention for ongoing symptoms compared with placebo) |
| Unlikely To Be Beneficial | • Humidification* |

| What are the effects of treatments in children with moderate to severe croup? | |
|---|---|
| Beneficial | • Budesonide, nebulised (compared with placebo)<br><br>• Dexamethasone, intramuscular or oral (compared with placebo) |
| Likely To Be Beneficial | • Adrenaline (epinephrine), nebulised (compared with placebo)<br><br>• Dexamethasone, intramuscular (improves croup scores compared with nebulised budesonide)<br><br>• Dexamethasone, oral (compared with nebulised budesonide)* |
| Unknown Effectiveness | • Dexamethasone (oral), higher dose versus lower dose (unclear which dose is most effective) |

|  | • Dexamethasone (intramuscular) versus dexamethasone (oral) (unclear which route of administration is most effective)<br><br>• Dexamethasone, oral (compared with oral prednisolone)<br><br>• Heliox (helium-oxygen mixture)<br><br>• L-adrenaline (epinephrine) compared with racemic adrenaline |
|---|---|
| **Unlikely To Be Beneficial** | • Dexamethasone (oral) plus budesonide (nebulised) versus either drug alone<br><br>• Humidification |

**Search date November 2013**

*Based on consensus.

**DEFINITION** Croup is characterised by the abrupt onset, most commonly at night, of a barking cough, inspiratory stridor, hoarseness, and respiratory distress due to upper airway obstruction. Croup symptoms are often preceded by symptoms like those of upper respiratory tract infection. The most important diagnoses to differentiate from croup include bacterial tracheitis, epiglottitis, and the inhalation of a foreign body. Some investigators distinguish subtypes of croup. Those most commonly distinguished are acute laryngotracheitis and spasmodic croup. Children with acute laryngotracheitis have an antecedent upper respiratory tract infection, are usually febrile, and are thought to have more persistent symptoms. Children with spasmodic croup do not have an antecedent upper respiratory tract infection, are afebrile, have recurrent croup, and are thought to have more transient symptoms. However, there is little empirical evidence that spasmodic croup responds differently from acute laryngotracheitis. **Population:** We have included children aged up to 12 years with croup; no attempt has been made to exclude spasmodic croup. We could not find definitions of clinical severity that are either widely accepted or rigorously derived. We have elected to use definitions derived by a committee consisting of a range of specialists and subspecialists during the development of a clinical practice guideline from Alberta Medical Association (Canada). The definitions of severity have been correlated with the Westley Croup Score, as it is the most widely used clinical score, and its validity and reliability have been well demonstrated. However, RCTs included in the review use a variety of croup scores. **Mild croup:** occasional barking cough; no stridor at rest; and no-to-mild suprasternal, intercostal indrawing (retractions of the skin of the chest wall), or both corresponding to a Westley Croup Score of 0–2. **Moderate croup:** frequent barking cough, easily audible stridor at rest, and suprasternal and sternal wall retraction at rest, but no or little distress or agitation, corresponding to a Westley Croup Score of 3–5. **Severe croup:** frequent barking cough, prominent inspiratory and, occasionally, expiratory stridor, marked sternal wall retractions, decreased air entry on auscultation, and significant distress and agitation, corresponding to a Westley Croup Score of 6–11. **Impending respiratory failure:** barking cough (often not prominent), audible stridor at rest (can occasionally be hard to hear), sternal wall retractions (may not be marked), usually lethargic or decreased level of consciousness, and often dusky complexion without supplemental oxygen, corresponding to a Westley Croup Score greater than 11. During severe respiratory distress, a young child's compliant chest wall 'caves in' during inspiration, causing unsynchronised chest and abdominal wall expansion (paradoxical breathing). By this classification scheme, about 85% of children attending general emergency departments with croup symptoms have mild croup, and less than 1% have severe croup (unpublished prospective data obtained from 21 Alberta general emergency departments).

**INCIDENCE/PREVALENCE** Croup has an average annual incidence of 3% and accounts for 5% of emergency admissions to hospital in children aged under 6 years in North America (unpublished population-based data from Calgary Health Region, Alberta, Canada, 1996–

*(continued over)*

*(from previous page)*

2000). One retrospective Belgian study found that 16% of children aged 5 to 8 years had suffered from croup at least once and 5% had experienced recurrent croup (>3 episodes). We are not aware of epidemiological studies establishing the incidence of croup in other parts of the world.

**AETIOLOGY/RISK FACTORS** One long-term prospective cohort study suggested that croup occurred most commonly in children aged between 6 months and 3 years, but can also occur in children as young as 3 months and as old as 12 to 15 years. Case-report data suggest that it is extremely rare in adults. Infections occur predominantly in late autumn, but can occur during any season. Croup is caused by a variety of viral agents and, occasionally, by *Mycoplasma pneumoniae*. Parainfluenza accounts for 75% of all cases, with the most common type being parainfluenza type 1. Prospective cohort studies suggest that the remaining cases are mainly respiratory syncytial virus, metapneumovirus, influenza A and B, adenovirus, coronavirus, and mycoplasma. Viral invasion of the laryngeal mucosa leads to inflammation, hyperaemia, and oedema. This leads to narrowing of the subglottic region. Children compensate for this narrowing by breathing more quickly and deeply. In children with more severe illness, as the narrowing progresses, their increased effort at breathing becomes counter-productive, airflow through the upper airway becomes turbulent (stridor), their compliant chest wall begins to cave in during inspiration, resulting in paradoxical breathing, and consequently the child becomes fatigued. With these events, if untreated, the child becomes hypoxic and hypercapnoeic, which eventually results in respiratory failure and arrest.

**PROGNOSIS** Croup symptoms resolve in most children within 48 hours. However, a small percentage of children with croup have symptoms that persist for up to a week. Rates of hospital admission vary significantly between communities but, on average, less than 5% of all children with croup are admitted to hospital. Of those admitted to hospital, only 1% to 3% are intubated. Mortality is low; in one 10-year study, less than 0.5% of intubated children died. Uncommon complications of croup include pneumonia, pulmonary oedema, and bacterial tracheitis.

Philip Hazell

## KEY POINTS

- Depression in children and adolescents may have a more insidious onset than in adults, with irritability a more prominent feature than sadness.

  Depression may affect 2% of children and 4% to 8% of adolescents, with a peak incidence around puberty.

  It may be self-limiting, but about 40% of affected children experience a recurrent attack, a third of affected children will make a suicide attempt, and 3% to 4% will die from suicide.

- Fluoxetine improves symptoms and may delay relapse over 7 to 12 weeks compared with placebo in children and adolescents.

  Fluoxetine may be more effective at improving symptoms compared with CBT. Combined fluoxetine plus CBT treatment may be more effective than CBT alone in adolescents.

  Fluvoxamine, citalopram, and escitalopram have not been shown to be beneficial in adolescents and children with depression. Paroxetine and sertraline may be unlikely to be beneficial.

  We don't know whether sertraline is as effective as CBT in the treatment of adolescents. We don't know whether sertraline and CBT as monotherapies are as effective as the combination of sertraline plus CBT.

  Tricyclic antidepressants have not been shown to reduce symptoms of depression and can be toxic in overdose, so their use is not recommended.

  We don't know whether mirtazapine, moclobemide, omega-3 polyunsaturated fatty acids, or St John's Wort are beneficial.

- CAUTION: SSRIs (other than fluoxetine) and venlafaxine have been associated with serious suicide-related events in people under 18 years of age.

- Group CBT in children and adolescents and interpersonal therapy in adolescents may improve symptoms in those with mild to moderate depression, but may not prevent relapse.

  We don't know whether other psychological treatments, individual CBT, group therapeutic support, interpersonal therapy in children, guided self-help, family therapy, or individual psychodynamic psychotherapy improve symptoms.

- We don't know whether electroconvulsive therapy or lithium are beneficial in children or adolescents with refractory depression.

 **Please visit http://clinicalevidence.bmj.com for full text and references**

| What are the effects of pharmacological treatments for depression in children and adolescents? | |
| --- | --- |
| Beneficial | • Fluoxetine (improves remission rates and prevents relapse) in children and adolescents |
| Unknown Effectiveness | • Citalopram/escitalopram in children and adolescents<br>• Fluvoxamine in children and adolescents<br>• MAOIs in children and adolescents<br>• Mirtazapine in children and adolescents |
| Unlikely To Be Beneficial | • Paroxetine in children and adolescents<br>• Sertraline in children and adolescents |
| Likely To Be Ineffective Or Harmful | • Tricyclic antidepressants (oral) in children and adolescents<br>• Venlafaxine in children and adolescents |

## What are the effects of psychological treatments for depression in children and adolescents?

| | |
|---|---|
| **Likely To Be Beneficial** | • CBT (group) in children and adolescents with mild to moderate depression<br><br>• Interpersonal therapy in adolescents with mild to moderate depression |
| **Unknown Effectiveness** | • CBT (individual) in children and adolescents with mild to moderate depression<br><br>• Family therapy in children and adolescents<br><br>• Group therapeutic support (other than CBT) in children and adolescents<br><br>• Guided self-help in children and adolescents<br><br>• Individual psychodynamic psychotherapy in children and adolescents<br><br>• Interpersonal therapy in children |
| **Unlikely To Be Beneficial** | • CBT (for relapse prevention) in children and adolescents |

## What are the effects of combination treatments for depression in children and adolescents?

| | |
|---|---|
| **Beneficial** | • Fluoxetine plus CBT in adolescents |
| **Unknown Effectiveness** | • Fluoxetine plus CBT in children<br><br>• Sertraline plus CBT in adolescents |

## What are the effects of complementary treatments for depression in children and adolescents?

| | |
|---|---|
| **Unknown Effectiveness** | • Omega-3 polyunsaturated fatty acids<br><br>• St John's Wort (*Hypericum perforatum*) in children and adolescents |

## What are the effects of treatments for refractory depression in children and adolescents?

| | |
|---|---|
| **Unknown Effectiveness** | • Electroconvulsive therapy in children and adolescents<br><br>• Lithium in children and adolescents |

Search date July 2011

**DEFINITION** Compared with adult depression (see reviews on depression in adults: drug and physical treatments, p 340 and depression in adults: psychological treatments and care pathways, p 343), depression in children (6–12 years) and adolescents (13–18 years) may have a more insidious onset, may be characterised more by irritability than by sadness, and occurs more often in association with other conditions such as anxiety, conduct disorder, hyperkinesis, and learning problems. The term "major depression" is used to distinguish discrete episodes of depression from mild, chronic (1 year or longer) low mood, or irritability, which is known as "dysthymia". The severity of depression may be defined by the level of impairment and the presence or absence of psychomotor changes and somatic symptoms (see review on depression in adults: drug and physical treatments, p 340). In some studies, severity of depression is defined according to cut-off scores on depression rating scales. Definitions of refractory depression (also known as treatment-resistant depression) vary, but in this review it refers to depression that has failed to respond, or has only partially responded, to an adequate trial of at least two recognised treatments.

**INCIDENCE/PREVALENCE** The prevalence of major depression is estimated to be approximately 2% in children and 4% to 8% in adolescents. Preadolescent boys and girls are affected equally by the condition, but in adolescents, depression is more common among girls than boys.

**AETIOLOGY/RISK FACTORS** Depression in children usually arises from a combination of genetic vulnerability, suboptimal early developmental experiences, and exposure to stresses. However, depressive syndromes sometimes occur as sequelae to physical illness, such as viral infection, and may overlap with fatigue syndromes. The heritability of depression may increase with age, but the findings from genetics studies are inconsistent. Recurrent depression seems to have a stronger familial association compared with single-episode depression. Depression-prone individuals have a cognitive style characterised by an overly pessimistic outlook on events. This cognitive style precedes the onset of depression and seems independent of recent life events and ongoing stresses. Stressful life events may trigger the first occurrence of depression, but are rarely sufficient on their own to cause depression. After a first incidence of depression, lower levels of stress are needed to provoke subsequent episodes of illness. Enduring problems in the relationship with the primary carers is an important risk factor for depression, but such difficulties also predispose to other psychiatric disorders.

**PROGNOSIS** In children and adolescents, the recurrence rate after a first depressive episode is 40%. Young people experiencing a moderate to severe depressive episode may be more likely than adults to have a manic episode within the following few years. Trials of treatments for child and adolescent depression have found high rates of response to placebo (as much as two-thirds of people in some inpatient studies), suggesting that episodes of depression may be self-limiting in many cases. One third of young people who experience a depressive episode will make a suicide attempt at some stage, and 3% to 4% of those who experience depression will die from suicide.

Leena D Mewasingh

## KEY POINTS

- Febrile seizures are defined as events in infancy or childhood usually occurring between 3 months and 5 years of age associated with a fever, but without evidence of intracranial infection or defined cause for the seizure.

  Simple febrile seizures are generalised in onset and have a brief duration. They do not occur more than once in 24 hours and resolve spontaneously. Complex seizures are longer lasting, have focal symptoms (at onset or during the seizure), and can recur within 24 hours or within the same febrile illness. This review only deals with simple febrile seizures.

  About 2% to 5% of children in the US and Western Europe, and 6% to 9% of infants and children in Japan will have experienced at least one febrile seizure by age 5 years.

  A very small number of children with simple febrile seizures may develop afebrile seizures, but simple febrile seizures are not associated with any permanent neurological deficits.

- Evidence is lacking on whether antipyretic drug treatments (paracetamol, ibuprofen) or physical methods of temperature reduction (tepid sponging, removing clothing, cooling room, direct fanning of child) are useful in treating episodes of fever to prevent seizure recurrence in children with one or more previous simple febrile seizures.

- Intermittent anticonvulsants (clobazam, diazepam) may be effective in reducing seizure recurrence at some time points, but the lack of consistency of results over time and weak methods of RCTs make it difficult to draw any definitive conclusions on their effectiveness, and any long-term clinical benefits are unclear.

  Also, adverse effects, such as hyperactivity, lethargy, ataxia, and sedation, may often be associated with the use of intermittent anticonvulsants (clobazam, diazepam, lorazepam).

 **Please visit http://clinicalevidence.bmj.com for full text and references**

| What are the effects of treatments given during episodes of fever in children (aged 6 months to 5 years) with one or more previous simple febrile seizures? | |
|---|---|
| Unknown Effectiveness | • Antipyretic drug treatments (paracetamol, ibuprofen) |
| | • Intermittent anticonvulsants (clobazam, diazepam, lorazepam) |
| | • Physical methods of temperature reduction (tepid sponging, removing clothing, cooling room, direct fanning of child) |

**Search date July 2013**

---

**DEFINITION** Febrile seizures are divided into three types: simple febrile seizures, complex febrile seizures, and febrile status epilepticus. This review focuses on children with simple febrile seizures. The National Institutes of Health (NIH) definition of a febrile seizure is "an event in infancy or childhood usually occurring between 3 months and 5 years of age associated with a fever, but without evidence of intracranial infection or defined cause for their seizure", after having excluded children with previous afebrile seizures. Another definition from the International League Against Epilepsy (ILAE) is that of "a seizure occurring in childhood after 1 month of age associated with a febrile illness not caused by an infection of the central nervous system (CNS), without previous neonatal seizures or a previous unprovoked seizure, and not meeting the criteria for other acute symptomatic seizures". In addition, following updates to ILAE classification and terminology, febrile seizures are now categorised under "conditions with epileptic seizures that are traditionally not diagnosed as a form of epilepsy per se". In working practice, the lower age limit for febrile seizures is generally taken to be 6 months, given concerns regarding the possibility of an underlying serious but treatable infection in younger infants masquerading as a febrile seizure (e.g., meningitis). A simple febrile seizure is a generalised seizure that has a brief duration. The American Academy of Pediatrics has defined this brief duration to be <15 minutes; whereas, in the UK, a maximum duration of 10 minutes is used. A simple febrile seizure does not occur more than once in 24 hours and resolves spontaneously. Treatment for the actual seizure is generally not indicated, given the short duration. In >80% of children the duration of the febrile seizure is <10 minutes, and in only about 9% of children do they last >15 minutes. Often, by the time the child presents to hospital, the seizure has already stopped. A febrile seizure may also be the presenting sign of a fever episode. This review does not include children experiencing complex febrile seizures, which are characterised by any of the following features: >10 or 15 minutes in duration (depending on the definition used), focal symptoms (at onset or during the seizure), and recurrence within 24 hours or within the same febrile illness. Investigations, including neuro-imaging and lumbar puncture, are often warranted. Also excluded from this review are children experiencing febrile status epilepticus, which lasts >30 minutes and requires treatment. Addressing parental anxiety forms a key part of the management of febrile seizures because parents' (unspoken) worry with a first seizure is often that their child might have died. It is good practice to support families with information on simple febrile seizures and contact details of medical services, and reassure them of the benign nature of simple febrile seizures.

**INCIDENCE/PREVALENCE** About 2% to 5% of children in the US and Western Europe, and 6% to 9% of infants and children in Japan will have experienced at least one febrile seizure, simple or complex, by the age of 5 years. Elsewhere the incidence varies: it ranges from 5% to 10% in India and is as high as 14% in Guam. There are no specific data available for simple febrile seizures.

**AETIOLOGY/RISK FACTORS** While the exact cause of simple febrile seizures is unknown, it is thought to be multifactorial, with both genetic and environmental factors having been shown to contribute to its pathogenesis. Increasingly, a genetic predisposition is recognised with febrile seizures occurring in families. However, the exact mode of inheritance is not known, and seems to vary between families. While polygenic inheritance is likely, there is a small number of families identified with an autosomal-dominant pattern of inheritance of febrile seizures, leading to the description of a 'febrile seizure susceptibility trait' with an autosomal-dominant pattern of inheritance with reduced penetrance. In addition, mutations in several genes have been found that account for enhanced susceptibility to febrile seizures. A familial epilepsy syndrome exists (generalised epilepsy with febrile seizures plus [GEFS+]), in which people can have classical febrile seizures, febrile seizures that persist beyond 5 years (hence FS+), and/or epilepsy. The revised ILAE classification refers to FS+ as an 'electroclinical syndrome' that usually starts in childhood but can occasionally have its onset in infancy. Similar genetic factors have been identified that are involved in both febrile seizures and FS+. Although the exact molecular mechanisms of febrile seizures are yet to be understood, underlying mutations have been found in genes encoding the gamma-aminobutyric acid A receptor and the sodium channel (e.g., sodium channel, voltage-gated, type I, alpha subunit [SCN1A]). The latter, in particular, is associated with an early epilepsy syndrome and epileptic encephalopathy called Dravet syndrome (also known as severe myoclonic epilepsy of infancy [SMEI]), which often begins with prolonged seizures triggered by fever or the first presentation of epilepsy. Certain SCN1A mutations have also been associated with increased susceptibility to febrile seizures and FS+. As most of the mutations in SCN1A-related epilepsies occur de novo, when an infant presents initially with febrile seizures, there is uncertainty as to whether they will have simple febrile seizures only, develop FS+, or develop severe epilepsy, such as Dravet syndrome. In the UK, genetic testing for SCN1A mutations is currently not routinely carried out in clinical practice for infants and children with simple febrile seizures, but it is increasingly being considered and performed in infants and children with complex febrile seizures, febrile status, and FS+. With regards to risk factors, febrile seizures are more frequent in children attending day-care centres, and in those with a first- or second-degree relative with a history of febrile seizures.

*(continued over)*

*(from previous page)*

The risk of another child having febrile seizures is 1 in 5 if one sibling is affected, and 1 in 3 if both parents and a previous child have had febrile seizures. Other risk factors associated with an increased rate of febrile seizure recurrence include young age at onset (<12 months), history of simple or complex febrile seizures, and body temperature at onset of <40°C. Among these, age at onset seems the most constant predictive factor, with 50% of children aged <12 months and 30% of children aged >12 months presenting with a recurrent febrile seizure. Positive family history of epilepsy is not consistently associated with increased simple febrile seizure recurrence.

**PROGNOSIS** A very small number of children with simple febrile seizures may develop afebrile seizures, but simple febrile seizures are not associated with any permanent neurological deficits. Furthermore, simple febrile seizures do not appear to have any known long-term adverse effects or sequelae. Whereas traditionally understood to be a 'benign' condition, the ILAE cautions against this terminology, stating that 'benign' can be misleading and leave physicians, patients, and families unaware of and unprepared to address the wide variety of brain disorders that may be associated with febrile seizures, such as cognitive, behavioural, and psychiatric illnesses, as well as sudden death and suicide. Nonetheless, there is very little evidence to suggest that simple febrile seizures have any adverse effects on behaviour or learning. The risk of developing epilepsy is increased further in children with a history of complex febrile seizures. A strong association exists between febrile status epilepticus or febrile seizures characterised by focal symptoms and later development of temporal lobe epilepsy.

Jacqueline R Dalby-Payne and Elizabeth J Elliott

## KEY POINTS

- Gastroenteritis in children worldwide is usually caused by rotavirus, which leads to considerable morbidity and mortality.

  Bacterial causes of gastroenteritis are more common in developing countries.

- Rotavirus vaccines are both safe and effective in preventing and minimising harm from gastroenteritis caused by rotavirus, particularly in preventing severe disease.

- Enteral rehydration solutions containing sugar or food plus electrolytes are as effective as intravenous fluids at correcting dehydration and reducing the duration of hospital stay, and may have fewer major adverse effects.

- Lactose-free feeds may reduce the duration of diarrhoea in children with mild to severe dehydration compared with feeds containing lactose, but studies have shown conflicting results.

- Loperamide can reduce the prevalence of acute diarrhoea in children in the first 48 hours after initiation of treatment, but there is an increased risk of adverse effects compared with placebo.

- Ondansetron reduces vomiting but increases diarrhoea in children with gastroenteritis compared with placebo.

- Zinc may reduce the duration of diarrhoea compared with placebo but may also increase the risk of vomiting; most studies were conducted in developing countries, with little evidence from developed countries.

- Probiotics may reduce the duration of diarrhoea and may reduce hospital stay, with most evidence for *Lactobacillus* species.

(i) **Please visit http://clinicalevidence.bmj.com for full text and references**

| What are the effects of interventions to prevent acute gastroenteritis in children? | |
|---|---|
| Beneficial | • Rotavirus vaccines (reduce episodes of gastroenteritis caused by rotavirus) |

| What are the effects of treatments for acute gastroenteritis in children? | |
|---|---|
| Beneficial | • Enteral (oral or gastric) rehydration solutions (as effective as intravenous fluids) <br> • Probiotics (reduce duration of diarrhoea) |
| Likely To Be Beneficial | • Lactose-free feeds (may reduce duration of diarrhoea) <br> • Ondansetron (reduces vomiting in children with acute gastroenteritis, but possible increased risk of diarrhoea) <br> • Zinc (reduces duration of diarrhoea; evidence mainly in developing countries) |
| Trade-off Between Benefits And Harms | • Loperamide (reduces duration of diarrhoea, but possible increased risk of adverse effects) |

Search date March 2010

**DEFINITION** Acute gastroenteritis results from infection of the gastrointestinal tract, most commonly with a virus. It is characterised by rapid onset of diarrhoea with or without vomiting, nausea, fever, and abdominal pain. In children, the symptoms and signs can be non-specific. Diarrhoea is defined as the frequent passage of unformed, liquid stools. Regardless of the cause, the mainstay of management of acute gastroenteritis is provision of adequate fluids to prevent and treat dehydration. The WHO also recommends administration of oral zinc. In this review, we examine the benefits and harms of interventions to prevent and treat gastroenteritis, irrespective of its cause.

**INCIDENCE/PREVALENCE** Worldwide, diarrhoea causes the death of about 2 million children under 5 years of age each year; of these deaths, up to 600,000 are caused by rotavirus. Gastroenteritis leads to hospital admission in 7/1000 children under 5 years of age each year in the UK, and diarrhoea results in hospital admission in 1/23 to 1/27 children in the US by the age of 5 years. In Australia, gastroenteritis accounts for 6% of all hospital admissions in children under 15 years. Acute gastroenteritis accounts for 204/1000 general practitioner consultations in children under 5 years in the UK. In the US, rotavirus results in hospital admission in 1/67 to 1/85 children by the age of 5 years.

**AETIOLOGY/RISK FACTORS** In developed countries, acute gastroenteritis is predominantly caused by viruses (87%), of which rotavirus is the most common. Worldwide, rotavirus causes almost 40% of cases of severe diarrhoea in infants. Rotavirus outbreaks show a seasonal pattern in temperate climates, and infections peak during winter months. In countries closer to the equator, seasonality is less noticeable, but the disease is more pronounced in the drier and cooler months. The reason for rotavirus seasonality is not known. Bacteria, predominantly *Campylobacter, Salmonella, Shigella,* and *Escherichia coli,* cause most of the remaining cases of acute gastroenteritis. In developing countries, where bacterial pathogens are more prevalent, rotavirus is still a major cause of gastroenteritis; 82% of worldwide deaths caused by rotavirus occur in these countries.

**PROGNOSIS** Acute gastroenteritis is usually self-limiting, but if untreated it can result in morbidity and mortality secondary to water loss, and electrolyte and acid–base disturbance. Acute diarrhoea causes 4 million deaths each year in children aged under 5 years in Asia (excluding China), Africa, and Latin America, and more than 80% of deaths occur in children under 2 years of age. Although death is uncommon in developed countries, dehydration secondary to gastroenteritis is a significant cause of morbidity and hospital admission.

Rajini Sarvananthan

## KEY POINTS

- Reflux of gastric contents into the oesophagus in infants and children may cause recurrent vomiting (usually before 6 weeks of age), epigastric and abdominal pain, feeding difficulties, failure to thrive, and irritability.

  At least half of infants regurgitate feeds at least once a day, but this only causes other problems in about 20% of infants, and most cases resolve spontaneously by 12 to 18 months of age. The majority of infants with regurgitation do not present with further symptoms or complications seen in gastro-oesophageal reflux disease (GORD). Reassurance and simple feed changes (small frequent feeds) are often all that is needed, and these infants do not need further investigations or treatment.

  Risk factors include infants born prematurely, lower oesophageal sphincter disorders, hiatus hernia, gastric distension, raised intra-abdominal pressure, and neurodevelopmental problems.

- We searched for evidence of effectiveness from RCTs and systematic reviews of RCTs.

- We extracted data from RCTs in our analysis of the selected interventions. We have focused on infants, including preterm infants, and children up to 12 years. Most of the evidence we found was in infants and very young children.

- Thickened feeds (with rice cereal, carob-bean gum, carob-seed flour, sodium carboxymethylcellulose, pre-thickened milk formula) may reduce the severity and frequency of regurgitation and vomiting in the short term compared with no thickeners/standard milk formula in infants and children younger than 2 years.

- We don't know if hydrolysed formula reduces symptoms of GORD in infants and young children compared with placebo or no treatment as we found no RCTs.

- Sodium alginate may be more effective in infants and children younger than 2 years at reducing the number of episodes of vomiting at 14 days, but we don't know whether it is more effective at reducing the number of regurgitation episodes.

  The high sodium content of sodium alginate makes it unsuitable for use in preterm babies as this may result in complications of hypernatraemia.

- Sleeping in the left lateral or prone position may improve oesophageal pH and number of episodes of reflux compared with sleeping supine or on the right side, but these positions increase the risk of sudden infant death syndrome (SIDS) compared with supine sleeping, and cannot be recommended in infants for that reason.

- We don't know whether sleeping in the head elevated position reduces symptoms of GORD compared with sleeping in the horizontal position. Due to the increased risk of SIDS, only the supine position is recommended for infants.

- We don't know whether metoclopramide is more effective than placebo or no treatment at reducing gastro-oesophageal reflux symptoms in infants and children up to 17 years old. However, a more serious consideration is the risk of adverse effects when used in the long term. Metoclopramide is now contraindicated for the treatment of GORD due to its adverse effects.

- We don't know whether $H_2$ antagonists reduce symptoms in babies and children with GORD, and they may cause adverse effects.

- Proton pump inhibitors may be no more effective than placebo at improving symptoms in infants and children younger than 12 months. We found no RCTs comparing proton pump inhibitors with placebo in older children.

- There is no evidence that domperidone reduces symptoms in children and we do not know whether domperidone reduces symptoms in infants. Domperidone is not recommended for long-term use due to its adverse effects on the heart.
- Weight loss is not a treatment option for infants and young children. We don't know whether weight loss reduces symptoms of GORD in older children as we found no RCTs.

(i) **Please visit http://clinicalevidence.bmj.com for full text and references**

## What are the effects of treatment for symptomatic gastro-oesophageal reflux in infants and children?

| Likely To Be Beneficial | • Feed thickeners in infants<br>• Sodium alginate |
|---|---|
| Trade-off Between Benefits And Harms | • Left lateral or prone sleep positioning |
| Unknown Effectiveness | • $H_2$ antagonists<br>• Head elevated sleep positioning<br>• Hydrolysed formula<br>• Proton pump inhibitors<br>• Weight loss |
| Likely To Be Ineffective Or Harmful | • Domperidone<br>• Metoclopramide |

**Search date October 2013**

**DEFINITION** Gastro-oesophageal reflux (GOR) is the passive retrograde transfer of gastric contents into the oesophagus due to relaxation of the lower oesophageal sphincter, which is a normal physiological process and causes effortless regurgitation in otherwise healthy infants and children. This does not cause additional symptoms and as such no investigations or treatment is required, only parental reassurance. Gastro-oesophageal reflux disease (GORD) occurs as a result of complications of GOR and results in more troublesome symptoms, such as unexplained crying, feeding refusal, choking or gagging, sleep disturbance, abdominal pain, poor weight gain, and respiratory symptoms. A survey of 69 children (median age 16 months) with GORD attending a tertiary referral centre found that presenting symptoms were recurrent vomiting (72%), epigastric and abdominal pain (36%), feeding difficulties (29%), failure to thrive (28%), and irritability (19%). However, results may not be generalisable to infants or children presenting in primary care, who make up the most of the cases. More than 90% of children with GORD have vomiting before 6 weeks of age. GORD symptoms often vary depending on the age of the child. Older children and adolescents may present with symptoms very similar to those in adults (see overview for GORD in adults, p 163).

**INCIDENCE/PREVALENCE** Gastro-oesophageal regurgitation is considered a problem if it is frequent, persistent, and associated with other symptoms such as increased crying, discomfort with regurgitation, and frequent back arching. A cross-sectional survey of parents of 948 infants attending 19 primary care paediatric practices found that regurgitation of at least one episode a day was reported in 51% of infants aged 0 to 3 months. 'Problematic' regurgitation occurred in significantly fewer infants (14% with problematic regurgitation *v* 51% with regurgitation of at least 1 episode a day; P <0.001). Peak regurgitation reported as 'problematic' was reported in 23% of infants aged 6 months. A prospective study of 2879 infants followed up from just after birth (from birth up to 2 weeks) to age 6 months by primary-care paediatricians found that regurgitation occurred in 23% of infants during the study period.

**AETIOLOGY/RISK FACTORS** Risk factors for GORD include immaturity of the lower oesophageal sphincter, chronic relaxation of the sphincter, increased abdominal pressure, gastric distension, hiatus hernia, and oesophageal dysmotility. Premature infants and children with severe neurodevelopmental problems or congenital oesophageal anomalies are particularly at risk.

**PROGNOSIS** Regurgitation is considered benign, and most cases resolve spontaneously by 12 to 18 months of age. The prevalence of 'problematic' regurgitation also reduced from 23% in infants aged 6 months to 3% in infants aged 10 to 12 months. One cohort study found that infants with frequent spilling in the first 2 years of life (at least 90 days in the first 2 years) were more likely to have symptoms of gastro-oesophageal reflux at 9 years of age than those with no spilling (RR 2.3, 95% CI 1.3 to 4.0). Rare complications of GORD include oesophagitis with haematemesis and anaemia, respiratory problems (such as cough, apnoea, and recurrent wheeze), and failure to thrive. A small comparative study (40 children) suggested that, when compared with healthy children, infants with GORD had slower development of feeding skills, and problems affecting behaviour, swallowing, food intake, and mother-child interaction.

Nick Peter Barnes

### KEY POINTS

- Diagnosis of migraine headache in children can be difficult as it depends on subjective symptoms; diagnostic criteria are broader than in adults.

  Migraine occurs in 3% to 10% of children and increases with age up to puberty.

  Migraine spontaneously remits after puberty in half of children, but if it begins during adolescence, it may be more likely to persist throughout adulthood.

- We don't know whether paracetamol or NSAIDs relieve the pain of migraine in children, as we found few good trials. Nevertheless, it is widely accepted good clinical practice that paracetamol, an NSAID such as ibuprofen, or both, should be the first-line agents for headache relief during acute attacks unless contraindicated.

- There is increasing RCT evidence that nasal sumatriptan is likely to be beneficial in reducing migraine headache pain at 2 hours in children aged 12 to 17 years with persisting headache.

  We found limited evidence that oral almotriptan may be more effective than placebo at reducing migraine headache pain at 2 hours, but not at reducing migraine recurrence within 24 hours.

  Oral rizatriptan seems to reduce nausea but we don't know if it reduces headache pain compared with placebo.

  We don't know whether oral zolmitriptan or eletriptan are effective; data regarding zolmitriptan are conflicting and data regarding eletriptan are limited.

- We don't know whether beta-blockers as prophylaxis are more effective than placebo in preventing migraine headache in children as the evidence is weak and inconclusive.

- We don't know whether flunarizine as prophylaxis is effective at reducing migraine symptoms in children.

- Pizotifen is widely used as prophylaxis in children with migraine, but we found no trials assessing its efficacy.

- Topiramate may be useful as prophylaxis in children with migraine when compared with placebo, but the evidence is limited.

  We don't know how prophylactic topiramate compares with prophylactic propranolol in reducing migraine headache in children as the evidence is inconsistent.

 **Please visit http://clinicalevidence.bmj.com for full text and references**

| **What are the effects of treatments for acute attacks of migraine headache in children?** | |
|---|---|
| Beneficial | • 5HT$_1$ agonists (most evidence of benefit for nasal sumatriptan; evidence is limited for other drugs in this class) |
| Likely To Be Beneficial | • NSAIDs<br>• Paracetamol |

| **What are the effects of pharmacological prophylaxis for migraine headache in children?** | |
|---|---|
| Unknown Effectiveness | • Beta-blockers<br>• Flunarizine |

| | • Pizotifen |
| | • Topiramate |

**Search date June 2014**

---

**DEFINITION** Migraine is defined by the International Headache Society (IHS) as a recurrent headache that occurs with or without aura and that lasts 2 to 72 hours. It is usually unilateral in nature, pulsating in quality, of moderate or severe intensity, and is aggravated by routine physical activity. Nausea, vomiting, photophobia, and phonophobia are common accompanying symptoms. This review focuses on migraine in children younger than 18 years of age. Diagnostic criteria for children are broader than criteria for adults, allowing for a broader range of duration and a broader localisation of the pain. Diagnosis can be more difficult in young children as the condition is defined by subjective symptoms. Studies that do not explicitly use criteria that are congruent with IHS diagnostic criteria (or revised IHS criteria in children <16 years of age) have been excluded from this review. Many children with a symptom cluster that includes headache may not perfectly match the IHS classification, but may benefit from medical interventions currently in use. A liberal approach to symptomatology is therefore likely to be beneficial in clinical practice.

**INCIDENCE/PREVALENCE** Migraine occurs in 3% to 10% of children, and currently affects 50/1000 school-age children in the UK and an estimated 7.8 million children in the EU. Studies in resource-poor countries suggest that migraine is the most common diagnosis among children presenting with headache to a medical practitioner. It is rarely diagnosed in children younger than 2 years of age because of the symptom-based definition, but it increases steadily with age thereafter. Migraine affects boys and girls similarly before puberty, but girls are more likely to suffer from migraine afterwards.

**AETIOLOGY/RISK FACTORS** The cause of migraine headaches is unknown. We found few reliable data identifying risk factors or measuring their effects in children. Suggested risk factors include stress, foods, menses, and exercise in genetically predisposed children. From a pathophysiological perspective, central neuronal hyper-excitability may underly a susceptibility to, and the development of, migraine episodes. The evidence base for this suggests multifactorial causation, with amino acids, magnesium depletion, calcium channels, and controlling genes all being implicated. Once triggered, a slowly propagating wave of neuronal depolarisation, 'cortical spreading dysfunction', may precipitate symptoms compounded by activation of trigeminal vascular afferents. These, in turn, may sensitise other peripheral/central afferent circuits to mechanical, chemical, and thermal stimuli, with stimulation of these circuits being painful. An abnormal cerebrovascular response to visual stimuli may also contribute. In support of this, people with migraine with aura exhibit a significantly higher cerebral blood flow than headache-free people in response to repetitive visual stimulation. In addition, people with migraine significantly lack habituation of this vascular response suggesting that they may have a reduced capacity to adapt to environmental stimuli (including light) and this may be part of the pathogenic process. The pathophysiological processes that precipitate the development of migraine in part support the logic in using calcium channel blockers therapeutically.

**PROGNOSIS** We found no reliable data about the prognosis of childhood migraine headache diagnosed by IHS criteria. Not all treatments work for every child; some will be non-responders to medicines with the clearest evidence available from controlled trials to support their use. It has been suggested that more than half of children will have spontaneous remission after puberty. Migraine that develops during adolescence often continues in adult life, although attacks tend to be less frequent and severe over time. We found one longitudinal study from Sweden (73 children with 'pronounced' migraine and mean age onset of 6 years) with more than 40 years' follow-up, which predated the IHS criteria for migraine headache. It found that migraine headaches had ceased before the age of 25 years in 23% of people. However, by the age of 50 years, more than half of people continued to have migraine headaches. We found no prospective data examining long-term risks in children with migraine.

Paul T. Heath and Luke Jardine

## KEY POINTS

- Early-onset neonatal sepsis, typically caused by group B streptococcal infection, usually begins within 24 hours of birth, affects up to 2 infants per 1000 live births, and leads to death if untreated.

  1 in 4 women carry group B streptococci vaginally, which can infect the amniotic fluid before delivery or infect the baby during delivery, causing sepsis, pneumonia, or meningitis.

  Very low-birthweight infants are at much higher risk of infection or mortality, with up to 3% infected, and mortality rates of up to 30%, even with immediate antibiotic treatment.

  Late-onset group B streptococcal infection begins from 7 days of age and usually causes fever or meningitis, but is less often fatal compared with early-onset infection.

- Routine antibiotic prophylaxis, either given to asymptomatic infants born to mothers with risk factors for neonatal infection or given to low-birthweight babies after birth, does not seem to be beneficial in reducing neonatal infection or mortality compared with close monitoring and selective antibiotics.

  We don't know which antibiotic regimen is most effective at preventing group B streptococcal infection in high-risk neonates.

- Increasing peripartum antibiotic prophylaxis may be associated with a shift in the pathogens causing sepsis in preterm and very low-birthweight infants, with *Escherichia coli* becoming a more prevalent cause.

 **Please visit http://clinicalevidence.bmj.com for full text and references**

### What are the effects of prophylactic treatment of asymptomatic neonates less than 7 days old with known risk factors for early-onset group B streptococcal infection?

| Unknown Effectiveness | • Different antibiotics |
| --- | --- |
| Unlikely To Be Beneficial | • Routine antibiotic prophylaxis (no more effective than monitoring and selective treatment) |

**Search date November 2013**

**DEFINITION** Early-onset neonatal sepsis usually occurs within the first 7 days of life, and is typically caused by infection with group B streptococcus. About 90% of cases present within 24 hours of birth. Group B streptococcus exists as part of the normal bacterial flora in the vagina and gastrointestinal tract. Infection can be transmitted by aspiration of group B streptococcus-infected amniotic fluid by the fetus. Symptoms of early-onset group B streptococcal infection may be non-specific, including temperature instability, poor feeding, excessive crying or irritability, and respiratory distress. Early-onset group B streptococcal infection typically presents with sepsis (69% of cases), pneumonia (26% of cases), respiratory distress (13% of cases), and, rarely, meningitis (11% of cases). Late-onset group B streptococcus infection occurs from 7 to 90 days of age, and differs from early-onset group B streptococcal infection in terms of group B streptococcus serotype, clinical manifestations, and outcome. Late-onset infection typically presents with fever or meningitis. This review deals with full-term and premature asymptomatic babies born with a known risk factor for group B streptococcal infection, but in whom a specific diagnosis of group B streptococcus (either by blood, urine, or cerebrospinal fluid) has not yet been made. The antenatal or intrapartum treatment of women with known group B streptococcal colonisation or infection is outside the scope of this review.

**INCIDENCE/PREVALENCE** The overall incidence of neonatal bacterial infections is between 1 and 8 infants per 1000 live births, and between 160 and 300 per 1000 very low-birthweight infants. Group B streptococcal infection accounts for nearly 50% of serious early-onset neonatal bacterial infections. Surveillance conducted between 2000 and 2001 estimated that there were 0.72 cases of group B streptococcal infection per 1000 live births in the UK and Ireland and that, of these, 0.48 cases per 1000 live births were early-onset, and 0.24 cases per 1000 live births were late-onset infection. Although the estimated incidence of early-onset group B streptococcal infection is 0.5 per 1000 births in the UK overall, incidence varies geographically from 0.21 per 1000 live births in Scotland to 0.73 per 1000 live births in Northern Ireland. Overall, the US and the UK currently have relatively similar incidences. Data from the US indicate that the rate of early-onset infection has decreased from 1.7 cases per 1000 live births in 1993 to 0.28 cases per 1000 live births in 2008. This is thought to be a result of the increasing use of maternal intrapartum antibiotic prophylaxis.

**AETIOLOGY/RISK FACTORS** The main risk factor for group B streptococcal infection in the baby is maternal group B streptococcal colonisation. Bacteria originating in the maternal genital tract can infect the amniotic fluid via intact or ruptured membranes. Neonatal infection can result from fetal aspiration or ingestion of the infected amniotic fluid. Infection of the neonate can also occur during birth, when the neonate moves through the vagina, with systemic infection then occurring via the umbilical cord, respiratory or gastrointestinal tract, or skin abrasions. Other risk factors for group B streptococcal infection include prematurity, low birthweight, prolonged rupture of membranes, intrapartum fever, chorioamnionitis, maternal ethnicity (black and Hispanic mothers are at increased risk compared with white mothers), endometritis, heavy maternal colonisation, and frequent vaginal examinations during labour and delivery. Lower maternal age (<20 years) and cigarette smoking may be associated with an increased risk of early-onset group B streptococcal infection, but these associations have not been shown consistently. Other factors that may increase the risk of group B streptococcal infection include lower socio-economic status, and maternal urinary tract infection during the third trimester. The role of group B streptococcal colonisation of fathers, siblings, and close household contacts in the development of late-onset group B streptococcal infection is unclear. Late-onset group B streptococcus infection is predominantly associated with serotype III.

**PROGNOSIS** Group B streptococcal infection is a frequent cause of neonatal morbidity and mortality. In the UK, one study has estimated that early-onset group B streptococcus infection causes more than 40 neonatal deaths and around 25 cases of long-term disability every year, whereas late-onset group B streptococcus infection causes around 16 deaths and 40 cases of long-term disability every year. In the US, the case fatality ratio of early-onset group B streptococcal disease declined from approximately 50% in the 1970s to 4% to 6% in recent years, primarily because of improved medical neonatal care. Mortality is higher among preterm infants; one prospective surveillance study (396,586 live births between February 2006 and December 2009) reported a mortality rate of 30% for preterm infants with early-onset group B streptococcus infection. Late-onset group B streptococcus infection typically presents as bacteraemia or meningitis. Less frequently, late-onset group B streptococcus infection may cause septic arthritis, cellulitis, or focal infections such as osteomyelitis. Late-onset group B streptococcal infection tends to have a less fulminant onset and is less often fatal than early-onset infection. One observational study reported a mortality rate of 14% with early-onset group B streptococcal infection compared with 4% with late-onset infection. Little information is available concerning long-term sequelae for survivors of neonatal group B streptococcal infection, except in the case of group B streptococcus meningitis, where nearly 50% of survivors may have long-term neurodevelopmental sequelae.

Luke Anthony Jardine and Paul Woodgate

## KEY POINTS

- About 50% of term and 80% of preterm babies develop jaundice, which usually appears 2 to 4 days after birth, and resolves spontaneously after 1 to 2 weeks.

    Jaundice is caused by bilirubin deposition in the skin. Most jaundice in newborn infants is a result of increased red cell breakdown and decreased bilirubin excretion.

    Breastfeeding, haemolysis, and some metabolic and genetic disorders also increase the risk of jaundice.

    Unconjugated bilirubin can be neurotoxic, causing an acute or chronic encephalopathy that may result in cerebral palsy, hearing loss, and seizures.

- Hospital phototherapy is provided by conventional or fibreoptic lights as a treatment to reduce neonatal jaundice.

- We assessed RCTs comparing light with different wavelengths used for hospital phototherapy for unconjugated hyperbilirubinaemia in term and preterm infants. Interventions compared included: conventional phototherapy (using halogen-quartz bulbs), daylight fluorescent lamps, standard blue fluorescent lamps, blue fluorescent lamps with a narrow spectral emission, green fluorescent lamps, blue-green fluorescent lamps, blue LED lamps, and blue-green LED lamps.

    Blue-green fluorescent light may be more effective than blue fluorescent light at reducing the requirement for phototherapy after 24 hours in healthy low birth weight babies with hyperbilirubinaemia in the first 4 days of life.

    Hospital phototherapy using blue LED lamps may be more effective at reducing the number of hours spent under phototherapy compared with conventional phototherapy (using halogen-quartz bulbs) in term and preterm infants.

    Apart from these two comparisons, we found no difference between the other wavelengths of light on the duration of phototherapy required.

    We don't know whether the various wavelengths of light studied differ in their effect on rate of decline in serum bilirubin levels.

    One small RCT found no significant difference in blue LED lamps compared with conventional phototherapy at reducing mortality in preterm infants requiring phototherapy.

- For different intensities of light:

    Close phototherapy compared with distant light-source phototherapy may reduce the duration of phototherapy and mean serum bilirubin level in infants with hyperbilirubinaemia.

    Double conventional phototherapy may be more effective than single conventional phototherapy at reducing the duration of treatment and mean serum bilirubin level in term infants of birth weight 2500 g or above with haemolysis included. However, we don't know if double phototherapy reduces the need for exchange transfusion.

    We don't know whether there is any additional benefit of triple phototherapy compared to double phototherapy.

- We assessed RCTs comparing light with different total doses used for hospital phototherapy for unconjugated hyperbilirubinaemia in term and preterm infants. Interventions included intermittent versus continuous phototherapy and increased skin exposure versus standard skin exposure phototherapy.

    We don't know whether there is any difference in effectiveness of intermittent phototherapy versus continuous phototherapy or increased skin exposure versus standard skin exposure phototherapy at reducing duration of phototherapy treatment or at improving the rate of decrease of serum bilirubin levels.

- We assessed RCTs comparing different thresholds for commencement of hospital phototherapy. This included comparing prophylactic phototherapy (commencement of phototherapy routinely according to specific criteria other than level of serum bilirubin) with threshold phototherapy (commencement of phototherapy when the serum bilirubin was above a certain predefined level).

  We only found one small RCT comparing prophylactic hospital phototherapy with threshold hospital phototherapy. It is generally accepted that phototherapy should only be applied once serum bilirubin levels reach predefined thresholds.

  Lower thresholds compared with higher thresholds in extremely low birth weight infants may reduce the proportion of infants with neurodevelopmental impairment, profound impairment, and severe hearing loss.

(i) **Please visit http://clinicalevidence.bmj.com for full text and references**

## What are the effects of different wavelengths of light in hospital phototherapy as treatment for unconjugated hyperbilirubinaemia in term and preterm infants?

| Likely To Be Beneficial | • Blue LED versus conventional quartz-halogen (blue LED may reduce hours spent in phototherapy; however, no significant difference in rate of bilirubin decline)<br><br>• Blue-green fluorescent versus blue fluorescent lamps (blue-green fluorescent light may be more effective at reducing duration of phototherapy than blue fluorescent light) |
|---|---|
| Unknown Effectiveness | • (Daylight) fluorescent versus blue fluorescent lamps<br><br>• Blue fluorescent versus green fluorescent lamps<br><br>• Blue-green LED versus conventional quartz-halogen |

## What are the effects of different intensities of light in hospital phototherapy as treatment for unconjugated hyperbilirubinaemia in term and preterm infants?

| Likely To Be Beneficial | • Close phototherapy versus distant light-source phototherapy (close phototherapy may reduce duration of treatment and serum bilirubin level)<br><br>• Double phototherapy versus single phototherapy (double phototherapy may reduce duration of treatment and serum bilirubin level) |
|---|---|
| Unknown Effectiveness | • Triple phototherapy versus double phototherapy |

## What are the effects of different total doses of light in hospital phototherapy as treatment for unconjugated hyperbilirubinaemia in term and preterm infants?

| Unknown Effectiveness | • Increased skin exposure versus standard skin exposure phototherapy<br><br>• Intermittent phototherapy versus continuous phototherapy |
|---|---|

## What are the effects of starting hospital phototherapy at different thresholds in term and preterm infants?

| Likely To Be Beneficial | • Low threshold versus high threshold phototherapy (low threshold may reduce neurodevelopmental impairment in extremely low birthweight infants; however, no difference in mortality or need for exchange transfusion) |
|---|---|
| Unknown Effectiveness | • Prophylactic phototherapy versus threshold phototherapy |

**Search date January 2014**

**DEFINITION** Neonatal jaundice refers to the yellow coloration of the skin and sclera of newborn babies that results from the deposition of bilirubin. This review focuses on phototherapy as treatment for unconjugated hyperbilirubinaemia in term and preterm infants; however, exchange transfusion is still the gold standard of treatment for severe hyperbilirubinaemia. Jaundice is usually seen first in the face, and progresses caudally to the trunk and extremities. However, visual estimation of the bilirubin levels can lead to errors, and a low threshold should exist for measuring serum bilirubin. There are devices that measure transcutaneous bilirubin, but these are generally for screening purposes.

**INCIDENCE/PREVALENCE** Jaundice is the most common condition requiring medical attention in newborn babies. About 50% of term and 80% of preterm babies develop jaundice in the first week of life. Jaundice is also a common cause of re-admission to hospital after early discharge of newborn babies. Jaundice usually appears 2 to 4 days after birth and disappears 1 to 2 weeks later, usually without the need for treatment.

**AETIOLOGY/RISK FACTORS** Jaundice occurs when there is accumulation of bilirubin in the skin and mucous membranes. In most infants with jaundice there is no underlying disease, and the jaundice is termed physiological. Physiological jaundice typically presents on the second or third day of life and results from the increased production of bilirubin (owing to increased circulating red cell mass and a shortened red cell lifespan) and the decreased excretion of bilirubin (owing to low concentrations of the hepatocyte binding protein, low activity of glucuronosyl transferase, and increased enterohepatic circulation) that normally occur in newborn babies. Breastfed infants are more likely to develop jaundice within the first week of life; this is thought to be an exacerbated physiological jaundice caused by a lower calorific intake and increased enterohepatic circulation of bilirubin. Prolonged unconjugated jaundice, persisting beyond the second week, is also seen in breastfed infants. The mechanism for this later 'breast milk jaundice syndrome' is still not completely understood. Non-physiological causes include blood group incompatibility (rhesus or ABO problems), other causes of haemolysis, sepsis, bruising, and metabolic disorders. Gilbert's and Crigler-Najjar syndromes are rare causes of neonatal jaundice.

**PROGNOSIS** In the newborn baby, unconjugated bilirubin can penetrate the blood-brain barrier and is potentially neurotoxic. Acute bilirubin encephalopathy consists of initial lethargy and hypotonia, followed by hypertonia (retrocollis and opisthotonus), irritability, apnoea, and seizures. Kernicterus refers to the yellow staining of the deep nuclei of the brain, namely, the basal ganglia (globus pallidus); however, the term is also used to describe the chronic form of bilirubin encephalopathy, which includes symptoms such as athetoid cerebral palsy, hearing loss, failure of upward gaze, and dental enamel dysplasia. The level at which unconjugated bilirubin becomes neurotoxic is unclear, and kernicterus at autopsy has been reported in infants in the absence of markedly elevated levels of bilirubin. Reports suggest a resurgence of kernicterus in countries in which this complication had virtually disappeared. This has been attributed mainly to early discharge of newborns from hospital.

Darcie Kiddoo

## KEY POINTS

- Nocturnal enuresis affects 15% to 20% of 5-year-old children, 5% of 10-year-old children, and 1% to 2% of people aged 15 years and older. Without treatment, 15% of affected children will become dry each year.

  Nocturnal enuresis is not diagnosed in children aged under 5 years, and treatment may be inappropriate for children aged less than 7 years.

- Overall, we found limited high-quality evidence on the effects of non-pharmacological interventions for nocturnal enuresis in children.

- Enuresis alarms increase the number of dry nights compared with no treatment.

  Combining the use of alarms with dry bed training may also increase the number of dry nights compared with no treatment.

- Acupuncture and laser acupuncture may be more effective than sham procedures at reducing enuresis and relapse rates; however, the evidence is weak.

- Hypnotherapy may be less effective than enuresis alarm at achieving dry nights or reducing relapse of enuresis; however, the evidence is weak.

- We don't know whether dry bed training alone or hypnotherapy are effective at increasing dry nights.

- Often, patients turn to alternative therapies after standard treatments fail; therefore, physicians are unable to judge the clinical effect of these therapies.

(i) **Please visit http://clinicalevidence.bmj.com for full text and references**

| What are the effects of non-pharmacological interventions for relief of symptoms of nocturnal enuresis? | |
|---|---|
| Beneficial | • Dry bed training plus enuresis alarm<br>• Enuresis alarm |
| Unknown Effectiveness | • Acupuncture<br>• Dry bed training<br>• Hypnotherapy |

**Search date October 2013**

**DEFINITION** Nocturnal enuresis is the involuntary discharge of urine at night in a child aged 5 years or older in the absence of congenital or acquired defects of the central nervous system or urinary tract. Pathological medical conditions that have bed-wetting as a symptom can be excluded by a thorough history, examination, and urinalysis. 'Monosymptomatic' nocturnal enuresis is characterised by night-time symptoms only and accounts for 85% of cases. Nocturnal enuresis is defined as primary if the child has not been dry for a period greater than 6 months, and secondary if such a period of dryness preceded the onset of wetting. Most management strategies are aimed at children aged 7 years and older.

**INCIDENCE/PREVALENCE** Between 15% and 20% of 5-year-olds, 7% of 7-year-olds, 5% of 10-year-olds, 2% to 3% of children aged 12 to 14 years, and 1% to 2% of people aged 15 years and older wet the bed twice a week on average.

**AETIOLOGY/RISK FACTORS** Nocturnal enuresis is associated with several factors, including small functional bladder capacity, nocturnal polyuria, and, most commonly, arousal dysfunction. Linkage studies have identified associated genetic loci on chromosomes 8q, 12q, 13q, and 22q11. More recent studies suggest that obstructive sleep apnoea and constipation may predispose to nocturnal enuresis. Treatment of these conditions may result in a resolution of the enuresis.

**PROGNOSIS** Nocturnal enuresis has widely differing outcomes, from spontaneous resolution to complete resistance to all current treatments. About 1% of children remain enuretic until adulthood. Without treatment, about 15% of children with enuresis become dry each year. We found no RCTs on the best age at which to start treatment in children with nocturnal enuresis. Behavioural treatments, such as moisture or wetting alarms, require motivation and commitment from the child and a parent. Anecdotal experience suggests that reassurance is sufficient below the age of 7 years. Anecdotal experience suggests that children under the age of 7 years may not have the commitment needed.

Dexter Canoy and Peter Bundred

## KEY POINTS

- Obesity is the result of long-term energy imbalances, where daily energy intake exceeds daily energy expenditure.

  Obesity in children is associated with physical as well as psychosocial problems. Long-term adverse health consequences of childhood obesity may include increased risk for cardiovascular and metabolic disease in adulthood.

  Most obese adolescents stay obese as adults.

- Obesity is increasing among children and adolescents, with 16.8% of boys and 15.2% of girls in the UK aged 2 to 15 years being obese in 2008.

- We don't know how lifestyle or surgical interventions help in improving quality of life of overweight and obese children or in reducing premature deaths associated with childhood overweight and obesity in the longer term.

- Multifactorial interventions (behavioural, dietary, and physical) may help overweight and obese children to lose weight.

  Multifactorial interventions may be more effective if they involve the family, are delivered in specialist settings, and combine changes in lifestyle habits, particularly diet and physical activity (generally involving behavioural management techniques).

- We don't know if behavioural, dietary, or physical interventions alone can help overweight and obese children lose weight.

- We don't know how effective surgical interventions are in treating obesity in children, as we found no high-quality RCTs.

(i) **Please visit http://clinicalevidence.bmj.com for full text and references**

| What are the effects of lifestyle interventions for the treatment of childhood obesity? | |
|---|---|
| Likely To Be Beneficial | • Multifactorial interventions |
| Unknown Effectiveness | • Behavioural interventions alone<br>• Diet alone<br>• Physical activity alone |

| What are the effects of surgical interventions for the treatment of childhood obesity? | |
|---|---|
| Unknown Effectiveness | • Bariatric surgery |

**Search date January 2010**

**DEFINITION** Obesity is a chronic condition characterised by an excess of body fat. It is most often defined by the body mass index (BMI), which is highly correlated with body fat. BMI is weight in kilograms divided by height in metres squared ($kg/m^2$). In children and adolescents, BMI varies with age and sex. It typically rises during the first months after birth, falls after the first year, and rises again around the sixth year of life. Thus, a given BMI value is usually compared against reference charts to obtain a ranking of BMI percentile for age and sex. The BMI percentile indicates the relative position of the child's BMI as compared with a historical reference population of children of the same age and sex. Worldwide, there is little agreement on the definition of overweight and obesity among children; however, a BMI above the 85th percentile is generally considered to be at least "at risk for overweight" in the USA and UK. A BMI above the 95th percentile is variably defined as overweight or obese but generally indicates a need for intervention. In this review, we have considered treatment of children for overweight and obesity, including children with a BMI above the 85th percentile for age and sex in a community setting. We have included interventions given to the children, their parents, or both.

**INCIDENCE/PREVALENCE** The prevalence of obesity (generally BMI >95th percentile) is steadily increasing among children and adolescents. In the UK in 2008, it was estimated that 16.8% of boys and 15.2% of girls aged 2 to 15 years were obese, which was an increase from 11.1% in boys and 12.2% in girls in 1995, but a decrease from 19.4% in boys and 18.5% in girls in 2004.

**AETIOLOGY/RISK FACTORS** Obesity is the result of long-term energy imbalances, where daily energy intake exceeds daily energy expenditure. Energy balance is modulated by a myriad of factors, including metabolic rate, appetite, diet, and physical activity. Although these factors are influenced by genetic traits in some children, the increase in obesity prevalence in the past few decades cannot be explained by changes in the human gene pool, and is more often attributed to environmental changes that promote excessive food intake and discourage physical activity. The risk of childhood obesity is related to childhood diet and sedentary time. Other risk factors are parental obesity, low parental education, social deprivation, infant feeding patterns, early or more rapid puberty (both a risk factor and an effect of obesity), extreme (both high and low) birth weights, and gestational diabetes. Specifically, physical activity levels have decreased over the years and now only 36% of children and adolescents in the USA are meeting recommended levels of physical activity. Among British children aged 4 to 15 years whose physical activity levels were objectively assessed using accelerometry, only 33% of boys and 21% of girls met the government recommendation for daily physical activity level. Less commonly, obesity may also be induced by drugs (e.g., high-dose glucocorticoids), neuroendocrine disorders (e.g., Cushing's syndrome), or inherited disorders (e.g., Down's syndrome and Prader–Willi syndrome).

**PROGNOSIS** Most obese adolescents will become obese adults. For example, a 5-year longitudinal study of obese adolescents aged 13 to 19 years found that 86% remained obese as young adults. Obesity is associated with a higher prevalence of insulin resistance, elevated blood lipids, increased blood pressure, and impaired glucose tolerance, which in turn may increase the risk of several chronic diseases in adulthood, including hypertension, dyslipidaemia, diabetes, cardiovascular disease, sleep apnoea, osteoarthritis, and some cancers. Perhaps a less recognised but important short-term comorbidity of overweight/ obesity, particularly in adolescent children, is functional impairment in several psychosocial domains, including social marginalisation, low self-esteem, and impaired quality of life. It is important that clinicians emphasise improvements in diet, physical activity, and health independently of changes in body weight.

Ian Williamson

## KEY POINTS

- Otitis media with effusion (OME, glue ear) usually presents with concerns about the child's behaviour, performance at school, or language development.

  Children usually only have mild hearing impairment and few other symptoms.

  Up to 80% of children have been affected by the age of 4 years, but prevalence declines beyond 6 years of age.

  Non-purulent middle-ear infections can occur in children or adults after upper respiratory tract infection or acute otitis media.

  Half or more of cases resolve within 3 months and 95% within 1 year, but complications such as tympanic membrane perforation, tympanosclerosis, otorrhoea, and cholesteatoma can occur.

- Risk of OME is increased with passive smoking, bottle feeding, low socioeconomic group, and exposure to many other children.

  However, there is no evidence to show whether interventions to modify these risk factors reduce the risk of OME.

- Autoinflation with purpose-manufactured devices may improve effusions over 2 weeks to 3 months, but long-term efficacy is unknown.

- We don't know whether non-purpose-manufactured devices are effective in treating otitis media with effusion. Children may find autoinflation difficult.

- Oral antibiotics, antihistamines plus oral decongestants, or mucolytics may be of no benefit in OME, and can cause adverse effects.

  Antibiotics can cause adverse effects in up to one third of children with OME.

  Antihistamines can cause behavioural changes, seizures, and blood pressure variability.

- Oral corticosteroids are unlikely to improve symptoms in OME, and can cause growth retardation.

  Intranasal corticosteroids are unlikely to be of benefit in children with bilateral OME.

- Ventilation tubes may improve short-term outcomes, but the clinical effect size is small. They may also increase the risk of tympanic membrane abnormalities.

  Ventilation tubes improve hearing for the first 2 years, but have no longer-term benefit, and may not improve cognition or language development.

  Adenoidectomy may improve hearing when performed with tympanostomy, but the clinical relevance of the improvements is unclear.

- Combination treatment with ventilation tubes plus adenoidectomy may be more effective than adenoidectomy alone.

(i) **Please visit http://clinicalevidence.bmj.com for full text and references**

| **What are the effects of interventions to prevent otitis media with effusion in children?** ||
|---|---|
| Unknown Effectiveness | • Modifying risk factors to prevent OME |

## What are the effects of pharmacological, mechanical, and surgical interventions to treat otitis media with effusion in children?

| | |
|---|---|
| **Trade-off Between Benefits And Harms** | • Corticosteroids (oral)<br>• Ventilation tubes<br>• Ventilation tubes plus adenoidectomy |
| **Unknown Effectiveness** | • Adenoidectomy alone<br>• Autoinflation using non-purpose-manufactured devices<br>• Autoinflation using purpose-manufactured devices |
| **Unlikely To Be Beneficial** | • Antibiotics (oral)<br>• Corticosteroids (intranasal)<br>• Mucolytics |
| **Likely To Be Ineffective Or Harmful** | • Antihistamines plus oral decongestants |

**Search date March 2010**

**DEFINITION** Otitis media with effusion (OME) or 'glue ear', is serous or mucoid, but not mucopurulent, fluid in the middle ear. Children usually present with hearing impairment and speech problems. By contrast with those with acute otitis media (see review on acute otitis media, p 67), children with OME do not suffer from acute ear pain, fever, or malaise. Hearing impairment is usually mild and often identified when parents express concern regarding their child's behaviour, performance at school, or language development.

**INCIDENCE/PREVALENCE** OME is commonly seen in paediatric practice, and accounts for 25% to 35% of all cases of otitis media. One study in the UK found that, at any time, 5% of children aged 5 years had persistent (at least 3 months) bilateral hearing impairment associated with OME. The prevalence declines considerably beyond 6 years of age. Studies in the USA and Europe have estimated that about 50% to 80% of children aged 4 years have been affected by OME at some time. One study in the USA estimated that, between the ages of 2 months and 2 years, 91% of young children will have one episode of middle-ear effusion, and 52% will have bilateral involvement. OME is the most common reason for referral for surgery in children in the UK. The number of general practitioner consultations for OME increased from 15.2 per 1000 (2–10 year olds) per year to 16.7 per 1000 per year between 1991 and 2001. Middle-ear effusions also occur infrequently in adults after upper respiratory tract infection or after air travel, and may persist for weeks or months after an episode of acute otitis media.

**AETIOLOGY/RISK FACTORS** Contributory factors include upper respiratory tract infection and narrow upper respiratory airways. Case-control studies have identified risk factors, including age 6 years or younger, day care centre attendance, large number of siblings, low socioeconomic group, frequent upper respiratory tract infection, bottle feeding, and household smoking. These factors may be associated with about twice the risk of developing OME.

**PROGNOSIS** Data from one prospective study of children aged 2 to 4 years showed that 50% of OME cases resolved within 3 months and 95% within 1 year. In 5% of preschool children, OME (identified by tympanometric screening) persisted for at least 1 year. One cohort study of 3-year-olds found that 65% of OME cases cleared spontaneously within 3 months. Most children aged 6 years or older will not have further problems. The disease is

*(continued over)*

*(from previous page)*

ultimately self-limiting in most cases. However, one large cohort study (534 children) found that middle-ear disease increased reported hearing difficulty at 5 years of age (OR 1.44, 95% CI 1.18 to 1.76) and was associated with delayed language development in children up to 10 years of age. Hearing impairment is the most common complication of OME. Most children with OME have fluctuating or persistent hearing deficits with mild to moderate degrees of hearing loss, averaging 27 decibels. The type of hearing impairment is usually conductive, but it may be sensorineural, or both. The sensorineural type is usually permanent. Tympanic membrane perforation, tympanosclerosis, otorrhoea, and cholesteatoma occur more frequently among children with OME than among those without OME.

Gerald W McGarry

**KEY POINTS**
- Up to 9% of children may have recurrent nosebleeds, usually originating from the anterior septum, but the majority grow out of the problem.

  Nosebleeds may be associated with local inflammation and trauma, including nose picking.

- Antiseptic cream (containing chlorhexidine hydrochloride plus neomycin sulfate) may reduce nosebleeds compared with no treatment, and may be as effective as silver nitrate cautery.

  Such creams may smell and taste unpleasant.

  Silver nitrate cautery is usually painful even if local anaesthesia is used.

  Simultaneous bilateral cautery is not recommended owing to the possible increased risk of perforation of the septum.

- Antiseptic cream (containing chlorhexidine hydrochloride plus neomycin sulfate) plus silver nitrate cautery may be more effective at reducing the frequency and severity of nosebleeds than antiseptic cream alone.

  We don't know whether petroleum jelly speeds up resolution of recurrent bleeding compared with no treatment.

 **Please visit http://clinicalevidence.bmj.com for full text and references**

| What are the effects of treatments for recurrent idiopathic epistaxis in children? | |
| --- | --- |
| Likely To Be Beneficial | • Antiseptic cream (containing chlorhexidine hydrochloride plus neomycin sulfate) |
| Unknown Effectiveness | • Petroleum jelly<br>• Silver nitrate cautery |

**Search date June 2013**

**DEFINITION** Recurrent idiopathic epistaxis is recurrent, self-limiting nasal bleeding for which no specific cause is identified. There is no consensus on the frequency or severity of recurrences. This review includes evidence on children aged 1 to 16 years with recurrent idiopathic epistaxis. Epistaxis caused by other specific local factors (e.g., tumours) or systemic factors (e.g., clotting disorders) is not considered here.

**INCIDENCE/PREVALENCE** A cross-sectional study of 1218 children (aged 11 to 14 years) found that 9% had frequent episodes of epistaxis. It is likely that only the most severe episodes are considered for treatment.

**AETIOLOGY/RISK FACTORS** In children, most epistaxis occurs from the anterior part of the septum in the region of Little's area (Kiesselbach's plexus). Initiating factors include local inflammation, mucosal drying, and local trauma (including nose picking).

**PROGNOSIS** Recurrent epistaxis is less common in people aged over 14 years, and many children 'grow out of' this problem.

Oliveiero Bruni and Luana Novelli

## KEY POINTS

- Sleep disorders may affect between 20% and 30% of young children, and include problems getting to sleep (dyssomnias) or undesirable phenomena during sleep (parasomnias), such as sleep terrors and sleepwalking.

  Children with physical or learning disabilities are at increased risk of sleep disorders. Other risk factors include the child being the first born, having a difficult temperament or having had colic, and increased maternal responsiveness.

- There is a paucity of evidence about effective treatments for sleep disorders in children, especially parasomnias, but behavioural interventions may be the best first-line approach.

- Extinction and graduated extinction in otherwise healthy children with dyssomnia may improve sleep quality and settling, and reduce the number of tantrums and wakenings compared with no treatment.

  Extinction and graduated extinction in children with physical disabilities, learning disabilities, epilepsy, or attention-deficit disorder with dyssomnia may be more effective at improving settling, reducing the frequency and duration of night wakings, and improving parental sleep compared with no treatment; however, we don't know whether it is more effective in improving sleep duration.

  Graduated extinction may be less distressing for parents, and therefore may have better compliance.

- Sleep hygiene for dyssomnia in otherwise healthy children may be more effective in reducing the number and duration of bedtime tantrums compared with placebo, but we don't know if it is more effective at reducing night wakenings, improving sleep latency, improving total sleep duration, or improving maternal mood.

  Sleep hygiene and graduated extinction seem to be equally effective at reducing bedtime tantrums in otherwise healthy children with dyssomnia.

  We don't know whether sleep hygiene for dyssomnia in children with physical disabilities, learning disabilities, epilepsy, or attention-deficit disorder is effective.

- Melatonin for dyssomnia in otherwise healthy children may be more effective at improving sleep-onset time, total sleep time, and general health compared with placebo.

  Evidence of improvements in dyssomnia with melatonin is slightly stronger in children with physical disabilities, learning disabilities, epilepsy, or attention-deficit disorder.

- Little is known about the long-term effects of melatonin, and the quality of the product purchased could be variable as melatonin is classified as a food supplement.

- Antihistamines for dyssomnia may be more effective than placebo at reducing night wakenings and decreasing sleep latency, but we don't know if they are more effective at increasing sleep duration. The evidence for antihistamines in dyssomnia comes from only one small, short-term study.

- We don't know whether behavioural therapy plus antihistamines, plus benzodiazepines, or plus chloral and derivatives, exercise, light therapy, or sleep restriction are effective in children with dyssomnia.

- We don't know whether antihistamines, behavioural therapy plus benzodiazepines or plus chloral and derivatives, benzodiazepines, 5-hydroxytryptophan, melatonin, safety/protective interventions, scheduled waking, sleep hygiene, or sleep restriction are effective in children with parasomnia.

 **Please visit http://clinicalevidence.bmj.com for full text and references**

## What are the effects of treatments for dyssomnias in children?

| Likely To Be Beneficial | • Extinction and graduated extinction for dyssomnia in children with physical disabilities, learning disabilities, epilepsy, or attention-deficit disorder<br><br>• Extinction and graduated extinction for dyssomnia in otherwise healthy children<br><br>• Sleep hygiene for dyssomnia in otherwise healthy children* |
| --- | --- |
| Trade-off Between Benefits And Harms | • Melatonin for dyssomnia in children with attention-deficit disorder, epilepsy, or neurodevelopmental disabilities<br><br>• Melatonin for dyssomnia in otherwise healthy children |
| Unknown Effectiveness | • Antihistamines for dyssomnia<br><br>• Behavioural therapy plus antihistamines<br><br>• Behavioural therapy plus benzodiazepines for dyssomnia<br><br>• Behavioural therapy plus chloral and derivatives for dyssomnia<br><br>• Exercise for dyssomnia<br><br>• Light therapy for dyssomnia<br><br>• Sleep hygiene for dyssomnia in children with physical disabilities, learning disabilities, epilepsy, or attention-deficit disorder<br><br>• Sleep restriction for dyssomnia |

## What are the effects of treatments for parasomnias in children?

| Unknown Effectiveness | • 5-hydroxytryptophan<br><br>• Antihistamines for parasomnias<br><br>• Behavioural therapy plus benzodiazepines for parasomnias<br><br>• Behavioural therapy plus chloral and derivatives for parasomnias<br><br>• Benzodiazepines<br><br>• Melatonin for parasomnias in healthy children or in children with attention-deficit disorder, epilepsy, neurodevelopmental disabilities, or physical disabilities |
| --- | --- |

- Safety/protective interventions for parasomnia
- Scheduled waking for parasomnias
- Sleep hygiene for parasomnias
- Sleep restriction for parasomnias

**Search date September 2009**

* Based on consensus; few RCT data

**DEFINITION** The International Classification of Sleep Disorders-2 (ICSD-2) defines more than 70 sleep disorders classified into 8 major categories: insomnia, sleep-related breathing disorders, hypersomnias of central origin, circadian rhythm sleep disorders, parasomnias, sleep-related movement disorders, isolated symptoms and normal variants, and other sleep disorders. For the purpose of this review we defined **dyssomnia** including only paediatric insomnia or excessive daytime sleepiness; and **parasomnias. Dyssomnia** Paediatric insomnia may be defined as difficulty initiating or maintaining sleep that is viewed as a problem by the child or carer. In the ICSD-2, paediatric insomnia is included in the category of 'Behavioral Insomnia of Childhood' divided in two types: sleep-onset association type and limit-setting type. Both types of insomnia are common and have an estimated prevalence of 10% to 30%. Sleep-onset association type occurs when a child associates falling asleep with an action (being held or rocked), object (bottle), or setting (parents' bed), and is unable to fall asleep if separated from that association. Limit-setting type occurs when a child stalls and refuses to go to sleep in the absence of strictly enforced bedtime limits. **Parasomnias** are defined as 'undesirable physical events or experiences that occur during entry into sleep, within sleep, or during arousals from sleep'. Parasomnias in childhood are common, more often benign, self-limited, and typically resolving in adolescence. Following the ICSD-2, they are subdivided into three groups: disorders of arousal (from NREM sleep); parasomnias usually associated with REM sleep; and other parasomnias. **Children with physical disabilities, learning disabilities, epilepsy, or attention-deficit disorder:** Sleep problems tend to be greater in prevalence and severity in this population. For example, pain is related to sleep disturbance, and attention paid to helping the child sleep better is likely to improve recovery. Across a range of physical problems, there are reports in the literature of sleep disturbance associated with them. In most cases, research is limited and the mechanisms are unclear. Children with visual impairment are prone to circadian rhythm problems: their light perception is poor and the primary cue for sleep onset is therefore lost. Many medications are known to cause sleep problems, such as severe drowsiness with many antiepileptic drugs. Learning disabilities vary considerably in the range of conditions covered by this global term. However, some conditions such as Smith–Magenis, Prader–Willi, and Williams syndrome have sleep disturbance as cardinal features. Others, such as Down's syndrome and mucopolysaccharidoses, are associated with sleep-related breathing problems. Treatment for these groups of children needs to be tailored to their particular problems, and may be problematic for anatomical and neurological reasons. Nevertheless, in large part, these sleep problems should be regarded as treatable, and careful investigation of these problems is required.

**INCIDENCE/PREVALENCE** Sleep problems, primarily settling problems and frequent night wakings, are experienced by about 20% to 30% of children aged 1 to 5 years, but cultural differences would seem to play at least some role. These sleep disturbances often persist in later childhood: 40% to 80% of children displaying sleep problems when aged 15 to 48 months were found to have persistent sleep disorders 2 to 3 years later. In toddlers, settling and night-waking problems are dominant, with rates about 20% to 25%. A second peak in sleep problems occurs in adolescence, where sleep-timing problems occur, including delayed sleep phase syndrome. Such children have difficulty getting off to sleep, and then problems getting up in the morning for school. Across the age range, sleep-related breathing problems occur at rates of about 2%. **Children with physical disabilities, learning disabilities, epilepsy, or attention-deficit disorder:** The prevalence of sleep disorders tends to be even greater in children with physical or learning disabilities: about 86% of children aged up to 6 years, 81% of children aged 6 to 11 years, and 77% of children aged 12 to 16 years with physical or learning disabilities suffer from severe sleep problems. Disorders of initiating and maintaining sleep, prolonged sleep latency, high number of night awakenings, and reduced total sleep time are also found in children with Angelman's syndrome compared with age-matched controls. Furthermore, children with autism are reported to have a shorter sleep duration, a longer sleep latency, and bed wetting compared with controls.

**AETIOLOGY/RISK FACTORS** Evidence of the aetiology of sleep disorders in children is generally limited. The vast majority of insomnia in infancy is behavioural insomnia, without a specific aetiology other than the altered interaction between parents and infants at bedtime. Factors related to sleep disorders are: having had colic, the child being the first born, and the child having a difficult temperament (e.g., low sensory threshold, negative mood, decreased adaptability). Other factors have been suggested, such as being born prematurely and low birth weight; however, evidence of such associations is contradictory. Recently, iron deficiency has also been related to the presence of insomnia, nocturnal hyperactivity, or restless leg syndrome, and therefore this kind of treatment could be considered in some forms of resistant insomnia in infancy and childhood. The factors described here may influence the onset of a sleep disorder, but the factors influencing the maintenance of a sleep problem are likely to be different. Increased maternal responsiveness is associated with the maintenance of sleep disorders in children. **Children with physical disabilities, learning disabilities, epilepsy, or attention-deficit disorder:** Children with physical disabilities, learning disabilities, epilepsy, or attention-deficit disorders may have other additional risk factors that include the influence of the specific cerebral lesions, the effect of medications (either antiepileptic drugs or stimulant drugs), the altered circadian phase, etc. Almost all children with brain diseases may be at risk for the development of sleep–wake rhythm disorders. The altered perception of 'common zeitgeber' (light–dark cycle, food schedule, maternal inputs, etc.) could lead to the development of irregular sleep habits and even to a free-running rhythm, not related to the 24-hour cycle. Children with learning disabilities or with brain damage/impairments may also exhibit endogenous dysfunction in hormone release. Hormone release synchronises circadian rhythms with sleep/wake alternation and can therefore interfere with the development of a normal sleep–wake cycle. It can be hypothesised that the difficulties in the perception of external stimuli and in their elaboration may be the first step in the development of disrupted sleep–wake organisation.

**PROGNOSIS** Children with excessive daytime sleepiness or night waking are likely to suffer from impaired daytime functioning without treatment, and their parents are likely to have increased stress. In addition to these effects, children with parasomnias are at serious risk of accidental injuries. Between 40% and 80% of children aged 15 to 48 months displaying sleep problems had persistent sleep problems 2 to 3 years later. **Children with physical disabilities, learning disabilities, epilepsy, or attention-deficit disorder:** Children with learning disabilities and sleep disorders are more likely to have greater challenging behaviour than those without sleep problems. This may affect the quality of life of the parents, frequently resulting in parental stress, parents displaying less affection for their children, and marital discord. For children with epilepsy, sleep disorders may exacerbate their condition: a persistent lack of sleep has been associated with an increased frequency of seizures.

James Larcombe

### KEY POINTS

- Up to 11% of girls and 7% of boys will have had a urinary tract infection (UTI) by the age of 16 years. Recurrent UTI is common.

- Vesicoureteric reflux (VUR) is identified in up to 40% of children being investigated for a first UTI, and it is a risk factor for, but weak predictor of, renal scarring.

- Renal parenchymal defects occur in 5% to 15% of children within 1 to 2 years of their first presentation with UTI, and it is associated with increased risks of progressive renal damage. The risk of parenchymal defects probably diminishes over time.

- Prophylactic antibiotics may be more effective than placebo at reducing the risk of recurrent UTI; however, they may increase microbial resistance to the prophylactic drug.

    Recent, well-conducted RCTs suggest a limited benefit of prophylaxis.

- Prophylactic antibiotics may be more effective than placebo at reducing renal parenchymal scarring in children with VUR.

- We found no systematic review or RCT evidence comparing different durations of antibiotics.

- Nitrofurantoin appears to be more effective than other prophylactic antibiotics, but this is balanced by the increased risk of side-effects and treatment drop-out.

 **Please visit http://clinicalevidence.bmj.com for full text and references**

### What are the effects of prophylactic antibiotics to prevent recurrent urinary tract infection in children?

| Trade-off Between Benefits And Harms | • Prophylactic antibiotics (compared to placebo or no treatment, may reduce UTI incidence and weak evidence may reduce scarring in children with VUR; however, antibiotics associated with resistance and other adverse effects) |
| --- | --- |
| Unknown Effectiveness | • Different durations of prophylactic antibiotics |

**Search date December 2013**

**DEFINITION** The presence of a pure growth of at least $10^7$ colony-forming units of bacteria per litre of urine indicates a diagnosis of UTI. Lower counts of bacteria may be clinically important, especially in boys, and in specimens obtained by urinary catheter. Any growth of typical urinary pathogens is considered clinically important if obtained by suprapubic aspiration. Different presentation and differential risk have often led to the stratification of children by age for clinical management and research. NICE guidance defines three age groups: under 3 months; 3 months to 3 years; and over 3 years. Other publications have defined risk groups as children aged up to 1 year, up to 7 years, and up to 12 to 16 years. Recurrent UTI is defined as a further infection by a new organism. Relapsing UTI is defined as a further infection with the same organism.

**INCIDENCE/PREVALENCE** Boys are more susceptible to UTI than girls before the age of 6 months; thereafter, the incidence is substantially higher in girls than in boys. Estimates of the true incidence of UTI depend on rates of diagnosis and investigation. Observational studies have found that UTIs have been diagnosed in Sweden in at least 2% of boys and girls by the age of 2 years, in 8% of girls and 2% of boys by age 7 years, and in the UK in 11% of girls and 7% of boys by age 16 years.

**AETIOLOGY/RISK FACTORS** The normal urinary tract is sterile. Contamination by bowel flora may result in urinary infection if a virulent organism is involved. In neonates, infection may originate from other sources. *Escherichia coli* accounts for about 75% of all pathogens. *Proteus* is more common in boys (one study found that *proteus* caused 33% of UTI infections in boys aged 1–16 years, compared with 0% of UTI infections in girls of the same age). In a study of children presenting with acute pyelonephritis, UTIs caused by non-*E coli* organisms were more likely to be associated with permanent renal damage than *E coli* (83% v 57%). **Obstructive anomalies** are found in up to 4%, and **vesicoureteric reflux (VUR)** in 8% to 40% of children being investigated for their first UTI. One meta-analysis of 12 cohort studies (537 children admitted to hospital for UTI, 1062 kidneys) found that 36% of all kidneys had parenchymal defects on dimercaptosuccinic acid (DMSA) scintigraphy, and that 59% of children with VUR on micturating cystourethrography had at least one scarred kidney (pooled positive likelihood ratio 1.96, 95% CI 1.51 to 2.54; pooled negative likelihood ratio 0.71, 95% CI 0.58 to 0.85). There was evidence of heterogeneity in likelihood ratios among studies. The authors concluded that VUR is a weak predictor of renal damage in children admitted to hospital. Thus, although VUR is a major risk factor for adverse outcome, other factors, some of which have not yet been identified, are also important. **Family history:** VUR itself runs in families. The mode of inheritance is autosomal dominance with variable penetrance and expressivity. In one review, the incidence of reflux in siblings ranged from 26% (a cohort of asymptomatic siblings) to 86% (siblings with a history of UTI). In another review, 32% of siblings had VUR, but only 2% was of a severe grade (Grade III and above). The rate in the general population has been calculated at 1% to 3%. Although some gene variants seem more common in children who suffer renal damage, no clear link has yet been established between specific genes and an adverse outcome. Local or systemic immune problems are also likely to be factors in the development of UTI.

**PROGNOSIS** **Recurrence:** A UK study found that 78% of girls and 71% of boys presenting with UTI within the first year of life experienced recurrence, and that 45% of girls and 39% of boys presenting after their first year of life developed further infections. **VUR:** In a longitudinal study, 84% of children (572 children with UTI and VUR) had spontaneous resolution during medical follow-up at between 5 and 15 years. **Renal parenchymal defects:** A systematic review of imaging in childhood UTI suggested that renal parenchymal defects (assessed with intravenous pyelogram [IVP] or DMSA scan) occurs in 5% to 15% of children within 1 to 2 years of their first diagnosed UTI. Between 32% and 70% of these parenchymal defects were noted at the time of initial assessment, suggesting a high level of pre-existing scarring, perhaps caused by previously unrecognised infection. This percentage did not substantially alter, despite an increasing referral rate, during the 3 years studied. A retrospective population-based study in the UK suggested that 4.3% of boys and 4.7% of girls develop parenchymal defects (2842 children assessed using DMSA scans after their first referral for UTI). **New or progressive renal parenchymal defects and recurrent UTI:** The systematic review reported on four studies that provided at least 2 years' follow-up: new renal parenchymal defects developed in 2% to 23% of children, and existing renal parenchymal defects progressed in 6% to 34%. It is unclear whether figures for new parenchymal defects included any children who were previously unscarred. The highest rates of renal parenchymal defects were associated with the highest rates of recurrent UTI. A further study showed that, in children aged 5 years or older, abnormal DMSA scans were noted in 64/118 (55%) children presenting with recurrent UTI, whereas 7/44 (15%) who presented with 'first UTI' had renal parenchymal defects (OR for recurrences causing renal parenchymal defects 6.3, 95% CI 2.6 to 15.2). However, recurrent UTI may be less important as a risk factor for renal parenchymal defects in older children. One study showed that, in children with initially normal scans at 3 or 4 years of age, 5/176 (3%) children aged 3 years at presentation, and 0/179 (0%) aged 4 years at presentation, had developed renal parenchymal defects between 2 and 11 years later. Of those children who developed renal parenchymal defects, 4/5 (80%) had a definite history of recurrent UTI, in all cases at least three episodes (OR for recurrences causing renal parenchymal defects 11.5, 95% CI 1.3 to 106.1). Another study (287 children with severe VUR treated either medically or surgically for any UTI) used serial DMSA scintigraphy to evaluate the risk of renal parenchymal defects over 5 years. It found that younger children (aged <2 years) were at greater risk of renal

*(continued over)*

*(from previous page)*

parenchymal defects than older children, regardless of treatment for the infection (deterioration in DMSA scan >5 years: 21/86 [24%] for younger children *v* 27/201 [13%] for older children; RR 1.82, 95% CI 1.09 to 3.03). It is likely that children who present when older, and who are found to have renal parenchymal defects, will have had at least one previous UTI that remained undiagnosed. Many children seem to lose their susceptibility to renal damage with age. **Consequences for longer term:** One long-term follow-up study in the UK found that children with renal parenchymal defects and vesicoureteric reflux at presentation, or with just one of these followed by documented UTI, were associated with an increased risk of progressive renal damage compared with children presenting without these features (RR of progressive renal damage 17, 95% CI 2.5 to 118). Persistent renal parenchymal defects may be associated with future complications, such as poor renal growth, recurrent adult pyelonephritis, impaired glomerular function, early hypertension, and end-stage renal failure. A combination of recurrent UTI, severe vesicoureteric reflux, and the presence of renal parenchymal defects at first presentation is associated with the worst prognosis.

Dereck L Hunt

## KEY POINTS

- Diabetic foot ulceration is full-thickness penetration of the dermis of the foot in a person with diabetes. Severity is classified using the Wagner system, which grades it from 1 to 5.

  The annual incidence of ulcers among people with diabetes is 2.5% to 10.7% in resource-rich countries, and the annual incidence of amputation for any reason is 0.25% to 1.8%.

  For people with healed diabetic foot ulcers, the 5-year cumulative rate of ulcer recurrence is 66% and of amputation is 12%.

- The most effective preventive measure for major amputation seems to be screening and referral to a foot-care clinic if high-risk features are present.

  Other interventions for reducing the risk of foot ulcers include wearing therapeutic footwear and increasing patient education for prevention, but we found no sufficient evidence to ascertain the effectiveness of these treatments.

- Pressure off-loading with total-contact casting or non-removable fibreglass casts successfully improves healing of ulcers.

  Removable-cast walkers rendered irremovable seem equally effective, but have the added benefit of requiring less technical expertise for fitting.

  We don't know whether pressure off-loading with felted foam or pressure-relief half-shoe is effective in treating diabetic foot ulcers.

- Human skin equivalent (applied weekly for a maximum of 5 weeks) seems better at promoting ulcer healing than saline-moistened gauze.

  Human cultured dermis does not seem effective at promoting healing.

- Topical growth factors seem to increase healing rates, but there has been little long-term follow-up of people treated with these factors.

- Systemic hyperbaric oxygen seems to be effective in treating people with severely infected ulcers, although it is unclear whether it is useful in people with non-infected, non-ischaemic ulcers.

- We don't know whether debridement or wound dressings are effective in healing ulcers.

  However, debridement with hydrogel and dimethyl sulfoxide wound dressings does seem to help ulcer healing.

  Debridement and wound dressings have been included together because the exact mechanism of the treatment can be unclear (e.g., hydrogel).

(i) Please visit http://clinicalevidence.bmj.com for full text and references

| What are the effects of interventions to prevent foot ulcers and amputations in people with diabetes? | |
|---|---|
| Likely To Be Beneficial | • Screening and referral to foot-care clinics |
| Unknown Effectiveness | • Education<br>• Therapeutic footwear |

| What are the effects of treatments in people with diabetes with foot ulceration? | |
|---|---|
| Likely To Be Beneficial | • Human skin equivalent |

| | |
|---|---|
| | • Pressure off-loading with total-contact or non-removable cast for plantar ulcers |
| | • Systemic hyperbaric oxygen (for infected ulcers) |
| | • Topical growth factors |
| Unknown Effectiveness | • Debridement or wound dressings |
| | • Pressure off-loading with felted foam or pressure-relief half-shoe |
| | • Systemic hyperbaric oxygen (for non-infected, non-ischaemic ulcers) |
| Unlikely To Be Beneficial | • Human cultured dermis |

**Search date September 2010**

---

**DEFINITION** Diabetic foot ulceration is full-thickness penetration of the dermis of the foot in a person with diabetes. Ulcer severity is often classified using the Wagner system. **Grade 1** ulcers are superficial ulcers involving the full skin thickness but no underlying tissues. **Grade 2** ulcers are deeper, penetrating down to ligaments and muscle, but not involving bone or abscess formation. **Grade 3** ulcers are deep ulcers with cellulitis or abscess formation, often complicated with osteomyelitis. Ulcers with localised gangrene are classified as **Grade 4**, and those with extensive gangrene involving the entire foot are classified as **Grade 5**.

**INCIDENCE/PREVALENCE** Studies conducted in Australia, Finland, the UK, and the USA have reported the annual incidence of foot ulcers among people with diabetes as 2.5% to 10.7%, and the annual incidence of amputation for any reason as 0.25% to 1.8%.

**AETIOLOGY/RISK FACTORS** Long-term risk factors for foot ulcers and amputation include duration of diabetes, poor glycaemic control, microvascular complications (retinopathy, nephropathy, and neuropathy), peripheral vascular disease, foot deformities, and previous foot ulceration or amputation. Strong predictors of foot ulceration are altered foot sensation, foot deformities, and previous foot ulcer or amputation of the other foot (altered sensation: RR 2.2, 95% CI 1.5 to 3.1; foot deformity: RR 3.5, 95% CI 1.2 to 9.9; previous foot ulcer: RR 1.6, 95% CI 1.2 to 2.3; previous amputation: RR 2.8, 95% CI 1.8 to 4.3).

**PROGNOSIS** In people with diabetes, foot ulcers frequently co-exist with vascular insufficiency (although foot ulcers can occur in people with no vascular insufficiency) and may be complicated by infection. Amputation is indicated if disease is severe or does not improve with conservative treatment. As well as affecting quality of life, these complications of diabetes account for a large proportion of the healthcare costs of dealing with diabetes. For people with healed diabetic foot ulcers, the 5-year cumulative rate of ulcer recurrence is 66%, and of amputation is 12%. Severe infected foot ulcers are associated with an increased risk of mortality.

Lalantha Leelarathna, Rustom Guzder, Koteshwara Muralidhara, and Mark L Evans

## KEY POINTS

- Type 1 diabetes occurs when destruction of the pancreatic islet beta cells, usually attributable to an autoimmune process, causes the pancreas to produce too little insulin or none at all.

   The prevalence of type 1 diabetes is 0.02% in people aged 0 to 14 years, and it is estimated that 479,000 people in this age group have type 1 diabetes worldwide.

   Although type 1 diabetes usually accounts for only a minority of the total burden of diabetes in a population, it is the predominant form of the disease in younger age groups in most resource-rich countries.

- Glycaemic control typically worsens in adolescence, owing to a combination of physical and psychological change and development.

- There is some evidence that educational and psychosocial interventions may improve glycaemic control and quality of life in adults and adolescents with type 1 diabetes.

- Intensive treatment programmes in adults and adolescents seem to improve glycaemic control compared with conventional treatment, and also seem to improve long-term outcomes (such as retinopathy, neuropathy, and macrovascular events), but they require a considerable investment of time and resources.

   Better glycaemic control is also associated with higher rates of hypoglycaemia, the risk of which may be reduced with the judicious use of modern technology such as continuous subcutaneous insulin infusion (CSII) and continuous glucose monitoring.

- While regular self-monitoring of blood glucose is recommended to adults with type 1 diabetes, outside the setting of intensive and structured insulin-management programmes, such as DAFNE (Dose Adjustment for Normal Eating training), there are no reliable data on which to base advice about optimum frequency of blood glucose self-testing.

- However, the use of continuous glucose monitoring (allowing real-time insulin dose adjustments) may improve glycaemic control in adults compared with intermittent/conventional monitoring.

- We don't know whether psychological interventions improve glycaemic control compared with control. They may improve some psychological outcomes; however, evidence was weak and inconsistent.

- Continuous subcutaneous insulin infusion seems effective at improving glycated haemoglobin levels and quality of life compared with multiple daily subcutaneous injections.

   The previously reported increased risk of diabetic ketoacidosis due to disconnection or malfunction of the pump is not reported in contemporary studies. People using CSII remain at increased risk of ketosis if the insulin delivery is interrupted for any reason.

   We found no evidence regarding the effects of CSII use on long-term complications/outcomes. A limitation of the current evidence is the limited number of trials that examined current insulin regimens.

Please visit http://clinicalevidence.bmj.com for full text and references

## What are the effects of intensive treatment programmes, psychological interventions, and educational interventions in adults and adolescents with type 1 diabetes?

| Likely To Be Beneficial | • Educational interventions (may improve glycaemic control compared with controls) |
|---|---|

|  | • Intensive treatment programmes (may improve glycaemic control and long-term outcomes compared with conventional treatment programmes) |
|---|---|
| **Unknown Effectiveness** | • Psychological interventions |

## What are the effects of different insulin regimens or frequency of blood glucose monitoring in adults and adolescents with type 1 diabetes?

| **Likely To Be Beneficial** | • Continuous blood glucose monitoring (may improve glycaemic control compared with conventional monitoring in adults aged 25 years or older) |
|---|---|
|  | • Continuous subcutaneous insulin infusion (may improve glycaemic control compared with multiple daily subcutaneous insulin injections) |

**Search date February 2010**

---

**DEFINITION** The term diabetes mellitus encompasses a group of disorders characterised by chronic hyperglycaemia with disturbances of carbohydrate, fat, and protein metabolism resulting from defects of insulin secretion, insulin action, or both. The WHO definition now recognises diabetes as a progressive disorder of glucose metabolism in which individuals may move between normoglycaemia, impaired glucose tolerance or impaired fasting glycaemia, and frank hyperglycaemia. Type 1 diabetes occurs when destruction of the pancreatic islet beta cells, usually attributable to an autoimmune process, causes the pancreas to produce too little insulin or none at all. Markers of autoimmune destruction (autoantibodies to islet cells, autoantibodies to insulin, or autoantibodies to both islet cells and insulin, and to glutamic acid decarboxylase) can be found in 85% to 90% of people with type 1 diabetes when hyperglycaemia is first detected. The definition of type 1 diabetes also includes beta-cell destruction, in people prone to ketoacidosis, for which no specific cause can be found. However, it excludes those forms of beta-cell destruction for which a specific cause can be found (e.g., cystic fibrosis, pancreatitis, pancreatic cancer). Type 2 diabetes results from defects in both insulin secretion and insulin action. Type 2 diabetes is not covered in this review. **Population:** For the purpose of this review, we have included adolescents and adults with type 1 diabetes, but have excluded pregnant women and people who are acutely unwell: for example, after surgery or MI.

**INCIDENCE/PREVALENCE** The prevalence of type 1 diabetes is 0.02% in people aged 0 to 14 years, and it is estimated that 479,000 people in this age group have type 1 diabetes worldwide, with annual increase in incidence of 3%. Each year, 75,000 new cases are diagnosed in this age group. Although type 1 diabetes usually accounts for only a minority of the total burden of diabetes in a population, in most resource-rich countries it is the predominant form of the disease in younger age groups. Nearly a quarter of people with diabetes come from the European region. There is a worldwide increase in the incidence of childhood diabetes with age of onset shifting to a younger age group. This younger age at onset means that complications appear at a younger age, and dependence on lifelong insulin imposes a heavy burden on people as well as on health services.

**AETIOLOGY/RISK FACTORS** Two main aetiological forms of type 1 diabetes are recognised. Autoimmune diabetes mellitus results from autoimmune-mediated destruction of the beta cells of the pancreas. The rate of destruction varies, but all people with this form of diabetes eventually become dependent on insulin for survival. Peak incidence of autoimmune diabetes is during childhood and adolescence, but it may occur at any age. There is a genetic predisposition, and people with this type of diabetes may have other autoimmune disorders. Certain viruses, including rubella, Coxsackie B, and cytomegalovirus, have been associated with beta-cell destruction. Other environmental factors are probably also contributory, but these are poorly defined and understood. Idiopathic diabetes (in which the cause is unidentified) is more common in individuals of African and Asian origin.

**PROGNOSIS** Untreated, most people with type 1 diabetes, particularly those with autoimmune diabetes mellitus, will experience increasing blood glucose levels, progressing to ketoacidosis resulting in coma and death. The course of idiopathic diabetes may be more varied, with some people experiencing permanent lack of insulin and a tendency to ketoacidosis, although in others the requirement for insulin treatment may fluctuate. However, most people with type 1 diabetes require insulin for survival, and are described as insulin dependent. The long-term effects of diabetes include retinopathy, nephropathy, and neuropathy. People with diabetes mellitus are also at increased risk of CVD, peripheral vascular disease, and cerebrovascular disease. Good glycaemic control can reduce the risk of developing diabetes-related complications.

# Diabetes: glycaemic control in type 2 (drug treatments)

Kees J Gorter, Floris Alexander van de Laar, Paul G H Janssen, Sebastian T Houweling, and Guy E H M Rutten

## KEY POINTS

- Diabetes mellitus affects about 6.5% of people aged 20 to 79 years worldwide. In 2010, an estimated 285 million people have diabetes, over 85% of whom have type 2 diabetes.

- Type 2 diabetes is often associated with obesity, hypertension, and dyslipidaemia, which are all powerful predictors of cardiovascular disease. For that reason, the treatment of type 2 diabetes requires a multifactorial approach, including lifestyle advice, treatment of hypertension, and lowering of lipid levels.

- Without adequate blood-glucose-lowering treatment, blood glucose levels may rise progressively over time in people with type 2 diabetes. Microvascular and macrovascular complications may develop.

- Metformin reduces HbA1c effectively compared with placebo.

  The UK Prospective Diabetes Study (UKPDS) RCT found that metformin may be moderately protective against mortality and cardiovascular morbidity, but further high-quality studies are needed.

  We found no evidence to suggest that metformin increases the risk of lactic acidosis.

- Sulphonylureas reduce HbA1c by 1% compared with placebo, and they may reduce microvascular complications compared with diet alone. They can cause weight gain and hypoglycaemia. One review found that the risk of hypoglycaemia was highest with glibenclamide compared with other second-generation sulphonylureas.

- The effectiveness of the combination of metformin and sulphonylurea on mortality and morbidity is unknown.

- Meglitinides reduce HbA1c by about 0.4–0.9% compared with placebo, but robust data are sparse.

- Alpha-glucosidase inhibitors reduce HbA1c by about 0.8% compared with placebo. We found no reports of dangerous adverse effects.

- Thiazolidinediones reduce HbA1c by 1% compared with placebo but may increase the risk of congestive heart failure and bone fractures. Rosiglitazone increases the risk of MI.

  DRUG ALERT: Rosiglitazone has been withdrawn from the market in many countries because the benefits of treatment are no longer thought to outweigh the risks.

- Dipeptidyl peptidase-4 (DPP-4) inhibitors reduce HbA1c by about 0.6–0.7% compared with placebo. We found no long-term data on effectiveness and safety.

- Glucagon-like peptide-1 (GLP-1) analogues reduce HbA1c compared with placebo and result in weight loss. We found no long-term data on effectiveness and safety.

- Combined oral drug treatment may reduce HbA1c levels more than monotherapy, but increases the risk of hypoglycaemia.

- Insulin improves glycaemic control in people with inadequate control of HbA1c on oral drug treatment, but is associated with weight gain, and an increased risk of hypoglycaemia.

- Adding metformin to insulin may reduce HbA1c levels compared with insulin alone, with less weight gain.

- Insulin analogues, short-acting, long-acting, and combined in various regimens, seem no more effective than conventional (human) insulin in reducing

HbA1c levels. However, in people presenting with recurrent hypoglycaemic episodes, long-acting insulin analogues may be preferred above human insulin.

- Long-acting insulin analogues seem equally effective at reducing HbA1c.
- There is lack of evidence about the effectiveness of various insulin analogue regimens after once-daily long-acting insulin has failed.
- The effectiveness of insulin basal bolus regimens is not well established.

 **Please visit http://clinicalevidence.bmj.com for full text and references**

## What are the effects of blood-glucose-lowering medications in adults with type 2 diabetes?

| | |
|---|---|
| **Beneficial** | • Metformin (may be moderately protective against mortality and cardiovascular morbidity; reduces HbA1c more effectively than placebo, and is comparably effective to sulphonylurea, alpha-glucosidase inhibitors, meglitinides, and insulin) |
| | • Sulphonylureas (lower the occurrence of microvascular disease; reduce HbA1c more effectively than placebo, may be marginally more effective than AGIs, and comparably effective to metformin, meglitinides, TZDs, and DPP-4 inhibitors) |
| **Likely To Be Beneficial** | • Alpha-glucosidase inhibitors (acarbose, miglitol only; AGIs) (reduction of HbA1c: more effective than placebo, may be comparably effective to metformin, meglitinides, and DDP-4 inhibitors, and may be slightly less effective than sulphonylureas; no evidence for an effect on disease-related mortality or morbidity) |
| | • Dipeptidyl peptidase-4 inhibitors (DPP-4 inhibitors) (reduction of HbA1c: more effective than placebo, may be comparably effective to sulphonylurea and AGIs, but may be less effective than metformin and TZDs; evidence on long-term effects is lacking) |
| | • Glucagon-like peptide-1 (GLP-1) analogues (reduction of HbA1c: more effective than placebo, may be comparably effective to insulin; evidence on long-term effects is lacking) |
| | • Insulin long-acting analogues versus each other (both effective; however, unclear whether one long-acting analogue is consistently more effective than the other) |
| | • Insulin plus metformin (more beneficial than insulin alone) |
| | • Meglitinides (reduction of HbA1c: more effective than placebo, and comparably or a little less effective than metformin, sulphonylurea, and AGIs; however, robust data are sparse) |
| **Trade-off Between Benefits And Harms** | • Thiazolidinediones (reduce HbA1c but increase the risk of congestive heart failure and bone |

| | |
|---|---|
| | fractures. Important note: this categorisation does not include rosiglitazone. Rosiglitazone has been associated with an increased risk of MI, has been withdrawn from the market in many countries, and is likely to be ineffective or harmful) |
| **Unknown Effectiveness** | • Continuation of insulin versus switching to metformin or gliclazide in people with severe hyperglycaemia who were hospitalised and treated with insulin as first-line treatment<br><br>• Metformin plus sulphonylurea (unclear effects on mortality and morbidity)<br><br>• One insulin analogue treatment regimen versus another insulin analogue treatment regimen (excluding long-acting analogue versus long-acting analogue) |
| **Unlikely To Be Beneficial** | • Various insulin analogue regimens compared with various conventional (human) insulin regimens |

**Search date February 2010**

---

**DEFINITION** The term diabetes mellitus encompasses a group of disorders characterised by chronic hyperglycaemia with disturbances of carbohydrate, fat, and protein metabolism resulting from defects of insulin secretion, insulin action, or both. Type 2 diabetes is the most common form of diabetes, and defects of both insulin action and insulin secretion are usually present by the time of diagnosis. WHO recognises diabetes as a progressive disorder of glucose metabolism in which individuals may proceed from normoglycaemia (fasting plasma venous glucose <5.5 mmol/L), impaired glucose tolerance (fasting plasma venous glucose <7.0 mmol/L and plasma glucose between 7.8 mmol/L and 11.1 mmol/L 2 hours after a 75 g oral glucose load, the oral blood glucose tolerance test [OGTT]), impaired fasting glycaemia (fasting venous plasma glucose between 5.6 mmol/L and 7.0 mmol/L), and diabetes. As a consequence of the inability of the body to use glucose as an energy source, blood glucose levels rise and symptoms such as thirst, polyuria, blurring of vision, or weight loss may develop. **Diagnosis:** Since 1965, WHO has published guidelines for the diagnosis and classification of diabetes. In 2006, WHO decided that the diagnostic criteria should be maintained. In the presence of symptoms, diabetes may be diagnosed on the basis of a single random elevated plasma glucose (11.1 mmol/L or more). In the absence of symptoms, the diagnosis should be based on blood glucose results in the diabetes range taken at different time points, either from a random sample, or fasting (plasma blood glucose 7.0 mmol/L or more), or from the OGTT (plasma blood glucose 11.1 mmol/L or more 2 hours after a 75 g glucose load). **Population:** For the purpose of this review, we have excluded pregnant women and acutely unwell adults (e.g., after surgery or MI), and people with secondary diabetes (e.g., those with hyperglycaemia based on temporal use of corticosteroids).

**INCIDENCE/PREVALENCE** It is estimated that about 285 million people between the ages of 20 and 79 years had diabetes worldwide in 2010, or 5% of the adult population. This number will increase to 438 million in 2030, an estimated prevalence of 7.7%, in the previously mentioned age category. By 2025, the region with the greatest number of people with diabetes is expected to be South-East Asia, with about 82 million people with type 2 diabetes. Incidence and prevalence figures for children and adolescents are unreliable, but there is some evidence that type 2 diabetes is becoming more common in adolescents and young adults, especially in resource-poor countries. The overall estimated prevalence of 6.5% for type 2 diabetes conceals considerable variation in prevalence, which ranges from less than 2% in some African countries to over 14% in some populations.

**AETIOLOGY/RISK FACTORS** By definition, the specific reasons for the development of the defects of insulin secretion and action that characterise type 2 diabetes are unknown. The risk of type 2 diabetes increases with age and lack of physical activity, and the disease occurs more frequently in people with obesity, hypertension, and dyslipidaemia (the metabolic syndrome). Type 2 diabetes also occurs more frequently in women with previous gestational diabetes and certain ethnic groups. There is also evidence of a familial, probably genetic, predisposition.

**PROGNOSIS** People with type 2 diabetes have blood glucose levels that have been shown to rise progressively from the time of diagnosis. During the UK Prospective Diabetes Study (UKPDS), HbA1c levels rose in newly diagnosed people with type 2 diabetes, irrespective of the type of treatment given. In 2011, primary care physicians in Denmark, the UK, and the Netherlands succeeded in lowering HbA1c levels in screen-detected type 2 diabetes patients for more than 5 years after diagnosis. Blood glucose levels above the normal range have been shown to be associated not only with the presence of symptoms, but also with an increased risk of long-term microvascular and macrovascular complications. Early treatment of hyperglycaemia in the UKPDS over 9 years resulted in a significant decrease in microvascular complications and a continued reduction in microvascular risk and emergent risk reductions for MI and death from any cause during 10 years of post-trial follow-up. However, in people with longstanding type 2 diabetes, the effects of treating hyperglycaemia are less positive or even absent. Data from a large General Practice Research Database show that both low and high mean HbA1c values are associated with increased all-cause mortality and cardiac events. Both intensive insulin treatment and the risk of hypoglycaemia have been linked to an increased death rate.

# 138 | Diabetes: managing dyslipidaemia

Jigisha Patel

## KEY POINTS

- Dyslipidaemia is characterised by decreased circulating levels of high-density lipoprotein cholesterol (HDL-C) and increased circulating levels of triglycerides and low-density lipoprotein cholesterol (LDL-C).

  Dyslipidaemia is a major contributor to the increased risk of heart disease found in people with diabetes.

  An increase of 1 mmol/L LDL-C is associated with a 1.57-fold increase in the risk of CHD in people with type 2 diabetes.

  A diagnosis of diabetic dyslipidaemia requiring pharmacological treatment is determined by the person's lipid profile and level of cardiovascular risk. The classification of cardiovascular risk and lipid targets for drug treatment differ between the USA and the UK, and the rest of Europe. We used the United Kingdom Prospective Diabetes Study (UKPDS) risk calculator to estimate 10-year cardiovascular risk, and categorised a 15% or more risk as 'higher risk', and 15% or less as 'lower risk' according to the UK clinical guidelines. We found no RCTs of a solely lower-risk population, although some studies were excluded because of insufficient data to calculate risk. In clinical practice, most people with diabetes are increasingly considered at high cardiovascular risk, regardless of the presence or absence of other risk factors.

- Statins are highly effective at improving cardiovascular outcomes in people with diabetes.

  Statins reduce cardiovascular mortality in people with type 2 diabetes with and without known CVD, and regardless of baseline total and LDL-C concentrations.

  Different statins seem to have similar efficacy at reducing LDL-C.

- Combining statins with other treatments (such as ezetimibe or a fibrate) seems to reduce LDL-C more than statin treatments alone.

  Combinations could be useful in people with mixed dyslipidaemia where one drug fails to control all lipid parameters.

- Fibrates seem to have a beneficial effect on cardiovascular mortality and morbidity by reducing triglyceride levels.

  In people with mixed dyslipidaemia, statins may also be required.

- Intensive-treatment programmes involving multiple interventions (people seen by a nurse every 4–6 weeks) seem better at reducing cholesterol than usual-care programmes.

- Fish oils may reduce triglyceride levels, but also seem to increase LDL-C levels, making them of limited benefit to most diabetic patients.

- Nicotinic acid seems effective at increasing HDL-C and may reduce triglycerides. However, in clinical practice, nicotinic acid alone is not the preferred treatment for hypertriglyceridaemia, but may be used in combination with a statin in people with mixed dyslipidaemia, or in those unable to tolerate fibrates.

  Nicotinic acid seems to increase the incidence of flushing, particularly in female patients.

- We don't know whether anion exchange resins or ezetimibe are useful in treating dyslipidaemia in people with diabetes, but they could be used in combination with a statin if the statin alone fails to achieve lipid targets.

(i) **Please visit http://clinicalevidence.bmj.com for full text and references**

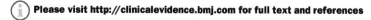

## What are the effects of interventions for dyslipidaemia in people with diabetes?

| | |
|---|---|
| **Beneficial** | • Statins |
| **Likely To Be Beneficial** | • Combined treatments (for lipid modification)<br>• Fibrates<br>• Intensive multiple-intervention treatment programmes (for lipid modification) |
| **Trade-off Between Benefits And Harms** | • Fish oil (for lipid modification)<br>• Nicotinic acid (for lipid modification) |
| **Unknown Effectiveness** | • Anion exchange resins<br>• Ezetimibe |

Search date June 2007

**DEFINITION** The term dyslipidaemia is used to describe a group of conditions in which there are abnormal levels of lipids and lipoproteins in the blood. Abnormalities of lipid metabolism are present in people with both type 1 and type 2 diabetes. The nature of these abnormalities is complex, but the core components of diabetic dyslipidaemia are elevated circulating levels of triglycerides and decreased circulating levels of high-density lipoprotein cholesterol (HDL-C). In addition, the number of small, dense lipoprotein particles is raised. Consequently — although the cholesterol content of these particles may be low — small, dense low-density lipoprotein cholesterol (LDL-C) is raised. Total cholesterol and LDL-C may be normal if glycaemic control is adequate. Triglycerides and cholesterol are the main lipids of interest. The main classes of lipoprotein considered in this review are low-density lipoproteins (LDL) and high-density lipoproteins (HDL). **Diagnosis:** A diagnosis of diabetic dyslipidaemia requiring drug treatment is determined by the person's lipid profile and level of cardiovascular risk. The classification of cardiovascular risk and lipid targets for drug treatment differ between the USA and the UK, and the rest of Europe. While it is accepted that people with diabetes are at high risk of CVD, in the UK and USA this high-risk group is stratified further to target those most likely to benefit from treatment. However, the European guidelines on CVD prevention classify as all high-risk people with type 2 diabetes, and with type 1 diabetes and microalbuminuria. It is acknowledged that in the USA, there is a case for offering drug treatment at lower lipid levels in people at high cardiovascular risk. In the USA, an 'optional' goal for LDL-C of 1.81 mmol/L (70 mg/dL) is considered in people with high cardiovascular risk; and the Canadian Diabetic Association recommends a goal for LDL-C of 2.0 mmol/L or less in similarly high-risk people. Although these targets apply to people with type 2 diabetes, in clinical practice they are often extrapolated to people with type 1 diabetes. **Population:** For this review, we have included studies of adults with type 1 and type 2 diabetes, including those with concurrent hypertension, and we have used UK (NICE) guidelines to determine level of risk. The UKPDS (United Kingdom Prospective Diabetes Study) tool, which includes data from people with diabetes, was used to calculate level of cardiovascular risk only. Subpopulations are described in detail in the description of individual studies where appropriate. Studies in children were excluded. Studies of adults with diabetes and microalbuminuria or nephropathy are covered in a separate review (see review on diabetic nephropathy, p 201).

**INCIDENCE/PREVALENCE Type 1 diabetes mellitus:** In people with well-controlled type 1 diabetes, the incidence of dyslipidaemia is comparable to that in the general population. However, there are no detailed data on the incidence and prevalence of dyslipidaemia in people with type 1 diabetes. **Type 2 diabetes mellitus:** Dyslipidaemia is common in people with type 2 diabetes. A survey of 498 adults with type 2 diabetes (representing a projected

*(continued over)*

*(from previous page)*

population size of 13,369,754 in the US adult general population) estimated that over 70% of people have an LDL-C greater than the US treatment goal of less than 2.6 mmol/L (<100 mg/dL; some have estimated this figure at >80%). Over half of men and two-thirds of women have an HDL-C level below US recommended goals of greater than 1.0 mmol/L, while over half of men and women have elevated triglyceride levels. Only 28.2% of people with diabetes were taking lipid-modifying drugs, and only 3% were controlled to US targets for all lipids.

**AETIOLOGY/RISK FACTORS** In people with diabetes mellitus, insulin insufficiency or insulin resistance can have an effect on lipid metabolism. **Type 1 diabetes mellitus:** Little is understood about the cause of dyslipidaemia in people with type 1 diabetes. In poorly controlled type 1 diabetes, and in nephropathy, the typical cluster of abnormalities seen in diabetic dyslipidaemia does occur, and is associated with a much greater cardiovascular risk than in people without diabetes. **Type 2 diabetes mellitus:** Impaired insulin action may not be the only cause of dyslipidaemia. Central/visceral obesity may increase the amount of free fatty acids released into the portal circulation, increasing hepatic triglyceride production, while high-fat meals — typical of a Western diet — may exacerbate postprandial hypertriglyceridaemia. Impaired insulin action in people with type 2 diabetes is thought to result in the loss of suppression of lipolysis (the breakdown of triglycerides into free fatty acids and glycerol) in adipose tissue. This leads to an increased release of free fatty acids into the portal circulation and, consequently, increased delivery of free fatty acids to the liver. This leads to increased production of triglycerides by the liver and a decreased production of HDL-C. In addition, there is impaired clearance of triglycerides from the circulation. This resulting hypertriglyceridaemia alters the activity of other enzymes, which leads to the formation of small, dense LDL particles, and increased catabolism of HDL.

**PROGNOSIS** CVD is 2 to 6 times more frequent in people with diabetes than in people without diabetes, and progresses more rapidly when it occurs. Overall, it is the most common cause of death in people with diabetes, with at least 50% of deaths in type 2 diabetes caused by CHD. Dyslipidaemia is one of the major contributors to this increased cardiovascular risk. Lipid abnormalities are important predictors of CHD in people with type 2 diabetes. High LDL-C, high triglycerides, and low HDL-C have all been reported as predictors for cardiovascular risk. A 1.57-fold increase in CHD risk has been reported to be associated with a 1 mmol/L increase in LDL-C, and a 15% decrease in risk with a 0.1 mmol/L increase in HDL-C concentration.

Sandeep Vijan

## KEY POINTS

- The age-adjusted prevalence of hypertension in US adults with diabetes is 59%, more than double the prevalence in those without diabetes.

  Major cardiac events occur in approximately 5% of people with diabetes and untreated hypertension each year, and the risk is higher in those with other risk factors, such as diabetic nephropathy.

- Most studies enrolled participants with type 2 diabetes.

- Early trials of blood pressure lowering in people with diabetes and hypertension, typically with systolic blood pressure targets of approximately 140–150 mmHg, reduced cardiovascular events and mortality in people with diabetes and hypertension.

- Results from studies with intensive (lower) systolic blood pressure targets (e.g., 120–130 mmHg) are inconsistent. In general, cardiovascular benefit appears to diminish, and the risk of treatment-related adverse effects increases, with intensive management. It is, therefore, difficult to specify precise blood pressure goals for people with diabetes and hypertension.

- We don't know whether more intensive (lower) blood pressure targets improve microvascular outcomes compared with less intensive (higher) targets.

- One large RCT found that targeting a systolic blood pressure of <120 mmHg in people with type 2 diabetes did not reduce cardiovascular mortality or cardiovascular events compared with a target of <140 mmHg.

- Few studies systematically report the adverse effects of treatment to reduce blood pressure in people with diabetes.

 **Please visit http://clinicalevidence.bmj.com for full text and references**

| What are the effects of different blood pressure targets in people with diabetes and hypertension? | |
|---|---|
| Likely To Be Beneficial | • More intensive (lower) blood pressure targets (in general, more effective than less intensive [higher] targets; however, optimum target is unclear) |

Search date October 2013

**DEFINITION** Hypertension in diabetes is classically defined as a systolic blood pressure of 140 mmHg or greater or a diastolic blood pressure of 90 mmHg or greater. Hypertension is divided into three stages. **Pre-hypertension** is a systolic blood pressure of 120 mmHg to 139 mmHg or a diastolic blood pressure of 80 mmHg to 89 mmHg. **Stage 1 hypertension** is a systolic blood pressure of 140 mmHg to 159 mmHg or diastolic blood pressure of 90 mmHg to 99 mmHg. **Stage 2 hypertension** is a systolic blood pressure of 160 mmHg or greater or a diastolic blood pressure of 100 mmHg or greater. However, guidelines now suggest that drug therapy should be instituted in any person with diabetes and hypertension, regardless of stage. This review focuses on adults with diabetes with stage 1 or 2 hypertension, but with no diagnosis of CHD, diabetic retinopathy, or nephropathy. The control of hypertension in people with diabetic retinopathy, p 222 and those with diabetic nephropathy, p 201 are described in separate reviews.

**INCIDENCE/PREVALENCE** Hypertension is highly prevalent among people with diabetes. It is about 1.5 to 3.0 times more common in people with type 2 diabetes than in the age-matched general population. Between 2007 and 2010, the age-adjusted prevalence of hypertension in US adults with diabetes was 59%, more than double the prevalence in those

*(continued over)*

*(from previous page)*

without diabetes. About 30% of people with type 1 diabetes eventually develop hypertension, usually after they develop diabetic nephropathy. The prevalence of hypertension varies depending on the population studied (see Aetiology).

**AETIOLOGY/RISK FACTORS** The cause of hypertension is multifactorial, complex, and not fully understood. In the general population, there are several major risk factors for hypertension; specific risk factors are not clearly different in the diabetic population. Age is the predominant factor; data suggest that prevalence increases with age. People with at least one parent with hypertension are about twice as likely to develop hypertension. African-American people have a 7% to 10% increase in prevalence compared with non-Hispanic white people from the US. Obese people also have greater risk: for each unit increase in BMI, the prevalence increases by about 1.0% to 1.5%. Insulin resistance is associated with development of hypertension.

**PROGNOSIS** Untreated hypertension in people with diabetes is associated with high rates of cardiovascular disease (such as MI, heart failure, and stroke) and microvascular disease (such as renal disease [including albuminuria, renal insufficiency, and end-stage renal disease] and diabetic retinopathy). In the placebo groups of major trials of hypertension control in type 2 diabetes, major cardiac events occurred in about 4% to 6% of people annually, and were substantially higher in populations with additional risk factors such as diabetic nephropathy.

Valerie Halpin

## KEY POINTS

- Acute cholecystitis causes unremitting right upper quadrant pain, anorexia, nausea, vomiting, and fever, and, if untreated, can lead to perforations, abscess formation, or fistulae.

  About 95% of people with acute cholecystitis have gallstones.

  It is thought that blockage of the cystic duct by a gallstone or local inflammation can lead to acute cholecystitis, but we don't know whether bacterial infection is also necessary.

- Early cholecystectomy within 7 days of onset of symptoms is the treatment of choice for acute cholecystitis.

  Early surgery reduces the duration of hospital admission compared with delayed surgery, but does not reduce mortality or complications.

  Up to one quarter of people scheduled for delayed surgery may require urgent operations because of recurrent or worsening symptoms.

- Laparoscopic cholecystectomy may reduce the duration of hospital admission and improve some intra-operative and postoperative outcomes compared with open cholecystectomy, but it may increase the risk of bile duct injury.

  Up to one quarter of people having laparoscopic cholecystectomy may need conversion to open surgery because of risks of complications or uncontrolled bleeding.

- We found limited evidence from one small RCT that percutaneous cholecystostomy plus early cholecystectomy may reduce time to symptomatic improvement and duration of hospital stay compared with medical treatment plus delayed cholecystectomy in people at high surgical risk.

  However, evidence was weak. We found no studies in people at normal surgical risk.

- Routine abdominal drainage in both uncomplicated laparoscopic and open cholecystectomy is associated with an increase in wound infections compared with no drainage.

(i) **Please visit http://clinicalevidence.bmj.com for full text and references**

| What are the effects of treatments for acute cholecystitis? | |
| --- | --- |
| Beneficial | • Early cholecystectomy (reduces hospital stay and the need for emergency surgery compared with delayed cholecystectomy)<br><br>• Laparoscopic cholecystectomy (reduces hospital stay and may improve some intra-operative and postoperative outcomes compared with open cholecystectomy) |
| Likely To Be Beneficial | • Percutaneous cholecystostomy within 8 hours plus early cholecystectomy compared with medical treatment followed by delayed cholecystectomy in people at high surgical risk (no evidence in people at normal surgical risk) |
| Trade-off Between Benefits And Harms | • Observation alone (associated with a 30% failure rate and a 36% rate of gallstone-related complications) |

- Open cholecystectomy (conversion from laparoscopic to open cholecystectomy necessary in 4%–27% of people but may increase some intra-operative and postoperative complications)

**Search date October 2013**

**DEFINITION** Acute cholecystitis results from obstruction of the cystic duct, usually by a gallstone, followed by distension and subsequent chemical or bacterial inflammation of the gallbladder. People with acute cholecystitis usually have unremitting right upper quadrant pain, anorexia, nausea, vomiting, and fever. About 95% of people with acute cholecystitis have gallstones (calculous cholecystitis) and 5% lack gallstones (acalculous cholecystitis). Severe acute cholecystitis may lead to necrosis of the gallbladder wall, known as gangrenous cholecystitis. This review does not include people with acute cholangitis, which is a severe complication of gallstone disease and generally a result of bacterial infection.

**INCIDENCE/PREVALENCE** The incidence of acute cholecystitis among people with gallstones is unknown. The incidence of acute cholecystitis is about 20% among people with biliary colic. Biliary colic occurs in 1% to 4% of people with gallstones. Of people admitted to hospital for biliary tract disease, 20% have acute cholecystitis. The number of cholecystectomies carried out for acute cholecystitis increased from the mid 1980s to the early 1990s, especially in older people. The number of cholecystectomies for acute cholecystitis has been decreasing as the rate of elective cholecystectomy has increased. Acute calculous cholecystitis is three times more common in women than in men up to the age of 50 years, and is about one and a half times more common in women than in men thereafter.

**AETIOLOGY/RISK FACTORS** Acute calculous cholecystitis seems to be caused by obstruction of the cystic duct by a gallstone, or local mucosal erosion and inflammation caused by a stone, but cystic duct ligation alone does not produce acute cholecystitis in animal studies. The role of bacteria in the pathogenesis of acute cholecystitis is not clear; positive cultures of bile or gallbladder wall are found in 50% to 75% of cases. The cause of acute acalculous cholecystitis is uncertain and may be multifactorial, including increased susceptibility to bacterial colonisation of static gallbladder bile.

**PROGNOSIS** Complications of acute cholecystitis include perforation of the gallbladder, pericholecystic abscess, and fistula caused by gallbladder wall ischaemia and infection. In the US, the overall mortality from untreated complications is about 20%.

Richard L. Nelson

## KEY POINTS

- Chronic anal fissures typically occur in the midline, with visible sphincter fibres at the fissure base, anal papillae, sentinel piles, and indurated margins.

  Anal fissures are a common cause of anal pain during, and for 1 to 2 hours after, defecation. The cause is not fully understood, but low intake of dietary fibre may be a risk factor.

  Chronic fissures typically have a cyclical history of intermittent healing and recurrence, but about 35% will eventually heal, at least temporarily, without intervention.

  Atypical features, such as multiple, large, or irregular fissures, or those not in the midline, may indicate underlying malignancy, sexually transmitted infections, inflammatory bowel disease, or trauma.

- Internal anal sphincterotomy is more effective than medical therapy for chronic anal fissure in adults. It improves fissure healing compared with treatment with nitric oxide donors (topical glyceryl trinitrate, topical isosorbide dinitrate), botulinum A toxin-haemagglutinin complex, and calcium channel blockers (nifedipine, diltiazem).

  Internal anal sphincterotomy also increases fissure healing compared with digital anal stretch, and anal stretch is more likely to cause flatus incontinence. One small RCT found limited evidence that controlled anal dilation may be equivalent to sphincterotomy in fissure healing, with negligible incontinence risk.

  We don't know whether anal dilation is more effective than topical glyceryl trinitrate at reducing the proportion of people with anal fissure.

  We don't know whether internal anal sphincterotomy is better or worse than anal advancement flap in improving fissure healing.

  Open partial lateral internal anal sphincterotomy may be equivalent to closed partial internal anal sphincterotomy in fissure healing.

  Longer internal anal sphincter division (to the dentate line, as opposed to the fissure apex only) may be more effective at reducing anal fissure.

- The risk of minor flatus or faecal incontinence is greater with internal anal sphincterotomy than with botulinum toxin. Topical glyceryl trinitrate increases the risk of headache compared with internal anal sphincterotomy.

- Post-surgical faecal incontinence may be confused with post-surgical leakage (a short-term adverse effect). Confirming post-surgical leakage requires long-term follow-up (at least 12 months).

 **Please visit http://clinicalevidence.bmj.com for full text and references**

| What are the effects of surgical treatments for chronic anal fissure? | |
|---|---|
| Beneficial | • Internal anal sphincterotomy (more effective than nitric oxide donors, botulinum A toxin-haemagglutinin complex, calcium channel blockers, or anal stretch) |
| Unknown Effectiveness | • Anal advancement flap (limited evidence that as effective as internal anal sphincterotomy based on one small RCT) |
| Unlikely To Be Beneficial | • Anal stretch (less effective than internal anal sphincterotomy) |

**Search date January 2014**

**DEFINITION** An anal fissure is an ulcer or tear in the squamous epithelium of the distal anal canal, usually in the posterior midline. People with an anal fissure usually experience pain during defecation and for 1 to 2 hours afterwards. Multiple fissures and large, irregular, or large and irregular fissures, or fissures off the midline are considered atypical. Atypical fissures may be caused by malignancy, chemotherapy, STIs, inflammatory bowel disease, or other traumas. Treatments for atypical fissures are not included in this review. It is not clear what the best treatment strategy is in people who present with a painless anal fissure and in whom an atypical aetiology has been ruled out. **Acute anal fissures** have sharply demarcated, fresh mucosal edges, often with granulation tissue at the base. Acute fissures are believed to often heal spontaneously. **Chronic anal fissures** Fissures persisting for longer than 4 weeks, or recurrent fissures, are generally defined as chronic. Chronic anal fissures have distinct anatomical features, such as visible sphincter fibres at the fissure base, anal papillae, sentinel piles, and indurated margins. Most published studies only require the presence of one of these signs or symptoms of chronicity to classify a fissure as chronic. This review deals only with chronic anal fissures.

**INCIDENCE/PREVALENCE** Anal fissures are a common cause of anal pain in all age groups, but we found no reliable evidence about precise incidence.

**AETIOLOGY/RISK FACTORS** The cause of anal fissure is not fully understood. Low intake of dietary fibre may be a risk factor for the development of acute anal fissure. People with anal fissure often have raised resting anal canal pressures with anal spasm, which may give rise to ischaemia.

**PROGNOSIS** Chronic anal fissure typically has a cyclical pain history, with intermittent healing and then recurrence. One systematic review found healing rates of about 35% without intervention, depending on the length of study follow-up.

Nigel D'Souza and Karen Nugent

## KEY POINTS

- Appendicitis is inflammation of the appendix that may lead to an abscess, ileus, peritonitis, or death, if untreated.

- Appendicitis is the most common abdominal surgical emergency.

- The current standard treatment for uncomplicated appendicitis is usually surgical removal of the appendix (appendicectomy), but there has been increasing evidence published on the use of antibiotics.

- The evidence comparing surgery with antibiotics is weak and confounded by factors such as inconsistencies with results and outcomes measured, which makes it difficult to compare these interventions.

- Appendicectomy may be associated with reduced overall treatment failure (including recurrence requiring surgery within 1 year) in the treatment of adults with acute appendicitis, but may also be associated with an increase in complications and sick days compared with antibiotics.

  We don't know whether appendicectomy and antibiotics differ with regard to hospital stay, or in improving quality of life scores.

  We found no studies reporting outcomes beyond 1 year, which is a major limitation of the available evidence.

  All of the evidence we found was in adults; we found no RCTs in children.

- At present, the weight of evidence does not suggest that antibiotics are superior to surgery for treating appendicitis.

- There is a lack of high-quality RCTs comparing what might be termed optimal current surgical techniques with optimal current antibiotic regimens. Further trials are currently under way, which may provide further information on how current surgical techniques compare with current antibiotic regimens when both treatment approaches are optimised.

 **Please visit http://clinicalevidence.bmj.com for full text and references**

## What are the effects of surgery compared with antibiotics for acute appendicitis?

| Likely To Be Beneficial | • Surgery versus antibiotics (increased initial treatment success and decreased recurrence with surgery compared with antibiotics in adults, but may be associated with some increased complications; we found no good evidence in children) |
|---|---|

Search date May 2014

**DEFINITION** Appendicitis is inflammation of the vermiform appendix. Progression of the inflammatory process can lead to abscess, ileus, peritonitis, or death if untreated. The term 'complicated' appendicitis refers to the presence of gangrene or perforation of the appendix. Free perforation into the peritoneal cavity can lead to purulent or faeculent peritonitis. A contained perforation can lead to appendix abscess or phlegmon (inflammatory mass).

**INCIDENCE/PREVALENCE** Appendicitis is the most common abdominal surgical emergency. The reported lifetime risk of appendicitis in the US is 8.6% in men and 6.7% in women, with an annual incidence of 9.38 per 100,000. In the US, it is estimated that around 326,000 operations for appendicitis were performed in 2007. In the UK, around 42,000 to 47,000 operations for appendicitis were performed yearly between 2007 and 2012. Large studies from the UK and US have shown that complicated appendicitis is found at surgery in around 16.5% to 24.4% of cases.

*(continued over)*

*(from previous page)*

**AETIOLOGY/RISK FACTORS** The cause of appendicitis is uncertain, although various theories exist. The predominant theories centre on luminal obstruction of the blind-ending appendix as the primary pathology. When goblet cell secretions are blocked from escaping by the luminal obstruction, the intra-luminal pressure within the appendix increases and leads to ischaemia of the appendix wall. The translocation of bacteria from the lumen across the compromised mucosa causes transmural inflammation. Ongoing tissue ischaemia and inflammation can then lead to infarction and perforation of the appendix (complicated appendicitis). Free perforation will lead to soiling of the intra-peritoneal cavity with pus or faeces. A perforation can also be enclosed by the surrounding soft tissues (omentum, mesentery, or bowel), thus leading to the development of an inflammatory mass. This inflammatory mass may contain pus (abscess) or it may not (phlegmon). There is some debate as to whether perforated appendicitis is a disease process distinct from uncomplicated appendicitis. Hyperplasia of the lymphoid tissue in the mucosa or submucosa has been posited as the most common mechanism causing obstruction of the appendix lumen. This may present with acute catarrhal appendicitis, with a gradual onset of symptoms. Lymphoid hyperplasia may be caused by infections (bacterial, viral, fungal, parasitic) or by inflammation, such as in inflammatory bowel disease. Other, rarer causes of obstruction may include parasites (more common in developing countries), fibrous bands, foreign bodies, or carcinoid and caecal carcinoma. A more abrupt course of symptoms has been described in acute obstructive appendicitis from faecoliths.

**PROGNOSIS** The prognosis of untreated appendicitis is unknown, since RCTs comparing treatment with no treatment would be unethical. Spontaneous resolution rate of radiologically confirmed appendicitis has been reported to range from around 4% to 20%. However, spontaneous resolution and recurrence of appendicitis (the 'grumbling appendix') remains a contentious issue among surgeons. The current standard treatment for uncomplicated appendicitis is usually surgical removal of the appendix (appendicectomy) to prevent potential complications from untreated appendicitis. There has been increasing evidence published on the use of antibiotics. Surgical treatment is performed either through an incision (open appendicectomy) or using keyhole surgery (laparoscopic appendicectomy). One systematic review found that wound infection was less likely with laparoscopic appendicectomy compared with open appendicectomy (OR 0.43, CI 0.34 to 0.54), but intra-abdominal abscess formation was more likely with laparoscopic appendicectomy (OR 1.87, CI 1.19 to 2.93). The incidences of both wound infection and abscess formation appear to be higher in complicated appendicitis. A perforated appendix in childhood does not seem to have subsequent negative consequences for female fertility.

# Chronic pancreatitis: dietary supplements

Hemant M. Kocher and Raghu Kadaba

## KEY POINTS

- **Chronic pancreatitis is characterised by long-standing inflammation of the pancreas due to a wide variety of causes, including recurrent acute attacks of pancreatitis.**

  **Chronic pancreatitis affects between 3 and 9 people in 100,000; 70% of cases are alcohol-induced.**

- **Pancreatic enzyme supplements reduce steatorrhoea in people with chronic pancreatitis, but they may have no effect on pain.**

- **We don't know whether calcium supplements or vitamin/antioxidant supplements are effective.**

 **Please visit http://clinicalevidence.bmj.com for full text and references**

| What are the effects of dietary supplements in people with chronic pancreatitis? | |
| --- | --- |
| Likely To Be Beneficial | • Pancreatic enzyme supplements (for reducing steatorrhoea) |
| Unknown Effectiveness | • Calcium supplements<br>• Vitamin/antioxidant supplements |

**Search date October 2014**

**DEFINITION** Pancreatitis is inflammation of the pancreas. The inflammation may be sudden (acute) or ongoing (chronic). Acute pancreatitis usually involves a single 'attack', after which the pancreas returns to normal. Chronic pancreatitis is characterised by long-standing inflammation of the pancreas owing to a wide variety of causes, including recurrent acute attacks of pancreatitis. Symptoms of chronic pancreatitis include recurring or persistent abdominal pain and impaired exocrine function. The most reliable test of exocrine function is the demonstration of increased faecal fat — although, this test is frequently not performed if imaging is consistent (particularly calcification of the pancreatic gland on computerised tomography scan). **Diagnosis:** There is no consensus on the diagnostic criteria for chronic pancreatitis. Typical symptoms include pain radiating to the back and people may present with malabsorption, malnutrition, and pancreatic endocrine insufficiency. However, these symptoms may be seen in people with more common disorders such as reflux disease and peptic ulcers (also more common in heavy drinkers), and also in people with more serious diseases such as pancreatic or periampullary cancers. Diagnostic tests for chronic pancreatitis include faecal elastase measurement (to prove pancreatic insufficiency) and imaging. Biopsy may be required to resolve diagnostic uncertainty.

**INCIDENCE/PREVALENCE** The annual incidence of chronic pancreatitis has been estimated in one prospective study and several retrospective studies to be between 3 and 9 cases/100,000 population. Prevalence is estimated at between 0.04% and 5%. Alcoholic chronic pancreatitis is usually diagnosed after a long history of alcohol abuse, and is the most common cause.

**AETIOLOGY/RISK FACTORS** The TIGAR-O system describes the main predisposing factors for chronic pancreatitis as: toxic-metabolic (which includes alcohol-induced [70% of all cases], smoking, hypercalcaemia, hyperlipidaemia, and chronic renal failure); idiopathic (which includes tropical pancreatitis and may form up to 20% of all cases); genetic (which includes cationic trypsinogen, CFTR, and SPINK1 mutation); autoimmune (which includes solitary and syndromic); recurrent and severe acute pancreatitis (which includes postnecrotic and radiation-induced); and obstructive (which includes pancreatic divisum and duct obstruction owing to various causes). Although 70% of people with chronic pancreatitis report excessive consumption of alcohol (>150 g/day) over a long period (>20 years), only 1

*(continued over)*

*(from previous page)*

in 10 heavy drinkers develop chronic pancreatitis, suggesting underlying genetic predisposition or polymorphism, although a link has not been established conclusively.

**PROGNOSIS** Mortality in people with chronic pancreatitis is higher than in the general population, with mortality at 10 years after diagnosis estimated at 70% to 80%. Diagnosis is usually made between 40 and 48 years of age. Reported causes of mortality in people with chronic pancreatitis are: complications of disease as well as treatment; development of pancreatic cancer or diabetes; and continual exposure to risk factors for mortality, such as smoking and alcohol.

David Humes, Janette K Smith, and Robin C Spiller

## KEY POINTS

- Diverticula (mucosal outpouching through the wall of the colon) are rare before the age of 40 years, after which prevalence increases steadily and reaches over 25% by 60 years and older. However, only 10% to 25% of affected people will develop symptoms such as lower abdominal pain.

  Recurrent symptoms are common, and 5% of people with diverticula eventually develop complications such as perforation, obstruction, haemorrhage, fistulae, or abscesses.

  Use of non-steroidal anti-inflammatory drugs (NSAIDs), corticosteroids, and opiate analgesics have been associated with an increased risk of perforation of diverticula, while calcium antagonists may protect against these complications.

- Dietary fibre supplementation using bran or ispaghula husk and laxatives such as methylcellulose and lactulose are widely used to treat uncomplicated diverticular disease, but we don't know whether they reduce symptoms or prevent complications.

  Antibiotics (rifaximin) plus dietary fibre supplementation may improve symptoms more than fibre alone, but increase the risk of adverse effects.

  We don't know whether mesalazine is also beneficial at improving symptoms in uncomplicated diverticular disease, or at reducing complications after acute diverticulitis, as no good-quality studies have been found.

  We don't know whether elective open or laparoscopic colonic resection, or antispasmodics improve symptoms in people with uncomplicated diverticular disease.

- Acute diverticulosis is often treated with intravenous fluids, limiting oral intake, and broad-spectrum antibiotic use. However, we don't know whether such medical treatment improves symptoms and cure rates in people with acute diverticulitis.

- Surgery is usually performed for people with peritonitis caused by perforated acute diverticulitis, but we don't know whether it improves outcomes compared with no surgery, or if any one surgical technique is better at preventing complications.

(i) **Please visit http://clinicalevidence.bmj.com for full text and references**

| What are the effects of treatments for uncomplicated diverticular disease? | |
|---|---|
| Likely To Be Beneficial | • Rifaximin (plus dietary fibre supplementation *v* dietary fibre supplementation alone) for uncomplicated disease |
| Unknown Effectiveness | • Antispasmodics for uncomplicated disease |
| | • Bran or ispaghula husk for uncomplicated disease |
| | • Elective surgery for uncomplicated disease |
| | • Lactulose for uncomplicated disease |
| | • Mesalazine for uncomplicated disease |
| | • Methylcellulose for uncomplicated disease |

## What are the effects of treatments to prevent complications of diverticular disease?

| Unknown Effectiveness | • Advice to increase fibre intake for preventing complications |
| | • Mesalazine for preventing complications |

## What are the effects of treatments for acute diverticulitis?

| Unknown Effectiveness | • Medical treatment for acute diverticulitis |
| | • Surgery for acute diverticulitis |

**Search date May 2010**

**DEFINITION** Colonic diverticula are mucosal outpouchings through the large bowel wall. They are often accompanied by structural changes (elastosis of the taenia coli, muscular thickening, and mucosal folding). They are usually multiple, and occur most frequently in the sigmoid colon. Most people with colonic diverticula are asymptomatic, with little to find on clinical examination, while 20% develop symptoms at some point. If diverticula are associated with symptoms, while then this is termed diverticular disease. If asymptomatic, then the condition is known as diverticulosis. People who go on to develop complications associated with diverticula (inflammation, perforation, fistulae, abscess formation, obstruction, or haemorrhage) are referred to as having complicated diverticular disease. People with uncomplicated diverticular disease may report abdominal pain (principally colicky left iliac fossa pain), bloating, and altered bowel habit, and may have mild left iliac fossa tenderness on examination. Acute diverticulitis occurs when a diverticulum becomes acutely inflamed. People with acute diverticulitis typically present with severe left iliac fossa pain associated with fever, malaise, and altered bowel habit with left iliac fossa tenderness, associated with general signs of infection, such as fever and tachycardia.

**INCIDENCE/PREVALENCE** In the UK, the incidence of diverticulosis increases with age; about 5% of people are affected in their fifth decade of life, 25% aged 60 years, and about 50% by their ninth decade. Diverticulosis is common in resource-rich countries, although there is a lower prevalence of diverticulosis in Western vegetarians consuming a diet high in fibre. Diverticulosis is almost unknown in rural Africa and Asia.

**AETIOLOGY/RISK FACTORS** There is an association between low-fibre diets and diverticulosis of the colon. Prospective observational studies have found that both physical activity and a high-fibre diet are associated with a lower risk of developing diverticular disease. Case-control studies have found an association between perforated diverticular disease and NSAIDs, corticosteroids, and opiate analgesics, and have found that calcium antagonists have a protective effect. People in Japan, Singapore, and Thailand develop diverticula that affect mainly the right side of the colon.

**PROGNOSIS** Inflammation will develop in 10% to 25% of people with diverticula at some point. It is unclear why some people develop symptoms and some do not. Even after successful medical treatment of acute diverticulitis, almost two-thirds of people suffer recurrent pain in the lower abdomen. Recurrent diverticulitis is observed in 7% to 42% of people with diverticular disease, and after recovery from the initial attack the calculated yearly risk of suffering a further episode is 3%. About 50% of recurrences occur within 1 year of the initial episode, and 90% occur within 5 years. Complications of diverticular disease (perforation, obstruction, haemorrhage, and fistula formation) are each seen in about 5% of people with colonic diverticula when followed up for 10 to 30 years. In the UK, the incidence of perforation is 4 cases per 100,000 people a year, leading to approximately 2000 cases annually. Intra-abdominal abscess formation is also a recognised complication.

Asad Qureshi, Anjali Verma, Paul Ross, and David Landau

## KEY POINTS

- Colorectal cancer is the third most common malignancy in the developed world, and about one fifth of people present with intestinal obstruction or perforation.

  Risk factors for colorectal cancer are mainly dietary and genetic.

  Overall 5-year survival is about 50%, with half of people having surgery experiencing recurrence of the disease.

- Adjuvant systemic chemotherapy reduces mortality compared with surgery alone in people who have Dukes' C colorectal cancer. We don't know whether adjuvant systemic chemotherapy improves mortality compared with surgery alone in people with Dukes' B colorectal cancer.

  It has been suggested that people with high-risk Dukes' B may derive some benefit with adjuvant systemic chemotherapy compared with surgery alone. However, we found no direct evidence on this group.

  We found some evidence that oral fluoropyrimidines (with or without leucovorin) may be as effective as intravenous fluorouracil (with or without leucovorin) regimens at reducing mortality.

  The addition of oxaliplatin to fluorouracil plus leucovorin improves disease-free survival at 3 and 4 years compared with fluorouracil plus leucovorin alone in people with Dukes' B or C colon cancer.

  Adding irinotecan to fluorouracil plus leucovorin does not reduce mortality any more than fluorouracil plus leucovorin alone in people with Dukes' C colorectal cancer and increases toxic effects.

- Preoperative radiotherapy may modestly reduce local tumour recurrence and mortality compared with surgery alone in people with rectal cancer.

  Preoperative radiotherapy may reduce local recurrence compared with postoperative radiotherapy. There may be no difference in overall survival between preoperative and postoperative radiotherapy.

- Routine intensive follow-up may reduce the time to detection of recurrence and may increase survival compared with less-intensive follow-up in people with colorectal cancer.

(i) **Please visit http://clinicalevidence.bmj.com for full text and references**

| What are the effects of treatments for colorectal cancer? | |
|---|---|
| Beneficial | • Adjuvant systemic chemotherapy<br>• Preoperative radiotherapy in people with rectal cancer |
| Likely To Be Beneficial | • Routine intensive follow-up |

**Search date August 2008**

**DEFINITION** Colorectal cancer is a malignant neoplasm arising from the lining (mucosa) of the large intestine (colon and rectum). About two-thirds of colorectal cancers occur in the colon and the remainder in the rectum. Colorectal cancer may be categorised as Dukes' stage A, B, or C. Some studies in this review have reported staging of colorectal cancer as stage I, II, or III. Stage I corresponds to Dukes' stage A–B1; stage II corresponds to Dukes' stage B2–B3; stage III corresponds to Dukes' stage C. In this review we have included

*(continued over)*

*(from previous page)*

people with Dukes' A, B, and C (stage I, II, III) and excluded people with distant metastatic disease (Dukes' stage D or stage IV).

**INCIDENCE/PREVALENCE** Colorectal cancer is the third most common cancer in the UK after breast and lung. There are about 36,000 new cases per year in the UK. It is the second highest cause of cancer death in the UK after lung cancer, with 16,000 deaths per year. Between 1979 and 1999 the incidence in men in the UK rose slowly before beginning to fall. Over the same period the incidence in women changed very little. In contrast to incidence trends, mortality has been falling since the early 1990s. Between 1997 and 2006 bowel cancer age-standardised mortality in the UK fell by 17%. The presentation of colorectal cancer can vary widely. Cancers of the proximal colon can present with weight loss and anaemia. Cancers of the distal colon and rectum are more likely to present with bleeding and altered bowel habit. In the UK, approximately one fifth of patients present with acute intestinal obstruction.

**AETIOLOGY/RISK FACTORS** Bowel cancer is generally more common in populations with a 'Westernised' diet. Several studies have shown an increased risk associated with increased consumption of red meat and alcohol. Conversely, a diet high in fibre, fresh fruit, vegetables, and fish has been shown to reduce the risk of colorectal cancer. A minority of cases are directly associated with known genetic risk factors. However, people with a first-degree relative with bowel cancer are at twice the risk of developing it themselves.

**PROGNOSIS** As a result of earlier diagnosis and better treatment 5-year overall survival rose from about 20% in the early 1970s to approximately 50% in early 2000. Surgery is undertaken in over 80% of people, but about half experience recurrence of their cancer.

Carmen Lewis

## KEY POINTS

- Colorectal cancer is a malignant neoplasm arising from the lining of the large intestine. Nearly two thirds of colorectal cancers occur in the rectum or sigmoid colon.

    It is the third most common cancer in resource rich countries, accounting for about 20,000 deaths each year in the UK, and 60,000 each year in the USA.

    Screening is defined (and distinguished from testing on demand) as any organised or systematic testing of asymptomatic people.

- Annual or biennial faecal occult blood testing, followed by further investigation in people with a positive test, decreases colorectal cancer-related mortality compared with no screening.

- We found no evidence examining combining faecal occult blood test plus flexible sigmoidoscopy for screening of colorectal cancer.

- A single flexible sigmoidoscopy (followed by an immediate colonoscopy and follow-up colonoscopies at 2 and 6 years in those found to have polyps on sigmoidoscopy screening) seems to reduce colorectal cancer rates, but not colorectal cancer mortality, compared with no screening.

- Flexible sigmoidoscopy can produce false positives by detecting polyps which do not have malignant potential, and has been reported by some people to be painful.

- We don't know how effective colonoscopy is in detecting colorectal cancer in healthy people, although the intervention is associated with rare but serious morbidity, including perforation and bleeding.

- Although we found no evidence examining either computed tomography colography or double contrast barium enema in healthy people, evidence in people at a high risk of colorectal cancer suggests that they may be useful diagnostic tools.

 **Please visit http://clinicalevidence.bmj.com for full text and references**

| What are the effects of screening for colorectal cancer? | |
| --- | --- |
| Beneficial | • Faecal occult blood test (annual or biennial testing, followed by further investigation if positive) |
| Likely To Be Beneficial | • Flexible sigmoidoscopy (single test, followed by colonoscopy if positive) |
| Unknown Effectiveness | • Colonoscopy |
| | • Combination of faecal occult blood test plus flexible sigmoidoscopy |
| | • Computed tomography colography |
| | • Double contrast barium enema |

Search date November 2006

**DEFINITION** Colorectal cancer is a malignant neoplasm arising from the lining (mucosa) of the large intestine (colon and rectum). Nearly two-thirds of colorectal cancers occur in the rectum or sigmoid colon. Colorectal cancer may be classified as A, B, or C Dukes'. More

*(continued over)*

*(from previous page)*

recently, stage D has been proposed to classify people with advanced and widespread regional involvement (metastasis). Screening is defined (and distinguished from testing on demand) as any organised or systematic testing of asymptomatic people. In this review, we have included studies of screening in men and women over 45 years of age (with no upper age limit) who are not known to be at high risk for colorectal cancer. People at high risk of colorectal cancer are defined as those with one or more first-degree relatives with colorectal cancer, or personal history of inflammatory bowel disease, polyps, or colorectal cancer.

**INCIDENCE/PREVALENCE** Colorectal cancer is the third most common cancer in resource-rich countries. It accounts for about 20,000 deaths each year in the UK, and 60,000 each year in the USA. Over most of the last 40 years the incidence of, and mortality from, colorectal cancer changed little. However, recently, both the incidence and mortality have fallen in the UK and the USA. In the UK, about one quarter of people with colorectal cancer present with either intestinal obstruction or perforation.

**AETIOLOGY/RISK FACTORS** Colon cancer affects almost equal proportions of men and women, most commonly between the ages of 60 and 80 years. Rectal cancer is more common in men. The pathogenesis of colorectal cancer involves genetic and environmental factors. The most important environmental factor is probably diet. People with a personal or family history of colorectal cancer or polyps, or a personal history of inflammatory bowel disease, are at higher risk of developing colorectal cancer.

**PROGNOSIS** Overall 5-year survival after colorectal cancer is about 50%. Disease-specific mortality in both UK and US cancer registries is decreasing, but the reasons for this are unclear. Surgery is undertaken with curative intent in over 80% of people, but about half experience cancer recurrence.

Michelle S. Y. Lau and Alexander C. Ford

## KEY POINTS

- People with idiopathic chronic constipation can be divided into two main categories: those with difficulty defecating (but with normal bowel motion frequency) and those with a transit abnormality (which can present as infrequent defecation).

    Although there are defined criteria for the diagnosis of constipation, in practice diagnostic criteria are less rigid and depend in part on the perception of normal bowel habit.

    Constipation is highly prevalent, with approximately 12 million general practitioner prescriptions for laxatives being written in England in 2001.

    Patients are often dissatisfied with laxatives, mainly due to concerns regarding their safety and efficacy.

    Emerging therapies have been tested, and meta-analyses pooling data from the relevant RCTs are reviewed in this overview.

- Lubiprostone, linaclotide, and prucalopride seem to be more effective than placebo at improving frequency of bowel movements and spontaneous complete bowel movements in people with chronic constipation.

- In terms of adverse events, lubiprostone is particularly associated with an increase in rates of nausea.

- The studies we found were conducted in secondary and tertiary care, and the patients were predominantly women; therefore, the results may not be truly applicable to all people, particularly men and patients being treated in primary care.

 **Please visit http://clinicalevidence.bmj.com for full text and references**

## What are the effects of medications in people with idiopathic chronic constipation?

| Likely To Be Beneficial | • Linaclotide |
| | • Lubiprostone |
| | • Prucalopride |

**Search date July 2014**

**DEFINITION** Bowel habits and perception of bowel habits vary widely within and among populations, making constipation difficult to define. People with constipation can be divided into two main categories: those with difficulty defecating (but normal bowel motion frequency) and those with a transit abnormality (which can present as infrequent defecation). The Rome III criteria is a standardised tool that diagnoses chronic constipation on the basis of two or more of the following symptoms for at least 12 weeks in the preceding 6 months: straining at defecation on at least one quarter of occasions, stools that are lumpy/hard on at least one quarter of occasions, sensation of incomplete evacuation, sensation of anorectal obstruction, or manual manoeuvres to facilitate defecation on at least one quarter of occasions, and three or less bowel movements per week. In practice, however, diagnostic criteria are less rigid and are in part dependent on perception of normal bowel habit. Typically, constipation is diagnosed when a person has bowel actions twice a week or less for two consecutive weeks, especially in the presence of features such as straining at stool, abdominal discomfort, and sensation of incomplete evacuation. **Population:** For the purposes of this overview, we included all RCTs stating that all participants had chronic constipation, whether or not this diagnosis was made according to strict Rome III criteria. Where the definitions of constipation in the RCTs differ markedly from those presented here,

*(continued over)*

*(from previous page)*

we have made this difference explicit. In this overview, we deal with chronic constipation not caused by a specific underlying disease (sometimes known as idiopathic constipation) in adults aged over 18 years, although we have included adults with pelvic floor dyssynergia. We excluded studies in pregnant women and in people with constipation associated with underlying specific organic diseases such as dehydration, autonomic neuropathy, spinal cord injury, bowel obstruction, irritable bowel syndrome, or paralytic ileus. We excluded people with Parkinson's disease and dementia, people who were postoperative, or people who were terminally ill. Opioid-induced constipation was also excluded (see overview on Constipation in people prescribed opioids, p 591). **Diagnosis:** The diagnosis of constipation is initially based on history (see above). Specific tests available for further investigation include thyroid function tests, calcium concentration, colonoscopy, defecation proctogram, anorectal manometry, and colon transit time studies.

**INCIDENCE/PREVALENCE** Twelve million general practitioner prescriptions were written for laxatives in England in 2001. Prevalence data are limited by small samples and problems with definition. One UK survey of 731 women found that 8.2% had constipation meeting Rome II criteria, and 8.5% defined themselves as being constipated. A larger survey (1892 adults) found that 39% of men and 52% of women reported straining at stool on more than one quarter of occasions. Prevalence rises in older people. Several surveys from around the world suggest that, in a community setting, prevalence among older people is about 20%. Levels of dissatisfaction with laxatives among patients with idiopathic chronic constipation are high.

**AETIOLOGY/RISK FACTORS** One systematic review suggested that factors associated with an increased risk of constipation included low-fibre diet and low fluid intake. One meta-analysis showed that the prevalence of constipation was higher in women (OR: 2.22; 95% CI 1.87 to 2.62) and increased with age.

**PROGNOSIS** Untreated constipation can lead to faecal impaction (with resulting faecal incontinence), particularly in older and confused people. Constipation has been suggested as a risk factor for haemorrhoids and diverticular disease; however, evidence of causality is lacking.

Sarah C Mills, Alexander C von Roon, Timothy R Orchard, and Paris P Tekkis

## KEY POINTS

- Crohn's disease is a chronic condition of the gastrointestinal tract.

  It is characterised by transmural, granulomatous inflammation that occurs in a discontinuous pattern, with a tendency to form fistulae.

  The cause is unknown but may depend on interactions between genetic predisposition, environmental triggers, and mucosal immunity.

- First-line treatment to induce remission of acute disease is corticosteroids.

  Budesonide is generally recommended in mild to moderate ileocaecal disease because it is only slightly less effective in inducing remission than prednisolone and has a superior adverse-effect profile.

  Prednisolone or methylprednisolone are generally recommended for severe or more extensive disease because of their superior efficacy.

- Azathioprine and mercaptopurine are effective in inducing remission and healing fistulae in Crohn's disease, provided that at least 17 weeks of treatment are given. Monitoring for myelosuppression is obligatory.

  Aminosalicylates (mesalazine, sulfasalazine) may reduce disease activity, but we don't know which regimen is best to induce remission.

  Methotrexate 25 mg weekly increases remission rates and has a corticosteroid-sparing effect. There is consensus that it is also effective for maintenance.

  Infliximab (a cytokine inhibitor) is effective in inducing and maintaining remission in Crohn's disease, but the long-term adverse-effect profile is unclear; infliximab is therefore generally reserved for treatment of disease that is refractory to treatment with corticosteroids or other immunomodulators.

  Antibiotics and ciclosporin are unlikely to be beneficial in inducing remission.

- Bowel-sparing surgery to induce remission may be preferable to extensive resection, to avoid short-bowel syndrome. Segmental and sub-total colectomy have similar remission rates.

- Laparoscopic resection may reduce postoperative hospital stay, but we don't know whether strictureplasty is effective.

- Azathioprine has been shown to be beneficial in maintaining remission in Crohn's disease, either alone or after surgery, and has a corticosteroid-sparing effect, but it is associated with important adverse effects.

  Ciclosporin, or oral corticosteroids, alone are unlikely to be beneficial in maintaining remission after medical treatment.

  Methotrexate and infliximab may also maintain remission compared with placebo.

  Smoking cessation reduces the risk of relapse, and enteral nutrition may be effective.

  Fish oil and probiotics have not been shown to be effective.

- Mesalazine seems effective in maintaining medically induced remission, but we don't know how effective other aminosalicylates are in maintaining remission.

(i) **Please visit http://clinicalevidence.bmj.com for full text and references**

## What are the effects of medical treatments to induce remission in adults with Crohn's disease?

| | |
|---|---|
| **Beneficial** | • Corticosteroids (oral) to induce remission<br><br>• Infliximab to induce remission |
| **Likely To Be Beneficial** | • Aminosalicylates to induce remission (improved Crohn's Disease Activity Index compared with placebo)<br><br>• Methotrexate to induce remission |
| **Trade-off Between Benefits And Harms** | • Azathioprine or mercaptopurine to induce remission |
| **Unlikely To Be Beneficial** | • Antibiotics to induce remission |
| **Likely To Be Ineffective Or Harmful** | • Ciclosporin to induce remission |

## What are the effects of surgical interventions to induce and maintain remission in adults with small bowel Crohn's disease?

| | |
|---|---|
| **Likely To Be Beneficial** | • Laparoscopic versus open ileocaecal resection (reduced postoperative hospital stay)<br><br>• Limited versus extended resection |
| **Unknown Effectiveness** | • Strictureplasty |

## What are the effects of surgical interventions to induce remission in adults with colonic Crohn's disease?

| | |
|---|---|
| **Likely To Be Beneficial** | • Segmental colectomy |

## What are the effects of medical interventions to maintain remission in adults with Crohn's disease?

| | |
|---|---|
| **Likely To Be Beneficial** | • Aminosalicylates to maintain remission (mesalazine seems more effective than placebo at maintaining medically induced remission; insufficient evidence to assess other aminosalicylates)<br><br>• Infliximab to maintain remission |

| | • Methotrexate to maintain remission |
|---|---|
| **Trade-off Between Benefits And Harms** | • Azathioprine to maintain remission |
| **Likely To Be Ineffective Or Harmful** | • Ciclosporin to maintain remission<br><br>• Corticosteroids (oral) to maintain remission |

## What are the effects of medical interventions to maintain remission after surgery in adults with Crohn's disease?

| **Likely To Be Beneficial** | • Aminosalicylates to maintain remission after surgery<br><br>• Azathioprine/mercaptopurine to maintain remission after surgery |
|---|---|

## What are the effects of lifestyle interventions to maintain remission in adults with Crohn's disease?

| **Beneficial** | • Smoking cessation |
|---|---|
| **Likely To Be Beneficial** | • Enteral nutrition (compared with unrestricted diet) |
| **Unknown Effectiveness** | • Fish oil<br><br>• Probiotics |

**Search date December 2009**

---

**DEFINITION** Crohn's disease is a chronic inflammatory condition of the gastrointestinal tract, characterised by transmural granulomatous inflammation, a discontinuous pattern of distribution, and fistulae. Although any part of the digestive tract from mouth to anus may be affected, Crohn's disease most frequently occurs in the terminal ileum, ileocaecal region, colon, and perianal region. The disease may be further classified into inflammatory, fistulating, and stricturing disease. The symptoms vary but commonly include diarrhoea, abdominal pain, weight loss, blood or mucus in the stool, perineal pain, discharge, and irritation resulting from perianal fistulae. Extraintestinal manifestations of the disease include arthritis, uveitis, and skin rash. **Diagnosis:** There is no single gold standard for the diagnosis of Crohn's disease. Diagnosis is made by clinical evaluation and a combination of endoscopic, histological, radiological, and biochemical investigations. Internationally accepted criteria for the diagnosis of Crohn's disease have been defined by Lennard-Jones. After exclusion of infection, ischaemia, irradiation, and malignancy as causes for intestinal inflammation, a combination of 3 or more of the following findings on clinical examination, radiological investigation, endoscopy, and histological examination of endoscopic biopsies or excised specimens is considered diagnostic: chronic inflammatory lesions of the oral cavity, pylorus or duodenum, small bowel or anus; a discontinuous disease distribution (areas of abnormal mucosa separated by normal mucosa); transmural inflammation (fissuring ulcer, abscess, or fistula); fibrosis (stricture); lymphoid aggregates or aphthoid ulcers; retention of colonic mucin on biopsy in the presence of active inflammation; and granulomata (of the non-caseating type and not caused by foreign bodies). Further macroscopic findings not included in the Lennard-Jones classification that are considered diagnostic for Crohn's disease include fat wrapping, cobblestoning, and thickening of the intestinal wall. Laboratory

*(continued over)*

*(from previous page)*

findings consistent with Crohn's disease include anaemia, thrombocytosis, raised C-reactive protein levels, and a raised erythrocyte sedimentation rate. It may be difficult to distinguish Crohn's disease from ulcerative colitis, particularly when only the colon is affected. In 10% to 15% of patients originally diagnosed as having Crohn's disease, the diagnosis changes to ulcerative colitis during the first year.

**INCIDENCE/PREVALENCE** Estimates of the incidence of Crohn's disease worldwide vary considerably. In Europe, incidence rates range from 0.7 (Croatia) to 9.8 (Scotland) new cases per 100,000 people per year, whereas in North America these range from 3.6 (California) to 15.6 (Manitoba, Canada). The incidence of Crohn's disease is increasing, with incidence rates in the UK, Italy, Iceland, Finland, and the USA having doubled between 1955 and 1995. Crohn's disease is most commonly diagnosed in late adolescence and early adulthood, but the mean age at diagnosis in North American studies ranges from 33.4 to 45 years. Crohn's disease appears to affect women more commonly than men. In a systematic review of North American cohort studies of Crohn's disease, the percentage of females affected by the disease varied from 48% to 66%, and was above 50% in 9 out of 11 studies.

**AETIOLOGY/RISK FACTORS** The true aetiology of Crohn's disease remains unknown. Current aetiological theories suggest that the disease results from a genetic predisposition, regulatory defects in the gut mucosal immune system, and environmental triggers. Defects in the gut mucosal immune system are mainly related to disordered activity of T cells (a type of white blood cell). Environmental triggers that have been linked with Crohn's disease include smoking, diet (high sugar intake), and the balance of beneficial and harmful bacteria in the gut. Finally, debate has raged since *Mycobacterium avium paratuberculosis* was cultured from intestinal tissue of people with Crohn's disease, with little agreement on whether this bacterium is an infective cause of Crohn's disease.

**PROGNOSIS** Crohn's disease is a lifelong condition, with periods of active disease alternating with periods of remission. The disease causes significant disability, with only 75% of sufferers being fully capable of work in the year of diagnosis, and 15% of people unable to work after 5 to 10 years of disease. At least 50% of people with Crohn's disease require surgical treatment during the first 10 years of disease, and approximately 70% to 80% will require surgery during their lifetime. People with Crohn's disease are at higher risk than those without the disease of developing colorectal and small bowel cancer. **Mortality:** Mortality rates among people with Crohn's disease are slightly higher than in those without it. A systematic review of 7 population-based cohort studies found that estimates of standardised mortality ratios were >1 in 6 of the 7 studies, with estimates ranging from 0.72 (95% CI 0.49 to 1.01) to 2.16 (95% CI 1.54 to 2.94). The review also found that mortality rates in Crohn's disease have not changed during the past 40 years.

Paul Moayyedi and Brendan Delaney

## KEY POINTS

- Up to 25% of people have symptoms of GORD, but only 25% to 40% of these people have oesophagitis visible on endoscopy.

  Although obesity, smoking, alcohol, or certain foods are considered risk factors, we don't know that they are actually implicated in GORD.

  About 80% of people with GORD will have recurrent symptoms if they stop treatment, and severe oesophagitis may result in oesophageal stricture or Barrett's oesophagus.

- Proton pump inhibitors (PPIs) increase healing in oesophagitis compared with placebo and $H_2$ receptor antagonists, but we don't know whether one specific PPI is more effective than the others.

  $H_2$ receptor antagonists increase oesophagitis healing rate compared with placebo, and may improve symptoms more than antacids.

- We don't know whether antacids/alginates, motility stimulants, or lifestyle advice to either lose weight or to raise the head of the bed are effective in either improving symptoms of GORD or in preventing recurrence.

  The motility stimulant cisapride has been associated with heart rhythm problems.

- Both standard- and low-dose proton pump inhibitors reduce relapse of oesophagitis and reflux symptoms compared with placebo or $H_2$ receptor antagonists, but we don't know which is the optimum drug regimen.

  $H_2$ receptor antagonists may reduce the risk of relapse of reflux symptoms compared with placebo, although they have not been shown to prevent recurrence of oesophagitis.

- Laparoscopic or open surgery (Nissen fundoplication) may improve endoscopic oesophagitis compared with medical treatment, although studies have given conflicting results.

  Laparoscopic surgery seems as effective as open surgery, with lower risks of operative morbidity and shorter duration of admission, but both types of surgery may have serious complications.

(i) **Please visit http://clinicalevidence.bmj.com for full text and references**

| What are the effects of initial treatment of GORD associated with oesophagitis? | |
|---|---|
| **Beneficial** | • $H_2$ receptor antagonists (increase healing of oesophagitis compared with placebo, but not as effective as proton pump inhibitors) <br><br> • Proton pump inhibitors (increase healing of oesophagitis compared with placebo and $H_2$ receptor antagonists; insufficient evidence to compare effects of different proton pump inhibitors) |
| **Unknown Effectiveness** | • Antacids/alginates <br><br> • Lifestyle advice/modification <br><br> • Motility stimulants (with the exception of cisapride) |

| **What are the effects of maintenance treatment of GORD associated with oesophagitis?** | |
|---|---|
| Beneficial | • Proton pump inhibitors (reduce relapse of oesophagitis and reflux symptoms at 6–12 months compared with placebo or $H_2$ receptor antagonists) |
| Likely To Be Beneficial | • $H_2$ receptor antagonists (reduce relapse of oesophagitis and reflux symptoms at 6–12 months compared with placebo, but not as effective as proton pump inhibitors) |
| Trade-off Between Benefits And Harms | • Laparoscopic surgery<br>• Open surgery |
| Unknown Effectiveness | • Antacids/alginates<br>• Lifestyle advice/modification<br>• Motility stimulants (with the exception of cisapride) |

**Search date July 2007**

**DEFINITION** Gastro-oesophageal reflux disease (GORD) is defined as reflux of gastroduodenal contents into the oesophagus, causing symptoms sufficient to interfere with quality of life. People with GORD often have symptoms of heartburn and acid regurgitation. GORD can be classified according to the results of upper gastrointestinal endoscopy. Currently, the most validated method is the Los Angeles classification, in which an endoscopy showing mucosal breaks in the distal oesophagus indicate the presence of oesophagitis, which is graded in severity from grade A (mucosal breaks of <5 mm in the oesophagus) to grade D (circumferential breaks in the oesophageal mucosa). Alternatively, severity may be graded according to the Savary–Miller classification (grade I: linear, non-confluent erosions, to grade IV: severe ulceration or stricture).

**INCIDENCE/PREVALENCE** Surveys from Europe and the USA suggest that 20% to 25% of people have symptoms of GORD, and 7% have heartburn daily. In primary-care settings, about 25% to 40% of people with GORD have oesophagitis on endoscopy, but most have endoscopy-negative reflux disease.

**AETIOLOGY/RISK FACTORS** We found no evidence of clear predictive factors for GORD. Obesity is reported to be a risk factor, but epidemiological data are conflicting. Smoking and alcohol are also thought to predispose to GORD, but observational data are limited. It has been suggested that some foods, such as coffee, mints, dietary fat, onions, citrus fruits, and tomatoes, may predispose to GORD. However, we found insufficient data on these factors. We found limited evidence that drugs that relax the lower oesophageal sphincter, such as calcium channel blockers, may promote GORD. Twin studies suggest that there may be a genetic predisposition to GORD.

**PROGNOSIS** GORD is a chronic condition, with about 80% of people relapsing once medication is discontinued. Therefore, many people require long-term medical treatment or surgery. Endoscopy-negative reflux disease remains stable, with a minority of people developing oesophagitis over time. However, people with severe oesophagitis may develop complications, such as oesophageal stricture or Barrett's oesophagus.

George E Reese, Alexander C von Roon, and Paris P Tekkis

## KEY POINTS

- Haemorrhoids are cushions of submucosal vascular tissue located in the anal canal starting just distal to the dentate line. Haemorrhoidal disease occurs when there are symptoms such as bleeding, prolapse, pain, thrombosis, mucus discharge, and pruritus.

  Incidence is difficult to ascertain as many people with the condition will never consult with a medical practitioner, although one study found 10 million people in the USA complaining of the disease.

- First- and second-degree haemorrhoids are classically treated with some form of non-surgical ablative/fixative intervention, third-degree treated with rubber band ligation or haemorrhoidectomy, and fourth-degree with haemorrhoidectomy.

- Rubber band ligation is known to be highly effective in treating first-, second-, and some third-degree haemorrhoids.

  Rubber band ligation can produce some immediate adverse effects, and the clinician should therefore always gain informed consent.

- Closed haemorrhoidectomy seems an effective treatment for relieving symptoms in people with first- to fourth-degree haemorrhoids.

  Although effective, closed haemorrhoidectomy does appear to be associated with greater postoperative complications than haemorrhoidal artery ligation.

- Open excisional haemorrhoidectomy may also be effective in treating all grades of haemorrhoids, although it produces similar levels of adverse effects to closed haemorrhoidectomy.

- Infrared coagulation may be as effective as rubber band ligation and injection sclerotherapy in the treatment of first- and second-degree haemorrhoids.

- We found insufficient evidence to judge the effectiveness of injection sclerotherapy, radiofrequency ablation, or haemorrhoidal artery ligation.

- While stapled haemorrhoidectomy seems effective in treating people with more severe haemorrhoids, some of the adverse effects are potentially life threatening, and so the procedure should only ever be carried out by a fully trained colorectal surgeon.

(i) **Please visit http://clinicalevidence.bmj.com for full text and references**

| What are the effects of treatments for haemorrhoidal disease? | |
|---|---|
| Beneficial | • Rubber band ligation |
| Likely To Be Beneficial | • Closed haemorrhoidectomy |
| | • Infrared coagulation/photocoagulation |
| | • Open excisional (Milligan–Morgan/diathermy) haemorrhoidectomy |
| | • Stapled haemorrhoidectomy |
| Unknown Effectiveness | • Haemorrhoidal artery ligation |
| | • Injection sclerotherapy |
| | • Radiofrequency ablation |

**Search date May 2008**

**DEFINITION** Haemorrhoids are cushions of submucosal vascular tissue located in the anal canal starting just distal to the dentate line. These vascular cushions are a normal anatomical structure of the anal canal, and their existence does not necessarily indicate haemorrhoidal disease. Haemorrhoidal disease occurs when there are symptoms such as bleeding, prolapse, pain, thrombosis, mucus discharge, and pruritus. Rectal bleeding is the most common manifestation of haemorrhoidal disease. The bleeding tends to be bright red in nature and occurs on the toilet tissue or drips into the toilet bowl. Haemorrhoids can occur internally, externally, or can be mixed (internal and external components). If prolapse occurs, a perianal mass may be evident with defecation. Haemorrhoids are traditionally graded into four degrees. **First degree (or grade):** The haemorrhoids bleed with defecation but do not prolapse. First-degree haemorrhoids associated with mild symptoms are usually secondary to leakage of blood from mildly inflamed, thin-walled veins or arterioles. Conservative management with dietary manipulation (addition of fibre) and attention to anal hygiene is often adequate. Recurrent rectal bleeding may require ablation of the vessels with non-surgical ablative techniques, such as injection sclerotherapy, infrared coagulation, or rubber band ligation. Infrared coagulation is used infrequently in clinical practice in the UK today, whereas rubber band ligation and injection sclerotherapy are commonly used. **Second degree:** The haemorrhoids prolapse with defecation and reduce spontaneously. Second-degree haemorrhoids can be treated with rubber band ligation or other non-surgical ablative techniques. **Third degree:** The haemorrhoids prolapse and require manual reduction. In third-degree haemorrhoids, where there is significant destruction of the suspensory ligaments, relocation and fixation of the mucosa to the underlying muscular wall is generally necessary. Prolapse can be treated with rubber band ligation initially, but haemorrhoidectomy may be required, especially if prolapse is seen in more than one position. **Fourth degree:** The haemorrhoids prolapse and cannot be reduced. If treatment is necessary, fourth-degree haemorrhoids require haemorrhoidectomy. Haemorrhoids are thought to be associated with chronic constipation, straining to defecate, pregnancy, and low dietary fibre. Frequency, duration, and severity of haemorrhoidal symptoms, such as bleeding, prolapse, or both, determine the type of treatment. Often, absent or episodic symptoms do not require treatment, and the presence of symptoms does not mandate invasive treatment. Some people decline treatment if they can be appropriately reassured that there is no other, more serious reason for their symptoms.

**INCIDENCE/PREVALENCE** Haemorrhoids are thought to be common in the general population, but we found no reliable data regarding incidence. Data from the National Center for Health Statistics found that 10 million people in the USA complained of haemorrhoids, leading to a prevalence rate of 4.4%. However, a true figure for prevalence of haemorrhoids is unknown, as many people with the condition never consult a medical practitioner.

**AETIOLOGY/RISK FACTORS** The cause of haemorrhoids remains unknown, but the downward slide of the anal vascular cushions is considered the most likely explanation. Other possible causes include straining to defecate, erect posture, and obstruction of venous return from raised intra-abdominal pressure: for example, in pregnancy. It is thought that there may be a hereditary predisposition in some people, possibly due to a congenital weakness of the venous wall.

**PROGNOSIS** The prognosis is generally excellent, as many symptomatic episodes will often settle with conservative measures only. If further intervention is required, the prognosis remains good, although symptoms may recur. Early in the clinical course of haemorrhoids, prolapse reduces spontaneously. Later, the prolapse may require manual reduction, and might result in mucus discharge, which can cause pruritus ani. Pain is usually not a symptom of internal haemorrhoids unless the haemorrhoids are prolapsed. Pain may be associated with thrombosed external haemorrhoids. Death from bleeding haemorrhoids is extremely rare.

Grigorios I Leontiadis, Alexander C Ford, and Paul Moayyedi

## KEY POINTS

- The principal effect of *Helicobacter pylori* infection is lifelong chronic gastritis, affecting up to 20% of younger adults but 50% to 80% of adults born before 1950 in resource-rich countries.

  *H pylori* infection can be identified indirectly by the C13 urea breath test and stool antigen tests, which are more accurate than serology.

  Transmission and prevalence rates are higher in areas of childhood poverty. Adult reinfection rates are less than 1% a year.

  In people with *H pylori* infection, about 15% will develop a peptic ulcer and 1% will develop gastric cancer during their lifetime.

- Eradication of *H pylori* makes healing of duodenal ulcers more likely and reduces the risk of bleeding with gastric and duodenal ulcers, either alone or when added to antisecretory drug treatment. Eradication also greatly reduces the risk of recurrence of a duodenal ulcer.

  Eradication reduces recurrence after healing of a gastric ulcer; however, we don't know whether it increases healing of gastric ulcers.

  Eradication of *H pylori* may reduce the risk of NSAID-related ulcers in people without previous ulcers; however, we don't know whether it reduces NSAID-related ulcers or bleeding in people with previous ulcers.

- In areas of low prevalence of *H pylori*, few ulcers are caused by *H pylori* infection. Eradication may be less effective in preventing ulcers in these areas compared with higher-prevalence areas.

- Eradication of *H pylori* reduces symptoms of dyspepsia, but not of GORD.

  Eradicating *H pylori* has been shown to reduce dyspeptic symptoms in people with non-ulcer dyspepsia or uninvestigated dyspepsia compared with placebo.

- Despite the association between *H pylori* infection and gastric cancer, no studies have shown a reduced risk after eradication treatment.

  Gastric B cell lymphoma lesions may regress after *H pylori* eradication, but we don't know this for sure.

- Quadruple and triple regimens seem equally effective at eradicating *H pylori* as first-line treatments. Quadruple regimens may be more effective as second-line treatment than triple regimens when a first-line triple regimen has failed to eradicate the infection. However, the evidence is limited in that, in comparisons of second-line quadruple versus triple regimens, most triple regimens did not contain a nitroimidazole.

- Ten-day sequential therapy may be more effective at eradicating *H pylori* than a 7-day triple regimen.

- Nitroimidazole-based triple regimens and amoxicillin-based triple regimens seem equally effective at eradicating *H pylori*. High-dose clarithromycin within an amoxicillin-based triple regimen seems more effective at eradicating *H pylori* than low-dose clarithromycin. However, the dose of clarithromycin within a nitroimidazole-based triple regimen does not seem to have an effect on eradication rates.

- Triple regimens using different proton pump inhibitors seem equally effective at eradicating *H pylori*.

  Pre-treatment with a proton pump inhibitor before triple regimen does not seem to increase *H pylori* eradication rates compared with no pre-treatment.

  Two-week triple proton pump inhibitor regimens may be more effective than 1-week regimens for eradicating *H pylori*.

- Lower eradication rates are achieved in people infected with strains of *H pylori* that are resistant to antibiotics included in the eradication regimen than are achieved in people infected with sensitive strains of *H pylori*.

- Antibiotics can cause adverse effects such as nausea and diarrhoea. Bismuth may turn the stools black.

(i) **Please visit http://clinicalevidence.bmj.com for full text and references**

## What are the effects of *H pylori* eradication treatment in people with a confirmed duodenal ulcer?

| Beneficial | • *H pylori* eradication for healing and preventing recurrence of duodenal ulcer |
|---|---|

## What are the effects of *H pylori* eradication treatment in people with a confirmed gastric ulcer?

| Beneficial | • *H pylori* eradication for preventing recurrence of gastric ulcer |
|---|---|

## What are the effects of *H pylori* eradication treatment in people with NSAID-related peptic ulcers?

| Unknown Effectiveness | • *H pylori* eradication for healing of NSAID-related peptic ulcers |
|---|---|

## What are the effects of *H pylori* eradication treatment for preventing recurrence of NSAID-related peptic ulcers in people with previous ulcers or dyspepsia?

| Unknown Effectiveness | • *H pylori* eradication for prevention of NSAID-related peptic ulcers in people with previous ulcers or dyspepsia |
|---|---|

## What are the effects of *H pylori* eradication treatment for preventing NSAID-related peptic ulcers in people without previous ulcers?

| Likely To Be Beneficial | • *H pylori* eradication for the prevention of NSAID-related peptic ulcers in people without previous ulcers (more effective than placebo and as effective as antisecretory treatment) |
|---|---|

## What are the effects of *H pylori* eradication treatment in people with confirmed GORD?

| Unlikely To Be Beneficial | • *H pylori* eradication in *H pylori*-positive people with GORD |
|---|---|

## What are the effects of *H pylori* eradication treatment in people with localised B cell lymphoma of the stomach?

| Unknown Effectiveness | • *H pylori* eradication for localised gastric B cell lymphoma |
|---|---|

## What are the effects of *H pylori* eradication treatment on the risk of developing gastric cancer?

| Unknown Effectiveness | • *H pylori* eradication for prevention of gastric cancer |
|---|---|

## What are the effects of *H pylori* eradication treatment in people with confirmed non-ulcer dyspepsia?

| Beneficial | • *H pylori* eradication for non-ulcer dyspepsia |
|---|---|

## What are the effects of *H pylori* eradication treatment in people with uninvestigated dyspepsia?

| Beneficial | • *H pylori* eradication in people with uninvestigated dyspepsia (more effective than placebo)* |
|---|---|

## Do *H pylori* eradication treatments differ in their effects?

| Likely To Be Beneficial | • Quadruple regimen (likely to be more effective than triple regimen that does not contain a nitroimidazole as second-line treatment)<br><br>• Sequential regimens (may be more effective than triple regimens as first-line treatment)<br><br>• Two-week triple regimen (more effective than 1-week triple regimen as first-line treatment) |
|---|---|
| Unknown Effectiveness | • Different triple regimens versus each other (all effective as first-line treatment but relative effects of different triple drug combinations on clinical outcomes unclear) |
| Unlikely To Be Beneficial | • Quadruple regimen (no more effective than triple regimen as first-line treatment) |

**Search date September 2007**

*Endoscopy should not be delayed in people at risk of malignancy.

**DEFINITION** *Helicobacter pylori* is a gram-negative flagellated spiral bacterium found in the stomach. Infection with *H pylori* is predominantly acquired in childhood. *H pylori* infection is not associated with a specific type of dyspeptic symptom. The organism is associated with lifelong chronic gastritis and may cause other gastroduodenal disorders. **Diagnosis:** *H pylori* can be identified indirectly by serology or by the C13 urea breath test. The urea breath test is more accurate than serology, with a sensitivity and specificity greater than 95%, and indicates active infection, whereas serology may lack specificity and cannot be used reliably as a test of active infection. Thus, the urea breath test is the test of choice where prevalence (and hence predictive value of serology) may be low, or where a 'test of cure' is required. In some areas, stool antigen tests that have a similar performance to the urea breath test are now available. **Population:** This review focuses on *H pylori*-positive people throughout.

**INCIDENCE/PREVALENCE** In the developed world, *H pylori* prevalence rates vary with year of birth and social class. Prevalence in many resource-rich countries tends to be much

*(continued over)*

*(from previous page)*

higher (50–80%) in individuals born before 1950 compared with prevalence (<20%) in individuals born more recently. In many resource-poor countries, the infection has a high prevalence (80–95%) irrespective of the period of birth. Adult prevalence is believed to represent the persistence of a historically higher rate of infection acquired in childhood, rather than increasing acquisition of infection during life.

**AETIOLOGY/RISK FACTORS** Overcrowded conditions associated with childhood poverty lead to increased transmission and higher prevalence rates. Adult reinfection rates are low — less than 1% a year.

**PROGNOSIS** *H pylori* infection is believed to be causally related to the development of duodenal and gastric ulceration, B cell gastric lymphoma, and distal gastric cancer. About 15% of people infected with *H pylori* will develop a peptic ulcer, and 1% of people will develop gastric cancer during their lifetime. One systematic review of observational studies (search date 2000; 16 studies, 1625 people) found that the frequency of peptic ulcer disease in people taking non-steroidal anti-inflammatory drugs (NSAIDs) was greater in those who were *H pylori* positive than in those who were *H pylori* negative (peptic ulcer: 341/817 [42%] in *H pylori*-positive NSAID users v 209/808 [26%] in *H pylori*-negative NSAID users; OR 2.12, 95% CI 1.68 to 2.67).

Andre Chow, Sanjay Purkayastha, Thanos Athanasiou, Paris Tekkis, and Ara Darzi

**KEY POINTS**

- The main risk factors for inguinal hernia are male sex and increasing age.

  Complications of inguinal hernia include strangulation, intestinal obstruction, and infarction. Recurrence can occur after surgery.

- The consensus is that surgery is the treatment of choice for inguinal hernia, although few good-quality studies have compared surgery with expectant management.

- Open suture repair is a well-established surgical treatment for people with unilateral inguinal hernia, but seems less effective at preventing recurrence, and prolongs recovery, compared with other techniques.

  Open mesh repair reduces the risk of recurrence compared with open suture repair, without increasing the rate of surgical complications.

  Totally extraperitoneal (TEP) laparoscopic repair may lead to less pain, faster recovery, and similar recurrence rates compared with open mesh repair, but studies have given inconclusive results.

  Transabdominal preperitoneal (TAPP) laparoscopic repair reduces pain and speeds up recovery compared with open mesh repair, but both procedures have similar recurrence rates.

- Open suture repair may be associated with longer recovery times compared with open mesh repair or TAPP laparoscopic repair in people with bilateral inguinal hernia.

  Open mesh repair seems as effective as TEP laparoscopic repair, but may prolong recovery and increase complication rates compared with TAPP laparoscopic repair.

- Open suture repair may be associated with an increased recovery time compared with open mesh repair in people with recurrent inguinal hernia.

  We don't know how open suture repair compares with TEP or TAPP laparoscopic repair in people with recurrent inguinal hernia.

  TAPP and TEP laparoscopic repair may both reduce recovery time compared with open mesh repair, but complication rates seem to be similar.

Please visit http://clinicalevidence.bmj.com for full text and references

| What are the effects of elective treatments for primary unilateral inguinal hernia in adults? | |
| --- | --- |
| Beneficial | • Open mesh repair (reduced recurrence compared with open suture repair, with no increase in surgical complications)<br>• Totally extraperitoneal (TEP) laparoscopic repair (reduced pain and time to return to usual activities compared with open repair)<br>• Transabdominal preperitoneal (TAPP) laparoscopic repair (reduced pain and time to return to usual activities compared with open repair) |
| Likely To Be Beneficial | • Open suture repair (conventional, well-established surgical technique, but less effective for improving clinically important outcomes than open mesh repair, laparoscopic repair)* |
| Unknown Effectiveness | • Expectant management |

## What are the effects of elective treatments for primary bilateral inguinal hernia in adults?

| Likely To Be Beneficial | • Open mesh repair (may reduce length of hospital stay compared with open suture repair) |
| --- | --- |
| | • Open suture repair (conventional, well-established surgical technique, but may be less effective in improving clinically important outcomes than open mesh repair or transabdominal preperitoneal [TAPP] laparoscopic repair)* |
| | • Totally extraperitoneal (TEP) laparoscopic repair (similar outcomes to open mesh repair) |
| | • Transabdominal preperitoneal (TAPP) laparoscopic repair (may reduce time to return to normal activities compared with open repair) |
| Unknown Effectiveness | • Expectant management |

## What are the effects of elective treatments for recurrent inguinal hernia in adults?

| Likely To Be Beneficial | • Open mesh repair (slightly reduced length of hospital stay compared with open suture repair; other effects uncertain) |
| --- | --- |
| | • Open suture repair (conventional, well-established surgical technique, but may be less effective than open mesh repair or transabdominal preperitoneal [TAPP] laparoscopic repair in improving clinically important outcomes)* |
| | • Totally extraperitoneal (TEP) laparoscopic repair (may reduce time to return to normal activities compared with open mesh repair) |
| | • Transabdominal preperitoneal (TAPP) laparoscopic repair (may reduce time to return to normal activities compared with open repair; other effects uncertain) |
| Unknown Effectiveness | • Expectant management |

**Search date September 2007**

*Based on clinical experience and consensus.

**DEFINITION** Inguinal hernia is an out-pouching of the peritoneum, with or without its contents, which occurs through the muscles of the anterior abdominal wall at the level of the inguinal canal in the groin. It almost always occurs in men because of the inherent weakness of the abdominal wall where the spermatic cord passes through the inguinal canal. A portion of bowel may become caught in the peritoneal pouch and present as a lump in the groin. The hernia may extend into the scrotum and can cause discomfort or ache. Primary hernias relate to the first presentation of a hernia, and are distinct from recurrent hernias. A hernia is described as reducible if it occurs intermittently (e.g., on straining or standing) and can be pushed back into the abdominal cavity, or irreducible if it remains permanently outside the abdominal cavity. Inguinal hernia is usually a long-standing condition and the diagnosis is made clinically, on the basis of these typical symptoms and signs. The condition may occur in one groin (unilateral hernia) or both groins simultaneously (bilateral hernia), and may recur after treatment (recurrent hernia). Inguinal hernias are frequently classified as direct or indirect, depending on whether the hernia sac bulges directly through the posterior wall of the inguinal canal (direct hernia), or whether it passes through the internal inguinal ring alongside the spermatic cord and follows the course of the inguinal canal (indirect hernia). Occasionally, hernia may present acutely because of complications (see prognosis below). Clinical experience and consensus suggest that surgical intervention is an effective treatment for inguinal hernia. However, surgery is associated with complications. Therefore, much of this review examines the relative effectiveness and safety of different surgical techniques. None of the studies that we identified distinguished between direct and indirect types of inguinal hernia. Identified studies gave little detail about the severity of hernia among included participants. In general, studies explicitly excluded people with irreducible or complicated hernia, large hernia (extending into the scrotum), or serious comorbidity, and those at high surgical risk (e.g., because of coagulation disorders). In this review, we deal only with non-acute uncomplicated inguinal hernias in adults.

**INCIDENCE/PREVALENCE** Inguinal hernia is usually repaired surgically in resource-rich countries. Therefore, surgical audit data provide reasonable estimates of incidence. We found one nationally mandated guideline, which reported that in 2001–2002 there were about 70,000 inguinal hernia surgeries performed in England, involving 0.14% of the population, and requiring over 100,000 NHS hospital-bed days. Of these procedures, 62,969 were for the repair of primary hernias and 4939 were for the repair of recurrent hernias. A similar number of inguinal hernia repairs were undertaken in public healthcare settings in England in 2002–2003. In the USA, estimates based on cross-sectional data suggest that about 700,000 inguinal hernia repairs were undertaken in 1993. A national survey of general practices, covering about 1% of the population of England and Wales in 1991–1992, found that about 95% of people presenting to primary-care settings with inguinal hernia were male. It found that the incidence rose from about 11/10,000 person-years in men aged 16 to 24 years to about 200/10,000 person-years in men aged 75 years and over.

**AETIOLOGY/RISK FACTORS** Age and male sex are risk factors. Chronic cough and manual labour involving heavy lifting are conventionally regarded as risk factors because they lead to high intra-abdominal pressure. Obesity has also been suggested as a risk factor.

**PROGNOSIS** Strangulation, intestinal obstruction, and infarction are the most important acute complications of untreated hernia, and are potentially life-threatening. National statistics from England found that 5% of primary inguinal hernia repairs were undertaken as emergencies (presumably because of acute complications) in 1998–1999. Older age, longer duration of hernia, and longer duration of irreducibility are thought to be risk factors for acute complications.

# Irritable bowel syndrome: dietary interventions

Alexander Charles Ford and Per Olav Vandvik

## KEY POINTS

- The key features of irritable bowel syndrome (IBS) are chronic, recurrent abdominal pain or discomfort, associated with disturbed bowel habit, in the absence of any structural abnormality to account for these symptoms.

  The prevalence of IBS varies depending on the criteria used to diagnose it, but it ranges from about 5% to 20%.

  IBS is associated with abnormal GI motor function, enhanced visceral perception, abnormalities in central pain processing, and altered gut flora, as well as psychosocial and genetic factors.

  People with IBS often have other bodily and psychiatric symptoms, and have an increased likelihood of having unnecessary surgery compared with people without IBS.

  A positive symptom-based diagnosis and a graded general treatment approach are cornerstones in the management of people with IBS.

  Pharmacological agents, including antispasmodics, antidepressants, and secretagogues, are effective therapies in IBS, but none have been shown to alter the long-term natural history of the condition.

  Some people with IBS believe that certain foods trigger their symptoms and would, therefore, rather try dietary modification as a first-line approach instead of taking drugs, which may have side effects.

- We searched for RCTs and systematic reviews of RCTs on gluten-free diets or diets low in fermentable oligosaccharides, disaccharides, monosaccharides, and polyols (low- FODMAP diet) compared with normal diet or general dietary advice, or compared with standard usual care (e.g., antispasmodic treatment).

- We don't know if a gluten-free diet is more effective than a normal gluten-containing diet in controlling symptoms in IBS, as there were few studies, and results were inconsistent.

  RCTs recruited people with IBS, in whom coeliac disease had already been excluded by either serological testing or small intestinal biopsy. The RCTs were conducted in specialist centres, so the results may not be generalisable to patients seen in primary care.

  Adverse events are unlikely in the short-term and, for people who are keen to avoid pharmacological therapies due to concerns about side effects (particularly those in whom pain or bloating is the predominant symptom), a trial of a gluten-free diet, instituted with the help of a trained dietitian, may be worthwhile.

- We don't know if a low-FODMAP diet is more effective than a normal diet in controlling symptoms in IBS, as there was only one trial providing evidence of low quality for a clinically significant benefit.

  As with gluten-free diets, adverse events are unlikely in the short-term and, for people who are keen to avoid pharmacological therapies due to concerns about side effects (particularly those in whom pain or bloating is the predominant symptom), a trial of a low-FODMAP diet may be worthwhile.

(i) **Please visit http://clinicalevidence.bmj.com for full text and references**

## What are the effects of dietary modification (gluten-free diet; a diet low in fermentable oligosaccharides, disaccharides, monosaccharides, and polyols [FODMAPs]) in people with irritable bowel syndrome?

| Unknown Effectiveness | • Diet low in fermentable oligosaccharides, disaccharides, monosaccharides, and polyols (FODMAPs)<br><br>• Gluten-free diet |
|---|---|

**Search date June 2014**

**DEFINITION** Irritable bowel syndrome (IBS) is a chronic functional condition of the lower GI tract characterised by abdominal pain or discomfort and disordered bowel habit (diarrhoea, constipation, or fluctuation between the two). There is no known structural or biochemical explanation for the symptoms. Symptom-based criteria, such as the Manning criteria and the latest revision of the Rome criteria, the Rome III criteria, aid diagnosis, but their main use is in recruiting patients for clinical trials. The Rome III criteria subcategorise IBS according to predominant symptom (diarrhoea, constipation, or alternating bowel habit). In practice, the division between constipation-predominant and diarrhoea-predominant IBS may not be clear-cut in all people, particularly as individuals often change subcategory during follow-up. Restriction of trial entry to a subcategory of IBS limits the generalisability of some RCT results.

**INCIDENCE/PREVALENCE** Estimates of incidence and prevalence of IBS vary depending on the diagnostic criteria used to define the condition. One cross-sectional survey conducted in the UK defined IBS as recurrent abdominal pain on more than six occasions during the previous year plus two or more of the Manning criteria. It estimated prevalence in the UK to be 17% overall, with 23% among women and 11% among men. An Australian study reported the prevalence to be 14% using the Manning criteria, 7% using the Rome I criteria, and 4% using the Rome II criteria. A cross-sectional survey of almost 4000 individuals in the UK with 10 years of follow-up estimated the incidence of IBS, defined using the Manning criteria, to be 1.5% a year.

**AETIOLOGY/RISK FACTORS** The pathophysiology of IBS is uncertain, and it is unlikely that a single unifying mechanism explains the condition, but abnormal GI motor function, enhanced visceral perception, and abnormalities of central pain processing seem important. Other determinants include psychosocial factors such as a history of childhood abuse, genetic predisposition, a history of exposure to acute enteric infection, so-called post-infectious IBS, and abnormalities in gut flora.

**PROGNOSIS** A retrospective study reviewed the medical records of people with IBS (112 people aged 20–64 years when diagnosed with IBS at the Mayo Clinic, US, between 1961 and 1963). IBS was defined as the presence of abdominal pain associated with either disturbed defecation or abdominal distension, and the absence of organic bowel disease. Over a 32-year period, less than 10% of people developed organic GI disease subsequently, and death rates were similar among people with IBS compared with age- and sex-matched controls. In another study conducted in the US, individuals meeting diagnostic criteria for IBS were followed up for between 10 and 13 years, during which time almost 50% had undergone subsequent investigation of the lower GI tract, yet this had not led to a revision of the diagnosis of IBS in any of the patients. Other investigators have reported that people with IBS are two to three times more likely to undergo unnecessary surgical procedures, such as cholecystectomy, hysterectomy, or appendicectomy.

# Pancreatic cancer

Wasfi Alrawashdeh and Hemant M Kocher

## KEY POINTS

- Pancreatic cancer is the fourth most common cause of cancer death in higher-income countries, with 5-year survival only 10% (range 7%–25%), even in people presenting with early-stage cancer.

  Risk factors include age, smoking, chronic pancreatitis, a family history, and dietary factors. Diabetes mellitus may also increase the risk.

- In people with pancreatic cancer considered suitable for complete tumour resection, pancreaticoduodenectomy (Kausch–Whipple procedure) or pylorus-preserving pancreaticoduodenectomy (Traverso–Longmire procedure) may prolong survival compared with non-surgical treatment, although no large RCTs have been found.

  Pylorus-preserving pancreaticoduodenectomy may lead to similar quality of life and survival compared with Kausch–Whipple pancreaticoduodenectomy.

  Extended lymphadenectomy is associated with increases in adverse effects compared with standard lymphadenectomy, without conferring any survival benefit.

- Somatostatin and its analogues, particularly octreotide, prevent complications (pancreatic leak and intra-abdominal collections) of pancreatic surgery but do not reduce mortality.

  We don't know which anastomosis (pancreaticogastrostomy or pancreaticojejunostomy) is more effective for preventing pancreatic leak.

  Pancreatic duct occlusion does not assist in preventing complications associated with pancreatic leak when added to anastomosis. When used alone, duct occlusion increases pancreatic fistula and pancreatic endocrine and exocrine insufficiency, and cannot therefore be recommended.

  We don't know whether fibrin glue is effective for preventing pancreatic leak.

- Adjuvant fluorouracil-based chemotherapy increases median and 5-year survival in people with completely resected pancreatic cancer compared with no chemotherapy.

  Adjuvant chemoradiotherapy does not seem to improve survival in people with resected pancreatic cancer.

  We don't know whether adjuvant gemcitabine-based chemotherapy increases survival compared with no chemotherapy in people with resected pancreatic cancer. Trials are under way and we await their results.

- In people with non-resectable pancreatic cancer, gemcitabine or fluorouracil monotherapy seem preferable to combination chemotherapy based on either drug.

  We found insufficient evidence to recommend chemoradiation over chemotherapy alone in people with non-resectable pancreatic cancer.

(i) **Please visit http://clinicalevidence.bmj.com for full text and references**

## What are the effects of surgical treatments in people with pancreatic cancer considered suitable for complete tumour resection?

| Unknown Effectiveness | • Extended (radical) versus standard lymphadenectomy in people having pancreaticoduodenectomy |
| --- | --- |
| | • Pancreaticoduodenectomy versus non-surgical treatment |

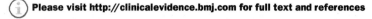

| | • Pylorus-preserving pancreaticoduodenectomy versus Kausch–Whipple pancreaticoduodenectomy |
|---|---|

## What are the effects of interventions to prevent pancreatic leak after pancreaticoduodenectomy in people with pancreatic cancer considered suitable for complete tumour resection?

| Likely To Be Beneficial | • Somatostatin and somatostatin analogues |
|---|---|
| Unknown Effectiveness | • Fibrin glue<br><br>• Pancreaticojejunostomy (unclear how it compares with pancreaticogastrostomy) |
| Likely To Be Ineffective Or Harmful | • Pancreatic duct occlusion |

## What are the effects of adjuvant treatments in people with completely resected pancreatic cancer?

| Beneficial | • Fluorouracil-based chemotherapy (adjuvant) for resected pancreatic cancer (increases survival compared with surgery alone) |
|---|---|
| Unknown Effectiveness | • Chemoradiotherapy for resected pancreatic cancer<br><br>• Gemcitabine-based chemotherapy (adjuvant) for resected pancreatic cancer |

## What are the effects of interventions in people with non-resectable (locally advanced or advanced) pancreatic cancer?

| Beneficial | • Fluorouracil-based chemotherapy for non-resectable pancreatic cancer (increases survival compared with supportive care) |
|---|---|
| Likely To Be Beneficial | • Fluorouracil monotherapy for non-resectable pancreatic cancer (may be less effective than gemcitabine monotherapy; as effective as fluorouracil-based combination chemotherapy, with fewer adverse effects)<br><br>• Gemcitabine monotherapy for non-resectable pancreatic cancer (may be more effective than fluorouracil monotherapy and as effective as gemcitabine-based combination chemotherapy, with fewer adverse effects) |

| Unknown Effectiveness | • Chemoradiotherapy |
|---|---|

**Search date August 2009**

*RCTs comparing surgery versus no surgery may be considered unethical in people with pancreatic cancer considered suitable for complete tumour resection.

**DEFINITION** In this review, the term 'pancreatic cancer' refers to primary ductal adenocarcinoma of the pancreas. Other pancreatic malignancies such as neuroendocrine and serous cystic tumours of the pancreas are not considered. Symptoms of pancreatic cancer include pain, jaundice, nausea, weight loss, anorexia, and symptoms associated with GI obstruction and diabetes. Pancreatic cancer is staged using the tumour, node, metastasis (TNM) and American Joint Committee on Cancer (AJCC) classification systems. A pancreatic tumour is considered resectable if the tumour appears to be localised to the pancreas, without invasion into major blood vessels or distant spread to liver, lungs, or bone. Earlier detection of tumours increases the possibility of resection. Other factors that influence resectability include perceived perioperative risk based on other comorbidities.

**INCIDENCE/PREVALENCE** Pancreatic cancer is the eighth most common cancer in the UK, with an annual incidence in England and Wales of about 12/100,000. It is the fourth most common cause of cancer death in higher-income countries, responsible for about 30,000 deaths each year in the USA. Prevalence is similar in men and women, with 5% to 10% presenting with resectable disease.

**AETIOLOGY/RISK FACTORS** Pancreatic cancer is more likely to develop in people who smoke and have high alcohol intake. Dietary factors, such as lack of fruit and vegetables, are also reported risk factors. One population-based cohort study of more than 2000 people suggested that there was a 1% chance of developing pancreatic cancer within 3 years of diagnosis in people diagnosed with new-onset diabetes mellitus. However, estimates of the magnitude of increased risk of pancreatic cancer in people with diabetes vary. Additional risk factors include chronic sporadic pancreatitis — which carries a five-fold increased risk of developing pancreatic cancer — and, in some cases, a family history of pancreatic cancer.

**PROGNOSIS** Prognosis in people with pancreatic cancer is poor. The overall median survival worldwide is less than 6 months, with an overall 5-year survival rate of 0.4% to 5.0%. The surgical resection rate worldwide is between 2.6% and 9.0%, with a median survival of 11 to 20 months and a 5-year survival of rate of 7% to 25%, with few long-term survivors. Tumour resection is graded from R0 to R2, with R0 meaning that no tumour remains after surgery (confirmed by histology); R1 meaning that the surgeon believes no tumour remains but histology demonstrates positive margins; and R2 meaning that the surgeon was unable to remove all macroscopic tumour completely.

Charles Bailey

## KEY POINTS

- Stomach cancer is usually an adenocarcinoma arising in the stomach and includes tumours arising at or just below the gastro-oesophageal junction (type II and III junctional tumours). Only non-metastatic stomach cancers are considered in this review.

  The incidence varies among countries and by sex, with about 80/100,000 cases per year in Japanese men, 30/100,000 in Japanese women, 18/100,000 in British men, and 10/100,000 in British women.

- With regard to surgical resection, subtotal gastrectomy seems as effective as total gastrectomy.

  In practice, surgeons sometimes recommend total gastrectomy 'de principe' in people with poorly differentiated 'diffuse' cancer, to prevent infiltration of microscopic tumour deposits into the proximal resection margin.

- Removal of adjacent organs (spleen and distal pancreas) is associated with increased morbidity and mortality compared with gastrectomy alone.

  Current consensus is that adjacent organs should only be removed to ensure complete tumour removal, or when required because of trauma during surgery.

- Radical lymphadenectomy seems no more effective than conservative lymphadenectomy at increasing survival and increases operative mortality and postoperative morbidity.

- Adjuvant chemoradiotherapy seems to improve survival compared with surgery alone in people with resectable stomach adenocarcinoma.

- Adjuvant chemotherapy is also more effective at reducing mortality than surgery alone.

(i) **Please visit http://clinicalevidence.bmj.com for full text and references**

| What are the effects of radical versus conservative surgical resection in people with stomach cancer? | |
|---|---|
| Likely To Be Beneficial | • Subtotal gastrectomy for resectable distal tumours (as effective as total gastrectomy) |
| Unlikely To Be Beneficial | • Radical lymphadenectomy (no better than conservative lymphadenectomy at increasing survival and increases adverse effects) |
| Likely To Be Ineffective Or Harmful | • Removal of adjacent organs |

| What are the effects of adjuvant chemotherapy in people with stomach cancer? | |
|---|---|
| Likely To Be Beneficial | • Adjuvant chemoradiotherapy |
| | • Adjuvant chemotherapy |

**Search date April 2010**

**DEFINITION** Stomach cancer is usually an adenocarcinoma arising in the stomach, and includes tumours arising at or just below the gastro-oesophageal junction (type II and III junctional tumours). Tumours are staged according to degree of invasion and spread. Only non-metastatic stomach cancers are considered in this review.

**INCIDENCE/PREVALENCE** The incidence of stomach cancer varies among countries and by sex (incidence per 100,000 population a year in Japanese men is about 80, Japanese women 30, British men 18, British women 10, white American men 11, and white American women 7). Incidence has declined dramatically in North America, Australia, and New Zealand since 1930, but the decline in Europe has been slower. In the USA, stomach cancer remains relatively common among particular ethnic groups, especially Japanese-American people, and some Hispanic groups. The incidence of cancer of the proximal stomach and gastro-oesophageal junction is rising rapidly in many European populations and in North America. The reasons for this are poorly understood.

**AETIOLOGY/RISK FACTORS** Distal stomach cancer is strongly associated with lifelong infection with *Helicobacter pylori* and poor dietary intake of antioxidant vitamins (A, C, and E). In Western Europe and North America, distal stomach cancer is associated with relative socioeconomic deprivation. Proximal stomach cancer is strongly associated with smoking (OR about 4), and is probably associated with GORD, obesity, high fat intake, and medium to high socioeconomic status.

**PROGNOSIS** Invasive stomach cancer (stages T2–T4) is fatal without surgery. Mean survival without treatment is less than 6 months from diagnosis. Intramucosal or submucosal cancer (stage T1) may progress slowly to invasive cancer over several years. In the USA, over 50% of people recently diagnosed with stomach cancer have regional lymph node metastasis or involvement of adjacent organs. The prognosis after macroscopically and microscopically complete resection (R0) is related strongly to disease stage, particularly penetration of the serosa (stage T3) and lymph node involvement. Five-year survival rates range from over 90% in intramucosal cancer to about 20% in people with stage T3N2 disease. In Japan, the 5-year survival rate for people with advanced disease is reported to be about 50%, but the explanation for the difference remains unclear. Comparisons between Japanese and Western practice are confounded by factors such as age, fitness, and disease stage, as well as by tumour location, because many Western series include gastro-oesophageal junction adenocarcinoma, which is associated with a much lower survival rate after surgery.

Peter Morris

## KEY POINTS

- Chronic suppurative otitis media (CSOM) causes recurrent or persistent discharge (otorrhoea) through a perforation in the tympanic membrane, and can lead to thickening of the middle-ear mucosa and mucosal polyps. It usually occurs as a complication of persistent acute otitis media with perforation in childhood.

  CSOM is a common cause of hearing impairment, disability, and poor scholastic performance. Occasionally it can lead to fatal intracranial infections and acute mastoiditis, especially in developing countries.

- In children with CSOM, topical antibiotics may improve symptoms compared with antiseptics. The benefits of ear cleansing are unknown, although this treatment is usually recommended for children with ear discharge.

- We don't know whether topical antiseptics, topical or systemic antibiotics, or topical corticosteroids, alone or in combination with antibiotics, improve symptoms in children with CSOM compared with placebo or other treatments.

- In adults with CSOM, topical antibiotics either alone or in combination with topical corticosteroids may improve symptoms compared with placebo or either treatment alone, although we found few adequate studies. There is consensus that topical antibiotics should be combined with ear cleansing so that the antibiotics are able to reach the middle ear space.

  We don't know whether topical antiseptics, topical corticosteroids, or systemic antibiotics are beneficial in reducing symptoms.

  It is possible that antibiotics against gram-negative bacteria may reduce ear discharge more than other classes of antibiotics or placebo.

- We don't know whether tympanoplasty with or without mastoidectomy improves symptoms compared with no surgery or other treatments in adults or children with CSOM.

- Cholesteatoma is an abnormal accumulation of squamous epithelium usually found in the middle ear cavity and mastoid process of the temporal bone. Granulation tissue and ear discharge are often associated with secondary infection of the desquamating epithelium.

- Cholesteatoma can be either congenital (behind an intact tympanic membrane) or acquired. If untreated, it may progressively enlarge and erode the surrounding structures.

  We don't know the beneficial effects of surgery, whether surgery can be delayed, or which surgical techniques are associated with the best outcomes in children or adults with cholesteatoma.

(i) **Please visit http://clinicalevidence.bmj.com for full text and references**

| What are the effects of treatments for chronic suppurative otitis media in adults? | |
|---|---|
| **Likely To Be Beneficial** | • Antibiotics (topical) in adults |
| | • Antibiotics (topical) plus corticosteroids (topical) in adults |
| **Unknown Effectiveness** | • Antibiotics (systemic) in adults (unclear if as effective as topical) |
| | • Antibiotics (topical plus systemic) in adults (unclear if more effective than topical alone) |
| | • Antiseptics (topical) in adults |

- Corticosteroids (topical) in adults
- Ear cleansing in adults
- Tympanoplasty (with or without mastoidectomy) in adults

## What are the effects of treatments for chronic suppurative otitis media in children?

| Unknown Effectiveness | • Antibiotics (systemic) in children |
|---|---|
| | • Antibiotics (topical) in children |
| | • Antibiotics (topical) plus corticosteroids (topical) in children |
| | • Antiseptics (topical) in children |
| | • Corticosteroids (topical) in children |
| | • Ear cleansing in children |
| | • Tympanoplasty (with or without mastoidectomy) in children |

## What are the effects of treatments for cholesteatoma in adults?

| Unknown Effectiveness | • Surgery for cholesteatoma in adults |
|---|---|

## What are the effects of treatments for cholesteatoma in children?

| Unknown Effectiveness | • Surgery for cholesteatoma in children |
|---|---|

**Search date May 2010**

**DEFINITION** Chronic suppurative otitis media (CSOM) is persistent inflammation of the middle ear or mastoid cavity. Synonyms include 'chronic otitis media', chronic mastoiditis, and chronic tympanomastoiditis. CSOM is characterised by recurrent or persistent ear discharge (otorrhoea) over 2 to 6 weeks through a perforation of the tympanic membrane. CSOM usually begins as a complication of persistent acute otitis media (AOM) with perforation in childhood. Typical findings may also include thickened granular middle-ear mucosa and mucosal polyps. Occasionally, CSOM will be associated with a cholesteatoma within the middle ear. CSOM is differentiated from chronic otitis media with effusion, in which there is an intact tympanic membrane with fluid in the middle ear but no active infection. CSOM does not include chronic perforations of the eardrum that are dry, or only occasionally discharge, and have no signs of active infection. Cholesteatoma is an abnormal accumulation of squamous epithelium usually found in the middle ear cavity and mastoid process of the temporal bone. Granulation tissue and ear discharge are often associated with secondary infection of the desquamating epithelium. Cholesteatoma is most often detected by careful otoscopic examination in children or adults with persistent discharge that does not respond to treatment.

**INCIDENCE/PREVALENCE** The worldwide prevalence of CSOM is 65 to 330 million people, and 39 to 200 million (60%) have clinically significant hearing impairment. Cholesteatoma can be either congenital (behind an intact tympanic membrane) or acquired. The overall incidence is estimated to be around 9 per 100,000 people. At least 95% of cholesteatomas are acquired. The incidence is similar in children and adults.

**AETIOLOGY/RISK FACTORS** CSOM is usually a complication of persistent AOM, but the risk factors for CSOM vary in different settings. Frequent upper respiratory tract infections and poor socioeconomic conditions (overcrowded housing and poor hygiene and nutrition) are often associated with the development of CSOM. In developed countries and advantaged populations, previous insertion of tympanostomy tubes is now probably the single most important aetiological factor. Of those children with tympanostomy tubes in place, a history of recurrent AOM, older siblings, and attendance at child care centres all increase the risk of developing CSOM. In developing countries and disadvantaged populations, poverty, over-crowding, family history, exposure to smoke, and being Indigenous are important. Improvement in housing, hygiene, and nutrition in Maori children was associated with a halving of the prevalence of CSOM between 1978 and 1987 (see also review on acute otitis media, p 67). The most commonly isolated microorganisms are *Pseudomonas aeruginosa* and *Staphylococcus aureus*; *P aeruginosa* has been particularly implicated in the causation of bony necrosis and mucosal disease. One systematic review found a lack of studies assessing the role of prophylactic antibiotics in preventing the progression of disease to CSOM. Most cholesteatomas are thought to occur as a complication of a retraction pocket in the tympanic membrane. They are associated with recurrent or persistent middle ear disease, family history, and craniofacial abnormalities. If untreated, a cholesteatoma may progressively enlarge and erode the surrounding structures.

**PROGNOSIS** The natural history of CSOM is poorly understood. The perforation may close spontaneously in an unknown portion of cases, but it persists in others leading to mild to moderate hearing impairment (about 26–60 dB increase in hearing thresholds), based on surveys among children in Africa, Brazil, India, and Sierra Leone, and among the general population in Thailand. In many developing countries, CSOM represents the most frequent cause of moderate hearing loss (40–60 dB). Persistent hearing loss during the first 2 years of life may increase learning disabilities and poor scholastic performance. Progressive hearing loss may occur among those in whom infection persists and discharge recurs. Less frequently, spread of infection may lead to life-threatening complications such as intracranial infections and acute mastoiditis. The frequency of serious complications fell from 20% in 1938 to 2.5% in 1948 worldwide and is currently estimated to be about 0.7% to 3.2% worldwide. This is believed to be associated with increased use of antibiotic treatment, tympanoplasty, and mastoidectomy. Otitis media was estimated to have caused 3599 deaths and a loss of almost 1.5 disability-adjusted life years in 2002, 90% of which were in developing countries. Most of these deaths were probably owing to CSOM, because AOM is a self-limiting infection (see review on acute otitis media, p 67).

# Ear wax

Tony Wright

## KEY POINTS

- Ear wax only becomes a problem if it causes a hearing impairment, or other ear-related symptoms.

  Ear wax is more likely to accumulate and cause a hearing impairment when normal extrusion is prevented (for example, by hearing aids or by the use of cotton buds to clean the ears).

  Ear wax can visually obscure the ear drum, and may need to be removed for diagnostic purposes.

- For such a commonly occurring condition, there is little high-quality evidence available to guide practice. All procedures for removing wax should be essentially pain free.

- Ear irrigation (syringing) is generally considered to be effective, but evidence is limited.

  Irrigation is usually performed using a motorised pump with a governable pressure.

  Ear irrigation may be associated with vertigo and tympanic membrane perforation in some people. Pain, damage to the skin of the ear canal, and otitis externa are other possible adverse effects.

  Ear irrigation may rarely cause permanent deafness; therefore, people with hearing in only one ear should not have this ear irrigated.

- Other mechanical methods of removing ear wax by trained staff using instruments, such as microsuction, are probably effective, although the evidence is limited.

  Mechanical removal of wax with suction, probes, or forceps is considered effective, but can cause trauma to the ear canal, depending on the experience and training of the operator and the adequacy of visualisation.

- Overall, we found limited high-quality evidence on the effects of proprietary wax softeners.

- With regard to the use of wax softeners prior to irrigation, we found very weak evidence that wax softeners may be better than no treatment.

  However, we found no good evidence that wax softeners improved wax clearance after irrigation compared with saline.

  We found no good evidence that any one type of wax softener was better than any other type of wax softener.

- With regard to the use of wax softeners alone, we found very weak evidence that wax softeners may be better than no treatment.

  We found no consistent evidence that wax softeners alone improved wax clearance compared with sterile water or normal saline.

  We also found no good evidence that any one type of wax softener was better than any other type of wax softener.

(i) **Please visit http://clinicalevidence.bmj.com for full text and references**

## What are the effects of methods to remove ear wax?

| | |
|---|---|
| **Trade-off Between Benefits And Harms** | • Ear irrigation (syringing) (considered to be effective; however, irrigation may be associated with adverse effects)* |
| **Unknown Effectiveness** | • Manual removal (other than ear irrigation)<br>• Wax softeners alone<br>• Wax softeners prior to irrigation |

Search date July 2014

*Although we found no RCTs, there is consensus that irrigation is effective at removing ear wax.

**DEFINITION** The external ear canal in adults is about 24 mm long. The outer third has cartilaginous and soft tissue walls, while the deep two-thirds has continuous bony walls. There is no soft tissue between the ear canal skin and the bone, and this gives the ear canal resonance properties that enhance the usual range of sounds we hear at the tympanic membrane. To prevent the deep ear canal becoming filled with dead skin cells, this skin is migratory and moves from the deep canal outwards. In the outer part of the canal are modified sweat glands (ceruminous glands), which secrete a modified sweat that has bacteriocidal and fungicidal properties, and sebaceous glands that produce an oily material and usually discharge in the hair follicles at the outside of the canal. Wax is a mixture of all three components, with keratin being predominant. Overall wax is sticky, waterproof, and protective, and there should be a thin coating of wax near the external opening of the canal. To cause a significant conductive hearing loss, the wax must completely occlude the ear canal. However, partial blockage of the canal alters the resonant properties and the quality of the hearing. Accumulation can reduce the efficiency of hearing aids. When wax gets wet, the keratin swells and can lead to the sudden onset of complete occlusion of the canal and a hearing loss. The wet, dead keratin can become infected and an otitis externa develop. Wax may obscure the view of the tympanic membrane and may need to be removed for diagnostic reasons. Impacted wax can become adherent to the ear canal skin and tympanic membrane and make removal more difficult. Since the deep ear canal may be wider than the opening, a large plug of dry, hard wax deep in the canal can be particularly difficult to remove. If wax needs to be removed, then various options are available: irrigation (syringing with unregulated manual syringes should no longer be used), wax softeners/solvents, irrigation following wax softeners, mechanical removal, or microsuction.

**INCIDENCE/PREVALENCE** We found four surveys of the prevalence of impacted wax. The studies were carried out in a variety of populations, and used a variety of definitions of impacted wax. Prevalence ranged from 7% to 35%. It is unclear how these figures relate to prevalence in the general population.

**AETIOLOGY/RISK FACTORS** Accumulation of wax occurs for many different reasons relating to the over- or underproduction of the three major components, a failure to self-clear because of slow skin migration especially in the dermatitides, or because of mechanical issues such as the use of cotton buds or hearing aid moulds.

**PROGNOSIS** Most ear wax emerges from the external canal spontaneously; one small RCT that included a no-treatment group found that 32% of ears with impacted wax showed some degree of spontaneous resolution after 5 days (26% described as moderately clear; 5% described as completely clear). Without impaction or adherence to the drum, there is likely to be minimal, if any, hearing loss.

# Hay fever in adolescents and adults

Aziz Sheikh, Sukhmeet Singh Panesar, and Sarah Salvilla

## KEY POINTS

- Hay fever causes sneezing, with an itchy, blocked, and/or running nose, and affects up to 25% of people in developed countries.

  Symptoms are caused by an IgE-mediated type 1 hypersensitivity reaction to airborne allergens such as pollen or fungal spores, and may also cause eye, sinus, respiratory, and systemic problems.

- Oral antihistamines reduce symptoms and improve quality of life compared with placebo, but they can cause drowsiness, particularly with older preparations.

  CAUTION: astemizole and terfenadine may be associated with cardiac adverse effects.

  Intranasal antihistamines improve symptoms compared with placebo. Intranasal azelastine seems as effective as oral antihistamines.

  We don't know whether oral decongestants reduce symptoms compared with placebo, but combined treatment with pseudoephedrine plus oral antihistamines may be more effective than either treatment alone.

- Intranasal corticosteroids improve symptoms compared with placebo, are more effective at improving nasal symptoms, and appear to be equally effective at improving ocular symptoms compared with oral antihistamines.

  Systemic corticosteroids improve symptoms compared with placebo, and are associated with mild adverse effects when used for short periods. Long-term or repeated use of systemic corticosteroids is associated with a range of well-documented, potentially serious adverse effects.

- The oral leukotriene receptor antagonist montelukast improves symptoms and quality of life compared with placebo, but combination treatment with montelukast plus loratadine may be no more effective than either treatment alone.

  We don't know whether intranasal ipratropium bromide reduces symptoms, as no studies were found.

(i) **Please visit http://clinicalevidence.bmj.com for full text and references**

| What are the effects of treatments for hay fever in adolescents and adults? | |
|---|---|
| **Beneficial** | • Intranasal antihistamines (azelastine) |
| | • Intranasal corticosteroids |
| | • Oral antihistamines (acrivastine, azatadine, brompheniramine, cetirizine, levocetirizine, ebastine, fexofenadine, loratadine, desloratadine, rupatadine, and mizolastine) |
| | • Oral antihistamines plus pseudoephedrine (reduce nasal symptom severity compared with antihistamines alone) |
| **Likely To Be Beneficial** | • Intranasal antihistamines (levocabastine and olopatadine) |
| | • Leukotriene receptor antagonists (oral) |

| | |
|---|---|
| | • Systemic corticosteroids |
| **Unknown Effectiveness** | • Intranasal ipratropium bromide<br>• Oral decongestants |
| **Unlikely To Be Beneficial** | • Oral antihistamines plus leukotriene receptor antagonists (seem no more effective than either treatment alone) |
| **Likely To Be Ineffective Or Harmful** | • Oral antihistamines (astemizole; associated with cardiac adverse effects)<br>• Oral antihistamines (terfenadine; associated with cardiac adverse effects) |

**Search date April 2008**

**DEFINITION** Hay fever is a symptom complex that may affect several organ systems. Symptoms typically consist of seasonal sneezing, nasal itching, nasal blockage, and watery nasal discharge. Eye symptoms (red eyes, itchy eyes, and tearing) are also common. Other symptoms may include peak seasonal coughing, wheezing and shortness of breath, oral allergy syndrome (manifesting as an itchy, swollen oropharynx on eating stoned fruits), and systemic symptoms such as tiredness, fever, a pressure sensation in the head, and itchiness. Confirming the presence of pollen hypersensitivity using objective allergy tests, such as skin prick tests, detection of serum-specific IgE, and nasal provocation challenge testing, may improve diagnostic accuracy. This review focuses on people aged 12 years and over.

**INCIDENCE/PREVALENCE** Hay fever is found throughout the world. Epidemiological evidence suggests considerable geographical variation in its prevalence. Prevalence is highest in socioeconomically developed countries, where the condition may affect as much as 25% of the population. Prevalence and severity are increasing. It is thought that improved living standards and reduced risk of childhood infections may lead to immune deviation of T helper cells in early life, which may, in turn, increase susceptibility to hay fever (the so-called "hygiene hypothesis"). Although people of all ages may be affected, the peak age of onset is adolescence.

**AETIOLOGY/RISK FACTORS** The symptoms of hay fever are caused by an IgE-mediated type 1 hypersensitivity reaction to grass, tree, or weed pollen. Allergy to other seasonal aeroallergens such as fungal spores may also provoke symptoms. Typically, symptoms become worse during the relevant pollen season, and outdoors when pollen exposure is increased. Risk factors include a personal or family history of atopy or other allergic disorders, male sex, birth order (increased risk being seen in first born), and small family size.

**PROGNOSIS** Hay fever may impair quality of life, interfering with work, sleep, and recreational activities. Other allergic problems such as asthma and eczema frequently coexist, adding to the impact of rhinitis.

# Menière's disease

Adrian James and Marc Thorp

## KEY POINTS

- Menière's disease causes recurrent vertigo, hearing loss, tinnitus, and fullness or pressure in the ear, which mainly affects adults aged 40 to 60 years.

  Menière's disease is at first progressive but fluctuating, and episodes can occur in clusters.

  Vertigo usually resolves but hearing deteriorates, and symptoms other than hearing loss and tinnitus usually improve regardless of treatment.

- We do not know whether anticholinergic drugs, benzodiazepines, phenothiazines, cinnarizine, or betahistine improve symptoms in an acute attack of Menière's disease, as no good-quality studies have been found.

- Betahistine seems to be no more effective than placebo at preventing hearing loss in people with Menière's disease.

  We don't know whether betahistine reduces the frequency or severity of vertigo, tinnitus or aural fullness.

  We do not know whether diuretics, trimetazidine, dietary modification, psychological support, or vestibular rehabilitation improve tinnitus or hearing, or reduce the frequency of attacks of Menière's disease.

 **Please visit http://clinicalevidence.bmj.com for full text and references**

## What are the effects of treatments for acute attacks of Menière's disease?

| Unknown Effectiveness | • Anticholinergics<br>• Benzodiazepines<br>• Betahistine<br>• Cinnarizine<br>• Phenothiazines |
|---|---|

## What are the effects of interventions to prevent attacks and delay disease progression of Menière's disease?

| Unknown Effectiveness | • Betahistine (for vertigo or tinnitus or aural fullness)<br>• Dietary modification<br>• Diuretics<br>• Psychological support<br>• Trimetazidine<br>• Vestibular rehabilitation |
|---|---|
| Unlikely To Be Beneficial | • Betahistine (for hearing loss) |

**Search date January 2006**

**DEFINITION** Menière's disease is characterised by recurrent episodes of spontaneous rotational vertigo, sensorineural hearing loss, tinnitus, and a feeling of fullness or pressure in the ear. It may be unilateral or bilateral. Acute episodes can occur in clusters of about 6 to 11 a year, although remission may last several months. The diagnosis is made clinically. It is important to distinguish Menière's disease from other types of vertigo that might occur independently with hearing loss and tinnitus, and respond differently to treatment (e.g., benign positional vertigo, acute labyrinthitis). Strict diagnostic criteria help to identify the condition. In this review, we have applied the classification of the American Academy of Otolaryngology — Head and Neck Surgery to assess the diagnostic rigour used in RCTs.

**INCIDENCE/PREVALENCE** Menière's disease is most common between 40 to 60 years of age, although younger people may be affected. In Europe, the incidence is about 50 to 200/100,000 a year. A survey of general practitioner records of 27,365 people in the UK in the 1950s found an incidence of 43 affected people in a 1-year period (157/100,000). Diagnostic criteria were not defined in this survey. A survey of over 8 million people in 1973 in Sweden found an incidence of 46/100,000 a year with diagnosis strictly based on the triad of vertigo, hearing loss, and tinnitus. From smaller studies, the incidence appears to be lower in Japan (17/100,000, based on national surveys of hospital attendances in 1977, 1982, and 1990) and in Uganda.

**AETIOLOGY/RISK FACTORS** Menière's disease is associated with endolymphatic hydrops (raised endolymph pressure in the membranous labyrinth of the inner ear), but a causal relationship remains unproved. Specific disorders associated with hydrops (such as temporal bone fracture, syphilis, hypothyroidism, Cogan's syndrome, and Mondini dysplasia) can produce symptoms similar to those of Menière's disease.

**PROGNOSIS** Menière's disease is at first progressive but fluctuates unpredictably. It is difficult to distinguish natural resolution from the effects of treatment. Significant improvement in vertigo is usually seen in the placebo arm of RCTs. Acute attacks of vertigo often increase in frequency during the first few years after presentation and then decrease in frequency in association with sustained deterioration in hearing. In most people, vertiginous episodes eventually cease completely. In one 20-year cohort study in 34 people, 28 (82%) people had at least moderate hearing loss (mean pure tone hearing loss >5 dB) and 16 (47%) developed bilateral disease. Symptoms other than hearing loss improve in 60% to 80% of people irrespective of treatment.

# Middle-ear pain and trauma during air travel

Tony Wright

## KEY POINTS

- Changes in air pressure during flying can cause eardrum pain and perforation, vertigo, and hearing loss.

  It has been estimated that 10% of adults and 22% of children might have changes to the eardrum after a flight, although perforation is rare.

  Symptoms usually resolve spontaneously.

- We did not find any RCT evidence assessing nasal balloon inflation, but non-RCT evidence suggests that it may prevent symptoms of barotitis in people during air travel compared with controls.

- Oral pseudoephedrine compared with placebo may prevent symptoms in adults with previous ear pain during flights.

  We don't know whether oral pseudoephedrine is also beneficial in children, but it may cause drowsiness.

- We don't know whether topical nasal decongestants can prevent symptoms of barotrauma compared with placebo.

 **Please visit http://clinicalevidence.bmj.com for full text and references**

## What are the effects of interventions to prevent middle-ear pain during air travel?

| Likely To Be Beneficial | • Nasal balloon inflation*<br>• Pseudoephedrine (oral) in adults |
|---|---|
| Unknown Effectiveness | • Nasal decongestants (topical)<br>• Pseudoephedrine (oral) in children |

**Search date July 2014**

*Categorisation based on non-RCT evidence.

**DEFINITION** The normal middle ear and mastoid is filled with air at atmospheric pressure, and the tympanic membrane (eardrum) is most efficient at absorbing sound when the air pressures are the same both sides (i.e., the membrane is not stretched). The air in the middle ear comes from the nasopharynx by way of the Eustachian tube. This is about 36 mm long, with the outer (ear) third having a rigid bony wall tapering to a diameter of less than 1 mm, where it meets the inner (nasopharyngeal) two-thirds, with walls made of cartilage, soft tissue, and muscles. The tube is lined with respiratory epithelium containing goblet cells and mucus glands, and has a carpet of ciliated cells along its floor. The Eustachian tube is usually closed, but may open on swallowing and usually on yawning to allow air to move from the nasopharynx to the middle ear and mastoid to replace the oxygen that has been absorbed by the respiratory mucosa. During ascent in an aeroplane flight, the external pressure drops and it is relatively easy for air to escape from the middle ear down its pressure gradient into the nasopharynx. As the plane starts to descend, the external pressure increases and the Eustachian tube has to open to allow the relatively low middle ear pressures to equalise. This is not so easy, as the increasing external pressures tend to hamper the opening of the Eustachian tube. The increasing external pressure causes the eardrum to be stretched inwards, but the strength and elastic properties of the normal eardrum may be enough to physically withstand this pressure difference — although pain develops. On landing, the pain gradually resolves but observation of the ear usually shows dilated blood vessels running down the handle of the malleus and sometimes slight bruising of the front parts of the membrane. These are common, transient changes that resolve completely and do not cause damage. This is barotitis. Occasionally, there comes a point called the 'critical closing pressure', when the tube cannot open and the pressure differential in the middle ear increases to the extent that changes occur. One such point may occur if there is an outpouring of fluid into the middle ear from the mucosa lining it. The fluid is an exudate or blood or both. Thus, the middle ear fills to a greater or lesser extent with fluid and the pressure on the membrane is relieved (Boyle's Law: $P_1V_1 = P_2V_2$). The downside of this is that the individual's hearing becomes significantly reduced, and this may persist for 1 month or more. The alternative is that, in a membrane with a healed perforation, the thin scar gives way and a new perforation develops, thereby instantly overcoming the pressure differential but again leaving some hearing loss and possibly an additional blood-stained discharge. These two complications are called barotrauma and are uncommon given the many plane flights each year. Both of these problems can result in a balance problem with unsteadiness. However, vertigo, with a prolonged sense of unreal movement (which is usually rotary), is very rare and suggests some disruption of the inner ear with a possible perilymph leak.

**INCIDENCE/PREVALENCE** The prevalence of symptoms depends on the altitude, type of aircraft, and characteristics of the passengers. One point prevalence study found that, in commercial passengers, 20% of adult and 40% of child passengers had negative pressure in the middle ear after flight, and that 10% of adults and 22% of children had otoscopic evidence of changes to the eardrum. We found no data on the incidence of perforation, which seems to be extremely rare in commercial passengers.

**AETIOLOGY/RISK FACTORS** The factors predisposing to barotrauma include the quality of cabin pressurisation and the speed of descent (short-haul flights are worse in general), the individual's anatomy and Eustachian tube function, the state of the respiratory mucosa at the time of the flight (with inflammation from colds, allergies, or sensitivities), and being awake or asleep (asleep is worse because the individual swallows much less). Because of this huge variability, good studies are very hard to perform.

**PROGNOSIS** Experience in military aviation shows that most perforations will heal spontaneously in adults.

Daniel Hajioff and Samuel Mackeith

## KEY POINTS

- Otitis externa is thought to affect 10% of people at some stage, and can present as acute, chronic, or necrotising forms. While milder forms of acute otitis externa are often short-lived isolated episodes, a substantial proportion of cases can persist for weeks or even months, despite intensive treatment. Once resolved, there is a significant risk of recurrence. Because of the risk of chronicity or recurrence, we have excluded studies with follow-up periods of less than 1 month; optimal treatment should not just transiently suppress early symptoms.

  Otitis externa may be associated with eczema or psoriasis of the ear canal or conchal bowl. It is more common in swimmers, in humid environments, in people with narrow ear canals, in hearing-aid users, and after mechanical trauma or ear syringing.

  The most common pathogens are *Pseudomonas aeruginosa* and *Staphylococcus aureus*.

  Fungal overgrowth can occur, especially after prolonged antibiotic use.

- Topical aluminium acetate may be as effective as a topical antibacterial-corticosteroid at improving cure rates in people with acute otitis externa.

- Topical antibacterial agents are likely to improve signs and symptoms of otitis externa.

  Combining topical antibacterial agents and corticosteroids (methylprednisolone-neomycin drops) is likely to be more effective than placebo in reducing signs and symptoms of otitis externa over 28 days.

  We don't know whether any one topical antibacterial regimen should be used in preference to another.

- There is a lack of evidence for corticosteroids when used alone; however, they are likely to be beneficial when used in combination with antibacterials.

  Consensus suggests that topical corticosteroids alone may reduce signs and symptoms of otitis externa, but few good-quality studies have been found assessing these agents alone in this population.

- There is a lack of evidence to demonstrate the benefit of specialist aural toilet use in otitis externa despite the fact there is consensus that it is likely to be beneficial and it is a key treatment used in the secondary care setting, particularly in cases where topical therapy alone has failed.

- We don't know whether topical antifungal agents improve symptoms of otitis externa. However, consensus would suggest that it is inferior as a first-line empirical agent, given that the most common pathogens implicated are bacterial; although, this may not be the case in tropical climates.

- Oral antibiotics have not been shown to be beneficial.

  Consensus suggests that adding oral antibiotics to topical anti-infective agents will not improve symptoms compared with topical agents alone.

- Topical acetic acid is likely to increase cure of otitis externa when used with topical anti-infective agents and corticosteroids, but is of unknown effectiveness when used alone.

- Preservatives in some topical ear products may potentially cause discomfort or contact dermatitis. Patient choice of generic topical ear drops may, therefore, be informed by the preservative used in a preparation.

- Overall, there is a relative lack of high-quality trials to assess each of these treatments, so meta-analysis is often not possible. In general, the outcomes of the various topical treatments available, and their combinations, are similar.

- Most of the studies have been performed in a secondary care setting, where aural toilet has also been provided. It is not clear how applicable these findings are to the primary care setting, where most cases of otitis externa are managed.

(i) **Please visit http://clinicalevidence.bmj.com for full text and references**

## What are the effects of empirical treatments for otitis externa?

| Likely To Be Beneficial | • Aluminium acetate (topical; as effective as topical antibacterial-corticosteroid)<br>• Antibacterials (topical; with or without corticosteroids)<br>• Specialist aural toilet* |
|---|---|
| Unknown Effectiveness | • Acetic acid (topical)<br>• Antibiotics (oral)<br>• Antifungals (topical; with or without corticosteroids)<br>• Corticosteroids (topical; likely to be beneficial when used in combination with antibacterials; unknown effectiveness when used alone)† |
| Unlikely To Be Beneficial | • Antibiotics (oral) plus anti-infective agents (topical) compared with topical anti-infective agents alone* |

Search date October 2013

*Based on consensus.
†Please see option on Antibacterials (topical; with or without corticosteroids).

**DEFINITION** Otitis externa is inflammation of the external ear canal, often with infection. This inflammation is usually generalised throughout the ear canal, so it is often referred to as 'diffuse otitis externa'. This review excludes localised inflammations, such as furuncles. Otitis externa has acute (<6 weeks), chronic (>3 months), and necrotising (malignant) forms. While milder forms of acute otitis externa are often short-lived isolated episodes, a substantial proportion of cases can persist for weeks or even months, despite intensive treatment. And, once resolved, there is a significant risk of recurrence. It causes pain with aural discharge and associated hearing loss. If the ear canal is visible, it appears red and inflamed. *Pseudomonas aeruginosa* and *Staphylococcus aureus* are the most frequent bacterial pathogens in otitis externa. Fungal overgrowth (e.g., with *Aspergillus niger* and *candida*) is also common, especially after prolonged antibiotic treatment. Chronic otitis externa may result in canal stenosis with associated hearing loss, for which it may be difficult to fit hearing aids. Necrotising otitis externa is defined by destruction of the temporal bone, usually in people with diabetes or in people who are immunocompromised, and can be life threatening. Making an accurate diagnosis can be challenging, firstly to differentiate between otitis media and otitis externa (although these may co-exist) and secondly to decide on the most likely underlying cause (e.g., bacterial, fungal, dermatitis), so that the most appropriate treatment can be started. In this review, we look at the empirical treatment of only acute and chronic otitis externa. Topical treatment refers to drops, ointment, solution, cream, or spray. The population studied included adults and children.

*(continued over)*

*(from previous page)*

**INCIDENCE/PREVALENCE** Otitis externa is common worldwide. The exact incidence is unknown, but 10% of people are thought to have been affected at some time. The condition does affect children, but is more common in adults. It accounts for a large proportion of the workload in otolaryngology departments, but milder cases are often managed in primary care.

**AETIOLOGY/RISK FACTORS** Otitis externa may be associated with dermatological disease of the ear canal and conchal bowl, such as eczema and, less commonly, psoriasis. It is more common in swimmers, in humid environments, in people with narrow external ear canals, in hearing-aid users, and after mechanical trauma or ear syringing. Many clinicians suggest prophylactic measures for patients with recurrent otitis externa. These include water precautions to keep the ears dry, topical corticosteroids to treat underlying eczema, or regular antiseptic agents (e.g., acetic acid or aluminium acetate) to reduce the pH of the ear canal, thus maintaining an unfavourable milieu for microbes. The rationale for these measures is reasonable, given that moisture and eczema are risk factors for otitis externa. The evidence to determine the efficacy of these practices is, however, lacking and does not form part of this review.

**PROGNOSIS** We found few reliable data. Many cases of otitis externa resolve spontaneously over several weeks or months. Acute episodes tend to recur, although risk of recurrence is unknown. Experience suggests that chronic inflammation affects a small proportion of people after a single episode of acute otitis externa and can, rarely, lead to canal stenosis.

Kim Ah-See

## KEY POINTS

- Acute rhinosinusitis is defined pathologically by transient inflammation of the mucosal lining of the paranasal sinuses lasting less than 4 weeks.

   It affects 1% to 5% of the adult population each year in Europe.

   Characteristic symptoms include nasal congestion, rhinorrhoea, facial pain, hyposmia, sneezing, and, if more severe, additional malaise and fever.

   The diagnosis is usually made clinically without radiological or bacteriological investigation. Clinically diagnosed acute rhinosinusitis is less likely to be caused by bacterial infection than acute rhinosinusitis confirmed by radiological or bacteriological investigation.

- This review examines evidence from RCTs and systematic reviews of RCTs in adults with clinically diagnosed acute rhinosinusitis only. We excluded studies in people with acute rhinosinusitis confirmed by radiological or bacteriological investigation.

- In clinically diagnosed acute rhinosinusitis, intranasal corticosteroids may reduce symptoms compared with placebo.

- We found little RCT evidence to support the use of amoxicillin, co-amoxiclav, or doxycycline in people with clinically diagnosed acute rhinosinusitis.

- We found no RCTs comparing cephalosporins or macrolides with placebo in people with clinically diagnosed acute rhinosinusitis.

- The balance between little evidence of benefit from antibiotics versus increased adverse effects should be discussed when considering prescribing antibiotics for people with mild-to-moderate clinically diagnosed acute rhinosinusitis.

   Incidence of adverse effects is higher in people prescribed antibiotics compared with placebo.

   The clinical response from cefotiam (a cephalosporin) appears to be the same after a 5-day course versus a 10-day course. However, this single RCT did not compare outcome with placebo.

   We found no RCTs on the effects of antibiotics in people with severe clinically diagnosed acute rhinosinusitis.

- We found no good-quality RCTs examining the effectiveness of decongestants or saline nasal washes in acute rhinosinusitis diagnosed clinically.

 **Please visit http://clinicalevidence.bmj.com for full text and references**

## What are the effects of treatments in people with clinically diagnosed acute rhinosinusitis?

| Likely To Be Beneficial | • Corticosteroids (intranasal) |
|---|---|
| Unknown Effectiveness | • Decongestants (xylometazoline, phenylephrine, pseudoephedrine) |
| | • Saline nasal washes |
| | • Selected antibiotics (amoxicillin, amoxicillin-clavulanic acid [co-amoxiclav], doxycycline, cephalosporins, macrolides only; limited evidence compared with placebo in people with |

mild-to-moderate acute rhinosinusitis, but may be associated with increased adverse effects)

**Search date October 2013**

**DEFINITION** Acute rhinosinusitis is defined pathologically by transient inflammation of the mucosal lining of the paranasal sinuses lasting less than 4 weeks. Clinically, it is characterised by nasal congestion, rhinorrhoea, facial pain, hyposmia, sneezing, and, if more severe, by additional malaise and fever. The diagnosis is usually made clinically (on the basis of history and examination, but without radiological or bacteriological investigation). Clinically diagnosed acute rhinosinusitis is less likely to be caused by bacterial infection than acute rhinosinusitis confirmed by radiological or bacteriological investigation. In this review, we have excluded studies in people with acute rhinosinusitis confirmed by bacteriological or radiological investigation, in children (younger than 16 years of age), in people with symptoms for longer than 4 weeks (chronic sinusitis) or recurrent sinusitis (may indicate a structural problem in the nasal cavity), and in people with symptoms after facial trauma.

**INCIDENCE/PREVALENCE** Each year in Europe, 1% to 5% of adults are diagnosed with acute rhinosinusitis by their general practitioners. Extrapolated to the British population, this is estimated to cause 6 million restricted working days per year. Most people with acute rhinosinusitis are assessed and treated in a primary-care setting. The prevalence varies according to whether diagnosis is made on clinical grounds or on the basis of radiological or bacteriological investigation.

**AETIOLOGY/RISK FACTORS** One systematic review (search date 1998) reported that about 50% of people with a clinical diagnosis of acute rhinosinusitis have bacterial sinus infection. The usual pathogens in acute bacterial rhinosinusitis are *Streptococcus pneumoniae* and *Haemophilus influenzae*, with occasional infection with *Moraxella catarrhalis*. Preceding viral upper respiratory-tract infection is often the trigger for acute bacterial rhinosinusitis, with about 0.5% of common colds becoming complicated by the development of acute rhinosinusitis.

**PROGNOSIS** One meta-analysis of RCTs found that up to two-thirds of people with acute rhinosinusitis had spontaneous resolution of symptoms without active treatment. One non-systematic review reported that people with acute rhinosinusitis are at risk of chronic rhinosinusitis and irreversible damage to the normal mucociliary mucosal surface. One further non-systematic review reported rare life-threatening complications, such as orbital cellulitis and meningitis, after acute rhinosinusitis. However, we found no reliable data to measure these risks.

Julian Savage and Angus Waddell

## KEY POINTS

- Up to 18% of people in industrialised societies are mildly affected by chronic tinnitus, and 0.5% report tinnitus having a severe effect on their daily life.

  Tinnitus can be associated with hearing loss, acoustic neuromas, drug toxicity, ear diseases, or depression.

  Tinnitus can last for many years, and can interfere with sleep and concentration.

- We found insufficient evidence to show that antidepressant drugs improve tinnitus symptoms.

  Antidepressant drugs can improve depression in people with tinnitus.

  Tricyclic antidepressants (TCAs) are associated with adverse effects such as dry mouth, blurred vision, and constipation.

- Psychotherapy (CBT) may be no more effective than placebo at reducing tinnitus loudness, but it may improve overall symptoms of tinnitus at 12 months.

  CBT may be more effective at improving anxiety, depression, quality of life, and annoyance scores for people with tinnitus.

  We don't know whether CBT plus a tinnitus-masking device is more effective than waiting-list control at improving depression or tinnitus annoyance scores in people with tinnitus.

- We don't know whether benzodiazepines, acupuncture, hypnosis, electromagnetic stimulation, hearing aids, or tinnitus-masking devices are effective in people with tinnitus.

- Ginkgo biloba may be no more effective than placebo at improving overall symptoms of tinnitus at 3 months. However, evidence was limited and inconsistent.

- Acamprosate may be more effective than placebo at improving overall symptom scores at 3 months in people with tinnitus. However, evidence was weak and it is unclear whether the improvement was clinically important.

- Carbamazepine may be no more effective than placebo at improving symptoms of tinnitus, and is associated with adverse effects such as dizziness, nausea, and headache.

ⓘ Please visit http://clinicalevidence.bmj.com for full text and references

| What are the effects of treatments for chronic tinnitus? | |
|---|---|
| Unknown Effectiveness | • Acamprosate |
| | • Acupuncture |
| | • Antidepressant drugs |
| | • Benzodiazepines (alprazolam) |
| | • CBT plus tinnitus-masking device (tinnitus re-training therapy) |
| | • Electromagnetic stimulation |
| | • Hearing aids |
| | • Hypnosis |
| | • Psychotherapy |

| | |
|---|---|
| | ● Tinnitus-masking devices |
| **Unlikely To Be Beneficial** | ● Ginkgo biloba |
| **Likely To Be Ineffective Or Harmful** | ● Carbamazepine (may be associated with adverse effects) |

**Search date November 2013**

**DEFINITION** Tinnitus is the perception of sound in the ear or head that does not arise from the external environment, from within the body (e.g., vascular sounds), or from auditory hallucinations related to mental illness. This review is concerned with tinnitus for which tinnitus is the only, or the predominant, symptom in an affected person.

**INCIDENCE/PREVALENCE** Up to 18% of the general population in industrialised countries are mildly affected by chronic tinnitus, and 0.5% report tinnitus having a severe effect on their ability to lead a normal life.

**AETIOLOGY/RISK FACTORS** Tinnitus can occur as an isolated idiopathic symptom, or in association with any type of hearing loss. Tinnitus can be a particular feature of presbycusis (age-related hearing loss), noise-induced hearing loss, Menière's disease (see review on Menière's disease, p 188), or the presence of an acoustic neuroma. In people with toxicity from aspirin or quinine, tinnitus can occur with hearing thresholds remaining normal. Tinnitus is also associated with depression, although it can be unclear whether the tinnitus is a manifestation of the depressive illness or a factor contributing to its development. Studies involving people with tinnitus caused by Menière's disease, acoustic neuroma, chronic otitis media, head injury, barotraumas, or other clear pathology have been excluded from this review. This review is principally concerned with idiopathic tinnitus with or without degenerative sensorineural hearing loss.

**PROGNOSIS** Tinnitus can have an insidious onset, with a long delay before clinical presentation. It can persist for many years or decades, particularly when associated with a sensorineural hearing loss. Tinnitus can cause disruption of sleep patterns, an inability to concentrate, and depression.

Christos C. Georgalas, Neil S. Tolley, and Antony Narula

## KEY POINTS

- Diagnosis of acute tonsillitis is clinical, and it can be difficult to distinguish viral from bacterial infections.

    Rapid antigen testing has a very low sensitivity in the diagnosis of bacterial tonsillitis, but more accurate tests take longer to deliver results.

    Bacteria are cultured from few people with tonsillitis. Other causes include infectious mononucleosis from Epstein-Barr virus infection, cytomegalovirus, toxoplasmosis, HIV, hepatitis A, and rubella.

- Acute tonsillitis with group A beta-haemolytic streptococci can occasionally cause rheumatic fever and acute glomerulonephritis, which can be prevented by treatment with penicillin.

    In resource-rich countries, these complications are so rare that routine aggressive antibiotic use cannot be justified.

- Tonsillectomy, with or without adenoidectomy, is one of the most frequently performed surgical procedures in the UK.

- In adults, we found limited evidence from one small RCT that surgery may reduce sore throats at 5 to 6 months, but we found no longer-term evidence. Tonsillectomy may be associated with morbidity.

- In children, the effectiveness of tonsillectomy has to be judged against the potential harms. Tonsillectomy is more beneficial in children with severe symptoms, while in populations with a low incidence of tonsillitis, the modest benefit may be outweighed by the morbidity associated with the surgery.

- The use of diathermy in tonsillectomy in adults or children is associated with reduced rates of primary bleeding, but increased rates of secondary and overall bleeding.

    Overall, cold-steel dissection tonsillectomy seems to have the lowest rates of postoperative haemorrhage and pain, although it is associated with slightly increased intra-operative bleeding. The use of diathermy in tonsillectomy must be weighed against its potential harms.

    Adequate training in the appropriate use of diathermy during tonsillectomy is important. In deciding which method to apply, the surgeon should consider the underlying characteristics of patients, as well as the relative importance of secondary compared with primary bleeding and intra-operative blood loss compared with postoperative pain.

 **Please visit http://clinicalevidence.bmj.com for full text and references**

| What are the effects of tonsillectomy in children and adults with acute recurrent or chronic throat infections? | |
| --- | --- |
| Beneficial | • Cold-steel tonsillectomy (better peri- and postoperative outcomes than diathermy tonsillectomy in adults and children) |
| Trade-off Between Benefits And Harms | • Tonsillectomy (may reduce sore throat frequency in adults compared with no surgery but associated with morbidity)<br><br>• Tonsillectomy (reduces tonsillitis in children compared with no surgery but associated with morbidity) |

Search date April 2014

**DEFINITION** The definition of severe recurrent throat infections is arbitrary, but recent criteria have defined severe tonsillitis as: five or more episodes of true tonsillitis a year; symptoms for at least 1 year; and episodes that are disabling and prevent normal functioning. However, in most cases, the severity of recurrent throat infections depends on many factors and cannot be judged solely on the basis of its incidence. This definition does not include tonsillitis caused by infectious mononucleosis, which usually occurs as a single episode. However, acute tonsillitis in this situation may be followed by recurrent tonsillitis in some people. Tonsillitis may occur in isolation or as part of a generalised pharyngitis. The clinical distinction between tonsillitis and pharyngitis is unclear in the literature, and the condition is often referred to simply as 'acute sore throat'. A sore throat lasting for 24 to 48 hours as part of the prodrome of minor upper respiratory tract infection is excluded from this definition. Diagnosis of acute tonsillitis is primarily clinical, with the main interest being in whether the illness is viral or bacterial — this being of relevance if antibiotics are being considered. Studies have attempted to distinguish viral from bacterial sore throat on clinical grounds, but the results are conflicting, suggesting a lack of reliable diagnostic criteria. Investigations to assist with this distinction include throat swabs and serological tests, including the rapid antigen test and the antistreptolysin O titre. Rapid antigen testing is convenient and popular in North America, but has doubtful sensitivity (61%–95%), at least when measured against throat swab results, although specificity is higher (88%–100%). However, the inevitable delay in reporting of both swabs and the antistreptolysin O titre reduce their value in the routine clinical situation.

**INCIDENCE/PREVALENCE** Recurrent sore throat has an incidence in general practice in the UK of 100 per 1000 population per year. Acute tonsillitis is more common in childhood.

**AETIOLOGY/RISK FACTORS** Common bacterial pathogens include beta-haemolytic and other streptococci. Bacteria are cultured from only a minority of people with tonsillitis. The role of viruses is uncertain. In tonsillitis associated with infectious mononucleosis, the most common infective agent is the Epstein-Barr virus (present in 50% of children and 90% of adults with the condition). Cytomegalovirus infection may also result in the clinical picture of infectious mononucleosis, and the differential diagnosis also includes toxoplasmosis, HIV, hepatitis A, and rubella.

**PROGNOSIS** We found no good data on the natural history of tonsillitis or recurrent sore throat in children or adults. People in RCTs randomised to medical treatment (courses of antibiotics as required) have shown a tendency towards improvement over time. Recurrent severe tonsillitis results in considerable morbidity, including time lost from school or work. The most common complication of acute tonsillitis is peritonsillar abscess, but we found no good evidence on its incidence. Rheumatic fever and acute glomerulonephritis are recognised complications of acute tonsillitis associated with group A beta-haemolytic streptococci. These diseases are rare in resource-rich countries, but do occasionally occur. They are still a common problem in certain populations, notably Australian aboriginal people, and may be effectively prevented in closed communities by the use of penicillin. A systematic review found that antibiotics reduced the incidence of these diseases. However, in resource-rich countries, these diseases are so rare that routine aggressive antibiotic use is not justified. The review also found that antibiotics shorten the duration of illness by about 16 hours overall.

Michael Shlipak

## KEY POINTS

- Up to one third of people with type 1 or 2 diabetes will develop microalbuminuria or macroalbuminuria after 20 years. Smoking, poor glycaemic control, male sex, older age, and ethnicity are also risk factors.

  Microalbuminuria can also be caused by hypertension, which often complicates type 2 diabetes and makes the diagnosis more difficult.

  Diabetic nephropathy increases the risk of end-stage renal disease and mortality, and is associated with increased cardiovascular risk.

- In people with type 1 diabetes, angiotensin-converting enzyme (ACE) inhibitors reduce progression of early nephropathy while, in people with late nephropathy, they reduce the risk of end-stage renal failure and death.

  Intensive glycaemic control reduces progression of nephropathy compared with conventional control in people with early renal disease, but we don't know whether glycaemic control is effective in people with late nephropathy.

  We don't know whether angiotensin II receptor blockers (ARBs), dietary protein restriction, or tight control of blood pressure reduce the risks of renal or cardiovascular disease, or improve survival, in people with early or late nephropathy.

- In people with type 2 diabetes, ACE inhibitors reduce progression from early to late nephropathy and may reduce cardiovascular events, but we don't know whether they are beneficial in late nephropathy.

  ARBs may reduce progression of nephropathy in people with early or late nephropathy.

  Lowering of diastolic blood pressure, even if not raised initially, reduces the risk of progression of early nephropathy, but we don't know whether it is effective in late nephropathy.

  We don't know whether protein restriction or tight glycaemic control are beneficial in early or late nephropathy.

(i) **Please visit http://clinicalevidence.bmj.com for full text and references**

| What are the effects of treatments to prevent progression of nephropathy in people with type 1 diabetes and early nephropathy? | |
|---|---|
| **Beneficial** | • ACE inhibitors in early nephropathy, type 1 diabetes (reduce progression to late nephropathy)<br><br>• Intensive glycaemic control in early nephropathy, type 1 diabetes (reduces progression to late nephropathy) |
| **Unknown Effectiveness** | • Angiotensin II receptor blockers in early nephropathy, type 1 diabetes<br><br>• Protein restriction in early nephropathy, type 1 diabetes<br><br>• Tight control of blood pressure in early nephropathy, type 1 diabetes |

## What are the effects of treatments to prevent progression of nephropathy in people with type 1 diabetes and late nephropathy?

| Beneficial | • Captopril in late nephropathy, type 1 diabetes |
|---|---|
| Unknown Effectiveness | • Angiotensin II receptor blockers in late nephropathy, type 1 diabetes<br><br>• Glycaemic control in late nephropathy, type 1 diabetes<br><br>• Protein restriction in late nephropathy, type 1 diabetes<br><br>• Tight control of blood pressure in late nephropathy, type 1 diabetes |

## What are the effects of treatments to prevent progression of nephropathy in people with type 2 diabetes and early nephropathy?

| Beneficial | • ACE inhibitors in early nephropathy, type 2 diabetes<br><br>• Angiotensin II receptor blockers in early nephropathy, type 2 diabetes<br><br>• Tight control of blood pressure in early nephropathy, type 2 diabetes (reduced progression to late nephropathy) |
|---|---|
| Unknown Effectiveness | • Glycaemic control in early nephropathy, type 2 diabetes<br><br>• Protein restriction in early nephropathy, type 2 diabetes |

## What are the effects of treatments to prevent progression of nephropathy in people with type 2 diabetes and late nephropathy?

| Beneficial | • Angiotensin II receptor blockers in late nephropathy, type 2 diabetes |
|---|---|
| Unknown Effectiveness | • ACE inhibitors in late nephropathy, type 2 diabetes<br><br>• Glycaemic control in late nephropathy, type 2 diabetes<br><br>• Protein restriction in late nephropathy, type 2 diabetes<br><br>• Tight control of blood pressure in late nephropathy, type 2 diabetes |

**Search date November 2009**

**DEFINITION** Diabetic nephropathy is a clinical syndrome in people with diabetes, characterised by albuminuria on at least two occasions separated by 3 to 6 months. Diabetic nephropathy is usually accompanied by hypertension, progressive rise in proteinuria, and decline in renal function. In type 1 diabetes, five stages have been proposed. Of these, **stages 1 and 2** are equivalent to pre-clinical nephropathy, and are detected only by imaging or biopsy. **Stage 3** is synonymous with early nephropathy — the clinical term used in this review. **Stage 4** nephropathy is also known clinically as late nephropathy, and this term will be used for the remainder of this review. **Stage 5** represents the progression to end-stage renal disease. **Population:** For the purpose of this review, we have included people with diabetes and both early and late nephropathy. Early nephropathy presents as microalbuminuria, usually defined by albuminuria level of 30 to 300 mg a day (or albumin/creatinine ratio of 30 to 300 mg/g [3.4–34.0 mg/mmol]). Late nephropathy presents as macroalbuminuria, characterised by albuminuria greater than 300 mg a day (or albumin/creatinine ratio >300 mg/g [34 mg/mmol]). The treatment of people with diabetes and end-stage renal disease is not covered in this review.

**INCIDENCE/PREVALENCE** After 20 years of type 1 or 2 diabetes, the cumulative risk of proteinuria is 27% to 28% and the overall prevalence of microalbuminuria and macroalbuminuria is 30% to 35%. In addition, the incidence of diabetic nephropathy is increasing, partly due to the growing epidemic of type 2 diabetes, and because of increased life expectancies: for example, in the USA, the incidence has increased by 150% in the past decade.

**AETIOLOGY/RISK FACTORS** Duration of diabetes, older age, male sex, smoking, and poor glycaemic control have all been found to be risk factors in the development of nephropathy. In addition, certain ethnic groups seem at greater risk (see prognosis). Microalbuminuria is less pathognomonic of nephropathy among people with type 2 diabetes because hypertension, which is a common complication of type 2 diabetes, can also cause microalbuminuria. Hypertension can also cause renal insufficiency; so, the time to development of renal insufficiency can be shorter in type 2 diabetes than in type 1. For people who have an atypical course, renal biopsy may be advisable. In addition, there are some differences in the progression of type 1 and type 2 diabetic nephropathy. In people with type 2 diabetes, albuminuria is more often present at diagnosis. Hypertension is also more common in type 2 diabetic nephropathy. Finally, microalbuminuria is less predictive of late nephropathy in people with type 2 diabetes compared with type 1.

**PROGNOSIS** People with microalbuminuria are at increased risk for progression to macroalbuminuria and end-stage renal disease. The natural history of diabetic nephropathy is better defined in type 1 than type 2 diabetes. In type 2 diabetes, the course can be more difficult to predict, primarily because the date of onset of diabetes is less commonly known, and comorbid conditions can contribute to renal disease. Without specific interventions, about 80% of people with type 1 diabetes, and 20% to 40% of people with type 2 diabetes with microalbuminuria, will progress to macroalbuminuria. Diabetic nephropathy is associated with poor outcomes. In the USA, diabetes accounts for 48% of all new cases of end-stage renal disease (ESRD). In the UK, it is the most common cause of ESRD, accounting for 20% of cases. People with type 1 diabetes and proteinuria have been found to have a 40-fold greater risk of mortality than people without proteinuria. The prognostic significance of proteinuria is less extreme in type 2 diabetes, although people with proteinuria have a fourfold risk of death compared with people without proteinuria. In addition, increased cardiovascular risk has been associated with albuminuria in people with diabetes. African-American, Native American, and Mexican-American people have a much higher risk of developing ESRD in the setting of diabetes compared with white people. In the USA, African-American people with diabetes progress to ESRD at a much more rapid rate than white people with diabetes. In England, the rates for initiating treatment for ESRD are 4.2 times higher for African-Caribbean people and 3.7 times higher for Indo-Asian people than for white people. Native American people of the Pima tribe, in southwestern USA, have much higher rates of diabetic nephropathy than white people, and also progress to ESRD at a faster rate.

Birte Nygaard

## KEY POINTS

- Hyperthyroidism is characterised by high levels of serum thyroxine and triiodothyronine, and low levels of thyroid-stimulating hormone (TSH).

  Thyrotoxicosis is the clinical effect of high levels of thyroid hormones, whether or not the thyroid gland is the primary source.

  The main causes of hyperthyroidism in pregnancy are Graves' disease and chorionic gonadotrophin (hCG)-mediated hyperthyroidism.

- Untreated severe hyperthyroidism in pregnancy is associated with obstetric and maternal complications.

- We found no RCTs on the effects of antithyroid drugs (carbimazole/thiamazole and propylthiouracil) in hyperthyroidism in pregnancy. However, there is consensus that they are effective.

  Observational studies have shown an increased risk of congenital malformation in children born to mothers taking antithyroid drugs.

- There have been alerts on the risk of hepatotoxicity with propylthiouracil.

(i) **Please visit http://clinicalevidence.bmj.com for full text and references**

| **What are the effects of antithyroid drug treatments for hyperthyroidism in pregnancy?** | |
|---|---|
| Unknown Effectiveness | • Carbimazole or thiamazole |
| | • Propylthiouracil |

**Search date June 2014**

**DEFINITION** Hyperthyroidism is characterised by high levels of serum thyroxine ($T_4$), high levels of serum triiodothyronine ($T_3$), or both, and low levels of thyroid-stimulating hormone (TSH, also known as thyrotrophin <0.05 mU/L). Subclinical hyperthyroidism is characterised by decreased levels of TSH (<0.1 mU/L) but with levels of $T_4$ and $T_3$ within the normal range. Healthy pregnancy can be characterised by a low or suppressed TSH (even <0.1 mU/L) in the first trimester. The terms hyperthyroidism and thyrotoxicosis are often used synonymously; however, they refer to slightly different conditions. Hyperthyroidism refers to overactivity of the thyroid gland leading to excessive production of thyroid hormones. Thyrotoxicosis refers to the clinical effects of unbound thyroid hormones, whether or not the thyroid gland is the primary source. Hyperthyroidism in pregnancy is most commonly caused by Graves' disease (diffusely enlarged thyroid gland on palpation, ophthalmopathy, and dermopathy), toxic multinodular goitre (thyrotoxicosis and increased radioiodine uptake with multinodular goitre on palpation), but can also be due to toxic adenoma (benign hyperfunctioning thyroid neoplasm presenting as a solitary thyroid nodule), or chorionic gonadotrophin (hCG)-mediated hyperthyroidism. **Diagnosis:** Most pregnant women with hyperthyroidism are diagnosed prior to conception. The diagnosis of hyperthyroidism is established by a raised serum total or free $T_4$ or $T_3$ hormone levels, reduced TSH level, and high radioiodine uptake in the thyroid gland along with features of thyrotoxicosis. During pregnancy, radioactive iodine testing is contraindicated. Diagnosis is, therefore, usually by other laboratory tests (elevated $T_4$ and the presence of thyrotrophin receptor stimulating antibodies). The usual symptoms are irritability, heat intolerance and excessive sweating, palpitations, weight loss with increased appetite, increased bowel frequency, and oligomenorrhoea. As many of these may be part of normal pregnancy, diagnosing new Graves' disease in pregnancy may be difficult.

**INCIDENCE/PREVALENCE** In pregnancy, the most common causes of hyperthyroidism are Graves' disease and human chorionic gonadotrophin (hCG)-mediated hyperthyroidism. Graves' disease is seen in 0.1% to 1.0% (0.4% clinical and 0.6% subclinical) of pregnant women. HCG-mediated hyperthyroidism is transient and mild and usually does not require treatment; it is seen in 1% to 3% of pregnant women.

**AETIOLOGY/RISK FACTORS** Smoking is a risk factor, with an increased risk of both Graves' disease (OR 2.5, 95% CI 1.8 to 3.5) and toxic nodular goitre (OR 1.7, 95% CI 1.1 to 2.5). In areas with high iodine intake, Graves' disease is the major cause; whereas in areas of low iodine intake, the major cause is nodular goitre. A correlation between diabetes mellitus and thyroid dysfunction has been described. In a Scottish population with diabetes, the overall prevalence of thyroid disease was found to be 13%, highest in women with type 1 diabetes (31%). As a result of screening, new thyroid disease was diagnosed in 7% of people with diabetes (hyperthyroidism in 1%). Around 50% of women who experience hyperemesis gravidarum have elevated $T_4$ levels.

**PROGNOSIS** Obstetric and medical complications are directly related to control of hyperthyroidism in pregnancy. Poor control is associated with miscarriages, prematurity, low birth weight, intrauterine growth restriction, stillbirth, thyroid storm, and maternal congestive heart failure. Pregnant women with Graves' disease usually show remission in the third trimester, allowing them to stop taking antithyroid drugs. In cases where remission does not occur, there is an increased risk of neonatal thyrotoxicosis.

Birte Nygaard

## KEY POINTS

- Primary hypothyroidism is defined as low levels of blood thyroid hormone due to destruction of the thyroid gland. This destruction is usually caused by autoimmunity or an intervention such as surgery, radiolodine, or radiation.

  It can be classified as clinical (overt) when diagnosed by characteristic clinical features, raised levels of thyroid stimulating hormone (TSH), and reduced levels of $T_4$; or subclinical when serum TSH is raised, but serum $T_4$ is normal, and there are no symptoms of thyroid dysfunction.

  Hypothyroidism is six times more common in women, affecting up to 40 in 10,000 each year (compared with 6 per 10,000 men).

- There is consensus that levothyroxine is effective in treating clinical (overt) hypothyroidism, but evidence is sparse.

  Treatment can lead to hyperthyroidism, reduction of bone mass in post-menopausal women, and increased risk of atrial fibrillation if the person is over-treated.

  We found no evidence from RCTs that levothyroxine plus liothyronine improves symptoms more than levothyroxine alone.

- We don't know how effective levothyroxine is in treating people with subclinical hypothyroidism, as trials have been too small to detect any clinically relevant improvements in outcomes.

 **Please visit http://clinicalevidence.bmj.com for full text and references**

### What are the effects of treatments for clinical (overt) hypothyroidism?

| | |
|---|---|
| Likely To Be Beneficial | • Levothyroxine (L-thyroxine)* |
| Unlikely To Be Beneficial | • Levothyroxine (L-thyroxine) plus liothyronine compared with levothyroxine alone** |

### What are the effects of treatments for subclinical hypothyroidism?

| | |
|---|---|
| Unknown Effectiveness | • Levothyroxine (L-thyroxine) |

**Search date July 2013**

*No RCT evidence, but there is clinical consensus that levothyroxine is beneficial in clinical (overt) hypothyroidism. A placebo-controlled trial would be considered unethical.
**We don't know whether a subgroup of people with thyroid hormone pathway polymorphisms improve with combination treatment levothyroxine plus liothyronine compared with levothyroxine alone.

**DEFINITION** Hypothyroidism is characterised by low levels of blood thyroid hormone. **Clinical (overt) hypothyroidism** is diagnosed on the basis of characteristic clinical features (e.g., mental slowing, depression, dementia, weight gain, constipation, dry skin, hair loss, cold intolerance, hoarse voice, irregular menstruation, infertility, muscle stiffness and pain, bradycardia, hypercholesterolaemia) and a serum TSH above and $T_4$ (and/or $T_3$) below the reference range. A number of guidelines quote serum TSH of 5–10 mU/L as mild, and >10 mU/L as severe hypothyroidism. **Subclinical hypothyroidism** is a biochemical diagnosis with findings of a serum TSH above the reference range and serum $T_4$ (and/or $T_3$) within the reference range. **Primary hypothyroidism** occurs after destruction of the thyroid gland because of autoimmunity (the most common cause) or medical intervention such as surgery, radioiodine, and radiation. **Secondary hypothyroidism** occurs after pituitary or hypothalamic damage, and is caused by insufficient production caused by pituitary or hypothalamic hypofunction. Secondary hypothyroidism is not covered in this review. **Euthyroid sick syndrome** is diagnosed when tri-iodothyronine ($T_3$) levels are low, serum $T_4$ is low, and TSH levels are normal or low. Euthyroid sick syndrome is not covered in this review.

**INCIDENCE/PREVALENCE** Hypothyroidism is more common in women than in men (in the UK, female:male ratio of 6:1). One study (2779 people in the UK with a median age of 58 years) found that the incidence of clinical (overt) hypothyroidism was 40 in 10,000 women a year and 6 in 10,000 men a year. The prevalence was 9.3% in women and 1.3% in men. In areas with high iodine intake, the incidence of hypothyroidism can be higher than in areas with normal or low iodine intake. In Denmark, where there is moderate iodine insufficiency, the overall incidence of hypothyroidism is 1.4 in 10,000 a year, increasing to 8 in 10,000 a year in people over 70 years. The incidence of subclinical hypothyroidism increases with age. Up to 10% of women over the age of 60 years have subclinical hypothyroidism (evaluated from data from the Netherlands and US).

**AETIOLOGY/RISK FACTORS** Primary thyroid gland failure can occur as a result of chronic autoimmune thyroiditis, radioactive iodine treatment, or thyroidectomy. Other causes include drug adverse effects (e.g., amiodarone and lithium), transient hypothyroidism due to silent thyroiditis, subacute thyroiditis, or postnatal thyroiditis.

**PROGNOSIS** In people with subclinical hypothyroidism, the risk of developing clinical (overt) hypothyroidism is described in the UK Whickham survey (25 years follow-up; for women: OR 8, 95% CI 3 to 20; for men: OR 44, 95% CI 19 to 104; if both a raised TSH and positive antithyroid antibodies were present; for women: OR 38, 95% CI 22 to 65; for men: OR 173, 95% CI 81 to 370). For women, the survey found an annual risk of 4.3% a year (if both raised serum TSH and antithyroid antibodies were present) and 2.6% a year (if raised serum TSH was present alone); the minimum number of people with raised TSH and antithyroid antibodies who would need treating to prevent this progression to clinical (overt) hypothyroidism in one person over 5 years is five to eight. **Cardiovascular disease:** A large cross-sectional study (25,862 people with serum TSH 5.1–10.0 mU/L) found significantly higher mean total cholesterol concentrations in people who were hypothyroid compared with people who were euthyroid (5.8 mmol/L v 5.6 mmol/L). Another study (124 elderly women with subclinical hypothyroidism, 931 women who were euthyroid) found a significantly increased risk of MI in women with subclinical hypothyroidism (OR 2.3, 95% CI 1.3 to 4.0) and of aortic atherosclerosis (OR 1.7, 95% CI 1.1 to 2.6). **Mental health:** Subclinical hypothyroidism is associated with depression. People with subclinical hypothyroidism may have depression that is refractory to both antidepressant drugs and thyroid hormone alone. Memory impairment, hysteria, anxiety, somatic complaints, and depressive features without depression have been described in people with subclinical hypothyroidism.

David DeLaet and Daniel Schauer

## KEY POINTS

- About one third of the US population and one quarter of the UK population are obese, with increased risks of hypertension, dyslipidaemia, diabetes, CVD, osteoarthritis, and some cancers.

  Fewer than 10% of overweight or obese adults aged 40 to 49 years revert to a normal body weight after 4 years.

  Nearly 5 million US adults used prescription weight-loss medication between 1996 and 1998, but one quarter of all users were not overweight.

- Orlistat, phentermine, and sibutramine may promote modest weight loss (an additional 1–7 kg lost) compared with placebo in obese adults having lifestyle interventions, but they can all cause adverse effects.

  Sibutramine may be more effective at promoting weight loss compared with orlistat, although not in obese people with type 2 diabetes or hypertension.

  We don't know whether combining orlistat and sibutramine treatment leads to greater weight loss than with either treatment alone.

  We don't know whether diethylpropion and mazindol are effective at promoting weight loss in people with obesity.

  Orlistat has been associated with GI adverse effects.

  Phentermine has been associated with heart and lung problems.

  Sibutramine has been associated with cardiac arrhythmias and cardiac arrest. In January 2010, the European Medicines Agency suspended marketing authorisation of sibutramine in the European Union because of the increased risk of non-fatal myocardial infarctions and strokes.

  In October 2010, the FDA requested the withdrawal of sibutramine from the US market because of the increased risk of adverse cardiovascular events.

  Rimonabant has been associated with an increased risk of psychiatric disorders.

- Bariatric surgery (gastric bypass, vertical banded gastroplasty, biliopancreatic diversion, or gastric banding) may increase weight loss compared with no surgery in people with morbid obesity.

- Compared with each other, we don't know whether gastric bypass, vertical banded gastroplasty, biliopancreatic diversion, or gastric banding is the most effective surgery or the least harmful.

  We don't know whether sleeve gastrectomy is effective.

  Bariatric surgery may result in loss of >20% of body weight, which may be largely maintained for 10 years.

  Operative and postoperative complications are common, and on average 0.28% of people die within 30 days of surgery. Mortality may be as high as 2% in some high-risk populations. However, surgery may reduce long-term mortality compared with no surgery.

 **Please visit http://clinicalevidence.bmj.com for full text and references**

| What are the effects of drug treatments in adults with obesity? | |
|---|---|
| Trade-off Between Benefits And Harms | • Orlistat |
| | • Phentermine |
| | • Sibutramine |
| | • Sibutramine plus orlistat (insufficient evidence to assess combination *v* either intervention alone, |

| | however sibutramine is associated with cardiovascular adverse effects) |
|---|---|
| **Unknown Effectiveness** | • Diethylpropion<br>• Mazindol |

## What are the effects of bariatric surgery in adults with morbid obesity?

| | |
|---|---|
| **Likely To Be Beneficial** | • Bariatric surgery (more effective than non-surgical treatment for clinically important weight loss in morbidly obese adults, but operative complications common)<br>• Biliopancreatic diversion<br>• Gastric banding<br>• Gastric bypass<br>• Vertical banded gastroplasty |
| **Unknown Effectiveness** | • Sleeve gastrectomy |

**Search date September 2010**

---

**DEFINITION** Obesity is a chronic condition characterised by an excess of body fat. It is most often defined by the BMI, a mathematical formula that is highly correlated with body fat. BMI is weight in kilograms divided by height in metres squared ($kg/m^2$). Worldwide, adults with a BMI of 25 $kg/m^2$ to 30 $kg/m^2$ are categorised as overweight, and those with a BMI above 30 $kg/m^2$ are categorised as obese. Nearly 5 million US adults used prescription weight-loss medication between 1996 and 1998. One quarter of users were not overweight. Inappropriate use of prescription medication is more common among women, white people, and Hispanic people. The National Institutes of Health (NIH) in the US has issued guidelines for obesity treatment, which indicate that all obese adults (BMI >30 $kg/m^2$), and all adults with a BMI of 27 $kg/m^2$ or more and with obesity-associated chronic diseases are candidates for drug treatment. Morbidly obese adults (BMI >40 $kg/m^2$), and all adults with a BMI of 35 $kg/m^2$ or more and with obesity-associated chronic diseases are candidates for bariatric surgery.

**INCIDENCE/PREVALENCE** Obesity has increased steadily in many countries since 1900. In the UK in 2002, it was estimated that 23% of men and 25% of women were obese. In the past decade alone, the prevalence of obesity in the US has increased from 22.9% between 1988 and 1994, to 34% in 2006.

**AETIOLOGY/RISK FACTORS** Obesity is the result of long-term mismatches in energy balance, where daily energy intake exceeds daily energy expenditure. Energy balance is modulated by a myriad of factors, including metabolic rate, appetite, diet, and physical activity. Although these factors are influenced by genetic traits, the increase in obesity prevalence in the past few decades cannot be explained by changes in the human gene pool, and it is more often attributed to environmental changes that promote excessive food intake and discourage physical activity. Less commonly, obesity may also be induced by drugs (e.g., high-dose glucocorticoids, antipsychotics, antidepressants, oral hypoglycaemic agents, and antiepileptic drugs), or be secondary to various neuroendocrine disorders, such as Cushing's syndrome and PCOS.

**PROGNOSIS** Obesity is a risk factor for several chronic diseases, including hypertension, dyslipidaemia, diabetes, CVD, sleep apnoea, osteoarthritis, and some cancers. The relationship between increasing body weight and mortality is curvilinear, where mortality is

*(continued over)*

*(from previous page)*

highest among adults with very low body weight (BMI <18.5 kg/m$^2$) and among adults with the highest body weight (BMI >35 kg/m$^2$). Obese adults have more annual admissions to hospitals, more outpatient visits, higher prescription drug costs, and worse health-related quality of life than normal-weight adults. Fewer than 10% of overweight or obese adults aged 40 to 49 years revert to a normal body weight after 4 years.

Jennifer Arnold and Wilson Heriot

## KEY POINTS

- Sight-threatening (late) age-related macular degeneration (AMD) occurs in 2% of people aged over 50 years in industrialised countries, with prevalence increasing with age.

  Early-stage disease is marked by normal vision, but retinal changes (drusen and pigment changes). Disease progression leads to worsening central vision, but peripheral vision is preserved.

  85% of cases are atrophic (dry) AMD, but exudative (wet) AMD, marked by choroidal neovascularisation, leads to a more rapid loss of sight.

  The main risk factor is age. Hypertension, smoking, and a family history of AMD are also risk factors.

- High-dose antioxidant vitamin and zinc supplementation may reduce progression of moderate AMD, but there is no evidence of benefit in people with no, or mild AMD, or in those with established late AMD in both eyes.

- CAUTION: Beta-carotene, an antioxidant vitamin used in AMD, has been linked to an increased risk of lung cancer in people at high risk of this disease.

- Photodynamic treatment with verteporfin reduces the risk of developing moderate or severe loss of visual acuity and legal blindness in people with vision initially better than 20/100 or 20/200, compared with placebo.

  Photodynamic treatment is associated with an initial loss of vision and photosensitive reactions in a small proportion of people.

- Thermal laser photocoagulation can reduce severe visual loss in people with exudative AMD. It is frequently associated with an immediate and permanent reduction in visual acuity if the lesion involves the central macula, but it remains a proven effective treatment for extrafoveal choroidal neovascularisation.

  About half of people treated with thermal lasers show recurrent choroidal neovascularisation within 3 years.

  We don't know whether laser treatment of drusen prevents progression of disease, and it may increase short-term rates of choroidal neovascularisation.

- Antiangiogenesis treatment using vascular endothelial growth factor (VEGF) inhibitors such as ranibizumab or pegaptanib reduces the risk of moderate vision loss, and may improve vision at 12 and 24 months.

  Antiangiogenesis treatment using anecortave acetate may be as effective as photodynamic therapy in reducing vision loss.

- Studies investigating external beam radiotherapy have given contradictory results, and have failed to show an overall benefit in AMD.

- Subcutaneous interferon alfa-2a and submacular surgery have not been shown to improve vision, and are associated with potentially severe adverse effects.

- We found no RCT evidence on the effects of transpupillary thermotherapy.

(i) **Please visit http://clinicalevidence.bmj.com for full text and references**

| What are the effects of interventions to prevent progression of early- or late-stage AMD? | |
|---|---|
| **Likely To Be Beneficial** | • Antioxidant vitamin plus zinc supplementation |
| **Unknown Effectiveness** | • Laser to drusen |

## What are the effects of treatments for exudative AMD?

| | |
|---|---|
| **Beneficial** | • Antiangiogenesis treatment using pegaptanib (reduces moderate vision loss compared with placebo)<br><br>• Antiangiogenesis treatment using ranibizumab (reduces moderate vision loss and increases vision gain and visual acuity compared with placebo or photodynamic therapy)<br><br>• Photodynamic treatment with verteporfin |
| **Likely To Be Beneficial** | • Antiangiogenesis treatment using anecortave acetate |
| **Trade-off Between Benefits And Harms** | • Thermal laser photocoagulation |
| **Unknown Effectiveness** | • External beam radiation<br><br>• Transpupillary thermotherapy |
| **Likely To Be Ineffective Or Harmful** | • Antiangiogenesis treatment using interferon alfa-2a (subcutaneous)<br><br>• Submacular surgery |

**Search date March 2006**

**DEFINITION** Age-related macular degeneration (AMD) typically affects those aged 50 years and older. It has two clinical stages: **early AMD**, marked by drusen and pigmentary change, and usually associated with normal vision; and **late or sight-threatening AMD**, associated with a decrease in central vision. Late-stage AMD has two forms: **atrophic (or dry) AMD**, characterised by geographic atrophy; and **exudative (or wet) AMD**, characterised by choroidal neovascularisation (CNV), which eventually causes a disciform scar.

**INCIDENCE/PREVALENCE** AMD is a common cause of blindness registration in industrialised countries. Atrophic AMD is more common than the more sight-threatening exudative AMD, affecting about 85% of people with AMD. Late (sight-threatening) AMD is found in about 2% of all people aged over 50 years, and prevalence rises with age (0.7–1.4% of people aged 65–75 years; 11–19% of people above 85 years).

**AETIOLOGY/RISK FACTORS** Proposed hypotheses for the cause of atrophic and exudative AMD involve vascular factors and oxidative damage, coupled with genetic predisposition. Age is the strongest risk factor. Systemic risk factors include smoking, and a family history of AMD. Complement factor H (HF1), a major inhibitor of the alternative complement pathway, seems to play a major role in the pathogenesis of AMD blindness. Haplotype analysis reveals that multiple HF1 variants confer elevated or reduced risk of AMD (proportion of people with 1 at-risk haplotype: 50% of AMD cases $v$ 29% of controls; OR 2.46, 95% CI 1.95 to 3.11; proportion of people with homozygotes for this halotype: 24% of AMD cases $v$ 8% of controls; OR 3.51, 95% CI 2.13 to 5.78). These results are supported by other laboratories, and suggest that retinal and pigment epithelial destruction may be related to defective protection from immunological activity, rather than senescence or oxidative injury alone. However, the trigger for complement activation is unknown. A link between a genetic trait (Y402H variant of CFH) and a modifiable lifestyle risk — smoking — has been established by logistic regression modelling of gene–gene and gene–environment interactions in a case-controlled data set. The study authors estimated that CFH, LOC387715, and cigarette smoking together explain 61% of the patient-attributable risk of AMD, with adjusted percentage estimates of 20% for smoking, 36% for LOC387715, and 43% for CFH. Ocular risk factors for the development of exudative AMD include the presence of soft drusen, macular pigmentary change, CNV in the other eye, and previous cataract surgery. Hypertension, diet (especially intake of antioxidant micronutrients), and oestrogen are suspected as causal agents for atrophic and exudative AMD, but the effects of these factors remain unproved.

**PROGNOSIS** AMD impairs central vision, which is required for reading, driving, face recognition, and all fine visual tasks. **Atrophic AMD** progresses slowly over many years, and time to legal blindness is highly variable (usually about 5–10 years). **Exudative AMD** is more often threatening to vision; 90% of people with serious visual loss caused by AMD have the exudative type. This condition usually manifests with a sudden worsening and distortion of central vision. One study estimated (based on data derived primarily from cohort studies) that the risk of developing exudative AMD in people with bilateral soft drusen was 1–5% at 1 year and 13–18% at 3 years. The observed 5-year rate in a population survey was 7%. Most eyes (estimates vary from 60% to 90%) with exudative AMD progress to legal blindness and develop a central defect (scotoma) in the visual field. Peripheral vision is preserved, allowing the person to be mobile and independent. The ability to read with visual aids depends on the size and density of the central scotoma, and the degree to which the person retains sensitivity to contrast. Once exudative AMD has developed in one eye, the other eye is at high risk (cumulative estimated incidence: 10% at 1 year, 28% at 3 years, and 42% at 5 years).

Stephanie West and Cathy Williams

## KEY POINTS

- Amblyopia is reduced visual acuity not immediately correctable by glasses, in the absence of ocular pathology.

  It is commonly associated with squint (strabismic amblyopia), refractive errors resulting in different visual inputs to each eye during the sensitive period of visual development (refractive amblyopia), or with cataract or ptosis (stimulus deprivation amblyopia).

  The cumulative incidence is estimated at 2% to 4% in children aged up to 15 years.

- Vision screening before school entry may increase detection rates of amblyopia. However, preschool screening may not improve treatment outcomes at 7 years compared with school-entry screening.

  We don't know whether children with a higher risk of eye problems should be targeted for vision screening.

- Most evidence is available for children aged <7 years, in whom wearing glasses for up to 30 weeks can improve amblyopia and may cure it. Children with suspected amblyopia who have clinically important refractive error are prescribed glasses; therefore, most data available on other interventions assess their effectiveness in combination with glasses.

- Occlusion (covering the fellow eye using a patch) may be more effective than glasses alone in children up to 13 years of age not fully treated with glasses. Further data assessing occlusion in combination with near-vision tasks, such as encouraging the child to do close work while wearing their patch, confirm that combined interventions are more effective than glasses alone in younger children.

  Some older children might improve with treatment, although there are few data available to support this.

  We don't know whether prescribing occlusion of the fellow eye for longer periods every day is more effective than prescribing for shorter periods of daily occlusion, but success rates do increase in proportion to objectively measured compliance.

  Penalisation with atropine may be as effective as occlusion when given in combination with other interventions for improving amblyopia in children aged <7 years who are not fully treated with glasses.

  We don't know whether near-vision tasks are effective alone as adjuvant treatment to glasses for amblyopia. Near-vision tasks may further enhance visual acuity when added to occlusion or penalisation, but the contribution of near-vision tasks to the effects of these combination interventions remains unclear.

 **Please visit http://clinicalevidence.bmj.com for full text and references**

| What are the effects of interventions to detect amblyopia early? | |
|---|---|
| Likely To Be Beneficial | • Screening versus usual care |
| Unknown Effectiveness | • Targeted vision screening versus mass screening |

| What are the effects of medical treatments for amblyopia? | |
|---|---|
| Beneficial | • Occlusion (patching) alone or in combination with near-vision tasks in younger children wearing glasses (more effective than glasses alone) |
| Likely To Be Beneficial | • Glasses*<br><br>• Penalisation (may be as effective as occlusion when given as part of combination treatment in children not fully treated by glasses) |
| Unknown Effectiveness | • Near-vision tasks alone |

**Search date May 2010**

*Categorisation based on consensus. Limited RCT evidence available.

**DEFINITION** Amblyopia is reduced visual acuity not immediately correctable by glasses, in the absence of ocular pathology. It is associated with complete or partial lack of clear visual input to one eye (stimulus deprivation amblyopia or unilateral/anisometropic refractive amblyopia), or, less often, to both eyes (bilateral refractive amblyopia), or to conflicting visual inputs to the two eyes (strabismic amblyopia). The severity of amblyopia is often classified according to the visual acuity in the affected eye, using visual acuity testing. 'Mild' amblyopia is often classified as being visual acuity of 6/9 to 6/12, 'moderate' amblyopia as being worse than 6/12 to 6/36, and 'severe' amblyopia as being worse than 6/36. Different studies use different definitions of severity, but most assume normal vision (6/6 or better) in the fellow eye. One line of letters or symbols (usually 4 or 5) in a visual acuity chart constitutes 0.1 logMAR units. A change in 0.2 logMAR units is often quoted as being the smallest clinically important change in visual acuity, although some studies use a change of 0.1 logMAR units or greater, which might be considered clinically marginal. **Diagnosis:** Amblyopia is diagnosed by testing visual acuity in each eye separately, with the person wearing an adequate refractive correction, and after exclusion of ocular pathology. Amblyopia is defined in terms of visual acuity, but other visual functions are affected as well.

**INCIDENCE/PREVALENCE** It is estimated that the cumulative incidence is 2% to 4% in children up to 15 years of age. The population prevalence is affected by whether there have been any interventions to prevent or treat the condition.

**AETIOLOGY/RISK FACTORS** Amblyopia is associated with degraded visual input, either caused by high refractive error (unilateral refractive amblyopia, also known as ametropic amblyopia), by different refractive errors in each eye (anisometropic amblyopia), or by conflicting visual inputs between the eyes because of squint (strabismic amblyopia). Amblyopia can also be associated with an obstruction to the visual axis — for example, by ptosis or cataract (known as stimulus deprivation amblyopia). In a multicentre RCT of 409 children aged 3 to 6 years treated for amblyopia, 38% were strabismic, 37% were anisometropic, and 24% were both strabismic and anisometropic. Whereas strabismus and anisometropia are common causes of amblyopia, less-common causes include ptosis, congenital cataract, and corneal injury or dystrophy, accounting for only up to 3% of cases.

**PROGNOSIS** Amblyopia is commonly regarded as untreatable after 7 to 8 years of age, although there is some evidence that treatment can be effective in children aged 7 to 12 years. Recovery of normal vision becomes progressively less likely in older children. Successfully treated amblyopia might regress in about one quarter of children. The lifetime risk of blindness because of loss of the better-seeing eye is 1.2% (95% CI 1.1% to 1.4%). If the better-seeing eye is lost, the visual acuity of 10% of amblyopic eyes can improve.

John Epling

## KEY POINTS

- Conjunctivitis causes irritation, itching, foreign body sensation, and watering or discharge of the eye.

    Most cases in adults are probably due to viral infection, but children are more likely to develop bacterial conjunctivitis than viral forms. The main bacterial pathogens are *Staphylococcus* species in adults, and *Haemophilus influenzae*, *Streptococcus pneumoniae*, and *Moraxella catarrhalis* in children.

    A bacterial cause is more likely if there is gluing of the eyelids and no itch.

    Contact lens wearers may be more likely to develop gram-negative infections. Bacterial keratitis occurs in up to 30 per 100,000 contact lens wearers.

    Gonococcal ophthalmia neonatorum can occur in up to 10% of infants exposed to gonorrhoeal exudate during delivery despite prophylaxis, and can be associated with bacteraemia and meningitis.

    Otitis media can occur in 25% of children with *H influenzae* conjunctivitis, and meningitis can develop in 18% of people with meningococcal conjunctivitis.

- Conjunctivitis resolves spontaneously within 2 to 5 days in more than half of people without treatment, but infectious complications can occur rarely.

- Topical antibiotics may speed up clinical and microbiological cure of bacterial conjunctivitis, but the benefit is small.

    In people with suspected, but not confirmed, bacterial conjunctivitis, empirical treatment with topical antibiotics may be beneficial. However, this benefit is marginal, so it is advisable to suggest that patients take antibiotics only if symptoms do not resolve after 1 to 2 days.

    Clinical and microbiological cure rates are increased in the first week in people with culture-positive bacterial conjunctivitis, but there is no good evidence of a longer-term benefit from topical antibiotics.

    Adverse effects of topical antibiotics are mild, but their effect on bacterial resistance is unknown.

- Parenteral antibiotics may cure gonococcal ophthalmia neonatorum, although we don't know whether they are beneficial in children in developed countries, as we only found studies from Africa. Neonates will usually require investigation for concomitant infections and complications.

    We don't know whether ocular decongestants, saline, or warm compresses are beneficial in people with suspected or confirmed bacterial or gonococcal conjunctivitis.

 **Please visit http://clinicalevidence.bmj.com for full text and references**

| What are the effects of empirical treatment in adults and children with suspected bacterial conjunctivitis? | |
|---|---|
| Likely To Be Beneficial | • Empirical treatment with topical antibiotics in people with suspected bacterial conjunctivitis (given to patient with advice to use after 1–2 days if symptoms do not resolve) |
| Unknown Effectiveness | • Empirical treatment with ocular decongestants in people with suspected bacterial conjunctivitis<br><br>• Empirical treatment with oral antibiotics in people with suspected bacterial conjunctivitis |

- Empirical treatment with saline in people with suspected bacterial conjunctivitis

- Empirical treatment with warm compresses in people with suspected bacterial conjunctivitis

## What are the effects of treatment in adults and children with bacteriologically confirmed bacterial conjunctivitis?

| Beneficial | • Antibiotics (topical) in people with culture-positive non-gonococcal bacterial conjunctivitis |
|---|---|
| Unknown Effectiveness | • Ocular decongestants in people with confirmed bacterial conjunctivitis<br><br>• Saline in people with confirmed bacterial conjunctivitis<br><br>• Warm compresses in people with confirmed bacterial conjunctivitis |

## What are the effects of treatment in adults and children with clinically confirmed gonococcal conjunctivitis?

| Likely To Be Beneficial | • Antibiotics (parenteral alone or combined with topical) in people with suspected or confirmed gonococcal conjunctivitis* |
|---|---|
| Unknown Effectiveness | • Antibiotics (oral) in people with suspected or confirmed gonococcal conjunctivitis<br><br>• Ocular decongestants in people with suspected or confirmed gonococcal conjunctivitis<br><br>• Saline in people with suspected or confirmed gonococcal conjunctivitis<br><br>• Warm compresses in people with suspected or confirmed gonococcal conjunctivitis |

**Search date July 2011**

*Categorisation based on consensus.

**DEFINITION** Conjunctivitis is any inflammation of the conjunctiva, generally characterised by irritation, itching, foreign body sensation, and watering or discharge. Treatment is often based on clinical suspicion that the conjunctivitis is bacterial, without waiting for the results of microbiological tests. In this review, therefore, we have distinguished the effects of empirical treatment from effects of treatment in people with culture-positive bacterial conjunctivitis. Bacterial conjunctivitis in contact lens wearers is of particular concern because of the risk of bacterial keratitis — an infection of the cornea accompanying acute or subacute corneal trauma, which is more difficult to treat than conjunctivitis and can threaten vision. Conjunctivitis caused by *Neisseria gonorrhoeae* — referred to as ophthalmia neonatorum — is primarily a disease of neonates, caused by exposure of the neonatal conjunctivae to the cervicovaginal exudate of infected women during delivery. **Diagnosis:** The traditional criteria differentiating bacterial from other types of conjunctivitis have been: a yellow-white mucopurulent discharge; a papillary reaction (small bumps with fibrovascular cores on the palpebral conjunctiva, appearing grossly as a fine velvety surface); and bilateral

*(continued over)*

*(from previous page)*

infection. One systematic review was unable to find any quality research basis for these criteria, but a follow-up study performed by the authors of the review found that glued eyes and the absence of itching were predictive of a bacterial cause. A history of recent conjunctivitis argued against a bacterial cause. If eye pain is moderate or severe and visual acuity is reduced, more serious causes need to be considered. Gonococcal ophthalmia neonatorum is diagnosed by a persistent and increasingly purulent conjunctivitis in exposed infants, beginning from 3 to 21 days after delivery.

**INCIDENCE/PREVALENCE** We found no good evidence on the incidence or prevalence of bacterial conjunctivitis. Bacterial keratitis is estimated to occur in 10 to 30 per 100,000 contact lens wearers. Gonococcal ophthalmia neonatorum occurs at rates of 0% to 10% in infants who received antibiotic prophylaxis after delivery to mothers with gonorrhoea infection, and in 2% to 48% of exposed infants without prophylaxis.

**AETIOLOGY/RISK FACTORS** Conjunctivitis may be infectious (causes include bacteria and viruses) or allergic. In adults, bacterial conjunctivitis is less common than viral conjunctivitis, although estimates vary widely (viral conjunctivitis has been reported to account for 8% to 75% of acute conjunctivitis). *Staphylococcus* species are the most common pathogens for bacterial conjunctivitis in adults, followed by *Streptococcus pneumoniae* and *Haemophilus influenzae*. In children, bacterial conjunctivitis is more common than the viral form, and is mainly caused by *H influenzae*, *S pneumoniae*, and *Moraxella catarrhalis*. One prospective study (428 children from southern Israel with a clinical diagnosis of conjunctivitis) found that in 55% of the children, conjunctivitis was caused by *S pneumoniae*, *H influenzae*, or *M catarrhalis*. Narrative reviews suggest that the causative agents of bacterial conjunctivitis and keratitis in contact lens wearers are more frequently gram-negative bacteria (such as *Pseudomonas aeruginosa*), but may include all of the above agents. *Acanthamoeba* spp. infections can be particularly difficult to diagnose and treat, and are most common in contact lens wearers.

**PROGNOSIS** Most bacterial conjunctivitis is self-limiting. One systematic review (search date 2004) found clinical cure or significant improvement with placebo within 2 to 5 days in 65% of people. Some organisms cause corneal or systemic complications, or both. Otitis media may develop in 25% of children with *H influenzae* conjunctivitis, and systemic meningitis may complicate primary meningococcal conjunctivitis in 18% of people. Untreated gonococcal ophthalmia neonatorum can cause corneal ulceration, perforation of the globe, and panophthalmitis. Investigations to detect concomitant infections, as well as gonococcal bacteraemia and meningitis, and admission to hospital for parenteral treatment of the eye infection, are frequently required.

David Allen

## KEY POINTS

- Cataracts are cloudy or opaque areas in the lens of the eye that can impair vision. Age-related cataracts are defined as those occurring in people >50 years of age, in the absence of known mechanical, chemical, or radiation trauma.

  Cataract accounts for over 47% of blindness worldwide, causing blindness in about 17.3 million people in 1990.

  Surgery for cataract in people with glaucoma may affect glaucoma control.

  There is contradictory evidence about the effect of cataract surgery on the development or progression of age-related macular degeneration (ARMD).

- Expedited phaco extracapsular extraction may be more effective at improving visual acuity compared with waiting list control in people with cataract without ocular comorbidities.

  When combined with foldable posterior chamber intraocular lens implant (IOL), phaco extracapsular extraction seems more effective than manual large-incision extracapsular extraction at improving vision, and has fewer complications.

  This procedure has largely superseded manual large-incision extracapsular cataract extraction in developed countries.

- Manual large-incision extracapsular extraction has also been shown to be successful in treating cataracts.

  Combined with IOL, manual large-incision extracapsular extraction is significantly better at improving vision compared with intracapsular extraction plus aphakic glasses.

  Small-incision manual extracapsular extraction (manual SICS) techniques and phaco extracapsular extraction techniques are similarly beneficial at improving visual acuity for advanced cataracts at 6 months, with few complications.

  This finding may be particularly relevant to treatment in developing countries.

- Intracapsular extraction is likely to be better at improving vision compared with no extraction, although it is not as beneficial as manual (large or small) incision extracapsular extraction.

  The rate of complications is also higher with this technique compared with extracapsular extraction.

- In people with glaucoma and cataract, concomitant cataract surgery (phaco or manual large-incision extracapsular extraction) and glaucoma surgery seems more beneficial than cataract surgery alone, in that they both improve vision to a similar extent, but the glaucoma surgery additionally improves intraocular pressure.

  We found no trials comparing different types of cataract surgery in people with glaucoma.

- In people with diabetic retinopathy and cataract, phaco extracapsular extraction may improve visual acuity and reduce postoperative inflammation compared with manual large-incision extraction.

  Performing procedures in the order of cataract surgery first followed by pan retinal photocoagulation may be more effective than the opposite order at improving visual acuity and reducing the progression of diabetic macular oedema in people with cataract and diabetic retinopathy secondary to type 2 diabetes. However, these results come from one small RCT.

- One of the possible harms of cataract surgery is cystoid macular oedema, which people with uveitis also frequently suffer from.

We found no trials comparing different types of cataract surgery in people with chronic uveitis.

We don't know whether intravitreal triamcinolone acetonide is more effective than orbital floor injection of triamcinolone acetonide in improving outcomes after cataract surgery in people with chronic uveitis as we found few trials.

(i) **Please visit http://clinicalevidence.bmj.com for full text and references**

## What are the effects of surgery for age-related cataract without other ocular comorbidity?

| | |
|---|---|
| Beneficial | • Manual large- or small-excision extracapsular extraction (manual large-excision extracapsular extraction more effective than intracapsular extraction, but less effective than phaco extracapsular extraction; unclear how manual small-excision [SICS] compares with phaco extracapsular extraction)<br><br>• Phaco extracapsular extraction (improved visual acuity with fewer complications than manual large-incision extracapsular extraction; unclear how it compares with manual small-incision extracapsular extraction [manual SICS]) |
| Likely To Be Beneficial | • Intracapsular extraction (more effective than no extraction;* less effective than manual large-incision extracapsular extraction and has more complications) |

## What are the effects of treatment for age-related cataract in people with glaucoma?

| | |
|---|---|
| Likely To Be Beneficial | • Concomitant cataract plus concomitant glaucoma surgery (reduced intraocular pressure compared with cataract surgery alone) |
| Unknown Effectiveness | • Cataract surgery alone<br><br>• Cataract surgery plus non-concomitant glaucoma surgery |

## What are the effects of surgical treatments for age-related cataract in people with diabetic retinopathy?

| | |
|---|---|
| Likely To Be Beneficial | • Cataract surgery in people with diabetic retinopathy |
| Unknown Effectiveness | • Adding diabetic retinopathy treatment to cataract surgery |

## What are the effects of surgical treatments for age-related cataract in people with chronic uveitis?

| Unknown Effectiveness | • Cataract surgery (phaco or manual extracapsular extraction) in people with chronic uveitis |
|---|---|
| | • Different methods of medical control of uveitis at the time of cataract surgery |

**Search date May 2010**

*Based on consensus.

**DEFINITION** **Cataracts** are cloudy or opaque areas in the lens of the eye (which should usually be completely clear). This results in changes that can impair vision. **Age-related (or senile) cataract** is defined as cataract occurring in people >50 years of age, in the absence of known mechanical, chemical, or radiation trauma. This review covers treatment for age-related cataract in 4 different populations: people without ocular comorbidity, people with glaucoma, people with diabetic retinopathy, and people with chronic uveitis. Surgery for cataracts in people with glaucoma may affect glaucoma control and, in people with diabetic retinopathy, visual acuity after surgery for cataracts may be lower; the optimal strategy for treating these conditions when they co-exist is not clear. See also reviews on glaucoma, p 225, diabetic retinopathy, p 222, and uveitis, p 236.

**INCIDENCE/PREVALENCE** Cataract accounts for over 47% of blindness worldwide, causing blindness in about 17.3 million people in 1990. A cross-sectional study in a representative sample of an urban population in New South Wales, Australia, in 1997 (3654 people aged 49–96 years) found that the prevalence of late cataract (of all types) in people aged 65 to 74 years was 21.6%, and in people aged 85 years and older it was 67.3%. This rate excluded those people who had already had cataract surgery. The incidence of non age-related cataract within this population is so small that this can be taken as the effective incidence of age-related cataract. Glaucoma has an overall prevalence of about 2.0% rising to about 4.5% in people aged 70 years and older (the peak age for cataract surgery). In 2006, the 5-year incidence of nuclear cataract with open-angle glaucoma in people aged >50 years was estimated to be 25%.

**AETIOLOGY/RISK FACTORS** Diet, smoking, and exposure to ultraviolet light are thought to be risk factors in the development of age-related cataract. In addition, some people may have a genetic predisposition to development of age-related cataract. Oxidative stress is also thought to be a factor in cataract development, although the impact of dietary anti-oxidants on cataract development remains uncertain.

**PROGNOSIS** Age-related cataract progresses with age, but at an unpredictable rate. Cataract surgery is indicated when the chances of significant visual improvement outweigh the risks of a poor surgical outcome. It is not dependent on reaching a specific visual-acuity standard. Cataract surgery may also be indicated where the presence of cataract makes it hard to treat or monitor concurrent retinal disease, such as diabetic retinopathy.

Quresh A Mohamed, Adam Ross, and Colin J Chu

## KEY POINTS

- Diabetic retinopathy is the most common cause of blindness in the UK, with older people and those with worse diabetes control, hypertension, and hyperlipidaemia most at risk.

  Diabetic retinopathy can cause microaneurysms, haemorrhages, exudates, changes to blood vessels, and retinal thickening.

- Peripheral retinal laser photocoagulation reduces the risk of severe visual loss compared with no treatment in people with preproliferative (moderate/ severe non-proliferative) retinopathy and maculopathy.

  We don't know if any one type of laser treatment is superior to another.

  We don't know whether peripheral laser photocoagulation is effective in people with background or preproliferative (non-proliferative) retinopathy without maculopathy because we found no RCTs assessing it in this population.

- The benefits of laser photocoagulation are more notable in people with proliferative retinopathy than in those with maculopathy.

  Focal macular laser photocoagulation reduces the risk of moderate visual loss in eyes with clinically significant macular oedema plus mild to moderate preproliferative (moderate/severe non-proliferative) diabetic retinopathy, compared with no treatment.

  Grid photocoagulation to zones of retinal thickening may improve visual acuity in eyes with diffuse maculopathy.

  Photocoagulation is unlikely to be beneficial in eyes with maculopathy but without clinically significant macular oedema.

- Intravitreal triamcinolone acetonide improves visual acuity and reduces macular thickness in eyes with macular oedema refractory to previous macular laser photocoagulation, but repeated injections are needed to maintain benefit.

  Secondary ocular hypertension and progression of cataract are common complications with intravitreal triamcinolone; infectious endophthalmitis is rare.

- Intravitreal vascular endothelial growth factor (VEGF) inhibitors pegaptanib and bevacizumab improve visual acuity and reduce macular thickness in eyes with centre-involving diabetic macular oedema and vision loss, but repeat intravitreal injections are needed to maintain benefit.

  Bevacizumab is not licensed for intraocular use.

  We don't know the long-term ocular and systemic safety of bevacizumab.

  We don't know if any one intravitreal VEGF inhibitor or treatment regimen is superior to another.

  We don't know whether combination treatment with VEGF inhibitor injection plus macular laser photocoagulation is effective as we found only one trial assessing ranibizumab as part of combined treatment.

- Vitrectomy can reduce visual loss if performed early in people with vitreous haemorrhage, especially if they have severe proliferative retinopathy.

  We don't know whether vitrectomy is effective in people with vitreous haemorrhage plus maculopathy as we found no RCTs assessing it.

 **Please visit http://clinicalevidence.bmj.com for full text and references**

## What are the effects of laser treatments in people with diabetic retinopathy?

| Beneficial | • Focal macular photocoagulation in people with clinically significant macular oedema |
|---|---|

| | • Peripheral retinal laser photocoagulation in people with proliferative retinopathy |
|---|---|
| **Likely To Be Beneficial** | • Grid photocoagulation to zones of retinal thickening in people with diffuse maculopathy |
| | • Peripheral retinal laser photocoagulation in people with preproliferative (moderate/severe non-proliferative) retinopathy and maculopathy |
| **Unknown Effectiveness** | • Peripheral retinal laser photocoagulation in people with background or preproliferative (non-proliferative) retinopathy without maculopathy |
| **Unlikely To Be Beneficial** | • Focal macular photocoagulation in people with maculopathy but without clinically significant macular oedema |

## What are the effects of drug treatments for diabetic retinopathy?

| **Likely To Be Beneficial** | • Corticosteroids (intravitreal) |
|---|---|
| | • Vascular endothelial growth factor inhibitors (injection) |

## What are the effects of treatments for vitreous haemorrhage?

| **Beneficial** | • Vitrectomy in people with severe vitreous haemorrhage and proliferative retinopathy (if performed early) |
|---|---|
| **Unknown Effectiveness** | • Vitrectomy in people with vitreous haemorrhage and maculopathy |

**Search date June 2010**

---

**DEFINITION** Diabetes is a major health problem estimated to affect 285 million people or 6.4% of the world's population as of 2010 (International Diabetes Federation atlas) and 2.6 million people or 4.9% of the population in the UK. This is expected to rise to 438 million people or 7.8% of the world's population by 2030. Diabetic retinopathy — a specific microvascular complication of diabetes — is the most common cause of blindness in working-age adults. Almost half of those with diabetes will have some degree of retinopathy at any given time. Diabetic retinopathy can be classified into non-proliferative (NPDR) and proliferative diabetic retinopathy (PDR). The earliest visible signs in NPDR are microaneurysms and retinal haemorrhages. With increasing ischaemia, cotton wool spots, venous beading, and intraretinal microvascular abnormalities develop (moderate/severe NPDR). Vision loss is primarily from the development of abnormal new retinal vessels (PDR), which can lead to haemorrhage, fibrosis, traction, and retinal detachment. Diabetic macular oedema, which can occur at any stage of diabetic retinopathy, is characterised by increased vascular permeability, central retinal thickening, and the deposition of hard exudates. When this is present close to or at the central macula, it is termed clinically significant macular oedema. Diabetic macular oedema is now the principal cause of vision loss in people with diabetes.

*(continued over)*

---

*(from previous page)*

**INCIDENCE/PREVALENCE** Diabetic eye disease is the most common cause of blindness in the UK, responsible for 12% of registrable blindness in people aged 16 to 64 years.

**AETIOLOGY/RISK FACTORS** Duration of diabetes is the strongest factor influencing the development of retinopathy. There are a number of modifiable systemic risk factors strongly associated with retinopathy, including glycaemic control; evidence from several well-conducted RCTs and observational studies show that tight glycaemic control reduces the incidence and progression of retinopathy. For type 1 diabetes, the Diabetes Control and Complications Trial (DCCT) showed that each 1% decrease in HbA1c (e.g., 9% to 8%) reduces the risk of retinopathy by 39%, and this beneficial effect persists long after the period of intensive control. In type 2 diabetes, the UK Prospective Diabetes Study (UKPDS) showed that each 10% decrease in HbA1c reduces the risk of microvascular events, including retinopathy, by 25%. There is also strong evidence that tight control of blood pressure in patients with diabetes who have hypertension is beneficial in reducing visual loss from diabetic retinopathy. The UKPDS showed that each 10 mmHg decrease in systolic blood pressure reduces the risk of microvascular complications by 13%, independent of glycaemic control. The benefit of blood pressure treatment in normotensive diabetic patients is less clear. There is emerging evidence that normalising blood lipid levels may reduce the risk of retinopathy. The ACCORD Eye study showed that combination lipid therapy with fenofibrate and simvastatin reduced the progression of retinopathy by about one third, from 10.2% to 6.5% over 4 years, compared with simvastatin treatment alone. Diabetic retinopathy needs a combined multidisciplinary approach with individualised treatment to optimise glycaemic control, blood pressure, and serum cholesterol and triglyceride levels. Other risk factors include pregnancy, renal impairment, race, and genetic influences.

**PROGNOSIS** Natural history studies from the 1960s found that at least half of people with proliferative diabetic retinopathy progressed to Snellen visual acuity of less than 6/60 (20/200) within 3 to 5 years. After 4 years' follow-up, the rate of progression to less than 6/60 (20/200) visual acuity in the better eye was 1.5% in people with type 1 diabetes, 2.7% in people with non-insulin-dependent type 2 diabetes, and 3.2% in people with insulin-dependent type 2 diabetes.

Rajiv Shah and Richard P L Wormald

## KEY POINTS

- Glaucoma is characterised by progressive optic neuropathy and peripheral visual field loss. It affects 1% to 2% of white people aged over 40 years and accounts for 8% of new blind registrations in the UK.

  The main risk factor for glaucoma is raised intraocular pressure (IOP), but up to 40% of people with glaucoma have normal IOP and only about 10% of people with raised IOP are at risk of optic-nerve damage.

  Glaucoma is more prevalent, presents earlier, and is more difficult to control in black people (especially those of West African descent) than in white populations.

  Blindness from glaucoma results from gross loss of visual field or loss of central vision and, when the optic nerve is vulnerable, can progress quickly without treatment.

- Lowering IOP by laser trabeculoplasty plus topical medical treatment may be more effective at reducing progression of glaucoma in people with primary open-angle or pseudoexfoliation glaucoma, compared with no treatment.

- Topical medical treatment may reduce the risk of developing glaucoma in people with ocular hypertension, compared with placebo.

- We don't know whether topical medical treatment, laser trabeculoplasty, or surgical trabeculectomy is more effective at maintaining visual fields and acuity in primary open-angle glaucoma. Surgery may increase the risk of developing cataracts.

- We don't know whether reducing IOP with medical treatment alone or in combination with other treatments including surgery is more effective than no treatment at reducing progression of visual field loss in people with normal-tension glaucoma.

- There is a consensus that medical and surgical treatments are beneficial in people with acute angle-closure glaucoma, although we don't know this for sure because it is unethical to withhold pressure-lowering treatment.

- The consensus about how laser treatments compare with medical or surgical treatments in people with acute angle-closure glaucoma is currently uncertain, and more high-quality evidence is needed.

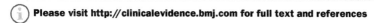 Please visit http://clinicalevidence.bmj.com for full text and references

| What are the effects of treatments for established primary open-angle glaucoma, ocular hypertension, or both? | |
|---|---|
| Likely To Be Beneficial | • Laser trabeculoplasty plus topical medical treatment (more effective than no initial treatment at reducing progression of glaucoma; in people with primary open-angle glaucoma)<br><br>• Topical medical treatment (in people with primary open-angle glaucoma, ocular hypertension, or both) |
| Trade-off Between Benefits And Harms | • Surgical trabeculectomy (in people with primary open-angle glaucoma, ocular hypertension, or both) |
| Unknown Effectiveness | • Laser trabeculoplasty in people with primary open-angle glaucoma (currently uncertain compared with surgical trabeculectomy or topical medical treatments) |

## What are the effects of lowering intraocular pressure in people with normal-tension glaucoma?

| Unknown Effectiveness | • Medical treatment in people with normal-tension glaucoma (currently uncertain as insufficient data of adequate quality)<br><br>• Surgical treatment in people with normal-tension glaucoma (currently uncertain as insufficient data of adequate quality) |
| --- | --- |

## What are the effects of treatment for acute angle-closure glaucoma?

| Likely To Be Beneficial | • Medical treatment* (any route; in acute angle-closure glaucoma)<br><br>• Surgical treatment* (any type; in acute angle-closure glaucoma) |
| --- | --- |
| Unknown Effectiveness | • Laser treatment (iridotomy or iridoplasty; currently uncertain compared with surgical or medical treatments) |

**Search date May 2010**

*No placebo-controlled RCTs, but a strong consensus that treatments are effective.

**DEFINITION** Glaucoma is a group of diseases characterised by progressive optic neuropathy. It is usually bilateral but asymmetrical, and may occur at any intraocular pressure (IOP). All forms of glaucoma show optic-nerve damage (cupping, pallor, or both) associated with peripheral visual field loss. **Primary open-angle glaucoma** occurs in people with an open anterior chamber drainage angle and no secondary identifiable cause. Knowledge of the natural history of these conditions is incomplete, but it is thought that the problem starts with an IOP that is too high for the optic nerve. However, in a large proportion of people with glaucoma (about 40% at first testing) IOP is within the statistically defined normal range. The term **normal-tension glaucoma** is often used to describe this condition. It exhibits the same clinical picture as primary open-angle glaucoma with some additional risk factors. The division between the two conditions is an artificial one based on IOP, but they are really two diseases at different ends of a spectrum. The term 'ocular hypertension' (OHT) generally applies to eyes with an IOP greater than the statistical upper limit of normal (about 21 mmHg). A thicker cornea leads to an overestimate of the IOP. Conversely, a thinner cornea may lead to underestimation of IOP and may be a risk factor for progression from OHT to glaucoma. Only a relatively small proportion of eyes with raised IOP have an optic nerve that is vulnerable to its effects (about 10%). Previously, trialists were anxious about withholding active treatment in overt primary open-angle glaucoma, and so several placebo or no-treatment trials selected people just with OHT. Trials comparing treatments often include both people with primary open-angle glaucoma and people with OHT, but in these the outcome is usually IOP alone. **Acute angle-closure glaucoma** is glaucoma resulting from a rapid and severe rise in IOP caused by physical obstruction of the anterior chamber drainage angle. Subacute and chronic angle-closure glaucoma also occur, but are not considered in this review.

**INCIDENCE/PREVALENCE** Glaucoma occurs in 1% to 2% of white people aged over 40 years, rising to 5% at 70 years. Primary open-angle glaucoma accounts for two-thirds of those affected, and normal-tension glaucoma for about one quarter. Glaucoma is more prevalent, presents at a younger age with higher IOPs, is more difficult to control, and is the main irreversible cause of blindness in black populations, especially those of West African origin. Glaucoma-related blindness is responsible for 8% of new blind registrations in the UK.

Angle-closure glaucoma occurs at about one tenth of the frequency of open-angle glaucoma in white Europeans but is more common in Chinese people and Native American people — especially the Inuit.

**AETIOLOGY/RISK FACTORS** The major risk factor for developing primary open-angle glaucoma is raised IOP. In one RCT (90 people with IOP >22 mmHg, another glaucoma risk factor, and normal visual fields; mean age 55–56 years), three baseline risk factors were identified to be independently associated with glaucomatous field loss. These were higher IOP ($P = 0.047$; IOP per mmHg), suspect discs ($P = 0.007$), and older age ($P = 0.034$; age per year). Lesser risk factors include family history and ethnic origin. The relationship between systemic blood pressure and IOP may be an important determinant of blood flow to the optic-nerve head and, as a consequence, may represent a risk factor for glaucoma. Systemic hypotension, vasospasm (including Raynaud's disease and migraine), and a history of major blood loss have been reported as risk factors for normal-tension glaucoma in hospital-based studies. Risk factors for acute angle-closure glaucoma include family history, female sex, being long-sighted, and cataracts. One systematic review (search date 1999, 6 observational studies, 594,662 people with mydriasis) found no evidence supporting the theory that routine pupillary dilatation with short-acting mydriatics was a risk factor for acute angle-closure glaucoma.

**PROGNOSIS** Advanced visual field loss is found in about 20% of people with primary open-angle glaucoma at diagnosis and is an important prognostic factor for glaucoma-related blindness. Blindness from glaucoma is caused initially by loss of the peripheral visual field and ultimately by loss of central vision. Once early field defects have appeared, and where the IOP is greater than 30 mmHg, untreated people may lose the remainder of the visual field in 3 years or less. As the disease progresses, people with glaucoma have difficulty moving from a bright room to a darker room, and judging steps and kerbs. Progression of visual field loss is often slower in normal-tension glaucoma. Acute angle glaucoma leads to rapid loss of vision, initially from corneal oedema and subsequently from ischaemic optic neuropathy. Once optic-nerve damage has occurred, it cannot be repaired.

Nigel H Barker

## KEY POINTS

- Ocular infection with HSV can cause inflammation of the eyelids, conjunctivae, iris, retina, and cornea.

  Infection is common and usually acquired early in life, with 50% of people from higher and 80% from lower socioeconomic groups in the USA having antibodies by the age of 30 years.

  HSV epithelial keratitis tends to resolve spontaneously within 1–2 weeks, while stromal keratitis is more likely to result in corneal scarring and loss of vision. Stromal keratitis or iritis occurs in about 25% of people after epithelial keratitis.

  Recurrence of ocular herpes (epithelial or stromal) for people with one episode is 10% at 1 year, 23% at 2 years, and 50% at 10 years.

- Topical antiviral agents and topical interferons increase healing of epithelial keratitis compared with placebo.

  Physicochemical debridement or interferon may speed up healing if added to antiviral agents, but we don't know whether debridement is effective when used alone.

- When added to topical antiviral agents, topical corticosteroids reduce progression and shorten the duration of stromal keratitis compared with placebo.

  Adding oral aciclovir to topical corticosteroids plus topical antiviral treatment may not increase healing compared with topical treatment alone.

- Long-term oral aciclovir treatment in people with previous ocular epithelial or stromal keratitis reduces recurrence after 1 year compared with placebo.

  Short-term prophylaxis (for 3 weeks) with oral aciclovir does not seem to reduce the risk of recurrence.

- We don't know whether oral aciclovir reduces recurrence of ocular herpes simplex infection after corneal grafts.

(i) **Please visit http://clinicalevidence.bmj.com for full text and references**

| What are the effects of treatments in people with epithelial keratitis? | |
|---|---|
| **Beneficial** | • Antiviral agents (topical) |
| | • Interferons (topical) |
| **Unknown Effectiveness** | • Debridement |

| What are the effects of treatments in people with stromal keratitis? | |
|---|---|
| **Beneficial** | • Adding topical corticosteroids to topical antiviral agents |
| **Unlikely To Be Beneficial** | • Adding oral aciclovir to topical corticosteroids plus topical antiviral agents to treat stromal keratitis |

## What are the effects of interventions to prevent recurrence of epithelial or stromal ocular herpes simplex?

| Beneficial | • Aciclovir (oral) for 1 year to prevent recurrence |
|---|---|
| Unlikely To Be Beneficial | • Aciclovir (oral) for 3 weeks to prevent recurrence |

## What are the effects of interventions to prevent recurrence of ocular herpes simplex in people with corneal grafts?

| Unknown Effectiveness | • Aciclovir (oral) to prevent recurrence after corneal grafts |
|---|---|

**Search date July 2007**

**DEFINITION** Ocular herpes simplex is usually caused by herpes simplex virus type 1 (HSV-1) but also occasionally by the type 2 virus (HSV-2). Ocular manifestations of HSV are varied and include blepharitis (inflammation of the eyelids), canalicular obstruction, conjunctivitis, corneal complications, iritis, and retinitis. Corneal complications are of two main types: **epithelial keratitis** is inflammation of the cells that form the surface layer of the cornea, and **stromal keratitis** is inflammation of the middle layer (stroma) of the cornea. HSV infections are classified as neonatal, primary (HSV in a person with no previous viral exposure), and recurrent (previous viral exposure with humoral and cellular immunity present).

**INCIDENCE/PREVALENCE** Infections with HSV are usually acquired in early life. A US study found antibodies against HSV-1 in about 50% of people with high socioeconomic status and 80% of people with low socioeconomic status by age 30 years. It quoted a report which suggested overcrowding as a causal factor. However, only about 20–25% of people with HSV antibodies had any history of clinical manifestations of ocular or cutaneous herpetic disease. Ocular HSV is the most common cause of corneal blindness in high-income countries, and is the most common cause of unilateral corneal blindness worldwide. A 33-year study of the population of Rochester, Minnesota found that the annual incidence of new cases of ocular herpes simplex was 8.4/100,000 (95% CI 6.9/100,000 to 9.9/100,000), and the annual incidence of all episodes (new and recurrent) was 20.7/100,000 (95% CI 18.3/100,000 to 23.1/100,000). The prevalence of ocular herpes was 149/100,000 population (95% CI 115/100,000 to 183/100,000). Twelve percent of people had bilateral disease.

**AETIOLOGY/RISK FACTORS** Epithelial keratitis results from productive, lytic viral infection of the corneal epithelial cells. Stromal keratitis and iritis are thought to result from a combination of viral infection and compromised immune mechanisms. Observational evidence (346 people with ocular HSV in the placebo arm of an RCT) showed that a previous history of stromal keratitis was a significant risk factor for the recurrence of stromal keratitis (proportion of people with recurrence: 6/174 [4%] without previous stromal keratitis v 53/172 [32%] with previous stromal keratitis; RR 10.0, 95% CI 4.3 to 23.0; P less than 0.001). Age, sex, ethnicity, and previous history of non-ocular HSV disease were not associated with an increased risk of recurrence.

**PROGNOSIS** HSV epithelial keratitis tends to resolve spontaneously within 1–2 weeks, while stromal keratitis is more likely to result in corneal scarring and loss of vision. In a trial of 271 people treated with topical trifluorothymidine and randomly assigned to receive either oral aciclovir or placebo, the epithelial lesion had resolved completely or was at least less than 1 mm after 1 week of treatment with placebo in 89% of people, and after 2 weeks in 99% of people. Stromal keratitis or iritis occurs in about 25% of people after epithelial keratitis. The effects of HSV stromal keratitis include scarring, tissue destruction, neovascularisation, glaucoma, and persistent epithelial defects. The rate of recurrence of ocular herpes (epithelial or stromal) for people with one episode is 10% at 1 year, 23% at 2 years, and 50% at 10 years. The risk of recurrent ocular HSV infection (epithelial or stromal) also

*(continued over)*

*(from previous page)*

increases with the number of previous episodes reported (2 or 3 previous episodes: RR 1.41, 95% CI 0.82 to 2.42; 4 or more previous episodes: RR 2.09, 95% CI 1.24 to 3.50). Of penetrating corneal grafts performed in Australia over a 22-year period, 4% were in people with visual disability, with active corneal disease, or with actual or impending perforation after stromal ocular herpes simplex. Of the penetrating corneal grafts reported by The Australian Corneal Graft Registry that failed, the ocular herpes simplex was a cause for failure in 4% of cases.

David Steel

## KEY POINTS

- Rhegmatogenous retinal detachment (RRD) is the most common form of retinal detachment, where a retinal 'break' allows the ingress of fluid from the vitreous cavity to the subretinal space, resulting in retinal separation. It occurs in about 1 in 10,000 people a year.

  This review considers only acute progressive RRD.

- There is consensus that scleral buckling, pneumatic retinopexy, and vitrectomy are all effective for treating RRD.

  We found insufficient evidence to assess effects of scleral buckling compared with pneumatic retinopexy.

  The effects of scleral buckling compared with primary vitrectomy are unclear. There is limited evidence that, in phakic RRD, scleral buckling improves visual acuity and is associated with a reduced risk of development or progression of cataract. However, we don't know whether scleral buckling is more effective than primary vitrectomy at increasing re-attachment rates in people with pseudophakic and aphakic RRD.

- In people undergoing vitrectomy for RRD with severe proliferative vitreoretinopathy (occurring as a complication of retinal detachment or previous treatment for retinal detachment), silicone oil and long-acting gas are equally effective for increasing re-attachment rates and improving visual acuity; silicone oil is better than short-acting gas.

- We found insufficient evidence assessing the effects of fluorouracil plus heparin, corticosteroids, or daunorubicin given during vitrectomy surgery for proliferative vitreoretinopathy.

 **Please visit http://clinicalevidence.bmj.com for full text and references**

| What are the effects of different surgical interventions in people with rhegmatogenous retinal detachment? | |
|---|---|
| Unknown Effectiveness | • Scleral buckling versus pneumatic retinopexy (there is consensus that both surgical techniques are effective: insufficient evidence to compare effects of scleral buckling versus pneumatic retinopexy) |
| | • Scleral buckling versus primary vitrectomy (there is consensus that both surgical techniques are effective, but effects of scleral buckling compared with vitrectomy are unclear: in pseudophakic or aphakic rhegmatogenous retinal detachment [RRD], rate of retinal re-attachment after one operation may be lower post-scleral buckling compared with post-vitrectomy, but scleral buckling is associated with a lower rate of development or progression of cataract in phakic RRD) |

## What are the effects of interventions to treat rhegmatogenous retinal detachment associated with proliferative vitreoretinopathy?

| Likely To Be Beneficial | • Silicone oil or long-acting gas tamponade (silicone oil and long-acting gas are equally effective in people receiving vitrectomy for RRD with severe proliferative vitreoretinopathy [PVR]; silicone oil is more effective than short-acting gas at increasing re-attachment rates) |
|---|---|
| Unknown Effectiveness | • Corticosteroid injection during vitrectomy surgery<br><br>• Daunorubicin infusion during vitrectomy surgery<br><br>• Fluorouracil plus low molecular weight heparin added to infusion solution during vitrectomy surgery |

**Search date September 2013**

**DEFINITION** Retinal detachment can be defined as the separation of the neurosensory retina from the underlying retinal pigment epithelium (RPE). Direct apposition of the retina to the RPE is essential for normal retinal function, and retinal detachment involving the foveal centre leads to profound loss of vision in the affected eye. **Rhegmatogenous retinal detachment (RRD)** is the most common form of retinal detachment, where a retinal 'break' allows the ingress of fluid from the vitreous cavity to the subretinal space, resulting in retinal separation. Retinal break refers to a full-thickness defect in the neurosensory retina. Retinal breaks that develop from a tear in the retina at the time of posterior vitreous detachment (PVD) are usually referred to as retinal tears. Lattice degeneration can lead to the formation of circular retinal holes, which are typically referred to as atrophic holes. Retinal breaks can also develop as a result of trauma to and inflammation of the eye; examples include retinal dialysis, which is typically secondary to blunt trauma, and tears associated with retinal necrosis, resulting from trauma or inflammation. Rarer causes of retinal detachment include tractional retinal detachment, secondary to fibrous tissue on the surface of the retina; exudative retinal detachment, as a result of choroidal tumours that produce increased fluid flow through the subretinal space; and ocular inflammatory conditions. Retinal detachments can also be a mixture of two or more of the above types. Asymptomatic and non-progressive chronic retinal detachment can also occur. This review considers only acute progressive RRD. **Diagnosis:** RRD is often, but not universally, associated with symptoms of flashes of light (retinal photopsia), visual floaters, and peripheral and usually progressive visual field loss. It is diagnosed by ophthalmoscopy. Acute RRD is seen as an oedematous folded retina with loss of the normal retinal transparency. The detachment can assume a bullous configuration that moves when the eye moves. There can be associated signs of PVD, as well as vitreous haemorrhage or RPE cells circulating in the vitreous cavity after retinal break formation. The presence of pigment cells in the anterior vitreous — visible on slit-lamp biomicroscopy (termed 'Shafer's sign') — is a sensitive indicator of the presence of a retinal break in a person presenting with an acute PVD. Chronic retinal detachments can be associated with retinal cyst formation and 'tidemarks' demarcating the extent of the detachment, as well as subretinal fibrosis.

**INCIDENCE/PREVALENCE** RRD can occur at any age, but reaches peak prevalence in people aged 60 to 70 years. It affects men more than women, and white people more than black people. Observational studies from the US, Europe, and New Zealand found that non-traumatic, phakic (lens intact) RRD occurred in about 6 to 18 in 100,000 people a year (i.e., about 1/10,000).

**AETIOLOGY/RISK FACTORS** The occurrence of retinal detachment is related to the interplay between predisposing retinal lesions and vitreoretinal traction, and occurs when fluid moves from the vitreous cavity through a retinal break into the subretinal space. Most (80%–90%) retinal detachments are associated with retinal-break formation at the time of PVD. PVD is a naturally occurring phenomenon, with a rapidly increasing prevalence in the

60- to 70-year-old age group. Most (70%) retinal breaks, formed at the time of PVD, are seen as tears in the retina or as holes with a free-floating retinal operculum. Retinal breaks can occur in areas of previously abnormal retina; for example, lattice degeneration. Symptoms and signs of acute PVD are known to be associated with a higher risk of immediate progression to RRD in people with predisposing retinal lesions. However, people with established (chronic) PVD and predisposing retinal lesions who have not immediately progressed to RRD are at lower risk than those without a PVD. Symptomatic retinal tears with persistent vitreoretinal traction (not a complete PVD) have a high rate of progression to retinal detachment (>50% if left untreated). The risk of retinal detachment is increased to a variable extent in people with a symptomatic pre-existing retinal disease or lesions, especially retinal-flap tears, operculated retinal holes after separation of a retinal flap, atrophic retinal holes, lattice degeneration (areas of retinal thinning with abnormal vitreoretinal adhesion), and retinal dialyses. Autopsy studies have shown that about 6% to 11% of people aged over 20 years have retinal breaks in one form or another. However, the chances of an RRD occurring in an asymptomatic eye with a retinal break and with no history of fellow-eye RRD is 0.5% over a follow-up period of 11 years. Similarly, 7% to 8% of adults have areas of lattice degeneration, but only a small proportion of these lesions progress to RRD. Asymptomatic retinal dialysis is thought to have a high risk of progression to retinal detachment, especially after trauma. Increased risk of RRD is associated with several factors. There is a higher prevalence of RRD in short-sighted (myopic) people, with around a 10-fold increased incidence in people with over three dioptres of myopia. Approximately 50% of phakic RRD cases are myopic. The fellow eye in people with an RRD is at a higher risk, with 2% to 10% of RRDs being bilateral. Although some RRD occurring in a fellow eye will develop from pre-existing retinal lesions, most subsequent RRD (at least 50%, and possibly as high as 80%–90%) in the fellow eye will occur from ophthalmoscopically normal areas of retina, and so prophylaxis to visible abnormal areas may not completely reduce the incidence of fellow-eye RRD. There is also a higher incidence of RRD in people with a family history of retinal detachment, especially in conditions such as Stickler's syndrome. People who have had previous cataract surgery also have a higher incidence of RRD, and about 1 in 5 patients presenting with RRD in the UK will have had cataract surgery. About 0.5% to 0.6% of people experience RRD after phacoemulsification surgery for cataracts, with the risk being increased by 15 to 20 times with rupture of the posterior capsule. About 10% of RRDs are associated with trauma. There are other conditions which, more rarely, increase the risk of RRD, including uveitis — especially CMV retinitis — and other degenerative retinal conditions, such as retinoschisis. Idiopathic macular holes may cause RRD in highly myopic eyes, but rarely in emmetropic or hypermetropic eyes.

**PROGNOSIS** On presentation, retinal detachment is usually divided into 'macula on', when the fovea is still attached, and 'macula off', where the retina is detached centrally. People with macula-on retinal detachments typically have good initial visual acuity and a better prognosis with successful surgery. Rapidly progressive cases are therefore treated as a matter of urgency. Macula-off retinal detachments have worse initial visual acuity, and have a worse prognosis even with successful re-attachment of the retina. Overall, about 95% of people have anatomically successful repair of RRD, with 70% to 90% achieving this in one operation. In 90% of successfully repaired macula-on retinal detachments, vision is 6/12 or better. However, in those with macula-off retinal detachments, only 50% of eyes achieve a visual acuity of 6/15, and, if the macula has been detached for 1 week or more, this level of visual acuity is rarely achieved. Reasons for anatomical failure of surgery include new or missed retinal breaks and proliferative vitreoretinopathy (PVR). PVR is classified based on extent, position, and type of PVR: the American Retina Society proposed the first classification of PVR in 1983, and, although updated in 1991 following the Silicone Oil Study, this classification system continues to be widely used. Causes of poor visual acuity after successful repair include macular epiretinal membranes (fibrosis), cystoid macular oedema, and foveal photoreceptor degeneration in macula-off retinal detachments.

## 234 | Trachoma

Anthony W Solomon and David CW Mabey

### KEY POINTS

- Active trachoma is caused by chronic infection of the conjunctiva by *Chlamydia trachomatis*, and is the world's leading infectious cause of blindness.

  Infection can lead to scarring of the tarsal conjunctiva, shortening and inversion of the upper eyelid (entropion), and scarring of the eye by eyelashes (trichiasis), leading to blindness.

  Trachoma is a disease of poverty, overcrowding, and poor sanitation. Active disease mainly affects children, but adults are at increased risk of scarring.

- Public health interventions to improve hygiene may reduce the risks of developing trachoma, but studies have given conflicting results.

  Face-washing plus topical antibiotics may be beneficial, but we don't know whether face-washing alone is effective.

  Fly control using insecticide alone, insecticide plus mass antibiotics, or by providing pit latrines, may reduce the risks of trachoma, but is unlikely to be a feasible large-scale approach.

- We don't know whether oral or topical antibiotics reduce the risk of active trachoma compared with placebo or with each other, as few comparable studies have been found.

- Lid-rotation surgery with bilamellar tarsal rotation or tarsal advance and rotation may be effective at correcting entropion and trichiasis compared with other types of surgery.

- We don't know whether posterior lamellar tarsal rotation plus azithromycin is more effective than posterior lamellar tarsal rotation alone at correcting entropion and trichiasis.

(i) **Please visit http://clinicalevidence.bmj.com for full text and references**

| What are the effects of interventions to prevent scarring trachoma by reducing the prevalence of active trachoma? | |
|---|---|
| Likely To Be Beneficial | • Face-washing plus topical tetracycline<br>• Fly control using insecticide alone |
| Unknown Effectiveness | • Antibiotics<br>• Face-washing alone<br>• Fly control through the provision of pit latrines<br>• Fly control using insecticide plus antibiotics<br>• Health education |

| What are the effects of eyelid surgery for treating entropion and trichiasis? | |
|---|---|
| Likely To Be Beneficial | • Bilamellar tarsal rotation or tarsal advance and rotation (compared with other types of eyelid surgery) |
| Unlikely To Be Beneficial | • Posterior lamellar tarsal rotation plus azithromycin (compared with surgery alone) |

**Search date January 2007**

**DEFINITION** **Active trachoma** is chronic inflammation of the conjunctiva caused by infection with *Chlamydia trachomatis*. The WHO simplified trachoma grading scheme defines active trachoma as TF and/or TI, where TF (trachomatous inflammation — follicular) is the presence of five or more follicles in the central part of the upper tarsal conjunctiva, each at least 0.5 mm in diameter, and TI (trachomatous inflammation — intense) is pronounced inflammatory thickening of the upper tarsal conjunctiva that obscures more than half of the normal deep vessels. **Cicatricial trachoma** is caused by repeated infection with *C trachomatis*; it includes the presence of visible scars on the tarsal conjunctiva (trachomatous scarring), shortening and inversion of the upper eyelid (entropion), and malposition of the lashes so that they abrade the eye (trichiasis). Trachomatous scarring can be present without entropion/trichiasis, but if entropion/trichiasis is present because of trachoma, there will be scarring. Trachoma blindness results from corneal opacification, which occurs because of the mechanical trauma wrought by entropion/trichiasis. **Diagnosis** of trachoma is by clinical examination, using the criteria set out in either the modified WHO grading system or the WHO simplified grading system. The simplified grading system is now the most commonly employed.

**INCIDENCE/PREVALENCE** Trachoma is the world's leading cause of infectious blindness. Globally, active trachoma affects an estimated 84 million people, most of them children. About 7.6 million people are blind or at risk of blindness as a consequence. Trachoma is a disease of poverty, regardless of geographical region. Cicatricial trachoma is prevalent in large regions of Africa, the Middle East, Asia, and Aboriginal communities in Australia, and there are also small foci in Central and South America. In areas where trachoma is constantly present at high prevalence, active disease is found in more than 50% of preschool children, and may have a prevalence as high as 60–90%, and as many as 75% of women and 50% of men aged over 45 years may show signs of scarring disease. The prevalence of active trachoma decreases with increasing age. Although similar prevalences of active disease are observed in boys and girls, the later sequelae of trichiasis, entropion, and corneal opacification are usually more common in women than men.

**AETIOLOGY/RISK FACTORS** Active trachoma is associated with youth, poor access to water and sanitation, and close contact between people. Discharge from the eyes and nose may facilitate transmission of ocular *C trachomatis* infection. Sharing a bedroom with someone who has active trachoma is a risk factor for infection. The density of eye-seeking flies in a community is associated with active trachoma. Flies important to trachoma transmission lay their eggs on human faeces lying exposed on the soil, suggesting that access to improved sanitation might help control trachoma.

**PROGNOSIS** Corneal damage from trachoma is caused by multiple processes. Scarring trachoma damages glandular structures and may cause an inadequate tear film; a dry eye may be more susceptible to damage from inturned lashes and superadded infection by other bacteria and fungi, leading to corneal opacification.

Niaz Islam and Carlos Pavesio

## KEY POINTS

- Anterior uveitis is inflammation of the uveal tract, and includes iritis (inflammation of the iris) and iridocyclitis (inflammation of both iris and ciliary body).

  It is usually rare, with an annual incidence of 12 per 100,000 population, although it is more common in Finland (annual incidence of 23/100,000), probably because of genetic factors such as high frequency of HLA-B27 in the population.

  It is often self-limiting but can, in some cases, lead to complications such as posterior synechiae, cataract, glaucoma, cystoid macular oedema, and chronic uveitis.

- This review searched for RCTs examining the effects of the listed interventions. In fact, we found few such studies to inform clinical practice. There is a need for further high-quality RCTs in this field.

- Corticosteroid eye drops have been the standard treatment for uveitis since the early 1950s, although RCT evidence supporting their effectiveness is somewhat sparse.

  Widely known adverse effects of topical corticosteroid eye drops include local irritation, hyperaemia, raised intraocular pressure (steroid responder), and blurred vision.

  We found seven RCTs comparing different corticosteroid eye drops versus each other. Overall, RCTs were small and evidence was limited, and we were unable to draw robust conclusions.

  We found no RCTs on the effects of oral corticosteroids or subconjunctival corticosteroid injections.

- The studies examining the effects of NSAID eye drops were either too small or of insufficient quality to allow us to judge their effectiveness in treating anterior uveitis.

- We found no RCTs on the effects of mydriatics.

(i) **Please visit http://clinicalevidence.bmj.com for full text and references**

| What are the effects of interventions on acute anterior uveitis? | |
|---|---|
| **Likely To Be Beneficial** | • Corticosteroids* |
| **Unknown Effectiveness** | • Mydriatics (different drugs or potencies)<br>• NSAID eye drops |

**Search date August 2014**

*Based on consensus; placebo-controlled RCTs unlikely to be conducted.

**DEFINITION** Anterior uveitis is inflammation of the uveal tract, and includes iritis and iridocyclitis. It can be classified according to its clinical course into acute or chronic anterior uveitis or according to its clinical appearance into granulomatous or non-granulomatous anterior uveitis. **Acute anterior uveitis** is characterised by an extremely painful red eye, often associated with photophobia, and occasionally with decreased visual acuity. **Chronic anterior uveitis** is defined as inflammation lasting more than 6 weeks. It is usually asymptomatic but many people have mild symptoms during exacerbations.

**INCIDENCE/PREVALENCE** Acute anterior uveitis is rare, with an annual incidence of 12 per 100,000 population. It is particularly common in Finland (annual incidence 22.6/100,000 population, prevalence 68.7/100,000 population), probably because of genetic factors such as the high frequency of HLA-B27 in the Finnish population. It is equally common in men and women, and more than 90% of cases occur in people older than 20 years of age.

**AETIOLOGY/RISK FACTORS** No cause is identified in 60% to 80% of people with acute anterior uveitis. This most common category is also termed 'idiopathic anterior uveitis'. Systemic disorders that may be associated with acute anterior uveitis include ankylosing spondylitis, Reiter's syndrome, Kawasaki's disease, infectious uveitis, Behçet's syndrome, inflammatory bowel disease, interstitial nephritis, sarcoidosis, Vogt-Koyanagi-Harada syndrome, and masquerade syndromes. Acute anterior uveitis also occurs in association with HLA-B27 expression not linked to any systemic disease. Acute anterior uveitis may occur after surgery, or as an adverse drug or hypersensitivity reaction.

**PROGNOSIS** Acute anterior uveitis is often self-limiting, but we found no evidence about how often it resolves spontaneously, in which people, or over what length of time. Complications include posterior synechiae, cataract, glaucoma, cystoid macular oedema, and chronic uveitis. In a study of 154 people (232 eyes) with acute anterior uveitis (119 people HLA-B27 positive), visual acuity was better than 20/60 in 209 of 232 eyes (90%), and 20/60 or worse in 23 of 232 (10%) eyes, including worse than 20/200 (classified as legally blind) in 11 of 232 (5%) eyes.

Martin Talbot

### KEY POINTS

- Infection with HIV usually leads to 8–10 years of asymptomatic infection before immune function deteriorates and AIDS develops.

  Without treatment, about 50% of infected people will die of AIDS over 10 years. With treatment, prognosis depends on age, CD4 cell count, and initial viral load.

- Concurrent STDs increase the risk of transmission of HIV infection. Treating STDs may reduce the risk of an individual acquiring HIV, but we don't know whether it is effective on a population level.

- Antiretroviral treatment (especially combinations including zidovudine) may reduce the risk of HIV infection among healthcare workers who have been exposed to the infection.

- Triple antiretroviral treatments are now standard for people with HIV infection.

  Boosted protease inhibitor-based regimens may be more effective than standard protease-based triple regimens at reducing viral load and preventing HIV progression and death.

  Non-nucleoside reverse transcriptase inhibitor- (NNRTI: efavirenz or nevirapine) based triple regimens seem to increase viral suppression compared with standard protease inhibitor-based triple regimens, although HIV progression rates may not be reduced.

  Standard protease inhibitor-based triple regimens may be less effective than NNRTI-based triple regimens at reducing viral load.

  Nucleoside reverse transcriptase inhibitor- (NRTI) based triple regimens offer similar viral suppression to standard protease inhibitor based triple regimens. Some NRTIs (stavudine) may be associated with lipodystrophy.

- We do not know whether combination treatments containing either chemokine (C-C motif) receptor 5 inhibitors or fusion inhibitors (enfuvirtide), orearly initiation of antiretroviral treatment using triple regimens improves long-term survival.

  The decision about when to start treatment currently depends on severity of symptoms, and on CD4 lymphocyte count, so that likely benefits can be balanced against risks of adverse effects of treatment.

(i) **Please visit http://clinicalevidence.bmj.com for full text and references**

| What are the effects of interventions to prevent transmission of HIV? | |
|---|---|
| Likely To Be Beneficial | • Early diagnosis and treatment of STDs (in regions with emerging HIV epidemics) |
| | • Postexposure prophylaxis in healthcare workers* |
| Unknown Effectiveness | • Presumptive mass treatment of STDs |

| What are the effects of different antiretroviral drug treatment regimens in HIV infection? | |
|---|---|
| Beneficial | • Boosted protease inhibitor-based triple regimens (may be more effective than standard protease-based triple regimens at reducing viral load, but may be less effective than non-nucleoside |

| | |
|---|---|
| | reverse transcriptase inhibitor- [NNRTI] based triple regimens at virological suppression) |
| | • Non-nucleoside reverse transcriptase inhibitor- (NNRTI) based triple regimens (may increase viral suppression compared with boosted protease inhibitor-based triple regimens but may not affect progression; may be more effective than standard protease inhibitor-based triple regimens at reducing viral load) |
| Likely To Be Beneficial | • Nucleoside reverse transcriptase inhibitor- (NRTI) based triple regimens (similar viral suppression to standard protease inhibitor-based triple regimens) |
| | • Standard protease inhibitor-based triple regimens (similar rate of disease progression and mortality to non-nucleoside reverse transcriptase inhibitor- [NNRTI] based triple regimens; similar viral suppression to nucleoside reverse transcriptase inhibitor- [NRTI] based triple regimens but less effective than NNRTI-based triple regimens at reducing viral load; may also be less effective than boosted protease inhibitor-based regimens) |
| Unknown Effectiveness | • Combination treatments containing chemokine (C-C motif) receptor 5 inhibitors |
| | • Combination treatments containing fusion inhibitors (enfuvirtide) |
| | • Early versus delayed antiretroviral treatment using triple antiretroviral regimens |

**Search date June 2007**

*No RCTs: based on consensus and known effectiveness of antiretroviral drugs in the treatment setting

**DEFINITION** HIV infection refers to infection with HIV type 1 or type 2. Clinically, this is characterised by a variable period (usually about 8–10 years) of asymptomatic infection, followed by repeated episodes of illness of varying and increasing severity as immune function deteriorates, resulting in AIDS. The type of illness varies by country, availability of specific treatments for HIV, and prophylaxis for opportunistic infections. Current treatments interrupt the life cycle of the virus without effecting a cure: mutations in the viral genome result in gradual resistance drift and increasing ineffectiveness of drug treatments.

**INCIDENCE/PREVALENCE** Worldwide estimates suggest that, by November 2007, about 33.2 million people were living with HIV. In 2007, there were estimated to be 2.5 million new cases of HIV and 2.1 million deaths from AIDS. About 95% of HIV infections occur in resource-poor countries. By 1999, occupationally acquired HIV infection in healthcare workers had been documented in at least 102 definite and 217 possible cases, although this is likely to be an underestimate.

**AETIOLOGY/RISK FACTORS** The major risk factor for transmission of HIV is unprotected heterosexual or homosexual intercourse. Other risk factors include needlestick injury, sharing drug-injecting equipment, and blood transfusion. A woman infected with HIV may also transmit the virus to her baby transplacentally, during birth, or through breast milk. This has been reported in 15–30% of pregnant women with HIV infection. Mother-to-child transmission of HIV is dealt with in a separate review (HIV: mother-to-child transmission, p 241). Not

*(continued over)*

*(from previous page)*

everyone exposed to HIV will become infected, although risk increases if exposure is repeated, is at high dose, or occurs through blood. There is at least a two- to fivefold greater risk of HIV infection among people with STDs.

**PROGNOSIS** Without treatment, about 50% of people infected with HIV will become ill and die from AIDS over about 10 years. A meta-analysis of 13 cohort studies from Europe and the USA looked at 12,574 treatment-naive people starting highly active antiretroviral therapy (HAART) with a combination of at least three drugs. A lower baseline CD4 cell count and higher baseline HIV-1 viral load were associated with an increased probability of progression to AIDS or death. Other independent predictors of poorer outcome were advanced age, infection through injection drug use, and a previous diagnosis of AIDS. The CD4 cell count at initiation was the dominant prognostic factor in people starting HAART. People with the most favourable prognostic factors (aged below 50 years old, not infected through injection drug use, viral load below 100,000 copies/mL, and CD4 cell count above 350 cells/mL on initiation of HAART) were estimated to have a 3.5% chance of progression to AIDS or death within 3 years. People with the least favourable prognostic factors (aged at least 50 years old, infected through intravenous drug use, viral load at least 100,000 copies/mL, and CD4 cell count below 50 cells/mL on initiation of HAART) had an estimated 50% chance of progression to AIDS or death within 3 years. Genetic factors have been shown to affect response to antiretroviral treatment, but were not considered in the meta-analysis. We found one non-systematic review assessing prognosis in people in Africa. It identified one study conducted in rural Uganda, which found similar survival rates (a median 9.8 years from the time of HIV-1 seroconversion) but found that progression to symptomatic disease was faster in Uganda than in resource-rich countries, owing largely to the high background level of morbidity. The review reported that most people in hospital in Africa with HIV have the clinical features of AIDS just before they die, and many are severely immunosuppressed. The review also suggested that morbidity was similar to that in resource-rich countries before the introduction of HAART.

Chloe Teasdale, Ben Marais, and Elaine Abrams

## KEY POINTS

- Without active intervention, the risk of mother-to-child transmission (MTCT) of HIV-1 is high, especially in populations where prolonged breastfeeding is the norm.

  Without antiviral treatment, the risk of transmission of HIV from infected mothers to their children is approximately 15% to 30% during pregnancy and labour, with an additional transmission risk of 10% to 20% associated with prolonged breastfeeding.

  HIV-2 is rarely transmitted from mother to child.

  Transmission is more likely in mothers with high viral loads, advanced HIV disease, or both.

  Without antiretroviral treatment (ART), 15% to 35% of vertically infected infants die within the first year of life.

  The long-term treatment of children with ART is complicated by multiple concerns regarding the complications associated with life-long treatment, including adverse effects of antiretroviral drugs, difficulties of adherence across the developmental trajectory of childhood and adolescence, and the development of resistance.

  From a paediatric perspective, successful prevention of MTCT and HIV-free survival for infants remain the most important focus.

- Antiretroviral drugs given to the mother during pregnancy or labour, to the baby immediately after birth, or to the mother and baby reduce the risk of intrauterine and intrapartum MTCT of HIV-1 and when given to the infant after birth and to the mother or infant during breastfeeding reduce the risk of postpartum MTCT of HIV-1.

- Reductions in MTCT are possible using multidrug ART regimens.

  Longer courses of ART are more effective, but the greatest benefit is derived from treatment during late pregnancy, labour, and early infancy.

  Suppression of the maternal viral load to undetectable levels (below 50 copies/mL) using highly active antiretroviral therapy (HAART) offers the greatest risk reduction, and is currently the standard of care offered in most resource-rich countries, where MTCT rates have been reduced to 1% to 2%.

  Alternative short-course regimens have been tested in resource-limited settings where HAART is not yet widely available. There is evidence that short courses of antiretroviral drugs have confirmed efficacy for reducing MTCT. Identifying optimal short-course regimens (drug combination, timing, and cost effectiveness) for various settings remains a focus for ongoing research.

  The development of viral resistance in mothers and infants after single-dose nevirapine and other short-course regimens that include single-dose nevirapine is of concern. An additional short-course of antiretrovirals with a different regimen during labour and early postpartum, and the use of HAART, may decrease the risk of viral resistance in mothers, and in infants who become HIV-infected despite prophylaxis.

  WHO guidelines recommend starting prophylaxis with antiretroviral drugs from as early as 14 weeks' gestation, or as soon as possible if women present late in pregnancy, in labour, or at delivery.

- Elective caesarean section at 38 weeks may reduce vertical transmission rates (apart from breast-milk transmission).

  The potential benefits of this intervention need to be balanced against the increased risk of surgery-associated complications, high cost, and feasibility issues. These reservations are particularly relevant in resource-limited settings.

- Immunotherapy with HIV hyperimmune globulin seems no more effective than immunoglobulin without HIV antibody at reducing HIV-1 MTCT risk.
- Vaginal microbicides have not been demonstrated to reduce HIV-1 MTCT risk.
- There is no evidence that supplementation with vitamin A reduces the risk of HIV-1 MTCT, and there is concern that postnatal vitamin A supplementation for mother and infant may be associated with increased risk of mortality.
- We don't know whether micronutrients are effective in prevention of MTCT of HIV as we found no RCT evidence on this outcome.
- Avoidance of breastfeeding prevents postpartum transmission of HIV, but formula feeding requires access to clean water and health education.

  The risk of breastfeeding-related HIV transmission needs to be balanced against the multiple benefits that breastfeeding offers. In resource-poor countries, breastfeeding is strongly associated with reduced infant morbidity and improved child survival.

  Exclusive breastfeeding during the first 6 months may reduce the risk of HIV transmission compared with mixed feeding, while retaining most of its associated benefits.

  In a population where prolonged breastfeeding is usual, early, abrupt weaning may not reduce MTCT or HIV-free survival at 2 years compared with prolonged breastfeeding, and may be associated with a higher rate of infant mortality for those infants diagnosed as HIV-infected at <4 months of age.

  Antiretrovirals given to the mother or the infant during breastfeeding can reduce the risk of HIV transmission in the postpartum period.

  WHO guidelines recommend that HIV-positive mothers should exclusively breastfeed for the first 6 months, after which time appropriate complementary foods can be introduced. Breastfeeding should be continued for the first 12 months of the infant's life, and stopped only when an adequate diet without breast milk can be provided.

  Heat- or microbicidal-treated expressed breast milk may offer value in particular settings.

(i) **Please visit http://clinicalevidence.bmj.com for full text and references**

## What are the effects of measures to reduce mother-to-child transmission of HIV?

| | |
|---|---|
| Beneficial | • Antiretroviral drugs to prevent intrauterine and intrapartum transmission of HIV<br><br>• Antiretroviral drugs to prevent postpartum transmission of HIV (extended regimens for the infant may be more effective than shorter regimens in reducing postpartum transmission) |
| Likely To Be Beneficial | • Elective caesarean section |
| Trade-off Between Benefits And Harms | • Avoiding breastfeeding (the risk of breastfeeding-related HIV transmission needs to be balanced against the multiple benefits that breastfeeding offers) |
| Unknown Effectiveness | • Micronutrient supplements |

|  | • Vaginal microbicides |
|---|---|
| **Unlikely To Be Beneficial** | • Immunotherapy |
| **Likely To Be Ineffective Or Harmful** | • Vitamin supplements (vitamin A seems no more effective than placebo at reducing the risk of transmission) |

Search date October 2009

**DEFINITION** Mother-to-child transmission (MTCT) of HIV infection is defined as transmission of HIV from an infected mother to her child during gestation, labour, or postpartum through breastfeeding. HIV-1 infection is frequently transmitted from mother to child, although HIV-2 is rarely transmitted in this way. Infected children rarely have symptoms or signs of HIV at birth, but usually develop them over subsequent months.

**INCIDENCE/PREVALENCE** A review of 13 cohort studies estimated the risk of MTCT of HIV in the absence of antiretroviral treatment (ART) to be 15% to 20% in Europe, 15% to 30% in the USA, and 25% to 35% in Africa. The risk of transmission is estimated to be 15% to 30% during pregnancy, with an additional transmission risk of 10% to 20% associated with prolonged breastfeeding. The Joint United Nation's Programme on HIV/AIDS (UNAIDS) estimates that more than 2 million children are infected with HIV-1 worldwide, and that more than 1000 new HIV infections are transmitted daily from mothers to infants. Of these, more than 80% are in sub-Saharan Africa, where almost 400,000 children were newly infected with HIV in 2008 alone.

**AETIOLOGY/RISK FACTORS** Transmission of HIV to infants is more likely if the mother has a high viral load. Based on polymerase chain reaction (PCR) results of infants at 6 weeks of age, a Tanzanian study reported that a maternal viral load of 50,000 copies/mL or more at delivery was associated with a 4-fold increase in the risk of early transmission (OR 4.21, 95% CI 1.59 to 11.13; P = 0.004). Other maternal risk factors include low CD4+ count, advanced HIV disease, sexually transmitted diseases, chorioamnionitis, prolonged rupture of membranes, vaginal mode of delivery, and obstetric events with bleeding (episiotomy, perineal laceration, and intrapartum haemorrhage). Estimations of the timing of MTCT of HIV-1 during pregnancy indicate that the probability of transmission in non-breastfeeding populations (80%) is highest during late pregnancy (3% at <14 weeks, 3% at 14–28 weeks, 14% at 28–36 weeks, 50% at 36 weeks to labour, and 30% during labour). Prolonged breastfeeding poses a significant additional risk for MTCT, with about 60% of total transmissions occurring during pregnancy, and 40% via breast milk in breastfeeding populations. With the use of effective drug regimens to reduce pre-partum and intrapartum MTCT of HIV, prolonged breast or mixed feeding without continued antiretroviral prophylaxis or treatment becomes the predominant route of transmission. Observational studies have found that mixed feeding (breast milk in combination with other liquids or solids) is associated with a significantly higher risk of postnatal transmission compared with exclusive breastfeeding; prospective cohort studies have reported early mixed feeding (during the infants' first 6 months) to be associated with increased risk of postnatal MTCT of 4.03 (95% CI 0.98 to 16.61; 2060 infants in Zimbabwe who were HIV-negative at 6 weeks) and 6.30 (95% CI 1.1 to 36.4; 622 infants from Cote d'Ivoire who were HIV-negative at or after 30 days). One study also found that prolonged exclusive breastfeeding (beyond 6 months) was associated with an increased risk of postnatal MTCT compared with formula feeding (622 infants from Cote d'Ivoire who were HIV-negative at or after 30 days; increase in risk of MTCT of 7.5, 95% CI 2.0 to 28.2; P = 0.003). Late postnatal transmission (beyond 6 months) contributes substantially to overall MTCT, with prolonged breastfeeding (beyond 6 months) and maternal disease progression (as measured by CD4+ count) identified as risk factors. Data from a small retrospective case series in China (104 women who acquired HIV-1 through postnatal blood transfusion) showed a potential increased risk of MTCT when mothers seroconverted during breastfeeding after becoming infected with HIV-1 through postnatal blood transfusion (MTCT risk 35.8%, 95% CI 26.7% to 44.9%). Data from a

*(continued over)*

*(from previous page)*

meta-analysis of individual patient data found a two-fold increase in the risk of postnatal transmission among women with CD4+ counts of less than 200 cells/mm$^3$.

**PROGNOSIS** The natural history of HIV infection in infancy is variable. It has been estimated that 25% of infants infected with HIV progress rapidly to AIDS or death within the first year of life, although some survive beyond 12 years of age, even in the absence of ART. One collaborative European study that documented the natural history of disease in the absence of ART reported 15% mortality during infancy, and 28% mortality by the age of 5 years. In one prospective cohort study carried out in France, 2% of perinatally infected children (data reported for 348 HIV-1-infected children) displayed no immunological or clinical symptoms by the age of 10 years. The study found that the mother's clinical status during pregnancy, prematurity of the infant, and the child's initial CD4+ and CD8+ counts were associated with disease progression. However, the prognosis of African children with vertically acquired HIV infection seems significantly worse. One meta-analysis of individual patient data for children born to HIV-infected mothers in Africa (3468 children in analysis) estimated that, of the 707 HIV-infected children, 35.2% would have died by 1 year of age, and 52.5% by 2 years of age. By comparison, the study estimated that 4.9% of uninfected children would have died by 1 year of age and 7.6% by 2 years of age. Stage of disease was a significant predictor of mortality; a prospective cohort study (213 infants with HIV) from Zambia found that infants infected with HIV in the intrauterine (0–3 days postpartum) or intrapartum/early postpartum (4–40 days) periods had a significantly higher risk of mortality at 12 months compared with children with late postpartum infection (>40 days) (HR for late postpartum infection *v* intrauterine infection 0.27, 95% CI 0.15 to 0.50; for intrapartum/early postpartum *v* late postpartum infection; P = 0.006). On a population level, HIV accounts for 4% of overall child deaths in sub-Saharan Africa, and each year causes 210,000 child deaths across the continent. Five countries (Botswana, Namibia, Swaziland, Zambia, and Zimbabwe) reported HIV-attributable mortality in excess of 30/1000 in children under the age of 5 years.

Brendan Payne and Richard Bellamy

## KEY POINTS

- Tuberculosis is a major opportunistic infection and cause of death in people with HIV, and often presents as non-pulmonary disease.

  In people infected with both HIV and *Mycobacterium tuberculosis*, the annual risk of developing active tuberculosis is 5% to 10%, more than 10 times the rate for people with *Mycobacterium tuberculosis* infection but without HIV.

  Untreated, mortality from tuberculosis in people with HIV is likely to be very high, and over 5% of people relapse after successful treatment.

- Conventional antituberculous treatment (2 months of rifampicin plus isoniazid plus pyrazinamide, with or without ethambutol, followed by 4–7 months of rifampicin plus isoniazid) is considered beneficial in people with HIV and is standard treatment. Placebo-controlled RCTs of active tuberculosis would therefore be considered unethical and are unlikely to be performed.

  We don't know whether antituberculous treatment regimens containing rifabutin or quinolones are more effective compared with conventional regimens.

  Regimens containing thiacetazone may be less effective at producing negative sputum cultures compared with conventional regimens and may have more adverse effects, including fatal mucocutaneous reactions.

  We don't know whether regimens lasting longer than 6 months are more effective than shorter regimens, but regimens that use rifampicin for at least 5 months are less likely to lead to recurrence compared with regimens that use 3 months or less of rifampicin.

- Adjuvant immunotherapy with *Mycobacterium vaccae* does not increase cure rates or survival compared with placebo vaccination.

- Adjuvant immunotherapy with corticosteroids may not increase survival or decrease tuberculosis recurrence in HIV-positive people with pulmonary or pleural tuberculosis compared with placebo. RCTs found that corticosteroids caused an increased risk of high blood glucose and high blood pressure.

  We don't know whether adjuvant immunotherapy with corticosteroids increases survival in HIV-positive people with tuberculous meningitis or tuberculous pericarditis compared with placebo.

  We don't know whether early initiation of highly active antiretroviral treatment (HAART) improves tuberculosis cure rates compared with delayed initiation of HAART, and there is a risk of interaction with antituberculous drugs.

  We don't know whether directly observed therapy improves cure rates compared with unsupervised treatment in people with HIV.

- We don't know which antimycobacterial treatment combinations are most effective in people with HIV who have failed first-line treatment.

- Secondary prophylaxis with antituberculous drugs after successful completion of conventional antituberculous treatment reduces the risk of tuberculosis recurrence in people with HIV, who are not receiving HAART, compared with placebo.

  We don't know whether secondary prophylaxis with antituberculous drugs reduces mortality.

(i) **Please visit http://clinicalevidence.bmj.com for full text and references**

### What are the effects of first-line treatments for tuberculosis in HIV-positive people?

| | |
|---|---|
| **Beneficial** | • Conventional antituberculous treatment* |
| **Unknown Effectiveness** | • Adjuvant immunotherapy with corticosteroids<br><br>• Antituberculous treatment containing quinolones (compared with alternative regimens)<br><br>• Antituberculous treatment containing rifabutin (compared with alternative regimens)<br><br>• Directly observed therapy, short course (compared with unsupervised treatment)<br><br>• Early initiation of highly active antiretroviral treatment (compared with delayed initiation of highly active antiretroviral treatment)<br><br>• Longer courses of antituberculous treatment (compared with conventional short-course treatment) |
| **Unlikely To Be Beneficial** | • Adjuvant immunotherapy with *Mycobacterium vaccae* |
| **Likely To Be Ineffective Or Harmful** | • Antituberculous treatment containing 3 months or less of rifampicin (compared with rifampicin for 5 months or more)<br><br>• Antituberculous treatment containing thiacetazone |

### What are the effects of second-line treatments for tuberculosis in HIV-positive people?

| | |
|---|---|
| **Unknown Effectiveness** | • Antimycobacterial treatment combinations (comparative benefits of different regimens unclear)<br><br>• Secondary prophylaxis with antituberculous drugs versus placebo after successful completion of conventional antituberculous treatment |

**Search date July 2009**

*Categorisation based on consensus.

**DEFINITION** HIV infection kills more people than any other infectious disease. Infection with *Mycobacterium tuberculosis* is among the most important HIV-related opportunistic infections, in both resource-rich and resource-poor countries. The WHO estimates that tuberculosis is the cause of death in 13% of people who die from AIDS. HIV infection compromises the host's immune defences and can lead to failure to control latent *M tuberculosis* infection, with the subsequent development of active (i.e., symptomatic) tuberculosis. The HIV pandemic has been a major contributing factor in the spread of tuberculosis in many countries. Tuberculosis most commonly affects the lungs, but can also affect many other organs, such as lymph nodes, kidneys, liver, GI tract, and the central nervous system. In a study of 132 HIV-positive people with tuberculosis in San Francisco, 50 (38%) had solely pulmonary disease, 40 (30%) had solely extrapulmonary disease, and 42 (32%) had both pulmonary and extrapulmonary disease. In Africa and South America, 40% to 80% of HIV-positive people presenting with tuberculosis have pulmonary disease. The specific symptoms of tuberculosis depend on the site of infection. Pulmonary disease characteristically presents with cough, haemoptysis, chest pain, and systemic symptoms, such as weight loss and night sweats. This review deals with the treatment of active tuberculosis (both pulmonary and extrapulmonary) in people with HIV.

**INCIDENCE/PREVALENCE** About one third of the world's population has latent *Mycobacterium tuberculosis* infection. Each year about 741,000 cases of active tuberculosis occur in people who are HIV positive, resulting in 248,000 deaths. HIV infection has been a major factor in the increase in the number of cases of tuberculosis occurring worldwide. Most people infected with HIV live in sub-Saharan Africa. In several countries of this region, over 40% of people who develop tuberculosis are infected with HIV. Tuberculosis is the most frequent cause of death in people infected with HIV in the Democratic Republic of Congo. Reliable data on cause of death in people in other sub-Saharan African countries are rare, but tuberculosis is probably a frequent cause of death among people with HIV.

**AETIOLOGY/RISK FACTORS** Risk factors for tuberculosis include social factors such as poverty, overcrowding, and homelessness, and medical factors such as corticosteroid treatment. In people co-infected with HIV and *Mycobacterium tuberculosis*, the annual risk of developing active tuberculosis is about 5% to 10% — more than 10 times greater than for HIV-negative people infected with *M tuberculosis*. The annual risk of tuberculosis in co-infected people may be higher in resource-poor countries than in established market economies because of additional risk factors, such as poor nutrition and poverty. Without preventive treatment, about 30% of HIV-positive people with latent tuberculosis will develop active tuberculosis. Preventive treatment aims to reduce this risk.

**PROGNOSIS** Without treatment, active tuberculosis would probably be fatal in a person infected with HIV. For ethical reasons, no studies have examined the prognosis of active tuberculosis without treatment in people infected with HIV. In one study in the era before highly active antiretroviral treatment in the USA, the median survival of HIV-positive people treated for tuberculosis was 16 months. However, only 13/99 (13%) of the deaths were attributed to tuberculosis. The other common causes of death were *Pneumocystis carinii* pneumonia (24%), bacterial pneumonia (14%), wasting syndrome (9%), and Kaposi's sarcoma (9%). In Malawi, 47% of HIV-positive people with tuberculosis died during 32 months' follow-up. The most common causes of death among people with HIV in sub-Saharan Africa are wasting syndrome, chronic diarrhoea, cryptococcal meningitis, and chest infection. The differences in cause of death between sub-Saharan Africa and the USA may be attributable to the availability of diagnostic tests as much as to genuine differences in the underlying causes. Recurrence of tuberculosis after completion of treatment is more common among people with HIV than among HIV-negative people. In one study in New York, 83/1530 (5.4%) people with HIV who completed tuberculosis treatment had a recurrence of disease, compared with 21/1413 (1.5%) HIV-negative people who completed tuberculosis treatment. One cohort study in 326 South African mineworkers successfully treated for tuberculosis found a higher recurrence rate of tuberculosis in HIV-positive people, with 16.0 cases per 100 person-years of follow-up compared with 6.4 cases per 100 person-years of follow-up among HIV-negative people. In a randomised trial in Haiti, the tuberculosis recurrence rate among HIV-positive people not receiving post-treatment isoniazid was 7.8 cases per 100 person-years of follow-up compared with 0.4 per 100 person-years of follow-up in HIV-negative people.

## 248 | Amoebic dysentery

Chelsea Marie and William Arthur Petri Jr.

### KEY POINTS

- Invasive infection with the parasite *Entamoeba histolytica* can be asymptomatic, or can cause diarrhoea with blood and mucus, abdominal pains, and fever.
- Amoebic dysentery is transmitted in areas where poor sanitation allows contamination of drinking water and food with faeces. In these areas, up to 40% of people with diarrhoea may have amoebic dysentery.
- Fulminant amoebic dysentery is often fatal. Other complications include perforation of the colon, colonic ulcers, amoeboma, or chronic carriage.
- Metronidazole may be less effective than tinidazole at reducing clinical symptoms, but may be as effective at clearing parasites. Metronidazole may be more likely than tinidazole to cause adverse effects such as nausea.
- Ornidazole may be effective at curing amoebic dysentery compared with placebo, but can cause nausea and vomiting.
- Secnidazole, tinidazole, and metronidazole may be as effective as ornidazole at curing amoebic dysentery.
- Nitazoxanide is likely to be more effective than placebo at reducing clinical failure. Nitazoxanide may not be more effective than placebo at preventing parasitological failure.
- We don't know whether emetine, paromomycin, diloxanide, or diiodohydroxyquinoline are effective in treating amoebic dysentery as we found no trials. However, paromomycin, diloxanide, and diiodohydroxyquinoline are luminal amoebicides and there is consensus that they have insufficient tissue penetration to be effective against invasive intestinal disease.

(i) **Please visit http://clinicalevidence.bmj.com for full text and references**

| What are the effects of drug treatments for amoebic dysentery in endemic areas? | |
|---|---|
| Likely To Be Beneficial | • Metronidazole* <br> • Nitazoxanide <br> • Ornidazole <br> • Secnidazole* <br> • Tinidazole* |
| Unknown Effectiveness | • Emetine |
| Unlikely To Be Beneficial | • Diiodohydroxyquinoline* <br> • Diloxanide* <br> • Paromomycin* |

**Search date June 2013**

* Categorisation based on consensus.

**DEFINITION** Amoebic dysentery is caused by the protozoan parasite *Entamoeba histolytica*. Invasive intestinal parasitic infection can result in symptoms of fulminant dysentery, such as fever, chills, bloody or mucous diarrhoea, and abdominal discomfort. The dysentery can alternate with periods of constipation or remission. This review focuses on amoebic dysentery only, and includes populations with both suspected and documented disease in endemic areas where levels of infection do not exhibit wide fluctuations through time. The term "amoebic dysentery" encompasses people described as having symptomatic intestinal amoebiasis, amoebic colitis, amoebic diarrhoea, or invasive intestinal amoebiasis. Extraintestinal amoebiasis (e.g., amoebic liver abscess) and asymptomatic amoebiasis are not covered.

**INCIDENCE/PREVALENCE** We found no accurate global prevalence data for *E histolytica* infection and amoebic dysentery. Estimates on the prevalence of *Entamoeba* infection range from 1% to 40% of the population in Central and South America, Africa, and Asia, and from 0.2% to 10.8% in endemic areas of developed countries such as the US. However, these estimates are difficult to interpret, mainly because infection can remain asymptomatic or go unreported, and because many older reports do not distinguish *E histolytica* from the non-pathogenic, morphologically identical species *Entamoeba dispar*. Development and availability of more sophisticated methods (such as the enzyme-linked immunosorbent assay [ELISA]-based test) to differentiate the two species might give a more accurate estimate of its global prevalence. Infection with *E histolytica* is a common cause of acute diarrhoea in developing countries. One survey conducted in Egypt found that 38% of people with acute diarrhoea in an outpatient clinic had amoebic dysentery.

**AETIOLOGY/RISK FACTORS** Ingestion of cysts from food or water contaminated with faeces is the main route of *E histolytica* transmission. Low standards of hygiene and sanitation, particularly those related to crowding, tropical climate, contamination of food and water with faeces, and inadequate disposal of faeces, all account for the high rates of infection seen in developing countries. In developed countries, risk factors include communal living, oral and anal sex, compromised immune system, and migration or travel from endemic areas.

**PROGNOSIS** Amoebic dysentery may progress to amoeboma, fulminant colitis, toxic megacolon, and colonic ulcers, and may lead to perforation. Amoeboma may be mistaken for colonic carcinoma or pyogenic abscess. Amoebic dysentery may also result in chronic carriage and the chronic passing of amoebic cysts. Fulminant amoebic dysentery is reported to have 55% to 88% mortality. It is estimated that more than 500 million people are infected with *E histolytica* worldwide. Between 40,000 and 100,000 will die each year, placing this infection second to malaria in mortality caused by protozoan parasites.

## 250 | Chickenpox: treatment

Jonathan Cohen and Judith Breuer

### KEY POINTS

- Chickenpox is caused by primary infection with the varicella zoster virus. In healthy people, it is usually a mild, self-limiting illness, characterised by low-grade fever, malaise, and a generalised, itchy, vesicular rash.

  Disease can be severely complicated by pneumonitis or disseminated disease in some individuals, such as neonates, pregnant women, and those who are immunocompromised.

- Treatment of chickenpox with oral aciclovir given within 24 hours of onset of rash may be more effective than placebo in otherwise healthy children. It also seems to be more effective than placebo at treating chickenpox in otherwise healthy adults.

  When given later than 24 hours after onset of rash, aciclovir does not seem so effective at treating chickenpox compared with placebo, although the evidence for this is sparse.

  In clinical practice, intravenous aciclovir is used to treat severe disease irrespective of time of onset of rash. However, this is not based on evidence from placebo-controlled RCTs, as such studies would be considered unethical.

- Intravenous aciclovir may be more effective than placebo at reducing time to full crusting and clinical deterioration from chickenpox in children with malignancy and receiving chemotherapy.

  We found no evidence comparing intravenous aciclovir and placebo in other immunocompromised children.

- We found no evidence assessing aciclovir for the treatment of chickenpox in immunocompromised adults.

  Placebo-controlled RCTs assessing antivirals, such as aciclovir, in treating immunocompromised adults are unlikely to be carried out, as this is now considered unethical. However, the treatment effects of aciclovir are likely to be the same for immunocompromised adults as they are for immunocompromised children.

  In clinical practice, treatment of chickenpox in immunocompromised adults is usually initiated with intravenous aciclovir due to the poor absorption of oral aciclovir and the potential risk of rapid disease progression.

 **Please visit http://clinicalevidence.bmj.com for full text and references**

| What are the effects of treatment for chickenpox in healthy adults and children (including neonates) within 24 hours after onset of rash? | |
|---|---|
| Likely To Be Beneficial | • Aciclovir |

| What are the effects of treatment for chickenpox in healthy adults and children (including neonates) later than 24 hours after onset of rash? | |
|---|---|
| Unlikely To Be Beneficial | • Aciclovir (unlikely to be beneficial in people without severe disease, but intravenous aciclovir may be used in people with severe disease) |

## What are the effects of treatment for chickenpox in immunocompromised adults and children (including neonates)?

| Likely To Be Beneficial | • Aciclovir for treatment in immunocompromised adults* |
|---|---|
| | • Aciclovir for treatment in immunocompromised children (including neonates) |

**Search date January 2014**

*Based on consensus.

**DEFINITION** Chickenpox is caused by primary infection with varicella zoster virus. In healthy people, it is usually a mild, self-limiting illness, characterised by low-grade fever, malaise, and a generalised, itchy, vesicular rash. However, severe disease can develop leading to pneumonitis, hepatitis, thrombocytopenia, or encephalitis. Risk of severe disease is higher in pregnancy, in neonates (<28 days of life), and in people who are immunocompromised due to medication or disease. In most people, infection is uncomplicated. The most common complication in immunocompetent people is secondary bacterial skin infection, often seen in children younger than 5 years of age. Less commonly, acute cerebellar ataxia can occur in older children. At all ages, infection can be complicated by soft tissue or deeper invasive group A streptococcal infection. Following primary infection, the varicella zoster virus remains latent in the body. Subsequently, it can re-activate to cause herpes zoster (shingles). The prevention and treatment of herpes zoster is outside the scope of this review (see review on Postherpetic neuralgia, p 286).

**INCIDENCE/PREVALENCE** Chickenpox is extremely contagious. More than 90% of unvaccinated people will become infected during their lifetime, but infection occurs at different ages in different parts of the world. In the US, the UK, and Japan, more than 80% of people have been infected by the age of 10 years, and by the age of 20 to 30 years in India, South East Asia, and the Caribbean.

**AETIOLOGY/RISK FACTORS** Chickenpox is caused by primary infection with the varicella zoster virus.

**PROGNOSIS Infants and children:** In healthy children, the illness is usually mild, self-limiting, and uncomplicated. In the US, mortality in infants and children (aged 1–14 years) with chickenpox was about 7/100,000 in infants, and 1.4/100,000 in children. However, mortality has fallen with the introduction of universal varicella vaccination in the US. In Australia, mortality from chickenpox is about 0.5 to 0.6/100,000 in children aged 1 to 11 years, and about 1.2/100,000 in infants. Bacterial skin sepsis is the most common complication in children under 5 years of age, and acute cerebellar ataxia is the most common complication in older children; both cause hospital admission in 2–3/10,000 children. **Adults:** Mortality in adults is higher, at about 31/100,000, reflecting the more severe clinical course seen overall in this age group. Varicella pneumonia is the most common manifestation of severe disease, causing 20 to 30 hospital admissions/10,000 adults. Activation of latent varicella zoster virus infection can cause herpes zoster, also known as shingles (see review on Postherpetic neuralgia, p 286). **Cancer chemotherapy:** One case series found that more children receiving chemotherapy developed progressive chickenpox with multiple organ involvement compared with those in remission (19/60 [32%] of children receiving chemotherapy v 0/17 [0%] of children in remission), and more children died (4/60 [7%] of children receiving chemotherapy v 0/17 [0%] of children in remission). **HIV infection:** One retrospective case series (45 children with AIDS; no treatment reported) found that one in four (25%) children with AIDS who acquired chickenpox in hospital developed pneumonia, and 5% died. In a retrospective cohort study (73 children with HIV and chickenpox; 83% with symptomatic HIV; 14 children received varicella zoster immunoglobulin, of which nine received varicella zoster immunoglobulin within 48 hours of exposure), infection beyond 2 months occurred in 10 children (14%), and recurrent varicella zoster virus infections occurred in 38 children (55%). There was a strong association

*(continued over)*

*(from previous page)*

between an increasing number of recurrences and low CD4 cell counts. Half of recurrent infections involved generalised rashes, and the other half had zoster. **Newborns:** Newborns are at high risk if they develop chickenpox within the first 28 days of life. Exposure in these cases is often from a mother who has been infected with the varicella zoster virus in late pregnancy. If the mother develops a rash between 7 days before to 7 days after delivery, there will be no passive transfer of protective antibody from the mother to the baby, putting the neonate at high risk. We found no cohort studies of untreated children with perinatal exposure to chickenpox. One cohort study (281 neonates receiving varicella zoster immunoglobulin because their mothers had developed a chickenpox rash during the month before or after delivery) found that 134 (48%) developed a chickenpox rash and 19 (14%) developed severe chickenpox. Sixteen (84%) of the 19 cases of severe chickenpox occurred in neonates of mothers whose rash had started between 4 days before and 2 days after delivery. **Pregnancy:** There is a higher risk of severe chickenpox at all stages of pregnancy. During the first trimester there is a risk of developing fetal varicella syndrome which may lead to fetal death, even with non-severe maternal disease.

Jeffrey Kravetz

## KEY POINTS

- Infection with *Toxoplasma gondii* is asymptomatic or mild in immunocompetent people, and leads to lifelong immunity, but it can have serious consequences in pregnancy.

  About 5 per 1000 non-immune pregnant women may acquire toxoplasma infection, with a 10% to 100% risk of transmission to the baby.

  Infection is usually acquired from undercooked meat, or from fruit and vegetables contaminated with cat faeces.

  Fetal infection can cause eye and brain damage, growth retardation, and intrauterine death.

  Risks of transmission to the baby are higher later in pregnancy, but risks of infection causing harm to the baby are greater earlier in pregnancy.

  Children with subclinical infection at birth may have cognitive, motor, or visual defects that may be difficult to diagnose in early childhood.

- We don't know whether treating infected pregnant women with spiramycin, pyrimethamine–sulfonamides, or both reduces the risk of fetal infection, as the few trials we found have produced conflicting results.

  It is possible that treatment of infection in pregnancy may save the pregnancy without preventing infection, which could increase the prevalence of congenital disease.

- We don't know whether antiparasitic drugs given to neonates who have been infected prenatally are effective, although there is consensus that infected infants should be treated with pyrimethamine and sulfadiazine for 6 to 12 months.

 **Please visit http://clinicalevidence.bmj.com for full text and references**

| What are the effects on mother and baby of treating toxoplasmosis during pregnancy to reduce risk of vertical transmission and treat fetal infection? | |
| --- | --- |
| Unknown Effectiveness | • Antiparasitic drugs in pregnancy |

| What are the effects of treating toxoplasmosis in neonates infected with toxoplasmosis prenatally? | |
| --- | --- |
| Unknown Effectiveness | • Antiparasitic drugs in neonates |

**Search date June 2013**

**DEFINITION** Toxoplasmosis is caused by the parasite *Toxoplasma gondii*. Infection is asymptomatic or unremarkable in immunocompetent individuals, but leads to a lifelong antibody response. During pregnancy, toxoplasmosis can be transmitted across the placenta and may cause intrauterine death, neonatal growth retardation, mental retardation, ocular defects, and blindness in later life. Congenital toxoplasmosis (confirmed infection of the fetus or newborn) can also present at birth: either as subclinical disease, which may evolve with neurological or ophthalmological disease later in life, or as a disease of varying severity, ranging from mild ocular damage to severe mental retardation.

**INCIDENCE/PREVALENCE** Reported rates of toxoplasma seroprevalence vary among and within countries, as well as over time. The risk of primary infection is highest in young

*(continued over)*

*(from previous page)*

people, including young women during pregnancy. We found no cohort studies describing annual seroconversion rates in women of childbearing age or incidence of primary infection. One systematic review (search date 1996) identified 15 studies that reported rates of seroconversion in non-immune pregnant women ranging from 2.4/1000 to 16/1000 in Europe and from 2/1000 to 6/1000 in the US. France began screening for congenital toxoplasmosis in 1978; during the period from 1980 to 1995, the seroconversion rate during pregnancy in non-immune women was 4/1000 to 5/1000.

**AETIOLOGY/RISK FACTORS** Toxoplasma infection is usually acquired by ingesting either sporocysts (from unwashed fruit or vegetables contaminated by cat faeces) or tissue cysts (from raw or undercooked meat). The risk of contracting toxoplasma infection varies with eating habits, contact with cats and other pets, and occupational exposure.

**PROGNOSIS** One systematic review of studies conducted from 1983 to 1996 found no population-based prospective studies of the natural history of toxoplasma infection during pregnancy. One systematic review (search date 1997; 9 controlled, non-randomised studies) found that untreated toxoplasmosis acquired during pregnancy was associated with infection rates in children of between 10% and 100%. We found two European studies that correlated gestation at time of maternal seroconversion with risk of transmission and severity of disease at birth. Risk of transmission increased with gestational age at maternal seroconversion, reaching 70% to 90% when seroconversion occurred after 30 weeks' gestation. By contrast, the risk of the infant developing clinical disease was highest when maternal seroconversion occurred early in pregnancy. The highest risk of developing early signs of disease (including chorioretinitis and hydrocephaly) was about 10%, recorded when seroconversion occurred between 24 and 30 weeks' gestation. Infants with congenital toxoplasmosis and generalised neurological abnormalities at birth develop mental retardation, growth retardation, blindness or visual defects, seizures, and spasticity. Children with subclinical infection at birth may have cognitive, motor, and visual deficits, which may go undiagnosed for many years. One case control study (845 school children in Brazil) found mental retardation and retinochoroiditis to be significantly associated with positive toxoplasma serology (population-attributable risk 6–9%).

Marissa Alejandria

## KEY POINTS

- Infection with the dengue virus, transmitted by the *Aedes* mosquito, ranges from asymptomatic or undifferentiated febrile illness to fatal haemorrhagic fever, and affects up to 100 million people per year worldwide.

  Non-severe dengue fever is characterised by a sudden onset of high fever associated with any of the following signs and symptoms: rash, severe aches and pains, and any of the following warning signs, abdominal pain or tenderness, persistent vomiting, clinical fluid accumulation, mucosal bleeding, lethargy, restlessness, liver enlargement greater than 2 cm, and an increase in haematocrit concurrent with rapid decrease in platelet count. Presence of warning signs warrants strict observation.

  Severe dengue haemorrhagic fever (previously dengue haemorrhagic fever and dengue shock syndrome) is characterised by severe plasma leakage, severe bleeding, and severe organ involvement manifested as elevated liver enzymes, impaired sensorium, and myocarditis. Severe plasma leakage is manifested by a rise or drop in haematocrit, fluid in the lungs or abdomen leading to respiratory distress, and dengue shock syndrome.

  Dengue haemorrhagic fever and dengue shock syndrome are major causes of hospital admission and mortality in children. If untreated, mortality can be as high as 20%. With appropriate case management, mortality can be reduced to less than 1%, depending on the availability of appropriate supportive care.

- Crystalloids seem as effective as colloids in children with moderately severe dengue shock syndrome. We found no RCTs comparing crystalloids versus colloids in children with severe dengue shock syndrome.

- There is consensus that blood component transfusion (fresh frozen plasma, packed red blood cells, or platelets) should be added to intravenous fluids in children with coagulopathy or bleeding. The optimal time for beginning transfusion is unclear.

- We don't know whether adding corticosteroids or intravenous immunoglobulin to standard intravenous fluids reduces the risks of shock, pleural effusion, or mortality.

(i) **Please visit http://clinicalevidence.bmj.com for full text and references**

| What are the effects of supportive treatments for dengue haemorrhagic fever or dengue shock syndrome in children? | |
|---|---|
| Likely To Be Beneficial | • Adding blood component transfusion to standard intravenous fluids* <br><br> • Crystalloids compared with colloids (evidence crystalloids as effective as colloids in moderately severe dengue shock syndrome; evidence insufficient in severe dengue shock syndrome) |
| Unknown Effectiveness | • Adding corticosteroids to standard intravenous fluids <br><br> • Adding intravenous immunoglobulin to standard intravenous fluids |

Search date March 2014

*Categorisation based on consensus.

**DEFINITION** Dengue infection is a mosquito-borne arboviral infection. An important criterion to consider in the diagnosis of dengue infection is history of travel or residence in a dengue-endemic area within 2 weeks of the onset of fever. The spectrum of dengue virus infection ranges from an asymptomatic or undifferentiated febrile illness to severe infection. In 2009, the classification of dengue into **dengue fever**, **dengue haemorrhagic fever**, and **dengue shock syndrome** was simplified into **non-severe** and **severe dengue**. Non-severe dengue is further divided into two subgroups — patients with warning signs and those without warning signs. This revised classification is aimed at guiding clinicians in deciding where and how patients should be observed and managed. Criteria for diagnosis of probable dengue include history of travel or residence in a dengue-endemic area, plus high-grade fever of acute onset and two of the following signs and symptoms: nausea/vomiting, rash, severe aches and pains (also called 'breakbone fever'), positive tourniquet test, leukopenia, and any warning sign. Presence of any of the following warning signs — abdominal pain or tenderness, persistent vomiting, clinical fluid accumulation, mucosal bleeding, lethargy, restlessness, liver enlargement greater than 2 cm, and an increase in haematocrit concurrent with rapid decrease in platelet count — will require strict observation and medical intervention. Criteria for severe dengue fever include severe plasma leakage, severe bleeding as evaluated by the clinician, and severe organ involvement. Severe plasma leakage is manifested by a rise or drop in haematocrit, fluid in the lungs or abdomen leading to respiratory distress, and dengue shock syndrome. Haemorrhagic manifestations include skin haemorrhages, mucosal and gastrointestinal tract bleeding, and pulmonary haemorrhage. Severe organ involvement is manifested by any of the following: elevated liver enzymes (AST, ALT >1000), impaired consciousness (dengue encephalopathy), and dengue myocarditis. The illness usually begins abruptly, occurring in three phases: febrile, critical, and recovery. The critical phase sets in during defervescence, when capillary permeability is increased accompanied by haemoconcentration, leading to hypovolaemic shock that can result in organ impairment, metabolic acidosis, disseminated intravascular coagulation, and severe haemorrhage. This review deals with interventions for dengue haemorrhagic fever and dengue shock syndrome in children.

**INCIDENCE/PREVALENCE** Dengue fever and dengue haemorrhagic fever are public health problems worldwide, particularly in low-lying areas where *Aedes aegypti*, a domestic mosquito, is present. Cities near to the equator but high in the Andes are generally free from dengue because *Aedes* mosquitoes do not survive at high altitudes. However, variations in the climate system (particularly climate warming) has increased the geographic distribution of *Aedes* mosquitoes. The highest published elevation records for *Aedes aegypti* in the Americas are 1700 to 2130 m for Mexico and 2200 m for Colombia. Worldwide, an estimated 50–100 million cases of dengue fever, and hundreds of thousands of dengue haemorrhagic fever, occur yearly. Recent estimates using novel mapping techniques (based on an extensive database of 10,000 clinical records) provided a global estimate of 390 million new infections per year, with symptomatic and asymptomatic dengue case burden at 96 and 294 million, respectively. Endemic regions are the Americas, South East Asia, the western Pacific, Africa, and the eastern Mediterranean. Major global demographic changes and their consequences (particularly, increases in the density and geographic distribution of the vector with declining vector control, unreliable water supply systems, increasing non-biodegradable container and poor solid waste disposal, increased geographic range of virus transmission due to increased air travel, and increased population density in urban areas) are responsible for the resurgence of dengue in the past century. The WHO estimates that global temperature rises of 1.0 to 3.5°C may increase transmission of dengue fever by shortening the extrinsic incubation period of viruses within the mosquito, adding 20,000 to 30,000 more fatal cases annually.

**AETIOLOGY/RISK FACTORS** Dengue virus serotypes 1 to 4 (DEN 1, 2, 3, 4) belonging to the flavivirus genus are the aetiological agents. These serotypes are closely related, but antigenically distinct. *Aedes aegypti*, the principal vector, transmits the virus to and between humans. Dengue haemorrhagic fever and dengue shock syndrome typically occur in children under the age of 15 years, although dengue fever primarily occurs in adults and older children. Important risk factors influencing who will develop dengue haemorrhagic fever or severe disease during epidemics include the virus strain and serotype, immune status of the host, age, and genetic predisposition. There is evidence that sequential infection or pre-existing antidengue antibodies increases the risk of dengue haemorrhagic fever through antibody-dependent enhancement. **Diagnosis:** To confirm dengue infection, identification of virus/viral RNA/viral antigen and the detection of an antibody response are preferred than either approach alone. During the first 4 to 5 days of illness, while the patient is febrile, dengue infections may be diagnosed by virus isolation in cell culture, by detection of viral RNA by nucleic acid amplification tests, or by detection of viral antigens by ELISA or rapid antigen detection tests using serum or plasma and other tissues. After day 5, dengue viruses and antigens disappear from the blood co-incident with the appearance of specific antibodies. Hence, at the end of the acute phase of infection, serology is the method of choice for diagnosis. Antibody response to infection differs according to the immune status of the host. In primary dengue infection, the antibodies rise slowly. IgM antibodies are the first to appear, detectable in 50% of patients by days 3 to 5 after onset of illness, increasing to 80% by day 5, and 99% by day 10. IgM levels peak about 2 weeks after the onset of symptoms and then decline to undetectable levels over 2 to 3 months. Anti-dengue serum IgG is detectable at low titres at the end of the first week of illness, increasing slowly thereafter. Serum IgG remains detectable after several months, and probably even for life. During a secondary dengue infection antibody titres rise rapidly with IgG as the dominant immunoglobulin. IgG is detectable at high levels, even in the acute phase, and persists for periods lasting from 10 months to life. Early convalescent stage IgM levels are significantly lower in secondary infections than in primary ones and may be undetectable in some cases, depending on the test used. To distinguish primary and secondary dengue infections, IgM/IgG antibody ratios are commonly used.

**PROGNOSIS** Dengue fever is an incapacitating disease, but prognosis is favourable in previously healthy adults, although dengue haemorrhagic fever and dengue shock syndrome are major causes of hospital admission and mortality in children. Dengue fever is generally self-limiting, with less than 1% case fatality. The acute phase of the illness lasts for 2 to 7 days, but the convalescent phase may be prolonged for weeks associated with fatigue and depression, especially in adults. Prognosis in dengue haemorrhagic fever and dengue shock syndrome depends on prevention, or early recognition and treatment of shock. Once shock sets in, fatality may be as high as 12% to 44%. However, in centres with appropriate intensive supportive treatment, fatality can be less than 1%. There is no specific antiviral treatment. The standard treatment is to give intravenous fluids to expand plasma volume. People usually recover after prompt and adequate fluid and electrolyte supportive treatment. The optimal fluid regimen, however, remains the subject of debate. This is particularly important in dengue, where one of the management difficulties is to correct hypovolaemia rapidly without precipitating fluid overload. WHO guidelines published in 2009 provide guidance on fluid management and blood transfusions.

Christopher S. Heather

## KEY POINTS

- Diarrhoea is an alteration in normal bowel movement, characterised by increased frequency, volume, and water content of stools, often defined clinically as an increase in stool frequency to three or more liquid or semi-formed motions in 24 hours.

- It is estimated that approximately 30% to 70% of international travellers will develop diarrhoea during their travels or after returning home.

- Risk of developing diarrhoea depends on destination, season of travel, and length of stay.

- Travellers to resource-poor countries in Africa, Asia, the Middle East, and South America are at higher risk than travellers to high-income countries.

- Travellers' diarrhoea is frequently self-limiting in otherwise-healthy adults and children and may require only supportive treatment unless symptoms are prolonged or severe.

- However, treatment with the aim of reducing symptom duration and severity should be considered, given the potential inconvenience associated with diarrhoea while travelling.

- This review examines the effects of treatments in adults with travellers' diarrhoea.

- Antibiotics and antimotility agents seem to be effective in treating people from resource-rich countries who have travellers' diarrhoea.

    Antibiotics plus antimotility agents may be more effective than antibiotics or antimotility agents alone at reducing the duration of diarrhoea and increasing cure rates in people with travellers' diarrhoea.

    Although we searched for all antimotility agents, we only found evidence for loperamide in people with travellers' diarrhoea.

    Efficacy of individual antibiotics could not be assessed due to the limited geographical restriction of most studies reviewed. Antibiotic efficacy may be affected by local antimicrobial resistance profiles and aetiological agent.

- Bismuth subsalicylate is effective in treating travellers' diarrhoea, but less so than loperamide, and with more adverse effects (primarily black tongue and black stools).

- We don't know the effectiveness of the antisecretory agent racecadotril, oral rehydration solutions, or restricting diet in reducing symptoms of diarrhoea in people travelling to resource-poor countries.

(i) **Please visit http://clinicalevidence.bmj.com for full text and references**

| **What are the effects of treatments for mild-to-moderate diarrhoea in adults from resource-rich countries travelling to resource-poor countries?** | |
|---|---|
| Likely To Be Beneficial | • Antibiotics (empirical use for mild-to-moderate diarrhoea) |
| | • Antibiotics plus antimotility agents |
| | • Antimotility agents |

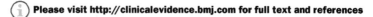

©BMJ Publishing Group Ltd 2015

| | |
|---|---|
| | • Bismuth subsalicylate (reduced duration of diarrhoea compared with placebo, but less effective than loperamide) |
| **Unknown Effectiveness** | • Diet<br>• Oral rehydration solutions<br>• Racecadotril |

**Search date September 2014**

---

**DEFINITION** Diarrhoea is an alteration in normal bowel movement, characterised by increased frequency, volume, and water content of stools. It is often clinically defined as an increase in stool frequency to three or more liquid or semi-formed motions in 24 hours. Acute diarrhoea is usually defined as diarrhoea of 14 days' duration or less, while persistent diarrhoea is of over 14 days' duration. Diarrhoea of over 30 days' duration is frequently defined as 'chronic'. This review examines the effects of treatments for travellers' diarrhoea in adults. For the purposes of this review, travellers' diarrhoea is defined as diarrhoea occurring during or shortly after travel in people who have crossed a national boundary from a resource-rich to a resource-poor country.

**INCIDENCE/PREVALENCE** It is estimated that 30% to 70% of international travellers will develop a diarrhoeal illness during or after their travel. Incidence of diarrhoea in travellers is dependent on season of travel and destination country, with people travelling to Africa, Asia, Mexico, Central and South America, and the Middle East at highest risk. The epidemiology of travellers' diarrhoea is not well understood. Incidence is higher in travellers visiting resource-poor countries, but it varies widely by location and season of travel.

**AETIOLOGY/RISK FACTORS** The cause of diarrhoea depends on geographical location, standards of food hygiene, sanitation, water supply, and season. No pathogens are identified in more than half of people with diarrhoea. In returning travellers, about 50% of episodes are caused by bacteria such as enterotoxigenic *Escherichia coli*, *Salmonella*, *Shigella*, *Campylobacter*, *Vibrio*, enteroadherent *E coli*, *Yersinia*, and *Aeromonas*.

**PROGNOSIS** Diarrhoea in travellers returning to resource-rich countries is usually self-limiting. However, severe or prolonged symptoms may develop in some people. Furthermore, travellers' diarrhoea may be incapacitating, causing significant inconvenience while travelling. It may, therefore, be desirable to treat mild-to-moderate diarrhoea in this setting.

Suzanne Norris and Abdul Hadi Mohsen

## KEY POINTS

- Nearly a third of the world's population has been infected by hepatitis B at some point, and at least 350 million people have become chronic carriers. Progressive liver damage occurs in up to 25% of carriers.

    In areas of high endemicity, transmission occurs largely in childhood, from an infected mother to her baby, or between members of a household.

    In areas of low endemicity, transmission usually occurs as a result of sexual activity, intravenous drug use, or occupational exposure.

    The risk of developing hepatitis B depends largely on the vaccination policy of the country of residence, and routine vaccination of all infants is recommended by the WHO.

- Selective vaccination of infants with recombinant or plasma-derived vaccines in countries with high endemicity of hepatitis B reduces occurrence and chronic carrier state.

    Combining vaccine with hepatitis B immunoglobulin is more effective than vaccine alone.

- Universal vaccination of infants with recombinant or plasma-derived vaccines, in countries with high endemicity of hepatitis B, reduces the risk of acute hepatitis, chronic carrier state, and complications of chronic infection, and may be more effective than selective vaccination of high-risk individuals.

    Vaccination of children born to hepatitis B surface antigen (HBsAg)-positive mothers prevents development of a chronic carrier state compared with placebo.

- Universal vaccination of infants or adolescents in low-endemic areas may reduce the risk of infection, or of developing a chronic carrier state, but we don't know how different vaccination strategies compare, as no studies have been done.

- Selective vaccination of high-risk individuals in countries with low hepatitis B endemicity may prevent acute infection and development of a chronic carrier state.

    Uptake of vaccination may be low, even in high-risk groups.

- Vaccination is associated generally with mild adverse effects, although more serious autoimmune adverse effects can occur rarely.

- We don't know whether selective vaccination of people with known chronic liver disease not caused by hepatitis B reduces subsequent infection rates, as few studies have been done.

- The evidence reported here is the best available evidence for this type of intervention, and further research is unlikely to change the conclusions reached.

 **Please visit http://clinicalevidence.bmj.com for full text and references**

### What are the effects of vaccination against hepatitis B infection in countries with high endemicity?

| Beneficial | • Selective vaccination of high-risk individuals (evidence only for children born to HBsAg-positive mothers; plasma-derived vaccine and recombinant vaccine are equally effective, more so when combined with hepatitis B immunoglobulin) |
| --- | --- |

- Universal vaccination of infants (more effective than placebo or no treatment; limited evidence that it may be better than selective vaccination of high-risk individuals)

## What are the effects of vaccination against hepatitis B infection in countries with low endemicity?

| | |
|---|---|
| Likely To Be Beneficial | • Selective vaccination of high-risk individuals |
| | • Universal vaccination of adolescents |
| | • Universal vaccination of infants |
| Unknown Effectiveness | • Selective vaccination of people with known chronic liver disease not caused by hepatitis B |

**Search date June 2008**

**DEFINITION** Hepatitis B is a viral infectious disease with an incubation period of 40 to 160 days. Acute hepatitis B infection is characterised by anorexia, vague abdominal discomfort, nausea and vomiting, jaundice, and occasional fever. Illness is associated with deranged liver function tests (especially raised alanine transaminases) and the presence of serological markers of acute hepatitis B infection (e.g., hepatitis B surface antigen [HBsAg] or antibody to hepatitis B core antigen [anti-HBc IgM]).

**INCIDENCE/PREVALENCE** The incidence of acute hepatitis B, and prevalence of its chronic carrier state, varies widely across the globe. In areas with high endemicity (HBsAg prevalence 8% or more; e.g., Southeast Asia and Africa), more than half of the population becomes infected at some point. In countries with low endemicity (HBsAg prevalence <2%; e.g., North America, Western Europe, and Australia), most of the population does not become infected. Nearly a third of the world's population has been infected by hepatitis B at some point, and at least 350 million people (5–6% of the world's population) are currently chronic carriers of hepatitis B infection.

**AETIOLOGY/RISK FACTORS** In countries with high endemicity, most transmissions occur during childhood from an infected mother to her baby (vertical transmission) or from one family member to another (horizontal transmission). Horizontal transmission is thought to be an important route of hepatitis B infection during early childhood, and probably occurs mainly through unnoticed contact with blood from infected family members. In countries with high endemicity, the proportion of chronic HBsAg carriage attributable to vertical transmission has been estimated at 5% to 50%. The proportion of chronic HBsAg carriage attributable to horizontal transmission is not known, although one survey in China found that 27.2% of families had one or more HBsAg-positive members. In countries with low endemicity, most hepatitis B infections occur later — from sexual activity, intravenous drug use, or occupational exposure. Less frequent causes of infection include household contact, regular haemodialysis, transmission from a healthcare professional, and receipt of infected organs or blood products. The vaccination policy of a country is a large determinant of the risk of developing hepatitis B. Since the development of plasma-derived hepatitis B vaccine in the early 1980s, subsequently replaced by recombinant vaccine, many countries have adopted a policy of universal vaccination of infants. On the basis of disease burden, the WHO recommended that the hepatitis B vaccine be incorporated into routine infant and childhood vaccination programmes in countries with high endemicity by 1995 and in all countries by 1997. However, in many countries with low endemicity, universal vaccination policy remains controversial and has still not been adopted. Some of these countries have adopted a policy of selective vaccination of high-risk individuals. Others have adopted a universal adolescent vaccination policy.

**PROGNOSIS** Hepatitis B infection resolves after the acute infection in 90% to 95% of cases. In the remainder, it may result in several serious sequelae. Massive hepatic necrosis occurs

*(continued over)*

*(from previous page)*

in 1% of people with acute viral hepatitis, leading to a serious and often fatal condition called acute fulminant hepatitis. Between 2% and 10% of those infected as adults become chronic carriers, indicated by HBsAg persistence for more than 6 months. Chronic carriage is more frequent in those infected as children, and reaches up to 90% in those infected during the perinatal period. Between 20% and 25% of chronic carriers develop a progressive chronic liver disease. In about one quarter to one third of cases, this progresses to cirrhosis and hepatocellular carcinoma. These complications usually arise in older adults, and are major causes of mortality in populations with high hepatitis B endemicity. Observational studies suggest that, in these countries, almost 80% of chronic liver disease and cirrhosis are attributed to hepatitis B, and these complications lead to at least 1 million deaths every year worldwide.

Alan Hoi Lun Yau, Vladimir Marquez-Azalgara, and Eric M. Yoshida

## KEY POINTS

- Chronic hepatitis C virus (HCV) infection is defined as persistent, detectable serum HCV RNA for a period greater than 6 months, with or without derangement in liver function tests.

  About 60% to 85% of people infected with HCV will go on to develop chronic hepatitis C, which is now believed to affect 3% of the world's population.

  Complications of chronic HCV infection include cirrhosis, compensated and decompensated liver disease, and hepatocellular carcinoma.

  Many people chronically infected with HCV remain asymptomatic, including a significant proportion of those who progress to cirrhosis, so routine screening of people in high-risk groups is advisable.

- This overview deals only with chronic HCV infection without liver decompensation.

- The landscape of HCV antiviral therapy has changed rapidly in the past 3 years. The limited efficacy and tolerability of interferon-based antiviral regimens has prompted the recent development of direct-acting antiviral agents, such as sofosbuvir, simeprevir, and ledipasvir. During this time, several different direct-acting antiviral agents have been approved by the FDA as oral therapies for the treatment of hepatitis C.

- Recommendations in major national clinical guidelines in this field are often based on both RCT and non-RCT evidence and should be referred to for guidance on current routine clinical practice. However, for this overview, in line with most other *BMJ Clinical Evidence* overviews, we have only reported on evidence from RCTs and systematic reviews of RCTs. We have reported on selected direct-acting antiviral agents, but in this fast-moving field, we will consider broadening this list of interventions in future updates.

- The following points are based on our search for evidence from RCTs and systematic reviews of RCTs.

- In treatment-naïve people with HCV without cirrhosis:

  Sofosbuvir plus ribavirin may be more effective than placebo at reducing HCV RNA levels at the end of treatment, and increasing sustained virological response at up to 12 weeks (SVR12) after the end of treatment in treatment-naïve people with HCV genotypes 2 or 3 without cirrhosis. However, this effect appears to be greater for HCV genotype 2 than for genotype 3.

- In treatment-naïve people with HCV with cirrhosis:

  Sofosbuvir plus ribavirin may be more effective than placebo at reducing HCV RNA levels at the end of treatment in treatment-naïve people with HCV genotypes 2 or 3 with cirrhosis.

  Sofosbuvir plus ribavirin may be more effective than placebo at increasing sustained virological response at up to 12 weeks (SVR12) after the end of treatment in treatment-naïve people with HCV genotypes 2 and 3 with cirrhosis. However, this effect appears to be greater for HCV genotype 2 than for genotype 3.

- Sofosbuvir plus ribavirin appears to be safe and well-tolerated, with an adverse event profile consistent with ribavirin alone.

- We found no RCTs assessing the effectiveness of sofosbuvir alone, sofosbuvir plus simeprevir, or sofosbuvir plus ledipasvir in treatment-naïve people with chronic HCV with or without cirrhosis.

- The Q80K polymorphism, associated with genotype 1a, confers resistance to simeprevir. Therefore, testing for this genetic variation may be important before considering treatment with this drug.

(i) **Please visit http://clinicalevidence.bmj.com for full text and references**

## What are the effects of interferon-free treatments in treatment-naïve people with chronic hepatitis C infection without cirrhosis?

| | |
|---|---|
| **Likely To Be Beneficial** | • Sofosbuvir plus ribavirin versus placebo/no treatment (in genotype 2 and genotype 3) |
| **Unknown Effectiveness** | • Sofosbuvir alone<br>• Sofosbuvir plus ledipasvir (with or without ribavirin)<br>• Sofosbuvir plus ribavirin versus peginterferon plus ribavirin<br>• Sofosbuvir plus ribavirin versus sofosbuvir plus peginterferon plus ribavirin<br>• Sofosbuvir plus simeprevir (with or without ribavirin) |

## What are the effects of interferon-free treatments in treatment-naïve people with chronic hepatitis C infection with cirrhosis?

| | |
|---|---|
| **Likely To Be Beneficial** | • Sofosbuvir plus ribavirin versus placebo/no treatment (in genotype 2; efficacy in genotype 3 is less clear) |
| **Unknown Effectiveness** | • Sofosbuvir alone<br>• Sofosbuvir plus ledipasvir (with or without ribavirin)<br>• Sofosbuvir plus ribavirin versus peginterferon plus ribavirin<br>• Sofosbuvir plus ribavirin versus sofosbuvir plus peginterferon plus ribavirin<br>• Sofosbuvir plus simeprevir (with or without ribavirin) |

**Search date August 2014**

---

**DEFINITION** Hepatitis C virus (HCV), identified in 1989, is a member of the *flaviviridae* family of spherical, enveloped, positive-strand RNA viruses. There are six different HCV genotypes with variable distribution worldwide; some genotypes have multiple subtypes. Genotype 1 is the most common and the most resistant to treatment. Chronic HCV infection is defined as persistent, detectable serum HCV RNA for a period greater than 6 months, with or without derangement in liver function tests. This is in contrast to acute HCV infection, in which serum HCV RNA clears within 6 months. Prospective studies have shown that 60% to 85% of HCV-infected people will develop chronic infection. This review only deals with chronic HCV infection without liver decompensation. The effect of treatment is measured by the presence or absence of detectable serum HCV RNA. The loss of detectable HCV RNA at the end of the treatment period is defined as the end of treatment virological response (EOTR). The loss of detectable HCV RNA 24 weeks or greater after the completion of treatment is termed the sustained virological response (SVR24). The loss of detectable HCV RNA 12 weeks after the completion of treatment is termed SVR12, and this has been recommended by the FDA as the primary efficacy endpoint in recent clinical trials as it has a positive predictive value of

98% for SVR24. Response to treatment is defined as the loss of detectable serum HCV RNA. Non-response is defined as a failure to clear serum HCV RNA during the treatment period. A relapse from treatment is defined as loss of serum HCV RNA during treatment, which reappears during the follow-up period, typically within 24 weeks of treatment episode.

**INCIDENCE/PREVALENCE** HCV has emerged as a major viral pandemic over the past two decades, with about 3% of the world's population chronically infected. HCV prevalence varies throughout the world, with the highest number of infections reported in Egypt (6%–28%). In the US, an estimated four million people are positive for HCV antibodies, reflecting a prevalence rate of 2%; and about 35,000 new HCV infections are estimated to occur each year. In Europe, the prevalence of HCV infection ranges from about 0.5% to 2%. Diagnosis of HCV infection is often the result of active screening, because many people chronically infected with HCV remain asymptomatic, including a significant number of those who progress to cirrhosis. The true incidence of HCV is, therefore, difficult to calculate accurately, because this relates to the prevalence of risk factors for HCV transmission, in particular injection drug use.

**AETIOLOGY/RISK FACTORS** HCV is mainly blood borne, and transmission occurs primarily through exposure to infected blood. This exposure may occur because of infected needles used for injection drug use, blood transfusion or solid organ transplantation from infected donors in the absence of universal screening procedures, maternal (vertical) transmission, unsafe medical practices, and occupational exposure to infected blood. As a result of HCV screening, the absolute risk of acquiring infection through blood components or products is now small — less than 1/400,000 units of blood transfused. HCV vertical transmission is uncommon, with a transmission rate of less than 6%. Poverty, high-risk sexual behaviour, and having less than 12 years of education are linked to an increased risk of infection. However, in some cases, no risk factors can be identified. Of the six known HCV genotypes, genotype 1 is the most common in developed countries, with values of 47% to 72%. In North America (unlike Europe and Asia), genotype 1a is the most common and is associated with Q80K polymorphism in 30% to 47% of people. The Q80K polymorphism confers resistance to the drug simeprevir (a second-generation NS3/4A protease inhibitor), which leads to a considerably lower SVR, such that testing for this genetic variation is recommended before commencement of treatment.

**PROGNOSIS** The spectrum of liver disease and the rate of disease progression vary in people with chronic HCV infection. Complications of chronic HCV infection include cirrhosis, compensated and decompensated liver disease, and hepatocellular carcinoma. Studies suggest that one third of people with chronic HCV infection are 'rapid progressors' (time from infection to cirrhosis <20 years); one third are 'intermediate progressors' (time to cirrhosis 20–50 years); and one third are 'slow or non-progressors' (time to cirrhosis >50 years). Factors associated with disease progression include: older age at acquisition; male sex; co-infection with HIV, hepatitis B virus, or both; co-existing liver disease; and excessive alcohol consumption. In people who develop cirrhosis, the 5-year risk of decompensation is 15% to 20%; the 5-year risk of hepatocellular carcinoma is 10%; and the annual risk of hepatocellular carcinoma is 1% to 5% per year.

Eliana Ferroni and Tom Jefferson

### KEY POINTS

- Influenza viruses are constantly altering their antigenic structure, and every year the WHO recommends which strains of influenza should be included in vaccines.

  During the autumn–winter months, influenza circulates more frequently (influenza seasons), causing a greater proportion of influenza-like illness and sometimes serious seasonal epidemics.

  The incidence of symptoms depends on the underlying immunity of the population.

- When a significantly different form of influenza occurs by mutation, it can greatly increase infection rates as well as morbidity and mortality (a pandemic).

- Influenza and influenza-like illness (caused by a range of other viruses) are clinically indistinguishable.

  Trials of vaccines assess how to prevent the symptoms and consequences of both, as well as assessing infection rates.

  Many of the studies we found were industry sponsored or written by employees of vaccine companies.

- Vaccines are effective in reducing symptoms and school absence in children >2 years old, but we found no evidence that they reduce hospitalisation, pneumonia, or death.

- Influenza vaccines have a modest effect in reducing influenza symptoms and working days lost in healthy adults. We found no evidence that they affect complications, such as pneumonia or hospitalisations. However, vaccines may be associated with adverse effects.

- Owing to the poor quality of the evidence, we cannot draw conclusions about the effects of influenza vaccines in people aged 65 years and older.

- Single studies reporting data for one or two seasons are difficult to interpret and not easy to generalise from, because of the marked variability of viral circulation.

- Owing to concerns regarding the completeness of evidence on some antivirals, we have omitted the questions on antiviral chemoprophylaxis and treatment from the review at this update. These questions will be reinstated at the next update following publication of further data.

 **Please visit http://clinicalevidence.bmj.com for full text and references**

| What are the effects of vaccines to prevent influenza? | |
|---|---|
| Likely To Be Beneficial | • Vaccines in adults (prevention of cases)<br>• Vaccines in children (prevention of symptoms and/or infection) |
| Unknown Effectiveness | • Vaccines in older people |

**Search date March 2011**

**DEFINITION** Influenza is an acute respiratory illness caused by infection with influenza A and B viruses. The illness can affect both the upper and lower respiratory tract and is often accompanied by systemic signs and symptoms, such as: abrupt onset of fever, chills, non-productive cough, myalgias, headache, nasal congestion, sore throat, and fatigue.

**Diagnosis:** Not everyone infected with influenza viruses will become symptomatic, and not everyone with the above symptoms will have influenza. This is because different viral and bacterial circulating agents cause an influenza-like illness with a clinical picture each year that is indistinguishable from influenza. Between 40% and 85% of infections with influenza result in clinical illness, depending on age and pre-existing immunity to the virus. One systematic review (search date 2004; 6 RCTs in Europe, North America, and the southern hemisphere; 7164 people) of symptoms of influenza found that, in all age groups, the likelihood of influenza was decreased by the absence of fever (OR 0.40, 95% CI 0.25 to 0.66), cough (OR 0.42, 95% CI 0.31 to 0.57), or nasal congestion (OR 0.49, 95% CI 0.42 to 0.59). It found that, in people aged 60 years or older, the probability of influenza was increased by the combination of fever, cough, and acute onset (OR 5.4, 95% CI 3.8 to 7.7); fever and cough (OR 5.0, 95% CI 3.5 to 6.9); fever alone (OR 3.8, 95% CI 2.8 to 5.0); malaise (OR 2.6, 95% CI 2.2 to 3.1); or chills (OR 2.6, 95% CI 2.0 to 3.2); the review also found that influenza was less likely if sneezing was present (OR 0.47, 95% CI 0.24 to 0.92). Although influenza is usually diagnosed clinically, genuine influenza infection can only be diagnosed with laboratory confirmation, either by culture, by serological responses, or by bedside testing. The rapid bedside diagnostic tests available on the market are mainly antigen detection immunoassays, and (unlike laboratory tests, such as culture or reverse transcription–polymerase chain reaction) can be carried out within 30 minutes. However, the results must be interpreted with caution. During times of low influenza viral circulation, the positive predictive value is low, leading to an increased proportion of false-positive results. In times of high viral circulation, the negative predictive value is low, leading to an increased proportion of false negatives. It is also impractical to test all potential influenza cases. If a good surveillance system is in place, with quick feedback, the positive predictive value of clinical diagnosis alone (based on high fever and a cough) will be similar to the bedside test (79–87%). **Population:** For the purpose of this review, we have included trials that assessed both influenza-like illness and influenza, which are clinically indistinguishable, in people with no comorbid conditions. Where appropriate, the applicability of data to influenza pandemics has been discussed. **Changes to the interventions covered at this update:** Owing to concerns regarding the completeness of evidence on some antivirals, we have omitted the questions on antiviral chemoprophylaxis and antiviral treatment from the review at this update. These questions will be reinstated at the next update following publication of further data.

**INCIDENCE/PREVALENCE Seasonal influenza:** Circulation of seasonal influenza viruses can vary between years, seasons, and even settings. In temperate areas, seasonal influenza activity typically peaks between late December and early March in the northern hemisphere, and between May and September in the southern hemisphere. In tropical areas, there is no temporal peak in influenza activity through the year. The annual incidence of influenza varies, and depends partly on the underlying level of population immunity to circulating influenza viruses. The incidence statistic for influenza is commonly estimated from virological testing of symptomatic people (so-called viral circulation). Patients presenting to a physician typically have a syndrome (influenza-like illness, or ILI) that can be caused by various agents, and only a proportion of these syndromes is caused by influenza A and B viruses. A way to determine (not estimate) the incidence of influenza is represented by virological testing of a truly random sample of people with ILI, together with the testing for all other major causal agents. This is not typically done, as it is not known how many people have ILI at a given time. For this reason, at present, the only method to determine influenza incidence with a high level of accuracy is to use the control arms of influenza vaccine and antiviral studies. Based on studies in The Cochrane Library, incidence of influenza is estimated at around 7%. However, the control arms of the 95 studies identified evaluate people with ILI. Therefore, 7% is not the absolute incidence of influenza in the general population, but is rather the portion of ILI that is caused by influenza, making the incidence of influenza much smaller in the general population (approximately 0.5%). **Pandemic influenza:** The incidence of symptomatic influenza depends on, among other factors, the susceptibility of the host. Occasionally, a new type of influenza virus appears, generated either by direct mutation or by reassortment of the viral genome. Because immunity to this new virus is low, it is able to behave in an aggressive way, causing morbidity and mortality on a global scale, mainly because of the body's inability to prevent the creation of a high viral load, the cytopathic effect of the new virus, and the complications in target organs, such as lungs and airways. Widespread epidemics are known as pandemics. In the 20th century, three pandemics were

*(continued over)*

*(from previous page)*

caused by different influenza A viral subtypes (see aetiology): in 1918–1919 (H1N1), 1957 (H2N2), and 1968 (H3N2). **Avian influenza:** Influenza infection may also appear as a zoonotic infection, with direct spread of the avian virus to humans. In April 2003, 87 people in the Netherlands were infected with avian virus H7N7. In most cases, the only symptom was conjunctivitis. However, a 57-year-old vet dealing with veterinary public-health interventions died of acute respiratory distress. An avian virus (H5N1) has been transmitted from bird to human (and occasionally from human to human) sporadically since 1997. Such transmission has frequently taken place in situations of poor hygiene and close proximity between birds and humans.

**AETIOLOGY/RISK FACTORS Viral classification:** The influenza virus is composed of a protein envelope around an RNA core. On the surface of the envelope are two antigens: neuraminidase (N antigen) and haemagglutinin (H antigen). The influenza virus has a marked propensity to mutate its external antigenic composition to escape the host's immune defences. Given this extreme mutability, a classification of viral subtype A based on H and N typing has been introduced. **Transmission:** Influenza viruses are transmitted primarily from person to person through respiratory droplets disseminated during sneezing, coughing, and talking, and through contact with contaminated surfaces. The incubation period of influenza is 1 to 4 days, and infected adults are usually contagious from the day before symptom onset until 5 days after symptom onset. **Pandemic influenza:** Pandemics are thought to originate mostly in southern China, where ducks (the animal reservoir and breeding ground for new strains), pigs (thought to be the biological intermediate host, or 'mixing vessel'), and humans live in close proximity. Pigs are considered plausible intermediate hosts because their respiratory epithelial cells have receptors for both avian (i.e., duck) and human viral haemagglutinins. Minor changes in viral antigenic configurations, known as 'drift', cause local or more circumscribed epidemics.

**PROGNOSIS** The symptoms of uncomplicated influenza usually resolve within 1 week, although cough and fatigue may persist. Complications include otitis media, bacterial sinusitis, secondary bacterial pneumonia, and, less commonly, viral pneumonia, respiratory failure, and exacerbations of underlying disease. In the UK, 1.3% of people with influenza-like illness are hospitalised each year (95% CI 0.6% to 2.6%). It is estimated that 300 to 400 deaths each year are attributable to influenza, rising to over 29,000 during an epidemic. The risk of hospitalisation is highest in people aged 65 years or older, in young children, and in people with chronic medical conditions. More than 90% of influenza-related deaths during recent seasonal epidemics in the USA have been in people aged 65 years or older. During influenza pandemics, morbidity and mortality may be high in younger age groups. Severe illness is more common with influenza A infections than with influenza B infections. For pandemic influenza, see incidence.

W Cairns S Smith and Paul Saunderson

## KEY POINTS

- Leprosy is a chronic granulomatous disease caused by *Mycobacterium leprae*, primarily affecting the peripheral nerves and skin.

  The WHO field leprosy classification is based on the number of skin lesions: paucibacillary leprosy (1–5 skin lesions), and multibacillary leprosy (>5 skin lesions).

  Worldwide, about 250,000 new cases of leprosy are reported each year, and about 2 million people have leprosy-related disabilities.

- Chemoprophylaxis given to contacts of index cases is moderately effective in preventing leprosy.

  Chemoprophylaxis with single-dose rifampicin reduces the incidence of leprosy in contacts of new cases, although the effect is only seen in the first 2 years.

- Vaccination is the most efficient method of preventing the contraction of leprosy.

  Vaccination with Bacillus Calmette–Guerin (BCG) vaccine, either alone or in combination with killed *M leprae*, reduces the incidence of leprosy. BCG and BCG plus killed *M leprae* seem to be as effective as each other at reducing the incidence of leprosy.

  ICRC vaccine prevents leprosy and produces few adverse effects, although its formulation is unclear and we only found evidence in one geographical area.

  *Mycobacterium w* vaccine reduces the incidence of leprosy compared with placebo.

- Leprosy is generally treated with multidrug programmes.

  Despite sparse good RCT or cohort study evidence, there is consensus that multidrug treatment (rifampicin plus clofazimine plus dapsone) is highly effective for treating multibacillary leprosy. Placebo-controlled trials of multidrug treatment would now be considered unethical.

  Multidrug treatment with rifampicin plus dapsone is believed to improve skin lesions, nerve impairment, and relapse rates in people with paucibacillary leprosy, despite a lack of good evidence.

  Multiple-dose treatments with rifampicin monthly plus dapsone daily for 6 months are more effective than single-dose treatments with rifampicin plus minocycline plus ofloxacin for treating people with single skin lesions (although both achieve high cure rates).

 Please visit http://clinicalevidence.bmj.com for full text and references

| What are the effects of interventions to prevent leprosy? | |
|---|---|
| Beneficial | • Bacillus Calmette–Guerin (BCG vaccination is beneficial, but the value of BCG revaccination is uncertain) |
| | • Bacillus Calmette–Guerin plus killed *Mycobacterium leprae* vaccine |
| | • Chemoprophylaxis with single-dose rifampicin |
| Likely To Be Beneficial | • ICRC vaccine |
| | • *Mycobacterium w* vaccine |

## What are the effects of treatments for leprosy?

| Likely To Be Beneficial | • Multidrug treatment for multibacillary leprosy* |
|---|---|
| | • Multidrug treatment for paucibacillary leprosy* |
| | • Multiple-dose compared with single-dose treatment for single skin lesion leprosy (both achieve high cure rates but multiple-dose is likely to achieve a higher rate) |

**Search date September 2009**

*Categorisation based on observational evidence and consensus; RCTs unlikely to be conducted.

**DEFINITION** Leprosy is a chronic granulomatous disease caused by *Mycobacterium leprae*, primarily affecting the peripheral nerves and skin. The clinical picture depends on the individual's immune response to *M leprae*. At the tuberculoid end of the Ridley–Jopling scale, individuals have good cell-mediated immunity and few skin lesions. At the lepromatous end of the scale, individuals have low reactivity for *M leprae*, causing uncontrolled bacterial spread and skin and mucosal infiltration. Peripheral nerve damage occurs across the spectrum. Nerve damage may occur before, during, or after treatment. Some people have no nerve damage, while others develop anaesthesia of the hands and feet, which puts them at risk of developing neuropathic injury. Weakness and paralysis of the small muscles of the hands, feet, and eyes put people at risk of developing deformity and contractures. Loss of the fingers and toes is caused by repeated injury in a weak, anaesthetic limb. These visible deformities cause stigmatisation. Classification is based on clinical appearance and bacterial index of lesions. The WHO field leprosy classification is based on the number of skin lesions: paucibacillary leprosy (1–5 skin lesions) and multibacillary leprosy (>5 skin lesions).

**INCIDENCE/PREVALENCE** Worldwide, about 250,000 new cases of leprosy are reported each year, and about 2 million people have leprosy-related disabilities. Three major endemic countries (India, Brazil, and Indonesia ) account for 77% of all new cases. Cohort studies show a peak of disease presentation between 10 and 20 years of age. After puberty, there are twice as many cases in males as in females.

**AETIOLOGY/RISK FACTORS** *M leprae* is discharged from the nasal mucosa of people with untreated lepromatous leprosy, and spreads, via the recipient's nasal mucosa, to infect their skin and nerves. It is a hardy organism and has been shown to survive outside human hosts in India for many months. Risk factors for infection, when known, include household contact with a person with leprosy. We found no good evidence of an association with HIV infection, nutrition, or socioeconomic status.

**PROGNOSIS** Complications of leprosy include nerve damage, immunological reactions, and bacillary infiltration. Without treatment, tuberculoid infection eventually resolves spontaneously. Most people with borderline tuberculoid and borderline lepromatous leprosy gradually develop lepromatous infection. Many people have peripheral nerve damage at the time of diagnosis, ranging from 15% in Bangladesh to 55% in Ethiopia. Immunological reactions can occur with or without antibiotic treatment. Further nerve damage occurs through immune-mediated reactions (type 1 reactions) and neuritis. Erythema nodosum leprosum (type 2 reactions) is an immune complex-mediated reaction causing fever, malaise, and neuritis, which occurs in 20% of people with lepromatous leprosy, and in 5% with borderline lepromatous leprosy. Secondary impairments (wounds, contractures, and digit resorption) occur in 33% to 56% of people with established nerve damage. We found no recent information on mortality.

Ashley M. Croft

## KEY POINTS

- This review examines evidence from RCTs and systematic reviews of RCTs on non-drug interventions to prevent malaria.

  For this review, travellers are defined as visitors from a malaria-free area to a malaria-endemic area, who stay in the endemic area for less than 1 year.

- Malaria transmission occurs most frequently in environments with a humidity greater than 60% and ambient temperature of 25°C to 30°C. Risks increase with longer visits, and depend on activity.

  Infection can follow a single mosquito bite. Incubation is usually 10 to 14 days, but can be up to 18 months depending on the strain of parasite.

  Complications are usually due to delayed or inappropriate treatment, but up to 88% of previously healthy travellers recover fully with prompt treatment. Older people have a worse prognosis.

  Malaria is more common and more severe in pregnancy. Contracting malaria significantly increases the likelihood of miscarriage.

- Many of the studies on prevention of malaria have been performed on people other than travellers, such as residents of endemic malaria areas.

- Prevention of malaria in travellers employs an integrated treatment approach of drug prophylaxis and non-drug interventions. Drug prophylaxis is of key importance to the prevention strategy. However, this review focuses on non-drug interventions for travellers as additional options to drug interventions, but which are not intended to be used in place of antimalaria drug prophylaxis.

- Various non-drug preventive measures may be effective, but some may have adverse effects.

  Using insecticide-treated nets or clothing in non-pregnant adults may be beneficial.

  Long-lasting insecticidal nets (LLINs) are likely to have an extended duration of action compared with conventionally treated bed nets.

  There is a consensus that skin-applied chemical repellents containing diethyltoluamide (DEET) reduce the risk of insect bites. Picaridin is a newer and possibly more effective repellent than DEET, but it has not yet been evaluated against clinical outcomes.

  Children may be at risk of encephalopathic adverse effects from topical insect repellents containing DEET.

  We don't know whether insecticide sprays, lifestyle changes (such as wearing full-length clothing), dietary supplementation, use of air conditioning or electric fans, mosquito coils or vapourising mats, bath or chemical-base oils, skin-applied plant-based repellents, electronic mosquito repellents, outdoor smoke, or biological control measures can reduce the risk of malaria infection. Mosquito coils and vapourising mats should not be used in a confined space in which there are people asleep.

- Insecticide-treated bed nets may be effective in preventing malaria in pregnant women.

  We found no RCT evidence about insecticide-treated clothing in pregnant women, but evidence in non-pregnant adults that it is effective is likely to be generalisable to pregnant women. However, there are attendant risks.

  Skin-applied insect repellents may be effective in preventing malaria in pregnant travellers (generalised from evidence in non-pregnant adults). However, there is a potential risk of mutagenicity from DEET and, therefore, plant-derived skin-applied insect repellents may be safer.

(i) **Please visit http://clinicalevidence.bmj.com for full text and references**

### What are the effects of non-drug interventions to prevent malaria in non-pregnant adult travellers?

| Likely To Be Beneficial | • Insecticide-treated clothing in non-pregnant adult travellers<br>• Insecticide-treated nets in non-pregnant adult travellers*<br>• Skin-applied chemical repellents (containing DEET or picaridin) in non-pregnant adult travellers* |
|---|---|
| Unknown Effectiveness | • Aerosol insecticides in non-pregnant adult travellers<br>• Air conditioning and electric fans in non-pregnant adult travellers<br>• Bath or chemical-base oils in non-pregnant adult travellers<br>• Biological control measures in non-pregnant adult travellers<br>• Dietary supplementation in non-pregnant adult travellers<br>• Electronic mosquito repellents in non-pregnant adult travellers<br>• Lifestyle changes (including full-length clothing, light-coloured clothing, behaviour modification) in non-pregnant adult travellers<br>• Mosquito coils and vapourising mats in non-pregnant adult travellers<br>• Outdoor smoke in non-pregnant adult travellers<br>• Skin-applied plant-based repellents in non-pregnant adult travellers |

### What are the effects of non-drug interventions to prevent malaria in child travellers?

| Trade-off Between Benefits And Harms | • Topical (skin-applied) insect repellents containing DEET in child travellers* |
|---|---|

### What are the effects of non-drug interventions to prevent malaria in pregnant travellers?

| Likely To Be Beneficial | • Insecticide-treated clothing in pregnant travellers**<br>• Insecticide-treated nets in pregnant travellers** |
|---|---|
| Trade-off Between Benefits And Harms | • Skin-applied insect repellents in pregnant travellers* |

**Search date November 2013**

*Categorisation based on consensus.
**Categorisation based on evidence in non-pregnant adults or pregnant long-term residents.

**DEFINITION** Malaria is an acute parasitic disease of the tropics and subtropics, caused usually by the invasion and destruction of red blood cells by one or more of four species of the genus *Plasmodium: P falciparum, P vivax, P ovale,* and *P malariae.* The clinical presentation of malaria varies according to the infecting species, and according to the genetics, immune status, and age of the infected person. The most severe form of human malaria is caused by *P falciparum*, in which variable clinical features include spiking fevers, chills, headache, muscular aching and weakness, vomiting, cough, diarrhoea, and abdominal pain. Other symptoms related to organ failure may supervene, such as acute renal failure, generalised convulsions, and circulatory collapse, followed by coma and death. *P falciparum* accounts for more than 50% of malaria infections in most East Asian countries, more than 90% in sub-Saharan Africa, and almost 100% in Hispaniola. Travellers are defined here as visitors from a malaria-free area to a malaria-endemic area, who stay in the endemic area for less than 1 year.

**INCIDENCE/PREVALENCE** Malaria is the most dangerous parasitic disease of humans, infecting about 5% of the world's population, and causing about one million deaths each year. The disease is strongly resurgent, owing to the effects of war, climate change, large-scale population movements, increased breeding opportunities for vector mosquitoes, rapidly spreading drug and insecticide resistance, and neglect of public-health infrastructure. Malaria is currently endemic in more than 100 countries, which are visited by more than 125 million international travellers each year. Cases of malaria acquired by international travellers from industrialised countries probably number 25,000 annually. Of these, about 10,000 are reported and 150 are fatal.

**AETIOLOGY/RISK FACTORS** Humans acquire malaria from sporozoites transmitted by the bite of infected female anopheline mosquitoes. Of about 3200 mosquito species so far described, some 430 belong to the genus *Anopheles*. Of these, about 70 anopheline species are known to transmit malaria, with about 40 species considered important vectors. When foraging, blood-thirsty female mosquitoes fly upwind searching for the scent trail of an attractive host. Female anophelines are attracted to their human hosts over a range of 7 to 20 m, through a variety of stimuli, including exhaled carbon dioxide, lactic acid, other host odours, warmth, and moisture. Larger people tend to be bitten by mosquitoes more than smaller individuals. Women receive significantly more mosquito bites in trials than men. Children secrete lower levels of chemical attractants than adults and, therefore, usually receive fewer mosquito bites than adults. Malaria transmission does not usually occur at temperatures less than 16°C or greater than 35°C or at altitudes greater than 3000 m above sea level at the equator (lower elevations in cooler climates) because sporozoite development in the mosquito cannot take place. The optimal conditions for transmission are a humidity of greater than 60% and an ambient temperature of 25°C to 30°C. Most of the important vectors of malaria breed in small temporary collections of fresh surface water exposed to sunlight and with little predation, and in sites such as residual pools in drying river beds. Although rainfall provides breeding sites for mosquitoes, excessive rainfall may wash away mosquito larvae and pupae. Conversely, prolonged droughts may be associated with increased malaria transmission if they reduce the size and flow rates of large rivers sufficiently to produce suitable *Anopheles* breeding sites. Anopheline mosquitoes vary in their preferred feeding and resting locations, although most bite in the evening and at night. The *Anopheles* mosquito will feed by day only if unusually hungry. *Anopheles* adults usually fly not more than 2 to 3 km from their breeding sites, although a flight range of up to 7 km has been observed. One cross-sectional study of about 7000 children under the age of 10 years found that, during months of peak transmission, living within 3 km of an *Anopheles* breeding site significantly increased the risk of malaria compared with living 8 to 10 km away (RR 21.00, 95% CI 2.87 to 153.00). Very occasionally, strong winds may carry *Anopheles* up to 30 km or more. In travellers, malaria risk is related to destination, activity, and duration of travel. A retrospective cohort study (5898 confirmed cases) conducted in Italian travellers between 1989 and 1997 found that the malaria incidence was 1.5 per 1000 for travel to Africa, 0.11 per 1000 for travel to Asia, and 0.04 per 1000 for travel to Central and South America. A survey of approximately 170,000 Swedish travellers found that the prevalence of malaria was lowest among travellers to Central America and the Caribbean (0.01/1000), and higher among travellers to East, Central, and West Africa (prevalence among travellers to East Africa 2.4/1000, Central Africa 3.6/1000, and West Africa 3.0/1000). A survey of

*(continued over)*

*(from previous page)*

2131 German travellers to sub-Saharan Africa found that solo travellers were at almost a ninefold greater risk of infection than those on package tours. A case control study (46 cases, 557 controls) reported that a visit to the tropics for more than 21 days doubled the malaria risk compared with visits lasting 21 days or less.

**PROGNOSIS** Malaria can develop after just one anopheline mosquito bite. Long-term residents of malaria-endemic areas acquire partial immunity to infected mosquito bites, with only a small proportion of such bites progressing to a new infection (in children aged 6 months to 6 years, monitored for 18 months in western Kenya, only 7.5% of infected bites produced a clinical episode of malaria). In non-immune travellers, the likelihood of malaria infection after a single infected bite is much higher (US marines who spent 1–14 nights in Liberia experienced a 44% malaria acquisition rate). Human malaria has a usual incubation period that ranges from 10 to 14 days (*P falciparum*, *P vivax*, and *P ovale*) to about 28 days (*P malariae*). Certain strains of *P vivax* and *P ovale* can have a much longer incubation period of 6 to 18 months. About 90% of malaria attacks in travellers occur at home. About 36% of cases that develop after returning home do so more than 2 months after the traveller's return. People returning from an endemic area with any fever pattern should be considered to have malaria until proved otherwise. Once malaria infection occurs, older travellers are at greater risk of poor clinical outcomes and death. In US travellers between 1966 and 1987, the case fatality rate was 0.4% for people aged 0 to 19 years, 2.2% for ages 20 to 39 years, 5.8% for ages 40 to 69 years, and 30.3% for those aged 70 to 79 years. Complications and death from malaria are mainly due to inappropriate treatment, or to delayed initiation of treatment. If malaria is diagnosed and treated promptly, about 88% of previously healthy travellers will recover completely. Malaria is more common and more severe in pregnancy. Contracting malaria significantly increases the likelihood of miscarriage.

Susanne H Sheehy and Brian J Angus

## KEY POINTS

- Severe malaria mainly affects children under 5 years old, non-immune travellers, migrants to malarial areas, and people living in areas with unstable or seasonal malaria.

  Cerebral malaria, causing encephalopathy and coma, is fatal in around 20% of children and adults, and neurological sequelae may occur in some survivors.

  Severe malarial anaemia may have a mortality rate of over 13%.

- International consensus has historically regarded quinine as standard treatment for severe falciparum malaria. RCTs will generally compare new treatments against this standard.

  We found no clear evidence on the best quinine treatment regimen or route of administration to use, although high initial dose quinine clears parasites more rapidly compared with lower-dose quinine. However, higher doses increase the risk of adverse effects.

  Intravenous artesunate is more effective than quinine in reducing mortality from severe malaria.

  Intramuscular artemether and rectal artemisinin, artemether, artesunate, and dihydroartemisinin may be as effective as quinine in reducing mortality from severe malaria.

  Routine use of phenobarbitone in cerebral malaria may reduce convulsions compared with placebo, but may be associated with higher mortality.

  Dexamethasone has not been shown to reduce mortality from severe malaria, and it increases the risk of gastrointestinal bleeding and seizures.

- We don't know whether initial blood transfusion or exchange blood transfusion reduce mortality from severe malaria as no adequate-quality trials have been found. Blood transfusion is associated with adverse effects, but is clinically essential in some circumstances.

- We don't know how intravenous or intramuscular dihydroartemisinin compare with quinine, how dihydroartemisinin and artesunate compare with each other when given either intravenously or intramuscularly, or how rectal administration of artemisinin derivatives compares with administering them intramuscularly or intravenously as we found insufficient evidence.

(i) **Please visit http://clinicalevidence.bmj.com for full text and references**

| What are the effects of antimalarial treatments for complicated falciparum malaria in non-pregnant people? | |
|---|---|
| **Beneficial** | • Artesunate (intravenous) (reduced mortality compared with quinine) |
| **Likely To Be Beneficial** | • Artemether (intramuscular) (as effective as quinine)<br><br>• Artemisinin and its derivatives given rectally versus quinine<br><br>• High initial dose quinine (reduced parasite and fever clearance times, but no significant difference in mortality compared with standard regimens) |

| | |
|---|---|
| | • Quinine* |
| **Unknown Effectiveness** | • Artemisinin derivatives given rectally versus artemisinin derivatives given intramuscularly |
| | • Artemisinin derivatives given rectally versus artemisinin derivatives given intravenously |
| | • Dihydroartemisinin (intramuscular) versus artesunate (intramuscular) |
| | • Dihydroartemisinin (intramuscular) versus quinine |
| | • Dihydroartemisinin (intravenous) versus artesunate (intravenous) |
| | • Dihydroartemisinin (intravenous) versus quinine |
| | • Quinine given intramuscularly versus quinine given intravenously |

## What are the effects of adjunctive treatment for complicated falciparum malaria in non-pregnant people?

| | |
|---|---|
| **Unknown Effectiveness** | • Exchange blood transfusion |
| | • Initial blood transfusion |
| **Likely To Be Ineffective Or Harmful** | • Dexamethasone |
| | • Phenobarbitone |

**Search date December 2009**

*Based on consensus. Placebo-controlled RCTs would be considered unethical.

**DEFINITION** Falciparum malaria is caused by protozoan infection of red blood cells with *Plasmodium falciparum* and comprises a variety of syndromes. This review deals with clinically complicated malaria (i.e., malaria that presents with life-threatening conditions, including coma, severe anaemia, renal failure, respiratory distress syndrome, hypoglycaemia, shock, spontaneous haemorrhage, and convulsions). The diagnosis of cerebral malaria should be considered when there is encephalopathy in the presence of malaria parasites. A strict definition of cerebral malaria requires the presence of unrousable coma and no other cause of encephalopathy (e.g., hypoglycaemia, sedative drugs), in the presence of *P falciparum* infection. This review does not currently cover the treatment of malaria in pregnancy.

**INCIDENCE/PREVALENCE** Malaria is a major health problem in the tropics, with an estimated 250 million clinical cases occurring annually and an estimated 1 million deaths each year as a result of severe malaria. Over 90% of deaths occur in children under 5 years old, mainly from cerebral malaria and anaemia. In areas where the rate of malaria transmission is stable (endemic), those most at risk of acquiring severe malaria are children under 5 years old, because adults and older children have partial immunity, which offers some protection. In areas where the rate of malaria transmission is unstable (non-endemic), severe malaria affects both adults and children. Non-immune travellers and migrants are also at risk of developing severe malaria.

**AETIOLOGY/RISK FACTORS** Malaria is transmitted by the bite of infected female anopheline mosquitoes. Certain haemoglobins such as haemoglobin S and haemoglobin C are protective against severe malaria (see aetiology in review on malaria: prevention in travellers, p 271).

**PROGNOSIS** In children under 5 years of age with cerebral malaria, the estimated case fatality of treated malaria is 19%, although reported hospital case fatality may be as high as 40%. Neurological sequelae persisting for more than 6 months may occur in some survivors, and include ataxia, hemiplegia, speech disorders, behavioural disorders, epilepsy, and blindness. Severe malarial anaemia may have a case fatality rate higher than 13%. In adults, mortality of cerebral malaria is 20%; this rises to 50% in pregnancy.

David Taylor-Robinson, Katharine Jones, Paul Garner, and David Sinclair

## KEY POINTS

- **Uncomplicated malaria is where the person has symptomatic infection with malaria parasites, but no signs of vital organ disturbance.**

  Uncomplicated malaria can progress to severe malaria, become chronic, or resolve, depending on host immunity and prompt access to appropriate treatment.

  Severe malaria is more likely to develop in people with no prior immunity, and accounts for over 1 million deaths worldwide each year.

  The choice between treatment regimens depends partly on background drug-resistance patterns in the relevant country or region.

- **In most RCTs, artemether–lumefantrine was more effective than amodiaquine plus sulfadoxine–pyrimethamine. However, it was not more effective in all RCTs.**

- **Artesunate plus amodiaquine is more effective at curing a current infection than amodiaquine plus sulfadoxine–pyrimethamine, but, in terms of people being parasite free at day 28, there is little to choose between them, since the risk of new infections appears greater with artesunate plus amodiaquine.**

- **Amodiaquine plus sulfadoxine–pyrimethamine achieved higher cure rates than artesunate plus sulfadoxine–pyrimethamine. Gametocyte clearance was better with artesunate plus sulfadoxine–pyrimethamine.**

- **Evidence suggests that a six-dose regimen of artemether–lumefantrine is more effective than a four-dose regimen.**

- **Both artemether–lumefantrine (6 doses) and artesunate plus amodiaquine were effective, but artemether–lumefantrine (6 doses) was superior in some trials.**

- **Artesunate plus mefloquine performs better than artemether–lumefantrine in terms of cure in some areas where this has been studied.**

- **The choice between artesunate plus amodiaquine and artesunate plus sulfadoxine–pyrimethamine depends on background drug-resistance patterns in the relevant country or region.**

- **We found insufficient evidence on the effects of artemer–lumefantrine (6 doses) versus artesunate plus sulfadoxine–pyrimethamine, artesunate plus mefloquine versus artesunate plus amodiaquine, or artesunate plus mefloquine versus artesunate plus sulfadoxine–pyrimethamine.**

(i) **Please visit http://clinicalevidence.bmj.com for full text and references**

## Are artemisinin combination treatments more effective than non-artemisinin combination treatments in people living in endemic areas (excluding South-East Asia)?

| | |
|---|---|
| **Likely To Be Beneficial** | • Artemether–lumefantrine (6 doses) (probably more effective than amodiaquine plus sulfadoxine–pyrimethamine)<br><br>• Artesunate (3 days) plus amodiaquine (possibly more effective than amodiaquine plus sulfadoxine–pyrimethamine) |
| **Unlikely To Be Beneficial** | • Artesunate (3 days) plus sulfadoxine–pyrimethamine (possibly less effective than amodiaquine plus sulfadoxine–pyrimethamine) |

## Which artemisinin combination treatment is most effective in people living in endemic areas?

| | |
|---|---|
| **Likely To Be Beneficial** | • Artemether–lumefantrine (6 doses) (6-dose regimen more effective than a 4-dose regimen)<br><br>• Artemether–lumefantrine (6 doses) (possibly more effective than artesunate plus amodiaquine) |
| **Unknown Effectiveness** | • Artemether–lumefantrine (6 doses) versus artesunate plus sulfadoxine–pyrimethamine<br><br>• Artesunate plus amodiaquine versus artesunate plus sulfadoxine–pyrimethamine (relative benefits unclear)<br><br>• Artesunate plus mefloquine versus artesunate plus amodiaquine<br><br>• Artesunate plus mefloquine versus artesunate plus sulfadoxine–pyrimethamine |
| **Unlikely To Be Beneficial** | • Artemether–lumefantrine (6 doses) (possibly less effective than artesunate [3 days] plus mefloquine) |

**Search date December 2007**

**DEFINITION** Malaria is a parasite transmitted by *Anopheles* mosquitoes. There are four types of human malaria: *falciparum*, *vivax*, *ovale*, and *malariae*. The *falciparum* type is the most important cause of illness and death, and *Plasmodium falciparum*, the responsible organism, is known to develop resistance to antimalarial drugs. This review covers treatments for *falciparum* malaria only, in a population of adults and children living in endemic malarial areas exposed (seasonally or all year round) to malaria. It does not cover treatment of malaria in non-immune travellers, pregnant women, and people infected with HIV. Repeated episodes of *falciparum* malaria result in temporary and incomplete immunity. Therefore, adults living in areas where malaria is common are often found to be "semi-immune" — presenting with asymptomatic or chronic forms of malaria, with clinical episodes attenuated by their immunity. **"Severe malaria"** is defined as a form of symptomatic malaria with signs of vital organ disturbance (WHO 2000). Any person with symptomatic malaria who does not develop any such signs is defined as having **"uncomplicated malaria"**. This review assesses the effectiveness of antimalarial drugs only in people with uncomplicated malaria.

**INCIDENCE/PREVALENCE** Malaria is a major health problem in the tropics, with 300 to 500 million new clinical cases annually, most of them cases of uncomplicated malaria. An estimated 1.1 to 2.7 million deaths occur annually as a result of severe *falciparum* malaria.

**AETIOLOGY/RISK FACTORS** The malaria parasite is transmitted by infected *Anopheles* mosquitoes. Risk factors for developing the disease include exposure to infected mosquitoes (living in an endemic area; housing that allows mosquitoes to enter and absence of mosquito nets; and living in an area where *Anopheles* mosquitoes can thrive). Risk factors in relation to severity of the illness relate to host immunity, determined mainly by exposure to the parasite, and therefore varying with level of transmission in the area, and the age of the host. Malaria is uncommon in the first 6 months of life (fetal haemoglobin is protective); it is, however, common in children over 6 months of age. In areas of intense transmission, infection is attenuated by host immunity in older age groups; however, morbidity and mortality can also be high in adults in areas of less-intense transmission.

**PROGNOSIS** Uncomplicated malaria may progress to severe malaria, become chronic, or resolve with effective treatment or the development of improved immunity. The outcome is therefore dependent on host immunity and prompt access to effective treatment. In the

*(continued over)*

*(from previous page)*

absence of effective treatment, people with no or low immunity are at increased risk of developing severe malaria (see review on malaria: severe, life-threatening, p 275) resulting in high morbidity and mortality.

Suzanne F Bradley

## KEY POINTS

- Methicillin-resistant *Staphylococcus aureus* (MRSA) has a gene that makes it resistant to methicillin as well as other beta-lactam antibiotics, including flucloxacillin, cephalosporins, and carbapenems.

  MRSA can be part of the normal body flora (colonisation), especially in the nose, but it can cause infection, especially in people with prolonged hospital admissions, with underlying disease, or after antibiotic use.

  Bloodstream infection due to MRSA is an all-too-common problem worldwide.

- Mupirocin nasal ointment may improve eradication of colonised MRSA compared with placebo, and may be as effective as topical fusidic acid plus oral trimethoprim–sulfamethoxazole (co-trimoxazole) and more effective than tea tree oil, although studies have given conflicting results.

  We don't know whether antiseptic body washes, chlorhexidine–neomycin nasal cream, other topical antimicrobials, or systemic antimicrobials are effective at clearing MRSA colonisation.

 Please visit http://clinicalevidence.bmj.com for full text and references

| What are the effects of treatment for MRSA nasal or extra-nasal colonisation in adults? | |
|---|---|
| Likely To Be Beneficial | • Mupirocin nasal ointment versus placebo |
| Unknown Effectiveness | • Antiseptic body washes<br>• Chlorhexidine–neomycin nasal cream<br>• Systemic antimicrobials<br>• Tea tree oil preparations<br>• Topical antimicrobials other than mupirocin nasal ointment, antiseptic body washes, chlorhexidine-neomycin nasal cream, and tea tree oil preparations |

Search date January 2010

**DEFINITION** Methicillin-resistant *Staphylococcus aureus* (MRSA) is an organism resistant to methicillin by means of the *mecA* gene. This confers resistance to all beta-lactam antibiotics, including flucloxacillin, oxacillin, cephalosporins, and carbapenems. Antimicrobial resistance is defined as the failure of the antimicrobial to reach a concentration in the infected tissue high enough to inhibit the growth of the infecting organism. MRSA presents in the same way as susceptible *S aureus*. It can be part of the normal flora (colonisation), or it can cause infection. The phenomena of colonisation and infection should be treated as separate entities. In many countries worldwide, a preponderance of *S aureus* bloodstream isolates are resistant to methicillin. **MRSA colonisation:** growth of MRSA from a body fluid or swab from any body site. The most common site of colonisation is the anterior nares, but MRSA can also be found in other areas such as the axillae, abnormal skin (e.g., eczema, wounds), urine, rectum, and throat. There should be no signs or symptoms of infection. The colonised site may act as a reservoir of MRSA, which then causes infection at another site or can be passed on to others. Although the colonised patient (or staff member) does not need treatment, a course of decolonisation treatment may be given in order to eradicate carriage and prevent future infections or transmission. In this review, we have included adults aged

*(continued over)*

*(from previous page)*

18 years or older in hospitals and residential homes, outpatients, and healthcare workers.

**INCIDENCE/PREVALENCE** The incidence of MRSA varies from country to country. The UK, Ireland, and southern Europe (e.g., Spain, Italy, and Greece) have a high incidence when compared with northern Europe and Scandinavia. The most objective measure of incidence is the percentage of *S aureus* found in blood cultures that are resistant to methicillin. Rates may exceed 40% in many countries.

**AETIOLOGY/RISK FACTORS** Traditional risk factors for MRSA colonisation include: prolonged stay in hospital, severe underlying disease, prior antibiotics, exposure to colonised people, and admission to a high risk unit (critical care, renal unit, etc). MRSA has primarily been a problem associated with exposure to the healthcare system. More recently, MRSA strains have emerged in the community (so-called community-associated MRSA [CA-MRSA] strains) that have no relationship with healthcare-related strains. These strains may colonise and cause infection among young, healthy people.

**PROGNOSIS** The virulence, or ability, of MRSA to cause death and severe infection seems to be greater than that of methicillin-susceptible *S aureus* strains. A meta-analysis of 31 cohort studies found that mortality associated with MRSA bacteraemia was significantly higher than that of methicillin-susceptible *S aureus* bacteraemia (mean mortality not reported; OR 1.93, 95% CI 1.54 to 2.42).

Dilip Nathwani, Peter Garnet Davey, and Charis Ann Marwick

## KEY POINTS

- Methicillin-resistant *Staphylococcus aureus* (MRSA) has a gene that makes it resistant to methicillin as well as other beta-lactam antibiotics including flucloxacillin, cephalosporins, and carbapenems.

  MRSA can be part of the normal body flora (colonisation), especially in the nose, but it can cause infection, especially in people with prolonged hospital admissions, with underlying disease, or after antibiotic use.

  About 20% of *S aureus* in blood cultures in England, Wales, and Northern Ireland is resistant to methicillin.

- Glycopeptides (teicoplanin, vancomycin) and linezolid seem to have similar efficacy at curing MRSA infection. However, they have all been associated with adverse effects.

- We found limited evidence that tigecycline may have similar cure rates as vancomycin, however effectiveness is not yet clear.

- Trimethoprim–sulfamethoxazole (co-trimoxazole; TMP-SMX) may be as effective as vancomycin at curing MRSA infection in injecting drug users, with similar toxicity. However, we cannot draw conclusions on the effects of this drug in other populations.

- We don't know whether macrolides (azithromycin, clarithromycin, erythromycin), quinolones (ciprofloxacin, levofloxacin, moxifloxacin), tetracyclines (doxycycline, minocycline, oxytetracycline), clindamycin, daptomycin, fusidic acid, pristinamycin, quinupristin–dalfopristin, rifampicin, and trimethoprim are effective at curing MRSA infection, because we found no adequate RCTs.

  Ciprofloxacin has been used in combination with rifampicin or fusidic acid for MRSA bone and joint infections but we cannot confirm its effectiveness from adequate studies. Fusidic acid or rifampicin should not be used as monotherapy because resistance rapidly develops.

  Clindamycin may be used in preference to macrolides in susceptible MRSA infections, as bioavailability may be better and resistance less likely, however we found no adequate trials.

  Oral tetracyclines may be recommended for minor MRSA infections; however, we found no adequate trials.

 Please visit http://clinicalevidence.bmj.com for full text and references

| What are the effects of treatment for MRSA infections at any body site? | |
|---|---|
| Trade-off Between Benefits And Harms | • Linezolid (compared with glycopeptides) |
| | • Teicoplanin, vancomycin (glycopeptides) (compared with linezolid) |
| Unknown Effectiveness | • Azithromycin, clarithromycin, erythromycin (macrolides) |
| | • Ciprofloxacin, levofloxacin, moxifloxacin (quinolones) |
| | • Clindamycin |
| | • Daptomycin |
| | • Doxycycline, minocycline, oxytetracycline (tetracyclines) |
| | • Fusidic acid |

- Pristinamycin

- Quinupristin–dalfopristin

- Rifampicin

- Tigecycline (limited evidence that it may have similar cure rates as vancomycin, however effectiveness is not yet clear)

- Trimethoprim

- Trimethoprim–sulfamethoxazole

**Search date November 2009**

**DEFINITION** *Staphylococcus aureus* mainly colonises the nasal passages, but it may be found regularly in most other anatomical sites. Carrier rates in adults vary from 20% to 50% with people being persistent carriers, intermittent carriers, or non-carriers. Methicillin-resistant *Staphylococcus aureus* (MRSA) is an organism resistant to methicillin by means of the *mecA* gene. This confers resistance to all beta-lactam antibiotics, including flucloxacillin, oxacillin, cephalosporins, and carbapenems. Antimicrobial resistance is defined as the failure of the antimicrobial drug to reach a concentration in the infected tissue that is high enough to inhibit the growth of the infecting organism. Like methicillin-sensitive *S aureus* (MSSA), MRSA can be part of the normal flora (colonisation) or it can cause infection. For MRSA to cause infection, it must be transmitted to the individual, colonise the individual, and gain entry to the host or target tissues. Infection is dependent on the balance between the host defences and the virulence of the infectious agent. Therefore, it is important to recognise the difference between colonisation and infection because they are entirely different entities in terms of clinical management. **MRSA infection:** Growth of MRSA from a sterile body site (e.g., blood culture or cerebrospinal fluid, joint aspirate or pleural fluid) or growth of MRSA from a non-sterile body site (e.g., wound, skin, urine, or sputum) usually in the presence of symptoms or signs of infection. The presence of viable bacteria in blood without a documented primary source of infection is termed primary bacteraemia whereas secondary bacteraemia is the presence of viable bacteria in the blood secondary to a localised focus of infection. The majority of strains of MRSA in the UK are associated with the healthcare setting (healthcare-associated MRSA [HA-MRSA]). These are strains that are transmitted to and circulate between individuals who have had contact with healthcare facilities. These infections can present in the hospital or healthcare setting (hospital or healthcare onset) or in the community (community onset), for example after hospital discharge. These MRSA strains are resistant to the isoxazolyl penicillins (such as methicillin, oxacillin, and flucloxacillin), beta-lactam/beta-lactamase inhibitor combinations, cephalosporins, and carbapenems. They also show a variable level of resistance to other groups of antibiotics such as quinolones, macrolides, and others. MRSA is also becoming an increasingly important cause of community-acquired infection in people who have not been recently admitted to healthcare facilities or had medical problems. This is termed community-associated or community-acquired MRSA (CA-MRSA). This is defined as MRSA strains isolated from patients in an outpatient or community setting (community onset), or within 48 hours of hospital admission (hospital onset), who have no previous history of MRSA infection or colonisation, no history of hospital admission, surgery, dialysis, or residence in a long-term care facility within 1 year of the MRSA culture date, and absence of an indwelling catheter or percutaneous device at the time of culture. These infections are generally less severe and primarily cause skin and soft-tissue infections, although cases of fulminant disseminated disease and necrotising pneumonia are increasingly reported. We have primarily excluded this population from this review. However, the boundaries between HA-MRSA and CA-MRSA are becoming blurred because of the movement of people and infections between hospitals and the community. For example, nosocomial outbreaks of CA-MRSA following admission of colonised or infected patients have been reported. In the US, where CA-MRSA is now common, it is becoming increasingly difficult to distinguish between CA-MRSA and HA-MRSA on clinical and epidemiological assessment. Since HA-MRSA and CA-MRSA strains are often genotypically and phenotypically different, the microbiological characteristics of staphylococcal isolates may help to distinguish between healthcare-associated and community-associated infections.Our population of interest in this review is primarily people with HA-MRSA, although we have included people with CA-MRSA from studies in which most people (>50%) had HA-MRSA infections. The investigation of treatment strategies for community-acquired compared with nosocomial MRSA is ongoing, and will not be covered here. **Population:** We include adults with predominantly nosocomial or healthcare-acquired MRSA infection; we exclude children under 16 years.

**INCIDENCE/PREVALENCE** The incidence of MRSA varies from country to country. The UK, Ireland, and southern Europe (e.g., Spain, Italy, and Greece) have a high incidence when compared with northern Europe and Scandinavia. The most objective measure of incidence is the percentage of S aureus found in blood cultures that are resistant to methicillin. At the time of writing this review this stands at about 20% in the UK.

**AETIOLOGY/RISK FACTORS** A case-control study (121 people with MRSA infection, 123 people with MSSA infection) found that the following characteristics were associated with a significantly increased risk of MRSA infection: more comorbidities, longer length of hospital stay, greater exposure to antibiotics, previous hospitalisation, enteral feedings, and surgery. A systematic review (search date 2006, 10 observational studies, 1170 people colonised, 791 colonised by MSSA, and 379 colonised by MRSA) found that MRSA colonisation was associated with a 4-fold increased risk of infection compared with MSSA colonisation (OR 4.08, 95% 2.1 to 7.44).

**PROGNOSIS** The virulence of MRSA has been found to be equal to that of MSSA in animal models. However, a meta-analysis of 31 cohort studies found that mortality associated with MRSA bacteraemia was significantly higher than that associated with MSSA bacteraemia (mean mortality not reported; OR 1.93, 95% CI 1.54 to 2.42). A subsequent cohort study (438 people, predominantly men, with S aureus infection complicated by bacteraemia, 193 [44%] of whom had MRSA) also found higher S aureus-related mortality with MRSA compared with MSSA in people without pneumonia (HR [adjusted for age, comorbidities, and pneumonia] 1.8, 95% CI 0.2 to 3.0; P <0.01). However, these studies had various methodological weaknesses including no specific data given on the adequacy of treatment administered or severity of illness, or other confounders not consistently available or considered. A more recent prospective cohort study (1194 episodes of S aureus bacterae-mia, 450 of these MRSA) found that MRSA infection was not an independent predictor of death and commented that the increased mortality associated with this invasive infection may be partly due to suboptimal treatment. Another retrospective cohort study (334 adults with S aureus bacteraemia, 77 due to MRSA) found that empirical treatment was inadequate significantly more often with MRSA bacteraemia than it was with MSSA bacteraemia (proportion of people with inadequate empirical treatment with antimicrobials: 54/257 [21%] in people with MSSA v 40/77 [52%] in people with MRSA; P <0.001). However, it found that MRSA was not associated with increased mortality rates at 30 days. Therefore, one cannot assume that invasive infection with MRSA *per se* is associated with a poorer clinical outcome. A range of confounders is likely to influence clinical outcome, and timeliness of treatment, among others, may be a factor.

# Postherpetic neuralgia

Peter Watson

## KEY POINTS

- Pain that occurs after resolution of acute herpes zoster infection can be severe. It may be accompanied by itching and follows the distribution of the original infection. All definitions of postherpetic neuralgia (PHN) are arbitrary and range from 1 month to 6 months after the rash. For clinical trials, neuralgia of 3 months or more has become the most common definition, because resolution of neuralgia after 3 months is slow.

  The main risk factor for postherpetic neuralgia is increasing age; it is uncommon in people aged <50 years, but develops in 20% of people aged 60 to 65 years who have had acute herpes zoster, and in >30% of those people aged >80 years.

  Up to 2% of people with acute herpes zoster may continue to have postherpetic pain for 5 years or more.

- Oral antiviral agents (aciclovir, famciclovir, valaciclovir, and netivudine), taken during acute herpes zoster infection, may reduce the duration of postherpetic neuralgia compared with placebo.

  We don't know whether topical antiviral drugs, tricyclic antidepressants, or corticosteroids taken during an acute attack reduce the risk of postherpetic neuralgia, as we found few good-quality studies.

  Corticosteroids may cause dissemination of herpes zoster infection.

  We don't know whether the use of dressings, oral opioids, or gabapentin during an acute attack reduces the risk of postherpetic neuralgia, as we found no studies.

  There is limited evidence that gabapentin and oxycodone may reduce the acute pain of herpes zoster.

  Gabapentin and tricyclic antidepressants (amitriptyline, nortriptyline) and some opioids (oxycodone, morphine, methadone) may reduce pain at up to 8 weeks in people with established postherpetic neuralgia compared with placebo.

  Topical lidocaine may be more effective than placebo in treating postherpetic neuralgia.

  Adverse effects of tricyclic antidepressants are dose related and may be less frequent in postherpetic neuralgia compared with depression, as lower doses are generally used.

  Opioid analgesic drugs are likely to be effective in reducing pain associated with postherpetic neuralgia, but they can cause sedation and other well-known adverse effects.

  We don't know whether dextromethorphan is effective at reducing postherpetic neuralgia.

  We don't know whether topical counterirritants such as capsaicin reduce postherpetic neuralgia.

  The zoster vaccine should be used as the primary prevention for herpes zoster and postherpetic neuralgia in people aged >60 years.

  We don't know whether serotonin–norepinephrine reuptake inhibitors (SNRIs; duloxetine, venlafaxine) or selective serotonin reuptake inhibitors are effective at reducing postherpetic neuralgia.

(i) **Please visit http://clinicalevidence.bmj.com for full text and references**

| What are the effects of interventions aimed at preventing herpes zoster and subsequent postherpetic neuralgia? | |
| --- | --- |
| Beneficial | • Herpes zoster vaccines |

## What are the effects of interventions during an acute attack of herpes zoster aimed at preventing postherpetic neuralgia?

| | |
|---|---|
| Unknown Effectiveness | • Antiviral agents (oral aciclovir, famciclovir, valaciclovir, netivudine) for preventing PHN<br><br>• Antiviral agents (topical idoxuridine) for preventing PHN<br><br>• Dressings for preventing PHN<br><br>• Gabapentin for preventing PHN<br><br>• Opioid analgesic drugs (oral) for preventing PHN<br><br>• Tricyclic antidepressants (amitriptyline) for preventing PHN |
| Likely To Be Ineffective Or Harmful | • Corticosteroids for preventing PHN |

## What are the effects of interventions to relieve established postherpetic neuralgia after the rash has healed?

| | |
|---|---|
| Beneficial | • Gabapentin for treating PHN<br><br>• Tricyclic antidepressants to treat postherpetic neuralgia |
| Likely To Be Beneficial | • Lidocaine (topical)<br><br>• Oral opioid analgesic drugs (oxycodone, morphine, methadone, tramadol) |
| Unknown Effectiveness | • Capsaicin (topical)<br><br>• Dextromethorphan<br><br>• Selective serotonin reuptake inhibitors<br><br>• Serotonin-norepinephrine reuptake inhibitors |

**Search date December 2009**

---

**DEFINITION** Postherpetic neuralgia (PHN) is pain that often follows resolution of acute herpes zoster and healing of the zoster rash. Herpes zoster is caused by reactivation of latent varicella zoster virus (human herpes virus 3) in people who have been rendered partially immune by a previous attack of chickenpox. Herpes zoster infects the sensory ganglia and their areas of innervation. It is characterised by pain in the distribution of the affected nerve, and crops of clustered vesicles over the area. Pain may occur days before rash onset, or no rash may appear (zoster sine herpete), making the diagnosis difficult. PHN is thought to arise following nerve damage caused by herpes zoster. PHN can be severe, accompanied by itching, and it follows the distribution of the original infection. All definitions of PHN are arbitrary and range from 1 month to 6 months after the rash. For clinical trials, neuralgia of 3 months or more has become the most common definition, because resolution of neuralgia after 3 months is slow. Thus, the number of people required for parallel and crossover trial designs is limited, and there is less risk of a period effect in a crossover trial.

*(continued over)*

---

*(from previous page)*

**INCIDENCE/PREVALENCE** In a UK general practice survey of between 3600 and 3800 people, the annual incidence of herpes zoster was 3.4/1000. Incidence varied with age. Herpes zoster was relatively uncommon in people aged <50 years (<2/1000/year), but rose to between 5/1000 and 7/1000 per year in people aged 50 to 79 years, and 11/1000 in people aged 80 years and older. A population-based study in the Netherlands reported a similar incidence (3.4/1000/year) and a similar increase of incidence with age (3–10/1000/year in people aged >50 years). Prevalence of PHN depends on when it is measured after acute infection. There is no agreed time point for diagnosis. About 10% of all ages will have PHN 1 month after the rash, but, as there is a direct relationship to age, about 50% will continue to suffer at age 60 years.

**AETIOLOGY/RISK FACTORS** The main risk factor for PHN is increasing age. In a UK general practice study (involving 3600–3800 people, 321 cases of acute herpes zoster) there was little risk in those aged <50 years, but PHN developed in >20% of people who had had acute herpes zoster aged 60 to 65 years, and in 34% of those aged >80 years. No other risk factor has been found to predict consistently which people with herpes zoster will experience continued pain. In a general practice study in Iceland (421 people followed for up to 7 years after an initial episode of herpes zoster), the risk of PHN was 1.8% (95% CI 0.6% to 4.2%) for people aged <60 years, and the pain was mild in all cases. The risk of severe pain after 3 months in people aged >60 years was 1.7% (95% CI 0% to 6.2%). Other risk factors for PHN (defined as moderate pain daily 3 months after herpes) are severe pain with herpes zoster, greater rash severity, increased neurological abnormalities in the affected dermatome (sensory loss), the presence of a prodrome, a more pronounced immune response, and psychosocial factors.

**PROGNOSIS** About 2% of people with acute herpes zoster in the UK general practice survey had pain for >5 years. Prevalence of pain falls as time elapses after the initial episode. Among 183 people aged >60 years in the placebo arm of a UK trial, the prevalence of pain was 61% at 1 month, 24% at 3 months, and 13% at 6 months after acute infection. In one RCT, the prevalence of postherpetic pain in the placebo arm at 6 months was 35% in 72 people aged >60 years. After PHN has persisted for >1 year, about 50% of people will have significant pain, and 50% will recover or be controlled with medication at a median of 2 years' follow-up.

Liliya Eugenevna Ziganshina and Michael Eisenhut

## KEY POINTS

- In 2013, an estimated 9.0 million people developed tuberculosis (TB) and 1.5 million died from the disease.

  Most people who inhale *Mycobacterium tuberculosis* contain the infection and become skin-test positive.

  Some people develop latent infection: persistent bacterial presence that is asymptomatic and not infectious.

  About one third of the world's population has immunological evidence of previous exposure to *M tuberculosis*.

  Drug treatments can reduce the risk of active TB in people at high risk of infection.

  Active infection is more likely in people affected by social factors (such as poverty, drug misuse, overcrowding, imprisonment, homelessness, and inadequate health care) or with reduced immune function (such as with HIV infection).

  Social factors associated with active infection have been associated with reduced adherence to antituberculous treatment.

- Directly observed treatment (DOT) has been developed to ensure adherence to treatment in patients treated for *M tuberculosis* infection. It involves the engagement of an appointed agent (health worker, community volunteer, family member) who directly monitors people swallowing their antituberculous drugs.

  DOT does not seem to increase cure rates compared with self-administered treatment. However, it may increase treatment compliance.

  We don't know how different types of support mechanisms for DOT compare with each other.

(i) **Please visit http://clinicalevidence.bmj.com for full text and references**

| What are the effects of directly observed treatment (DOT) versus self-administered treatment (SAT) in people with tuberculosis without HIV infection? | |
| --- | --- |
| Unknown Effectiveness | • Directly observed treatment compared with self-administered treatment (DOT may increase treatment compliance but there is no evidence that it increases cure rates, and there is a lack of trials in high-risk and under-served populations) |

| What are the effects of support mechanisms for DOT in people with tuberculosis without HIV infection? | |
| --- | --- |
| Likely To Be Beneficial | • Complex support interventions versus usual treatment<br><br>• Mobile phone reminders versus usual treatment<br><br>• Participant-chosen site plus financial incentive versus participant-chosen site alone |
| Unknown Effectiveness | • Clinic-based support versus home-based support<br><br>• Community-based health worker support versus family member support |

- Food incentives versus usual treatment
- Participant-chosen site versus designated site

Search date June 2014

**DEFINITION** Tuberculosis (TB) is caused by *Mycobacterium tuberculosis* and can affect many organs. Specific symptoms relate to site of infection, and are generally accompanied by fever, sweats, and weight loss. This review focuses on TB in people who do not have HIV. (For TB in people with HIV, see our separate review on TB in people with HIV, p 245.)

**INCIDENCE/PREVALENCE** The *M tuberculosis* organism kills more people than any other infectious agent. The global incidence of TB per capita peaked around 2003 and seems to have stabilised or begun to decline. Incidence per 100,000 population is approximately stable in the European Region and is falling in all of the five other WHO regions. It is also falling in all nine subregions, with the possible exception of African countries with low HIV prevalence (Africa — low HIV). The downward trend was fastest in the Latin America and Caribbean subregion (–3.4% per year, 2001–2006). Globally, the slow decline in incidence per capita is more than offset by population growth. This means that the number of new cases was still increasing between 2005 and 2006, from 9.1 to 9.2 million (an increase of 0.6%). The increases in numbers of new cases were in the African, Eastern Mediterranean, European, and South-East Asian Regions.

**AETIOLOGY/RISK FACTORS** The chief route of infection is through inhalation of airborne bacteria released by people with active respiratory TB by cough, sneeze, or speech. Inhaled mycobacteria reach the lung, and grow slowly over several weeks. The immune systems of most healthy exposed people (80%–90%) contain the bacteria, with only a positive skin test left as a marker of exposure. In a proportion of people infected, a defensive barrier is built around the infection, but the TB bacteria are not killed and lie dormant. This is known as latent TB, where the person is asymptomatic and not infectious. In the rest of those infected, active TB develops either immediately or after reactivation of the dormant bacteria. **Risk factors:** Social factors include poverty, overcrowding, homelessness, and inadequate health services. Medical factors include HIV infection and immunosuppression.

**PROGNOSIS** Prognosis varies widely and depends on treatment. In 2013, an estimated 9.0 million people developed TB and 1.5 million died from the disease. Cure rates in TB depend on adherence to treatment. Poor adherence to antituberculous treatment may lead to treatment failure and relapse and to drug resistance; prolonged and expensive therapy of drug-resistant TB is less likely to be successful than the treatment of drug-susceptible TB. Measures to improve adherence include: directly observed treatment, short course (DOTS) (staff motivation and supervision, reminder systems and late patient tracers in the diagnosis and management of tuberculosis, education and counselling for promoting adherence to the treatment of active tuberculosis); incentives and reimbursements (money or cash in kind to reimburse expenses of attending services or to improve the attractiveness of visiting the service); contracts (written or verbal agreements to return for an appointment or course of treatment); and peer assistance (people from the same social group helping someone with tuberculosis return to the health service by prompting or accompanying them). The cure rate among cases registered under DOTS worldwide was 77.6%, and a further 7.1% completed treatment (no laboratory confirmation of cure), giving a reported overall treatment success rate of 84.7% — very close to the 85% target. This means that 49% of the smear-positive cases estimated to have occurred in 2005 were treated successfully by DOTS programmes. Recurrence after successful treatment ranged from 0% to 14% in one systematic review (search date 2006), which identified RCT and observational studies assessing recurrence after successful treatment; little is known about the long-term efficacy of this strategy.

John A Kellum, Mark L Unruh, and Raghavan Murugan

## KEY POINTS

- Acute renal failure (also called acute kidney injury) is characterised by abrupt and sustained decline in GFR, which leads to accumulation of urea and other chemicals in the blood.

  It can be classified according to a change from baseline serum creatinine or urine output, with 'Risk' being defined by either a 50% increase in serum creatinine, or a urine output of <0.5 mL/kg/hour for at least 6 hours; and 'Failure' being defined by a three-fold increase in serum creatinine, or a urine output of <0.3 mL/kg/hour for 24 hours.

- In people at high risk of developing acute renal failure, intravenous sodium chloride (0.9%) reduces incidences of acute renal failure compared with unrestricted oral fluids or 0.45% intravenous sodium chloride solution.

  N-acetylcysteine plus intravenous fluids may reduce contrast nephropathy compared with intravenous fluids alone in people undergoing contrast nephrography, although data about prevention of renal failure are inconclusive.

  Sodium bicarbonate may be as effective as sodium chloride but the evidence is conflicting so we cannot draw conclusions.

  Low-osmolality contrast medium is less nephrotoxic compared with high-osmolality media, and iso-osmolar contrast media has similar nephrotoxicity to low-osmolar contrast media.

  We found insufficient evidence on the effects of prophylactic renal replacement therapy.

  Single-dose aminoglycosides seem as beneficial as multiple doses for treating infections, but are less nephrotoxic.

  Lipid formulations of amphotericin B may cause less nephrotoxicity than standard formulations, although the evidence for this is somewhat sparse.

  Mannitol, theophylline, aminophylline, fenoldopam, and calcium channel blockers do not seem useful treatments for people at high risk of acute renal failure.

- We don't know whether continuous renal replacement therapy is any more effective than intermittent renal replacement therapy. High-dose continuous renal replacement therapy was ineffective in treatment of people critically ill with acute kidney injury, and is also associated with an increased risk of hypophosphataemia, hypokalaemia, and hypotension.

  Synthetic dialysis membranes may be associated with improved survival compared with cellulose-based membranes for treating people with acute renal failure; however, evidence is inconclusive and of variable quality.

  Loop diuretics plus fluids seem to increase the risk of developing acute renal failure compared with fluids alone, both in high-risk and critically ill people, and do not seem to improve renal function or mortality compared with placebo in people with acute renal failure, but may increase the risks of ototoxicity and volume depletion.

  We found no evidence that examined whether intravenous albumin supplementation improved the effects of loop diuretics, or whether continuous infusion was any more effective than bolus injection in the treatment of people critically ill with acute renal failure.

- Neither natriuretic peptides nor dopamine seem beneficial in either high-risk or critically ill people, and both are associated with significant adverse effects.

- We don't know whether early versus late renal replacement therapy or extended daily dialysis improve outcomes in people critically ill with acute kidney injury.

(i) **Please visit http://clinicalevidence.bmj.com for full text and references**

## What are the effects of interventions to prevent acute kidney injury in people at high risk?

| | |
|---|---|
| **Beneficial** | • Contrast media (low-osmolality more effective than high-osmolality contrast media) |
| **Likely To Be Beneficial** | • Aminoglycosides (single dose as effective as multiple doses for treating infection, but with reduced nephrotoxicity)<br>• Amphotericin B (lipid formulations may cause less nephrotoxicity than standard formulations)*<br>• Sodium chloride-based fluids |
| **Unknown Effectiveness** | • Contrast media (iso-osmolar may be more effective than low-osmolality contrast media)<br>• N-Acetylcysteine<br>• Renal replacement therapy (prophylactic haemofiltration/dialysis)<br>• Sodium bicarbonate-based fluids |
| **Unlikely To Be Beneficial** | • Fenoldopam<br>• Mannitol<br>• Natriuretic peptides<br>• Theophylline or aminophylline |
| **Likely To Be Ineffective Or Harmful** | • Calcium channel blockers (for early allograft dysfunction)<br>• Dopamine<br>• Loop diuretics |

## What are the effects of treatments for critically ill people with acute kidney injury?

| | |
|---|---|
| **Unknown Effectiveness** | • Albumin supplementation plus loop diuretics (intravenous)<br>• Continuous renal replacement therapy versus intermittent renal replacement therapy (unclear whether CRRT or IRRT is more effective)<br>• Dialysis membranes (unclear if synthetic or cellulose-based membranes more effective)<br>• Early versus late renal replacement therapy<br>• Extended daily dialysis<br>• Loop diuretics (unclear if continuous infusion more effective than bolus injection) |
| **Unlikely To Be Beneficial** | • Loop diuretics |
| **Likely To Be Ineffective Or Harmful** | • Continuous high-dose renal replacement therapy versus continuous low-dose renal replacement therapy (reduced mortality with high dose compared with low dose) |

| | • Dopamine |
| --- | --- |
| | • Natriuretic peptides |

**Search date December 2009**

*Categorisation based on consensus.

**DEFINITION** Acute renal failure is characterised by abrupt and sustained decline in glomerular filtration rate (GFR), which leads to accumulation of urea and other chemicals in the blood. Most studies define it biochemically as a serum creatinine of 2 mg/dL to 3 mg/dL (200–250 micromol/L), an elevation of >0.5 mg/dL (45 micromol/L) over a baseline creatinine below 2 mg/dL, or a two-fold increase of baseline creatinine. An international interdisciplinary consensus panel has classified acute renal failure (now termed acute kidney injury) according to a change from baseline serum creatinine or urine output. The three-level classification begins with 'Risk' (defined by either a 50% increase in serum creatinine or a urine output of <0.5 mL/kg/hour for at least 6 hours), and concludes with 'Failure' (defined by a 3-fold increase in serum creatinine or a urine output of <0.3 mL/kg/hour for 24 hours). Acute renal failure is usually additionally classified according to the location of the predominant primary pathology (prerenal, intrarenal, and postrenal failure). Critically ill people are clinically unstable and at imminent risk of death, which usually implies that they need to be in, or have been admitted to, the intensive care unit (ICU).

**INCIDENCE/PREVALENCE** Two prospective observational studies (2576 people) found that established acute renal failure affected nearly 5% of people in hospital, and as many as 15% of critically ill people, depending on the definitions used.

**AETIOLOGY/RISK FACTORS General risk factors:** Risk factors for acute renal failure that are consistent across multiple causes include: age; hypovolaemia; hypotension; sepsis; pre-existing renal, hepatic, or cardiac dysfunction; diabetes mellitus; and exposure to nephrotoxins (e.g., aminoglycosides, amphotericin, immunosuppressive agents, NSAIDs, ACE inhibitors, intravenous contrast media). **Risk factors/aetiology in critically ill people:** Isolated episodes of acute renal failure are rarely seen in critically ill people, but are usually part of multiple organ dysfunction syndromes. Acute renal failure requiring dialysis is rarely seen in isolation (<5% of people). The kidneys are often the first organs to fail. In the perioperative setting, risk factors for acute renal failure include prolonged aortic clamping, emergency rather than elective surgery, and use of higher volumes (>100 mL) of intravenous contrast media. One study (3695 people) using multiple logistic regression identified the following independent risk factors: baseline creatinine clearance below 47 mL/minute (OR 1.20, 95% CI 1.12 to 1.30), diabetes (OR 5.5, 95% CI 1.4 to 21.0), and a marginal effect for doses of contrast media above 100 mL (OR 1.01, 95% CI 1.00 to 1.01). Mortality of people with acute renal failure requiring dialysis was 36% while in hospital. Prerenal acute renal failure is caused by reduced blood flow to the kidney from renal artery disease, systemic hypotension, or maldistribution of blood flow. Intrarenal acute renal failure is caused by parenchymal injury (acute tubular necrosis, interstitial nephritis, embolic disease, glomerulonephritis, vasculitis, or small-vessel disease). Postrenal acute renal failure is caused by urinary tract obstruction. Observational studies (in several hundred people from Europe, North America, and West Africa with acute renal failure) found a prerenal cause in 40% to 80%, an intrarenal cause in 10% to 50%, and a postrenal cause in the remaining 10%. Prerenal acute renal failure is the most common type of acute renal failure in critically ill people. Intrarenal acute renal failure in this context is usually part of multisystem failure, most frequently caused by acute tubular necrosis due to ischaemic or nephrotoxic injury, or both.

**PROGNOSIS** One retrospective study (1347 people with acute renal failure) found that mortality was <15% in people with isolated acute renal failure. One prospective study (>700 people) found that, in people with acute renal failure, overall mortality (72% in ICU v 32% in non-ICU; P = 0.001) and the need for dialysis (71% in ICU v 18% in non-ICU; P <0.001) were higher in an ICU than in a non-ICU setting, despite no significant difference between the groups in mean maximal serum creatinine (5.21 ± 2.34 mg/dL in ICU v 5.82 ± 3.26 mg/dL in non-ICU). One large study (>17,000 people admitted to Austrian ICUs) found that acute renal failure was associated with a higher than 4-fold increase in mortality. Even after

*(continued over)*

*(from previous page)*

controlling for underlying severity of illness, mortality was still significantly higher in people with acute renal failure (62.8% in people with acute renal failure *v* 38.5% in people with no acute renal failure), suggesting that acute renal failure is independently responsible for increased mortality, even if dialysis is used. However, the exact mechanism that leads to increased risk of death is uncertain. A systematic review including 80 articles and a total of 15,897 people with acute renal failure from 1970 to 2004 found mortality unchanged at about 50%, and exceeding 30% in most studies. An observational study including 54 sites and 23 countries screened 29,269 people, and found that 1738 (6%) had severe acute renal failure warranting renal replacement therapy. Overall hospital mortality among people with severe acute renal failure was 60.3% (95% CI 58.0% to 62.6%).

Maaz Abbasi, Glenn M Chertow, and Yoshio N Hall

## KEY POINTS

- End-stage renal disease (ESRD) affects >1500 people per million population in countries with a high prevalence, such as the US and Japan. About two-thirds of people with ESRD receive haemodialysis, one quarter have kidney transplants, and one tenth receive peritoneal dialysis.

  Risk factors for ESRD include advanced age; hypertension; diabetes mellitus; obesity; a history of renal disease; and tobacco, heroin, or analgesic use.

  ESRD leads to fluid retention, anaemia, disturbances of bone and mineral metabolism, and increased risk of cardiovascular disease (CVD).

- Increasing the dose of peritoneal dialysis does not seem to reduce mortality.

- In people receiving haemodialysis, there seems no difference in mortality for high membrane-flux compared with low membrane-flux, or increased-dose haemodialysis compared with standard dose.

- Erythropoietin and darbepoetin may help maintain haemoglobin levels in people with ESRD, although normalising haemoglobin levels in people with both ESRD and CVD may increase mortality.

- Disorders of calcium and phosphate metabolism may contribute to the increased risk of CVD in people with ESRD.

  Phosphate binders (sevelamer) may slow down arterial calcification, and may reduce serum low-density lipoprotein cholesterol levels, but we don't yet know whether this reduces cardiovascular events or mortality.

  Cinacalcet is more effective than placebo at improving control of secondary hyperparathyroidism, but we don't know whether it reduces cardiovascular events or mortality.

- Mupirocin reduces *Staphylococcus aureus* infections compared with placebo or no treatment.

- The use of statins in people with ESRD does not seem to reduce mortality or cardiovascular events.

 Please visit http://clinicalevidence.bmj.com for full text and references

| What are the effects of different doses for peritoneal dialysis? | |
| --- | --- |
| Unlikely To Be Beneficial | • Increased-dose peritoneal dialysis (no more effective than standard-dose dialysis in reducing overall mortality) |

| What are the effects of different doses and membrane fluxes for haemodialysis? | |
| --- | --- |
| Unlikely To Be Beneficial | • High membrane-flux haemodialysis (no more effective than low membrane-flux haemodialysis in reducing all-cause mortality)<br>• Increased-dose haemodialysis (no more effective than standard-dose haemodialysis in reducing all-cause mortality) |

| What are the effects of interventions aimed at preventing secondary complications? | |
| --- | --- |
| Likely To Be Beneficial | • Cinacalcet (improves control of secondary hyperparathyroidism compared with placebo) |

|  | • Mupirocin (reduces *Staphylococcus aureus* catheter infections compared with placebo or no treatment)<br><br>• Sevelamer (reduces progression of coronary artery and aortic calcification compared with calcium salts) |
|---|---|
| **Trade-off Between Benefits And Harms** | • Erythropoietin or darbepoetin (maintain haemoglobin levels but associated with increased mortality and cardiovascular events in people with cardiovascular disease) |
| **Unknown Effectiveness** | • Statins in people with end-stage renal disease and normal lipid profiles |

**Search date October 2009**

**DEFINITION** End-stage renal disease (ESRD) is defined as irreversible decline in a person's own kidney function, which is severe enough to be fatal in the absence of dialysis or transplantation. ESRD is included under stage 5 of the National Kidney Foundation Kidney Disease Outcomes Quality Initiative classification of chronic kidney disease (CKD), where it refers to individuals with an estimated glomerular filtration rate <15 mL per minute per 1.73 $m^2$ body surface area, or those requiring dialysis irrespective of glomerular filtration rate. Reduction in or absence of kidney function leads to a host of maladaptive changes including fluid retention (extracellular volume overload), anaemia, disturbances of bone and mineral metabolism, dyslipidaemia, and protein energy malnutrition. This review deals with ESRD in adults only. **Fluid retention** in people with ESRD contributes significantly to the hypertension, ventricular dysfunction, and excess cardiovascular events observed in this population. **Anaemia** associated with CKD is normocytic and normochromic, and is most commonly attributed to reduced erythropoietin synthesis by the affected kidneys. Additional factors contribute to the anaemia, including: iron deficiency from frequent phlebotomy, blood retention in the dialyser and tubing, and gastrointestinal bleeding; severe secondary hyperparathyroidism; acute and chronic inflammatory conditions (e.g., infection); and shortened red blood cell survival. **Disturbances of bone and mineral metabolism** such as hyperparathyroidism, hyperphosphataemia, and hypo- or hypercalcaemia, are common in people with CKD. If untreated, these disturbances can cause pain, pruritus, anaemia, bone loss, and increased fracture risk, and can contribute to hypertension and cardiovascular disease (CVD).

**INCIDENCE/PREVALENCE** According to the US Renal Data System 2009 annual report, there were 111,000 new cases of ESRD in 2007 — equivalent to an annual incidence of 361 cases per million population. The prevalence of ESRD in the US in 2007 was 527,283 (1698 cases per million population). According to international comparative data published in the US Renal Data System 2009 annual report, the highest incidence (415 per million population) and prevalence (2288 cases per million population) rates of ESRD in 2007 worldwide occurred in Taiwan. In 2007, Japan also observed relatively high incidence (285 per million population) and prevalence (2060 cases per million population) of ESRD, which included only people receiving maintenance dialysis. In comparison, the incidence of treated ESRD among all registries reporting to the European Renal Association–European Dialysis and Transplant Association Registry (ERA-EDTA) was 116 per million population in 2007. The overall prevalence of treated ESRD in 2007 among all registries reporting to the ERA-EDTA Registry was 662 per million population. In 2007, the Australia and New Zealand Dialysis and Transplant Registry reported an annual incidence of treated ESRD of 110 people per million population in Australia and 109 people per million population in New Zealand. The prevalence of treated ESRD in 2007 was 797 people per million population for Australia and 793 people per million population for New Zealand.

**AETIOLOGY/RISK FACTORS** The amount of daily proteinuria remains one of the strongest predictors of progression to ESRD. Hypertension is a strong independent risk factor for progression to ESRD, particularly in people with proteinuria. Age is also a predictor for ESRD; people aged >65 years have a four- to fivefold increase in risk of ESRD compared with people <65 years of age. Additional risk factors for developing ESRD include a history of chronic renal insufficiency, diabetes mellitus, heroin abuse, tobacco or analgesic use, non-white race or ethnicity, lower socioeconomic status, obesity, hyperuricaemia, and a family history of kidney disease.

**PROGNOSIS** The overall prognosis of untreated ESRD remains poor. Most people with ESRD eventually die from complications of CVD, infection, or, if dialysis is not provided, progressive uraemia (hyperkalaemia, acidosis, malnutrition, altered mental functioning). Precise mortality estimates, however, are unavailable because international renal registries omit individuals with ESRD who do not receive renal replacement therapy. Among people receiving renal replacement therapy, CVD is the leading cause of mortality, and accounts for >40% of deaths in this population. Extracellular volume overload and hypertension — which are common among people with chronic kidney disease — are known predictors of left ventricular hypertrophy and cardiovascular mortality in this population. Even after adjustment for age, sex, race, or ethnicity, and the presence of diabetes, annual cardiovascular mortality remains roughly an order of magnitude higher in people with ESRD than in the general population, particularly among younger people.

# Kidney stones

Timothy Y Tseng and Glenn M Preminger

## KEY POINTS

- Kidney stones develop when crystals separate from the urine and aggregate within the kidney papillae, renal pelvis, or ureter.

  The age of peak incidence for stone disease is 20 to 40 years, although stones are seen in all age groups. There is a male to female ratio of 3:2.

- The RCT evidence is somewhat sparse regarding the best treatments for people with asymptomatic kidney stones.

  Both percutaneous nephrolithotomy (PCNL) and extracorporeal shockwave lithotripsy (ESWL) may reduce the need for further invasive surgery. However, they are not without risk, and the risks and benefits should be weighed carefully in asymptomatic people.

  We found no RCT evidence assessing ureteroscopy in people with asymptomatic kidney stones.

- For symptomatic kidney stones, PCNL, ureteroscopy, and ESWL are all options for treatment.

  PCNL seems more effective than ESWL in removing symptomatic kidney stones, but it is associated with more complications.

  In very highly selected, uncomplicated cases, tubeless (no nephrostomy but stented) and totally tubeless (no nephrostomy or stent) PCNL seems to give an improved recovery profile.

  Ureteroscopy seems as effective as ESWL in removing symptomatic kidney stones, but it is associated with more complications.

  With ESWL, a slower shock rate of 60 per minute may result in greater treatment success.

  People with larger stones are likely to take longer to pass stone fragments after ESWL; in these cases PCNL may be a more suitable option.

  Open nephrolithotomy has been largely superseded by PCNL in developed countries.

- For symptomatic ureteric stones, ureteroscopy seems to increase overall stone-free rates and decrease time to becoming stone free compared with ESWL.

- Medical expulsive therapy with alpha-blockers seems to increase stone-free rates and decrease time to stone passage compared with standard treatment.

  We found no RCT evidence examining ureterolithotomy (either open or laparoscopic) in people with symptomatic ureteric stones.

(i) **Please visit http://clinicalevidence.bmj.com for full text and references**

| What are the effects of interventions for stone removal in people with asymptomatic kidney stones? | |
|---|---|
| Likely To Be Beneficial | • Extracorporeal shockwave lithotripsy (ESWL) in people with asymptomatic renal or ureteric stones<br><br>• Percutaneous nephrolithotomy (PCNL) in people with asymptomatic renal or ureteric stones |
| Unknown Effectiveness | • Ureteroscopy in people with asymptomatic renal or ureteric stones |

## What are the effects of interventions for the removal of symptomatic renal stones?

| Likely To Be Beneficial | • Extracorporeal shockwave lithotripsy (ESWL) in people with symptomatic renal stones <20 mm<br><br>• Percutaneous nephrolithotomy (PCNL) in people with symptomatic renal stones |
|---|---|
| Unknown Effectiveness | • Open nephrolithotomy in people with symptomatic renal stones<br><br>• Ureteroscopy in people with symptomatic renal stones |

## What are the effects of interventions to remove symptomatic ureteric stones?

| Likely To Be Beneficial | • Alpha-blockers in people with symptomatic ureteric stones<br><br>• Extracorporeal shockwave lithotripsy (ESWL) in people with mid- and distal symptomatic ureteric stones<br><br>• Extracorporeal shockwave lithotripsy (ESWL) in people with symptomatic proximal ureteric stones<br><br>• Ureteroscopy in people with mid- and distal symptomatic ureteric stones<br><br>• Ureteroscopy in people with symptomatic proximal ureteric stones |
|---|---|
| Unknown Effectiveness | • Ureterolithotomy (open or laparoscopic) in people with symptomatic ureteric stones |

## What are the effects of interventions for the management of acute renal colic?

| Likely To Be Beneficial | • NSAIDs (indometacin and diclofenac) in people with acute renal colic<br><br>• Opioid analgesics in people with acute renal colic* |
|---|---|
| Unknown Effectiveness | • Antispasmodic agents in people with acute renal colic<br><br>• Fluids (intravenous or oral) in people with acute renal colic |

Search date June 2011

*Based on consensus opinion.

**DEFINITION** Nephrolithiasis is the presence of stones within the kidney; urolithiasis is a more general term for stones anywhere within the urinary tract. Urolithiasis is usually

*(continued over)*

*(from previous page)*

categorised according to the anatomical location of the stones (i.e., renal calyces, renal pelvis, ureteric, bladder, and urethra). Ureteric urolithiasis is described further by stating in which portion (proximal, middle, or distal) the stone is situated. This review assesses the effects of treatments only for the removal of asymptomatic or symptomatic renal and ureteric stones. It excludes pregnant women, in whom some diagnostic procedures and treatments for stone removal may be contraindicated, and people with significant comorbidities (including severe cardiovascular and respiratory conditions) who may be at increased risk when having general anaesthesia. **Diagnosis:** Diagnosis is usually based on clinical history, supported by investigations with diagnostic imaging. One third of all kidney stones become clinically evident, typically causing pain (often severe in nature), renal angle tenderness, haematuria, or digestive symptoms (e.g., nausea, vomiting, or diarrhoea). The onset of pain is usually sudden, typically felt in the loin, and radiating to the groin and genitalia (scrotum or labia). People are typically restless, find the pain excruciating, and describe it as the worst pain ever experienced. The cause and chemical composition of a stone may have some bearing on its diagnosis, management, and particularly on prevention of recurrence. Although the choices for surgical management in general remain the same for all types of stone disease, the recognition of a specific cause, such as recurrent infection with a urease-producing organism for struvite stones, or cystinuria for cystine stones, will inform further management. **Differential diagnosis:** Bleeding within the urinary tract may present with identical symptoms to kidney stones, particularly if there are blood clots present within the renal pelvis or ureter. Other differential diagnoses include urinary tract infection (which may be concurrent), ureteropelvic junction obstruction, and urothelial carcinoma. Patients with papillary cell necrosis (which may occur in diabetes or sickle cell disease) may also present with renal colic.

**INCIDENCE/PREVALENCE** The age of peak incidence for stone disease is 20 to 40 years, although stones are seen in all age groups. The male predominance of stone disease may be decreasing, with recent reports of male to female ratio being approximately 3:2. In North America, calcium oxalate stones (the most common variety) have a recurrence rate of 10% at 1 year and 35% at 5 years after the first episode of kidney stone disease.

**AETIOLOGY/RISK FACTORS** Kidney stones develop when crystals precipitate out from the urine and aggregate within the kidney papillae, renal pelvis, or ureter. The most common type of stones are calcium-containing stones, which are usually formed of calcium oxalate, and less commonly of calcium phosphate. Other metabolic stones include uric acid, cystine, and xanthine stones. There are also infection stones, or 'struvite' stones, which contain a mixture of magnesium, ammonium, and phosphate, and are associated with urease-forming organisms such as *Klebsiella* or *Proteus* species. Predisposing factors for stone formation include dehydration, lifestyle, geographical location (dry arid climate), and certain specific risk factors. These factors may include anatomical/structural abnormalities (e.g., ureteropelvic junction obstruction, urinary diversion surgery, horseshoe kidney, calyceal diverticulum), and underlying metabolic conditions (e.g., cystinuria, oxaluria, gout), certain drugs, and urease-producing infective organisms.

**PROGNOSIS** Most kidney stones pass within a few days to several weeks with expectant treatment (including adequate fluid intake and analgesia). Others may take longer to pass and an observation period of 4 to 6 weeks is appropriate. Ureteric stones <5 mm in diameter will pass spontaneously in about 90% of people, compared with 50% of ureteric stones between 5 mm and 10 mm. Expectant (conservative) management is considered on an individual basis in people with stones that are asymptomatic, mildly symptomatic, small, or in people with significant comorbidities, for whom the risks of treatment may outweigh the benefits. A stone causing chronic constriction of a ureter may lead to hydronephrosis and renal atrophy. Ureteral obstruction may also result in serious complications including urinary infection, perinephric abscess, or urosepsis. Drainage of an infected obstructed kidney is a medical emergency. Infection may also occur after invasive procedures for stone removal. Some of these complications may cause kidney damage and compromised renal function.

Catherine M. Clase and Andrew Smyth

## KEY POINTS

- Chronic kidney disease (CKD) is usually first recognised by an elevated serum creatinine or low estimated glomerular filtration rate (GFR).

  Continued progression of kidney disease will lead to renal function too low to sustain healthy life. In developed countries, such people will be offered renal replacement therapy in the form of dialysis or renal transplantation. Requirement for dialysis or transplantation is termed end-stage renal disease (ESRD).

  Diabetes, glomerulonephritis, hypertension, pyelonephritis, renovascular disease, polycystic kidney disease, and certain drugs may cause chronic kidney disease.

- We searched for RCTs of 6 months' or longer duration on the effects of low-sodium diets or low-protein diets in people with CKD.

- Because sodium intake affects blood pressure in some people, and because blood pressure control is considered to be important in preventing progression of kidney disease, it has been hypothesised that reduction in dietary sodium intake would reduce the progression of kidney disease in people with CKD. However, we found no RCTs on the effects of low-sodium diets.

- We found RCTs and systematic reviews on the effects of low-protein diets in adults without diabetes, in children, and in adults with diabetic nephropathy.

  The low-protein diets and control diets examined in RCTs varied widely, and most individual studies and reviews did not report on harms.

  Individual large RCTs and long-term follow-up of participants in RCTs found no benefit for low-protein diet in terms of prevention of death or ESRD in adults without diabetes or in children.

  One meta-analysis suggested a large difference in the composite outcome death or ESRD in adults without diabetes; however, the findings were only significant for very low-protein diets but not for low-protein diets as usually implemented in clinical practice.

- One meta-analysis found an improvement in GFR or creatinine clearance with low-protein diet in adults with diabetic nephropathy, but the evidence was difficult to interpret, and we found no evidence on mortality or disease progression (dialysis or transplantation) in this group.

- We found no good evidence on cardiovascular effects or quality of life measures.

- The greatest clinical concern is malnutrition, because people with CKD, especially those who are older, are at risk for malnutrition from CKD and comorbidity, and spontaneous caloric and protein intake is lower in people with lower GFR.

- In children in carefully supervised settings we found no evidence of increased risk of malnutrition or poor growth with low-protein diet, but the evidence mainly derives from one RCT of around 200 children.

- Adult participants in RCTs have mean ages in the 50s to 60s, whereas many people in clinical practice with CKD are in their 70s and 80s. Older people and those with higher levels of comorbidity may be more likely to have cognitive impairment, face financial or practical challenges in implementing dietary advice, and be at greater risk from malnutrition from poorly-understood or poorly-implemented alterations to their diet.

(i) **Please visit http://clinicalevidence.bmj.com for full text and references**

| **What are the effects of a low-sodium diet to reduce progression rate of chronic kidney disease?** | |
|---|---|
| Unknown Effectiveness | • Low-sodium diet versus usual diet |

| **What are the effects of a low-protein diet to reduce progression rate of chronic kidney disease?** | |
|---|---|
| Unknown Effectiveness | • Low-protein diet (low-protein diet or very low-protein diet) versus usual diet |

**Search date September 2014**

**DEFINITION** Chronic kidney disease (CKD) is usually first recognised by an elevated serum creatinine or low estimated glomerular filtration rate (GFR). Since 2002, the Kidney Disease Improving Global Outcomes (KDIGO) statement and subsequent reiterations define low GFR as a GFR of <60 mL/minute/1.73 m² on two occasions at least 3 months apart, and CKD as low GFR, or urinary abnormalities, or clinically important structural abnormalities present for more than 3 months. Low GFR corresponds approximately to serum creatinine concentration >137 micromol/L in men and >104 micromol/L in women. Current KDIGO guidelines, published in 2012, further classify people with low GFR as follows: G3a (GFR 45–59 mL/minute); G3b (GFR 30–44 mL/minute); G4 (GFR 15–29 mL/minute); and G5 CKD (GFR <15 mL/minute or a need for dialysis). The term end-stage renal disease (ESRD) is commonly used to refer to people treated with some form of renal replacement therapy (i.e., dialysis or transplantation). The terms chronic renal insufficiency and chronic renal failure, once widespread in the literature, usually referred to people with low GFR not treated with dialysis, but lacked a clear definition. **For the purposes of this overview, chronic renal failure, chronic renal insufficiency, and chronic kidney failure will be considered synonymous.** Sometimes the term 'CKD' is used synonymously with 'low GFR'; this is particularly prevalent in renal subgroup analyses of RCTs where CKD is often defined based on the 'G' category information alone, and would be more accurately described as low GFR. CKD is actually a broader concept that encompasses not only low GFR but also any clinically important abnormality of kidney structure or abnormality on urine analysis (e.g., protein or blood). In the latest iteration of the international classification of CKD, proteinuria is graded by assessment of albuminuria, ideally as albumin:creatinine ratio, into A1 (normal to mildly increased), <3 mg/mmol; A2 (moderately increased), 3–30 mg/mmol; and A3 (severely increased), >30 mg/mmol. These terms replace the previous equivalent terms 'normal', 'microalbuminuria', and 'macroalbuminuria'. People are classified according to their G and A stage of kidney disease, because level of GFR and degree of proteinuria or albuminuria are well established as independent predictors of both renal and cardiovascular outcomes. Progression of chronic renal failure refers to further decline in renal clearance or GFR over time. This is often assessed as an event (such as increase in serum creatinine to 50% or 100% more than previous values) or — less meaningfully from a clinical perspective — as the rate of decline of clearance (measured or estimated creatinine clearance or GFR). KDIGO further defines a certain fall in GFR (i.e., definite progression) as a change of at least 25%, accompanied by a change in G category, although whether category change should be included in the definition has been questioned. Rapid progression is defined as loss of GFR of >5 mL/min/year. Continued progression of renal failure, in the absence of the competing event of death, will lead to renal function too low to sustain healthy life. In developed countries, people with this problem will usually be offered renal replacement therapy in the form of dialysis or renal transplantation. **Diagnosis:** The diagnosis of CKD is established by the finding, on at least two occasions separated by at least 3 months, of elevated serum creatinine, low GFR, low creatinine clearance, or increased proteinuria, albuminuria, or persistent haematuria. GFR and creatinine clearance may be measured directly or calculated from clinical variables and serum creatinine, and many laboratories now provide an estimated GFR with all reports of serum creatinine. Normal values for creatinine or GFR are the subject of some controversy. In the Framingham study of predominantly white American men and women, a subset (consisting of 3241 people who were free of known renal disease, CVD, hypertension, and diabetes) was used to define a healthy reference sample. The upper 95th percentiles for serum creatinine levels in the healthy reference sample were 136 micromol/L for men and 120 micromol/L for women. In terms of GFR, on the basis of prospective longitudinal studies of healthy ageing, normal kidney function had generally been considered as a creatinine clearance of 150 mL/minute (standard deviation 20 mL/minute) for men aged 20–30 years, and to decline by 0.75 mL/minute a year. Average clearances of 90–100 mL/minute were expected in healthy older people. However, in participants in the third US National Health and Nutrition Examination Survey (NHANES III), a large proportion of the older population had low GFR (e.g., 15% of people in their 80s without diabetes had a GFR of 60–80 mL/minute/1.73 $m^2$, and a further 3% had a GFR of 30–60 mL/minute/1.73 $m^2$). The distinction between decline in GFR caused by ageing and that caused by disease in older people remains controversial. KDIGO defines a GFR of <60 mL/minute/1.73 $m^2$ as indicative of disease. Creatinine calibration varies greatly between laboratories, further increasing the difficulty in setting absolute thresholds for the definition of chronic renal failure, either in terms of creatinine values or in terms of estimates of GFR calculated from serum creatinine. Few studies have been conducted on the cost-effective assessment of people with a new diagnosis of CKD. The rate of change of renal function, and the presence of known risk factors for CKD (e.g., diabetes, hypertension, known autoimmune or connective tissue disease, urinary tract obstruction, and family history of specific renal diseases), can be helpful diagnostically. Proteinuria and haematuria on urinalysis make glomerular or inflammatory tubulointerstitial disease more likely. Ultrasound may be useful to exclude urinary tract obstruction. Direct evidence about the measurement properties of clinical features or diagnostic tests in the diagnosis of unselected people with CKD is lacking, and detailed discussion of this issue is beyond the scope of this overview. An opinion-based account of an approach to this problem can be found within the NKF-KDOQI guidelines.

**INCIDENCE/PREVALENCE** Few data are available on the incidence of CKD. In one UK study of clinical laboratory serum creatinine values, the incidence of new chronic renal failure (defined as a single creatinine value of >180 micromol/L in men or >135 micromol/L in women [corresponding to a GFR of about 30 mL/minute/1.73 $m^2$]) was 0.244% a year. Studies suggest prevalence rises dramatically with age. In the UK, the 2010 Health Survey of England found a prevalence of CKD of 6% in men and 5% in women. New Opportunities for Early Renal Intervention by Computerised Assessment (NEOERICA), also in the UK, identified a prevalence of 6% in men and 11% in women (based on clinically-ordered laboratory testing). In the US, by national survey, the prevalence of CKD was: 1.8% for G1 A2–3 (see Definition); 3.2% for G2 A2–3; 7.6% for G3 A1–3; and 0.4% for G4 A1–3. Repeated national surveys in the US suggest that prevalence is increasing over time, beyond the expected increase associated with the changing age structure of the population.

**AETIOLOGY/RISK FACTORS** Little is known about the epidemiology of the underlying cause of CKD in people without diabetes in the community or in primary care. In people managed at referral centres, and in people who progress to ESRD, glomerulonephritis, hypertension or renovascular disease, and polycystic kidney disease are the most common diagnoses, with a smaller proportion of people having tubulointerstitial disease or vasculitis. In people with CKD who progress to ESRD in Canada, diabetes is the most common cause (24%), followed by glomerulonephritis (20%), unknown (14%), hypertension (10%), pyelonephritis (7%), renovascular disease (7%), polycystic kidney disease (6%), and drug-induced disease (commonly by lithium, analgesics, and NSAIDs, 2%).

**PROGNOSIS** A 10-year, community-based cohort study in Japan found that higher serum creatinine levels may lead to an increase in the risk of developing ESRD. In a community-based cohort in Tromsø, Norway, the 10-year cumulative incidence of renal failure (identified through clinical laboratory screening as having a GFR of 30–60 mL/minute/1.73 $m^2$) was 4% (95% CI 3% to 6%) and mortality was 51% (95% CI 48% to 55%). In a 5-year follow-up of a cohort identified through the laboratories of a large managed care organisation in the US, the rate of ESRD was 1% and mortality 24% for people with a GFR of 30–60 mL/minute/1.73 $m^2$, and ESRD was 20% and mortality 46% for those with a GFR of 15–30 mL/minute/1.73 $m^2$. In a cohort study of men with serum creatinine >300 micromol/L and women with serum creatinine >250 micromol/L, identified through clinical laboratories, 80% reached ESRD at follow-up of 55 to 79 months. In a UK community-based study of clinical laboratory serum creatinine values, chronic renal failure was defined as a single creatinine

*(continued over)*

*(from previous page)*

value of >180 micromol/L in men or >135 micromol/L in women (corresponding to a GFR of about 30 mL/minute/1.73 m$^2$). In those people meeting this definition, but who had not been referred to a nephrologist, and in whom repeat serum creatinine levels were obtained, the annual rate of decline in GFR was <2 mL/minute/year in 79% of people and 5 mL/minute/year or greater in 8% of people. In NHANES III (conducted between 1986–1994), 4.3% of the group had a low GFR (30–60 mL/minute/1.73 m$^2$) and 0.2% had a very low GFR (15–30 mL/minute/1.73 m$^2$). In addition, in the United States Renal Data Survey (USRDS) for 1990, 0.06% of the group required renal replacement therapy. The data from these two studies strongly suggest that many unreferred people with a low GFR do not have progressive disease, or are either of an age or carrying a burden of comorbidity such that the competing risk of death outweighs the risk of ESRD. Proteinuria is a consistent multivariable risk factor for progression of renal failure and for ESRD and can be classified in many ways. In addition to the classification by urine albumin:creatinine ratio (A1 [normal to mildly increased], <3 mg/mmol; A2 [moderately increased], 3–30 mg/mmol; and A3 [severely increased], >30 mg/mmol) recommended for initial assessment of CKD, proteinuria may be quantified by dipstick (0, 1+, 2+, and 3+), by 24-hour collection (non-proteinuric, <300 mg/day; non-nephrotic range proteinuria, 300–3000 mg/day; and nephrotic range proteinuria, >3000 mg/day), and by protein:creatinine ratio. Hypertension and cigarette smoking have also been shown to be risk factors for progression to ESRD. People referred to nephrologists differ from those in primary care in both prognostic markers and rates of progression. For example, in the Modification of Diet in Renal Disease (MDRD) study A (GFR 25–55 mL/minute/1.73 m$^2$), 27% of participating people had >1000 mg daily proteinuria, whereas in NHANES III only 3% of participants with a GFR of 30–60 mL/minute/1.73 m$^2$ showed >288 mg daily of albuminuria. Rate of progression also seems to differ between referred and unreferred people. In a review summarising studies of mostly referred people, the weighted mean loss of GFR was 7.56 mL/minute/year. By contrast with this, in a community-based study of unreferred people conducted in the UK, only 21% of people showed evidence of progression of renal disease (defined as at least 2.0 mL/minute/1.73 m$^2$ a year), and the remaining 79% showed no evidence of progression.

Tom McNicholas and Roger Kirby

## KEY POINTS

- Symptomatic benign prostatic hyperplasia (BPH) may affect up to 30% of men in their early 70s, causing urinary symptoms of bladder outlet obstruction.

  Symptoms can improve without treatment, but the usual course is a slow progression of symptoms, with acute urinary retention occurring in 1% to 2% of men with BPH a year.

- Alpha-blockers improve symptoms compared with placebo and more rapidly than with finasteride, and may be most effective in men with more severe symptoms of BPH or with hypertension.

  CAUTION: A drug safety alert has been issued on risk of intraoperative floppy iris syndrome during cataract surgery with tamsulosin and probably other alpha-blockers. People taking an alpha-blocker should inform their eye surgeon.

- 5 alpha-reductase inhibitors (finasteride and dutasteride) improve symptoms (especially with longer duration of treatment) and reduce the risk of complications of BPH occurring compared with placebo, and are more effective in men with larger prostates.

  CAUTION: A drug safety alert has been issued on the risk of male breast cancer with finasteride. Changes in breast tissue such as lumps, pain, or nipple discharge should be promptly reported for further assessment.

- Saw palmetto plant extracts may be no more effective than placebo at improving symptoms. However, evidence was weak and further good-quality long-term RCTs are needed.

- Beta-sitosterol plant extract may improve symptoms of BPH compared with placebo in the short term.

- We don't know whether rye grass pollen extract or *Pygeum africanum* are also beneficial, as few studies were found.

- Transurethral resection of the prostate (TURP) improves symptoms of BPH more than watchful waiting, and has been shown not to increase the risk of erectile dysfunction or incontinence.

  Some less invasive surgical techniques such as transurethral incision, laser ablation, transurethral Holmium laser enucleation (HoLEP), and transurethral electrovaporisation seem to be as effective as TURP at improving symptoms.

  TURP may be more effective at improving symptoms and preventing re-treatment compared with transurethral microwave thermotherapy, but causes more complications.

  Transurethral microwave thermotherapy reduces symptoms compared with sham treatment or with alpha-blockers, but long-term effects are unknown.

  We don't know whether transurethral needle ablation is effective.

(i) Please visit http://clinicalevidence.bmj.com for full text and references

| What are the effects of medical treatments in men with benign prostatic hyperplasia? | |
|---|---|
| Beneficial | • 5 alpha-reductase inhibitors |
| | • Alpha-blockers |

## What are the effects of herbal treatments in men with benign prostatic hyperplasia?

| | |
|---|---|
| Likely To Be Beneficial | • Beta-sitosterol plant extract |
| Unknown Effectiveness | • *Pygeum africanum*<br><br>• Rye grass pollen extract |
| Unlikely To Be Beneficial | • Saw palmetto plant extracts |

## What are the effects of surgical treatments in men with benign prostatic hyperplasia?

| | |
|---|---|
| Beneficial | • Transurethral resection (improves symptoms compared with no surgery) |
| Likely To Be Beneficial | • Transurethral Holmium laser enucleation of the prostate (HoLEP) (may be as effective as transurethral resection; however, unclear how it compares with no surgery or with other surgical techniques)<br><br>• Transurethral electrovaporisation of the prostate (TUEVP) (may be as effective as transurethral resection; however, unclear how it compares with no surgery or with other surgical techniques)<br><br>• Transurethral microwave thermotherapy (TUMT) (improves symptoms compared with no surgery; may be less effective than transurethral resection at improving symptoms) |
| Unknown Effectiveness | • Transurethral needle ablation (unclear how it compares with no surgery or with other surgical techniques) |

**Search date July 2009**

**DEFINITION** Benign prostatic hyperplasia (BPH) is defined histologically. Several terms such as 'prostatism', 'symptoms of BPH', and 'clinical BPH' have previously been used to describe male lower urinary tract symptoms (LUTS). These descriptions incorrectly imply that urinary symptoms in the male arise from the prostate. The acronym 'LUTS' was introduced in order to avoid this. Increasingly, scientific communications on this syndrome use the term LUTS and avoid the use of the global term BPH. Nevertheless, BPH remains familiar to and commonly used by general practitioners, other clinicians, and patients when searching for clinical information and guidance. Clinically, the syndrome is characterised by lower urinary tract symptoms (urinary frequency, urgency, a weak and intermittent stream, needing to strain, a sense of incomplete emptying, and nocturia) and can lead to complications, including acute urinary retention.

**INCIDENCE/PREVALENCE** Estimates of the prevalence of symptomatic BPH range from 10% to 30% for men in their early 70s, depending on how BPH is defined.

**AETIOLOGY/RISK FACTORS** The mechanisms by which BPH causes symptoms and complications are unclear, although bladder outlet obstruction is an important factor. The best documented risk factors are increasing age and normal testicular function.

**PROGNOSIS** Community- and practice-based studies suggest that men with LUTS can expect slow progression of symptoms. However, symptoms can wax and wane without treatment. In men with LUTS secondary to BPH, rates of acute urinary retention range from 1% to 2% a year.

Diana K. Bowen, Elodi Dielubanza, and Anthony J. Schaeffer

### KEY POINTS

- Chronic prostatitis is a syndrome of pain and urinary symptoms, and occurs either with recurrent bacterial infection (chronic bacterial prostatitis [CBP]) or as pain without evidence of bacterial infection (chronic pelvic pain syndrome [CPPS]). Occasionally, there may be positive bacterial cultures from prostatic secretions in CPPS, but no evidence that these are causative of the men's symptoms.

    Bacterial infection can result from urinary tract instrumentation, but the cause and natural history of CPPS are unknown.

- CBP has identifiable virulent micro-organisms in prostatic secretions.

    Oral antimicrobial drugs are beneficial for CBP, although trials comparing them with placebo or no treatment have not been found.

    Clinical success rates with oral antimicrobials have reached about 70% to 90% at 6 months in studies comparing different regimens.

    Trimethoprim and quinolones are most commonly used. These should be used above other antibiotics given their ability to penetrate the prostate, except in circumstances where specific bacterial sensitivities indicate otherwise.

    Although we don't know from clinical trials whether local injections of antimicrobial drugs or transurethral resection of the prostate improve symptoms compared with no treatment in people with CBP, these should be considered for those that fail oral antibiotics.

- Effective treatment regimens for CPPS remain to be defined, and strategies are based on symptomatic control and anxiety relief.

    Alpha-blockers have been found in some RCTs to have some efficacy in symptom relief of CPPS; however, there are studies that show no effect. To date, we don't know how effective alpha-blockers are in people with CPPS.

    We don't know whether 5 alpha-reductase inhibitors, NSAIDs, pentosan polysulfate, allopurinol, transurethral microwave thermotherapy, sitz baths, mepartricin, or quercetin reduce symptoms in men with CPPS.

(i) **Please visit http://clinicalevidence.bmj.com for full text and references**

| **What are the effects of treatments for chronic bacterial prostatitis?** | |
|---|---|
| **Beneficial** | • Antimicrobial drugs (oral) for CBP* |
| **Unknown Effectiveness** | • Antimicrobial drugs (locally injected) for CBP |
| | • Transurethral resection of the prostate for CBP |

| **What are the effects of treatments for chronic pelvic pain syndrome?** | |
|---|---|
| **Unknown Effectiveness** | • 5 alpha-reductase inhibitors for CPPS |
| | • Allopurinol for CPPS |
| | • Alpha-blockers for CPPS (better than placebo; however, considerable heterogeneity in trials and of borderline clinical importance for some outcomes) |
| | • Mepartricin for CPPS |
| | • NSAIDs for CPPS |

- Pentosan polysulfate for CPPS
- Quercetin for CPPS
- Sitz baths for CPPS
- Transurethral microwave thermotherapy for CPPS

**Search date February 2014**

* No RCTs; categorised on the basis of consensus and non-RCT evidence.

**DEFINITION** Chronic bacterial prostatitis (CBP) is characterised by recurrent infections with documented positive cultures of expressed prostatic secretions. It is asymptomatic until the patient has a urinary tract infection with associated symptoms such as suprapubic, lower back, or perineal pain, with or without mild urgency and increased frequency of urination and dysuria. However, it will be asymptomatic between acute infective episodes. **Chronic pelvic pain syndrome (CPPS)** is characterised by pelvic or perineal pain in the absence of pathogenic bacteria in expressed prostatic secretions. It is often associated with irritative and obstructive voiding symptoms including urgency, frequency, hesitancy, and poor interrupted flow. Symptoms can also include pain in the suprapubic region, lower back, penis, testes, or scrotum and painful ejaculation. CPPS may be inflammatory (white cells present in prostatic secretions) or non-inflammatory (white cells absent in prostatic secretions). A classification system for the prostatitis syndromes has been developed by the US National Institutes of Health (NIH).

**INCIDENCE/PREVALENCE** One community-based study in the US (cohort of 2115 men aged 40–79 years) estimated that 9% of men have a diagnosis of either type of prostatitis at any one time. Another observational study found that, in men presenting with genito-urinary symptoms, 8% of those presenting to urologists and 1% of those presenting to primary-care physicians were diagnosed as having CBP or CPPS. However, most cases were abacterial; therefore, these studies are generally examining the prevalence of CPPS (formerly known as 'abacterial prostatitis'). CBP, although easy to diagnose, is rare.

**AETIOLOGY/RISK FACTORS** Organisms commonly implicated in bacterial prostatitis include *Escherichia coli*, other gram-negative enterobacteriaceae, occasionally *Pseudomonas* species, and, rarely, gram-positive enterococci. Risk factors for chronic bacterial prostatitis include urethral catheterisation or instrumentation, condom drainage, dysfunctional voiding (high-pressure urination), and unprotected anal intercourse. The cause of CPPS is unclear, although it has been suggested that it may be caused by undocumented infections with *Chlamydia trachomatis*, *Ureaplasma urealyticum*, *Mycoplasma hominis*, and *Trichomonas vaginalis*. Viruses, *Candida* (in immunosuppressed people), and parasites have also rarely been implicated. Non-infectious factors might also be involved, including inflammation, autoimmunity, hormonal imbalances, pelvic floor tension myalgia, intraprostatic urinary reflux, and psychological disturbances. In one case-control study (463 men with CPPS; 121 asymptomatic age-matched controls), when compared with controls, men with CPPS reported a significantly higher lifetime prevalence of non-specific urethritis; CVD; neurological disease; psychiatric conditions; and haematopoietic, lymphatic, or infectious disease (non-specific urethritis: 12% with CPPS *v* 4% with no CPPS; P = 0.008; CVD: 11% with CPPS *v* 2% with no CPPS; P = 0.004; neurological disease: 41% with CPPS *v* 14% with no CPPS; P <0.001; psychiatric conditions: 29% with CPPS *v* 11% with no CPPS; P <0.001; haematopoietic, lymphatic, or infectious disease: 41% with CPPS *v* 20% with no CPPS; P <0.001). Further studies are necessary to determine whether these factors play a role in the pathogenesis of CPPS.

**PROGNOSIS** The natural histories of untreated CBP and CPPS remain ill-defined. CBP usually causes recurrent UTI in men, whereas CPPS does not. Several investigators have reported an association between CBP, CPPS, and infertility. One study found that CPPS had an impact on quality of life similar to that of angina, Crohn's disease, or a previous MI.

Mohit Khera and Irwin Goldstein

## KEY POINTS

- Erectile dysfunction may affect 30% to 50% of men aged 40 to 70 years, with age, smoking, and obesity being the main risk factors, although 20% of cases have psychological causes.

- Sildenafil improves erections and increases the likelihood of successful intercourse in men with erectile dysfunction (any cause) and in specific populations of men with erectile dysfunction and diabetes mellitus, heart disease, spinal cord injury, prostate cancer, or after radical prostatectomy.

  Tadalafil and vardenafil also improve erections in men with erectile dysfunction (any cause). They are also effective in specific populations of men with erectile dysfunction, for example in those with diabetes, or in men with prostate cancer or after radical prostatectomy; however, fewer studies were found than with sildenafil, and no high-quality evidence was found in other specific populations such as in men with cardiovascular disease.

- CAUTION: sildenafil, tadalafil, and vardenafil are contraindicated in men who are taking nitrates, as combined treatment has been associated with severe hypotension and death.

- Intracavernosal, intraurethral, and topical alprostadil improve erections compared with placebo, but can cause penile pain in up to 40% of men.

  Intracavernosal alprostadil may improve erections compared with intraurethral alprostadil and intracavernosal papaverine.

  Intracavernosal alprostadil may be as effective as sildenafil and bimix.

  Adding phentolamine to intracavernosal papaverine (bimix) may increase effectiveness compared with papaverine alone, and adding alprostadil to bimix (trimix) may be more effective again. However, papaverine injections may cause altered liver function, and penile bruising and fibrosis.

- Ginseng and yohimbine may increase successful erections and intercourse compared with placebo.

- Vacuum devices may be as effective as intracavernosal papaverine, phentolamine, and alprostadil (trimix) at increasing rigidity, but less effective for orgasm, and may block ejaculation.

  There is consensus that penile prostheses may be beneficial, but they can cause infections and are only used if less invasive treatments have failed.

- Psychosexual counselling and cognitive behavioural therapy may improve sexual functioning in men with psychological erectile dysfunction, but we found few good-quality studies. Several studies have demonstrated benefit of combination therapy (i.e., sex therapy and sildenafil or sex therapy and vacuum erection device) compared with monotherapy without sex therapy.

(i) **Please visit http://clinicalevidence.bmj.com for full text and references**

| What are the effects of phosphodiesterase inhibitors in men with erectile dysfunction of any cause? | |
|---|---|
| Beneficial | • Sildenafil in men with erectile dysfunction of any cause |
| | • Tadalafil in men with erectile dysfunction of any cause |
| | • Vardenafil in men with erectile dysfunction of any cause |

## What are the effects of phosphodiesterase inhibitors on erectile dysfunction in men with diabetes?

| | |
|---|---|
| Beneficial | • Sildenafil in men with diabetes |
| Likely To Be Beneficial | • Tadalafil in men with diabetes<br>• Vardenafil in men with diabetes |

## What are the effects of phosphodiesterase inhibitors on erectile dysfunction in men with cardiovascular disease?

| | |
|---|---|
| Beneficial | • Sildenafil in men with cardiovascular disease |
| Unknown Effectiveness | • Tadalafil in men with cardiovascular disease<br>• Vardenafil in men with cardiovascular disease |

## What are the effects of phosphodiesterase inhibitors on erectile dysfunction in men with spinal cord injury?

| | |
|---|---|
| Likely To Be Beneficial | • Sildenafil in men with spinal cord injury<br>• Tadalafil in men with spinal cord injury |
| Unknown Effectiveness | • Vardenafil in men with spinal cord injury |

## What are the effects of phosphodiesterase inhibitors on erectile dysfunction in men with prostate cancer or undergoing prostatectomy?

| | |
|---|---|
| Likely To Be Beneficial | • Sildenafil in men with prostate cancer or undergoing prostatectomy<br>• Tadalafil in men with prostate cancer or undergoing prostatectomy<br>• Vardenafil in men with prostate cancer or undergoing prostatectomy |

## What are the effects of drug treatments other than phosphodiesterase inhibitors in men with erectile dysfunction of any cause?

| | |
|---|---|
| Trade-off Between Benefits And Harms | • Alprostadil (intracavernosal) in men with erectile dysfunction of any cause<br>• Alprostadil (intraurethral) in men with erectile dysfunction of any cause<br>• Alprostadil (topical) in men with erectile dysfunction of any cause<br>• Papaverine in men with erectile dysfunction of any cause<br>• Papaverine plus phentolamine (bimix) in men with erectile dysfunction of any cause |

| | • Papaverine plus phentolamine plus alprostadil (trimix) in men with erectile dysfunction of any cause |
|---|---|

## What are the effects of devices in men with erectile dysfunction of any cause?

| Likely To Be Beneficial | • Penile prosthesis in men with erectile dysfunction of any cause* |
|---|---|
| Unknown Effectiveness | • Vacuum devices in men with erectile dysfunction of any cause |

## What are the effects of psychological/behavioural treatments in men with erectile dysfunction of any cause?

| Likely To Be Beneficial | • Psychosexual counselling in men with erectile dysfunction of any cause |
|---|---|
| Unknown Effectiveness | • Cognitive behavioural therapy in men with erectile dysfunction of any cause* |

## What are the effects of alternative treatments in men with erectile dysfunction of any cause?

| Likely To Be Beneficial | • Ginseng in men with erectile dysfunction of any cause • Yohimbine in men with erectile dysfunction of any cause |
|---|---|

### Search date August 2009

*Categorisation based on consensus; RCTs unlikely to be conducted.

**DEFINITION** Erectile dysfunction is defined as the persistent inability to obtain or maintain sufficient rigidity of the penis to allow satisfactory sexual performance. The term erectile dysfunction has largely replaced the term "impotence". For the purposes of this review we included only men with normal testosterone and gonadotrophin levels, who could gain an erection while asleep. We also included men with comorbid conditions such as cardiovascular disorders, prostate cancer, diabetes, and spinal cord injury. We excluded men with drug-induced sexual dysfunction. Because the cause of erectile dysfunction in men with cardiovascular disease is unclear (the disease or treatment drugs), we included them.

**INCIDENCE/PREVALENCE** Cross-sectional epidemiological studies from around the world reveal that 30% to 50% of men aged 40 to 70 years report some degree of erectile dysfunction. About 150 million men worldwide are unable to achieve and maintain an erection adequate for satisfactory sexual intercourse. Age is the variable most strongly associated with erectile dysfunction; between the ages of 40 to 70 years, the incidence of moderate erectile dysfunction doubles from 17% to 34%, whereas that of severe erectile dysfunction triples from 5% to 15%.

**AETIOLOGY/RISK FACTORS** About 80% of cases are believed to have an organic cause, the rest being psychogenic in origin. Most cases of erectile dysfunction are believed to be multifactorial and secondary to disease, stress, trauma (such as spinal cord injury, pelvic and prostate surgery), or drug adverse effects that interfere with the coordinated psychological, neurological, endocrine, vascular, and muscular factors necessary for normal erections. Risk factors include increasing age, smoking, obesity, and sedentary lifestyle. The prevalence of erectile dysfunction also increases in people with diabetes mellitus, hypertension, heart disease, anxiety, and depression.

**PROGNOSIS** We found no good evidence on prognosis in untreated organic erectile dysfunction.

Peter Chung and Padraig Warde

### KEY POINTS

- More than half of painless solid swellings of the body of the testis are malignant, with a peak incidence in men aged 25 to 35 years.

  Most testicular cancers are germ cell tumours and about half of these are seminomas, which tend to affect older men and have a good prognosis.

- In men with seminoma confined to the testis (stage 1), standard treatment is orchidectomy followed by radiotherapy, chemotherapy, or surveillance. All three management options are associated with cure rates approaching 100% because of successful salvage therapy.

  Adjuvant chemotherapy reduces the risk of relapse after orchidectomy compared with surveillance, but is associated with short-term adverse effects (nausea, diarrhoea, and indigestion) and possible long-term risks of reduced fertility and development of second malignancies.

  We don't know which is the most effective chemotherapy regimen, or the optimum number of cycles to use. The high cure rate with standard therapy makes it difficult to show which alternative therapy is superior.

  Toxicity is lower, but efficacy the same, with adjuvant irradiation of 20 Gy in 10 fractions compared with 30 Gy in 15 fractions, or with irradiation to para-aortic nodes compared with ipsilateral iliac nodes.

- In men with good-prognosis non-stage 1 seminoma who have had orchidectomy, radiotherapy may improve survival and be less toxic than chemotherapy, except in men with large-volume disease, in whom chemotherapy may be more effective.

  Combined chemotherapy may be more effective than single agents, but three cycles seem to be as effective as four and with less toxicity.

  A standard radiotherapy treatment comprises 30 to 36 Gy in 15 to 18 fractions (2 Gy per fraction), although we don't know whether this is more effective than other regimens.

- In men who are in remission after orchidectomy plus chemotherapy for good-prognosis, non-stage 1 seminoma, further chemotherapy is unlikely to reduce relapse rates or increase survival.

  Chemotherapy increases survival in men with intermediate-prognosis seminomas who have had orchidectomy; although evidence for this is derived mostly from treatment of intermediate-prognosis non-seminoma, it is likely to be generalisable to intermediate-prognosis seminoma.

 **Please visit http://clinicalevidence.bmj.com for full text and references**

| What are the effects of treatments in men with stage 1 seminoma (confined to testis) who have undergone orchidectomy? | |
| --- | --- |
| **Beneficial** | • Adjuvant irradiation of 20 Gy in 10 fractions to para-aortic area compared with 30 Gy in 15 fractions to para-aortic area and iliac nodes (similarly effective but less toxicity) |
| **Trade-off Between Benefits And Harms** | • Adjuvant chemotherapy (reduced risk of relapse compared with surveillance, increased immediate toxicity, and possible long-term fertility problems and development of secondary malignancies)* |
| | • Adjuvant radiotherapy (reduced risk of relapse compared with surveillance, increased immediate |

| | |
|---|---|
| | toxicity, and possible long-term fertility problems and development of secondary malignancies)*<br><br>● Surveillance (avoids toxicity associated with adjuvant radiotherapy or chemotherapy, increased risk of relapse)* |
| **Unknown Effectiveness** | ● Comparative effects of different drug combinations for adjuvant chemotherapy<br><br>● Comparative effects of different number of cycles of adjuvant chemotherapy |

## What are the effects of treatments in men with good-prognosis non-stage 1 seminoma who have undergone orchidectomy?

| | |
|---|---|
| **Likely To Be Beneficial** | ● Chemotherapy using bleomycin added to vinblastine plus cisplatin (reduced relapse rates and mortality compared with two-drug regimen of vinblastine plus cisplatin alone)<br><br>● Chemotherapy using etoposide plus cisplatin with or without bleomycin (increased relapse-free survival compared with other combined regimens)<br><br>● Radiotherapy (30–36 Gy in 15–18 fractions)*<br><br>● Three cycles of chemotherapy compared with four cycles (no significant difference in survival; reduced toxicity) |
| **Trade-off Between Benefits And Harms** | ● Radiotherapy versus chemotherapy (less toxicity with radiotherapy compared with chemotherapy; higher risk of relapse)* |
| **Unknown Effectiveness** | ● Adding higher compared with lower doses of cisplatin or vinblastine to a two-drug chemotherapy regimen |
| **Unlikely To Be Beneficial** | ● Chemotherapy using single-agent carboplatin (may be less effective than combined chemotherapy in increasing relapse-free survival) |

## What are the effects of maintenance chemotherapy in men who are in remission after orchidectomy and chemotherapy for good-prognosis non-stage 1 seminoma?

| | |
|---|---|
| **Unlikely To Be Beneficial** | ● Maintenance chemotherapy |

## What are the effects of treatments in men with intermediate-prognosis non-stage 1 seminomas who have undergone orchidectomy?

| Unknown Effectiveness | • Chemotherapy |
|---|---|

**Search date June 2010**

*No RCTs. Based on observational evidence and consensus.

**DEFINITION** Although testicular symptoms are common, testicular cancer is relatively rare. Solid swellings affecting the body of the testis have a high probability (>50%) of being due to cancer. The most common presenting symptom of cancer is a painless lump or swelling (>85%). About 10% of men present with acute pain and 20% to 30% experience a heavy dragging feeling or general ache. These symptoms may lead the cancer to be initially wrongly diagnosed as epididymitis or acute testicular torsion. A small percentage present with symptoms of metastatic disease and infertility. Testicular germ cell tumours are divided into **seminomas**, which make up about half of all testicular tumours and which occur in older patients; and **non-seminomatous tumours**, comprising teratomas, mixed tumours, and other cell types, which tend to occur in younger patients. Several staging systems for testicular cancer have been developed. The most commonly used system for metastatic disease in current practice is the International Germ Cell Consensus Classification, which classifies testicular tumours as good prognosis, intermediate prognosis, or poor prognosis. This system is less useful in seminoma, as 90% are classified as good prognosis and the majority of men with seminoma present with disease confined to the testis. Thus we have further divided good-prognosis seminoma into stage 1 (confined to testis) and non-stage 1, based on the Royal Marsden and TNM staging systems.

**INCIDENCE/PREVALENCE** There are about 1400 new cases of testicular cancer (seminomas, non-seminomas) in the UK annually, with the peak incidence in men aged 25 to 35 years. This cancer comprises 1% of all cancers in men and is the most common tumour in young men. Incidence varies markedly with geography; a study among 10 cancer registries in northern Europe identified a 10-fold variation, with the highest incidence rate in Denmark (7.8 per 100,000) and lowest in Lithuania (0.9 per 100,000). Recent reviews of the incidence of testicular cancer have reported a clear trend towards increased incidence during the past 30 years in the majority of industrialised countries in North America, Europe, and Oceania.

**AETIOLOGY/RISK FACTORS** There seem to be both individual and environmental risk factors for testicular cancer. Having a close relative who has had testicular cancer increases the risk of getting the disease. Inherited genetic factors may play a role in up to 1 in 5 cancers. Men are more at risk of developing testicular cancer if they have a history of developmental abnormality (e.g., maldescent or gonadal dysgenesis); previous cancer in the opposite testis; HIV infection, AIDS, or both; torsion; trauma (although this may be coincidental); and Klinefelter's syndrome. The wide geographical variation and changes over time in incidence rates imply that there are likely to be important environmental factors, because the individual risk factors described above do not explain global disease patterns.

**PROGNOSIS** Testicular tumours generally have a good prognosis. The International Germ Cell Consensus Classification classifies 90% of all seminomas as 'good prognosis'. These include tumours confined to the testis (stage 1 of the Royal Marsden or TNM system) as well as tumours with nodal but no non-pulmonary visceral metastases. The remaining 10% of seminomas, including those with non-pulmonary visceral metastases, are classified as 'intermediate prognosis'. No seminomas are classified as 'poor prognosis'. Untreated disease will progress over time, leading to large local tumours and distant spread. The first site of spread is the lymphatic system, particularly the para-aortic and pelvic lymph nodes. Haematological spread leading to lung, liver, and brain metastases is less common in seminomas; 75% of men present with stage 1 disease. Overall survival in the 'good prognosis' category is expected to be in the order of 86% at 5 years, and of the 10% who present as 'intermediate prognosis', 5-year survival is in the order of 72%. However, these data are based mainly on people with non-seminomas. Seminoma is a radio-sensitive tumour, and the standard treatment for stage 1 seminoma is orchidectomy followed by adjuvant radiotherapy, adjuvant chemotherapy, or surveillance. Clinical observation suggests that, with these approaches, cure rates are nearly 100%.

Rebecca Macleod, Chandra Shekhar Biyani, Jon Cartledge, and Ian Eardley

## KEY POINTS

- The prevalence of varicocele varies considerably between the general population and infertile men. It usually occurs only on the left side, and is often asymptomatic. If symptoms do occur, they may include testicular ache or distress about cosmetic appearance.

  There is little evidence that varicocele reduces male fertility, although it is found in 15% of the general male population and in 35% (19%-42%) of men with primary infertility.

- Varicocele is caused by dysfunction of the valves in the spermatic vein.

- We searched for evidence of effectiveness from RCTs and systematic reviews of RCTs.

- We reported on clinical outcomes such as spontaneous pregnancy rate, spontaneous live birth rates, pain or discomfort, quality of life, and adverse effects. We excluded non-clinical outcomes such as sperm count, testicular temperature, and blood flow.

- Overall, we found insufficient evidence from RCTs to support the concept that successful varicocele treatment will increase the chance of spontaneous pregnancy.

  We do not know whether surgical ligation or embolisation of the spermatic vein increase pregnancy rates or reduce symptoms of varicocele.

  Sclerotherapy may be no more effective than no treatment at improving pregnancy rates. We don't know whether it reduces symptoms of varicocele.

  We don't know how expectant management and embolisation compare, as we found no evidence from RCTs.

 Please visit http://clinicalevidence.bmj.com for full text and references

| What are the effects of treatments in adult males with varicocele? | |
|---|---|
| Unknown Effectiveness | • Embolisation |
| | • Expectant management |
| | • Sclerotherapy |
| | • Surgical ligation |

Search date November 2013

**DEFINITION** Varicocele is a dilation of the pampiniform plexus of the spermatic cord. Severity is commonly graded as follows: **grade 0 (subclinical)** only demonstrable by imaging investigation; **grade 1** palpable or visible only on Valsalva manoeuvre (straining); **grade 2** palpable but not visible when standing upright at room temperature; and **grade 3** visible when standing upright at room temperature. Varicocele is unilateral and left-sided in at least 85% of cases. In most of the remaining cases, the condition is bilateral. Unilateral right-sided varicocele is rare. Many men who have a varicocele have no symptoms. Symptoms may include testicular ache or discomfort, and distress about cosmetic appearance. This overview deals with varicocele in adult males only.

**INCIDENCE/PREVALENCE** We found few data on the prevalence of varicocele. Prevalence of varicocele varies considerably between the general population and infertile men. One study suggests states that varicocele is found in 15% of the male general population and in 35% (19%–41%) of men with primary infertility. One multicentre study found that, in couples with subfertility, the prevalence of varicocele in male partners was about 12%. In men with abnormal semen analysis, the prevalence of varicocele was about 25%.

**AETIOLOGY/RISK FACTORS** We found few reliable data on epidemiological risk factors for varicocele, such as a family history or environmental exposures. An increased incidence has been reported in first-degree relatives. A small study showed a higher prevalence in tall and heavy men. Anatomically, varicoceles are caused by dysfunction of the valves in the spermatic vein, which allows pooling of blood in the pampiniform plexus. This is more likely to occur in the left spermatic vein than in the right because of normal anatomical asymmetry. Varicocele is present in one quarter of men with abnormal semen analyses. However, the precise association between male subfertility and varicocele is unclear.

**PROGNOSIS** Varicocele is believed to be associated with male subfertility, although reliable evidence is sparse. The natural history of varicocele is unclear.

320 | **Alcohol misuse**

Simon Coulton

**KEY POINTS**

- Alcohol use is a leading cause of mortality and morbidity internationally, and is ranked by the WHO as one of the top 5 risk factors for disease burden.

  Without treatment, approximately 16% of hazardous or harmful alcohol users will progress to more dependent patterns of alcohol consumption.

- This review covers interventions in hazardous or harmful (but not dependent) alcohol users.

  Hazardous alcohol consumption is defined as a pattern of alcohol consumption that increases the individual's risk of alcohol-related harm, but is not currently causing alcohol-related harm.

  Harmful alcohol consumption is a pattern of consumption likely to have already led to alcohol-related harm.

- Single- or multiple-session brief intervention reduces alcohol consumption over 1 year in hazardous drinkers treated in the primary-care setting, but we don't know how it affects mortality.

- Brief intervention (single or multiple session) is also effective at reducing alcohol consumption in people treated in the emergency department, although the evidence is not as strong.

- Adding universal screening to brief intervention enhances its benefits when given in primary care.

  We found insufficient RCT evidence to assess whether universal screening and brief intervention is any more effective than usual care in emergency departments.

  We don't know whether targeted screening is effective, as we found no RCT evidence assessing its use in primary or emergency care.

(i) **Please visit http://clinicalevidence.bmj.com for full text and references**

| What are the effects of interventions in hazardous or harmful drinkers in the primary-care setting? | |
|---|---|
| Beneficial | • Brief intervention (single or multiple session) in primary care (more effective than usual care) |
| Likely To Be Beneficial | • Adding universal screening to brief interventions in primary care (more effective than brief intervention alone) |
| Unknown Effectiveness | • Adding targeted screening to brief intervention in primary care |

| What are the effects of interventions in hazardous or harmful drinkers in the emergency-department setting? | |
|---|---|
| Likely To Be Beneficial | • Single-session brief intervention (more effective than usual care in people presenting to emergency departments with injuries related to alcohol consumption) |
| Unknown Effectiveness | • Targeted screening plus brief intervention in emergency departments |

> • Universal screening plus brief intervention in emergency departments

**Search date September 2010**

**DEFINITION** This review covers interventions in hazardous and harmful alcohol users aged 18 years and older being treated in primary care or in emergency departments. In defining hazardous and harmful alcohol consumption, we have used the WHO categorisation of alcohol-use disorders. Dependent drinkers (who have more serious alcohol misuse problems than harmful or hazardous drinkers) are not covered by this review. It is important to note that threshold levels of hazardous and harmful consumption often vary by country and culture. **Hazardous alcohol consumption** is defined as a pattern of alcohol consumption that increases the individual's risk of alcohol-related harm, but is not currently causing alcohol-related harm. The quantity and frequency of alcohol consumption that constitutes hazardous consumption is usually specified using threshold levels of consumption. In the UK, these levels are specified as: in excess of 14 standard drinks for women and 21 standard drinks for men in any week, where a standard drink constitutes 10 mL by volume or 8 g by weight of pure ethanol. **Harmful alcohol consumption** is a pattern of consumption likely to have already led to alcohol-related harm. In the ICD-10, alcohol consumption is defined as harmful if: there is clear evidence that alcohol is responsible for physical or psychological harm; the nature of the harm is identifiable; alcohol consumption has persisted for at least 1 month over the previous 12 months; and the individual does not meet the criteria for alcohol dependence. Harmful alcohol consumption is also conceptualised in terms of a pattern of alcohol consumption in excess of specified limits, which currently stands in the UK as 35 standard drinks for women and 50 standard drinks for men in any week. Hazardous and harmful alcohol users are unlikely to seek treatment specifically for alcohol-related problems, but they may come to the attention of health services through opportunistic screening for alcohol use, or, in the case of people with harmful levels of alcohol consumption, because they exhibit alcohol-related harm at presentation. Alcohol-related harm may be acute (such as alcohol-related accidents, alcohol poisoning, or acute pancreatitis), and may also be chronic (such as hypertension, cirrhosis, depression and anxiety, fetal alcohol syndrome, and fetal alcohol effects). **Diagnosis:** Clinical presentations in primary and emergency care that are associated with excessive alcohol use include hypertension, accidental injury, hand tremors, duodenal ulcers, gastrointestinal bleeding, cognitive impairments, anxiety, and depression. There are several short paper-based screening instruments available for use in primary-care populations. The Alcohol Use Disorder Identification Test (AUDIT) is a 10-item questionnaire that addresses quantity and frequency of alcohol use, alcohol-related problems, and symptoms of mild alcohol dependence. It exhibits high levels of sensitivity (92%) and specificity (94%). A score of 8 or more is indicative of hazardous alcohol use, and a score of 16 or more indicative of harmful alcohol use. Several shortened versions of the AUDIT exist. AUDIT-C incorporates the first three questions of AUDIT, and measures the quantity and frequency of alcohol consumption; it also has acceptable levels of sensitivity and specificity in primary-care populations (sensitivity: 78% for males, 50% for females; specificity: 75% for males, 93% for females). The FAST alcohol screening test is a short AUDIT derivative specifically developed for use in emergency departments. It identifies 90% of the hazardous alcohol users identified by the 10-item AUDIT questionnaire. Other short screening instruments include the Michigan Alcohol Screening Test, CAGE, and the Paddington Alcohol Test (PAT). A number of biological markers of alcohol use can be used in the diagnosis of hazardous or harmful use. These include elevations in mean red blood cell volume (MCV), serum gamma glutamyl transferase (GGT), and carbohydrate deficient transferrin (CDT). While the results of biochemical tests may be useful as motivating factors in addressing an individual's alcohol consumption, they are less sensitive and specific than screening questionnaires in identifying hazardous and harmful alcohol use.

**INCIDENCE/PREVALENCE** Alcohol use is a leading cause of mortality and morbidity internationally, and is ranked as one of the top 5 risk factors for disease burden by the WHO. On the basis of data from 28 countries in Europe between 1992 and 1996, the prevalence of hazardous alcohol consumption was estimated at between 5% and 41% for men, and 1% to 21% for women. Research in England in 2005 estimated that 7.1 million people, or 23%

*(continued over)*

*(from previous page)*

of the adult population (32% of men and 15% of women), could be categorised as hazardous or harmful alcohol users. The prevalence of hazardous and harmful consumption was highest in people aged 16 to 24 years, and while the prevalence has remained relatively stable in the male population, between 1984 and 2006 it had increased by 50% in the female population. In England, 150,000 hospital admissions annually result from acute or chronic alcohol use, and alcohol use is implicated in 33,000 deaths each year.

**AETIOLOGY/RISK FACTORS** The causes of hazardous and harmful alcohol consumption are uncertain and complex. There is some evidence that genetic susceptibility may have a role, particularly in terms of an individual's response to alcohol consumption. Other approaches address issues of psychological predisposition — particularly the roles of learning theories, expectancies, and self-efficacy. Another approach emphasises the role of market forces and social norms in increasing the availability of alcohol and the acceptability of its use within society. Integrated models that address the complex interplay between genetic, physiological, psychological, and social factors are probably the most reliable approach to understanding the aetiology of alcohol-use disorders.

**PROGNOSIS** Some hazardous and harmful alcohol users reduce their consumption to 'safe' levels without intervention, and others move in and out of different consumption patterns throughout their lives. Approximately 16% of hazardous or harmful alcohol users will progress to more dependent patterns of alcohol consumption. Harmful alcohol consumption is associated with damage to the liver, increased blood pressure, increased risk of haemorrhagic stroke, cardiomyopathy and arrhythmias, cancer of the oesophagus, gastrointestinal bleeding, and pancreatitis. Psychiatric comorbidities include increased risk of depression, anxiety, suicide, and parasuicide. Alcohol use accounts for 1700 accidental deaths a year and, in the elderly, may be associated with an increased risk for falls. Alcohol use also contributes to the early onset of age-related cognitive deficits, dementia, and Parkinson's disease. From a social perspective, increased alcohol use is associated with increased rates of relationship breakdown, domestic violence, child neglect, and negative impact on neonates — for example, fetal alcohol syndrome.

Kathleen Kara Fitzpatrick and James Lock

## KEY POINTS

- Anorexia nervosa is characterised by a low body mass index (BMI), fear of gaining weight, denial of current low weight and its impact on health, and amenorrhoea.

  Estimated prevalence is highest in teenage girls, and the condition may affect up to 0.7% of this group.

  Anorexia nervosa is related to family, sociocultural, genetic, and other biological factors. Psychiatric and personality disorders such as depression, anxiety disorders, obsessive compulsive disorder, and perfectionism are commonly found in people who have anorexia nervosa.

  Most people with anorexia nervosa recover completely or partially, but about 5% die from the condition and 20% develop a chronic eating disorder.

  Young women with anorexia nervosa are at increased risk of fractures later in life.

  Population assessment indicates that risks to fertility may be overstated in those who reach a healthy BMI, but children born to mothers who have recovered from anorexia nervosa seem to have lower birth weights.

- There is no strong RCT evidence that any treatments work well for anorexia nervosa. However, there is a gradual accumulation of evidence suggesting that early intervention is effective. Increasing evidence suggests that working with the family may also interrupt the development of a persistent form of the illness, when this work begins early in the disease.

- Evidence on the benefits of psychotherapy is unclear.

- Refeeding is a necessary and effective component of treatment, but is not sufficient alone.

  Very limited evidence from a quasi-experimental study suggests that a lenient approach to refeeding is as effective and more acceptable compared with a more strict approach.

  Refeeding may be as effective in an outpatient setting as during hospital admission.

  Nasogastric refeeding has been used to speed up weight gain in inpatient observational studies, although it is rarely studied in RCTs. Very limited RCT evidence suggests that adding nasogastric feeding to oral nutrition can increase weight gain and reduce relapse in the short term more than oral nutrition alone, but these gains are not maintained at 1 year post-discharge. Given ethical and medical concerns with tube feeding, this approach is encouraged with caution.

  Nutritional supplements, including zinc, have only limited evidence for their effectiveness, and additional evaluations of these measures are warranted.

- We don't know whether inpatient or outpatient treatment is more effective in people with anorexia nervosa.

- Limited evidence from small RCTs has not shown significant weight gain from SSRIs or tricyclic antidepressants, some of which may cause serious adverse effects.

  Tricyclic antidepressants may cause drowsiness, dry mouth, blurred vision, and a prolonged QT interval in people who have anorexia nervosa.

  SSRIs have not been shown to be beneficial, but the evidence remains very limited; in the 4 RCTs we found, conclusions were limited because of small trial size and high rates of withdrawal.

- Older-generation antipsychotic drugs may prolong the QT interval, increasing the risk of ventricular tachycardia, torsades de pointes, and sudden death.

Atypical antipsychotics have been evaluated for their potential role in reducing agitation and anxiety related to refeeding, as well as for potentially increasing appetite. Increasing observational data (case series) have suggested that they may decrease obsessiveness and agitation. However, further evidence from large, well-conducted RCTs is necessary to draw reliable conclusions.

Newer atypical antipsychotics, in particular olanzapine, do not seem to be associated with the same cardiac risks as older-generation antipsychotic drugs, but the known association between olanzapine and weight gain may impact compliance in people with anorexia nervosa. However, further research needs to be done.

- We found insufficient RCT evidence assessing benzodiazepines or cyproheptadine for treating anorexia nervosa.

- Oestrogen treatment has been hypothesised to reduce the negative effects on bone mineral density associated with anorexia nervosa. However, three small RCTs have failed to demonstrate clinically relevant changes in bone mineral density after treatment with oestrogen either HRT or oral contraceptives), and these results are supported by 2-year longitudinal data, which found similar lack of improvement.

(i) **Please visit http://clinicalevidence.bmj.com for full text and references**

## What are the effects of treatments in anorexia nervosa?

| Likely To Be Beneficial | • Refeeding* |
|---|---|
| Unknown Effectiveness | • Atypical antipsychotic drugs<br>• Benzodiazepines<br>• Cyproheptadine<br>• Inpatient versus outpatient treatment setting (unclear how they compare at improving anorexia symptoms)<br>• Psychotherapy<br>• SSRIs |
| Likely To Be Ineffective Or Harmful | • Older-generation antipsychotic drugs<br>• Tricyclic antidepressants |

## What are the effects of interventions to prevent or treat complications of anorexia nervosa?

| Unknown Effectiveness | • Oestrogen treatment (HRT or oral contraceptives) |
|---|---|

**Search date April 2010**

*Not based on RCT evidence; RCTs unlikely to be conducted.

**DEFINITION** Anorexia nervosa is characterised by a refusal to maintain weight at or above a minimally normal weight (<85% of expected weight for age and height, or body mass index

[BMI] <17.5 kg/m$^2$), or a failure to show the expected weight gain during growth. There is also often an intense fear of gaining weight, preoccupation with weight, denial of current low weight and its adverse impact on health, and amenorrhoea. Two subtypes of anorexia nervosa, binge–purge and restricting, have been defined.

**INCIDENCE/PREVALENCE** One population-based study using consultation data from the General Practitioner Database in the UK found a mean incidence for anorexia nervosa of 4/100,000 in people aged 10 to 39 years. One systematic review (5 studies) assessing prevalence in European people aged over 19 years found a 12-month prevalence of 0.2% to 0.7%. Little is known about the incidence or prevalence in Asia, South America, or Africa. Population studies on the incidence of anorexia nervosa among adult ethnic-minority populations in the USA have found a 12-month prevalence of 0.02% in Asian-Americans, 0.03% in Latinos, and 0.05% in African-American and Caribbean adults.

**AETIOLOGY/RISK FACTORS** Anorexia nervosa has been related to family, biological, social, and cultural factors. Studies have found that the condition is associated with a family history of anorexia nervosa (adjusted HR 11.4, 95% CI 1.1 to 89.0), bulimia nervosa (adjusted HR 3.5, 95% CI 1.1 to 14.0), depression, generalised anxiety disorder, obsessive compulsive disorder, or obsessive compulsive personality disorder (adjusted RR 3.6, 95% CI 1.6 to 8.0). A twin study suggested that anorexia nervosa may be related to genetic factors, but it was unable to estimate reliably how non-shared environmental factors contributed. Specific aspects of childhood temperament thought to be related include perfectionism, negative self-evaluation, and extreme compliance. Perinatal factors include prematurity, particularly if the baby was small for gestational age (prematurity: OR 3.2, 95% CI 1.6 to 6.2; prematurity and small for gestational age: OR 5.7, 95% CI 1.1 to 28.7). In a prospective cohort study (51 adolescents with the condition), people with anorexia nervosa were significantly more likely to have an affective disorder than were controls matched for sex, age, and school (lifetime risk of affective disorder 96% in people with anorexia nervosa v 23% in controls; ARI 73%, 95% CI 60% to 85%). It is unclear whether affective disorders precede anorexia nervosa or occur as a consequence of starvation. Similarly, obsessive compulsive disorder was significantly more likely to be present in people with anorexia nervosa compared with controls (30% in people with anorexia nervosa v 10% in controls; ARI 20%, 95% CI 10% to 41%). However, in two-thirds of people with obsessive compulsive disorder and anorexia nervosa, obsessive compulsive disorder preceded the anorexia nervosa.

**PROGNOSIS** One prospective study followed up 51 people with teenage-onset anorexia nervosa, about half of whom received no or minimal treatment (fewer than 8 sessions). After 10 years, 14/51 (27%) people had a persistent eating disorder, three (6%) had ongoing anorexia nervosa, and 6 (12%) had experienced a period of bulimia nervosa. About half of all participants in the study continued to have poor psychosocial functioning after 10 years (assessed using the Morgan Russell scale and Global Assessment of Functioning Scale). An extended follow-up RCT of 38 participants, who completed either separate or conjoint family therapy, found that 75% of people had no eating disorder symptoms at 5-year follow-up. It found that those people who had good to intermediate outcomes at the end of treatment were more likely to have good outcomes at the end of the 5-year follow-up. A summary of treatment studies (119 studies published between 1953 and 1999, 5590 people, length of follow-up 1–29 years) found that 47% of people recover completely from anorexia nervosa (range 0–92%), 34% improve (range 0–75%), 21% develop a chronic eating disorder (range 0–79%), and 5% die from the condition (range 0–22%). Favourable prognostic factors include an early age at onset, and a short interval between onset of symptoms and the beginning of treatment. Family criticism, in particular maternal criticism, seems to influence the outcome of treatment. Unfavourable prognostic factors include vomiting, profound weight loss, chronicity, psychiatric comorbidity, psychosocial problems, and a history of premorbid developmental or clinical abnormalities. In particular, psychiatric comorbidities represent significant negative outcomes, with one review of outcomes indicating increased risk for personality disorders (in particular avoidant, dependent, obsessive-compulsive, and passive-aggressive personality disorders), obsessive compulsive disorder, and depression. The all-cause standardised mortality ratio of eating disorders (anorexia nervosa and bulimia nervosa) has been estimated at 538, which is about three times higher than that of other psychiatric illnesses. In studies published between 1970 and 1996, the average annual mortality was 0.59% a year for females in 10 eating-disorder populations (1322 people), with a minimum follow-up of 6 years. Mortality was higher for people with lower weight and older age at presentation. Mortality by suicide represents a significant threat to people who

*(continued over)*

*(from previous page)*

have anorexia nervosa and is reported as the second most common cause of death in this population. A review of studies published on suicide and suicide attempts in people who have eating disorders found that suicide rates were markedly elevated compared with the general population: between 3% and 20% of the inpatient and outpatient groups assessed had attempted suicide at some point. The elevated rates of suicide attempts and death by suicide are present for those receiving both inpatient and outpatient treatment, and seem to exist independently of BMI at the time of death. Assessment of suicide risk remains a critical feature in the evaluation and treatment of people who have anorexia nervosa, particularly among those with comorbid psychiatric illnesses. Young women who have anorexia nervosa are also at an increased risk of fractures later in life. Clinicians often report difficulties with fertility, birth weight, and pregnancy complications for those with active anorexia nervosa as well as for those recovered from anorexia. However, a controlled community-based study comparing outcomes after 18 years in 48 women with adolescent-onset anorexia nervosa with outcomes in 48 matched comparison cases indicated similar rates of pregnancy and delivery (although none of those with active anorexia had become mothers), although birth weights in babies born to women with a history of anorexia were significantly lower (P = 0.03). Feeding difficulties were similar between groups.

John Geddes and David Briess

## KEY POINTS

- Bipolar disorder, with mood swings between depression and mania, may affect up to 1.5% of adults, and increases the risk of suicide and disability.

  Most people improve over time, but two-thirds may have residual dysfunction, and at least 40% may have recurrent episodes.

- Lithium reduces symptoms of mania compared with placebo, and seems as effective as haloperidol, carbamazepine, and clonazepam, but can cause adverse effects including hypothyroidism.

- Older antipsychotic drugs such as chlorpromazine and haloperidol are widely used to treat mania, but few studies have been done to confirm their efficacy.

  Olanzapine, valproate, carbamazepine, and risperidone increase the likelihood of response in people with mania compared with placebo, and seem to have similar efficacy as each other, with different adverse-effect profiles.

  Ziprasidone, quetiapine, and clonazepam may also be beneficial, but few studies have been done to assess the effects of lamotrigine or gabapentin in mania.

  Topiramate is unlikely to be beneficial in mania.

  Antidepressants increase treatment response compared with placebo in people with bipolar depression. It is possible that selective serotonin reuptake inhibitors are more effective, and less likely to induce mania, compared with tricyclic antidepressants.

  Lamotrigine may increase response rates in people with depression compared with placebo, but can cause headache.

  Quetiapine may also improve depression compared with placebo.

  We don't know whether lithium, carbamazepine, valproate, or topiramate improve depression in people with bipolar disorder.

  We don't know whether psychological treatments are effective for people with bipolar depression, as we found no studies.

- Lithium reduces relapse in bipolar disorder compared with placebo.

  Valproate, carbamazepine, and lamotrigine seem as effective as lithium in reducing relapse.

  Cognitive therapy and patient or family education may reduce the risk of relapse, but studies have given conflicting results.

  We don't know whether antidepressants can prevent relapse, and they may induce mood instability or manic episodes.

  Olanzapine may reduce relapse, but long-term use may be associated with weight gain.

 Please visit http://clinicalevidence.bmj.com for full text and references

| What are the effects of treatments in people with mania associated with bipolar disorder? | |
|---|---|
| Beneficial | <ul><li>Lithium in mania</li><li>Olanzapine in mania</li><li>Risperidone in mania</li><li>Valproate in mania</li></ul> |
| Likely To Be Beneficial | <ul><li>Carbamazepine in mania</li><li>Clonazepam in mania</li></ul> |

| | |
|---|---|
| | • Haloperidol in mania |
| | • Quetiapine in mania |
| | • Ziprasidone in mania |
| **Unknown Effectiveness** | • Chlorpromazine in mania |
| | • Gabapentin in mania |
| | • Lamotrigine in mania |
| **Unlikely To Be Beneficial** | • Topiramate in mania |

## What are the effects of treatments in bipolar depression?

| | |
|---|---|
| **Likely To Be Beneficial** | • Antidepressants in bipolar depression |
| | • Lamotrigine in bipolar depression |
| | • Quetiapine in bipolar depression |
| **Unknown Effectiveness** | • Carbamazepine in bipolar depression |
| | • Lithium in bipolar depression |
| | • Psychological treatments in bipolar depression |
| | • Topiramate in bipolar depression |
| | • Valproate in bipolar depression |

## What are the effects of interventions to prevent relapse of mania or bipolar depression?

| | |
|---|---|
| **Beneficial** | • Lithium to prevent relapse |
| **Likely To Be Beneficial** | • Carbamazepine to prevent relapse |
| | • Cognitive therapy to prevent relapse |
| | • Education to recognise symptoms of relapse |
| | • Family-focused psychoeducation to prevent relapse |
| | • Lamotrigine to prevent relapse |
| | • Valproate to prevent relapse |
| **Trade-off Between Benefits And Harms** | • Olanzapine to prevent relapse |
| **Unknown Effectiveness** | • Antidepressant drugs to prevent relapse |

**Search date July 2006**

**DEFINITION** Bipolar disorder (bipolar affective disorder, manic depressive disorder) is characterised by marked mood swings between mania (mood elevation) and bipolar depression that cause significant personal distress or social dysfunction, and are not caused by drugs or known physical disorders. **Bipolar type I disorder** is diagnosed when episodes of depression are interspersed with mania or mixed episodes. **Bipolar type II disorder** is diagnosed when depression is interspersed with less severe episodes of elevated mood that do not lead to dysfunction or disability (hypomania). Bipolar disorder has been subdivided in several further ways.

**INCIDENCE/PREVALENCE** One 1996 cross-national community-based study (38,000 people) found lifetime prevalence rates of bipolar type I disorder ranging from 0.3% in Taiwan to 1.5% in New Zealand. It found that men and women were at similar risk, and that the mean age at first onset ranged from 19–29 years (average of 6 years earlier than first onset of major depression).

**AETIOLOGY/RISK FACTORS** The cause of bipolar disorder is uncertain, although family and twin studies suggest a genetic basis. The lifetime risk of bipolar disorder is increased in first-degree relatives of a person with bipolar disorder (40–70% for a monozygotic twin; 5–10% for other first-degree relatives). If the first episode of mania occurs in an older adult, it may be secondary mania caused by underlying medical or substance-induced factors.

**PROGNOSIS** Bipolar disorder is a recurring illness, and one of the leading causes of worldwide disability, especially in the 15–44 years age group. One 4-year inception cohort study (173 people treated for a first episode of mania or mixed affective disorder) found that 93% of people no longer met criteria for mania at 2 years (median time to recover from a syndrome 4.6 weeks), but that only 36% had recovered to premorbid function. It found that 40% of people had a recurrent manic (20%) or depressive (20%) episode within 2 years of recovering from the first episode. A meta-analysis, comparing observed versus expected rates of suicide in an age- and sex-matched sample of the general population, found that the lifetime prevalence of suicide in people with bipolar disorder was about 2% — or 15 times greater than expected.

Phillipa J. Hay and Angélica Claudino

### KEY POINTS

- Up to 1% of people at any one time may have bulimia nervosa, characterised by an intense preoccupation with body weight, binge-eating episodes, and use of extreme measures to counteract the feared effects of overeating.

  People with bulimia nervosa are of normal weight or are overweight, making the condition distinct from anorexia nervosa.

  Obesity has been associated with both an increased risk of bulimia nervosa and a worse prognosis, as have personality disorders and substance misuse.

  After 10 years, about half of people with bulimia nervosa will have recovered fully, one third will have made a partial recovery, and 10% to 20% will still have symptoms.

- In this review, we have considered interventions delivered online.

- With online therapies, it is often hard to make rigorous diagnoses as therapy is not being delivered in a clinic and, in the real world, such online therapies rely on a degree of self-referral and self-report of symptoms, especially where used for initial therapy versus relapse prevention.

- For the purposes of this review, we have included interventions delivered via the internet (including real-time videoconferencing), by e-mail, or by text, but not those delivered by other routes (such as by speaking by telephone) or delivered by other means without an internet component.

- The trials we found were generally small, included mixed populations, used different delivery systems, assessed different interventions, and reported different outcome measures. This makes it difficult to draw reliable conclusions or to generalise results.

- Although we have reported an ITT analysis where possible, some trials had large numbers of drop-outs, which may affect the robustness of results.

- We don't know whether online therapy involving contact with a person online is more effective than placebo, sham therapy, waiting list control, or no online therapy in people with bulimia nervosa or eating disorder not otherwise specified.

  We found insufficient evidence on an internet cognitive behavioural therapy (CBT)-based programme plus e-mail guidance compared with guided bibliotherapy plus e-mail guidance.

  We also found insufficient evidence on the effects of CBT delivered by telemedicine compared with face-to-face contact.

- One study found no evidence that a self-help therapeutic writing task delivered online was more effective than a control writing task delivered online. However, the trial was small, and participants did not need a formal diagnosis of bulimia nervosa.

- We found limited evidence that a 16-week text messaging intervention (SMS) that delivered a tailored feedback message may improve abstinence and reduce full bulimic symptoms at 8 months, compared with treatment as usual, in women who had been discharged after specialist inpatient care.

  However, the trial included a mixed population of women with full and sub-threshold bulimia nervosa as well as women with eating disorder not otherwise specified.

  In addition, the trial was limited to one hospital site and used a non-standard intervention, which may limit its generalisability.

- There is a need for further high-quality studies in this area.

 **Please visit http://clinicalevidence.bmj.com for full text and references**

## What are the effects of online interventions for people with bulimia nervosa?

| Unknown Effectiveness | • Apps or online programmes used as an adjunct to face-to-face therapy |
| | • Delivery of self-help online (not involving contact with a person as part of intervention) |
| | • Delivery of therapy online (involving contact with a person online) |

**Search date April 2014**

**DEFINITION** Bulimia nervosa is an intense preoccupation with body weight and shape, with regular episodes of overeating (binge eating) associated with extreme measures to counteract the feared effects of the overeating. If a person also meets the diagnostic criteria for anorexia nervosa, then the diagnosis of anorexia nervosa takes precedence. The latest version of the Diagnostic and Statistical Manual for Mental Disorders (DSM-5) has broadened the previous criteria in the DSM-IV used for diagnosing bulimia nervosa by including people with a lower frequency of bingeing and purging symptoms (now at least once a week for 3 months). This change allowed for many cases that were previously considered in DSM-IV as having an eating disorder not otherwise specified (EDNOS) and represented, in fact, less severe cases of bulimia nervosa (those presenting with lower than twice a week episodes), to now be diagnosed as having bulimia nervosa. For this reason, this review includes studies with mixed samples of participants with bulimia nervosa or EDNOS of bulimic type that were diagnosed before changes to DSM-5. Bulimia nervosa can be difficult to identify because of extreme secrecy about binge eating and purgative behaviour. While current weight may be normal, there is often a history of anorexia nervosa or of restrictive dieting and weight suppression. Some people alternate between anorexia nervosa and bulimia nervosa. Nearly all cases of bulimia nervosa identified in a national community survey featured an additional psychiatric disorder, and common comorbidities were mood, anxiety, impulse control, and substance-misuse disorders. Some RCTs included people with sub-threshold bulimia nervosa, or with a related eating disorder, binge-eating disorder. Where possible, only results relevant to bulimia nervosa are reported in this review. In this review, we have considered interventions delivered online. For the purposes of this review, we have included interventions delivered via the internet (including real-time videoconferencing), by e-mail, or by text. We have not included interventions delivered by other means, such as by speaking by telephone or by CD/DVD delivered without an internet component.

**INCIDENCE/PREVALENCE** In community-based studies, the point prevalence of bulimia nervosa is between 0.5% and 1.0% in people, with a lifetime prevalence of up to 2% in women and with an even social-class distribution. About 90% of people diagnosed with bulimia nervosa are women. The numbers presenting with bulimia nervosa in industrialised countries increased during the decades after its recognition in the late 1970s, although the incidence has plateaued or even fallen since then, with an incidence of new diagnoses at 6.6 per 100,000 in 2000 in young women from the general population, and around 20.7 per 100,000 new cases in females aged 10 to 49 in UK primary care registers. A 'cohort effect', with an increasing incidence, has been reported in community surveys. The prevalence of eating disorder features such as weight/shape overconcern, as found in bulimia nervosa, appears to be increasing in non-industrialised populations but may vary across ethnic groups. African-American women have a lower rate of restrictive dieting compared with white American women, but they have a similar rate of recurrent binge eating.

**AETIOLOGY/RISK FACTORS** The aetiology of bulimia nervosa is complex, but sociocultural pressures to be thin and the promotion of dieting seem to increase risk. One community-based case-control study compared 102 people with bulimia nervosa with 204 healthy controls and found higher rates of obesity, mood disorder, sexual and physical abuse, parental obesity, substance misuse, low self-esteem, perfectionism, disturbed family dynamics, parental weight/shape concern, and early menarche in people with the eating

*(continued over)*

*(from previous page)*

disorder. Heritability is high, ranging from 28% to 83% in one review, although it has been suggested that genotypic variations map onto intermediate phenotypes, such as traits of affective instability and impulsivity, rather than onto a 'gross' bulimia nervosa phenotype. Personality traits such as perfectionism may thus be important moderators of clinical features of an eating disorder.

**PROGNOSIS** A large study (222 people) from a trial of antidepressants and structured, intensive group psychotherapy found that, after a mean follow-up of 11.5 years, 11% still met criteria for bulimia nervosa, whereas 70% were in full or partial remission. One study (102 women) of the natural course of bulimia nervosa found that 31% continued to have the disorder at 15 months and 15% continued to have the disorder at 5 years. Only 28% received treatment during the follow-up period. A 5-year naturalistic study of 23 people with bulimia nervosa found a 74% remission at 5 years, with a 47% probability of relapse within the 5-year follow-up study in those in remission. A large review of 79 studies found an overall recovery rate of 45%, 27% partial improvement, and 23% with a chronic course, and crude mortality rate of 0.32%. There are very few consistent predictors of long-term outcome. A systematic review found a family history of obesity to predict poor outcome for treatment of bulimia nervosa, and a good prognosis to be associated with shorter illness duration and good interpersonal relationships. However, on the whole there were many more inconsistent positive and negative predictors than consistent positive predictors of outcome. A consistent post-treatment predictor of a better outcome is an early response to treatment.

# Deliberate self-harm (and attempted suicide)

G. Mustafa Soomro and Sara Kakhi

## KEY POINTS

- Deliberate self-harm involves acts such as self-cutting or self-poisoning, carried out deliberately, with or without the intention of suicide.

  Lifetime prevalence of deliberate self-harm in Europe and the US is about 3% to 5% of the population, and has been increasing.

  Familial, biological, and psychosocial factors may contribute. Risks are higher in women and young adults, in people who are socially isolated or deprived, and in those with psychiatric or personality disorders.

- Around a quarter of people will repeat the self-harm within 4 years, and the long-term suicide risk is 3% to 7%.

  Younger adults are more likely to repeat non-fatal self-harm, while adults aged over 45 years are more likely to die by suicide, especially if the previous self-harm involved a violent method.

- Interventions for the treatment of deliberate self-harm may include pharmacological and non-pharmacological therapies. For this review, we have focused on non-pharmacological treatments only. We assessed outcomes of repetition of deliberate self-harm, improvement in underlying psychiatric symptoms, quality of life, and adverse effects.

- We searched for evidence from RCTs and systematic reviews of RCTs.

- The effects of psychological treatments following deliberate self-harm are unclear.

  Problem-solving therapy may reduce depression and hopelessness but it does not seem to be effective at preventing recurrence of self-harm, although one RCT found limited evidence of benefit in people whose index episode was a repeat of self-harm.

  Evidence for benefit from cognitive therapy, psychodynamic interpersonal therapy, or telephone contact following deliberate self-harm compared with usual care is unclear.

  Two RCTs of low quality found that cognitive therapy plus usual care reduces repetition of deliberate self-harm and improves some underlying symptoms compared with usual care alone.

  We were unable to find any evidence from RCTs meeting our inclusion criteria on the effects of dialectical behavioural therapy in people following deliberate self-harm.

  One large multicentre trial found brief intervention and contact (a form of intensive follow-up plus outreach) may be more effective at decreasing death from suicide in people presenting to the emergency department following an episode of deliberate self-harm compared with treatment as usual.

  However, intensive follow-up plus outreach may not reduce recurrent self-harm compared with usual care.

- Nurse-led management, emergency card, and hospital admission have not been shown to reduce recurrent self-harm compared with usual care.

- We found insufficient evidence on the effect of follow-up with the same therapist after hospital treatment for deliberate self-harm compared with follow-up with a different therapist (continuity of care).

(i) Please visit http://clinicalevidence.bmj.com for full text and references

## What are the effects of non-pharmacological treatments for deliberate self-harm in adolescents and adults?

| Unknown Effectiveness | • Cognitive therapy<br>• Continuity of care |
|---|---|

- Dialectical behavioural therapy
- Emergency card
- Hospital admission
- Intensive outpatient follow-up plus outreach (1 RCT found a reduced mortality due to suicide, although the same RCT and others found unclear effects on repetition of deliberate self-harm; interventions differed between studies)
- Nurse-led case management
- Problem-solving therapy
- Psychodynamic interpersonal therapy
- Telephone contact

**Search date August 2013**

**DEFINITION** Deliberate self-harm is an acute non-fatal act of self-harm carried out deliberately in the form of an acute episode of behaviour by an individual with variable motivation. The intention to end life may be absent or present to a variable degree. Other terms used to describe this phenomenon are 'attempted suicide' and 'parasuicide'. For the purpose of this review, the term deliberate self-harm will be used throughout. Common methods of deliberate self-harm include self-cutting and self-poisoning (e.g., by overdosing on medicines). Some acts of deliberate self-harm are characterised by high suicidal intent, meticulous planning (including precautions against being found out), and severe lethality of the method used. Other acts of deliberate self-harm are characterised by no or low intention of suicide, lack of planning and concealing of the act, and low lethality of the method used. The related term of 'suicide' is defined as an act with a fatal outcome, deliberately initiated and performed by the person with the knowledge or expectation of its fatal outcome. This review focuses on the literature in people aged at least 15 years who present with an episode of deliberate self-harm (with or without suicidal intent) as the main presenting problem and where this is the main (primary) sample selection and outcome criterion for the RCTs. Some people thus selected may have other accompanying conditions, such as borderline personality disorder or depression, which are considered as secondary criteria and outcomes. The review excludes RCTs where the main (primary) sample selection criterion is not deliberate self-harm but some other condition such as depression or borderline personality disorder, even though such trials may study deliberate self-harm as a secondary criterion and outcome. Deliberate self-harm is not defined in the DSM-IV or the ICD-10. The DSM-5 defines 'suicidal behaviour disorder' and 'nonsuicidal self-injury' (NSSI) as conditions for further research. In the 'suicidal behaviour disorder' an individual has made at least one suicide attempt in the last 24 months, where 'suicide attempt' is further defined as a self-initiated sequence of behaviours by an individual who at the time of initiation expected that the set of actions would lead to his or her own death. Conversely, NSSI is defined as intentional self-inflicted damage to the surface of the body of a sort that is likely to induce bleeding, bruising, or pain (e.g., cutting, burning, stabbing, hitting, excessive rubbing), with the expectation that injury will only lead to minor or moderate physical harm (i.e., there is no suicidal intent). However, these DSM-5 definitions do not cover the situation where self-poisoning is carried out with no suicidal intent.

**INCIDENCE/PREVALENCE** Based on the data from 16 European countries between 1989 and 1992, the lifetime prevalence of deliberate self-harm in people treated in hospital and other medical facilities, including general practice settings, is estimated at about 3% for women and 2% for men. A subsequent WHO/Euro survey carried out from 1995 to 1999 showed annual rates for females to be between 83/100,000 per year (in Italy) and 433/100,000 per year (in the UK); and for males to be 53/100,000 per year (in Sweden) to 337/100,000 per year (in the UK). The trend between the two surveys showed that there was an average decrease of 13% in men and 4% in women. However, over the last 50 years, there has been a longer-term trend showing a rise in the incidence of deliberate self-harm in the UK. A reasonable current estimate is about 400/100,000 population a year. In the two community studies in the US, 3% to 5% of responders said that they had made an attempt at deliberate self-harm at some time. The US National Comorbidity Survey (carried out from 1990–1992 using a nationally representative sample of 5877 respondents, aged between 15–54 years) showed prevalence of suicide attempts as 2.7% and suicide gestures as 1.9% — the former were characterised by male sex, fewer years of education, psychiatric diagnoses (including depressive, impulsive, and aggressive symptoms), and history of multiple physical and sexual assaults. An international survey using representative community samples of adults (aged 18–64 years) reported lifetime prevalence of self-reported deliberate self-harm of 3.8% in Canada, 5.9% in Puerto Rico, 5.0% in France, 3.4% in West Germany, 0.7% in Lebanon, 0.8% in Taiwan, 3.2% in Korea, and 4.4% in New Zealand. WHO carried out a multi-site survey in 2004 of random samples (n = 500 to 8794) of the general population of one city each in 10 countries and found the following lifetime prevalence of attempted suicide: Brazil 3.1%, China 2.4%, Estonia 3.6%, India 1.6%, Iran 4.2%, South Africa 3.4%, Sri Lanka 2.1%, Vietnam 0.4%, Australia 4.2%, and Sweden 4.0%. Self-poisoning using organophosphates is particularly common in resource-poor countries. A large hospital (catering for 900,000 people) in Sri Lanka reported 2559 adult hospital admissions and 41% occupancy of medical intensive care beds for deliberate self-harm with organophosphates over 2 years.

**AETIOLOGY/RISK FACTORS** Familial, biological, and psychosocial factors may contribute to deliberate self-harm. Evidence for genetic factors includes a higher risk of familial suicide, and greater concordance in monozygotic than dizygotic twins for deliberate self-harm. Evidence for biological factors includes reduced cerebrospinal fluid 5-hydroxyindoleacetic acid levels and a blunted prolactin response to the fenfluramine challenge test, indicating a reduction in the function of serotonin in the central nervous system. People who deliberately self-harm also show traits of impulsiveness and aggression, inflexible and impulsive cognitive style, and impaired decision making and problem solving. Other features suggested are emotional dysregulation, hopelessness, and over-general memory (i.e., problem with autobiographical memory preventing recall of reasons for living). Deliberate self-harm is more likely to occur in: women; young adults; people who are single or divorced; people with low education level; unemployed people; disabled people; people suffering from a psychiatric disorder (particularly depression); people with substance-misuse problems; people with borderline and antisocial personality disorders; people with severe anxiety disorders; and people with physical illness. A study based on a prospectively collected self-harm register from inner-city Manchester, UK, showed that the incidence of self-harm was positively correlated with area-level deprivation and unemployment. Further analysis using logistic regression modelling found that repetition of self-harm within the first 6 months was associated with factors such as a person's previous history of self-harm, being unemployed or registered sick, marital status (being single, separated, divorced, or widowed), or living in an area with a lower percentage of white population. However, a person's own ethnicity was not a distinguishing factor. In adults, SSRIs have been thought to be associated with an increased risk of suicidal behaviour compared with placebo, but not compared with tricyclic antidepressants.

**PROGNOSIS** Suicide is highest during the first year after deliberate self-harm. One systematic review found median rates of repetition of 16% (interquartile range [IQR] 12%–25%) within the first year, 21% (IQR 12%–30%) within 1 to 4 years, and 23% (IQR 11%–32%) within 4 years or longer. It found median mortality from suicide after deliberate self-harm of 1.8% (IQR 0.8%–2.6%) within the first year, 3.0% (IQR 2.0%–4.4%) within 1 to 4 years, 3.4% (IQR 2.5%–6.0%) within 5 to 10 years, and 6.7% (IQR 5.0%–11.0%) within 9 years or longer. The DSM-5 estimates that 20% to 30% of suicide attempters go on to make more attempts. Repetition of deliberate self-harm is more likely in people where the following factors are present: aged 25 to 49 years; unemployment; divorce; socio-economic disadvantage; history of substance misuse; depression; hopelessness; powerlessness; personality disorders; unstable living conditions or living alone; criminal record; previous psychiatric treatment; history of stressful traumatic life events; and history of coming from a broken home or of family violence. Other factors relevant to repetition are previous attempts, history of violence, and being single or separated. Factors associated with risk of suicide after deliberate self-harm are: being aged over 45 years; male sex; being unemployed, retired, separated, divorced, or widowed; living alone; having poor physical health; having a psychiatric disorder (particularly depression, alcoholism, schizophrenia, and sociopathic personality disorder); high suicidal intent in current episode including leaving a written note;

*(continued over)*

*(from previous page)*

violent method used in current episode; and history of previous deliberate self-harm. Also, the rate of non-suicidal death is higher in those with a history of attempted suicide; three cohort studies reported higher rates of non-suicidal deaths. The first cohort study investigated 302 people over 5 years and showed that deaths by motor vehicle accidents were 12 times higher than the expected. The second study investigated 4044 people over 10 years and showed that standardised mortality ratio for non-accidental death was 4.98 (95% CI 4.08 to 6.07). The third study investigated 1083 people over 4 to 7 years and showed standardised mortality ratio for non-suicidal mortality was 4.7.

Rob Butler and Raghavakurup Radhakrishnan

## KEY POINTS

- Dementia is characterised by chronic, global, non-reversible deterioration in memory, executive function, and personality. Speech and motor function may also be impaired.

- Median life expectancy for people with Alzheimer's and Lewy body dementia is about 6 years after diagnosis, although many people may live far longer.

- RCTs of dementia are often not representative of all people with dementia; most are of 6 months' duration or less, not in primary care, and in people with Alzheimer's disease. Few RCTs address vascular dementia, and fewer still Lewy body dementia.

- Some cognitive symptoms of dementia may be improved by acetylcholinesterase inhibitors (donepezil, galantamine, and rivastigmine).

   Acetylcholinesterase inhibitors may improve cognitive function and global function scores compared with placebo at 12 to 26 weeks in people with Alzheimer's disease. However, they may be associated with an increase in adverse effects, particularly GI symptoms (anorexia, nausea, vomiting, or diarrhoea).

- We don't know whether cognitive stimulation, music therapy, reminiscence therapy, omega 3 fish oil, statins, or NSAIDs are effective at improving cognitive outcomes in people with cognitive symptoms of dementia, as we found insufficient evidence.

- In people with cognitive symptoms, memantine may modestly improve cognitive function and global function scores in people with Alzheimer's disease over 24 to 28 weeks, and may modestly improve activities of daily living scores in people with moderate to severe Alzheimer's disease.

   Although memantine is associated with a statistically significant increase in cognition scores in some population groups, the clinical importance of some of these results is unclear.

- We found inconsistent evidence on the effects of ginkgo biloba on cognitive outcomes, which varied by the analysis performed.

   We found no evidence that ginkgo biloba improves activities of daily living outcomes, but the available evidence was weak.

- Acetylcholinesterase inhibitors may marginally improve neuropsychiatric symptoms compared with placebo in people with behavioural and psychological symptoms of dementia, but they are also associated with adverse effects.

- We don't know whether antidepressants (clomipramine, fluoxetine, imipramine, sertraline) improve depressive symptoms in people with Alzheimer's disease associated with depression.

   Many RCTs were small and short term, and adverse effects were sparsely reported.

- Memantine may be associated with a small improvement in neuropsychiatric symptoms compared with placebo in people with behavioural and psychological symptoms of dementia, but it is also associated with adverse effects.

- We don't know whether diazepam, lorazepam, aromatherapy, CBT, exercise, carbamazepine, or sodium valproate/valproic acid are effective at improving neuropsychiatric symptoms in people with behavioural and psychological symptoms of dementia, as we found insufficient evidence.

- Some antipsychotics may improve neuropsychiatric symptoms or aggression in people with behavioural and psychological symptoms of dementia, but antipsychotics are also associated with an increased risk of severe adverse events such as stroke, TIA, or death.

- **CAUTION: Regulatory bodies have issued alerts that both conventional and atypical antipsychotics are associated with an increased risk of death in older people treated for dementia-related psychosis.**

 **Please visit http://clinicalevidence.bmj.com for full text and references**

## What are the effects of treatments on cognitive symptoms of dementia (Alzheimer's, Lewy body, or vascular)?

| | |
|---|---|
| Likely To Be Beneficial | • Acetylcholinesterase inhibitors (donepezil, galantamine, rivastigmine)<br><br>• Memantine (evidence of statistical benefit, but results of unclear clinical importance) |
| Unknown Effectiveness | • Ginkgo biloba<br><br>• NSAIDs<br><br>• Non-pharmacological interventions (cognitive stimulation, music therapy, reminiscence)<br><br>• Omega 3 (fish oil)<br><br>• Statins |

## What are the effects of treatments on behavioural and psychological symptoms of dementia (Alzheimer's, Lewy body, or vascular)?

| | |
|---|---|
| Likely To Be Beneficial | • Acetylcholinesterase inhibitors (donepezil, galantamine, rivastigmine) (evidence of marginal benefit)<br><br>• Memantine (evidence of marginal benefit) |
| Trade-off Between Benefits And Harms | • Antipsychotic medications (limited evidence of effectiveness; however, associated with severe adverse effects including cerebrovascular events and death) |
| Unknown Effectiveness | • Antidepressants (clomipramine, fluoxetine, imipramine, sertraline) in people with depression and dementia<br><br>• Benzodiazepines (diazepam, lorazepam)<br><br>• Mood stabilisers (carbamazepine, sodium valproate/valproic acid)<br><br>• Non-pharmacological interventions (aromatherapy, CBT, exercise) |

Search date July 2011

**DEFINITION Dementia** is characterised by memory loss (initially of recent events), loss of executive function (such as the ability to make decisions or sequence complex tasks), other cognitive deficits, and changes in personality. This decline must be serious enough to affect social or occupational functioning, and reasonable attempts must be made to exclude other common conditions, such as depression and delirium. **Alzheimer's disease** is a type of dementia characterised by an insidious onset and slow deterioration, and involves impairments in memory, speech, personality, and executive function. It should be diagnosed after other systemic, psychiatric, and neurological causes of dementia have been excluded clinically and by laboratory investigation. **Vascular dementia** is often due to multiple large or small vessel disease. It often presents with a stepwise deterioration in cognitive function with or without language and motor dysfunction. It usually occurs in the presence of vascular risk factors (diabetes, hypertension, arteriosclerosis, and smoking). Characteristically, it has a more sudden onset and stepwise progression than Alzheimer's disease, and often has a patchy picture of cognitive deficits. **Lewy body dementia** is a type of dementia that involves insidious impairment of cognitive function with parkinsonism, visual hallucinations, and fluctuating cognitive abilities. Night-time disturbance is common and there is an increased risk of falls. Careful clinical examination of people with mild to moderate dementia and the use of established diagnostic criteria accurately identifies 70% to 90% of causes confirmed at post mortem. In all types of dementia, people will experience problems with cognitive functioning and are likely to experience behavioural and psychological symptoms of dementia. Where possible, we have divided outcomes into cognitive or behavioural/psychological, although there is often considerable crossover between these outcomes, both clinically and in research. This review deals solely with people with Alzheimer's disease, Lewy body dementia, or vascular dementia.

**INCIDENCE/PREVALENCE** About 6% of people aged >65 years and 30% of people aged >90 years have some form of dementia. Dementia is rare before the age of 60 years. Alzheimer's disease and vascular dementia (including mixed dementia) are each estimated to account for 35% to 50% of dementia, and Lewy body dementia is estimated to account for up to 5% of dementia in older people, varying with geographical, cultural, and racial factors. There are numerous other causes of dementia, all relatively rare, including frontotemporal dementia, alcohol-related dementia, Huntington's disease, normal pressure hydrocephalus, HIV infection, syphilis, subdural haematoma, and some cerebral tumours.

**AETIOLOGY/RISK FACTORS Alzheimer's disease:** The cause of Alzheimer's disease is unclear. A key pathological process is deposition of abnormal amyloid in the central nervous system. Another early change is abnormal phosphorylation of tau, an intracellular structural protein. This results in apoptosis and neurofibrillary tangles. Disease-modifying agents in development target both processes. Most people with the relatively rare condition of early-onset Alzheimer's disease (before age 60 years) exhibit an autosomal-dominant inheritance due to mutations in presenilin or amyloid precursor protein genes. Several gene mutations (on *APP*, *PS-1*, and *PS-2* genes) have been identified. Later-onset dementia is sometimes clustered in families, but specific gene mutations have not been identified. Down's syndrome, cardiovascular risks, and lower premorbid intellect may be risk factors for Alzheimer's disease. Alzheimer's disease and vascular pathology frequently co-exist. **Vascular dementia:** Vascular dementia is related to cardiovascular risk factors, such as smoking, arteriosclerosis, hypertension, and diabetes. **Lewy body dementia:** Lewy body dementia is characterised by the presence of Lewy bodies (abnormal intracellular inclusions consisting of alpha-synuclein) in the cortex. Brain acetylcholine activity is reduced in many forms of dementia, and the level of reduction correlates with cognitive impairment.

**PROGNOSIS Alzheimer's disease:** Alzheimer's disease usually has an insidious onset with progressive reduction in cerebral function. Diagnosis is difficult in the early stages. Median life expectancy after diagnosis is about 6 years, although many people live far longer. **Vascular dementia:** We found no reliable data on prognosis. **Lewy body dementia:** People with Lewy body dementia have an average life expectancy of about 6 years after diagnosis. Behavioural problems, depression, and psychotic symptoms are common in all types of dementia. Eventually, most people with dementia find it difficult to perform simple tasks without help.

Andrea Cipriani, Corrado Barbui, Rob Butler, Simon Hatcher, and John Geddes

## KEY POINTS

- Depression may affect up to 10% of the population, with half of affected people having recurrence of their symptoms.

- In mild to moderate depression, there is no reliable evidence that any one treatment is superior in improving symptoms of depression, but the strength of evidence supporting different treatments varies.

  In severe depression, only prescription antidepressants and electroconvulsive treatment are known to improve symptoms.

- Tricyclic antidepressants, selective serotonin reuptake inhibitors (SSRIs), monoamine oxidase inhibitors, and venlafaxine improve symptoms in the short term. However, long-term studies are lacking.

  No one class or individual antidepressant has been shown to be more effective than the others in the short term, but adverse effects vary between classes.

  St John's wort may have similar efficacy compared with antidepressants, but preparations vary and drug interactions can occur.

  We don't know if exercise is beneficial in people with mild to moderate depression.

- CAUTION: Some antidepressants may induce or worsen suicidal ideation and behaviour, and agitation after initiation of treatment.

- We don't know whether adding lithium or pindolol to other antidepressant drugs reduces symptoms in people with treatment-resistant depression.

- Continuing prescription antidepressant drugs reduces the risk of relapse after recovery.

 **Please visit http://clinicalevidence.bmj.com for full text and references**

## What are the effects of drug and physical treatments in mild to moderate or severe depression?

| | |
|---|---|
| **Beneficial** | • Electroconvulsive therapy (in severe depression)<br>• Monoamine oxidase inhibitors (MAOIs) versus other prescription antidepressant drugs in atypical depressive disorders<br>• Prescription antidepressant drugs (tricyclic antidepressants [including low-dose tricyclic antidepressants], SSRIs, monoamine oxidase inhibitors, or venlafaxine) (improved symptoms compared with placebo)<br>• SSRIs and related drugs versus each other and other prescription antidepressant drugs<br>• Tricyclic antidepressants versus each other and other prescription antidepressant drugs<br>• Venlafaxine versus other prescription antidepressant drugs |
| **Likely To Be Beneficial** | • St John's wort (more effective than placebo, may be as effective as other antidepressants in mild to moderate depression) |
| **Unknown Effectiveness** | • Exercise (in mild to moderate depression) |

## What are the effects of interventions in treatment-resistant depression?

| Unknown Effectiveness | • Lithium augmentation |
|---|---|
| | • Pindolol augmentation |

## Which interventions reduce relapse rates?

| Beneficial | • Continuing prescription antidepressant drugs (reduced risk of relapse after recovery) |
|---|---|

**Search date June 2009**

**DEFINITION** Depressive disorders are characterised by persistent low mood, loss of interest and enjoyment, and reduced energy. They often impair day to day functioning. Most RCTs assessed in this review classify depression using the *Diagnostic and statistical manual of mental disorders* (DSM-IV) or the *International classification of mental and behavioural disorders* (ICD-10). DSM-IV divides depression into major depressive disorder or dysthymic disorder. **Major depressive disorder** is characterised by one or more major depressive episodes (i.e., at least 2 weeks of depressed mood or loss of interest accompanied by at least 4 additional symptoms of depression). **Dysthymic disorder** is characterised by at least 2 years of depressed mood for more days than not, accompanied by additional symptoms that do not reach the criteria for major depressive disorder. ICD-10 divides depression into mild to moderate or severe depressive episodes. Mild to moderate depression is characterised by depressive symptoms and some functional impairment. Severe depression is characterised by additional agitation or psychomotor retardation with marked somatic symptoms. **Treatment-resistant depression** is defined as an absence of clinical response to treatment with a tricyclic antidepressant at a minimum dose of 150 mg daily of imipramine (or equivalent drug) for 4 to 6 weeks. In this review, we use both DSM-IV and ICD-10 classifications, but treatments are considered to have been assessed in severe depression if the RCT included inpatients. **Older adults:** Older adults are generally defined as people aged 65 years or older. However, some of the RCTs of older people in this review included people aged 55 years or over. The presentation of depression in older adults may be atypical: low mood may be masked and anxiety or memory impairment may be the principal presenting symptoms. Dementia should be considered in the differential diagnosis of depression in older adults. **Treating depressive disorders in adults:** Depressive disorders are generally treated with a range of drug, physical, and psychological treatments. For coverage of psychological treatments (including drug treatments v psychological treatments) and for coverage of combined drug and psychological treatment, see review on depression in adults: psychological treatments and care pathways, p 343. **Population:** This review does not cover intervention in women with depression in pregnancy, seasonal affective disorder, or depression owing to a physical illness such as stroke or substance abuse. See separate review on treatment of postnatal depression, p 486.

**INCIDENCE/PREVALENCE** Depressive disorders are common, with a prevalence of major depression between 5% and 10% of people seen in primary care settings. Two to three times as many people may have depressive symptoms but do not meet DSM-IV criteria for major depression. Women are affected twice as often as men. Depressive disorders are the fourth most important cause of disability worldwide, and are expected to become the second most important by 2020. **Older adults:** Between 10% and 15% of older people have depressive symptoms, although major depression is relatively rare in older adults.

**AETIOLOGY/RISK FACTORS** The causes of depression are uncertain, but are thought to include both childhood events and current psychosocial adversity. Studies suggest that genetic factors may also be important, indicating that several chromosomal regions may be involved. However, phenotypes do not seem to exhibit classic Mendelian inheritance. Psychiatric research has also focused on the role that psychosocial factors, such as social context and personality dimensions, have in depression. Many theories emphasise the importance of temperament (differences in the adaptive systems), which can increase

*(continued over)*

*(from previous page)*

vulnerability to mood disturbances. Impairment in social relationships, gender, socioeconomic status, and dysfunctional cognition may also have a role. It seems that integrative models, which take into account the interaction of biological and social variables, offer the most reliable way to approach the complex aetiology of depression.

**PROGNOSIS** About half of people suffering a first episode of major depressive disorder experience further symptoms in the next 10 years. **Older adults:** One systematic review (search date 1996, 12 prospective cohort studies, 1268 people, mean age 60 years) found that the prognosis may be especially poor in older people with a chronic or relapsing course of depression. Another systematic review (search date 1999, 23 prospective cohort studies in people aged 65 years and over, including 5 identified by the first review) found that depression in older people was associated with increased mortality (15 studies; pooled OR 1.73, 95% CI 1.53 to 1.95).

# Depression in adults: psychological treatments and care pathways | 343

Rob Butler, Simon Hatcher, Jonathan Price, and Michael Von Korff

## KEY POINTS

- Depression may affect up to 10% of the population, with symptoms recurring in half of affected people.

- In mild to moderate depression, there is no reliable evidence that any one treatment is superior in improving symptoms of depression, but the strength of evidence supporting different treatments varies.

- CBT and interpersonal psychotherapy reduce symptoms of mild to moderate depression, although many of the trials have been small.

    Combining psychological treatment with antidepressant drugs may be more effective than either treatment alone.

    Non-directive counselling may also be effective, but we don't know whether problem-solving therapy or befriending are beneficial.

    Care pathways may improve the effectiveness of treatment for depression.

- We don't know whether CBT or relapse prevention programmes are beneficial in reducing the risk of relapse after recovery.

 Please visit http://clinicalevidence.bmj.com for full text and references

| What are the effects of psychological treatments in mild to moderate or severe depression? | |
|---|---|
| Beneficial | • Cognitive therapy (improves symptoms in mild to moderate depression) <br><br> • Interpersonal psychotherapy (improves symptoms in mild to moderate depression) |
| Likely To Be Beneficial | • Combining prescription antidepressant drugs and psychological treatments (improves symptoms in mild to moderate and severe depression) <br><br> • Non-directive counselling (improves symptoms in mild to moderate depression) |
| Unknown Effectiveness | • Befriending (in mild to moderate depression) <br><br> • Problem-solving therapy (in mild to moderate depression) |

| What are the effects of psychological interventions to reduce relapse rates in mild to moderate or severe depression? | |
|---|---|
| Unknown Effectiveness | • Cognitive therapy (weak evidence that may reduce relapse over 1–2 years after stopping treatment in people with mild to moderate depression compared with antidepressant drugs or usual clinical management) <br><br> • Relapse prevention programme (improved symptoms over 1 year after recovery in people with mild to moderate depression but no significant difference in relapse rates) |

**What are the effects of psychological interventions to improve delivery of treatments in mild to moderate or severe depression?**

| Likely To Be Beneficial | • Care pathways (reduces relapse in mild to moderate depression) |
|---|---|

Search date April 2006

**DEFINITION** Depressive disorders are characterised by persistent low mood, loss of interest and enjoyment, and reduced energy. They often impair day to day functioning. Most of the RCTs assessed in this review classify depression using the DSM-IV or the ICD-10. DSM-IV divides depression into major depressive disorder or dysthymic disorder. **Major depressive disorder** is characterised by one or more major depressive episodes (i.e. at least 2 weeks of depressed mood or loss of interest accompanied by at least 4 additional symptoms of depression). **Dysthymic disorder** is characterised by at least 2 years of depressed mood for more days than not, accompanied by additional symptoms that do not reach the criteria for major depressive disorder. ICD-10 divides depression into mild to moderate or severe depressive episodes. Mild to moderate depression is characterised by depressive symptoms and some functional impairment. Severe depression is characterised by additional agitation or psychomotor retardation with marked somatic symptoms. **Treatment-resistant depression** is defined as an absence of clinical response to treatment with a tricyclic antidepressant at a minimum dose of 150 mg daily of imipramine (or equivalent drug) for 4–6 weeks. In this review, we use both DSM-IV and ICD-10 classifications, but treatments are considered to have been assessed in severe depression if the RCT included inpatients. **Older adults:** Older adults are generally defined as people aged 65 years or older. However, some of the RCTs of older people in this review included people aged 55 years or over. The presentation of depression in older adults may be atypical: low mood may be masked, and anxiety or memory impairment may be the principal presenting symptoms. Dementia should be considered in the differential diagnosis of depression in older adults. **Treating depressive disorders in adults:** Depressive disorders are generally treated with a range of drug, physical, and psychological treatments. For coverage of drug and other physical treatments, see review on depression adults: drug and physical treatments, p 340. Combined drug and psychological treatment and comparisons of psychological versus drug treatment are covered in this review. **Population:** This review does not cover intervention in women with postnatal depression (see review on postnatal depression, p 486), seasonal affective disorder, or depression because of a physical illness, such as stroke or substance abuse.

**INCIDENCE/PREVALENCE** Depressive disorders are common, with a prevalence of major depression between 5% and 10% of people seen in primary-care settings. Two to three times as many people may have depressive symptoms but do not meet DSM-IV criteria for major depression. Women are affected twice as often as men. Depressive disorders are the fourth most important cause of disability worldwide, and are expected to become the second most important cause by 2020. **Older adults:** Between 10% and 15% of older people have depressive symptoms, although major depression is less common among older adults.

**AETIOLOGY/RISK FACTORS** The causes of depression are uncertain, but are thought to include both childhood events and current psychosocial adversity. Recent studies suggest that genetic factors may also be important, indicating that several chromosomal regions may be involved. However, phenotypes do not seem to exhibit classic Mendelian inheritance. Psychiatric research has also focused on the role that psychosocial factors, such as social context and personality dimensions, have in depression. Many theories emphasise the importance of temperament (differences in the adaptive systems), which can increase vulnerability to mood disturbances. Impairment in social relationships, gender, socioeconomic status, and dysfunctional cognition may also be involved. It seems that integrative models, which take into account the interaction of biological and social variables, offer the most reliable way to approach the complex causes of depression.

**PROGNOSIS** About half of people suffering a first episode of major depressive disorder experience further symptoms in the subsequent 10 years. **Older adults:** One systematic review (search date 1996, 12 prospective cohort studies, 1268 people, mean age 60 years) found that the prognosis may be especially poor in elderly people with a chronic or relapsing course of depression. Another systematic review (search date 1999, 23 prospective cohort studies in people aged 65 years or over, including 5 identified by the first review) found that depression in older people was associated with increased mortality (15 studies; pooled OR 1.73, 95% CI 1.53 to 1.95).

# 346 | Generalised anxiety disorder

Christopher K Gale and Jane Millichamp

## KEY POINTS

- Generalised anxiety disorder (GAD) is excessive worry and tension about everyday events, on most days, for at least 6 months, to the extent that there is distress or difficulty in performing day-to-day tasks. However, diagnosing GAD accurately can be difficult.

  Up to 1 in 20 people may have GAD at any one time, and most have other health problems. Less than half of people have full remission after 5 years.

  GAD may have a genetic component, and has also been linked to previous psychological or other trauma.

- In adults:

- CBT (including exposure, relaxation, and cognitive restructuring) improves anxiety compared with waiting list control, treatment as usual, or enhanced usual care.

  It is unclear whether CBT is more effective than supportive therapy.

- Applied relaxation may be as effective as CBT, but we found insufficient RCT evidence about applied relaxation compared with no treatment.

- Various drug treatments, such as benzodiazepines, buspirone, hydroxyzine, antidepressants, and pregabalin may all reduce symptoms of anxiety in people with GAD, but they can have unpleasant adverse effects, and most trials have been short term.

  Benzodiazepines increase the risk of dependence, sedation, and accidents, and can cause adverse effects in neonates if used during pregnancy.

  Buspirone may be less effective if used in people who have recently been taking benzodiazepines.

  Antidepressants (imipramine, paroxetine, sertraline, escitalopram, venlafaxine, and opipramol) have been shown to reduce symptoms compared with placebo, but antidepressants can cause a variety of adverse effects including sedation, dizziness, falls, nausea, and sexual dysfunction.

  In general, comparisons between different antidepressants have shown similar effectiveness in reducing anxiety, although one RCT found limited evidence of an increased benefit with escitalopram compared with paroxetine.

- Antipsychotic drugs may reduce anxiety in people who have not responded to other treatments, but these drugs may have adverse effects including drowsiness, and movement disorders.

- We don't know whether abecarnil reduces anxiety as the RCTs we found reported inconsistent results.

- In children and adolescents:

- CBT improves symptoms compared with waiting list control or active control.

  Most RCTs of CBT in children and adolescents have included other anxiety disorders.

- We found limited RCT evidence regarding the efficacy of antidepressants for childhood GAD. SSRIs (fluvoxamine, fluoxetine, sertraline) have shown some promise, but antidepressants are associated with abdominal pain and nausea, and other well documented adverse effects.

- We found no RCT evidence on the effects of applied relaxation, benzodiazepines, buspirone, hydroxyzine, abecarnil, pregabalin, or antipsychotics in children and adolescents.

(i) **Please visit http://clinicalevidence.bmj.com for full text and references**

## What are the effects of treatments for generalised anxiety disorder in adults?

| | |
|---|---|
| **Beneficial** | • Antidepressants in adults (imipramine, duloxetine, paroxetine, sertraline, escitalopram, venlafaxine, and opipramol)<br>• CBT in adults |
| **Likely To Be Beneficial** | • Applied relaxation in adults<br>• Buspirone in adults<br>• Hydroxyzine in adults<br>• Pregabalin in adults |
| **Trade-off Between Benefits And Harms** | • Antipsychotics in adults<br>• Benzodiazepines in adults |
| **Unknown Effectiveness** | • Abecarnil in adults |

## What are the effects of treatments for generalised anxiety disorder in children and adolescents?

| | |
|---|---|
| **Beneficial** | • CBT in children and adolescents |
| **Trade-off Between Benefits And Harms** | • Antidepressants in children and adolescents (sertraline, fluvoxamine, fluoxetine, paroxetine, venlafaxine) |
| **Unknown Effectiveness** | • Abecarnil in children and adolescents<br>• Antipsychotics in children and adolescents<br>• Applied relaxation in children and adolescents<br>• Benzodiazepines in children and adolescents<br>• Buspirone in children and adolescents<br>• Hydroxyzine in children and adolescents<br>• Pregabalin in children and adolescents |

**Search date May 2011**

**DEFINITION** Generalised anxiety disorder (GAD) is defined as excessive worry and tension about everyday events and problems, on most days, for at least 6 months, to the point where the person experiences distress or has marked difficulty in performing day-to-day tasks. It may be characterised by the following symptoms and signs: increased motor tension (fatigability, trembling, restlessness, and muscle tension); autonomic hyperactivity (shortness of breath, rapid heart rate, dry mouth, cold hands, and dizziness); and increased vigilance and scanning (feeling keyed up, increased startling, and impaired concentration), but not by panic attacks. One non-systematic review of epidemiological and clinical studies found marked reduction in quality of life and psychosocial functioning in people with anxiety disorders, including GAD. It also found that people with GAD had low overall life satisfaction, and some impairment in ability to fulfil roles, social tasks, or both.

*(continued over)*

**http://clinicalevidence.bmj.com**

*(from previous page)*

**INCIDENCE/PREVALENCE** The most recent community surveys have used a newer version of the Composite International Diagnostic Interview (CIDI), which allows direct comparisons between different surveys. One observational survey in Europe completed in 2003, which included people from Belgium, France, Germany, Italy, the Netherlands, and Spain, estimated the 12-month prevalence of GAD at 1.0% (0.5% males, 1.3% females). An observational survey in New Zealand (12,800 people) estimated the 12-month prevalence of GAD at 2.0%, 95% CI 1.7% to 2.3% (men: 1.4%, 95% CI 1.1% to 1.8%; women: 2.6%, 95% CI 2.2% to 3.1%). In this survey, people aged >65 years had a markedly lower 12-month prevalence of GAD (1.0%, 95% CI 0.6% to 1.5%). The lifetime prevalence of GAD was estimated to be 6.0%, 95% CI 5.5% to 6.6%. An observational survey in the UK in 2000 of people aged 16 to 74 years used the Clinical Interview Schedule-Revised (CIS-R), followed by a Schedules for Clinical Assessment in Neuropsychiatry [SCAN] interview of a stratified sample. The survey estimated that 4.7% of people had GAD (men: 4.6%; women: 4.8%). A survey of children and adolescents aged 5 to 16 years in the UK in 2004, which used a similar methodology, estimated that 0.7% had GAD (boys: 0.6%; girls: 0.8%). In the European survey of adults, 76% of those people who had more than one mental disorder for 12 months had GAD. Those people who had GAD were significantly more likely to have other mental disorders which included (odds ratio to have the disorder): major depression (OR 37.1, 95% CI 23.2 to 59.1), social phobia (OR 13.5, 95% CI 7.8 to 23.6), specific phobia (OR 7.4, 95% CI 4.6 to 12.0), post-traumatic stress disorder (OR 16.4, 95% CI 9.1 to 29.8), agoraphobia (OR 26.6, 95% CI 10.8 to 65.1), panic disorder (OR 21.8, 95% CI 11.5 to 41.2), and alcohol dependence (OR 18.9, 95% CI 4.8 to 74.4). Another observational survey in 2004 found that people with GAD were also more likely to have physical health problems. In one systematic review (search date 2006), people with GAD had a significantly decreased quality of life (effect size [6 studies, 248 people, P <0.01). A non-systematic review (20 observational studies in younger and older adults) suggested that autonomic arousal to stressful tasks was decreased in older people, and that older people became accustomed to stressful tasks more quickly than younger people.

**AETIOLOGY/RISK FACTORS** GAD is believed to be associated with an increase in the number of minor life events, independent of demographic factors; however, this finding is also common in people with other diagnoses. One non-systematic review (5 case-control studies) of psychological sequelae to civilian trauma found that rates of GAD reported in 4 of the 5 studies were significantly increased compared with a control population (RR 3.3, 95% CI 2.0 to 5.5). One systematic review (search date 1997) of cross-sectional studies found that bullying (or peer victimisation) was associated with a significant increase in the incidence of GAD (effect size 0.21, CI not reported). One systematic review (search date not reported, 2 family studies, 45 index cases, 225 first-degree relatives) found a significant association between GAD in the index cases and in their first-degree relatives (OR 6.1, 95% CI 2.5 to 14.9). One systematic review of twin and family studies (search date 2003, 23 twin studies, 12 family studies) found an association between GAD, other anxiety disorders, and depression, and postulated that a common genetic factor was implicated.

**PROGNOSIS** One systematic review found that 25% of adults with GAD will be in full remission after 2 years, and 38% will have a remission after 5 years. The Harvard–Brown anxiety research programme reported 5-year follow-up of 167 people with GAD. During this period, the weighted probability for full remission was 38% and for at least partial remission was 47%; the probability of relapse from full remission was 27%, and of relapse from partial remission was 39%.

G Mustafa Soomro

## KEY POINTS

- Obsessions or compulsions that cause personal distress or social dysfunction affect about 1% of adult men and 1.5% of adult women. Prevalence in children and adolescents is 2.7%.

  About half of adults with obsessive compulsive disorder (OCD) have an episodic course, whereas the other half have continuous problems. Up to half of adults show improvement of symptoms over time. The disorder persists in about 40% of children and adolescents at mean follow-up of 5.7 years.

- In adults, CBT and behavioural therapy improve symptoms of OCD compared with a waiting list control or placebo treatments.

  Behavioural therapy may be as effective at improving symptoms as CBT, but we don't know how they compare with SRIs (SSRIs and clomipramine).

- SRIs improve symptoms of OCD in adults compared with placebo. Abrupt withdrawal of SRIs is associated with adverse effects.

- We don't know whether combining SRIs and cognitive therapy or behavioural therapy improves symptoms compared with each treatment alone.

- We don't know whether electroconvulsive therapy improves symptoms in adults with OCD.

- In children and adolescents, CBT and SRIs improve symptoms of OCD. We don't know whether CBT in combination with SRIs is more effective than CBT alone, but it may be more effective than SRIs alone.

- We don't know whether behavioural therapy improves symptoms in children and adolescents with OCD.

- We don't know which is the most effective SRI to use, or for how long maintenance treatment should continue in adults or children and adolescents.

- Adding antipsychotic drugs to SRIs may improve symptoms in adults who did not respond to SRIs alone, although RCTs have given conflicting results.

- We don't know whether psychosurgery improves OCD because we found no studies of sufficient quality to assess its effectiveness.

- Transcranial magnetic stimulation (rTMS) is not likely to improve symptoms of OCD. The quality of evidence is limited with trials being small.

- CAUTION: SSRIs have been associated with an increase in suicidal ideation in children and adolescents.

 Please visit http://clinicalevidence.bmj.com for full text and references

| What are the effects of initial treatments for obsessive compulsive disorder in adults? | |
|---|---|
| Beneficial | • SRIs (SSRIs and clomipramine) in adults |
| Likely To Be Beneficial | • Behavioural therapy in adults<br>• CBT in adults |
| Unknown Effectiveness | • Behavioural therapy or cognitive therapy plus SRIs (SSRIs and clomipramine) in adults (unclear if combination more effective than behavioural or cognitive therapy or SRI alone)<br>• Electroconvulsive therapy in adults |

## What are the effects of initial treatments for obsessive compulsive disorder in children and adolescents?

| Beneficial | • CBT in children and adolescents |
| --- | --- |
| Trade-off Between Benefits And Harms | • Behavioural therapy or cognitive therapy plus SRIs (SSRIs and clomipramine) in children and adolescents<br>• SRIs (SSRIs and clomipramine) in children and adolescents |
| Unknown Effectiveness | • Behavioural therapy in children and adolescents |

## What are the effects of maintenance treatment for obsessive compulsive disorder in adults?

| Unknown Effectiveness | • Ongoing SRIs (SSRIs and clomipramine) versus no ongoing treatment/placebo in adults |
| --- | --- |

## What are the effects of maintenance treatment for obsessive compulsive disorder in children and adolescents?

| Unknown Effectiveness | • Optimum duration of maintenance treatment with SRIs in children and adolescents |
| --- | --- |

## What are the effects of treatments for obsessive compulsive disorder in adults who have not responded to initial treatments?

| Likely To Be Beneficial | • Addition of antipsychotics to SRIs (SSRIs and clomipramine) in adults |
| --- | --- |
| Unknown Effectiveness | • Psychosurgery<br>• Transcranial magnetic stimulation |

**Search date April 2011**

**DEFINITION** Obsessive compulsive disorder (OCD) involves obsessions, compulsions, or both, that are not caused by drugs or by a physical disorder, and which cause significant personal distress or social dysfunction. The disorder may have a chronic or an episodic course. **Obsessions** are recurrent and persistent ideas, images, or impulses that cause pronounced anxiety, and that the person perceives to be self-produced. **Compulsions** are repetitive behaviours or mental acts performed in response to obsessions or according to certain rules, which are aimed at reducing distress or preventing certain imagined dreaded events. People with OCD may have insight into their condition, in that obsessions and compulsions are usually recognised and resisted. There are minor differences in the criteria for OCD between the DSM-III, DSM-III-R, and DSM-IV and the ICD-10.

**INCIDENCE/PREVALENCE In adults:** One national, community-based survey of OCD in the UK (1993, 10,000 people) found that 1.0% of men and 1.5% of women reported symptoms in the previous month. A survey of a random sample of people living in private households in the UK (2000, 8580 adults aged 16–74 years) found that 1.1% of those surveyed reported symptoms of OCD during the previous week. An epidemiological catchment area survey carried out in the US in 1984 (about 10,000 people) found an age- and sex-standardised annual prevalence of OCD in people aged 26 to 64 years of 1.3%, and a lifetime prevalence of 2.3%. Subsequent national surveys used a similar methodology to the survey in the US, and found broadly similar age- and sex-standardised annual and lifetime prevalence rates in Canada, Puerto Rico, Germany, Korea, and New Zealand, but a slightly lower prevalence in Taiwan. A subsequent national comorbidity survey replication was carried out between February 2001 to December 2003 in the US (nationally representative sample of 2073 people aged 18 years or older). It found lifetime prevalence of DSM-IV OCD to be 2.3% and 12 months' prevalence to be 1.2%. **In children and adolescents:** Prevalence in children and adolescents was 2.7% in the US in a community study conducted by the National Institute of Mental Health (NIMH) Methods for the Epidemiology of Child and Adolescent Mental Disorders (MECA) Study. The study evaluated a community sample of 1285 carer–child pairs, where both members of the pair were interviewed using structured interview DISC 2.3 with DSM-III-R criteria.

**AETIOLOGY/RISK FACTORS** The cause of OCD is uncertain. **In adults:** Behavioural, cognitive, genetic, and neurobiological factors have been implicated. Limited evidence from genetic studies in families, and in twins, suggests that genetic factors may be involved, at least in some groups. Risk factors include a family history of OCD, being single (which could be a consequence of the disorder), and belonging to a higher socioeconomic class. The risk of OCD in women is higher than in men in most countries. Other risk factors include cocaine abuse, not being in paid employment, past history of alcohol dependence, affective disorder, and phobic disorder. **In children and adolescents:** About half of children and adolescents displayed 'micro-episodes of OCD' characterised by excessive rigidity and repetitive rituals some years before developing the disorder. Tics in childhood also predicted an increase in OCD symptoms in late adolescence.

**PROGNOSIS In adults:** One study (144 people followed for a mean of 47 years) found that an episodic course of OCD was more common during the initial years of the disease (about 1–9 years), but that a chronic course was more common afterwards. Over time, the study found that 39% to 48% of people had symptomatic improvement. A 1-year prospective cohort study found that 46% of people had an episodic course and 54% had a chronic course. A prospective non-inception cohort study (214 adults with OCD, and follow-up of at least 1 year) found that the probability of full or partial remission after 2 years was 24%; older age of onset, lesser severity of illness, and being female predicted higher probability of full or partial remission. **In children and adolescents:** One systematic review (search date not reported; 22 studies with mean follow-up period of 5.7 years) examining the course of OCD in children and adolescents (mean age of onset 10.4 years; mean study entry age 13.3 years) found that the rate of persistent, full OCD was 41% and the rate of persistent, full, or subclinical OCD was 60%. Greater persistence was predicted by early onset of the disorder, increased OCD duration, and history of inpatient status.

Sara Kakhi and G. Mustafa Soomro

## KEY POINTS

- Obsessions or compulsions that cause personal distress or social dysfunction have been reported to affect about 3% of children and adolescents.

  In children the disorder often presents at around 10 years of age.

  The disorder persists in about 40% of children and adolescents at mean follow-up of 5.7 years.

  The disorder is disabling with adverse impact on functioning, including education and social/family life.

- We searched for evidence from RCTs and systematic reviews of RCTs.

- We do not know what the optimum duration of maintenance drug treatment with serotonin reuptake inhibitors (SRIs) is for children and adolescents with OCD, as we found no evidence.

  Current guidelines recommend a minimum duration of maintenance treatment as being 6 months.

- CAUTION: SSRIs have been associated with an increase in suicidal ideation in children and adolescents.

(i) **Please visit http://clinicalevidence.bmj.com for full text and references**

## What are the effects of maintenance drug treatment for obsessive compulsive disorder in children and adolescents?

| Unknown Effectiveness | • Optimum duration of maintenance drug treatment with serotonin reuptake inhibitors in children and adolescents |
|---|---|

**Search date June 2014**

**DEFINITION** Obsessive compulsive disorder (OCD) involves obsessions, compulsions (or both) that are not caused by drugs or by a physical disorder, and which cause significant personal distress or social dysfunction. The disorder may have a chronic or an episodic course. **Obsessions** are recurrent and persistent ideas, images, or impulses that cause pronounced anxiety, and that the person perceives to be self-produced. **Compulsions** are repetitive behaviours or mental acts performed in response to obsessions or according to certain rules, which are aimed at reducing distress or preventing certain imagined dreaded events. People with OCD may have insight into their condition, in that obsessions and compulsions are usually recognised and resisted. There are minor differences in the criteria for OCD between the DSM-III, DSM-III-R, DSM-IV, and DSM-5, and the ICD-10. Unlike other classification systems which refer to OCD as a type of anxiety disorder, the DSM-5 classifies OCD as a separate disorder under the category 'Obsessive-compulsive and related disorders'.

**INCIDENCE/PREVALENCE** In the US, prevalence of OCD in children and adolescents was reported to be about 3% in a community study conducted by the National Institute of Mental Health (NIMH) Methods for the Epidemiology of Child and Adolescent Mental Disorders (MECA) Study. The study evaluated a community sample of 1285 carer-child pairs, where both members of the pair were interviewed using structured interview DISC 2.3 with DSM-III-R criteria. In the UK, prevalence of OCD in children and adolescents was reported to be 0.25% in a UK nationwide epidemiological study that surveyed 10,438 children aged 5 to 15 years.

**AETIOLOGY/RISK FACTORS** About half of children and adolescents display 'micro-episodes of OCD', characterised by excessive rigidity and repetitive rituals some years before developing the disorder. Tics in childhood may also predict an increase in OCD symptoms in late adolescence. Age of onset of OCD is reported to be bi-modal with one peak at about 10 to 11 years of age, and another during early adulthood. Childhood OCD appears to be more common in boys. There is a strong co-morbidity with disruptive behavioural problems, developmental disorders (including autistic disorder), depression, and other anxiety disorders.

**PROGNOSIS** In children, OCD often presents around 10 years of age. One systematic review (search date not reported, 22 studies with mean follow-up period of 5.7 years) examining the course of OCD in children and adolescents (mean age of onset 10.4 years, mean study entry age 13.3 years) found that the rate of persistent, full OCD was 41% and the rate of persistent, full, or subclinical OCD was 60%. Greater persistence was predicted by early onset of the disorder, increased OCD duration, and history of inpatient status. The disorder is disabling with adverse impact on functioning, including education and social/family life.

## 354 | Opioid dependence

K Thyarappa Praveen, Fergus Law, Jacinta O'Shea, and Jan Melichar

### KEY POINTS

- Dependence on opioids is a multifactorial condition involving genetic and psychosocial factors.

- There are three stages to treating opioid dependence.

  Stabilisation is usually by opioid substitution treatments, and aims to ensure that the drug use becomes independent of mental state (such as craving and mood) and independent of circumstances (such as finance and physical location).

  The next stage is to withdraw (detox) from opioids.

  The final stage is relapse prevention.

- Methadone and buprenorphine help to stabilise opioid use, as they decrease heroin use and help to retain people in treatment programmes.

  Methadone and buprenorphine seem equally effective at stabilising opioid use.

- Methadone, buprenorphine, and alpha$_2$-adrenoceptor agonists (lofexidine, clonidine) can all help people to withdraw from dependence on illicit opioids.

  Lofexidine and clonidine may be less effective than methadone and buprenorphine in withdrawal, although evidence is weak.

  Ultra-rapid withdrawal can help in detoxification, although there are important safety risks in keeping people heavily sedated or under general anaesthesia for a day, or under general anaesthesia for a few hours, and outcomes are no better.

- Naltrexone can help to prevent relapse of heroin use if combined with psychosocial treatment.

 **Please visit http://clinicalevidence.bmj.com for full text and references**

### What are the effects of drug treatments for stabilisation (maintenance) in people with opioid dependence?

| Beneficial | • Buprenorphine for stabilisation |
| --- | --- |
| | • Methadone for stabilisation |
| Unknown Effectiveness | • Buprenorphine versus methadone for stabilisation (both beneficial and seem as effective as each other) |

### What are the effects of drug treatments for withdrawal in people with opioid dependence?

| Beneficial | • Buprenorphine for withdrawal |
| --- | --- |
| | • Methadone for withdrawal |
| Likely To Be Beneficial | • Lofexidine/clonidine for withdrawal |
| Unknown Effectiveness | • Ultra-rapid withdrawal (antagonist-assisted [naltrexone and naloxone only]) |

## What are the effects of drug treatments for relapse prevention in people with opioid dependence?

| Likely To Be Beneficial | • Naltrexone for relapse prevention |
| --- | --- |

**Search date March 2011**

---

**DEFINITION** Opioids (opiates) are highly addictive, and opioid dependence is a chronic relapsing disorder. Heroin is the most commonly abused opioid; others include morphine, buprenorphine, codeine, and methadone. Dependence is a cluster of physiological, behavioural, and cognitive phenomena in which the use of a substance takes on a much higher priority for a given individual than other behaviours that once had a greater value. **Diagnosis:** Diagnosis of dependence syndrome is usually made from a combination of history and examination including urinalysis to corroborate the history, looking for the presence of opioid metabolites (e.g., morphine) in the urine. A definite diagnosis of dependence should usually be made only if three or more of the following have been present together at some stage during the previous year: 1) a strong desire or compulsion to take opioids; 2) difficulties in controlling substance-taking behaviour in terms of its onset, termination, and levels of use; 3) a physiological withdrawal state; 4) evidence of tolerance; 5) progressive neglect of alternative pleasures or interests because of opioid use; and 6) persisting with substance use despite clear evidence of overtly harmful consequences. Physical examination can also provide evidence of acute intoxication, withdrawal, and chronic or physical consequences of drug administration, such as abscesses, malnutrition, poor dentition, and DVT. When commencing treatment, urinalysis should confirm the use of opioids, and some practitioners require a number of samples to be taken several days apart to confirm ongoing use. However, regular urinalysis might not be necessary with continuing treatment because studies report that, in situations where there is no coercion, self-reports of drug users are sufficiently reliable and valid to provide descriptions of drug use, drug-related problems, and the natural history of drug use. Random sampling is, however, still useful. **Population:** All patients reported in this review were 16 years and older.

**INCIDENCE/PREVALENCE** Opioid use/intravenous drug use rose substantially in the 1990s. New notifications to the Addicts Index (a register held by the UK Home Office) by physicians of people dependent on opioids increased over 30-fold, from approximately 600 in 1966 to >18,000 in 1996, and nearly tripled during the 1990s. The UK drug strategy reported 100,000 to 200,000 problem drug users in the mid-1990s. A pilot study of national estimation methods suggested that there were 143,000 to 266,000 problem drug users, with about 75,000 to 150,000 opioid users in England and Wales in 1996. More recently, the number of people becoming dependent on opioids in 2000 ranged from 13,000 (0.06/100 adults aged 15–44 years) to >26,000 (0.13/100 adults aged 15–44 years). A reduction in the supply of heroin in Australia has also led to a halving in the prevalence of opioid abuse and dependence between the late 1990s and the present. In 2008/9; a report from the National Drug Evidence centre estimated 262,428 problematic opiate users in England, suggesting a rate of 7.69 per 1000 population aged 15 to 64 years.

**AETIOLOGY/RISK FACTORS** Opioid dependence is a multifactorial condition involving genetic and psychosocial factors. Studies in twins report that both the genetic and shared environmental effects on risk for use and misuse are usually entirely non-specific in their effects. Environmental experiences unique to the person largely determine whether predisposed individuals will use or misuse opioids.

**PROGNOSIS** Addictive disorders are chronic relapsing conditions with no known 'cure'. Naturalistic studies have demonstrated that over a 5-year period, approximately half of individuals recover from the dependence.

Shailesh Kumar and Darren Malone

## KEY POINTS

- Panic disorder is characterised by recurrent, unpredictable panic attacks, making people worry about or change their behaviour to avert subsequent panic attacks or their consequences.

  Panic disorder occurs in up to 3% of the adult population at some time, and is associated with other psychiatric and personality disorders, and with drug and alcohol abuse.

  The risk of suicide and attempted suicide has been found to be higher in people with panic disorder than in people with other psychiatric illness, including depression.

- CBT is effective in reducing symptoms of panic disorder over 6 months or longer, but we don't know whether it is more effective than other psychological treatments.

  CBT is more effective than waiting list and other controls in reducing symptoms in panic disorder with or without mild to moderate agoraphobia.

  We don't know whether CBT alone is more effective than antidepressants alone, but weak evidence suggests that the effects of CBT may last longer. Combined treatment with CBT plus antidepressants has been shown to be more effective than CBT alone or antidepressants alone in reducing symptoms in the short term.

- Other forms of psychotherapy can also be beneficial in reducing symptoms associated with panic disorder, with or without drug treatments.

  Applied relaxation, client-centred therapy, cognitive restructuring, and exposure to the panic-inducing stimulus are all likely to be effective in reducing symptoms.

  Self-help using CBT techniques may be as effective as therapist-based CBT.

  Breathing retraining, couple therapy, insight-orientated therapy, psychoeducation, and brief dynamic psychotherapy may be beneficial, but we found insufficient evidence to be sure.

- SSRIs and tricyclic antidepressants are also effective at reducing the symptoms of panic disorder.

  Benzodiazepines can be effective in reducing symptoms in panic disorder, but their adverse-effect profile makes them unsuitable for long-term treatment.

  We don't know whether buspirone or MAOIs are effective.

(i) **Please visit http://clinicalevidence.bmj.com for full text and references**

| What are the effects of non-drug treatments for panic disorder? | |
|---|---|
| **Beneficial** | • CBT versus no treatment |
| **Likely To Be Beneficial** | • Applied relaxation |
| | • Client-centred therapy (no direct evidence versus no treatment, but may be as effective as other forms of CBT) |
| | • Cognitive restructuring |
| | • Exposure (external or interoceptive) |

| | • Self-help (may be as effective as other forms of CBT) |
|---|---|
| **Unknown Effectiveness** | • Breathing retraining |
| | • Brief dynamic psychotherapy |
| | • CBT versus antidepressants (unclear which more effective, but weak evidence that effects of CBT may last longer than those of antidepressants) |
| | • CBT versus other psychological treatments (unclear how CBT compares with other psychological treatments) |
| | • Couple therapy |
| | • Insight-orientated therapy |
| | • Psychoeducation |

### What are the effects of drug treatments for panic disorder?

| **Beneficial** | • SSRIs |
|---|---|
| | • Tricyclic antidepressants (imipramine) |
| **Trade-off Between Benefits And Harms** | • Benzodiazepines |
| **Unknown Effectiveness** | • Buspirone |
| | • MAOIs |

### What are the effects of combined drug and psychological treatments for panic disorder?

| **Likely To Be Beneficial** | • CBT plus antidepressants versus CBT alone (combination may be more effective in acute phase; unclear which is more effective with continued treatment, or 6–24 months after treatment discontinuation) |
|---|---|
| | • CBT plus antidepressants versus antidepressants alone (combination treatment may be more effective) |

**Search date June 2007**

**DEFINITION** A panic attack is a period in which there is sudden onset of intense apprehension, fear, or terror, often associated with feelings of impending doom. Panic disorder is classified by the DSM-IV as recurrent, unpredictable panic attacks followed by at least 1 month of persistent concern about having another panic attack, worry about the possible implications or consequences of the panic attacks, or a significant behavioural change related to the attacks. The term 'panic disorder' excludes panic attacks attributable to the direct physiological effects of a general medical condition, a substance, or another mental disorder. The ICD-10 classifies panic disorder as recurrent, unpredictable panic attacks, with sudden onset of palpitations, chest pain, choking sensations, dizziness, and feelings of unreality, often with associated fear of dying, losing control, or going mad, but

*(continued over)*

*(from previous page)*

without the requirement for the symptoms to have persisted for 1 month or longer. The DSM-IV classifies these conditions as primarily panic disorder with or without agoraphobia, whereas the ICD-10 classifies them as primarily agoraphobia with or without panic disorder. The diagnosis should not be made in people with co-morbid depression, when the panic is considered to be secondary to depression. **Diagnosis:** Although panic attacks are a necessary feature of panic disorder, panic attacks on their own are not enough to make the diagnosis. Panic attacks may happen in the context of specific situations such as social or specific phobia which are different from panic disorder. A diagnosis of panic disorder is made in the presence of recurrent unexpected panic attacks followed by at least 1 month of persistent concern about having another panic attack.

**INCIDENCE/PREVALENCE** Panic disorder often starts at about 20 years of age (between late adolescence and the mid-30s). Lifetime prevalence is 1–3%, and panic disorder is more common in women than in men. An Australian community study found 1-month prevalence rates for panic disorder (with or without agoraphobia) of 0.4% using ICD-10 diagnostic criteria, and of 0.5% using DSM-IV diagnostic criteria. One systematic review of observational data estimated the prevalence rate of panic disorder during the perinatal period at between 1.3–2.0%, and that, although the symptoms of panic during pregnancy may be identical to at other periods, they are often interpreted in the context of the perinatal state (for example, a woman may interpret panic attacks during pregnancy as an indication that something is wrong with the pregnancy).

**AETIOLOGY/RISK FACTORS** The onset of panic disorder tends to be preceded by stressful life events, although a negative interpretation of these events, in addition to their occurrence, has been suggested as an important causal factor. Panic disorder is associated with major depression, social phobia, generalised anxiety disorder, obsessive compulsive disorder, and a substantial risk of drug and alcohol misuse. It is also associated with avoidant, histrionic, and dependent personality disorders.

**PROGNOSIS** The severity of symptoms in people with panic disorder fluctuates considerably, and people commonly have periods of no attacks, or only mild attacks with few symptoms. There is often a long delay between the initial onset of symptoms and presentation for treatment. Recurrent attacks may continue for several years, especially if associated with agoraphobia. Reduced social or occupational functioning varies among people with panic disorder, and is worse in people with associated agoraphobia. Panic disorder is also associated with an increased rate of attempted suicide, with one study finding that it occured in 20% of people with panic disorder, compared with 12% of people with panic attacks alone, 6% of those with other psychiatric disorder, and 1% of those with no disorders. The odds ratio for attempted suicide was increased if there were co-morbid conditions. One study analysing data from RCTs and systematic reviews found that co-existence of anxiety and depressive features adversely affected treatment response at 12 years compared with treatment of panic disorder alone.

Jonathan Bisson

## KEY POINTS

- Post-traumatic stress disorder (PTSD) is characterised by disabling symptoms of re-experiencing a traumatic event, avoidance behaviour, and hyperarousal (e.g., irritability or hypervigilance), lasting at least 1 month.

  PTSD may affect 10% of women and 5% of men at some stage, and symptoms may persist for several years.

  Risk factors include major trauma, lack of social support, peritraumatic dissociation, and previous psychiatric or personality factors.

- Multiple-session trauma-focused CBT may be effective at preventing development of PTSD in people with psychological distress after a traumatic event.

  However, we don't know whether multiple-session trauma-focused CBT is beneficial for people who have experienced a traumatic event but have not been diagnosed with psychological distress.

- We don't know whether antiepileptic drugs, antihypertensive drugs, hydrocortisone, multiple-session collaborative trauma support, multiple-session education, single-session group debriefing, or temazepam are beneficial in preventing PTSD.

  Single-session individual debriefing may increase the rate of PTSD after a traumatic event compared with no debriefing, and supportive counselling may be less effective than multiple-session CBT at preventing onset of PTSD.

- In people with PTSD, trauma-focused CBT improves PTSD symptoms compared with no treatment or with other psychological interventions, including stress management and present-centred therapy. Eye movement desensitisation and reprocessing seems as effective as trauma-focused CBT in the treatment of chronic PTSD.

  We don't know whether other psychological treatments (affect management, drama therapy, group therapy, hypnotherapy, inpatient treatment regimens, Internet-based psychotherapy, psychodynamic psychotherapy, or supportive psychotherapy) are beneficial in people with PTSD.

- Paroxetine may improve symptoms in people with PTSD. However, venlafaxine does not seem effective at improving symptoms, and the benefits of fluoxetine are unclear.

  We found insufficient good evidence to assess the effects of sertraline, tricyclic antidepressants, or benzodiazepines.

  We found limited evidence that sertraline and nefazodone may be equally effective at improving symptoms of PTSD, but we don't know how other antidepressants compare with each other in the treatment of PTSD.

  We don't know whether antiepileptic drugs, antihypertensive drugs, brofaromine, nefazodone, olanzapine, phenelzine, mirtazapine, or risperidone are beneficial in people with PTSD.

 **Please visit http://clinicalevidence.bmj.com for full text and references**

| What are the effects of interventions to prevent post-traumatic stress disorder? | |
|---|---|
| Likely To Be Beneficial | • Multiple-session CBT to prevent PTSD in people with acute stress disorder (reduced PTSD compared with supportive counselling) |
| Unknown Effectiveness | • Antiepileptic drugs to prevent PTSD  • Antihypertensive drugs to prevent PTSD |

|  | • Hydrocortisone to prevent PTSD |
|  | • Multiple-session CBT to prevent PTSD in all people exposed to a traumatic event |
|  | • Multiple-session collaborative trauma support to prevent PTSD |
|  | • Multiple-session education to prevent PTSD |
|  | • Single-session group debriefing to prevent PTSD |
|  | • Temazepam to prevent PTSD |
| **Unlikely To Be Beneficial** | • Single-session individual debriefing to prevent PTSD |
|  | • Supportive counselling to prevent PTSD |

### What are the effects of interventions to treat post-traumatic stress disorder?

| **Beneficial** | • CBT to treat PTSD |
|  | • Eye movement desensitisation and reprocessing (EMDR) to treat PTSD |
| **Likely To Be Beneficial** | • Paroxetine to treat PTSD |
| **Unknown Effectiveness** | • Affect management to treat PTSD |
|  | • Antiepileptic drugs to treat PTSD |
|  | • Antihypertensive drugs to treat PTSD |
|  | • Benzodiazepines to treat PTSD |
|  | • Brofaromine to treat PTSD |
|  | • Drama therapy to treat PTSD |
|  | • Fluoxetine to treat PTSD |
|  | • Group therapy to treat PTSD |
|  | • Hypnotherapy to treat PTSD |
|  | • Inpatient treatment programmes to treat PTSD |
|  | • Internet-based psychotherapy to treat PTSD |
|  | • Mirtazapine to treat PTSD |
|  | • Nefazodone to treat PTSD |
|  | • Olanzapine to treat PTSD |
|  | • Phenelzine to treat PTSD |
|  | • Psychodynamic psychotherapy to treat PTSD |
|  | • Risperidone to treat PTSD |
|  | • SSRIs versus other antidepressants to treat PTSD |
|  | • Sertraline to treat PTSD |
|  | • Supportive psychotherapy to treat PTSD |

| | • Tricyclic antidepressants to treat PTSD |
|---|---|
| Unlikely To Be Beneficial | • Venlafaxine to treat PTSD |

**Search date March 2009**

**DEFINITION** Post-traumatic stress disorder (PTSD) can occur after any major traumatic event. Symptoms include upsetting thoughts and nightmares about the traumatic event, avoidance behaviour, numbing of general responsiveness, increased irritability, and hyper-vigilance. To fulfil the *Diagnostic and Statistical Manual-IV* (DSM-IV) criteria for PTSD, an individual must have been exposed to a traumatic event; have at least one re-experiencing, three avoidance, and two hyperarousal phenomena; have had the symptoms for at least 1 month; and the symptoms must cause clinically important distress or reduced day-to-day functioning. It is labelled as acute for the first 3 months and chronic if it lasts beyond 3 months. People with subsyndromal PTSD have all the criteria for PTSD except one of the re-experiencing, avoidance, or hyperarousal phenomena. **Acute stress disorder** occurs within the first month after a major traumatic event and requires the presence of symptoms for at least 2 days. It is similar to PTSD, but dissociative symptoms are required to make the diagnosis. Treatments for PTSD may have similar effects, regardless of the traumatic event that precipitated PTSD. However, great caution should be applied when generalising from one type of trauma to another.

**INCIDENCE/PREVALENCE** One large cross-sectional study in the USA found that 1/10 (10%) women and 1/20 (5%) men experience PTSD at some stage in their lives.

**AETIOLOGY/RISK FACTORS** Risk factors include major trauma, such as: rape; a history of psychiatric disorders; acute distress and depression after the trauma; lack of social support; and personality factors.

**PROGNOSIS** One large cross-sectional study in the USA found that over one third of people with previous PTSD continued to satisfy the criteria for PTSD 6 years after initial diagnosis. However, cross-sectional studies provide weak evidence about prognosis.

Sarah JE Barry, Tracey M Gaughan, and Robert Hunter

## KEY POINTS

- The lifetime prevalence of schizophrenia is approximately 0.7% and incidence rates vary between 7.7 and 43.0 per 100,000; about 75% of people have relapses and continued disability, and one third fail to respond to standard treatment.

  Positive symptoms include auditory hallucinations, delusions, and thought disorder. Negative symptoms (anhedonia, asociality, flattening of affect, and demotivation) and cognitive dysfunction have not been consistently improved by any treatment.

- Standard treatment of schizophrenia has been antipsychotic drugs, the first of which included chlorpromazine and haloperidol, but these so-called first-generation antipsychotics can all cause adverse effects such as extrapyramidal adverse effects, hyperprolactinaemia, and sedation. Attempts to address these adverse effects led to the development of second-generation antipsychotics.

- The second-generation antipsychotics amisulpride, clozapine, olanzapine, and risperidone may be more effective at reducing positive symptoms compared with first-generation antipsychotic drugs, but may cause similar adverse effects, plus additional metabolic effects such as weight gain.

- CAUTION: Clozapine has been associated with potentially fatal blood dyscrasias. Blood monitoring is essential, and it is recommended that its use be limited to people with treatment-resistant schizophrenia.

- Pimozide, quetiapine, aripiprazole, sulpiride, ziprasidone, and zotepine seem to be as effective as standard antipsychotic drugs at improving positive symptoms. Again, these drugs cause similar adverse effects to first-generation antipsychotics and other second-generation antipsychotics.

- CAUTION: Pimozide has been associated with sudden cardiac death at doses above 20 mg daily.

- We found very little evidence regarding depot injections of haloperidol decanoate, flupentixol decanoate, or zuclopenthixol decanoate; thus, we don't know if they are more effective than oral treatments at improving symptoms.

- In people who are resistant to standard antipsychotic drugs, clozapine may improve symptoms compared with first-generation antipsychotic agents, but this benefit must be balanced against the likelihood of adverse effects.

  We found limited evidence on other individual first- or second-generation antipsychotic drugs other than clozapine in people with treatment-resistant schizophrenia.

  In people with treatment-resistant schizophrenia, we don't know how second-generation agents other than clozapine compare with each other or first-generation antipsychotic agents, or how clozapine compares with other second-generation antipsychotic agents, because of a lack of evidence.

- We don't know whether behavioural interventions, compliance therapy, psychoeducational interventions, or family interventions improve adherence to antipsychotic medication compared with usual care because of a paucity of good-quality evidence.

- It is clear that some included studies in this review have serious failings and that the evidence base for the efficacy of antipsychotic medication and other interventions is surprisingly weak. For example, although in many trials haloperidol has been used as the standard comparator, the clinical trial evidence for haloperidol is less impressive than may be expected.

- By their very nature, systematic reviews and RCTs provide average indices of probable efficacy in groups of selected individuals. Although some RCTs limit inclusion criteria to a single category of diagnosis, many studies include individuals with different diagnoses such as schizoaffective disorder. In all RCTs, even in those recruiting people with a single DSM or ICD-10 diagnosis, there is considerable clinical heterogeneity.

- Genome-wide association studies of large samples with schizophrenia demonstrate that this clinical heterogeneity reflects, in turn, complex biological heterogeneity. For example, genome-wide association studies suggest that around 1000 genetic variants of low penetrance and other individually rare genetic variants of higher penetrance, along with epistasis and epigenetic mechanisms, are thought to be responsible, probably with the biological and psychological effects of environmental factors, for the resultant complex clinical phenotype. A more stratified approach to clinical trials would help to identify those subgroups that seem to be the best responders to a particular intervention.

- To date, however, there is little to suggest that stratification on the basis of clinical characteristics successfully helps to predict which drugs work best for which people. There is a pressing need for the development of biomarkers with clinical utility for mental health problems. Such measures could help to stratify clinical populations or provide better markers of efficacy in clinical trials, and would complement the current use of clinical outcome scales. Clinicians are also well aware that many people treated with antipsychotic medication develop significant adverse effects such as extrapyramidal symptoms or weight gain. Again, our ability to identify which people will develop which adverse effects is poorly developed, and might be assisted by using biomarkers to stratify populations.

- The results of this review tend to indicate that as far as antipsychotic medication goes, current drugs are of limited efficacy in some people, and that most drugs cause adverse effects in most people. Although this is a rather downbeat conclusion, it should not be too surprising, given clinical experience and our knowledge of the pharmacology of the available antipsychotic medication. All currently available antipsychotic medications have the same putative mechanism of action — namely, dopaminergic antagonism with varying degrees of antagonism at other receptor sites. More efficacious antipsychotic medication awaits a better understanding of the biological pathogenesis of these conditions so that rational treatments can be developed.

 **Please visit http://clinicalevidence.bmj.com for full text and references**

## What are the effects of drug treatments for positive, negative, or cognitive symptoms of schizophrenia?

| Trade-off Between Benefits And Harms | • Amisulpride |
| --- | --- |
| | • Aripiprazole |
| | • Chlorpromazine |
| | • Clozapine |
| | • Haloperidol |
| | • Olanzapine |
| | • Paliperidone |
| | • Pimozide |
| | • Quetiapine |
| | • Risperidone |

| | • Ziprasidone |
| | • Zotepine |
| Unknown Effectiveness | • Depot flupentixol decanoate |
| | • Depot haloperidol decanoate |
| | • Depot zuclopenthixol decanoate |
| | • Flupentixol |
| | • Sertindole |
| | • Sulpiride |
| | • Zuclopenthixol |

## What are the effects of drug treatments in people with schizophrenia who are resistant to standard antipsychotic drugs?

| Trade-off Between Benefits And Harms | • Clozapine (compared with first-generation antipsychotic drugs) |
| | • Clozapine (insufficient evidence to compare effectiveness versus other second-generation antipsychotic drugs) |
| Unknown Effectiveness | • Second-generation antipsychotics (other than clozapine) (insufficient evidence to compare effectiveness of drugs in this class) |
| | • Second-generation antipsychotics (other than clozapine) (insufficient evidence to compare effectiveness versus first-generation antipsychotics) |

## What are the effects of interventions to improve adherence to antipsychotic medication in people with schizophrenia?

| Unknown Effectiveness | • Behavioural therapy |
| | • Compliance therapy |
| | • Multiple-session family interventions |
| | • Psychoeducational interventions (brief group psychoeducational intervention may be more effective than usual care) |

**Search date May 2010**

---

**DEFINITION** Schizophrenia is a complex syndrome characterised by three major symptom domains: positive symptoms, such as auditory hallucinations, delusions, and thought disorder; negative symptoms, including anhedonia, social withdrawal, affective flattening, and demotivation; and cognitive dysfunction, particularly in the domains of attention, working memory, and executive function. Schizophrenia is typically a life-long condition characterised by acute symptom exacerbations and widely varying degrees of functional disability. Maintenance antipsychotic drug regimens for schizophrenia are intended to limit the frequency and severity of relapses, maximise the beneficial effects of treatment for persistent symptoms, and enhance adherence to recommended regimens. Antipsychotic medications are primarily effective for positive symptoms, and most people require psychosocial interventions to manage the disability that often results from negative symptoms and cognitive dysfunction. Adherence to prescribed antipsychotic regimens is typically low, and several psychosocial interventions have been developed to enhance adherence. About 20% of people with schizophrenia are resistant to standard antipsychotics, as defined by lack of clinically important improvement in symptoms after two to three regimens of treatment with standard antipsychotic drugs for at least 6 weeks; an additional 30% to 40% of people improve but are residually symptomatic despite antipsychotic treatment. Several pharmacological strategies have been advocated for this group of people. This review focuses on three key aspects of the management of schizophrenia: 1) What are the effects of drug treatments for positive, negative, or cognitive symptoms of schizophrenia? 2) What are the effects of interventions in people with schizophrenia who are resistant to standard antipsychotic drugs? and 3) What are the effects of interventions to improve adherence to antipsychotic medication in people with schizophrenia?

**INCIDENCE/PREVALENCE** The lifetime prevalence of schizophrenia is approximately 0.7% and incidence rates vary between 7.7 and 43.0 per 100,000. The onset of symptoms typically occurs in early adult life (average age 25 years), and occurs earlier in men than in women.

**AETIOLOGY/RISK FACTORS** Risk factors for schizophrenia include a family history (including genetic factors), obstetric complications, developmental difficulties, central nervous system infections in childhood, cannabis use, and acute life events. The precise contributions of these factors, and ways in which they may interact, are unclear.

**PROGNOSIS** About three-quarters of people with schizophrenia suffer recurrent relapse and continued disability. Outcome may be worse in people with insidious onset and delayed initial treatment, social isolation, or a strong family history; people living in industrialised countries; men; and in people who misuse drugs. Drug treatment is more successful in treating positive symptoms, but up to one third of people derive little benefit, and negative symptoms are difficult to treat. About half of people with schizophrenia do not adhere to treatment in the short term, and in the long term adherence is even lower.

Peter A. A. Struijs and Gino M. M. J. Kerkhoffs

## KEY POINTS

- Injury of the lateral ligament complex of the ankle joint occurs in about one in 10,000 people per day, accounting for a quarter of all sports injuries.

  Pain may be localised to the lateral side of the ankle.

  Residual complaints include joint instability, stiffness, and intermittent swelling, and are more likely to occur after more extensive cartilage damage.

  Recurrent sprains can add new damage and increase the risk of long-term degeneration of the joint.

- In this overview, we have searched for RCTs and systematic reviews of RCTs on the effects of non-steroidal anti-inflammatory drugs (NSAIDs) in people with acute ankle sprain.

- NSAIDs might be beneficial when used in combination with immobilisation for people with ankle sprain, although possible side effects should be taken into consideration.

- Oral NSAIDs may be more effective than placebo at improving pain and swelling in the short term up to 2 weeks, but we don't know about longer-term effects.

  We found insufficient evidence on the effects of selective COX-2 inhibitors versus other NSAIDs.

- Topical NSAIDs may be more effective than placebo at reducing pain in the short term at up to 2 weeks, but we don't know about swelling, or about longer-term effects.

- We found no RCTs comparing oral NSAIDs with topical NSAIDs.

 Please visit http://clinicalevidence.bmj.com for full text and references

| What are the effects of non-steroidal anti-inflammatory drugs (NSAIDs) in the treatment of acute ankle sprains? | |
|---|---|
| Likely To Be Beneficial | • Oral NSAIDs versus placebo (evidence of short-term improvement only; no longer-term evidence; possible adverse events)<br><br>• Topical NSAIDs versus placebo (evidence of short-term improvement only; no longer-term evidence) |
| Unknown Effectiveness | • Oral NSAIDs versus topical NSAIDs (no direct RCT evidence)<br><br>• Selective COX-2 inhibitors versus other NSAIDs (insufficient evidence to say if any difference in effectiveness) |

Search date April 2014

---

**DEFINITION** Ankle sprain is an injury of the lateral ligament complex of the ankle joint. The injury is graded on the basis of severity. Grade 1 is a mild stretching of the ligament complex without joint instability; grade 2 is a partial rupture of the ligament complex with mild instability of the joint (such as isolated rupture of the anterior talofibular ligament); and grade 3 involves complete rupture of the ligament complex with instability of the joint. This gradation has limited practical consequences because both grade 2 and 3 injuries are treated similarly, and grade 1 injuries need no specific treatment after diagnosis. In this review, we have included acute ankle injury in people who are skeletally mature (adults, >16 years of age), and excluded studies undertaken in children, in people with chronic ankle instability, or in people with congenital deformities or degenerative conditions.

**INCIDENCE/PREVALENCE** Ankle sprain is a common problem in acute medical care, occurring at a rate of about one injury per 10,000 people per day. Injuries of the lateral ligament complex of the ankle form a quarter of all sports injuries.

**AETIOLOGY/RISK FACTORS** The usual mechanism of injury is inversion and adduction (usually referred to as supination) of the plantar flexed foot. Predisposing factors are a history of ankle sprains, ligament hyperlaxity syndrome, and specific malalignment, such as crus varum and pes cavo-varus.

**PROGNOSIS** Some sports (e.g., basketball, football/soccer, volleyball) are associated with a particularly high incidence of ankle injuries. Pain and intermittent swelling are the most frequent residual problems, often localised on the lateral side of the ankle. Other residual complaints include mechanical instability and stiffness. People with more extensive cartilage damage have a higher incidence of residual complaints. In the long term, the initial traumatic cartilage damage can lead to degenerative changes, especially if there is persistent or recurrent instability. Every further sprain has the potential to add new damage.

Nigel L. Ashworth

## KEY POINTS

- Carpal tunnel syndrome (CTS) is a collection of clinical symptoms and signs caused by compression of the median nerve within the carpal tunnel.

  Classic symptoms include numbness, tingling, burning, or pain in at least two of the three digits supplied by the median nerve (i.e., the thumb and the index and middle fingers).

  Symptoms can resolve within 6 months in about one third of people, particularly younger people, whereas poor prognosis is often indicated by bilateral symptoms and a positive Phalen's test. However, the severity of symptoms and signs does not often correlate well with the extent of nerve compression.

- Local corticosteroid injections seem beneficial in treating CTS compared with placebo.

  Risks associated with local corticosteroid injections into the carpal tunnel include tendon rupture and injection into the median nerve.

- We don't know whether diuretics or non-steroidal anti-inflammatory drugs (NSAIDs) are effective in treating CTS because the RCTs identified have been too small to draw reliable conclusions.

- We don't know whether therapeutic ultrasound or wrist splints are effective in relieving symptoms of CTS.

- We found insufficient RCT evidence to assess whether surgery is more effective than no treatment. However, there is consensus that surgery is more effective than no treatment, but a trial of surgery versus sham surgery would be unethical.

  Surgery may improve clinical outcomes compared with wrist splints.

  We don't know whether surgery is as effective as local corticosteroid injections in treating CTS.

  Both endoscopic and open carpal tunnel release seem to improve symptoms, although the data are unclear as to which is more beneficial. Both may be associated with several adverse effects.

(i) **Please visit http://clinicalevidence.bmj.com for full text and references**

| What are the effects of drug treatments for carpal tunnel syndrome? | |
|---|---|
| Likely To Be Beneficial | • Corticosteroids (local injection) |
| Unknown Effectiveness | • Diuretics |
| | • NSAIDs |

| What are the effects of non-drug treatments for carpal tunnel syndrome? | |
|---|---|
| Unknown Effectiveness | • Therapeutic ultrasound |
| | • Wrist splints |

## What are the effects of surgical treatments for carpal tunnel syndrome?

| | |
|---|---|
| **Likely To Be Beneficial** | • Surgery (versus no treatment or placebo)* |
| **Trade-off Between Benefits And Harms** | • Endoscopic carpal tunnel release versus open carpal tunnel release (seem equally effective at improving symptoms but both associated with adverse effects)<br><br>• Surgery versus local corticosteroid injection (unclear which is most effective; both associated with adverse effects)<br><br>• Surgery versus wrist splint (surgery more effective but associated with adverse effects) |

**Search date October 2013**

*There is consensus that surgery is effective in people who haven't responded to non-surgical treatment.

**DEFINITION** Carpal tunnel syndrome (CTS) is a collection of clinical symptoms and signs caused by compression of the median nerve within the carpal tunnel. Classical symptoms of CTS include numbness, tingling, burning, or pain in at least two of the three digits supplied by the median nerve (i.e., the thumb and the index and middle fingers). The American Academy of Neurology has described diagnostic criteria that rely on a combination of symptoms and physical examination findings. Other diagnostic criteria include results from electrophysiological studies.

**INCIDENCE/PREVALENCE** A general population survey in Rochester, Minnesota, found the age-adjusted incidence of CTS to be 105 cases (95% CI 99 to 112) per 100,000 person-years. Age-adjusted incidence rates were 52 cases (95% CI 45 to 59) per 100,000 person-years for men and 149 cases (95% CI 138 to 159) per 100,000 person-years for women. The study found that incidence rates increased from 88 cases (95% CI 75 to 101) per 100,000 person-years between 1961 and 1965 to 125 cases (95% CI 112 to 138) per 100,000 person-years between 1976 and 1980. Incidence rates of CTS increased with age for men, whereas for women they peaked between the ages of 45 and 54 years. A general population survey in the Netherlands found prevalence to be 1% for men and 7% for women. A more comprehensive study in southern Sweden found that the general population prevalence for CTS was 3% (95% CI 2% to 3%). As in other studies, the overall prevalence in women was higher than in men (male to female ratio 1.0:1.4); however, among older people, the prevalence in women was almost four times that in men (age group 65–74 years: men 1%, 95% CI 0% to 4%; women 5%, 95% CI 3% to 8%). More than 50% of pregnant women developed symptoms of CTS. However, many trials exclude pregnant women, and we did not identify any RCTs assessing the treatment of pregnancy-induced CTS. The pathophysiology of idiopathic and pregnancy-induced CTS are likely to differ, with one key consideration in pregnancy-induced CTS being fluid retention. Therefore, strategies to reduce fluid retention will probably be of more benefit in pregnancy-induced CTS than they have been shown to be in idiopathic CTS.

**AETIOLOGY/RISK FACTORS** Most cases of CTS have no easily identifiable cause (idiopathic). Secondary causes of CTS include the following: space-occupying lesions (tumours, hypertrophic synovial tissue, fracture callus, and osteophytes), metabolic and physiological (pregnancy, hypothyroidism, and rheumatoid arthritis), infections, neuropathies (associated with diabetes mellitus or alcoholism), and familial disorders. One case-control study found that risk factors in the general population included repetitive activities requiring wrist extension or flexion, obesity, rapid dieting, shorter height, hysterectomy without oophorectomy, and recent menopause.

*(continued over)*

*(from previous page)*

**PROGNOSIS** One observational study (CTS defined by symptoms and electrophysiological study results) found that 34% of people with idiopathic CTS without treatment had complete resolution of symptoms (remission) within 6 months of diagnosis. Remission rates were higher for younger age groups and for women. One observational study in pregnant women found that, in most cases, pregnancy-induced CTS spontaneously improved after delivery. However, some women complained of symptoms of CTS 1 year after delivery. An observational study of untreated idiopathic CTS also found that symptoms can spontaneously resolve in some people. The main positive prognostic indicators were short duration of symptoms and young age, whereas bilateral symptoms and a positive Phalen's test were indicators of a poorer prognosis.

Steven Reid, Trudie Chalder, Anthony Cleare, Matthew Hotopf, and Simon Wessely

## KEY POINTS

- Chronic fatigue syndrome is characterised by severe, disabling fatigue, and other symptoms including musculoskeletal pain, sleep disturbance, impaired concentration, and headaches.

  CFS affects between 0.006% and 3% of the population depending on the criteria used, with women being at higher risk than men.

- Graded exercise therapy has been shown to effectively improve measures of fatigue and physical functioning.

  Educational interventions with encouragement of graded exercise (treatment sessions, telephone follow-ups, and an educational package explaining symptoms and encouraging home-based exercise) improve symptoms more effectively than written information alone.

- CBT is effective in treating chronic fatigue syndrome in adults.

  CBT may also be beneficial when administered by therapists with no specific experience of chronic fatigue syndrome, but who are adequately supervised.

  In adolescents, CBT can reduce fatigue severity and improve school attendance compared with no treatment.

- We don't know how effective antidepressants, corticosteroids, and intramuscular magnesium are in treating chronic fatigue syndrome.

  Antidepressants should be considered in people with affective disorders, and tricyclics in particular have potential therapeutic value because of their analgesic properties.

- Interventions such as dietary supplements, evening primrose oil, oral nicotinamide adenine dinucleotide, homeopathy, and prolonged rest have not been studied in enough detail in RCTs for us to draw conclusions on their efficacy.

- Based on a single large RCT galantamine seems no better than placebo at improving symptoms of chronic fatigue syndrome.

- Although there is some RCT evidence that immunotherapy can improve symptoms compared with placebo, it is associated with considerable adverse effects, and should therefore probably not be offered as a treatment for chronic fatigue.

(i) **Please visit http://clinicalevidence.bmj.com for full text and references**

| What are the effects of treatments for chronic fatigue syndrome? | |
|---|---|
| Beneficial | • CBT |
| | • Graded exercise therapy |
| Unknown Effectiveness | • Antidepressants |
| | • Corticosteroids |
| | • Dietary supplements |
| | • Evening primrose oil |
| | • Homeopathy |
| | • Magnesium (intramuscular) |
| | • Nicotinamide adenine dinucleotide (oral) |

| | |
|---|---|
| | • Prolonged rest |
| **Unlikely To Be Beneficial** | • Galantamine |
| **Likely To Be Ineffective Or Harmful** | • Immunotherapy |

**Search date March 2010**

**DEFINITION** Chronic fatigue syndrome (CFS) is characterised by severe, disabling fatigue, and other symptoms, including musculoskeletal pain, sleep disturbance, impaired concentration, and headaches. Two widely used definitions of CFS, from the US Centers for Disease Control and Prevention (CDC; current criteria issued in 1994, which superseded the CDC criteria issued in 1988) and from Oxford, UK, were developed as operational criteria for research. The principal difference between these definitions is the number and severity of symptoms, other than fatigue, that must be present. A third operational definition, the Australian criteria, is similar to the CDC diagnostic criteria, and has also been used in treatment trials. The 1994 CDC criteria were reviewed with the aim of improving case ascertainment for research. The exclusion criteria were clarified, and the use of specific instruments for the assessment of symptoms was recommended.

**INCIDENCE/PREVALENCE** Community-based and primary-care-based studies have reported the prevalence of CFS to be from 0.007% to 2.8% in the general adult population, and from 0.006% to 3.0% in primary care, depending on the criteria used.

**AETIOLOGY/RISK FACTORS** Despite considerable research effort and several hypotheses, the cause of CFS remains poorly understood. Endocrine and immunological abnormalities have been found in many people, although it is unclear whether these changes are causal, or are part of the course of the syndrome. Certain infectious illnesses, such as Epstein–Barr virus, Q fever, and viral meningitis, are associated with a greater risk of developing CFS, but many people have no evidence of viral infection, and there is no evidence of persistent infection. People with prior psychiatric disorders are more likely to report with CFS later in life (OR 2.7, 95% CI 1.3 to 5.6). Women are at higher risk than men (RR 1.3–1.7, depending on diagnostic criteria used; CIs not reported). Population surveys in the US have found that white people have a lower risk of CFS compared with Latin Americans, African-Americans, and Native Americans.

**PROGNOSIS** Studies have focused on people attending specialist clinics. A systematic review of studies of prognosis (search date 1996) found that children with CFS had better outcomes than adults: 54% to 94% of children showed definite improvement in symptoms (after up to 6 years' follow-up), whereas 20% to 50% of adults showed some improvement in the medium term (12–39 months) and only 6% returned to premorbid levels of functioning. Despite the considerable burden of morbidity associated with CFS, we found no evidence of increased mortality. The systematic review found that a longer duration of illness, fatigue severity, comorbid depression and anxiety, and a physical attribution for CFS are factors associated with a poorer prognosis. A more recent review found a median full recovery rate of 5% (range 0–31%), and the median proportion of patients who improved during follow-up to be 39.5% (range 8–63%). Good outcome was associated with less fatigue severity at baseline, a sense of control over symptoms, and not attributing the illness to a physical cause.

Peter Vestergaard, Leif Mosekilde, and Bente Langdahl

## KEY POINTS

- The lifetime risk of fracture in white women is 20% for the spine, 15% for the wrist, and 18% for the hip, with an exponential increase in risk beyond the age of 50 years.

  About 13% of people die in the year after a hip fracture, and most survivors lose some or all of their previous independence.

- Alendronate, risedronate, zoledronate, denosumab, and parathyroid hormone reduce vertebral and non-vertebral fractures compared with placebo.

  Etidronate, ibandronate, pamidronate, and raloxifene reduce vertebral fractures, but have not been shown to reduce non-vertebral fractures.

  Raloxifene protects against breast cancer, but increases venous thrombo-embolic events and stroke compared with placebo.

  Strontium ranelate reduces vertebral and, to some extent, non-vertebral fractures.

  Clodronate may reduce non-vertebral fractures at 3 years, but its effects on rate of vertebral fracture are unclear.

- CAUTION: Hormone replacement therapy may reduce fractures, but it increases the risk of breast cancer and cardiovascular events. The risks of adverse effects of treatment are thought to outweigh the beneficial effects of hormone replacement therapy in prevention of fractures.

- Combined calcium plus vitamin D or vitamin D analogues alone may reduce vertebral and non-vertebral fractures, but trials have given inconclusive results.

  Monotherapy with calcium or vitamin D has not been shown to reduce fractures, and calcium alone may potentially be associated with an increased risk of cardiovascular adverse effects.

- We don't know whether multifactorial non-pharmacological interventions including environmental manipulation or regular exercise reduce the risk of fractures.

  Hip protectors may reduce the risk of hip fractures in nursing-home residents, but compliance tends to be low.

- Calcitonin was included in an earlier version of this review. However, in light of a drug alert (http://www.ema.europa.eu/ema/) it was removed from this version because of new harms data. It will be covered in the next update of this review when these new harms data can be incorporated.

(i) **Please visit http://clinicalevidence.bmj.com for full text and references**

## What are the effects of bisphosphonates to prevent fractures in postmenopausal women?

| Beneficial | • Alendronate |
| | • Risedronate |
| | • Zoledronate |
| Likely To Be Beneficial | • Clodronate |
| | • Etidronate |
| | • Ibandronate |
| Unknown Effectiveness | • Pamidronate |

## What are the effects of pharmacological treatments other than bisphosphonates to prevent fractures in postmenopausal women?

| Beneficial | • Denosumab<br>• Parathyroid hormone<br>• Strontium ranelate |
|---|---|
| Likely To Be Beneficial | • Calcium plus vitamin D<br>• Vitamin D analogues (alfacalcidol or calcitriol) |
| Trade-off Between Benefits And Harms | • Raloxifene |
| Unlikely To Be Beneficial | • Vitamin D alone |
| Likely To Be Ineffective Or Harmful | • Calcium alone<br>• Hormone replacement therapy |

## What are the effects of non-pharmacological treatments to prevent fractures in postmenopausal women?

| Likely To Be Beneficial | • Hip protectors (likely to be beneficial in people in residential homes or nursing homes) |
|---|---|
| Unknown Effectiveness | • Exercise<br>• Multifactorial non-pharmacological interventions |

**Search date September 2010**

**DEFINITION** This review covers interventions to prevent fractures in postmenopausal women. A fracture is a break or disruption of bone or cartilage, and may be symptomatic or asymptomatic. Symptoms and signs may include immobility, pain, tenderness, numbness, bruising, joint deformity, joint swelling, limb deformity, and limb shortening. **Diagnosis:** Fracture is usually diagnosed on the basis of a typical clinical picture (see above) combined with results from an appropriate imaging technique. Usually, in trials dealing with osteoporosis, menopause is considered to be present 12 months after the last menstruation.

**INCIDENCE/PREVALENCE** The lifetime risk of fracture in white women is 20% for the spine, 15% for the wrist, and 18% for the hip. The incidence of postmenopausal fracture increases with age. Observational studies found that age-specific incidence rates for postmenopausal fracture of the hip increased exponentially beyond the age of 50 years. The incidence of fractures varies by ethnic group. The incidence of hip fractures is highest in white people and decreases successively in Hispanic, Asian, and African-American people. Publications have suggested that a decrease in the incidence of hip fractures has taken place.

**AETIOLOGY/RISK FACTORS** A fracture arises when load to the bone exceeds bone biomechanical competence (strength). Fractures usually arise from trauma, but may arise without any apparent injury. Risk factors are those factors that increase the risk of trauma, and that decrease bone biomechanical competence. An increased risk of trauma exists when the risk of falls is increased, such as in people with impaired vision, decreased postural balance, or neurological disorders (e.g., ataxia, stroke, epilepsy). Factors that decrease bone biomechanical competence, and so induce osteoporosis, include increasing age, low body mass index or weight, genetic predisposition, diseases (e.g., hyperthyroidism, hyperparathyroidism, and rheumatoid arthritis), drugs (e.g., corticosteroids), and environmental factors (e.g., smoking). Postmenopausal women are at increased risk of fracture compared with premenopausal women and men of all ages because of hormone-related bone loss.

**PROGNOSIS** Fractures may result in pain, short- or long-term disability, haemorrhage, thromboembolic disease (see thromboembolism review, p 58), shock, and death. Vertebral fractures are associated with pain, physical impairment, muscular atrophy, changes in body shape, loss of physical function, and lower quality of life. About 13% of people die in the first year after a hip fracture, representing a doubling of mortality compared with people of similar age and no hip fracture. Half of all older women who have previously been independent become partly dependent after hip fracture. One third becomes totally dependent. One systematic review (search date 2008, 8 RCTs) suggested that treatments for osteoporosis reduced mortality independent of the effect on hip fracture incidence.

Martin Underwood

## KEY POINTS

- Gout is characterised by deposition of urate crystals, causing acute monoarthritis and crystal deposits (tophi).

  Gout affects about 5% of men and 1% of women, with up to 80% of people experiencing a recurrent attack within 3 years.

  Definitive gout diagnosis is based on crystal identification in synovial fluid or tophus material. However, in routine practice, diagnosis is usually made clinically, supported by the presence of hyperuricaemia.

  Risk factors are those associated with hyperuricaemia, including older age; non-white ethnicity; obesity; excess consumption of alcohol, meat, and fish; and use of diuretics.

  Hyperuricaemia and gout may be independent risk factors for cardiovascular disease.

- There is a lack of evidence from RCTs on the effectiveness of non-steroidal anti-inflammatory drugs (NSAIDs) to reduce pain and tenderness in an acute attack of gout, although they are commonly used in clinical practice. They are associated with increased risks of gastrointestinal, and possible cardiovascular, adverse effects.

  Indometacin may be more effective than celecoxib, and equally effective as etoricoxib, at reducing pain in people with acute gout, although indometacin may be associated with an increased risk of adverse effects compared with etoricoxib.

- Colchicine may be more effective than placebo at improving symptoms in acute gout. Its use is limited by the high incidence of adverse effects, although these may be reduced with low-dose colchicine regimens.

  Low-dose colchicine may also be effective at reducing pain in gout and may produce fewer adverse effects than high-dose colchicine.

- There is a lack of evidence from RCTs concerning the effectiveness of intra-articular or parenteral corticosteroids to improve symptoms in acute gout.

  Oral corticosteroids seem as effective as NSAIDs and may have fewer short-term adverse events.

- It's not clear from the evidence from RCTs if xanthine oxidase inhibitors are effective at reducing the risk of recurrent attacks in the long term when compared with placebo or other treatments. Higher doses of febuxostat may increase the risks of gout attacks compared with placebo, and compared with allopurinol.

  Colchicine may reduce the risk of an attack in a person starting allopurinol treatment.

(i) **Please visit http://clinicalevidence.bmj.com for full text and references**

## What are the effects of treatments for acute gout?

| Likely To Be Beneficial | • Colchicine (oral) for treating acute gout (may be more effective than placebo; however, use, particularly of high-dose regimens, may be limited by adverse effects) |
|---|---|
| Unknown Effectiveness | • Corticosteroids <br> • NSAIDs |

## What are the effects of xanthine oxidase inhibitors to prevent gout in people with prior acute episodes?

| Unknown Effectiveness | • Xanthine oxidase inhibitors |
|---|---|

**Search date September 2013**

**DEFINITION** Gout is a syndrome caused by deposition of urate crystals. It typically presents as an acute monoarthritis of rapid onset. The first metatarsophalangeal joint is the most commonly affected joint (podagra). Gout also affects other joints; joints in the foot, ankle, knee, wrist, finger, and elbow are the most frequently affected. Crystal deposits (tophi) may develop around hands, feet, elbows, and ears. **Diagnosis:** Definitive gout diagnosis is based on crystal identification in synovial fluid or tophus material. However, in routine practice, diagnosis is usually made clinically, supported by presence of hyperuricaemia. The American College of Rheumatology (ACR) criteria for diagnosing gout are as follows: (1) characteristic urate crystals in joint fluid; (2) a tophus proved to contain urate crystals; or (3) the presence of six or more defined clinical laboratory and x-ray phenomena. We have included studies of people meeting the ACR criteria, studies in which the diagnosis was made clinically, and studies that used other criteria. Where possible, we have reported the study entry criteria.

**INCIDENCE/PREVALENCE** Gout is more common in older people and men. In people aged 65 to 74 years in the UK, the prevalence is about 50/1000 in men and about 9/1000 in women. The annual incidence of gout in people aged over 50 years in the US is 1.6/1000 in men and 0.3/1000 in women. One 12-year longitudinal study of 47,150 male health professionals with no previous history of gout estimated that annual incidence of gout ranged from 1.0/1000 for those aged 40 to 44 years to 1.8/1000 for those aged 55 to 64 years. The global prevalence of gout is 0.076% (95% uncertainty interval 0.072% to 0.082%). There are wide regional variations in prevalence. The highest prevalence is in Australasia (0.389%, 95% uncertainty interval 0.354% to 0.428%). This compares with a prevalence of 0.205% in Western Europe (95% uncertainty interval 0.178% to 0.245%) and 0.242% in North American high-income countries (95% uncertainty interval 0.217% to 0.279%). Gout may be becoming more common because of increasing longevity, obesity, meat and fish consumption, and use of diuretics. Although there has been little change in global (age-standardised) prevalence, the disability-adjusted life years (DALYs) attributable to gout increased by 49% from 76,000 (95% credibility interval 48,000 to 112,000) in 1990 to 114,000 (95% credibility interval 72,000 to 167,000) in 2010. In the global burden of disease 2010 study, gout was ranked 173 out of 291 conditions studied for overall burden (DALYs).

**AETIOLOGY/RISK FACTORS** Urate crystals form when serum urate concentration exceeds 0.42 mmol/L. Serum urate concentration is the principal risk factor for a first attack of gout, although 40% of people have normal serum urate concentration during an attack of gout. A cohort study of 2046 men followed up for about 15 years found that the annual incidence was about 0.4% in men with a urate concentration of 0.42 mmol/L to 0.47 mmol/L, rising to 4.3% when serum urate concentration was 0.45 mmol/L to 0.59 mmol/L. One 5-year longitudinal study of 223 asymptomatic men with hyperuricaemia estimated the 5-year cumulative incidence of gout to be 11% for those with baseline serum urate of 0.42 mmol/L to 0.47 mmol/L, 28% for baseline urate of 0.48 mmol/L to 0.53 mmol/L, and 61% for baseline urate levels of 0.54 mmol/L or more. The study found that a 0.6 mmol/L difference in baseline serum urate increased the odds of an attack of gout by a factor of 1.8 (OR adjusted for other risk factors for gout: 1.84, 95% CI 1.24 to 2.72). One 12-year longitudinal study (47,150 male health professionals with no history of gout) estimated that the relative risks of gout associated with one additional daily serving of various foods (weekly for seafood) were as follows: meat 1.21 (95% CI 1.04 to 1.41), seafood (fish, lobster, and shellfish) 1.07 (95% CI 1.01 to 1.12), purine-rich vegetables 0.97 (95% CI 0.79 to 1.19), low-fat dairy products 0.79 (95% CI 0.71 to 0.87), and high-fat dairy products 0.99 (95% CI 0.89 to 1.10). Alcohol consumption of more than 14.9 g daily significantly increased the risk of gout compared with no alcohol consumption (RR for 15.0–29.9 g/day 1.49, 95% CI 1.14 to 1.94; RR for 30.0–49.9 g/day 1.96, 95% CI 1.48 to 2.60; RR for at least 50 g/day 2.53,

*(continued over)*

*(from previous page)*

95% CI 1.73 to 3.70). The longitudinal study also estimated the relative risk of gout associated with an additional serving of beer (355 mL, 12.8 g alcohol), wine (118 mL, 11.0 g alcohol), and spirits (44 mL, 14.0 g alcohol). It found that an extra daily serving of beer or spirits was significantly associated with gout, but an extra daily serving of wine was not (RR for 355 mL/day beer 1.49, 95% CI 1.32 to 1.70; RR for 44 mL/day spirits 1.15, 95% CI 1.04 to 1.28; RR for 118 mL/day wine 1.04, 95% CI 0.88 to 1.22). Other suggested risk factors for gout include obesity, insulin resistance, dyslipidaemia, hypertension, dietary fructose intake, and cardiovascular disorders. Both hyperuricaemia and gout appear to be independently associated with cardiovascular and all-cause mortality in 2010.

**PROGNOSIS** We found few reliable data about prognosis or complications of gout. One study found that 3 of 11 (27%) people with untreated gout of the first metatarsophalangeal joint had spontaneous resolution after 7 days. A case series of 614 people with gout who had not received treatment to reduce urate levels, and who could recall the interval between first and second attacks, reported recurrence rates of 62% after 1 year, 78% after 2 years, and 84% after 3 years.

Jill Ferrari

## KEY POINTS

- Hallux valgus (bunions) are prominent and often inflamed metatarsal heads and overlying bursae, which cause pain and problems with walking and wearing normal shoes.

  Hallux valgus (where the great toe moves towards the second toe) is found in at least 2% of children aged 9 to 10 years and almost half of adults, with greater prevalence in women.

  We don't know what role footwear plays in the development of hallux valgus.

- We don't know whether night splints or orthoses (in adults or children) prevent deterioration of hallux valgus.

- Distal chevron osteotomy may be more effective than orthoses or no treatment at reducing pain and improving function. However, we found insufficient evidence comparing its effectiveness with scarf osteotomy and other types of distal or proximal osteotomies.

- We don't know whether minimally invasive surgery (percutaneous distal metatarsal osteotomy, SERI [Simple, Effective, Rapid, Inexpensive] distal metatarsal osteotomy) is beneficial in improving outcomes compared with non-minimally invasive types of osteotomy as we found insufficient evidence.

- We don't know whether other surgical procedures such as phalangeal (Akin) osteotomy or proximal osteotomy are beneficial in improving outcomes.

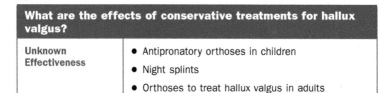 Please visit http://clinicalevidence.bmj.com for full text and references

| What are the effects of conservative treatments for hallux valgus? | |
|---|---|
| Unknown Effectiveness | • Antipronatory orthoses in children<br>• Night splints<br>• Orthoses to treat hallux valgus in adults |

| What are the effects of osteotomy for hallux valgus? | |
|---|---|
| Likely To Be Beneficial | • Distal chevron osteotomy (more effective than no treatment or orthoses, but insufficient evidence to compare with scarf osteotomy and other types of distal or proximal osteotomies) |
| Unknown Effectiveness | • Chevron osteotomy plus adductor tenotomy versus chevron osteotomy alone<br><br>• Minimally invasive surgery (percutaneous distal metatarsal osteotomy, SERI [Simple, Effective, Rapid, Inexpensive] distal metatarsal osteotomy)<br><br>• Phalangeal (Akin) osteotomy plus distal chevron osteotomy<br><br>• Proximal chevron osteotomy versus other types of proximal osteotomy<br><br>• Proximal osteotomy versus distal chevron osteotomy |

Search date October 2013

**DEFINITION** **Hallux valgus** is a deformity of the great toe, whereby the hallux (great toe) moves towards the second toe, overlying it in severe cases. This abduction (movement away from the midline of the body) is usually accompanied by some rotation of the toe so that the nail is facing the midline of the body (valgus rotation). With the deformity, the metatarsal head becomes more prominent, and the metatarsal is said to be in an adducted position as it moves towards the midline of the body. Radiological criteria for hallux valgus vary, but a commonly accepted criterion is to measure the angle formed between the metatarsal and the abducted hallux. This is called the metatarsophalangeal joint angle (also known as the hallux valgus angle, and hallux abductus angle), and it is considered abnormal when it is greater than 14.5°. **Bunion** is the lay term used to describe a prominent and often inflamed metatarsal head and overlying bursa. Symptoms include pain, limitation in walking, and problems with wearing normal shoes.

**INCIDENCE/PREVALENCE** The prevalence of hallux valgus varies in different populations. In a study of 6000 UK school children aged 9 to 10 years, 2.5% had clinical evidence of hallux valgus, and 2% met both clinical and radiological criteria for hallux valgus. An earlier study found hallux valgus in 48% of adults. Differences in prevalence may result from different methods of measurement, varying age groups, or different diagnostic criteria (e.g., older studies generally used a metatarsal joint angle of >10° as a diagnostic criterion, but more recent studies have used a threshold of >15°).

**AETIOLOGY/RISK FACTORS** Nearly all population studies have found that hallux valgus is more common in women. Footwear may contribute to the deformity, but studies comparing people who wear shoes with those who do not have found contradictory results. Hypermobility of the first ray and excessive foot pronation are associated with hallux valgus.

**PROGNOSIS** Prognosis seems uncertain. While progression of deformity and symptoms is rapid in some people, others remain asymptomatic. One study found that hallux valgus is often unilateral initially, but usually progresses to bilateral deformity.

Jo Jordan, Kika Konstantinou, and John O'Dowd

## KEY POINTS

- Herniated lumbar disc is a displacement of disc material (nucleus pulposus or annulus fibrosis) beyond the intervertebral disc space.

  The highest prevalence is among people aged 30 to 50 years, with a male to female ratio of 2:1.

- There is little high-quality evidence to suggest that drug treatments are effective in treating herniated disc.

  NSAIDs and cytokine inhibitors do not seem to improve symptoms of sciatica caused by disc herniation.

  We found no RCT evidence examining the effects of analgesics, antidepressants, or muscle relaxants in people with herniated disc.

  We found several RCTs that assessed a range of different measures of symptom improvement and found inconsistent results, so we are unable to draw conclusions on effects of epidural injections of corticosteroids.

- With regard to non-drug treatments, spinal manipulation seems more effective at relieving local or radiating pain in people with acute back pain and sciatica with disc protrusion compared with sham manipulation, although concerns exist regarding possible further herniation from spinal manipulation in people who are surgical candidates.

  Neither bed rest nor traction seem effective in treating people with sciatica caused by disc herniation.

  We found insufficient RCT evidence about advice to stay active, acupuncture, massage, exercise, heat, or ice to judge their efficacy in treating people with herniated disc.

- About 10% of people have sufficient pain after 6 weeks for surgery to become a consideration.

  Standard discectomy and microdiscectomy seem to increase self-reported improvement to a similar extent.

  We found insufficient evidence judging the effects of automated percutaneous discectomy, laser discectomy, or percutaneous disc decompression.

 **Please visit http://clinicalevidence.bmj.com for full text and references**

| What are the effects of drug treatments for herniated lumbar disc? | |
|---|---|
| Unknown Effectiveness | • Analgesics |
| | • Antidepressants |
| | • Corticosteroids (epidural injections) |
| | • Cytokine inhibitors |
| | • Muscle relaxants |
| Unlikely To Be Beneficial | • NSAIDs |

## What are the effects of non-drug treatments for herniated lumbar disc?

| Likely To Be Beneficial | • Spinal manipulation |
| --- | --- |
| Unknown Effectiveness | • Acupuncture<br>• Advice to stay active<br>• Exercise therapy<br>• Heat<br>• Ice<br>• Massage |
| Unlikely To Be Beneficial | • Bed rest<br>• Traction |

## What are the effects of surgery for herniated lumbar disc?

| Likely To Be Beneficial | • Microdiscectomy (as effective as standard discectomy)<br>• Standard discectomy (short-term benefit) |
| --- | --- |
| Unknown Effectiveness | • Automated percutaneous discectomy<br>• Laser discectomy<br>• Percutaneous disc decompression |

**Search date June 2010**

**DEFINITION** Herniated lumbar disc is a displacement of disc material (nucleus pulposus or annulus fibrosis) beyond the intervertebral disc space. The diagnosis can be confirmed by radiological examination. However, MRI findings of herniated disc are not always accompanied by clinical symptoms. This review covers treatment of people with clinical symptoms relating to confirmed or suspected disc herniation. It does not include treatment of people with spinal cord compression, or people with cauda equina syndrome, which require emergency intervention. The management of non-specific acute low back pain, p 390 and chronic low back pain, p 392 are covered elsewhere in *Clinical Evidence*.

**INCIDENCE/PREVALENCE** The prevalence of symptomatic herniated lumbar disc is about 1% to 3% in Finland and Italy, depending on age and sex. The highest prevalence is among people aged 30 to 50 years, with a male to female ratio of 2:1. In people aged 25 to 55 years, about 95% of herniated discs occur at the lower lumbar spine (L4/5 and L5/S1 level); disc herniation above this level is more common in people aged over 55 years.

**AETIOLOGY/RISK FACTORS** Radiographical evidence of disc herniation does not reliably predict low back pain in the future, or correlate with symptoms; 19% to 27% of people without symptoms have disc herniation on imaging. Risk factors for disc herniation include smoking (OR 1.7, 95% CI 1.0 to 2.5), weight-bearing sports (e.g., weight lifting, hammer throw), and certain work activities, such as repeated lifting. Driving a motor vehicle has been suggested to be a risk factor for disc herniation, although evidence is inconclusive (OR 1.7, 95% CI 0.2 to 2.7).

**PROGNOSIS** The natural history of disc herniation is difficult to determine, because most people take some form of treatment for their back pain, and a formal diagnosis is not always made. Clinical improvement is usual in most people, and only about 10% of people still have sufficient pain after 6 weeks to consider surgery. Sequential MRIs have shown that the herniated portion of the disc tends to regress over time, with partial to complete resolution after 6 months in two-thirds of people.

David Oliver, Richard Griffiths, James Roche, and Opinder Sahota

## KEY POINTS

- Between 12% and 37% of people will die in the year after a hip fracture, and 10% to 20% of survivors will move into a more dependent residence.

- Surgery is routinely used in the treatment of hip fracture.

    Surgical fixation leads to earlier mobilisation and less leg deformity compared with conservative treatment.

    In people with intracapsular hip fracture, internal fixation is associated with less operative trauma and deep wound sepsis, but is more likely to require subsequent revision surgery, compared with arthroplasty. We don't know the best method for internal fixation, or the best method of arthroplasty, for these fractures.

    Older fixed nail plates for extramedullary fixation of extracapsular fracture increase the risk of fixation failure compared with sliding hip screws. Short intramedullary cephalocondylic nails, Ender nails, and older fixed nail plates increase the risk of re-operation compared with extramedullary fixation with a sliding hip screw device, but we don't know whether other kinds of extramedullary devices are better than the sliding hip screw. We also don't know how different intramedullary devices compare with each other.

- Various perisurgical interventions may be used with the aim of improving surgical outcome and preventing complications.

    Routine preoperative traction to the injured limb has not been shown to relieve pain or to aid subsequent surgery.

    Antibiotic prophylaxis reduces wound infections, but we don't know which is the most effective regimen (regimens assessed are antibiotics given on the day of surgery and single-dose antibiotics versus multiple-dose regimens).

    Antiplatelet agents and heparin reduce the risk of deep vein thrombosis (DVT) when used prophylactically, but both treatments increase the risk of bleeding. We don't know how low molecular weight heparin and unfractionated heparin compare at reducing risk of DVT.

    Cyclical compression devices also reduce the risk of DVT, but we don't know whether graduated elastic compression stockings are effective.

    Oral protein and energy multinutrient feeds may reduce unfavourable outcomes after surgery.

    We don't know whether nerve blocks are effective in reducing pain post-surgery or the pain or requirement for analgesia after surgery. We don't how different anaesthetic regimens compare with each other.

    We don't know whether nasogastric feeds for nutritional supplementation are effective at improving outcomes after hip fracture.

- Various rehabilitation interventions and programmes aim to improve recovery after a hip fracture.

    Coordinated multidisciplinary care may improve outcomes compared with usual care, but we don't know which method is best.

    We don't know how effective mobilisation strategies, early supported discharge, or multidisciplinary home-based rehabilitation are at improving outcomes after hip surgery.

(i) **Please visit http://clinicalevidence.bmj.com for full text and references**

### What are the effects of surgical interventions in people with hip fracture?

| | |
|---|---|
| **Trade-off Between Benefits And Harms** | • Internal fixation versus arthroplasty for intracapsular hip fracture |
| **Unknown Effectiveness** | • Arthroplasties for intracapsular hip fracture versus each other<br>• Arthroplasty versus internal fixation for extracapsular hip fracture<br>• External fixation for extracapsular fracture<br>• Extramedullary implants (other than older fixed nail plates) versus sliding hip screw for extracapsular fracture<br>• Implants for internal fixation of intracapsular hip fracture versus each other<br>• Intramedullary fixation devices versus each other for extracapsular hip fracture (various intramedullary devices seem to be as effective as each other at improving postoperative outcomes) |
| **Unlikely To Be Beneficial** | • Conservative versus operative treatment for most types of hip fracture<br>• Intramedullary fixation with short cephalocondylic nail versus extramedullary fixation with sliding hip screw for extracapsular hip fracture (short cephalocondylic nails are associated with higher risk of fracture fixation complications) |
| **Likely To Be Ineffective Or Harmful** | • Intramedullary fixation with condylocephalic nails versus extramedullary fixation with sliding hip screw or fixed nail plate for extracapsular fracture<br>• Older fixed nail plates for extramedullary fixation of extracapsular fracture (increased risk of fixation failure compared with sliding hip screws) |

### What are the effects of perisurgical medical interventions on surgical outcome and prevention of complications in people with hip fracture?

| | |
|---|---|
| **Beneficial** | • Perioperative prophylaxis with antibiotics |
| **Likely To Be Beneficial** | • Cyclical compression of the foot or calf to reduce venous thromboembolism<br>• Oral multinutrient feeds for nutritional supplementation after hip fracture<br>• Perioperative prophylaxis with antiplatelet agents |
| **Trade-off Between Benefits And Harms** | • Perioperative prophylaxis with heparin to reduce venous thromboembolism |
| **Unknown Effectiveness** | • Graduated elastic compression to prevent venous thromboembolism |

|  | • Low molecular weight heparin versus unfractionated heparin to reduce venous thromboembolism after hip fracture surgery |
|  | • Nasogastric feeds for nutritional supplementation after hip fracture |
|  | • Nerve blocks for pain control before and after hip fracture |
|  | • Operative-day (<24 hours) versus longer-duration multiple-dose antibiotic regimens |
|  | • Regional versus general anaesthesia for hip fracture surgery |
|  | • Single-dose (long-acting) versus multiple-dose antibiotic regimens |
| **Unlikely To Be Beneficial** | • Preoperative traction to the injured limb |

## What are the effects of rehabilitation interventions and programmes after hip fracture?

| **Likely To Be Beneficial** | • Coordinated multidisciplinary approaches for inpatient rehabilitation of older people |
| **Unknown Effectiveness** | • Early supported discharge followed by home-based rehabilitation |
|  | • Mobilisation strategies applied soon after hip fracture surgery |
|  | • Systematic multicomponent home-based rehabilitation |

**Search date April 2009**

**DEFINITION** A hip or proximal femoral fracture refers to any fracture of the femur from the hip joint articular cartilage to a point 5 cm below the distal part of the lesser trochanter. Femoral head fractures are not included within this definition. Hip fractures are divided into two groups according to their relationship to the capsular attachments of the hip joint. **Intracapsular fractures** occur proximal to the point at which the hip joint capsule attaches to the femur, and can be subdivided into displaced and undisplaced fractures. Undisplaced fractures include impacted and adduction fractures. Displaced intracapsular fractures may be associated with disruption of the blood supply to the head of the femur, leading to avascular necrosis. **Extracapsular fractures** occur distal to the hip joint capsule. In the most distal part of the proximal femoral segment (below the lesser trochanter), the term 'subtrochanteric' fracture is used. Numerous further subclassifications of intracapsular and extracapsular fractures exist.

**INCIDENCE/PREVALENCE** Hip fractures may occur at any age, but are most common in older people (here defined as people aged 65 years and over). In industrialised societies, the mean age of people with hip fracture is about 80 years, and about 80% are female. In the US, the lifetime risk of hip fracture after 50 years of age is about 17% in white women and 6% in white men. A study in the US reported that prevalence increases from about 3/100 women aged 65 to 74 years to 12.6/100 women aged 85 years and above. The age-stratified incidence has also increased in some societies — not only are people living longer, but the incidence of fracture in each age group may have increased. An estimated 1.26 million hip fractures occurred in adults in 1990, with predictions of numbers rising to 7.3 million to 21.3 million by 2050.

**AETIOLOGY/RISK FACTORS** Hip fractures are usually sustained through a fall from standing height or less. The pattern of incidence is consistent with an increased risk of falling, loss of protective reflex mechanisms, and loss of skeletal strength from osteoporosis. All of these increased risks are associated with ageing.

**PROGNOSIS** Reported figures for mortality after a hip fracture in adults vary considerably. One-year mortality figures vary from 12% to 37%, with about 9% of these deaths directly attributed to the hip fracture. After a hip fracture, a 15% to 25% decline in the ability to perform daily activities is to be expected, and about 10% to 20% of the survivors will require a change to a more dependent residential status.

Gavin Young

## KEY POINTS

- Involuntary, localised leg cramps are common and typically affect the calf muscles at night.

    The causes of leg cramps are unclear, but risk factors include pregnancy, exercise, salt and electrolyte imbalances, disorders affecting peripheral nerves or blood vessels, renal dialysis, and some drugs.

- This review examined RCTs on the effects of interventions on idiopathic leg cramps and leg cramps in pregnancy. Overall, many of the RCTs were small and had weak methods.

- Idiopathic leg cramps:

- Quinine reduces the frequency of idiopathic leg cramps at night compared with placebo.

    CAUTION: quinine may be associated with cardiac arrhythmias, thrombocytopenia, and severe hypersensitivity reactions. It is a known teratogen and the risks are not outweighed by any potential benefits of its use in pregnancy. It may also be associated with fatal adverse effects.

- We don't know whether analgesics, anti-epileptic drugs, diltiazem, magnesium salts, stretching exercises, verapamil, vitamin B6, or vitamin E reduce idiopathic leg cramps.

- Leg cramps in pregnancy:

- We don't know whether magnesium is more effective than placebo at reducing leg cramps in pregnancy.

    The RCT evidence was weak and contradictory. Further well-conducted RCTs are needed.

- We don't know whether calcium salts, multivitamins and mineral supplements, sodium chloride, vitamin B6, or vitamin E reduce leg cramps in pregnant women.

(i) **Please visit http://clinicalevidence.bmj.com for full text and references**

| What are the effects of treatments for idiopathic leg cramps? | |
|---|---|
| **Trade-off Between Benefits And Harms** | • Quinine (may reduce leg cramps, but may be associated with occasional severe adverse effects) |
| **Unknown Effectiveness** | • Analgesics<br>• Anti-epileptic drugs<br>• Diltiazem<br>• Magnesium salts<br>• Stretching exercises<br>• Verapamil<br>• Vitamin B6 (pyridoxine)<br>• Vitamin E |

| What are the effects of treatments for leg cramps in pregnancy? | |
|---|---|
| **Unknown Effectiveness** | • Calcium salts |

- Magnesium salts (1 trial found some benefit, 2 other trials found no benefit, evidence is weak and unclear)
- Multivitamins and mineral supplements
- Sodium chloride
- Vitamin B6 (pyridoxine)
- Vitamin E

**Search date January 2014**

**DEFINITION** Leg cramps are involuntary, localised, and usually painful skeletal muscle contractions, which commonly affect calf muscles but can occur anywhere in the leg from foot up to the thigh. Leg cramps typically occur at night and usually last only seconds to minutes. Leg cramps may be idiopathic (of unknown cause) or may be associated with a definable process or condition such as pregnancy, renal dialysis, or venous insufficiency. This review does not currently cover leg cramps associated with renal dialysis or venous insufficiency.

**INCIDENCE/PREVALENCE** Leg cramps are common and their incidence increases with age. About half of people attending a general medicine clinic have had leg cramps within 1 month of their visit, and more than two-thirds of people aged over 50 years have experienced leg cramps.

**AETIOLOGY/RISK FACTORS** Little is known about the causes of leg cramps. Risk factors include pregnancy, exercise, electrolyte imbalances, salt depletion, renal dialysis, peripheral vascular disease (both venous and arterial), peripheral nerve injury, polyneuropathies, motor neurone disease, and certain drugs (including beta agonists and potassium-sparing diuretics). Other causes of acute calf pain include trauma, DVT (see review on Thromboembolism), p 58, and ruptured Baker's cyst.

**PROGNOSIS** Leg cramps may cause severe pain and sleep disturbance.

# Low back pain (acute): non-drug treatments

Greg McIntosh and Hamilton Hall

## KEY POINTS

- Low back pain is pain, muscle tension, or stiffness, localised below the costal margin and above the inferior gluteal folds, with or without referred or radicular leg pain (sciatica), and is defined as acute when pain persists for less than 12 weeks.

  Low back pain affects about 70% of people in resource-rich countries at some point in their lives.

  Acute low back pain may be self-limiting, although there is a high recurrence rate with less-painful symptoms recurring in 50% to 80% of people within 1 year of the initial episode; 1 year later, as many as 33% of people still experience moderate-intensity pain and 15% experience severe pain.

- We searched for evidence of effectiveness from RCTs and systematic reviews of RCTs.

- With regard to non-drug treatments, advice to stay active (be it as a single treatment or in combination with other interventions such as back schools, a graded activity programme, or behavioural counselling) may be effective.

- There is conflicting evidence as to whether spinal manipulation improves pain or function compared with sham treatments.

- We found insufficient evidence to judge the effectiveness of acupuncture, massage, multidisciplinary treatment programmes (for either acute or subacute low back pain), TENS, or temperature treatments in treating people with acute low back pain.

- Back exercises may decrease recovery time compared with no treatment, but there is considerable heterogeneity among studies with regard to the definition of back exercise. There is a large disparity in results among studies of generic exercise and among those of specific back exercise.

- Overall, the literature is full of methodological limitations. Inadequate design and reporting of trials frequently produce low- or very low-quality evidence. The results are often inconclusive, insufficient, or contradictory.

 **Please visit http://clinicalevidence.bmj.com for full text and references**

| What are the effects of non-drug treatments for acute low back pain? | |
|---|---|
| **Likely To Be Beneficial** | • Advice to stay active |
| **Unknown Effectiveness** | • Acupuncture |
| | • Back exercises (insufficient evidence for generic back exercises and conflicting evidence for specific back exercises) |
| | • Massage |
| | • Multidisciplinary treatment programmes (for acute low back pain) |
| | • Multidisciplinary treatment programmes (for subacute low back pain) |
| | • Spinal manipulation (unknown effectiveness due to conflicting evidence) |

- TENS
- Temperature treatments (short-wave diathermy, ultrasound, ice, heat)

**Search date October 2013**

**DEFINITION** Low back pain is pain, muscle tension, or stiffness, localised below the costal margin and above the inferior gluteal folds, with or without referred or radicular leg pain (sciatica). For this overview, acute low back pain is defined as pain that persists for less than 12 weeks. Non-specific low back pain is a meaningless term but is used by some people to label back pain that is not attributable to a recognisable pathology or symptom pattern (such as infection, tumour, osteoporosis, rheumatoid arthritis, fracture, or inflammation). This overview excludes acute low back pain with symptoms or signs at presentation that suggest a specific underlying pathoanatomical condition. Studies solely of sciatica (lumbosacral radicular syndrome), herniated discs, or both were also excluded. Unless otherwise stated, people included in this overview had a new episode of acute low back pain (i.e., of <12 weeks' duration). Some included RCTs further subdivided acute low back pain of less than 12 weeks' duration into acute (<6 weeks' duration) or subacute (6–12 weeks' duration).

**INCIDENCE/PREVALENCE** More than 70% of people in resource-rich countries will experience low back pain at some time in their lives. Each year, 15% to 45% of adults suffer low back pain, and 1/20 (5%) people present to a healthcare professional with a new episode. Low back pain is most common between the ages of 35 and 55 years. About 30% of European workers reported that their work caused low back pain. In a Canadian study, 67% of people (not involved in workers' compensation claims) struggled to name one specific cause or precipitating event that led to their symptoms. Prevalence rates from different countries range from 13% to 44%.

**AETIOLOGY/RISK FACTORS** Symptoms, pathology, and radiological appearances are poorly correlated. An anatomical source of pain cannot be identified in about 80% of people. About 4% of people with low back pain in primary care have compression fractures, and only about 1% have a tumour. The prevalence of prolapsed intervertebral disc is about 1% to 3%. Ankylosing spondylitis and spinal infections are less common. Risk factors for the development of back pain include heavy physical work; frequent bending, twisting, or lifting; and prolonged static postures, including sitting. Psychosocial risk factors include anxiety, depression, and mental stress at work.

**PROGNOSIS** Acute low back pain may be self-limiting, although acute low back pain has a high recurrence rate with symptoms recurring in 50% to 80% of people within 1 year; 1 year after the initial episode, as many as 33% of people still endure moderate-intensity pain and 15% experience severe pain. The longer the period of sick leave, the less likely return to work becomes.

Roger Chou

## KEY POINTS

- Over 70% of people in developed countries develop low back pain at some time, which usually improves within 2 weeks; however, about 10% remained off work and about 20% had persistent symptoms at 1 year.

- Non-steroidal anti-inflammatory drugs (NSAIDs) may be more effective than placebo at improving pain intensity in people with chronic low back pain.

- Opioid analgesics (with or without paracetamol) may improve pain and function compared with placebo. However, long-term use of NSAIDs or opioids may be associated with well-recognised adverse effects.

  We don't know whether antidepressants decrease chronic low back pain or improve function compared with placebo in people with or without depression.

  Benzodiazepines may improve pain, but studies of non-benzodiazepine muscle relaxants have given conflicting results.

- CAUTION: Since the last update of this review, a drug safety alert has been issued on increased suicidal behaviour with antidepressants (www.fda.gov/medwatch).

- We don't know whether epidural corticosteroid injections or local injections with corticosteroids and local anaesthetic improve chronic low back pain in people without sciatica.

  Facet-joint corticosteroid injections may be no more effective than placebo at reducing pain.

- Fusion surgery is more effective than standard rehabilitation for improving pain in people with chronic non-radicular low back pain, but it is no better than intensive rehabilitation with a cognitive behavioural component.

- Exercise improves pain and function compared with other conservative treatments.

- Intensive multidisciplinary treatment programmes improve pain and function compared with usual care, but less-intensive programmes do not seem beneficial.

- Acupuncture, back schools, behavioural therapy, and spinal manipulation may reduce pain in the short term, but effects on function are unclear.

- Massage may improve pain and function compared with sham or other active treatment.

- We don't know whether electromyographic biofeedback, lumbar supports, traction, or TENS improve pain relief.

- We also don't know whether intradiscal electrothermal therapy, radiofrequency denervation, or disc replacement improve pain relief or function.

(i) **Please visit http://clinicalevidence.bmj.com for full text and references**

| What are the effects of oral drug treatments for people with chronic low back pain? | |
|---|---|
| Trade-off Between Benefits And Harms | • Muscle relaxants<br>• NSAIDs |
| Unknown Effectiveness | • Analgesics<br>• Antidepressants |

### What are the effects of injection therapy for people with chronic low back pain?

| Unknown Effectiveness | • Epidural corticosteroid injections |
| --- | --- |
| | • Facet joint injections |
| | • Local injections |

### What are the effects of non-drug treatments for people with chronic low back pain?

| Beneficial | • Back exercises |
| --- | --- |
| Likely To Be Beneficial | • Acupuncture |
| | • Behavioural therapy |
| | • Intensive multidisciplinary treatment programmes (evidence of benefit for intensive programmes but none for less-intensive programmes) |
| | • Massage |
| | • Spinal manipulative therapy |
| Unknown Effectiveness | • Back schools |
| | • Electromyographic biofeedback |
| | • Lumbar supports |
| | • TENS |
| | • Traction |

### What are the effects of non-surgical treatments for chronic low back pain?

| Unknown Effectiveness | • Intradiscal electrothermal therapy (IDETT) |
| --- | --- |
| | • Radiofrequency denervation |

### What are the effects of surgical treatments for chronic low back pain?

| Likely To Be Beneficial | • Fusion surgery |
| --- | --- |
| Unknown Effectiveness | • Artificial disc replacement |

**Search date April 2009**

**DEFINITION** Low back pain is pain, muscle tension, or stiffness localised below the costal margin and above the inferior gluteal folds, with or without leg pain (sciatica), and is defined as chronic when it persists for 12 weeks or more (see definition of low back pain [acute], p 390). Non-specific low back pain is pain not attributed to a recognisable pathology (such as infection, tumour, osteoporosis, rheumatoid arthritis, fracture, or inflammation).

*(continued over)*

*(from previous page)*

This review excludes chronic low back pain with symptoms or signs at presentation that suggest a specific underlying condition. People solely with sciatica (lumbosacral radicular syndrome) and pain due to herniated discs, or both, are also excluded. People in this review have chronic low back pain (>12 weeks' duration).

**INCIDENCE/PREVALENCE** Over 70% of people in developed countries will experience low back pain at some time in their lives. Each year, between 15% and 45% of adults suffer low back pain, and 5% of people present to hospital with a new episode. About 10% remained off work and about 20% had persistent symptoms at 1 year.

**AETIOLOGY/RISK FACTORS** Symptoms, pathology, and radiological appearances are poorly correlated. Pain is non-specific in about 85% of people. About 4% of people with low back pain in primary care have compression fractures, and about 1% have a tumour. The prevalence of prolapsed intervertebral disc among people with low back pain in primary care is about 1% to 3%. Ankylosing spondylitis and spinal infections are less common. This review only covers chronic low back pain where a definitive diagnosis cannot be made. Risk factors include heavy physical work; frequent bending, twisting, and lifting; and prolonged static postures. Psychosocial risk factors include anxiety, depression, and mental stress at work. Having a previous history of low back pain and a longer duration of the present episode are significant risk factors for chronicity. One systematic review of prospective cohort studies found that some psychological factors (distress, depressive mood, and somatisation) are associated with an increased risk of chronic low back pain. Individual and workplace factors have also been reported to be associated with the transition to chronic low back pain.

**PROGNOSIS** Generally, the clinical course of an episode of low back pain appears favourable, but back pain among people in a primary-care setting typically has a recurrent course (characterised by variation and change), rather than an acute, self-limiting course. Most people with back pain have experienced a previous episode, and acute attacks often occur as exacerbations of chronic low back pain. In general, recurrences will occur more frequently and be more severe if people have had frequent or long-lasting low back pain complaints in the past. The course of sick leave caused by low back pain can be favourable; however, the longer the period of sick leave, the less likely the return to work becomes. Less than 50% of people with low back pain who have been off work for 6 months will return to work. After 2 years of work absenteeism, the chance of returning to work is almost zero.

Allan Binder

## KEY POINTS
- Non-specific neck pain has a postural or mechanical basis, and affects about two thirds of people at some stage, especially in middle age.

  Acute neck pain resolves within days or weeks, but becomes chronic in about 10% of people.

  Whiplash injuries follow sudden acceleration–deceleration of the neck, such as in road traffic or sporting accidents. Up to 40% of people continue to report symptoms 15 years after the accident.

- The evidence about the effects of individual interventions for neck pain is often contradictory because of poor-quality RCTs, and because of the tendency for interventions to be given in combination, and for RCTs to be conducted in diverse groups. This lack of consistency in study design makes it difficult to isolate which intervention may be of use in which type of neck pain.

- Stretching and strengthening exercise reduces chronic neck pain compared with usual care, either alone or in combination with manipulation, mobilisation, or infrared.

  Manipulation and mobilisation may reduce chronic pain more than usual care or less-active exercise. They seem likely to be as effective as each other or as exercise, and more effective than pulsed electromagnetic field (PEMF) treatment, or than heat treatment.

  Acupuncture may be more effective than some types of sham or inactive treatment at improving pain relief and quality of life at the end of treatment or in the short term.

- Analgesics, NSAIDs, antidepressants, and muscle relaxants are widely used to treat chronic neck pain, but we don't know whether they are effective.

- We don't know whether traction, PEMF treatment, TENS, heat or cold, biofeedback, spray and stretch, multimodal treatment, patient education, soft collars, or special pillows are better or worse than other treatments at reducing chronic neck pain.

- Early mobilisation may reduce pain in people with acute whiplash injury compared with immobilisation or rest with a collar.

  We don't know whether exercise, early return to normal activity, PEMF treatment, multimodal treatment, or drug treatment can reduce pain in people with acute whiplash injury.

- We don't know whether percutaneous radiofrequency neurotomy, multimodal treatment, or physical treatment reduce pain in people with chronic whiplash injury.

- We don't know whether surgery, analgesics, NSAIDs, muscle relaxants, or cervical epidural corticosteroid injections reduce pain in people with neck pain plus radiculopathy.

ⓘ **Please visit http://clinicalevidence.bmj.com for full text and references**

| **What are the effects of treatments for people with non-specific neck pain without severe neurological deficit?** | |
|---|---|
| Likely To Be Beneficial | • Acupuncture |
| | • Exercise and postural treatments (pilates, yoga, Alexander technique) for non-specific neck pain |

| | • Manipulation (with or without exercise or advice) |
| | • Mobilisation |
| **Unknown Effectiveness** | • Biofeedback |
| | • Different combinations of multimodal treatment for non-specific neck pain versus each other |
| | • Drug treatments (analgesics, antidepressants, epidural corticosteroids, epidural local anaesthetics, muscle relaxants, NSAIDs) for non-specific neck pain |
| | • Heat or cold |
| | • PEMF treatment for non-specific neck pain |
| | • Patient education |
| | • Soft collars and special pillows |
| | • Spray and stretch |
| | • TENS |
| | • Traction |

## What are the effects of treatments for acute whiplash injury?

| **Likely To Be Beneficial** | • Mobilisation (early) for acute whiplash injury |
| **Unknown Effectiveness** | • Drug treatments (analgesics, antidepressants, epidural corticosteroids, epidural local anaesthetics, muscle relaxants, NSAIDs) for acute whiplash injury |
| | • Early return to normal activity |
| | • Exercise for acute whiplash injury |
| | • Multimodal treatment for acute whiplash injury |
| | • PEMF treatment for acute whiplash injury |

## What are the effects of treatments for chronic whiplash injury?

| **Unknown Effectiveness** | • Multimodal treatment for chronic whiplash injury |
| | • Percutaneous radiofrequency neurotomy |
| | • Physical treatments |

## What are the effects of treatments for neck pain with radiculopathy?

| **Unknown Effectiveness** | • Drug treatments (analgesics, antidepressants, epidural corticosteroids, epidural local anaesthetics, muscle relaxants, NSAIDs) for neck pain with radiculopathy |
| | • Surgery versus conservative treatment |

**Search date May 2007**

**DEFINITION** In this review, we have differentiated non-specific (uncomplicated) neck pain from whiplash, although many studies, particularly in people with chronic pain (duration longer than 3 months), do not specify which types of pain are included. Most studies of acute pain (duration less than 3 months) are confined to whiplash. Non-specific neck pain is defined as pain with a postural or mechanical basis, often called cervical spondylosis. It does not include pain associated with fibromyalgia. Non-specific neck pain may include some people with a traumatic basis for their symptoms, but does not include people for whom pain is specifically stated to have followed sudden acceleration–deceleration injuries to the neck (whiplash). Whiplash is commonly seen in road traffic accidents and sports injuries. It is not accompanied by radiographic abnormalities or clinical signs of nerve root damage. Neck pain often occurs in combination with limited movement and poorly defined neurological symptoms affecting the upper limbs. The pain can be severe and intractable, and can occur with radiculopathy or myelopathy. We have included those studies involving people with predominantly radicular symptoms arising in the cervical spine under the section on neck pain with radiculopathy.

**INCIDENCE/PREVALENCE** About two thirds of people will experience neck pain at some time. Prevalence is highest in middle age, with women being affected more than men. The prevalence of neck pain varies widely between studies, with a mean point prevalence of 7.6% (range 5.9–38.7%) and mean lifetime prevalence of 48.5% (range 14.2–71.0%). About 15% of hospital-based physiotherapy in the UK, and 30% of chiropractic referrals in Canada are for neck pain. In the Netherlands, neck pain accounts for up to 2% of general practitioner consultations.

**AETIOLOGY/RISK FACTORS** The aetiology of uncomplicated neck pain is unclear. Most uncomplicated neck pain is associated with poor posture, anxiety and depression, neck strain, occupational injuries, or sporting injuries. With chronic pain, mechanical and degenerative factors (often referred to as cervical spondylosis) are more likely. Some neck pain results from soft-tissue trauma, most typically seen in whiplash injuries. Rarely, disc prolapse and inflammatory, infective, or malignant conditions affect the cervical spine, and present with neck pain with or without neurological features.

**PROGNOSIS** Neck pain usually resolves within days or weeks, but can recur or become chronic. In some industries, neck-related disorders account for as much time off work as low back pain (see review on low back pain [acute], p 390). The proportion of people in whom neck pain becomes chronic depends on the cause, but is thought to be about 10%, a similar proportion to low back pain. Neck pain causes severe disability in 5% of affected people. The clinical course of neck pain in the absence of formal treatment is not well documented. One systematic review assessing the outcome of control groups in RCTs of conservative management for chronic neck pain (outcome intervals ranging from 1–52 weeks) found that the change in pain score (visual analogue scale) with placebo or with no treatment was small, and did not seem to increase in the long-term (mean change in pain with placebo 0.5 at 10 weeks, 0.33 at 12–24 weeks; mean change in pain with no treatment 0.18 at 10 weeks, 0.4 at 12–52 weeks; P value not reported, reported as not significant). Whiplash injuries are more likely to cause disability compared with neck pain resulting from other causes: up to 40% of whiplash sufferers reported symptoms even after 15 years' follow-up. Factors associated with a poor outcome after whiplash are not well defined. The incidence of chronic disability after whiplash varies among countries, although reasons for this variation are unclear.

# NSAIDs

Peter C Gøtzsche

## KEY POINTS

- Non-steroidal anti-inflammatory drugs (NSAIDs) inhibit the cyclo-oxygenase (COX) enzyme to exert their anti-inflammatory, analgesic, and antipyretic effects.

- No important differences in efficacy have been demonstrated between different oral NSAIDs in the management of musculoskeletal disorders.

  There seems to be a plateau for effectiveness, with recommended doses close to those required for maximal effectiveness. However, the risk of adverse effects increases with increasing dose, with no plateau.

  Oral NSAIDs that selectively inhibit COX-2 have a reduced risk of causing gastrointestinal ulcers compared with less-selective NSAIDs. However, COX-2 inhibitors increase the risk of myocardial infarction and other cardiovascular events.

  Paracetamol is less effective than oral NSAIDs at reducing pain in osteoarthritis, but similarly effective for acute musculoskeletal pain.

- Misoprostol reduces serious NSAID-related gastrointestinal complications and symptomatic ulcers compared with placebo, but is itself associated with adverse effects including diarrhoea, abdominal pain, and nausea.

  Proton pump inhibitors and $H_2$ antagonists have been shown to reduce endoscopic ulcers in people taking NSAIDs, but their clinical benefits are less clear.

  We don't know which treatment is the most effective at reducing gastrointestinal adverse effects from oral NSAIDs.

- We don't know whether topical NSAIDs are beneficial.

(i) Please visit http://clinicalevidence.bmj.com for full text and references

### Are there any important differences among oral NSAIDs?

| Trade-off Between Benefits And Harms | • Differences in efficacy among oral NSAIDs |
| --- | --- |
| Unlikely To Be Beneficial | • Higher dose of oral NSAIDs (has very low benefit in terms of pain reduction and adverse effects increase in linear fashion with increase in dose) |

### What are the effects of co-treatments to reduce the risk of gastrointestinal adverse effects of oral NSAIDs?

| Trade-off Between Benefits And Harms | • Misoprostol in people who cannot avoid oral NSAIDs |
| --- | --- |
| Unknown Effectiveness | • $H_2$ blockers in people who cannot avoid oral NSAIDs |
| | • Proton pump inhibitors in people who cannot avoid oral NSAIDs |

### What are the effects of topical NSAIDs?

| Unknown Effectiveness | • NSAIDs (topical) |
| --- | --- |

- Topical versus oral NSAIDs or alternative analgesics

**Search date September 2009**

**DEFINITION** Non-steroidal anti-inflammatory drugs (NSAIDs) have anti-inflammatory, analgesic, and antipyretic effects, and they inhibit platelet aggregation. This review deals specifically with the use of NSAIDs for the treatment of the symptoms of musculoskeletal conditions. NSAIDs have no documented effect on the course of musculoskeletal diseases. NSAIDs inhibit the enzyme cyclo-oxygenase (COX), which has two known isoforms: COX-1 and COX-2. NSAIDs are often categorised according to their ability to inhibit the individual isoforms, with newer NSAIDs often predominantly inhibiting the COX-2 isoform and older NSAIDs often being less specific inhibitors.

**INCIDENCE/PREVALENCE** NSAIDs are widely used. Almost 10% of people in The Netherlands used a non-aspirin NSAID in 1987, and the overall use was 11 defined daily doses per 1000 population a day. In Australia in 1994, overall use was 35 defined daily doses per 1000 population a day, with 36% of the people receiving NSAIDs for osteoarthritis, 42% for sprain and strain or low back pain, and 4% for rheumatoid arthritis; 35% of the people receiving NSAIDs were aged over 60 years.

David Scott

## KEY POINTS

- The hip is the second most common large joint to be affected with osteoarthritis, affecting about 5% of people aged over 60 years, although few will need surgery.

  Osteoarthritis is characterised by focal areas of damage to the cartilage surface of the bone, with remodelling of the underlying bone and mild synovitis, leading to pain, bony tenderness, and crepitus.

  Osteoarthritis of the hip seems more likely in people who are obese, who participate in sporting activities such as running, or who have occupations requiring a heavy physical workload, such as farming or lifting heavy loads.

- Oral NSAIDs, including COX-2 inhibitors, reduce short-term pain in people with osteoarthritis of the hip compared with placebo.

  Long-term benefits of NSAIDs are not known, and they increase the risk of serious gastrointestinal adverse effects, including haemorrhage.

  We found no evidence on the effects of oral non-opioid analgesics in people with osteoarthritis of the hip.

  Combined NSAIDs plus paracetamol may be no more effective than NSAIDs alone.

- Chondroitin may reduce pain and improve function in people with osteoarthritis of the hip, but glucosamine may not be effective in improving pain and function. However, few studies have been performed on these treatments.

- The benefits of opioid analgesics, capsaicin, intra-articular injections, acupuncture, education to aid self-management, exercise, and physical aids remain unclear.

- Total hip replacement reduces pain and improves function in people with osteoarthritis of the hip, although we don't know which individuals are likely to respond.

- We don't know whether arthroscopic debridement, hip resurfacing, or osteotomy are effective in treating osteoarthritis of the hip.

(i) **Please visit http://clinicalevidence.bmj.com for full text and references**

| What are the effects of non-drug treatments for osteoarthritis of the hip? | |
|---|---|
| **Unknown Effectiveness** | • Acupuncture |
| | • Education to aid self-management |
| | • Exercise |
| | • Physical aids |

| What are the effects of drug treatments for osteoarthritis of the hip? | |
|---|---|
| **Beneficial** | • NSAIDs (oral, including COX-2 inhibitors) for short-term pain relief |
| **Unknown Effectiveness** | • Capsaicin |
| | • Chondroitin |
| | • Glucosamine |

- Intra-articular injections (of hyaluronan or corticosteroid)

- NSAIDs (oral) plus non-opioid analgesics (oral) or opioid analgesics (insufficient evidence to assess combination *v* either intervention alone)

- Non-opioid analgesics (oral; insufficient evidence to assess effects in people with osteoarthritis of the hip)

- Opioid analgesics

## What are the effects of surgical treatments for osteoarthritis of the hip?

| | |
|---|---|
| **Beneficial** | • Hip replacement |
| **Unknown Effectiveness** | • Arthroscopic debridement<br>• Hip resurfacing<br>• Osteotomy |

**Search date May 2007**

---

**DEFINITION** Osteoarthritis is a heterogeneous condition for which the prevalence, risk factors, clinical manifestations, and prognosis vary according to the joints affected. It most commonly affects knees, hips, hands, and spinal apophyseal joints. It is characterised by focal areas of damage to the cartilage surfaces of synovial joints, and is associated with remodelling of the underlying bone and mild synovitis. It is variously defined by a number of clinical and/or radiological features. Clinical features include pain, bony tenderness, and crepitus. When severe, there is often characteristic joint-space narrowing and osteophyte formation, with visible subchondral bone changes on radiography. The hip is the second most common large joint to be affected by osteoarthritis. It is associated with significant pain, disability, and impaired quality of life.

**INCIDENCE/PREVALENCE** Osteoarthritis is a common and important cause of pain and disability in older adults. Radiographical features are practically universal in at least some joints in people over 60 years old, but significant clinical disease probably affects 10% to 20% of people. Hip disease is not as prevalent as knee disease in people over 60 years old (about 5% *v* 10%). The actual impact that osteoarthritis has on an individual person is the result of a combination of physical (including comorbidities), psychological, cultural, and social factors, and this may influence outcomes found in research (for example, if comorbidities are not accounted for in analysis).

**AETIOLOGY/RISK FACTORS** There is moderate evidence for a positive association between osteoarthritis of the hip and obesity, participation in sporting activities (including running), and vocational activity, particularly involving a heavy physical workload, as characterised by farming (especially for >10 years) or lifting heavy loads (25 kg or more). Only limited evidence exists for a positive association between the occurrence of osteoarthritis of the hip and participation in athletics or presence of hip dysplasia in older people.

**PROGNOSIS** The natural history of osteoarthritis of the hip is poorly understood. Only a minority of people with clinical disease of the hip will progress to requiring surgery.

David Scott and Anna Kowalczyk

## KEY POINTS

- Osteoarthritis of the knee affects about 10% of adults aged over 60 years, with increased risk in those with obesity, and joint damage or abnormalities.

  Progression of disease on x rays is commonplace, but x ray changes don't correlate well with clinical symptoms.

  We don't know the long-term effectiveness of any non-surgical treatment in reducing pain and improving function.

- Exercise and physiotherapy, and joint bracing or taping reduce pain and disability in people with knee osteoarthritis, but we don't know whether patient education or insoles are beneficial.

- Oral and topical NSAIDs reduce pain in the short term compared with placebo, but can cause gastrointestinal, renal, and cardiac adverse effects.

  Paracetamol reduces pain in the short term compared with placebo, but may be less effective than NSAIDs.

  Opioid analgesics reduce pain in knee osteoarthritis, but they are associated with serious adverse effects, so are not recommended for first-line treatment.

- Intra-articular corticosteroids and intra-articular hyaluronan may improve pain, although most studies are of poor quality.

  We don't know whether acupuncture, capsaicin, glucosamine, or oral or intramuscular chondroitin improve symptoms in knee osteoarthritis.

- Consensus is that total knee replacement is the most clinically effective treatment for severe osteoarthritis of the knee.

  Unicompartmental knee replacement may be more effective than tricompartmental knee replacement in the long term.

  Tibial osteotomy may be as effective as unicompartmental knee replacement in reducing symptoms of medial compartment knee osteoarthritis.

(i) **Please visit http://clinicalevidence.bmj.com for full text and references**

| What are the effects of non-surgical treatments for osteoarthritis of the knee? | |
| --- | --- |
| Beneficial | • Exercise and physiotherapy (pain relief and improved function)<br>• NSAIDs (oral) for short-term pain relief |
| Likely To Be Beneficial | • Corticosteroids (intra-articular — short-term pain relief)<br>• Hyaluronan (intra-articular)<br>• Joint bracing<br>• NSAIDs (topical) for short-term pain relief<br>• Simple oral analgesics (short-term pain relief only)<br>• Taping |
| Trade-off Between Benefits And Harms | • Opioid analgesics |
| Unknown Effectiveness | • Acupuncture<br>• Capsaicin |

- Chondroitin
- Education (to aid self-management)
- Glucosamine
- Insoles

### What are the effects of surgical treatments for osteoarthritis of the knee?

| Likely To Be Beneficial | • Knee replacement |
|---|---|
| | • Osteotomy |

**Search date October 2006**

**DEFINITION** Osteoarthritis is a heterogeneous condition for which the prevalence, risk factors, clinical manifestations, and prognosis vary according to the joints affected. It most commonly affects knees, hips, hands, and spinal apophyseal joints. It is characterised by focal areas of damage to the cartilage surfaces of synovial joints, and is associated with remodelling of the underlying bone, and mild synovitis. It is variously defined by a number of clinical or radiological features, or both. Clinical features include pain, bony tenderness, and crepitus. When severe, there is often characteristic joint-space narrowing and osteophyte formation, with visible subchondral bone changes on radiography. Osteoarthritis of the knee is common, causes considerable pain and frequent instability, and, consequently, often results in physical disability. x Ray changes are not strongly associated with disability.

**INCIDENCE/PREVALENCE** Osteoarthritis is a common and important cause of pain and disability in older adults. Radiographical features are practically universal in people aged over 60 years in at least some joints, but significant clinical disease probably affects 10–20% of people. Knee disease is about twice as prevalent as hip disease in people aged over 60 years (about 10% knee *v* 5% hip). In a general practice setting. 1% of people aged over 45 years have a currently-recorded clinical diagnosis of knee osteoarthritis; 5% will have had the clinical diagnosis made at some point. A community-based cohort study showed that radiological features of knee osteoarthritis were very common: 13% of women aged 45–65 years developed new knee osteophytes — an incidence of 3% per year.

**AETIOLOGY/RISK FACTORS** Risk factors for osteoarthritis include abnormalities in joint shape, injury, and previous joint inflammation. Obesity is a major risk factor for osteoarthritis of the knee. Genetic factors modulate obesity and other risks.

**PROGNOSIS** The natural history of osteoarthritis of the knee is poorly understood. Radiological progression is commonplace, with 25% of osteoarthritic knees with initially normal joint space showing major damage after 10 years, although x ray progression is not related to clinical features. People with peripheral-joint osteoarthritis of sufficient severity to lead to hospital referral generally have bad outcomes, with high levels of physical disability, anxiety, and depression; they also have high levels of healthcare resources utilisation, including joint replacement, drugs, and walking aids.

# Plantar heel pain and fasciitis

Karl B Landorf and Hylton B Menz

## KEY POINTS

- Plantar heel pain causes soreness or tenderness of the sole of the foot under the heel, which sometimes extends into the medial arch.

   The prevalence and prognosis are unclear, but in most people the symptoms seem to resolve over time.

- Casted orthoses (custom-made insoles) may improve function (but not pain) at 3 months in people with plantar heel pain compared with a sham orthosis, but they may be no better than appropriate prefabricated orthoses.

- Supportive taping may improve pain in the short term at 1 week, but we found no evidence on its effectiveness beyond 1 week.

- We don't know whether heel pads, heel cups, or night splints reduce pain.

- Corticosteroid injections are commonly used to treat plantar heel pain, but we don't know whether they reduce pain compared with placebo or other treatments.

   Corticosteroid injections have been associated with long-term complications.

   We don't know whether local anaesthetic injections, alone or added to corticosteroids, improve pain relief compared with corticosteroids alone.

- Extracorporeal shock-wave therapy may reduce pain, but we don't know for sure that it is beneficial.

- We don't know whether laser treatment, ultrasound, or surgery reduce symptoms compared with sham treatment or no treatment.

- We don't know whether stretching exercises reduce pain compared with no treatment or other treatments.

 **Please visit http://clinicalevidence.bmj.com for full text and references**

| What are the effects of treatments for plantar heel pain? | |
|---|---|
| **Likely To Be Beneficial** | • Casted orthoses (custom-made insoles) (improved function [but not pain] at 3 months compared with sham orthosis, but no difference between casted [custom] orthosis and prefabricated orthosis at 3 months)<br><br>• Taping (limited evidence of reduced pain at 1 week; no evidence beyond 1 week) |
| **Unknown Effectiveness** | • Corticosteroid injection (in the short term)<br><br>• Corticosteroid injection plus local anaesthetic injection in the short term (with or without NSAIDs or heel pads)<br><br>• Extracorporeal shock-wave therapy (ESWT)<br><br>• Heel pads and heel cups<br><br>• Lasers<br><br>• Local anaesthetic injection<br><br>• Night splints plus NSAIDs<br><br>• Stretching exercises<br><br>• Surgery |

| | • Ultrasound |
|---|---|
| Likely To Be Ineffective Or Harmful | • Corticosteroid injection in the medium to long term (with or without heel pad)<br><br>• Corticosteroid injection plus local anaesthetic injection in the medium to long term (with or without NSAIDs or heel pads) |

**Search date January 2007**

**DEFINITION** Plantar heel pain is soreness or tenderness of the heel that is restricted to the sole of the foot. It often radiates from the central part of the heel pad or the medial tubercle of the calcaneum, but may extend along the plantar fascia into the medial longitudinal arch of the foot. Severity may range from an irritation at the origin of the plantar fascia, which is noticeable on rising after rest, to an incapacitating pain. This review excludes clinically evident underlying disorders; for example, calcaneal fracture, and calcaneal-nerve entrapment, which may be distinguished clinically — a calcaneal fracture may present after trauma, and calcaneal nerve entrapment gives rise to shooting pains and feelings of "pins and needles" on the medial aspect of the heel.

**INCIDENCE/PREVALENCE** The incidence and prevalence of plantar heel pain are uncertain. However, it has been estimated that 7% of people aged over 65 years report tenderness in the region of the heel, that plantar heel pain accounts for a quarter of all foot injuries relating to running, and that the diagnosis and treatment of plantar heel pain accounts for over 1 million visits a year to physicians in the USA. The condition affects both athletic and sedentary people, and does not seem to be influenced by gender.

**AETIOLOGY/RISK FACTORS** Unknown. Suggested risk factors include overweight, prolonged standing, and having a reduced range of motion in the ankle and 1st metatarsophalangeal joint.

**PROGNOSIS** One systematic review found that almost all of the included trials reported an improvement in discomfort regardless of the intervention received (including placebo), suggesting that the condition is at least partially self-limiting. A telephone survey of 100 people treated conservatively (average follow-up 47 months) found that 82 people had resolution of symptoms, 15 had continued symptoms but no limitations of activity or work, and three had persistent bilateral symptoms that limited activity or changed work status. Thirty-one people said that they would have seriously considered surgical treatment at the time that medical attention was sought. In addition, one recent RCT has observed marked improvement in pain and function over time in 45 people randomised to a sham intervention.

Ariane Herrick and Lindsay Muir

**KEY POINTS**

- Raynaud's phenomenon is episodic vasospasm of the peripheral vessels.

  It presents as episodic colour changes of the digits (sometimes accompanied by pain and paraesthesia), usually in response to cold exposure or stress. The classic change is white (ischaemia), then blue (deoxygenation), then red (reperfusion).

- Raynaud's phenomenon can be primary (idiopathic) or secondary to several different conditions and causes. When secondary (e.g., to systemic sclerosis), it can progress to ulceration of the fingers and toes. This review deals with secondary Raynaud's phenomenon.

- Most trials we found were in people with Raynaud's phenomenon secondary to systemic sclerosis.

- We found no RCT evidence on the effectiveness of botulinum toxin, simple debridement/surgical toilet of ulcers, peripheral sympathectomy (digital, digital plus ulnar and/or radial artery, ligation of the ulnar artery), cervical/thoracic sympathectomy, arterial reconstruction (venous graft, arterial graft, balloon angioplasty), or amputation at improving outcomes for people with complicated secondary Raynaud's phenomenon.

  The use of botulinum toxin in people with complicated secondary Raynaud's phenomenon is currently an off-license application that needs further research.

  Clinical experience suggests surgical debridement improves symptoms in people with systemic sclerosis-related secondary Raynaud's phenomenon and painful digital ulcers.

  Peripheral digital sympathectomy may have a role in the treatment of people with complicated secondary Raynaud's phenomenon. However, more research is required, especially for longer-term outcomes and the duration of any early effect.

  The evidence is no more certain for more radical sympathectomy than for local surgery.

  Amputation may be helpful in cases of refractory infection and provide pain relief in people with secondary Raynaud's phenomenon complicated by digital ulceration and/or critical ischaemia when other treatment options have failed.

 **Please visit http://clinicalevidence.bmj.com for full text and references**

| **What are the effects of surgical interventions in complicated secondary Raynaud's phenomenon?** | |
|---|---|
| Unknown Effectiveness | • Amputation (however, may be useful in cases of refractory infection or to provide pain relief when all other treatment options have failed) |
| | • Arterial reconstruction (arterial graft) |
| | • Arterial reconstruction (balloon angioplasty) |
| | • Arterial reconstruction (venous graft) |
| | • Botulinum toxin |
| | • Cervical/thoracic sympathectomy |
| | • Leriche sympathectomy (ligation of the ulnar artery) |

- Peripheral sympathectomy (digital plus ulnar and/or radial artery)
- Peripheral sympathectomy (digital)
- Simple debridement/surgical toilet of ulcers

**Search date March 2014**

**DEFINITION** Raynaud's phenomenon is episodic vasospasm of the peripheral vessels. It presents as episodic colour changes of the digits (sometimes accompanied by pain and paraesthesia), usually in response to cold exposure or stress. The classic triphasic colour change is white (ischaemia), then blue (deoxygenation), then red (reperfusion). Raynaud's phenomenon can be primary (idiopathic) or secondary to several different conditions or causes, including connective tissue diseases such as systemic sclerosis, extrinsic vascular obstruction (e.g., in thoracic outlet syndrome), certain drugs/chemicals (e.g., ergotamine, vinyl chloride), vibration exposure (hand-arm vibration syndrome), and hyperviscosity states. When secondary, Raynaud's phenomenon can progress to ulceration of the fingers and toes and, less commonly, critical digital ischaemia. This review excludes primary (idiopathic) Raynaud's phenomenon, and concerns the management of complicated secondary Raynaud's phenomenon. Most of the evidence we found on complicated secondary Raynaud's phenomenon was in people with systemic sclerosis.

**INCIDENCE/PREVALENCE** See Raynaud's phenomenon (primary), p 46. The prevalence of secondary Raynaud's depends on the associated disease or condition. For example, the prevalence of Raynaud's phenomenon in people with systemic sclerosis is almost 100%.

**AETIOLOGY/RISK FACTORS** Many different conditions can be associated with secondary Raynaud's phenomenon, and the pathogenesis and pathophysiology of Raynaud's phenomenon vary depending upon these underlying conditions. Abnormalities of the blood vessel wall, of the neural control of vascular tone, and intravascular factors may all have a role. Other factors have also been implicated, including smoking (in people with systemic sclerosis, smoking is associated with severity of digital ischaemia), hormonal factors (Raynaud's is more common in women than in men), and genetic factors.

**PROGNOSIS** Secondary Raynaud's phenomenon can be severe, and may progress to ulceration, scarring, and sometimes gangrene necessitating amputation. Therefore, prognosis depends, at least to some extent, on the underlying cause of Raynaud's phenomenon. Prognosis has been studied most successfully in people with systemic sclerosis who developed underlying structural vascular abnormalities affecting both the microcirculation and the digital arteries. One study found that, of 1168 people with systemic sclerosis, 203 people (17.4%) over an 18-month period had severe digital vasculopathy (Raynaud's phenomenon complicated by digital ulceration, critical digital ischaemia, gangrene, or requiring digital sympathectomy).

Karen Walker-Bone and Sarah Farrow

## KEY POINTS

- Rheumatoid arthritis is a chronic inflammatory disorder that mainly affects the peripheral joints and surrounding tissue.

  It usually starts as a symmetrical polyarthritis, and its course is marked by flares and remissions.

  The aims of treatment are to relieve pain and swelling, and to improve function. In addition, disease-modifying antirheumatic drugs (DMARDs) may reduce disease progression.

- The DMARD methotrexate is widely used as first-line treatment in people with rheumatoid arthritis because of consensus about its effectiveness in practice.

  Sulfasalazine and combined treatment with methotrexate and sulfasalazine are as effective as methotrexate in improving pain, joint swelling, and function in people with early rheumatoid arthritis who have not previously received DMARDs.

  Antimalarials may improve symptoms and function in DMARD-naïve people, and are reasonably well tolerated, but radiological evidence of erosion is more marked with antimalarials than with sulfasalazine.

- There is a variety of DMARDs available for second-line treatment of rheumatoid arthritis, and we found no clear evidence that one is superior.

  Methotrexate, sulfasalazine, penicillamine, and leflunomide cause similar improvements in symptoms and function when given to people as second-line DMARD treatment, although methotrexate causes fewer adverse effects.

  The combination of methotrexate plus sulfasalazine plus hydroxychloroquine is more effective in reducing measures of disease activity in people receiving second-line treatment than any of the drugs used alone. Adding the cytokine inhibitors infliximab or etanercept to methotrexate is more effective than using methotrexate alone.

  Although antimalarials and oral gold seem to improve clinical disease activity when given as second-line treatment, they are not as effective as methotrexate or sulfasalazine. Although parenteral gold is more effective than oral gold, it leads to higher levels of toxicity than most of the other commonly used DMARDs.

  Ciclosporin offers short-term control of rheumatoid arthritis when used as second-line treatment, but it is associated with nephrotoxicity.

  We don't know whether cyclophosphamide is as effective as other DMARDs for second-line treatment.

  Cytokine inhibitors may offer an alternative to traditional DMARDs for second-line treatment of rheumatoid arthritis, but more research is needed.

  Etanercept may be as effective as methotrexate at improving symptoms, function, and radiological evidence of progression, but more evidence for its effect is needed.

  Azathioprine is less effective and is less well tolerated than methotrexate.

  We don't know whether anakinra or adalimumab are as effective as other DMARDs for second-line treatment.

  Although widely used for the initial short-term relief of clinical disease activity in rheumatoid arthritis, we don't know how corticosteroids compare with other drugs for first- or second-line treatment.

 **Please visit http://clinicalevidence.bmj.com for full text and references**

### What are the effects of drug treatments in people with rheumatoid arthritis who have not previously received any disease-modifying antirheumatic drug treatment?

| Beneficial | • Methotrexate (first-line treatment)<br>• Sulfasalazine (first-line treatment) |
|---|---|
| Likely To Be Beneficial | • Antimalarial drugs (first-line treatment) |
| Unknown Effectiveness | • Corticosteroids (first-line treatment) |

### How do different drug treatments compare in people with rheumatoid arthritis who have either not responded or are intolerant of first-line disease-modifying antirheumatic drugs?

| Beneficial | • Infliximab plus methotrexate (second-line treatment)<br>• Leflunomide (second-line treatment)<br>• Methotrexate (second-line treatment)<br>• Methotrexate plus sulfasalazine plus hydroxychloroquine (second-line treatment)<br>• Penicillamine (second-line treatment)<br>• Sulfasalazine (second-line treatment) |
|---|---|
| Likely To Be Beneficial | • Antimalarial drugs (second-line treatment)<br>• Azathioprine (second-line treatment)<br>• Ciclosporin (second-line treatment)<br>• Etanercept (second-line treatment)<br>• Gold (oral) (second-line treatment) |
| Trade-off Between Benefits And Harms | • Gold (parenteral) (second-line treatment) |
| Unknown Effectiveness | • Adalimumab (second-line treatment)<br>• Anakinra (second-line treatment)<br>• Corticosteroids (second-line treatment)<br>• Cyclophosphamide (second-line treatment) |

**Search date June 2005**

---

**DEFINITION** Rheumatoid arthritis is a chronic inflammatory disorder. It is characterised by chronic pain and swelling that primarily affects the peripheral joints and related periarticular tissues. It usually starts as an insidious symmetrical polyarthritis, often with non-specific symptoms such as malaise and fatigue.

*(continued over)*

*(from previous page)*

**INCIDENCE/PREVALENCE** Studies from the US have suggested age-adjusted incidence rates of between 0.7 and 0.4 per 1000 person years at risk, but data from European studies suggest a slightly lower incidence rate (0.25/1000 person years). With the exception of some Native American populations where incidence is higher, there is marked consistency in the prevalence of rheumatoid arthritis worldwide. All studies suggest a female incidence rate between two and three times higher than the male rate, and that incidence rates increase progressively with age.

**AETIOLOGY/RISK FACTORS** The cause of rheumatoid arthritis is, as yet, unknown. Genetic factors, hormonal influences, obesity, diet, and cigarette smoking have all been implicated as risk factors. The most widely accepted cause of rheumatoid arthritis is an infection with a micro-organism in a genetically susceptible host.

**PROGNOSIS** Rheumatoid arthritis is a chronic condition. In most cases, it follows a course of relapses and remissions (polycyclic pattern). Relapses ('flares') are associated with generalised pain, swelling, and stiffness, which may affect most joints simultaneously. People with rheumatoid arthritis have reduced life expectancy compared with healthy controls, as shown by a longitudinal cohort study undertaken in the UK including 1010 people with rheumatoid arthritis (standardised all-cause mortality among men: 1.45, 95% CI 1.22 to 1.71; standardised all-cause mortality among women: 1.84, 95% CI 1.64 to 2.05). People with rheumatoid arthritis also have excess cardiovascular disease mortality (standardised cardiovascular mortality among men: 1.36, 95% CI 1.04 to 1.75; standardised cardiovascular mortality among women: 1.93, 95% CI 1.65 to 2.26).

Richard J Murphy and Andrew J Carr

## KEY POINTS

- Shoulder pain encompasses a diverse array of pathologies and can affect as many as one quarter of the population depending on age and risk factors.

  Shoulder pain may be due to problems with the neck, glenohumeral joint, acromioclavicular joint, rotator cuff, or other soft tissues around the shoulder.

- Rotator cuff problems are the most common source of shoulder pain, accounting for more than two-thirds of cases.

  Rotator cuff disorders are associated with musculoskeletal problems that affect the joints and muscles of the shoulder, cuff degeneration due to ageing and ischaemia, and overloading of the shoulder.

- Frozen shoulder (adhesive capsulitis) accounts for 2% of cases of shoulder pain.

  Risk factors for frozen shoulder include female sex, older age, shoulder trauma and surgery, diabetes, and cardiovascular, cerebrovascular, and thyroid disease.

- In many people, the cornerstone of treatment is achieving pain control to permit a return to normal functional use of the shoulder and encourage this with manual exercises. In people with acute post-traumatic tear, an early surgical option is warranted.

- We don't know whether topical NSAIDs, oral corticosteroids, oral paracetamol, or opioid analgesics improve shoulder pain, although oral NSAIDs may be effective in the short term in people with acute tendonitis/subacromial bursitis. If pain control fails, the diagnosis should be reviewed and other interventions considered.

- Physiotherapy may improve pain and function in people with mixed shoulder disorders compared with placebo.

- Intra-articular corticosteroid injections may reduce pain in the short term compared with physiotherapy and placebo for people with frozen shoulder, but their benefit in the long term and when compared with local anaesthetic is unclear.

- Platelet-rich plasma injections may improve the speed of recovery in terms of pain and function in people having open subacromial decompression for rotator cuff impingement, but further evidence is needed.

- Acupuncture may not improve pain or function in people with rotator cuff impingement compared with placebo or ultrasound.

- Extracorporeal shock wave therapy may improve pain in calcific tendonitis.

- We found some evidence that suprascapular nerve block, laser treatment, and arthroscopic subacromial decompression may be effective in some people with shoulder pain.

- We don't know whether autologous blood injections, intra-articular NSAID injections, subacromial corticosteroid injections, electrical stimulation, ice, ultrasound, rotator cuff repair, manipulation under anaesthesia, or shoulder arthroplasty are effective as we found insufficient evidence on their effects.

(i) **Please visit http://clinicalevidence.bmj.com for full text and references**

## What are the effects of oral drug treatment in people with shoulder pain?

| Likely To Be Beneficial | • NSAIDs (oral) (reduce pain in people with acute tendonitis, subacromial bursitis, or both) |
|---|---|
| Unknown Effectiveness | • Corticosteroids (oral)<br>• Opioid analgesics<br>• Paracetamol |

## What are the effects of topical drug treatment in people with shoulder pain?

| Unknown Effectiveness | • NSAIDs (topical) |
|---|---|

## What are the effects of local injections in people with shoulder pain?

| Likely To Be Beneficial | • Nerve block |
|---|---|
| Unknown Effectiveness | • Autologous whole blood injections<br>• Intra-articular NSAID injections<br>• Intra-articular corticosteroid injections<br>• Platelet-rich plasma injections<br>• Subacromial corticosteroid injections |

## What are the effects of non-drug treatment in people with shoulder pain?

| Likely To Be Beneficial | • Extracorporeal shock wave therapy<br>• Laser treatment<br>• Physiotherapy (manual treatment, exercises) |
|---|---|
| Unknown Effectiveness | • Acupuncture<br>• Electrical stimulation<br>• Ice<br>• Ultrasound |

## What are the effects of surgical treatment in people with shoulder pain?

| Likely To Be Beneficial | • Arthroscopic subacromial decompression |
|---|---|
| Unknown Effectiveness | • Excision of distal clavicle<br>• Manipulation under anaesthesia<br>• Rotator cuff repair |

● Shoulder arthroplasty

**Search date August 2009**

**DEFINITION** Shoulder pain arises in or around the shoulder from its joints and surrounding soft tissues. Joints include the glenohumeral, acromioclavicular, and sternoclavicular joints. Bursae and motion planes include the subacromial bursa and scapulothoracic plane. Regardless of the disorder, pain is the most common reason for consulting a practitioner. In frozen shoulder (adhesive capsulitis), pain is associated with pronounced restriction of movement. Rotator cuff disorders may affect one or more portions of the rotator cuff and can be further defined as subacromial impingement (rotator cuff tendonitis), rotator cuff tear (partial/full thickness), or calcific tendonitis. A subacromial/subdeltoid bursitis may be associated with any of these disorders, or may occur in isolation. Post-stroke shoulder pain and pain referred from the cervical spine are not addressed in this review. When selecting treatment options for shoulder pain a diagnosis of the specific pathology is rarely necessary. The most useful aspect of diagnosis is to define the source of pain as originating from the cervical spine, glenohumeral joint, rotator cuff, or acromioclavicular joint. A simple algorithm incorporating identification of red flag symptoms and signs, questions in the history, and simple shoulder tests can be followed to locate the source of the shoulder pain.

**INCIDENCE/PREVALENCE** Each year in primary care in the UK, about 1% of adults aged over 45 years present with a new episode of shoulder pain. Prevalence is uncertain, with estimates from 4% to 26%. One community survey (392 people) in the UK found a 1-month prevalence of shoulder pain of 34%. A second survey (644 people aged at least 70 years), in a community-based rheumatology clinic in the UK, reported a point prevalence of 21%, with a higher frequency in women than men (25% in women v 17% in men). Seventy percent of cases involved the rotator cuff. Further analysis of 134 people included in the survey found that 65% of cases were rotator cuff lesions, 11% were caused by localised tenderness in the pericapsular musculature, 10% involved acromioclavicular joint pain, 3% involved gleno-humeral joint arthritis, and 5% were referred pain from the neck. Another survey in Sweden found that, in adults, the annual incidence of frozen shoulder was about 2%, with those aged 40 to 70 years most commonly affected.

**AETIOLOGY/RISK FACTORS** Rotator cuff disorders are associated with excessive overloading, instability of the glenohumeral and acromioclavicular joints, muscle imbalance, adverse anatomical features (narrow coracoacromial arch and a hooked acromion), rotator cuff degeneration with ageing, ischaemia, and musculoskeletal diseases that result in wasting of the cuff muscles. Risk factors for frozen shoulder (adhesive capsulitis) include female sex, older age, shoulder trauma, surgery, diabetes, cardiorespiratory disorders, cerebrovascular events, thyroid disease, and hemiplegia. Arthritis of the glenohumeral joint can occur in numerous forms, including primary and secondary osteoarthritis, rheumatoid arthritis, and crystal arthritides. Shoulder pain can also be referred from other sites, in particular the cervical spine. It can also arise after stroke. Post-stroke shoulder pain and referred pain are not addressed in this review.

**PROGNOSIS** One survey in community of older people found that most people with shoulder pain were still affected 3 years after the initial survey. One prospective cohort study of 122 adults in primary care found that 25% of people with shoulder pain reported previous episodes and 49% reported full recovery at 18 months' follow-up.

Rajan Madhok and Olivia Wu

## KEY POINTS

- Systemic lupus erythematosus (SLE) is a chronic, multisystem, inflammatory connective tissue disorder of unknown cause that can involve joints, kidneys, serous surfaces, skin, and vessel walls. It occurs predominantly in young women, but also in children. The course of SLE is highly variable, involving non-organ-threatening symptoms (such as arthritis, arthralgia, and rashes), organ-threatening symptoms (such as lupus nephritis), and neuropsychiatric disorders (such as seizures and cognitive dysfunction).

- The prevalence of SLE varies widely worldwide, ranging from about 1 in 3500 women (regardless of race) in the UK, to 1 in 1000 women in China, to 1 in 250 African-American women in the USA.

- There is consensus that NSAIDs and corticosteroids are useful in relieving pain caused by arthralgia/arthritis, and pleuritis and pericarditis associated with SLE. We found no evidence that the well-documented adverse effects of NSAIDs differ in people with SLE.

   There is also consensus that corticosteroids and sunscreens are effective in reducing cutaneous manifestations of SLE.

- Hydroxychloroquine or chloroquine are likely to be effective in reducing arthritis, pleuritis, and pericarditis. They may also improve cutaneous symptoms.

   Methotrexate may also be effective for both joint and cutaneous symptoms, but is associated with adverse effects.

- Combining immunosuppressants plus corticosteroids may be more effective than corticosteroids alone in people with lupus nephritis, but with an increase in adverse effects.

   We don't know how corticosteroids alone compare with immunosuppressants alone in people with proliferative lupus nephritis.

- We don't know whether corticosteroids, immunosuppressants, plasmapheresis, or intravenous immunoglobulin are effective in people with neuropsychiatric symptoms of lupus.

   Most people with neuropsychiatric lupus and psychotic symptoms will be offered antipsychotic drugs to control symptoms unless there are contraindications, despite the lack of RCTs assessing their effectiveness.

(i) **Please visit http://clinicalevidence.bmj.com for full text and references**

| What are the effects of treatments on joint symptoms (arthralgia/arthritis) and other non-organ-threatening symptoms (such as serositis and fatigue) in people with systemic lupus erythematosus? | |
|---|---|
| Likely To Be Beneficial | • Hydroxychloroquine or chloroquine |
| Trade-off Between Benefits And Harms | • Corticosteroids (oral)* <br><br> • Methotrexate <br><br> • NSAIDs* |

### What are the effects of interventions for cutaneous involvement in people with systemic lupus erythematosus?

| | |
|---|---|
| **Likely To Be Beneficial** | • Hydroxychloroquine or chloroquine<br>• Sunblock* |
| **Trade-off Between Benefits And Harms** | • Corticosteroids*<br>• Methotrexate |
| **Unknown Effectiveness** | • Acitretin |

### What are the effects of treatments in people with proliferative lupus nephritis (WHO grades 3–5)?

| | |
|---|---|
| **Trade-off Between Benefits And Harms** | • Combination corticosteroids plus immunosuppressants (may be more effective than corticosteroids alone, but increases adverse effects) |
| **Unknown Effectiveness** | • Corticosteroids (unclear how they compare with immunosuppressants) |

### What are the effects of treatments for neuropsychiatric involvement in people with systemic lupus nephritis?

| | |
|---|---|
| **Unknown Effectiveness** | • Antipsychotic drugs<br>• Corticosteroids (unclear how they compare with immunosuppressants)<br>• Intravenous immunoglobulin<br>• Plasmapheresis |

**Search date December 2007**

*Based on consensus; RCTs unlikely to be conducted.

**DEFINITION** Systemic lupus erythematosus (SLE) is a chronic, multisystem, inflammatory connective tissue disorder of unknown cause that can involve joints, kidneys, serous surfaces, and vessel walls. It occurs predominantly in young women, but also in children. The course of SLE is highly variable, and may be characterised by exacerbations. **Non-organ-threatening symptoms** occur in most people with SLE during the course of active disease. These include: arthritis or arthralgia (84%), oral ulcers (24%), fever (52%), and serositis (pleuritis or pericarditis; 36%). **Lupus glomerulonephritis (lupus nephritis)** is the diagnosis applied to people with renal inflammation occurring in the context of SLE. It occurs in 39% of people. The WHO graded the disease in 1982, based on histological features, as follows: grade 1 = normal kidney or minor abnormalities; grade 2 = mesangial proliferation; grade 3 = focal proliferative glomerulonephritis; grade 4 = diffuse proliferative glomerulonephritis; grade 5 = membranous disease; and grade 6 = sclerosing glomerulonephritis. This review covers treatments of WHO grades 3 to 5. **Cutaneous involvement** may include malar rash (which occurs in 58% of people), photosensitivity (45%), discoid rash (10%), livedo reticularis (14%), and subacute cutaneous lesions (6%). **Neuropsychiatric involvement** occurs in 27% of people and has a wide variety of clinical presentations, including seizures,

*(continued over)*

*(from previous page)*

chronic headache, transverse myelitis, vascular brain disease, psychosis, and neural cognitive dysfunction. SLE is also characterised by haematological features, such as haemolytic anaemia (8%), thrombocytopenia (22%), and lymphadenopathy (12%), and cardiovascular complications, such as thrombosis (14%) and Raynaud's phenomenon (34%). Prevention and treatment of haematological and cardiovascular complications is not currently covered by this review. **Diagnosis:** The American College of Rheumatology (ACR) has developed classification criteria for SLE. For a diagnosis to be made, 4 of the following 11 criteria must be met: malar rash; discoid rash; photosensitivity; oral ulcers; arthritis; serositis; renal disorder; neuropsychiatric disorder; haematological disorder; immunological disorder; and antinuclear antibody.

**INCIDENCE/PREVALENCE** The prevalence of SLE worldwide varies greatly. From population-based epidemiological studies, it has been estimated that 1 in 3500 women (independent of race) in the UK, 1 in 250 African-American women in the USA, 1 in 1000 Chinese women, and 1 in 4200 white women in New Zealand may have SLE. Although the prevalence of SLE is higher in black people than in white people in the USA and UK, the prevalence of lupus is low in most African countries.

**AETIOLOGY/RISK FACTORS** Although the exact cause of SLE remains unclear, genetic, environmental, and hormonal influences are all thought to play a role.

**PROGNOSIS** The manifestations of SLE that determine survival include lupus nephritis, cardiovascular complications, and neuropsychiatric involvement. In cohort studies performed since 1980, survival at 5 years has exceeded 90%, a higher survival rate than in studies performed earlier than 1980. One multicentre study performed in Europe found a survival probability of 92% at 10 years after diagnosis. A lower survival probability was detected in those people who presented at the beginning of the study with nephropathy (88% in people with nephropathy *v* 94% in people without nephropathy; P = 0.045). When the causes of death during the initial 5 years of follow-up (1990–1995) were compared with those during the ensuing 5 years (1995–2000), active SLE and infections (29% each) seemed to be the most common causes during the initial 5 years, although thromboses (26%) became the most common cause of death during the last 5 years. Race is an independent predictor of mortality; black people in the USA have a worse prognosis than white people, as do Asian people in the UK compared with white people in the UK.

Leanne Bisset, Brooke Coombes, and Bill Vicenzino

## KEY POINTS

- Lateral pain in the elbow affects up to 3% of the population, and is usually an overload injury that often follows minor trauma to extensor forearm muscles.

  Although usually self-limiting, symptoms may persist for over 1 year in up to 20% of people.

- Corticosteroid injections improve pain, function, and global improvement from tennis elbow in the short term compared with placebo, local anaesthetic, orthoses, physiotherapy, and oral NSAIDs.

  We don't know which corticosteroid regimen leads to greatest pain relief.

  In the long term, physiotherapy or oral NSAIDs may be more effective than corticosteroid injections at reducing pain.

  Corticosteroid injections may increase the recurrence rate compared with physiotherapy and "wait and see".

  Repeated corticosteroid injections may lead to lower reduction in pain and greater need for surgery than single corticosteroid injection.

  Topical NSAIDs lead to short-term pain relief and better global improvement compared with placebo, but long-term effects are unknown.

- Extracorporeal shock wave therapy is unlikely to be more effective than placebo at improving pain, and may be less effective than injected corticosteroids.

  We don't know whether acupuncture or exercise and mobilisation reduce symptoms of tennis elbow as we found few trials, and they gave conflicting results.

  We don't know whether orthoses (braces) reduce symptoms compared with no treatment or other treatments, as we found few trials.

  We don't know whether manipulation improves pain and function, as we found few trials and they were of low quality.

  We also don't know whether open or percutaneous surgical techniques, exercise, combination physical therapies, ultrasound, iontophoresis, or pulsed electromagnetic field treatment improve pain and function, as we found insufficient good-quality evidence.

  Low-level laser therapy may be beneficial at improving pain in the short term when compared with placebo.

(i) **Please visit http://clinicalevidence.bmj.com for full text and references**

| What are the effects of oral drug treatment for tennis elbow? | |
|---|---|
| Unknown Effectiveness | • NSAIDs (oral) (for short-term pain relief) |

| What are the effects of topical drug treatment for tennis elbow? | |
|---|---|
| Likely To Be Beneficial | • NSAIDs (topical) (for short-term pain relief) |

### What are the effects of local injections for tennis elbow?

| Likely To Be Beneficial | • Corticosteroid injections (for short-term pain relief) |
|---|---|
| Unknown Effectiveness | • Autologous whole blood injections<br>• Platelet-rich plasma injections |

### What are the effects of non-drug treatment for tennis elbow?

| Likely To Be Beneficial | • Low-level laser therapy (for short-term pain relief and improvement of function) |
|---|---|
| Unknown Effectiveness | • Acupuncture (for short-term pain relief)<br>• Combination physical therapies<br>• Exercise<br>• Iontophoresis<br>• Manipulation<br>• Orthoses (bracing)<br>• Pulsed electromagnetic field treatment<br>• Surgery<br>• Ultrasound |
| Unlikely To Be Beneficial | • Extracorporeal shock wave therapy |

**Search date November 2009**

**DEFINITION** Tennis elbow has many analogous terms, including lateral elbow pain, lateral epicondylitis, lateral epicondylalgia, tendonitis of the common extensor origin, and peritendinitis of the elbow. Tennis elbow is characterised by pain and tenderness over the lateral epicondyle of the humerus, and pain on resisted dorsiflexion of the wrist, middle finger, or both. For the purposes of this review, tennis elbow is restricted to lateral elbow pain or lateral epicondylitis or lateral epicondylalgia.

**INCIDENCE/PREVALENCE** Lateral elbow pain is common (population prevalence 1–3%), with peak incidence occurring at 40 to 50 years of age. In women aged 42 to 46 years, incidence increases to 10%. In the UK, the Netherlands, and Scandinavia, the incidence of lateral elbow pain in general practice is 4–7/1000 people a year.

**AETIOLOGY/RISK FACTORS** Tennis elbow is considered an overload injury, typically after minor and often unrecognised trauma of the extensor muscles of the forearm. Despite the title tennis elbow, tennis is a direct cause in only 5% of people with lateral epicondylitis.

**PROGNOSIS** Although lateral elbow pain is generally self-limiting, in a minority of people symptoms persist for 18 months to 2 years, and in some cases for much longer. The cost, therefore, both in terms of lost productivity and healthcare use, is high. In a general practice trial of an expectant waiting policy, 80% of people with elbow pain of already >4 weeks' duration had recovered after 1 year.

David Murdoch

## KEY POINTS

- Up to half of people who ascend to heights above 2500 m may develop acute mountain sickness, pulmonary oedema, or cerebral oedema, with the risk being greater at higher altitudes, and faster rates of ascent.

  Symptoms of acute mountain sickness include headache, weakness, fatigue, nausea, insomnia, and decreased appetite.

  It is generally thought that symptoms resolve over a few days if no further ascent is attempted, but little is known about the long-term prognosis.

- We found little good-quality research on the prevention or treatment of this condition. There is consensus that slow ascent reduces the risk of acute mountain sickness.

- Acetazolamide and dexamethasone reduce the risk of developing acute mountain sickness compared with placebo, although we don't know whether they are more or less effective than each other or than other prophylactic treatments.

  Acetazolamide causes polyuria and paraesthesia in a high proportion of people, while in some people dexamethasone may cause depression after withdrawal of treatment.

- We don't know whether ginkgo biloba reduces the risk of acute mountain sickness compared with placebo, but it may be less effective than acetazolamide.

- Dexamethasone may reduce symptom scores in people with acute mountain sickness compared with placebo.

- We don't know whether acetazolamide is effective in the treatment of symptoms of acute mountain sickness.

- There is consensus that people who develop acute mountain sickness should descend if possible, but we don't know of any RCTs showing that this improves symptoms compared with resting at the same altitude.

(i) **Please visit http://clinicalevidence.bmj.com for full text and references**

| What are the effects of interventions to prevent acute mountain sickness? | |
|---|---|
| Beneficial | • Acetazolamide (prevention) |
| | • Dexamethasone (prevention) |
| Likely To Be Beneficial | • Slow ascent (or acclimatisation)* |
| Unknown Effectiveness | • Ginkgo biloba |

| What are the effects of treatments for acute mountain sickness? | |
|---|---|
| Likely To Be Beneficial | • Descent compared with resting at the same altitude* |

| | • Dexamethasone (treatment) |
|---|---|
| **Unknown Effectiveness** | • Acetazolamide (treatment) |

**Search date October 2009**

*Although we found no RCTs on the effects of these interventions, there is a general consensus that they are effective.

**DEFINITION** Altitude sickness (or high-altitude illness) includes acute mountain sickness, high-altitude pulmonary oedema, and high-altitude cerebral oedema. **Acute mountain sickness** typically occurs at altitudes >2500 m (about 8000 feet), and is characterised by the development of some or all of the symptoms of headache, weakness, fatigue, listlessness, nausea, insomnia, and suppressed appetite. Symptoms may take days to develop or may occur within hours, depending on the rate of ascent and the altitude attained. More severe forms of altitude sickness have been identified. **High-altitude pulmonary oedema** is characterised by symptoms and signs typical of pulmonary oedema, such as shortness of breath, coughing, and production of frothy or blood-stained sputum. **High-altitude cerebral oedema** is characterised by confusion, ataxia, and a decreasing level of consciousness. This review covers only acute mountain sickness.

**INCIDENCE/PREVALENCE** The incidence of acute mountain sickness increases with absolute height attained and with the rate of ascent. One survey in Taiwan (93 people ascending above 3000 m) found that 27% of people experienced acute mountain sickness. One survey in the Himalayas (278 unacclimatised hikers at 4243 m) found that 53% of people developed acute mountain sickness. One survey in the Swiss Alps (466 climbers at 4 altitudes between 2850 m and 4559 m) found the prevalence of two or more symptoms of acute mountain sickness to be 9% of people at 2850 m, 13% of people at 3050 m, 34% of people at 3650 m, and 53% of people at 4559 m.

**AETIOLOGY/RISK FACTORS** One survey in the Himalayas identified the rate of ascent and absolute height attained as the only risk factors for acute mountain sickness. It found no evidence of a difference in risk between men and women, or that previous episodes of altitude experience, load carried, or recent respiratory infections, affected risk. However, the study was too small to exclude these as risk factors, or to quantify risks reliably. One systematic review (search date 1999) comparing prophylactic agents versus placebo found that, among people receiving placebo, the incidence of acute mountain sickness was higher with a faster rate of ascent (54% of people at a mean ascent rate of 91 m/hour; 73% at a mean ascent rate of 1268 m/hour; 89% at a simulated ascent rate in a hypobaric chamber of 1647 m/hour). One survey in Switzerland (827 mountaineers ascending to 4559 m) examined the effects of susceptibility, pre-exposure, and ascent rate on acute mountain sickness. In this study, pre-exposure was defined as having spent >4 days above 3000 m in the preceding 2 months, and slow ascent was defined as ascending in >3 days. It found that, in susceptible people (who had previously had acute mountain sickness at high altitude), the prevalence of acute mountain sickness was 58% with rapid ascent and no pre-exposure, 29% with pre-exposure only, 33% with slow ascent only, and 7% with both pre-exposure and slow ascent. In non-susceptible people, the corresponding values were 31%, 16%, 11%, and 4%. The overall odds ratio for developing acute mountain sickness in susceptible compared with non-susceptible people was 2.9 (95% CI 2.1 to 4.1).

**PROGNOSIS** We found no reliable data on prognosis. It is widely held that if no further ascent is attempted, then the symptoms of acute mountain sickness tend to resolve over a few days. We found no reliable data about long-term sequelae in people whose symptoms have completely resolved.

N. Julian Holland and Jonathan M. Bernstein

### KEY POINTS

- Bell's palsy is an idiopathic, unilateral, acute paresis (partial weakness) or paralysis (complete palsy) of facial movement caused by dysfunction of the lower motor neurone of the facial nerve. Bell's palsy is a diagnosis of exclusion of other causes of facial nerve palsy.

  Most people with paresis make a spontaneous recovery within 3 weeks. Up to 30% of people, typically those with paralysis, have a delayed or incomplete recovery.

- Corticosteroids alone improve the rate of recovery and the proportion of people who make a full recovery, and reduce cosmetically disabling sequelae compared with placebo or no treatment.

- Antiviral treatment alone is no more effective than placebo at improving facial motor function and reducing the risk of disabling sequelae.

- We found no good evidence of significant benefit of combination corticosteroid-antiviral therapy over corticosteroid alone. However, there is a lack of data on people presenting with complete paralysis and any potential benefit of combination corticosteroid-antiviral therapy cannot be excluded.

- Hyperbaric oxygen may improve the time to recovery and the proportion of people who make a full recovery compared with corticosteroids. However, the evidence for this is weak and comes from one small RCT.

- Facial re-training may improve the recovery of facial motor function scores, including stiffness and lip mobility, and may reduce the risk of motor synkinesis in Bell's palsy, but the evidence is too weak to draw reliable conclusions.

 **Please visit http://clinicalevidence.bmj.com for full text and references**

### What are the effects of drug treatments for Bell's palsy in adults and children?

| | |
|---|---|
| **Likely To Be Beneficial** | • Corticosteroids |
| **Unknown Effectiveness** | • Corticosteroids plus antiviral treatment versus corticosteroids alone (inconclusive evidence that adding antivirals to corticosteroids provides any benefit over corticosteroids alone)<br>• Hyperbaric oxygen therapy |
| **Unlikely To Be Beneficial** | • Antiviral agents |

### What are the effects of physical treatments for Bell's palsy in adults and children?

| | |
|---|---|
| **Unknown Effectiveness** | • Facial re-training |

**Search date October 2013**

**DEFINITION** Bell's palsy is an idiopathic, unilateral, acute weakness of the face in a pattern consistent with peripheral facial nerve dysfunction, and may be partial or complete,

*(continued over)*

*(from previous page)*

occurring with equal frequency on either side of the face. Bell's palsy is idiopathic but there is weak evidence that Bell's palsy is caused by herpes simplex virus. Additional symptoms of Bell's palsy may include mild pain in or behind the ear, oropharyngeal or facial numbness, impaired tolerance to ordinary levels of noise, and disturbed taste on the anterior part of the tongue. Severe pain is more suggestive of herpes zoster virus infection and Ramsay Hunt syndrome. Bell's palsy is a diagnosis of exclusion. Other causes of lower motor neurone weakness include middle ear infection, parotid malignancy, malignant otitis externa, and lateral skull base tumours. Features such as sparing of movement in the upper face (central pattern), or weakness of a specific branch of the facial nerve (segmental pattern), suggest an alternative cause. Bell's palsy is less commonly the cause of facial palsy in children aged under 10 years (<50%).

**INCIDENCE/PREVALENCE** The incidence is about 20 in 100,000 people a year, with about 1 in 60 lifetime risk. Bell's palsy has a peak incidence between the ages of 15 and 40 years. Men and women are equally affected, although the incidence may be higher in pregnant women.

**AETIOLOGY/RISK FACTORS** The cause of Bell's palsy is uncertain. It is thought that reactivated herpes virus at the geniculate ganglion of the facial nerve may play a key role in the development of Bell's palsy. Herpes simplex virus (HSV)-1 has been detected in up to 50% of cases by some researchers. However, one study demonstrated the replication of HSV, herpes zoster virus (HZV), or both, in <20% of cases. Herpes zoster-associated facial palsy more frequently presents as zoster sine herpete (without vesicles), although 6% of people develop vesicles (Ramsay Hunt syndrome). Infection of the facial nerve by HZV initially results in reversible neuropraxia, but irreversible Wallerian degeneration may occur. Treatment plans for the management of Bell's palsy should recognise the possibility of HZV infection.

**PROGNOSIS** Overall, Bell's palsy has a fair prognosis without treatment. Clinically important improvement occurs within 3 weeks in 85% of people and within 3 to 5 months in the remaining 15%. People failing to show signs of improvement by 3 weeks may have suffered severe degeneration of the facial nerve, or may have an alternative diagnosis that requires identification by specialist examination or investigations, such as CT or MRI. Overall, 71% of people will experience complete recovery in facial muscle function (i.e., 61% of people with complete paralysis, 94% of people with partial paralysis). The remaining 29% have permanent mild to severe residual facial muscle weakness, 17% with contracture and 16% with hemifacial spasm or synkinesis. Incomplete recovery of facial expression has a long-term impact on quality of life and self-esteem. The prognosis for children with Bell's palsy is generally better, with a high rate (>90%) of spontaneous recovery, in part because of the higher frequency of paresis. However, children with paralysis have permanent facial muscle weakness as frequently as adults.

Nicola Rosenfelder and Vincent Khoo

## KEY POINTS

- Brain (cerebral) metastases may be either solitary or multiple, with or without disseminated disease elsewhere.

- They may present with focal or generalised symptoms, although up to one third of people may be asymptomatic.

  Headache is the most common presenting symptom. Focal weakness, mental change, and seizures are also common.

- The incidence of brain metastases is between 8 and 11/100,000 people a year.

  The lung is the most common primary site for brain metastases.

- This review only includes adults with brain metastases (cerebral hemispheres and posterior fossa structures) confirmed with a biopsy or by computed tomography (CT) or magnetic resonance imaging (MRI).

- We found no direct evidence from RCTs comparing corticosteroids versus no corticosteroids. Such RCTs are unlikely to be undertaken.

  Although we found no RCT evidence, there is consensus that corticosteroids are effective for the relief of symptoms.

- Whole-brain radiotherapy (external beam) (WBRT) may be effective in some selected people with brain metastases.

  However, there are adverse effects associated with the use of WBRT, which need to be weighed against any potential benefits on an individual basis.

- We don't know whether WBRT plus radiosurgery is more effective than WBRT alone at improving survival in people with between one and four brain metastases.

  However, subgroup analysis in one large RCT found that, in people with a single unresectable brain metastasis, WBRT plus radiosurgery may increase median survival compared with WBRT alone.

- We found insufficient evidence on the effects of systemic cytotoxic chemotherapy alone.

  Combining chemotherapy with WBRT may increase response rates compared with WBRT alone, but there seems no survival advantage and further data are needed to draw conclusions.

- We found little RCT evidence on the effects of surgery plus WBRT. However, surgical resection followed by WBRT is recommended for people with single, surgically accessible brain metastases who have controlled extracranial disease.

- We found insufficient evidence to assess surgery, radiosurgery, surgery plus radiosurgery, or surgery plus radiosurgery plus WBRT.

- Current evidence suggests that adding radiation sensitisers to WBRT is unlikely to produce any additional benefit compared with giving WBRT alone.

(i) **Please visit http://clinicalevidence.bmj.com for full text and references**

## What are the effects of interventions for managing brain metastases in adults?

| Likely To Be Beneficial | • Corticosteroids* |
|---|---|
| | • Surgery plus whole-brain radiotherapy (external beam) in people with single brain metastases* |
| | • Whole-brain radiotherapy (external beam) (addition of some other interventions to WBRT may be no |

| | more effective than WBRT alone; WBRT alone may be effective in selected people) <br><br> • Whole-brain radiotherapy (external beam) plus radiosurgery (some evidence of improved survival in people with a single unresectable brain metastasis with WBRT plus radiosurgery compared with WBRT alone; no evidence of improved survival in people with multiple brain metastases) |
|---|---|
| **Unknown Effectiveness** | • Cytotoxic chemotherapy (systemic) <br><br> • Radiosurgery (stereotactic LINAC radiotherapy or gamma knife) <br><br> • Surgery <br><br> • Surgery plus radiosurgery <br><br> • Surgery plus radiosurgery plus whole-brain radiotherapy (external beam) |
| **Unlikely To Be Beneficial** | • Whole-brain radiotherapy plus radiation sensitisers (no evidence that combination is more effective than WBRT alone) |

**Search date March 2010**

*Categorisation based on clinical consensus.

**DEFINITION** Metastases to the central nervous system may occur with tumours of any primary origin. Brain (cerebral) metastases may be either solitary or multiple, with or without disseminated disease elsewhere. Brain metastases may present with focal or generalised symptoms, although up to one third of people may be asymptomatic. A high index of suspicion is required when managing people with cancer. Headache is the most common presenting symptom (50% of people). Focal weakness, mental change, and seizures are also common. Although clinical signs can be helpful to localise the lesion(s), the initial diagnostic evaluation is commonly performed with pre- and post-contrast computed tomography (CT) scan. Although CT is commonly done, magnetic resonance imaging (MRI) is considered imaging modality of choice. MRI with gadolinium contrast is performed following the detection of a solitary lesion on CT, or if clinical suspicion remains high. MRI may detect lesions as small as 1.9 mm, and is superior to CT for detection of posterior fossa lesions. More than 10% of solitary lesions will not be metastatic and therefore biopsy may be warranted to confirm diagnosis. In the case of solitary or multiple metastases in the absence of known malignancy, further investigations are directed towards the identification of a primary lesion, most commonly from the chest. In this review, we have included only adults with brain metastases (cerebral hemispheres and posterior fossa structures) from any primary source that have been confirmed with biopsy or by CT or MRI, and excluded metastasis to the leptomeninges and peripheral nervous system, where management may be more case specific.

**INCIDENCE/PREVALENCE** The incidence of brain metastasis is 8 to 11/100,000 people a year. The proportion of people with primary cancers developing brain metastasis varies widely, between 9.6% and 50.0% depending on the series selected. The lung is the most common primary site, with 9.7% to 64.0% of people developing brain metastases, while melanoma (6.9–7.4%), renal (6.5–9.8%), breast (5.0–5.1%), and colorectal (1.2–1.9%) account for most of the remaining cases. Cancer of unknown primary origin represents 15% of cases of brain metastasis.

**AETIOLOGY/RISK FACTORS** Brain metastases are most common in the advanced stages of disseminated disease, but can occur in isolation. Tumour seeding of the brain parenchyma involves a number of steps, including intravasation (reaching the brain vasculature), breaching of the blood–brain barrier, and proliferation and neoangiogenesis (the formation of new blood vessels/vasculature) within the brain. These steps are dependent on the expression of specific regulatory molecules such as matrix metalloproteinases and growth factors.

**PROGNOSIS** People with untreated brain metastases have a median survival of about 4 weeks from diagnosis. The addition of corticosteroids may extend this by another 4 weeks. Whole-brain radiotherapy further extends median survival to 3 to 6 months. The additional benefit of surgery, radiotherapy, chemotherapy, and biological agents alone or in combination depends on tumour type. Prognostic factors predicting a better outcome are solitary lesions, surgical resection, and the use of combined chemotherapy and radiotherapy.

Manjit Matharu

### KEY POINTS

- The revised International Headache Society (IHS) criteria for cluster headache are: attacks of severe or very severe, strictly unilateral pain, which is orbital, supraorbital, or temporal pain, lasting 15 to 180 minutes and occurring from once every other day to eight times daily. The attacks are associated with one or more of the following, all of which are ipsilateral: conjunctival injection, lacrimation, nasal congestion, rhinorrhoea, forehead and facial sweating, miosis, ptosis, and eyelid oedema. Most people are restless or agitated during an attack. Cluster headache may be episodic or chronic.

  Cluster headache is rare, but the exact prevalence remains a matter of debate.

- The main focus of intervention is to abort attacks once they have begun and to prevent future attacks.

- Sumatriptan, used subcutaneously or intranasally, and zolmitriptan used intranasally reduce the severity and duration of cluster headache attacks once they have begun.

  Oral zolmitriptan reduces severity of attacks in people with episodic cluster headache, but we don't know how effective it is in people with chronic cluster headache.

  We don't know whether oral sumatriptan is effective.

- There is consensus that high-dose and high-flow-rate oxygen is effective for abortive treatment of episodic or chronic cluster headache. We don't know whether this consensus can be applied to hyperbaric oxygen, as little research has been conducted.

- There is also consensus that subcutaneous octreotide is effective for abortive treatment of cluster headache.

- We don't know whether intranasal lidocaine is effective for abortive treatment of cluster headache.

- There is consensus that both verapamil and lithium prevent cluster headache, but that verapamil is more effective than lithium, and causes fewer adverse effects.

  There is also consensus that corticosteroids and greater occipital nerve injections (betamethasone plus xylocaine) are effective for preventive treatment.

- We don't know whether baclofen, botulinum toxin, capsaicin, chlorpromazine, civamide, clonidine, ergotamine or dihydroergotamine, gabapentin, leuprolide, melatonin, methysergide, pizotifen, sodium valproate, oral sumatriptan, topiramate, or tricyclic antidepressants are effective for prevention of cluster headache. Some of these interventions are not routinely used in clinical practice.

(i) **Please visit http://clinicalevidence.bmj.com for full text and references**

| What are the effects of interventions to abort cluster headache? | |
|---|---|
| **Beneficial** | • Sumatriptan (subcutaneous and intranasal) for episodic or chronic cluster headache<br><br>• Zolmitriptan (intranasal) |
| **Likely To Be Beneficial** | • High-dose and high-flow-rate oxygen for episodic or chronic cluster headache* |

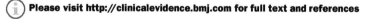

| | • Octreotide (subcutaneous)* |
| | • Zolmitriptan (oral) for aborting episodic cluster headache (unknown effectiveness for chronic cluster headache) |
| Unknown Effectiveness | • Hyperbaric oxygen |
| | • Lidocaine (intranasal) |
| | • Sumatriptan (oral) |

## What are the effects of interventions to prevent cluster headache?

| Likely To Be Beneficial | • Corticosteroids (oral)* |
| | • Greater occipital nerve injections (betamethasone plus xylocaine)* |
| | • Lithium (oral) (effective for preventing chronic cluster headache, but less so than verapamil and more adverse effects)* |
| | • Verapamil (more effective than lithium for preventing chronic cluster headache and fewer adverse effects)* |
| Unknown Effectiveness | • Baclofen (oral) |
| | • Botulinum toxin (intramuscular) |
| | • Capsaicin (intranasal) |
| | • Chlorpromazine |
| | • Civamide (intranasal) |
| | • Clonidine (transdermal) |
| | • Ergotamine and dihydroergotamine (oral or intranasal) |
| | • Gabapentin (oral) |
| | • Leuprolide |
| | • Melatonin |
| | • Methysergide (oral) |
| | • Pizotifen (oral) |
| | • Sodium valproate (oral) |
| | • Sumatriptan (oral) |
| | • Topiramate (oral) |
| | • Tricyclic antidepressants |

**Search date June 2009**

*Categorisation based on consensus.

**DEFINITION** The revised International Headache Society (IHS) criteria for cluster headache are: attacks of severe or very severe, strictly unilateral pain, which is orbital, supraorbital, or temporal pain, lasting 15 to 180 minutes, and occurring from once every other day to eight times daily. The attacks are associated with at least one of the following cranial autonomic features, all of which are ipsilateral: conjunctival injection, lacrimation, nasal congestion, rhinorrhoea, forehead and facial sweating, miosis, ptosis, and eyelid oedema. The revised IHS criteria allow the diagnosis of cluster headache to be made in the absence of ipsilateral cranial autonomic features, provided the person reports a sense of restlessness or agitation. Attacks usually occur in series (cluster periods) lasting for weeks or months, separated by remission periods usually lasting months or years. However, about 10% to 15% of people have chronic symptoms without remissions. Cluster headache is further subclassified according to the duration of the bout. Episodic cluster headache is diagnosed when cluster headache attacks occur in periods lasting 7 days to 1 year, separated by remissions lasting 1 month or longer. Chronic cluster headache is diagnosed when cluster headache attacks occur for more than 1 year without remission, or with remissions lasting less than 1 month. The term cluster headache is now widely accepted, although historically the condition has been known by several different names, including: migrainous neuralgia, Horton's headache, histaminic cephalalgia, sphenopalatine neuralgia, Sluder's neuralgia, petrosal neuralgia, red migraine, erythroprosopalgia of Bing, ciliary neuralgia, erythromelalgia of the head, Vidian neuralgia, hemicrania angioparalytica, hemicrania periodic neuralgiforms, syndrome of hemicephalic vasodilation of sympathetic origin, and autonomic faciocephalalgia.

**INCIDENCE/PREVALENCE** Cluster headache is rare, but the exact prevalence remains a matter of debate because of the remarkable variation of the estimated prevalence — between 56 and 401 per 100,000 population — in the various studies. Recent studies suggest that the prevalence of cluster headache is likely to be at least one person per 500. Cluster headache is more prevalent in men. The gender ratio in the various case series varies between 2.5:1 and 7.2:1.

**AETIOLOGY/RISK FACTORS** There is a small increased familial risk of cluster headache, suggesting a genetic role in causation. People with cluster headache may over indulge in non-essential consumption habits including smoking, intake of alcohol, and consumption of coffee. There is an increased incidence of previous head trauma in cluster headache, ranging between 5% and 37%, although there is often a long interval between the head trauma and the onset of the headaches.

**PROGNOSIS** Onset of symptoms most commonly occurs between the second and fourth decades of life, although cluster headache has been reported in all age groups. Although there is a paucity of literature on the long-term prognosis of cluster headache, the available evidence suggests that it is a lifelong disorder in most people. In one study, episodic cluster headache (ECH) evolved into chronic cluster headache (CCH) in about 10% of people, whereas CCH transformed into ECH in one third of people. Furthermore, a substantial proportion of people with cluster headache can expect to develop longer remission periods with increasing age.

Ailsa Snaith and Derick Wade

## KEY POINTS

- Dystonia is characterised by involuntary muscle contractions, resulting in abnormal postures and twisting of body parts.

  It is often a lifelong condition, with persistent pain and disability.

  Focal dystonia affects a single part of the body; generalised dystonia can affect most or all of the body.

  It is more common in women, and some types of dystonia are more common in people of Ashkenazi descent.

- Botulinum toxin is effective at relieving cervical dystonia in adults.

  Botulinum A toxin and botulinum B toxin are both effective treatments for focal dystonia.

  We don't know whether botulinum toxins are effective for generalised dystonia.

- Although we assessed other treatments, we primarily found evidence for botulinum toxin, and it is currently the mainstay of treatment for focal dystonia.

- We don't know whether any other drug treatments (amantadine, baclofen, benzatropine, bromocriptine, carbamazepine, carbidopa/levodopa, clonazepam, clozapine, diazepam, gabapentin, haloperidol, lorazepam, ondansetron, pregabalin, procyclidine, tizanidine, trazodone hydrochloride, and trihexyphenidyl) are effective for either focal or generalised dystonia.

- We don't know whether deep brain stimulation of thalamus and globus pallidus is effective for either focal or generalised dystonia. We don't know whether any other surgical interventions (selective peripheral denervation or myectomy) are effective for focal dystonia.

- Most people will see a physiotherapist after diagnosis, but there is no consistent approach to treatment. We don't know whether any other physical treatments (acupuncture, biofeedback, occupational therapy, or speech therapy) are effective for either focal or generalised dystonia.

(i) **Please visit http://clinicalevidence.bmj.com for full text and references**

| What are the effects of drug treatments for focal dystonia? | |
|---|---|
| Beneficial | • Botulinum toxins (in cervical dystonia; both A and B toxin beneficial compared with placebo and similarly effective when compared with each other) for focal dystonia |
| Unknown Effectiveness | • Amantadine for focal dystonia |
| | • Baclofen for focal dystonia |
| | • Benzatropine for focal dystonia |
| | • Bromocriptine for focal dystonia |
| | • Carbamazepine for focal dystonia |
| | • Carbidopa/levodopa for focal dystonia |
| | • Clonazepam for focal dystonia |
| | • Clozapine for focal dystonia |
| | • Diazepam for focal dystonia |
| | • Gabapentin for focal dystonia |

- Haloperidol for focal dystonia
- Lorazepam for focal dystonia
- Ondansetron for focal dystonia
- Pregabalin for focal dystonia
- Procyclidine for focal dystonia
- Tizanidine for focal dystonia
- Trazodone hydrochloride for focal dystonia
- Trihexyphenidyl for focal dystonia

## What are the effects of surgical treatments for focal dystonia?

| | |
|---|---|
| Unknown Effectiveness | • Deep brain stimulation of thalamus and globus pallidus for focal dystonia<br>• Myectomy for focal dystonia<br>• Selective peripheral denervation for focal dystonia |

## What are the effects of physical treatments for focal dystonia?

| | |
|---|---|
| Unknown Effectiveness | • Acupuncture for focal dystonia<br>• Biofeedback for focal dystonia<br>• Occupational therapy for focal dystonia<br>• Physiotherapy for focal dystonia<br>• Speech therapy for focal dystonia |

## What are the effects of drug treatments for generalised dystonia?

| | |
|---|---|
| Unknown Effectiveness | • Amantadine for generalised dystonia<br>• Baclofen for generalised dystonia<br>• Benzatropine for generalised dystonia<br>• Botulinum toxins for generalised dystonia<br>• Bromocriptine for generalised dystonia<br>• Carbamazepine for generalised dystonia<br>• Carbidopa/levodopa for generalised dystonia<br>• Clonazepam for generalised dystonia<br>• Clozapine for generalised dystonia<br>• Diazepam for generalised dystonia<br>• Gabapentin for generalised dystonia<br>• Haloperidol for generalised dystonia<br>• Lorazepam for generalised dystonia<br>• Ondansetron for generalised dystonia<br>• Pregabalin for generalised dystonia |

- Procyclidine for generalised dystonia
- Tizanidine for generalised dystonia
- Trazodone hydrochloride for generalised dystonia
- Trihexyphenidyl for generalised dystonia

## What are the effects of surgical treatments for generalised dystonia?

| Unknown Effectiveness | • Deep brain stimulation of thalamus and globus pallidus for generalised dystonia |
|---|---|

## What are the effects of physical treatments for generalised dystonia?

| Unknown Effectiveness | • Acupuncture for generalised dystonia |
|---|---|
| | • Biofeedback for generalised dystonia |
| | • Occupational therapy for generalised dystonia |
| | • Physiotherapy for generalised dystonia |
| | • Speech therapy for generalised dystonia |

**Search date September 2013**

---

**DEFINITION** Dystonia is a neurological disorder characterised by involuntary, abnormal muscle contractions that result in sustained abnormal postures, twisting, or both, and repetitive movements of body parts. It arises from dysfunction of the motor control system within the central nervous system. Dystonia is most simply classified by location: **focal dystonia** involves a single body part; **multifocal dystonia** involves two or more unrelated body parts; **segmental dystonia** affects two or more adjacent parts of the body; **hemidystonia** involves the arm and leg on the same side of the body; and **generalised dystonia** affects most or all of the body. For the purpose of this review we have classified dystonia into focal dystonia and generalised/other dystonia. However, studies in which dystonia has been classified according to other classification systems are also covered. In addition to focal and generalised dystonia, classification may also be based on age at onset (**early onset** or **late onset**), or according to the cause of the dystonia: **primary dystonia** where dystonia is the only sign and no cause can be identified; **dystonia-plus syndrome** where dystonia is associated with other pathology (e.g., dopa-responsive dystonia and myoclonus dystonia); **heredodegenerative dystonia** where dystonia is a sign associated with neurological conditions, such as Parkinson's disease and Huntington's disease; and **secondary dystonia** where a cause (usually environmental) can be identified, such as head injury and use of drugs (e.g., neuroleptic drugs and metoclopramide). Certain dystonias may also be classified as task specific; examples of task-specific focal hand dystonia include writer's cramp, typist's cramp, and musician's cramp (affects, for example, pianists and flautists). **Diagnosis:** The clinical diagnosis of dystonia is based on the hallmark features of the abnormal, involuntary, and prolonged muscle contractions with consistent directionality that lead to an abnormal posture of the area affected. There is no definitive diagnostic test for dystonia. Investigation typically involves history and clinical examination, laboratory tests, and imaging, to establish severity and potential cause. Laboratory tests and neuro-imaging may help to rule out metabolic or structural causes. Genetic testing, electrophysiological tests, and tissue biopsy may also be considered. The goal of accurate diagnosis is to facilitate treatment choice.

**INCIDENCE/PREVALENCE** Dystonia occurs worldwide, with prevalence estimates varying widely depending on study methodology. In the US, the prevalence of focal dystonia has been reported as 30 per 100,000 people. Cervical dystonia (torticollis or 'wry neck') is the most

*(continued over)*

*(from previous page)*

common adult form of focal dystonia, with a prevalence in Europe of 5.7 per 100,000. Other frequently occurring focal dystonias are blepharospasm (forceful eyelid closures), which affects 3.6 per 100,000 people, and limb dystonias (e.g., writer's cramp), which affect 1.4 per 100,000. In the US, the prevalence of generalised dystonia has been reported as 0.2 to 6.7 per 100,000 population; generalised dystonia affects more people of Ashkenazi descent. In Europe, the prevalence of primary dystonia has been estimated at 15.2 per 100,000. Studies identified to have rigorous methodology estimated the prevalence of early-onset (at <20 years of age) dystonia to be 11.1 per 100,000 for dystonia in people of Ashkenazi descent from the New York area, 60 per 100,000 for late-onset (at >20 years of age) dystonia in the overall population of Northern England, and 300 per 100,000 for late-onset dystonia in the Italian population (aged 50 years or older). Dystonia occurs more frequently in women.

**AETIOLOGY/RISK FACTORS** The pathophysiology of dystonia remains unclear. Dystonia may occur because of abnormal neurochemical transmission in the basal ganglia, brainstem, or both, resulting in abnormal execution of motor control. Focal dystonias have been associated with loss of inhibition, abnormal plasticity in the motor cortex, and impairments in spatial and temporal discrimination. There is debate on the extent to which psychological factors cause dystonia, although they can undoubtedly exacerbate it. Dystonia can be classified as primary (where underlying cause is unknown) or secondary (related to known disorders). The primary disorders may be further classified as hereditary or sporadic. Currently, 19 types of dystonia can be distinguished on a genetic basis, six of which are primary dystonias (*DYT1, 2, 4, 6, 7,* and *13*). The remainder are secondary dystonia, dystonia-plus syndromes, and paroxysmal dystonias.

**PROGNOSIS** Dystonia is often a lifelong disorder, once it has started, although a small minority experience complete remission. Most people with dystonia have a normal life expectancy, but with continued symptoms. The presence and severity of symptoms are unpredictable, as symptoms may fluctuate over time (e.g., stressful situations may make symptoms worse) or may disappear or stabilise for a time. Regardless of the cause, dystonic contractions may have a chronic course and may lead to severe persistent pain and disability. Also, embarrassment caused by the symptoms may lead to social withdrawal. Prognosis seems to depend on a number of factors, including age at onset, distribution, and cause. Focal dystonia may become generalised over time. Dystonia with a later age of onset has a lower likelihood of spreading compared with dystonia beginning in childhood. Similarly, dystonia starting in the neck is less likely to spread than dystonia starting in the limbs.

J. Helen Cross

## KEY POINTS

- Epilepsy is a group of disorders rather than a single disease.

- Seizures can be classified as generalised or focal. This review examines the effects of additional treatments in people with drug-resistant epilepsy characterised by generalised seizures.

- During their lifetime, about 3% of people will be diagnosed with epilepsy, but about 70% of people with epilepsy eventually go into remission.

- Adding lamotrigine seems to be more effective than adding placebo at reducing seizure frequency in people with drug-resistant epilepsy characterised by generalised seizures.

- Adding levetiracetam seems to be more effective than adding placebo at reducing seizure frequency in people with drug-resistant epilepsy characterised by generalised seizures.

- The RCTs we found were relatively short term (12–24 weeks) and we found no longer term studies. There is a need for further long-term studies to confirm the ongoing efficacy and safety of agents.

- We don't know about the benefits of adding lacosamide, perampanel, or zonisamide compared to adding placebo, as we found no systematic reviews or RCTs.

(i) **Please visit http://clinicalevidence.bmj.com for full text and references**

| What are the effects of additional treatments in people with drug-resistant epilepsy characterised by generalised seizures? | |
|---|---|
| Likely To Be Beneficial | • Addition of lamotrigine compared with adding placebo in people with drug-resistant epilepsy characterised by generalised seizures |
| | • Addition of levetiracetam compared with addition of placebo in people with drug-resistant epilepsy characterised by generalised seizures |
| Unknown Effectiveness | • Addition of lacosamide compared with adding placebo in people with drug-resistant epilepsy characterised by generalised seizures |
| | • Addition of perampanel compared with the addition of placebo in people with drug-resistant epilepsy characterised by generalised seizures |
| | • Addition of zonisamide compared with the addition of placebo in people with drug-resistant epilepsy characterised by generalised seizures |

**Search date April 2014**

**DEFINITION** Epilepsy is a group of disorders rather than a single disease. Seizures can be classified by type as generalised (generalised tonic clonic, absence, myoclonic, tonic, and atonic seizures) or focal (previously categorised as simple partial, complex partial, and secondary generalised tonic clonic seizures). A person is considered to have epilepsy if he/she has had two or more unprovoked seizures or has had a single seizure and is

*(continued over)*

*(from previous page)*

regarded as at significant risk of a second. When a diagnosis of epilepsy has been made, the epilepsy syndrome should be characterised if possible, dependent on the electroclinical features (e.g., childhood absence epilepsy is characterised by age of onset [5-10 years], frequent short absence seizures, and an EEG demonstrating 3 Hz spike and wave). The optimal first-line medication will be chosen, dependent on the syndrome; the intervention most likely to lead to benefit and least likely to cause aggravation of seizures. Valproate remains the most effective medication as first-line treatment in many of the epilepsies characterised by predominantly generalised seizures (e.g., genetic generalised epilepsy), especially those including generalised tonic clonic seizures. Ethosuximide may be the first drug of choice in generalised epilepsies characterised by absence seizures. Side effects of medication also need to be kept to a minimum. There has been emerging concern about the effect of valproate on the unborn child, specifically with regard to postnatal neurocognitive development. Consequently it is now not considered as treatment of choice in women of child-bearing age. This has led to wider use of levetiracetam and lamotrigine as alternative first-line treatment in this population. This review deals with additional pharmacological treatments for people with drug-resistant epilepsy characterised by generalised seizures. Status epilepticus is not covered in this review.

**INCIDENCE/PREVALENCE** Epilepsy is common, with an estimated average prevalence of 5.5/1000 people in Europe, 6.8/1000 people in the US, and 7.5/1000 people in Australia. Prevalence rates in developing countries vary widely, with studies carried out in sub-Saharan Africa reporting rates of 5.2 to 74.4/1000 people, studies in Asia reporting overall prevalence rates of 1.5 to 14.0/1000 people, and Latin America reporting rates of 17 to 22/1000 people. The worldwide incidence of epilepsy (defined as 2 or more unprovoked seizures occurring at least 24 hours apart) is 50.4/100,000 people per year. The incidence is approximately 45.0/100,000 per year for high-income countries and 81.7/100,000 per year for low- and middle-income countries. The worldwide incidence of single unprovoked seizures is 23 to 61/100,000 person-years. About 3% of people will be diagnosed with epilepsy at some time in their lives.

**AETIOLOGY/RISK FACTORS** Epilepsy is a symptom rather than a disease, and it may be caused by various disorders involving the brain. Where possible, an epilepsy will be described as an electroclinical syndrome. The causes/risk factors, however, remain wide and include birth/neonatal injuries, congenital or metabolic disorders, head injuries, tumours, infections of the brain or meninges, genetic defects, malformations of the brain, degenerative disease of the brain, cerebrovascular disease, or demyelinating disease; these may be grouped as genetic, structural/metabolic, or unknown.

**PROGNOSIS** After their first seizure, about 60% of untreated people have no further seizures in the following 2 years. Prognosis is good for most people with epilepsy. About 70% go into remission, defined as being seizure-free for 5 years on or off treatment. This leaves 20% to 30% who continue to have epileptic seizures, despite treatment with anti-epileptic drugs. This group are often treated with multiple anti-epileptic drugs.

Professor Helen Cross

## KEY POINTS

- During their lifetime, about 3% of people will be diagnosed with epilepsy. First-line treatment in the majority is anticonvulsant medication; about 70% of people with epilepsy respond to medication, or in the longer term go into spontaneous remission.

- Alternative treatments for epilepsy are sought where medication fails and surgery is not an option.

- We searched for good-quality RCTs on the effects of selected interventions.

  We found few studies, many of which were small or short-term, and most of which were methodically weak.

  There is a need for further high-quality trials in this field reporting longer-term outcomes.

  However, the difficulties of undertaking trials, particularly in people with refractory epilepsy, should not be underestimated.

- Educational programmes may improve some psychosocial functioning outcomes compared with control.

- We found insufficient evidence to draw robust conclusions on the effects of cognitive behavioural therapy (CBT) or of relaxation plus behavioural modification therapy.

- We found no RCTs of sufficient quality on the effects of relaxation therapy, yoga, biofeedback (electroencephalographic or galvanic skin response), or family counselling.

- We found evidence from two RCTs that a ketogenic diet or a modified-Atkins diet may improve seizure frequency compared with control in children aged 2 to 16 years who had tried at least two anticonvulsants and had at least daily seizures.

  A ketogenic diet may be associated with gastrointestinal (constipation, hunger, vomiting, etc.) and other adverse effects, so continued monitoring is required.

  There may also be issues of tolerability and family acceptance.

  We found no RCTs in adults or any longer-term data.

- We found five RCTs comparing different ketogenic diets, which were of varying methodological quality.

- No two trials compared the same interventions in the same population.

(i) **Please visit http://clinicalevidence.bmj.com for full text and references**

### What are the effects of behavioural and psychological treatments in people with epilepsy?

| Likely To Be Beneficial | • Educational programmes |
|---|---|
| Unknown Effectiveness | • Biofeedback |
| | • Cognitive behavioural therapy (CBT) |
| | • Family counselling |
| | • Relaxation plus behavioural modification therapy |
| | • Relaxation therapy |
| | • Yoga for people with epilepsy |

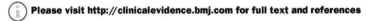

## What are the effects of ketogenic diet in people with epilepsy?

| | |
|---|---|
| Likely To Be Beneficial | • Ketogenic diet versus no change to treatment (improves seizure frequency in the short term in children not responding to anticonvulsants; no evidence in adults, or longer term) |
| Unknown Effectiveness | • Different implementation methods of ketogenic diet therapies versus each other (limited evidence on comparisons available from RCTs) |

**Search date April 2014**

**DEFINITION** Epilepsy should now be considered a group of disorders rather than a single disease. Seizures can be classified by type as focal (with or without evolution into a bilateral convulsive seizure, as with tonic clonic seizure) or generalised (categorised as generalised tonic clonic, absence, myoclonic, tonic, and atonic seizures). A person is considered to have epilepsy if they have had two or more unprovoked seizures. Accurate diagnosis is important both for epilepsy and for the type of epilepsy (epilepsy syndrome). Exact medication is based on the type of epilepsy and age of presentation, not only looking for the medication most likely to work but also avoiding aggravation of seizures. This review considers behavioural and psychological treatments of any epilepsy (generalised or focal). See also the separate related review on Epilepsy (generalised seizures), p 433 for information on pharmacological and surgical treatments of generalised epilepsy. Status epilepticus is not covered in this review.

**INCIDENCE/PREVALENCE** Epilepsy is common, with an estimated average prevalence of 5.5/1000 people in Europe, 6.8/1000 people in the US, and 7.5/1000 people in Australia. Prevalence rates in developing countries vary widely, with studies carried out in sub-Saharan Africa reporting rates of 5.2 to 74.4/1000 people, studies in Asia reporting overall prevalence rates of 1.5 to 14.0/1000 people, and studies in Latin America reporting rates of 17 to 22/1000 people. The annual incidence rates of epilepsy are 24 to 56/100,000 people in Europe, 44/100,000 in the US, 63 to 158/100,000 people in sub-Saharan Africa, 113 to 190/100,000 people in Latin America, and 28 to 60/100,000 people in Asia. The worldwide incidence of single unprovoked seizures is 23 to 61/100,000 person-years. About 3% of people will be diagnosed with epilepsy at some time in their lives.

**AETIOLOGY/RISK FACTORS** Epilepsy is a symptom rather than a disease, and it may be caused by various disorders involving the brain. The causes/risk factors include birth/ neonatal injuries, genetic abnormalities, structural or metabolic disorders (including brain malformations), tumours, infections of the brain or meninges, head injuries, degenerative disease of the brain, or cerebrovascular disease. Epilepsy can be classified by cause. A reorganisation of the epilepsies has considered that, on a diagnosis of epilepsy, the syndrome should be diagnosed where possible. The cause may then be considered according to whether it is genetic, structural, metabolic, immune, infectious, or unknown.

**PROGNOSIS** About 60% of untreated people have no further seizures during the 2 years after their first unprovoked seizure; however, community-based studies have suggested a lower percentage. Prognosis is good for most people with epilepsy. About 70% go into remission, defined as being seizure-free for 5 years on or off treatment. This leaves 20% to 30% who develop chronic epilepsy, which is often treated with multiple anticonvulsant drugs.

Joaquim Ferreira and Cristina Sampaio

### KEY POINTS

- Essential tremor refers to a persistent bilateral oscillation of both hands and forearms, or an isolated tremor of the head, without abnormal posturing, and when there is no evidence that the tremor arises from another identifiable cause.

    Essential tremor is one of the most common movement disorders throughout the world, with a prevalence of 0.4–3.9% in the general population.

    Although most people with essential tremor are only mildly affected, those who seek medical care are disabled to some extent, and most are socially handicapped by the tremor.

- Overall, we found few RCTs that assessed the long-term effects of drug treatments for essential tremor of the hand.

- Propranolol seems to effectively improve clinical scores, tremor amplitude, and self-evaluation of severity compared with placebo in people with hand tremor.

    We found insufficient evidence to judge the efficacy of other beta-blockers such as atenolol, metoprolol, nadolol, pindolol, and sotalol in treating essential tremor of the hand.

- Barbiturates, such as phenobarbital (phenobarbitone) and primidone, may improve hand tremor in the short term, but are associated with depression, and with cognitive and behavioural adverse effects.

- Benzodiazepines may improve hand tremor and function in the short term, but we were unable to draw reliable conclusions because of the weakness of the studies.

    Benzodiazepines are also associated with adverse effects such as dependency, sedation, and cognitive and behavioural effects.

- We don't know whether carbonic anhydrase inhibitors, dihydropyridene calcium channel blockers, flunarizine, clonidine, isoniazid, or gabapentin are useful in treating essential tremor of the hand, because the studies have all been too small to detect clinically important differences in symptoms.

- Botulinum A toxin-haemagglutinin complex and topiramate both appear to improve clinical rating scales for hand tremor in the short term, but are associated with frequent adverse effects.

    Botulinum A toxin-haemagglutinin complex is associated with hand weakness which is dose dependent and transient.

    The most common adverse effects of topiramate are appetite suppression, weight loss, and paraesthesia.

- Adding mirtazapine to antitremor drugs such as propranolol does not seem to improve outcomes further in people with essential tremor of the hand, and leads to more frequent adverse effects, such as drowsiness, confusion, dry mouth, and weight gain.

(i) **Please visit http://clinicalevidence.bmj.com for full text and references**

| What are the effects of drug treatments in people with essential tremor of the hand? | |
|---|---|
| **Likely To Be Beneficial** | • Propranolol |
| **Trade-off Between Benefits And Harms** | • Botulinum A toxin–haemagglutinin complex (improved clinical rating scales at 4–12 weeks, but associated with hand weakness) |

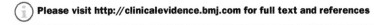

| | |
|---|---|
| | • Phenobarbital (may improve tremor at 5 weeks, but associated with depression and cognitive adverse effects)<br><br>• Primidone (may improve tremor and function at 5 weeks compared with placebo and at 1 year compared with baseline, but associated with depression, and with cognitive adverse effects)<br><br>• Topiramate (improved tremor scores after 24 weeks' treatment, but associated with appetite suppression, weight loss, and paraesthesia) |
| **Unknown Effectiveness** | • Benzodiazepines<br><br>• Beta-blockers other than propranolol (atenolol, metoprolol, nadolol, pindolol, and sotalol)<br><br>• Calcium channel blockers (dihydropyridine)<br><br>• Carbonic anhydrase inhibitors<br><br>• Clonidine<br><br>• Flunarizine<br><br>• Gabapentin<br><br>• Isoniazid |
| **Likely To Be Ineffective Or Harmful** | • Mirtazapine added to other antitremor drugs |

**Search date December 2006**

**DEFINITION** Tremor is a rhythmic, mechanical oscillation of at least one body region. The term essential tremor is used when there is either a persistent bilateral tremor of hands and forearms, or an isolated tremor of the head, without abnormal posturing, and when there is no evidence that the tremor arises from another identifiable cause. The diagnosis is not made if there are: abnormal neurological signs; known causes of enhanced physiological tremor; a history or signs of psychogenic tremor; sudden change in severity; primary orthostatic tremor; isolated voice tremor; isolated position-specific or task-specific tremors; and isolated tongue, chin, or leg tremor.

**INCIDENCE/PREVALENCE** Essential tremor is one of the most common movement disorders throughout the world, with a prevalence of 0.4–3.9% in the general population.

**AETIOLOGY/RISK FACTORS** Essential tremor is sometimes inherited with an autosomal dominant pattern. About 40% of people with essential tremor have no family history of the condition. Alcohol ingestion provides symptomatic benefit in 50–70% of people.

**PROGNOSIS** Essential tremor is a persistent and progressive condition. It usually begins during early adulthood and the severity of the tremor slowly increases. Only a small proportion of people with essential tremor seek medical advice, but the proportion in different surveys varies from 0.5% to 11%. Most people with essential tremor are only mildly affected. However, most of the people who seek medical care are disabled to some extent, and most are socially handicapped by the tremor. A quarter of people receiving medical care for the tremor change jobs or retire because of essential tremor-induced disability.

Anita Krishnan and Nicholas Silver

## KEY POINTS

- Chronic tension-type headache (CTTH) is a disorder that evolves from episodic tension-type headache, with daily or very frequent episodes of headache lasting minutes to days.

  It affects 4.1% of the general population in the US, and is more prevalent in women (up to 65% of cases).

- We found only limited evidence about the treatment of CTTH.

  Regular analgesics may lead to chronic headache symptoms and reduce the effectiveness of prophylactic treatment.

  Amitriptyline and mirtazapine may be equally effective in reducing the duration and frequency of CTTH, although amitriptyline may be associated with a less-favourable adverse-effect profile.

  We don't know whether tricyclic antidepressants other than amitriptyline are effective in treating CTTH.

  We found no evidence examining the effectiveness of noradrenergic and specific serotonergic antidepressants, other than mirtazapine, in CTTH.

  We don't know whether SSRIs are effective in treating CTTH.

  We don't know whether benzodiazepines are effective in treating CTTH, and they are commonly associated with significant adverse effects.

  We found no evidence examining the effectiveness of anticonvulsants, such as sodium valproate, topiramate, and gabapentin, in CTTH.

  Botulinum toxin does not seem to be a useful treatment for CTTH. It may be associated with several adverse effects, including facial weakness, difficulty in swallowing, and disturbed local sensation.

- We don't know whether non-drug treatments, such as CBT, relaxation or electromyographic biofeedback, or acupuncture, are effective in treating CTTH.

  We don't know whether chiropractic and osteopathic manipulations are effective in treating CTTH. These treatments have been associated with rare, but very serious, adverse effects; for example, arterial dissection causing stroke, other stroke syndromes, and cerebellar and spinal cord injuries.

(i) **Please visit http://clinicalevidence.bmj.com for full text and references**

| What are the effects of drug treatments for CTTH? | |
|---|---|
| Beneficial | • Amitriptyline |
| Likely To Be Beneficial | • Noradrenergic and specific serotonergic antidepressants (mirtazapine) |
| Unknown Effectiveness | • Anticonvulsant drugs (valproate, topiramate, or gabapentin)<br><br>• SSRI antidepressants<br><br>• Tricyclic antidepressants (other than amitriptyline) |
| Likely To Be Ineffective Or Harmful | • Benzodiazepines<br><br>• Botulinum toxin<br><br>• Regular analgesics (e.g., paracetamol, codeine, NSAIDs) |

## What are the effects of non-drug treatments for CTTH?

| | |
|---|---|
| Unknown Effectiveness | • Acupuncture<br>• CBT<br>• Indian head massage<br>• Relaxation or electromyographic biofeedback |
| Likely To Be Ineffective Or Harmful | • Spinal manipulation (chiropractic and osteopathic treatment) |

Search date March 2007

**DEFINITION** Chronic tension-type headache (CTTH) is a disorder that evolves from episodic tension-type headache, with daily or very frequent episodes of headache lasting minutes to days. The 2004 International Headache Society criteria for CTTH are: headaches on 15 or more days a month (180 days/year) for at least 3 months; pain that is bilateral, pressing, or tightening in quality and non-pulsating, of mild or moderate intensity, which does not worsen with routine physical activity (such as walking or climbing stairs); presence of no more than one additional clinical feature (mild nausea, photophobia, or phonophobia); and without moderate/severe nausea or vomiting. CTTH is generally regarded as a featureless headache. Not all experts agree that mild features more typically seen in migraine (photophobia, phonophobia, etc.) should be included in the operational definition of CTTH, and it is often difficult to distinguish mild migraine headache from tension-type headache. CTTH is to be distinguished from other causes of chronic daily headache that require different treatment strategies (e.g., new daily persistent headache, medication overuse headache, chronic migraine, hemicrania continua). Many people who develop chronic daily headache owing to chronic migraine or medication overuse also develop mild migrainous 'background' headaches that might be mistaken for coincidental CTTH. It is therefore extremely important to take a full headache history to elicit the individual features of the headache and look for prodromal or accompanying features that might indicate an alternative diagnosis. In contrast with CTTH, episodic tension-type headache can last from 30 minutes to 7 days, and occurs on fewer than 180 days a year. The greatest obstacle to studying tension-type headache is the lack of any single proved specific or reliable, clinical, or biological defining characteristic of the disorder. Terms based on assumed mechanisms (muscle contraction headache or tension headache) are not operationally defined. Old studies that used these terms may have included people with many different types of headache.

**INCIDENCE/PREVALENCE** The prevalence of chronic daily headache from a survey of the general population in the US was 4.1%. Half of sufferers met the International Headache Society criteria for CTTH. In a survey of 2500 undergraduate students in the US, the prevalence of CTTH was 2%. The prevalence of CTTH was 2.5% in a Danish population-based survey of 975 individuals. One community-based survey in Singapore (2096 people from the general population) found that the prevalence was 1.8% in women and 0.9% in men.

**AETIOLOGY/RISK FACTORS** Tension-type headache is more prevalent in women (65% of cases in 1 survey). Symptoms begin before the age of 10 years in 15% of people with CTTH. Prevalence declines with age. There is a family history of some form of headache in 40% of people with CTTH, although a twin study found that the risk of CTTH was similar for identical and non-identical twins.

**PROGNOSIS** The prevalence of CTTH declines with age.

Ian Maconochie and Mark Ross

## KEY POINTS

- Head injury in young adults is often associated with motor vehicle accidents, violence, and sports injuries. In older adults it is often associated with falls. This review covers only moderate to severe head injury.

  Severe head injury can lead to secondary brain damage from cerebral ischaemia resulting from hypotension, hypercapnia, and raised intracranial pressure.

  Poor outcome correlates with low post-resuscitation Glasgow Coma Scale (GCS) score, older age, eye pupil abnormalities, hypoxia or hypotension before definitive treatment, traumatic subarachnoid haemorrhage, and inability to control intracranial pressure.

  Severity of brain injury is assessed using the GCS. While about one quarter of people with severe brain injury (GCS score <8) will make a good recovery, about one third will die, and one fifth will have severe disability or be in a vegetative state.

- There is no strong evidence of benefit from any treatment in reducing the complications of moderate to severe head injury. Despite this, most clinicians implement various combinations of treatments discussed here.

- Hyperventilation and mannitol are frequently used to lower intracranial pressure. Anticonvulsants, barbiturates, antibiotics, and hypothermia are less commonly implemented.

  Evidence on hyperventilation, mild hypothermia, and mannitol has been inconclusive.

  Carbamazepine and phenytoin may reduce early seizures in people with head injury, but they have not been shown to reduce late seizures, neurological disability, or death.

  Barbiturates have not been shown to be effective in reducing intracranial pressure or in preventing adverse neurological outcomes after head injury.

  Prophylactic antibiotics have not been shown to reduce the risk of death or meningitis in people with skull fracture.

- CAUTION: Corticosteroids have been shown to increase mortality when used acutely in people with head injury.

  One large RCT (the CRASH trial) found that death from all causes and severe disability at 6 months were more likely in people with head injury given methylprednisolone infusion than in those given placebo. Corticosteroids are no longer used in the treatment of head injuries.

(i) **Please visit http://clinicalevidence.bmj.com for full text and references**

## What are the effects of interventions to reduce complications of moderate to severe head injury as defined by Glasgow Coma Scale?

| Unknown Effectiveness | • Antibiotics |
| | • Hyperventilation |
| | • Hypothermia |

| | • Mannitol |
|---|---|
| **Unlikely To Be Beneficial** | • Anticonvulsants |
| **Likely To Be Ineffective Or Harmful** | • Corticosteroids |

**Search date November 2009**

**DEFINITION** The basic operational components of a head injury are a history of blunt or penetrating trauma to the head — which may be followed by a period of altered consciousness — and the presence of physical evidence of trauma. The specific elements of a head injury are related to its severity. Some guidelines define head injury more broadly as any trauma to the head other than superficial injuries to the face. Head injuries are classified in a variety of ways: severity of injury as assessed by the Glasgow Coma Scale (GCS; mild, moderate, severe); mechanism (blunt or penetrating); or morphology (skull fractures or intracranial lesions). Since its introduction in 1974, the GCS has been widely used as an initial measure of the severity of brain injury. The scale incorporates neurological findings such as voluntary movements, speech, and eye movements, into a 3- to 15-point scale. GCS allows measurement of neurological findings, and it has been used to predict immediate and long-term outcome after head injury. A GCS of 8 or lower is considered representative of a **severe** brain injury, 9 to 13 of a **moderate** head injury, and 14 to 15 a **mild** head injury. The GCS is complicated by difficulties of communication and cooperation in the younger child. In children aged >5 years, the adult GCS can be used. In younger children the verbal response is modified, and in very young children the motor response is also modified because these children are unable to obey commands. In this review, we cover only moderate to severe head injury as classified by GCS. **Diagnosis and monitoring:** The Advanced Trauma Life Support (ATLS) and Advanced Paediatric Life Support (APLS) guidelines contain standardised protocols for the initial assessment of traumatic head-injured adults and children, respectively. Most moderate to severe head injuries will require investigations after standard history and physical examination. Computed tomography (CT) scan is the investigation of choice in people with traumatic head injuries. Numerous organisations, including the National Institute for Health and Clinical Excellence, the Scottish Intercollegiate Guidelines Network, and the Royal College of Paediatrics and Child Health, have developed evidence-based pathways to provide physicians with guidance regarding whether a CT scan is required, and how urgently it should be performed. Monitoring of people with head injury may range from monitoring of intracranial pressure (ICP) with ventricular drains in people with severe head injuries to regular clinical neurological observations in people with less-severe head injuries.

**INCIDENCE/PREVALENCE** Head injury remains the leading cause of death in trauma cases in Europe and the USA, and accounts for a disproportionate amount of morbidity in trauma survivors. Worldwide, several million people, mostly children and young adults, are treated each year for severe head injury. In the UK, 1.4 million people, 50% of whom are children, present to emergency departments every year after a head injury. This represents 11% of all new emergency department presentations. About 80% of people presenting to emergency departments can be categorised as having mild head injury, 10% as moderate, and 10% as severe.

**AETIOLOGY/RISK FACTORS** The main causes of head injury include injuries incurred from motor vehicle accidents (MVAs), falls, acts of violence, and sports injuries. MVAs account for most fatal and severe head injuries. Young adults (15–35 years old) are the most commonly affected group, reflecting increased risk-taking behaviour. A second peak occurs in older people (>70 years), related to an increased frequency of falls. For most age groups, with the exception of extremes of age, there is a 2:1 male predominance. Severe head injury marks the beginning of a continuing encephalopathic process — secondary brain damage from ongoing cerebral ischaemia closely linked to factors such as hypotension, hypercapnia, and elevated ICP is a potential cause of morbidity and mortality.

**PROGNOSIS** Head injury can result in death or a lifelong impairment in physical, cognitive, and psychosocial functioning. Several factors have been shown to correlate with poor outcome — including low post-resuscitation GCS score, older age, eye pupil abnormalities, hypoxia or hypotension before definitive treatment, traumatic subarachnoid haemorrhage, and inability to control ICP. Data from the Traumatic Coma Data Bank found that people with an initial GCS score of 3 had 78% mortality, whereas those with a GCS score of 8 had 11% mortality. Overall, prognoses for people with severe head injury (GCS score 3–8) were: good recovery 27%, moderate disability 16%, severe disability 16%, vegetative 5%, and mortality 36%. Despite such data, the role of GCS in determining prognosis in head injury remains controversial. The impacts of head injury range from mild cognitive and psychosocial changes to severe physical disability and cognitive and sensory losses.

Richard Nicholas and Waqar Rashid

**KEY POINTS**

- Multiple sclerosis is characterised by central nervous system lesions causing neurological dysfunction and other problems, such as fatigue, pain, depression, and anxiety.

  Early disease is usually relapsing and remitting, but most people develop secondary-progressive disease over time. No treatment has been shown to affect long-term outcome.

  Irreversible disability can occur, but life expectancy is generally not affected.

- In people with relapsing and remitting disease, glatiramer acetate and azathioprine may reduce relapse rates, but have not been shown to affect disease progression. Toxicity associated with azathioprine means that 10% of people cannot tolerate it at therapeutic doses.

  Interferon beta may reduce exacerbations and disease progression in relapsing and remitting multiple sclerosis, and may reduce the risk of conversion to clinically definite multiple sclerosis in people experiencing a first demyelinating event.

  Intravenous immunoglobulin may prevent relapse after a first demyelinating event, but we don't know whether it is effective in people with relapsing and remitting disease.

  Mitoxantrone may reduce exacerbations and disease progression.

  Natalizumab may increase the proportion of people who are relapse-free at 2 years in relapsing and remitting multiple sclerosis.

- CAUTION: Interferon beta and mitoxantrone have been associated with serious adverse effects. Natalizumab has been associated with progressive multifocal leukoencephalopathy (PML), and the long-term benefits and risks are still unknown.

- We don't know whether interferon beta, intravenous immunoglobulin, or methotrexate delay disease progression in people with secondary-progressive multiple sclerosis, as studies have given conflicting results.

- Corticosteroids (methylprednisolone or corticotropin) may improve symptoms in people with an acute exacerbation of multiple sclerosis compared with placebo.

  We don't know whether plasma exchange, intravenous immunoglobulin, or natalizumab are beneficial.

  We don't know whether amantadine, behavioural modification, modafinil, or exercise reduce fatigue. Exercise may help to maintain strength, fitness, mobility, and improve quality of life, but studies have been difficult to compare.

  We don't know whether botulinum toxin, gabapentin, intrathecal baclofen, oral antispasmodic drugs, or physiotherapy improve spasticity.

- Inpatient rehabilitation may improve function in the short term, but we don't know whether outpatient rehabilitation is also of benefit.

(i) **Please visit http://clinicalevidence.bmj.com for full text and references**

**What are the effects of interventions aimed at reducing relapse rates and disability in people with multiple sclerosis?**

| Likely To Be Beneficial | • Glatiramer acetate (parenteral) in people with relapsing and remitting or progressive multiple sclerosis |
|---|---|

| | |
|---|---|
| | • Interferon beta in people having a first demyelinating event or with relapsing and remitting multiple sclerosis<br><br>• Intravenous immunoglobulin in people having a first demyelinating event |
| **Trade-off Between Benefits And Harms** | • Azathioprine<br><br>• Mitoxantrone in people with relapsing and remitting multiple sclerosis<br><br>• Natalizumab in people with relapsing and remitting multiple sclerosis |
| **Unknown Effectiveness** | • Interferon beta in people with secondary-progressive multiple sclerosis<br><br>• Intravenous immunoglobulin in people with relapsing and remitting or secondary-progressive multiple sclerosis<br><br>• Methotrexate |

## What are the effects of interventions to improve symptoms during acute relapse in people with multiple sclerosis?

| | |
|---|---|
| **Likely To Be Beneficial** | • Corticosteroids (methylprednisolone, corticotropin, or dexamethasone) versus placebo |
| **Unknown Effectiveness** | • Corticosteroids (methylprednisolone, corticotropin, or dexamethasone) versus each other (insufficient evidence to compare effectiveness)<br><br>• Intravenous immunoglobulin in people with acute relapse of multiple sclerosis<br><br>• Natalizumab in people with acute relapse of multiple sclerosis<br><br>• Plasma exchange |

## What are the effects of treatments for fatigue in people with multiple sclerosis?

| | |
|---|---|
| **Unknown Effectiveness** | • Amantadine<br>• Behavioural modification<br>• Exercise<br>• Modafinil |

## What are the effects of treatments for spasticity in people with multiple sclerosis?

| | |
|---|---|
| **Unknown Effectiveness** | • Baclofen (intrathecal)<br>• Botulinum toxin<br>• Drug treatments (oral) other than gabapentin<br>• Gabapentin |

| | ● Physiotherapy |
|---|---|

## What are the effects of multidisciplinary care on disability in people with multiple sclerosis?

| Unknown Effectiveness | ● Inpatient rehabilitation |
|---|---|
| | ● Outpatient rehabilitation |

**Search date July 2011**

---

**DEFINITION** Multiple sclerosis is a chronic inflammatory disease of the central nervous system. Diagnosis requires evidence of lesions that are separated in both time and space, and the exclusion of other inflammatory, structural, or hereditary conditions that might give a similar clinical picture. The disease takes three main forms: relapsing and remitting multiple sclerosis, characterised by episodes of neurological dysfunction interspersed with periods of stability; primary-progressive multiple sclerosis, in which progressive neurological disability occurs from the outset; and secondary-progressive multiple sclerosis, in which progressive neurological disability occurs later in the course of the disease. Axonal loss is the major determinant of the accumulation of irreversible (progressive) disability as a result of inflammation during both the relapsing and remitting and progressive phases of multiple sclerosis, but also because of possible neurodegeneration through loss of trophic support. The emergence of treatment for multiple sclerosis has led to the recognition of a first demyelinating event or "clinically isolated syndrome" (CIS), a single episode of neurological dysfunction lasting for >24 hours, which can be a prelude to multiple sclerosis. Characteristic episodes include optic neuritis, solitary brainstem lesions, and transverse myelitis that, when associated with magnetic resonance imaging (MRI) changes, result in a 30% to 70% risk of developing multiple sclerosis. Increasingly recognised are other demyelinating syndromes thought to be distinct from multiple sclerosis; these include Devic's disease (neuromyelitis optica), relapsing optic neuritis, and relapsing myelitis. Other than episodes of neurological dysfunction, chronic symptoms produce much of the disability in multiple sclerosis. Symptoms include fatigue (main symptom in two-thirds of people), spasticity, bladder/bowel problems, ataxia/tremor, visual problems, pain, depression/anxiety, dysphagia, and sexual dysfunction.

**INCIDENCE/PREVALENCE** Prevalence varies with geography and racial group. It is highest in white populations in temperate regions. In Europe and North America, prevalence is 1/800 people, with an annual incidence of 2–10/100,000, making multiple sclerosis the most common cause of neurological disability in young adults. Age of onset is broad, peaking between 20 and 40 years.

**AETIOLOGY/RISK FACTORS** The cause remains unclear, although current evidence suggests that multiple sclerosis is an autoimmune disorder of the central nervous system resulting from an environmental stimulus in genetically susceptible individuals. Multiple sclerosis is currently regarded as a single disorder with clinical variants, but there is some evidence that it may consist of several related disorders with distinct immunological, pathological, and genetic features.

**PROGNOSIS** In 90% of people early disease is relapsing and remitting. Although some people follow a relatively benign course over many years, most develop secondary-progressive disease, usually 6–10 years after onset. In 10% of people, initial disease is primary progressive. Apart from a minority of people with "aggressive" multiple sclerosis, life expectancy is not greatly affected, and the disease course is often of >30 years' duration.

Arnar Astradsson and Tipu Z. Aziz

## KEY POINTS

- The mean age of onset of Parkinson's disease is about 65 years, with a median time of 9 years between diagnosis and death.

- As the efficacy of conventional drug treatment wears off, other treatments may be sought. Neural transplantation may be applicable to a subset of patients, in particular younger patients, with advanced disease and a prior good response to levodopa.

- We found two double-blind RCTs that compared fetal cell transplant with sham surgery. The RCTs included 74 people in total, all of whom had advanced Parkinson's disease.

    The RCTs found no good evidence that fetal cell transplant improved clinical outcomes, such as disease severity, or reduced the need for levodopa or other treatment at 1 to 2 years.

    Fetal cell transplant may improve the non-clinical outcome of putaminal fluoro-DOPA uptake, as measured by PET scan.

    Fetal cell transplant may be associated with adverse effects such as graft-induced dyskinesias.

    The findings of the RCTs were in contrast to more favourable outcomes suggested by earlier open-label and uncontrolled studies.

    However, it has been highlighted that some procedures in the two trials might not have been optimal, and follow-up time in at least one of the trials may have been too short.

    Larger-scale RCTs are currently under way to address the benefits and harms of fetal cell transplantation for Parkinson's disease.

- We don't know how fetal cell therapy versus deep brain stimulation, stem cell-derived therapy versus sham surgery, or stem cell-derived therapy versus deep brain stimulation compare as we found no studies addressing these comparisons.

 **Please visit http://clinicalevidence.bmj.com for full text and references**

## What are the effects of fetal cell or stem cell-derived therapy in people with Parkinson's disease?

| Unknown Effectiveness | • Fetal cell therapy versus deep brain stimulation |
| --- | --- |
| | • Fetal cell therapy versus sham surgery |
| | • Stem cell-derived therapy versus deep brain stimulation |
| | • Stem cell-derived therapy versus sham surgery |

**Search date September 2014**

**DEFINITION** Idiopathic Parkinson's disease is an age-related neurodegenerative disorder, which is associated with a combination of asymmetrical bradykinesia, hypokinesia, and rigidity, sometimes combined with rest tremor and postural changes. Clinical diagnostic criteria have a sensitivity of 80% and a specificity of 30% (likelihood ratio +ve test 1.14, –ve test 0.67) compared with the gold standard of diagnosis at autopsy. The primary pathology is progressive loss of cells that produce the neurotransmitter dopamine from the substantia nigra in the brainstem. Treatment aims to replace or compensate for the lost dopamine. A good response to treatment supports, but does not confirm, the diagnosis. Several other catecholaminergic neurotransmitter systems are also affected in Parkinson's disease. There

*(continued over)*

*(from previous page)*

is no consistent definition distinguishing early-stage from late-stage Parkinson's disease. In this review, we consider people with established Parkinson's disease who have had a good effect with conventional medical (e.g., levodopa) treatment.

**INCIDENCE/PREVALENCE** Parkinson's disease occurs worldwide, with a male to female ratio of 1.5:1.0. In 5% to 10% of people who develop Parkinson's disease, the condition appears before the age of 40 years (young onset). The mean age of onset is about 65 years. Overall age-adjusted prevalence is 1.0% worldwide, and 1.6% in Europe, rising from 0.6% at age 65 to 69 years to 3.5% at age 85 to 89 years.

**AETIOLOGY/RISK FACTORS** The cause for Parkinson's disease is unknown. Parkinson's disease may represent different conditions with a final common pathway. People may be affected differently by a combination of genetic and environmental factors (viruses, toxins, 1-methyl-4-phenyl-1, 2, 3, 6-tetrahydropyridine, well water, vitamin E, and smoking). First-degree relatives of affected people may have twice the risk of developing Parkinson's disease (17% chance of developing the condition in their lifetime) compared with the general population. However, purely genetic varieties probably affect a small minority of people with Parkinson's disease. The LRRK2 gene is the most prevalent gene associated with both familial and sporadic Parkinson's disease. Also, mutations in PARK genes, in particular the PARKIN-1 gene that encodes alpha-synuclein, may be associated with Parkinson's disease in families with at least one member with young-onset Parkinson's disease.

**PROGNOSIS** Parkinson's disease is currently incurable. Disability is progressive, and is associated with increased mortality (RR of death compared with matched control populations ranges from 1.6–3.0). Treatment can reduce symptoms, but rarely achieves complete control. Whether treatment reduces mortality remains controversial. Levodopa seemed to reduce mortality in the UK for 5 years after its introduction, before a 'catch-up' effect was noted and overall mortality rose towards previous levels. This suggested a limited prolonging of life. An Australian cohort study followed 130 people treated for 10 years. The standardised mortality ratio was 1.58 (P <0.001). At 10 years, 25% had been admitted to a nursing home, and only four people were still employed. The mean duration of disease until death was 9.1 years. In a similar Italian cohort study conducted over 8 years, the relative risk of death for affected people compared with healthy controls was 2.3 (95% CI 1.60 to 3.39). Age at initial census date was the main predictor of outcome (for people aged <75 years: RR of death 1.80, 95% CI 1.04 to 3.11; for people aged >75 years: RR of death 5.61, 95% CI 2.13 to 14.80).

Mohsen Javadpour and Nicholas Silver

## KEY POINTS

- Subarachnoid haemorrhage (SAH) may arise spontaneously or as a result of trauma. Spontaneous SAH accounts for about 5% of all strokes. Ruptured aneurysms are the cause of 85% of spontaneous SAH. This review deals with only spontaneous aneurysmal SAH.

   Without treatment, mortality rates of about 50% at 1 month after spontaneous aneurysmal SAH have been reported.

- Treatment is aimed at prevention of rebleeding from the same aneurysm. This can be performed by surgical clipping or by endovascular coiling.

   In people suitable for either procedure, endovascular coiling has lower rates of poor functional outcome compared with surgical clipping, but it is also associated with increased rate of recurrent haemorrhage from the treated aneurysm and a higher rate of retreatment for the same aneurysm. Most evidence is in small (<11 mm) aneurysms of the anterior circulation. Therefore, the conclusions cannot be applied to all aneurysms (particularly large and giant aneurysms, and aneurysms with broad necks).

   Factors that should be considered when deciding on the method of treatment include the morphology of the aneurysm, the age and clinical condition of the person, and the presence or absence of a space-occupying intracranial haematoma.

- We do not know the optimal timeframe for carrying out surgical clipping or endovascular coiling after aneurysmal SAH. However, early surgery will prevent rebleeding from the aneurysm, and is preferred in most people.

- Oral nimodipine reduces poor outcome (death or dependence), secondary ischaemia, and CT/MRI evidence of infarction after aneurysmal SAH.

- We found no evidence on the effects of intravenous nimodipine alone.

(i) **Please visit http://clinicalevidence.bmj.com for full text and references**

## What are the effects of surgical treatments for people with confirmed aneurysmal subarachnoid haemorrhage?

| | |
|---|---|
| Beneficial | • Endovascular coiling versus surgical clipping (endovascular coiling is associated with improved functional outcome and decreased risk of epilepsy in people in good clinical condition with small ruptured aneurysms that have suitable anatomy for both procedures, but increased risk of rebleed and retreatment) |
| Unknown Effectiveness | • Early surgery versus late surgery (insufficient evidence to assess optimal timing of surgery) |

## What are the effects of medical treatments to prevent delayed cerebral ischaemia in people with confirmed aneurysmal subarachnoid haemorrhage?

| | |
|---|---|
| Beneficial | • Nimodipine (oral) |
| Unknown Effectiveness | • Nimodipine (intravenous) |

**Search date March 2009**

**DEFINITION** Subarachnoid haemorrhage (SAH) is a type of haemorrhagic stroke in which there is bleeding into the subarachnoid space. It can be subdivided into traumatic SAH and spontaneous (non-traumatic) SAH. This review deals with only spontaneous aneurysmal SAH. **Diagnosis:** The most characteristic clinical feature is sudden-onset severe headache. Other features include vomiting, photophobia, neck stiffness, impaired level of consciousness, acute confusional state, agitation/restlessness, and focal neurological deficit or seizures, or both. As the headache may have insidious onset in some cases, or may even be absent, a high degree of suspicion is required to diagnose SAH with these less typical presentations. Examination findings may include a reduced level of consciousness, confusion/agitation, nuchal rigidity, retinal haemorrhage, or focal neurological signs (e.g., cranial nerve palsies and hemiplegia).When SAH is suspected, an unenhanced CT scan of the head should be obtained as soon as possible. However, CT scan does not always identify the haemorrhage, and the false-negative rate increases with time after the bleed. In a prospective observational study of 3451 people with confirmed SAH, 3% (51/1553) had a normal CT scan within 24 hours of ictus. By day 5, 27% (9/33) had a normal CT scan. Even if the CT scan is done within 12 hours of ictus, 2% (95% CI 0.2 to 6) of people have a normal scan. Therefore, a lumbar puncture should be performed in anyone with suspected SAH and a normal CT scan. CSF findings in SAH may include elevated opening pressure, uniformly blood-stained CSF across all tubes, excess red blood cell count, and elevated protein or lymphocytic cellular reaction, or both. However, to differentiate genuine SAH from a traumatic tap (blood introduced into the needle at the time of lumbar puncture), CSF must be analysed for presence of xanthochromia (yellow discoloration of supernatant after centrifugation of CSF, caused by the presence of bilirubin). It has been recommended that the lumbar puncture should be delayed until 12 hours after the onset of symptoms (unless meningitis is suspected) to allow sufficient time for haemoglobin to degrade into oxyhaemoglobin and bilirubin. Earlier sampling may produce false-negative results. The colour of the supernatant should be compared with water against a white background, in bright light. Yellow discoloration of the supernatant (xanthochromia) indicates SAH. To reduce the subjectivity of this test, it has been recommended that CSF should, in all cases, be examined for bilirubin and oxyhaemoglobin using spectrophotometry, rather than by visual inspection alone. In a study of 111 people with CT-confirmed SAH, the sensitivity of CSF spectrophotometry was reported to be 100% up to 2 weeks after the ictus. However, the false-negative rate of spectrophotometry in the diagnosis of SAH in CT-negative people is not known. If a person presents more than 2 weeks after the onset of symptoms, no test can rule out SAH with 100% certainty, although MRI (particularly fluid-attenuated inversion recovery [FLAIR] and gradient echo sequences) may be useful in detecting subarachnoid blood in some people. The sensitivity of CSF spectrophotometry drops significantly after 2 weeks, decreasing to 90% by 3 weeks' post-bleed. These people should be referred urgently to a neuroscience unit for consideration of further investigations. The correct diagnosis of SAH is pivotal to successful outcome. Pitfalls in diagnosis include: (1) the headache of SAH does not have any specific distinguishing features and may resemble migraine; (2) the pain of SAH may be relieved by migraine attack-treatments such as triptans — response to a triptan may provide false and unjustified reassurance; (3) there is an over-reliance on the classical presentation of the reported feeling of a 'sudden blow to the head'; (4) because SAH may often cause fever, some people may be misdiagnosed as having meningitis; (5) approximately 20% of people with SAH develop cardiac arrhythmia, and some people will have an ECG suggestive of ischaemia (thrombolysis can have disastrous consequences in this situation); (6) people may occasionally present with an isolated acute confusional state; (7) people may present in a coma; and (8) in some people the predominant feature may be vomiting, leading to GI investigations. Once SAH has been confirmed by CT scan or CSF examination, the source of haemorrhage must be identified. The gold-standard technique is catheter cerebral angiography. However, CT angiography (CTA) and magnetic resonance angiography (MRA) provide non-invasive means of diagnosing a cerebral aneurysm. A systematic review found that, for aneurysms larger than 3 mm, the sensitivity of CTA was 96% (95% CI 94% to 98%) and of MRA was 94% (95% CI 90% to 97%). For aneurysms 3 mm or smaller, the sensitivity of CTA was 61% (95% CI 51% to 70%) and of MRA was 38% (95% CI 25% to 53%). In people with confirmed SAH in whom CTA or MRA is negative, catheter angiography must be performed.

**INCIDENCE/PREVALENCE** Spontaneous SAH accounts for about 5% of all strokes. In most populations, the incidence of SAH is 7.8/100,000 population a year (95% CI 7.2/100,000 to 8.4/100,000). However, the incidence has been reported to be markedly higher in Finland (21.4/100,000 a year, 95% CI 19.5/100,000 to 23.4/100,000). The incidence in women is 1.6 times that in men (95% CI 1.1 to 2.3).

**AETIOLOGY/RISK FACTORS** Ruptured aneurysms are the cause of 85% of spontaneous SAHs. Other causes of spontaneous SAH include benign perimesencephalic SAH, other idiopathies, some drugs (e.g., amphetamines), coagulation disorders, vascular malformations, dural venous sinus thrombosis, tumours, and vasculitides. The exact aetiology of intracranial aneurysms remains unclear. Risk factors include smoking (RR 2.2, 95% CI 1.3 to 3.6), hypertension (RR 2.1, 95% CI 2.0 to 3.1), and excessive alcohol intake (RR 2.1, 95% CI 1.5 to 2.8). Genetic factors may also be involved. Aneurysms are associated with defined heritable disorders, including connective tissue disorders and autosomal dominant polycystic kidney disease. They may also occur in a familial setting.

**PROGNOSIS** Aneurysmal SAH has a poor prognosis, particularly if the aneurysm is not occluded. Observational studies from the 1960s reported mortality rates of 10% to 32% on day 1, 27% to 43% during the first week, and 49% to 56% at 1 month after SAH. Most deaths occur as a result of rebleeding from the same aneurysm. If untreated, rebleeding occurs in 15% of people on day 1, and in 40% of people by 1 month after SAH. The rate of rebleeding decreases with time to 3% a year after the initial 6 months. A systematic review of population-based studies found that the overall case fatality rate after aneurysmal SAH ranged from 32% to 67%. It also found that the case fatality rates had decreased by +0.5% a year (95% CI –0.1% to +1.2%) between 1960 and 1992, suggesting that improved management of people with SAH may be the reason for the better outcomes. A more recent population-based study found a case fatality rate of 39% (95% CI 34% to 44%). These reported case fatality rates include people who die before reaching hospital, which was found in a meta-analysis of population-based studies to be 12.4% (95% CI 11% to 14%). Between 10% and 20% of all people with SAH (17%–46% of survivors) become dependent. As well as physical disability, SAH results in cognitive impairment in a large number of people. In a population-based study, 105/230 (46%) of survivors interviewed at 1 year reported incomplete recovery, with ongoing problems with memory (50%), mood (39%), and speech (14%).

Joanna Zakrzewska and Mark E. Linskey

## KEY POINTS

- Trigeminal neuralgia is a sudden, unilateral, brief, stabbing, recurrent pain in the distribution of one or more branches of the fifth cranial nerve. The diagnosis is made on the history alone, based on characteristic features of the pain.

  Pain occurs in paroxysms, which can last from a few seconds to several minutes. The frequency of the paroxysms ranges from a few to hundreds of attacks a day.

  Periods of remission can last for months to years, but tend to get shorter over time.

  The condition can impair activities of daily living and lead to depression.

  The annual incidence in the UK (based on GP practice lists and rather liberal diagnostic criteria) has been reported to be 26.8 per 100,000. However, studies in other countries such as the US and the Netherlands, with stricter definitions, have reported much lower incidence rates ranging between 5.9 and 12.6 per 100,000.

  Experts find that symptoms worsen over time and become less responsive to medication despite dose increases and adding further agents.

- Treatment success is defined differently in studies of medical and surgical therapies for trigeminal neuralgia.

  Treatment success in medical studies is usually defined as at least 50% pain relief from baseline. However, complete pain relief is the measure of treatment success in surgical studies.

- Carbamazepine is considered the gold standard for the initial medical treatment of trigeminal neuralgia symptoms.

  Carbamazepine has been shown to increase pain relief compared with placebo, but also increases adverse effects, such as drowsiness, dizziness, rash, liver damage, and ataxia.

  Studies evaluating durability of response with carbamazepine are lacking, but consensus expert opinion suggests that it may have a greater than 50% failure rate for long-term (5-10 year) pain control.

  Based on the strength of published evidence, carbamazepine remains the best supported standard medical treatment for trigeminal neuralgia.

- There is consensus that oxcarbazepine is an effective treatment in people with trigeminal neuralgia and may have fewer adverse effects than carbamazepine, although there is a lack of RCT-based data to confirm this.

  Oxcarbazepine rarely provides complete or long-term pain relief, although studies evaluating durability of response with this drug are lacking.

- We found no sufficient evidence to judge the effectiveness of baclofen or lamotrigine.

  Lamotrigine is often used in people who cannot tolerate carbamazepine, but the dose must be increased slowly to avoid rashes, thus making it unsuitable for acute use.

  There is consensus that baclofen may be useful for people with multiple sclerosis who develop trigeminal neuralgia.

- We found no evidence comparing gabapentin versus placebo/no treatment or other treatments covered in this review in people with trigeminal neuralgia.

  Gabapentin does have support for use in treating other neuropathic pain conditions, particularly multiple sclerosis.

- Despite a lack of RCT data, observational evidence supports the use of microvascular decompression to relieve symptoms of trigeminal neuralgia.

Microvascular decompression has been shown in at least two prospective comparative cohort trials to have superiority over stereotactic radiosurgery for complete pain relief, durability of response (up to 5 years), and preservation of trigeminal sensation.

However, microvascular decompression requires general anaesthesia and can, albeit rarely, be associated with surgical complications, of which a less than 5% risk of ipsilateral hearing loss appears to be the most common.

Well-conducted observational studies have demonstrated that microvascular decompression has a greater magnitude of therapeutic effect than any medical and surgical therapy for trigeminal neuralgia. As such, this procedure is unlikely to be compared against best medical therapy in an RCT.

- We found no RCT evidence comparing percutaneous destructive neurosurgical techniques (radiofrequency thermocoagulation, glycerol rhizolysis, balloon compression) or non-percutaneous destructive neurosurgical techniques (stereotactic radiosurgery) versus placebo/no treatment or other treatments covered in this review in people with trigeminal neuralgia.

Observational data suggest that radiofrequency thermocoagulation may offer higher rates of complete pain relief than glycerol rhizolysis and stereotactic radiosurgery, but may also be associated with higher rates of complications (e.g., facial numbness and corneal insensitivity).

In contrast to stereotactic radiosurgery, pain relief with microvascular decompression and percutaneous destructive neurosurgical techniques is immediate, but they require sedation and/or anaesthesia to perform, which are not required for stereotactic radiosurgery.

**Please visit http://clinicalevidence.bmj.com for full text and references**

## What are the effects of ongoing treatments in people with trigeminal neuralgia?

| Likely To Be Beneficial | • Baclofen (in people with multiple sclerosis who develop trigeminal neuralgia)* |
|---|---|
| | • Carbamazepine |
| | • Oxcarbazepine* |
| Trade-off Between Benefits And Harms | • Microvascular decompression* |
| | • Non-percutaneous destructive neurosurgical techniques (stereotactic radiosurgery)* |
| | • Percutaneous destructive neurosurgical techniques (radiofrequency thermocoagulation, glycerol rhizolysis, or balloon compression)* |
| Unknown Effectiveness | • Gabapentin |
| | • Lamotrigine |

**Search date September 2013**

*Categorisation based on observational studies and/or consensus.

**DEFINITION** Trigeminal neuralgia is a characteristic pain in the distribution of one or more branches of the fifth cranial nerve. The diagnosis is made on the history alone, based on characteristic features of the pain. It occurs in paroxysms, with each pain lasting from a few seconds to several minutes. The frequency of paroxysms is highly variable, ranging from hundreds of attacks a day to long periods of remission that can last years. Between paroxysms, the person is asymptomatic. The pain is severe and described as intense, sharp, superficial, stabbing, or shooting — often like an electric shock. It can be triggered by light touch in any area innervated by the trigeminal nerve, including eating, talking, washing the face, or cleaning the teeth. The condition can impair activities of daily living and lead to depression. In some people there remains a background pain of lower intensity for 50% of the time. This has been termed atypical trigeminal neuralgia or type 2 trigeminal neuralgia. The International Classification for Headache Disorders (ICHD) refers to this condition as trigeminal neuralgia with concomitant pain. Other causes of facial pain may need to be excluded. In trigeminal neuralgia, the neurological examination is usually normal but sensory and autonomic symptoms may be reported, and people with longer histories may demonstrate subtle sensory loss on careful examination.

**INCIDENCE/PREVALENCE** Most evidence about the incidence and prevalence of trigeminal neuralgia is from the US. The annual incidence (age adjusted to the 1980 age distribution of the US) is 5.9 per 100,000 women and 3.4 per 100,000 men. The incidence tends to be slightly higher in women at all ages, and increases with age. In men aged over 80 years, the incidence is 45.2 per 100,000. One questionnaire survey of neurological disease in one French village found one person with trigeminal neuralgia among 993 people. A retrospective cohort study in UK primary care, which examined the histories of 6.8 million people, found that 8268 people had trigeminal neuralgia, giving it an incidence of 26.8 per 100,000 person-years. A similar primary care study carried out in the Netherlands reported an incidence of 12.6 per 100,000 person-years when trained neurologists reviewed the data. A population-based study in Germany reported a lifetime prevalence of 0.3%.

**AETIOLOGY/RISK FACTORS** The cause of trigeminal neuralgia remains unclear but the most common hypothesis is that of the ignition theory. More peripheral and central mechanisms may be involved, and trigeminal nerve microstructure may be altered. It is more common in people with multiple sclerosis (RR 20.0, 95% CI 4.1 to 59.0) and stroke. Hypertension is a risk factor in women (RR 2.1, 95% CI 1.2 to 3.4), but the evidence is less clear for men (RR 1.53, 95% CI 0.30 to 4.50).

**PROGNOSIS** One retrospective cohort study found no reduction in 10-year survival in people with trigeminal neuralgia. We found no evidence about the natural history of trigeminal neuralgia. However, the TNA Facial Pain Association continues to periodically receive individual isolated reports of people with trigeminal neuralgia who either die from overdose of medications, take their own life, or both. The illness is characterised by recurrences and remissions. Many people have periods of remission with no pain lasting months or years. At least 50% of people with trigeminal neuralgia will have remissions lasting at least 6 months in duration. Collective expert experience suggests that, in many people, trigeminal neuralgia becomes more severe and less responsive to treatment over time, despite increasing medication doses and adding additional agents. Most people with trigeminal neuralgia are initially managed medically, and a proportion eventually have a surgical procedure. We found no good evidence about the proportion of people who require surgical treatment for pain control. Anecdotal evidence indicates that pain relief is better after surgery than with medical treatment. Furthermore, responses from a questionnaire taken by people who had surgery for trigeminal neuralgia indicated that the majority of respondents wished they had surgery earlier.

Konrad Staines and Mark Greenwood

## KEY POINTS

- Recurrent aphthous ulcers are the most common cause of recurrent oral ulceration in otherwise-healthy individuals.

- Most people with recurrent aphthous ulcers develop a few ulcers less than 10 mm in diameter that heal after 7 to 10 days without scarring.

   In 10% of sufferers, lesions are more than 10 mm in diameter and can cause scarring.

   The majority of aphthous ulcers are idiopathic, although factors such as local physical trauma may trigger ulcers in susceptible people.

- Chlorhexidine mouth rinses may reduce the severity and pain of ulceration, although studies have reported inconclusive results about whether the incidence of new ulcers is reduced.

- Topical corticosteroids may reduce the number of new ulcers, reduce pain, and increase healing of ulcers without causing notable adverse effects.

- We don't know whether local analgesics or tetracycline mouthwash work, as evidence was weak.

 **Please visit http://clinicalevidence.bmj.com for full text and references**

| What are the effects of selected topical treatments for recurrent idiopathic aphthous ulcers? | |
|---|---|
| Likely To Be Beneficial | • Corticosteroids (topical)<br><br>• Topical antiseptic agents (chlorhexidine may be effective; insufficient evidence for other similar agents) |
| Unknown Effectiveness | • Analgesics (local)<br><br>• Tetracycline antibiotic mouthwash |

**Search date December 2013**

---

**DEFINITION** Recurrent aphthous ulcers (RAU) are superficial, rounded, painful mouth ulcers usually occurring in recurrent bouts at intervals of a few days to a few months in otherwise-well people. They are the most common cause of recurrent oral ulceration and may be classified as minor (<10 mm), major (>10 mm) or herpetiform aphthous ulcers.

**INCIDENCE/PREVALENCE** The point prevalence of recurrent aphthous ulcers in Swedish adults has been reported as 2%. Prevalence may be 5% to 10% in some groups of children. Up to 66% of young adults give a history consistent with recurrent aphthous ulceration. Frequency of RAU lessens with advancing age.

**AETIOLOGY/RISK FACTORS** The majority of aphthous ulcers are idiopathic with no known cause identified, although factors such as local physical trauma may trigger ulcers in susceptible people. Recurrent aphthous ulcers are uncommon on keratinised oral mucosal surfaces or with people who smoke tobacco. Aphthous-like ulcers may develop secondary to systemic diseases such as Behçet's disease, coeliac disease, inflammatory bowel disease, and haematinic deficiencies, or to drugs such as non-steroidal anti-inflammatory drugs (NSAIDS). Only idiopathic RAU are considered in this review.

**PROGNOSIS** Minor recurrent aphthous ulcers typically involve non-keratinised oral mucosa, are less than 10 mm in diameter, and persist over a 7- to 10-day period. Spontaneous healing without scarring is generally followed by a variable ulcer-free period and recurrence of the ulceration. The minor variant accounts for 80% of patients with RAU. Major recurrent

*(continued over)*

*(from previous page)*

aphthous ulcers may involve both keratinised and non-keratinised oral mucosa, may exceed 10 mm in diameter, may persist for 20 to 30 days, and heal with scarring. Herpetiform ulcers present as multiple (ranging from 1–100) pinpoint ulcers involving either keratinised or non-keratinised mucosa with the potential for these ulcers to merge into a larger area of ulceration. Most of the trials in this review have focused on the treatment of minor aphthous ulceration.

John Buchanan and Joanna Zakrzewska

## KEY POINTS

- **Burning mouth syndrome is characterised by discomfort or pain of the mouth, with no known medical or dental cause. It may affect up to one third of postmenopausal women and up to 15% of adults overall.**

  **Symptoms of burning mouth can also be caused by infections, allergies, vitamin deficiencies, and ill-fitting dentures, leading to problems identifying effective treatments.**

  **Psychogenic factors, such as anxiety, depression, or personality disorders, may be involved in some people.**

  **People with burning mouth syndrome may show altered sensory and pain thresholds, or other signs of neuropathy.**

  **Complete spontaneous remission occurs in only a small percentage of people, and up to 30% will note moderate improvement with or without treatment.**

- **CBT may improve symptom intensity compared with placebo, although we found no good-quality studies.**

- **Topical clonazepam may reduce pain compared with placebo, but it may be absorbed systemically, with increased risk of dependence over time.**

  **We don't know whether antidepressants, benzydamine hydrochloride, or HRT in postmenopausal women can improve symptoms of burning mouth, as we found few studies.**

  **Dietary supplements may be no more effective than placebo at reducing symptoms of burning mouth.**

 **Please visit http://clinicalevidence.bmj.com for full text and references**

| What are the effects of treatments for burning mouth syndrome? | |
|---|---|
| **Likely To Be Beneficial** | • CBT |
| **Trade-off Between Benefits And Harms** | • Benzodiazepines (topical clonazepam) |
| **Unknown Effectiveness** | • Anaesthetics (local)<br>• Antidepressants<br>• Benzydamine hydrochloride<br>• HRT in postmenopausal women |
| **Unlikely To Be Beneficial** | • Dietary supplements |

**Search date November 2009**

**DEFINITION** Burning mouth syndrome (BMS) is an idiopathic burning discomfort or pain affecting people with clinically normal oral mucosa, in whom a medical or dental cause has been excluded. Terms previously used to describe what is now called burning mouth syndrome include glossodynia, glossopyrosis, stomatodynia, stomatopyrosis, sore tongue, and oral dysaesthesia. A survey of 669 men and 758 women randomly selected from

*(continued over)*

*(from previous page)*

48,500 people aged 20 to 69 years found that people with burning mouth also have subjective dryness (66%), take some form of medication (64%), report other systemic illnesses (57%), and have altered taste (11%). Many studies of people with symptoms of burning mouth do not distinguish those with BMS (i.e., idiopathic disease) from those with other conditions (such as vitamin B deficiency), making results unreliable. Local and systemic factors (such as infections, allergies, ill-fitting dentures, hypersensitivity reactions, and hormone and vitamin deficiencies) may cause the symptom of burning mouth, and should be excluded before diagnosing burning mouth syndrome. This review deals only with idiopathic BMS.

**INCIDENCE/PREVALENCE** BMS mainly affects women, particularly after the menopause, when its prevalence may be 18% to 33%. One study in Sweden found a prevalence of 4% for the symptom of burning mouth without clinical abnormality of the oral mucosa (11/669 [2%] men, mean age 59 years; 42/758 [6%] women, mean age 57 years), with the highest prevalence (12%) in women aged 60 to 69 years. Reported prevalence in general populations varies from 1% to 15%. However, there may several aetiological factors behind BMS. One oral clinical examination survey in the general adult population in Finland found that 14.8% of the individuals surveyed had experienced BMS. However, when people with mucosal lesions, oral candidiasis, or both were excluded, the frequency decreased to 7.9%. Less than 1% (0.7%) of people reported continuous BMS complaints. Incidence and prevalence vary according to diagnostic criteria, and many studies have included people with the symptom of burning mouth, rather than with BMS as defined above.

**AETIOLOGY/RISK FACTORS** The cause is unknown, and we found no good aetiological studies. Possible causal factors include hormonal disturbances associated with the menopause, psychogenic factors (including anxiety, depression, stress, life events, person-ality disorders, and phobia of cancer), and neuropathy in so-called supertasters. Support for a neuropathic cause comes from studies that have shown altered sensory and pain thresholds in people with BMS. Two studies using blink reflex and thermal quantitative sensory tests have demonstrated signs of neuropathy in most people with BMS.

**PROGNOSIS** We found no prospective cohort studies describing the natural history of BMS. We found anecdotal reports of at least partial spontaneous remission in about 50% of people with BMS within 6 to 7 years. However, a retrospective study assessing 53 people with BMS (48 women and 5 men, mean duration of BMS 5.5 years, mean follow-up 56 months) found a complete spontaneous resolution of oral symptoms in 4% of people who received no treatment. Overall, 28% of people (15/53) experienced a moderate improvement with or without treatment.

Caroline L Pankhurst

## KEY POINTS

- Opportunistic infection with the fungus *Candida albicans* causes painful red or white lesions of the oropharynx, which can affect taste, speech, and the act of eating.

  *Candida* is present in the mouth of up to 60% of healthy people, but overt infection is associated with immunosuppression, diabetes, broad-spectrum antibiotics, corticosteroid use, haematinic deficiencies, and denture wear.

- In people with immunosuppression following cancer treatment, absorbed (ketoconazole, itraconazole, or fluconazole) or partially absorbed antifungal drugs (miconazole, clotrimazole) prevent oropharyngeal candidiasis compared with placebo or non-absorbed antifungal drugs. We don't know whether antifungal treatment is effective in this group.

  Non-absorbed antifungal drugs (nystatin or amphotericin B) may be no more effective than placebo at preventing candidiasis.

  We don't know whether antifungal prophylaxis is effective in adults having tissue transplants, as we found few studies.

- CAUTION: there have been drug safety alerts that oral ketoconazole can cause severe liver injury, adrenal gland problems, can lead to harmful drug interactions, and that the benefits do not outweigh the risks in treating fungal infections. It has been suspended in some countries and restrictions placed on its use in others.

- Prophylaxis with fluconazole is more effective than oral nystatin or amphotericin B at preventing candidiasis in immunocompromised infants and children, while treatment with fluconazole and miconazole increases cure rates compared with nystatin in both immunocompromised and immunocompetent infants and children.

- Antifungal drugs may increase clinical improvement or cure in people with oropharyngeal candidiasis caused by wearing dentures.

  We don't know whether denture hygiene or removing dentures at night reduces the risk of developing oropharyngeal candidiasis.

- Daily or weekly prophylaxis with fluconazole or itraconazole reduces the incidence of candidiasis in people with HIV infection. Prophylaxis with nystatin may not be effective.

  Topical treatments with clotrimazole lozenges and miconazole buccal slow-release tablets may be as effective as oral tablets/suspensions of oral antifungals (fluconazole/itraconazole/ketoconazole) at reducing symptoms of candidiasis in people with HIV infection.

  A single dose of fluconazole (750 mg) may be as effective as a 14-day course of fluconazole in reducing symptoms of candidiasis in people with HIV infection.

- Resistance to antifungal drugs, particularly azole drugs, is an increasing problem. Continuous prophylaxis with antifungal agents may not increase the risk of developing antifungal resistance compared with intermittent prophylaxis, but it may be no more effective at reducing the number of attacks in people with HIV infection, the majority of whom were receiving highly active antiretroviral treatment (HAART).

(i) **Please visit http://clinicalevidence.bmj.com for full text and references**

## What are the effects of interventions to prevent and treat oropharyngeal candidiasis in adults undergoing treatments that cause immunosuppression?

| Beneficial | • Antifungal prophylaxis with absorbed or partially absorbed antifungal drugs in adults having chemotherapy, radiotherapy, or both treatments for cancer (more effective than placebo or non-absorbed drugs) |
| --- | --- |
| Unknown Effectiveness | • Antifungal prophylaxis in adults having tissue transplants<br><br>• Antifungal treatment in adults having chemotherapy, radiotherapy, or both treatments for cancer |

## What are the effects of interventions to prevent and treat oropharyngeal candidiasis in infants and children?

| Beneficial | • Antifungal treatment with miconazole or fluconazole in immunocompetent and immunocompromised infants and children (more effective than nystatin) |
| --- | --- |
| Likely To Be Beneficial | • Antifungal prophylaxis with fluconazole in immunocompromised infants and children (more effective than oral nystatin or amphotericin B) |

## What are the effects of interventions to prevent and treat oropharyngeal candidiasis in people with dentures?

| Likely To Be Beneficial | • Antifungal treatment for denture stomatitis |
| --- | --- |
| Unknown Effectiveness | • Denture hygiene |

## What are the effects of interventions to prevent and treat oropharyngeal candidiasis in people with HIV infection?

| Beneficial | • Antifungal prophylaxis (fluconazole or itraconazole)<br><br>• Antifungal treatment |
| --- | --- |

## Which antifungal regimens reduce the risk of acquiring resistance to antifungal drugs?

| Unlikely To Be Beneficial | • Intermittent treatment in people with HIV infection and acute episodes of oropharyngeal candidiasis (no reduction in antifungal resistance compared with continuous prophylaxis) |
| --- | --- |

Search date July 2013

**DEFINITION** Oropharyngeal candidiasis is an opportunistic mucosal infection caused, in most cases, by the fungus *Candida albicans*. It can also be caused by other species such as *C glabrata*, *C tropicalis*, and *C krusei*. The four main types of oropharyngeal candidiasis are: (1) pseudomembranous (thrush), consisting of white, curd-like, discrete plaques on an erythematous background that is exposed after the removal of the plaque and found on the buccal mucosa, throat, tongue, or gingivae; (2) erythematous, consisting of smooth red patches on the hard or soft palate, dorsum of tongue, or buccal mucosa; (3) hyperplastic, consisting of white, firmly adherent patches or plaques that cannot be removed, usually bilaterally distributed on the buccal mucosa, tongue, or palate; and (4) denture-induced stomatitis, presenting as either a smooth or a granular erythema confined to the denture-bearing area of the hard palate and often associated with an angular cheilitis, which occurs as red, fissured lesions in the corners of the mouth. Symptoms vary, ranging from none to a sore and painful mouth with a burning tongue and altered taste. Oropharyngeal candidiasis can impair speech, nutritional intake, and quality of life. Oropharyngeal candidiasis is the most common oral manifestation of HIV infection. HIV-seropositive people with recurrent oropharyngeal candidiasis have overall lower levels of oral health as measured by a higher decayed, missing, and filled-teeth index; dry mouth; and taste problems.

**INCIDENCE/PREVALENCE** *Candida* species are commensals in the gastrointestinal tract. Most infections are endogenously acquired, although infections in neonates can be primary infections. Transmission can also occur directly from infected people or on fomites (objects that can harbour pathogenic organisms). *Candida* is found in the mouth of 18% to 60% of healthy people in high- and middle-income countries. One cross-sectional study in China (77 HIV-seropositive outpatients and 217 HIV-negative students) found no significant difference in the rates of asymptomatic *Candida* carriage reported in healthy and HIV-seropositive people (18% of healthy people v 29% of HIV-seropositive people; P = 0.07). Denture stomatitis associated with *Candida* is prevalent in 65% of denture wearers. Oropharyngeal candidiasis affects 15% to 60% of people with haematological or oncological malignancies during periods of immunosuppression. The prevalence of oral candidiasis during head and neck radiation therapy is similar to that during chemotherapy. Oropharyngeal candidiasis occurs in 7% to 48% of people with HIV infection and in >90% of those with advanced disease. In severely immunosuppressed people, relapse rates are high (30% to 50%) and relapse usually occurs within 14 days of stopping treatment.

**AETIOLOGY/RISK FACTORS** Risk factors associated with symptomatic oropharyngeal candidiasis include: local or systemic immunosuppression; haematological disorders; broad-spectrum antibiotic use; inhaled or systemic corticosteroids; xerostomia; diabetes; wearing dentures, obturators, or orthodontic appliances; and smoking. Smoking predisposes to oral carriage of *Candida*. In one study of 2499 men with HIV and a baseline CD4+ cell count >200 cells/microlitre, smoking increased the risk of pseudomembranous candidiasis by 40% (P less than or equal to 0.01). However, another study (139 people with HIV infection) suggested that smoking was not a risk factor for those with a baseline CD4+ cell count <200 cells/microlitre. The exact mechanism of action by which smoking predisposes to *Candida* is not known, but it may involve the impairment of local immunity by inducing cytokine changes and reducing epithelial cell-mediated anticandidal activity. The same *Candida* strain may persist for months or years in the absence of infection. In people with HIV infection, there is no direct correlation between the number of organisms and the presence of clinical disease. Candidal strains causing disease in people with HIV infection seem to be the same as those colonising HIV-negative people, and in most people do not change over time. Symptomatic oropharyngeal candidiasis associated with in-vitro resistance to fluconazole occurs in 5% of people with advanced HIV disease. Resistance to azole antifungal drugs is associated with severe immunosuppression (CD4+ cell count 50 cells/microlitre or less), more episodes treated with antifungal drugs, and longer median duration of systemic azole treatment.

**PROGNOSIS** In most people, untreated candidiasis persists for months or years unless associated risk factors are treated or eliminated. In neonates, spontaneous cure of oropharyngeal candidiasis usually occurs after 3 to 8 weeks. Protease inhibitors used in highly active antiretroviral treatment (HAART) regimens in HIV-seropositive people have been shown to directly attenuate the adherence of *Candida albicans* to epithelial cells in vitro by inhibiting the action of *Candida* virulence factors.

Crispian Scully, CBE

## KEY POINTS

- Halitosis can be caused by oral disease or by respiratory tract conditions such as sinusitis, tonsillitis, and bronchiectasis, but an estimated 40% of affected people have no underlying organic disease.

  The main chemicals causing the odour seem to be volatile sulfur compounds, but little is known about the cause of physiological halitosis.

- Regular use of a mouthwash may reduce breath odour compared with placebo.

- Zinc toothpastes seem to reduce breath odour compared with placebo for people with halitosis.

- We don't know whether tongue cleaning, sugar-free chewing gums, or artificial saliva reduce halitosis, as no studies of adequate quality have been found.

 Please visit http://clinicalevidence.bmj.com for full text and references

| What are the effects of treatments in people with physiological halitosis? | |
|---|---|
| Likely To Be Beneficial | • Regular-use mouthwash (containing chlorhexidine, zinc, hydrogen peroxide, or other antimicrobial agents)<br><br>• Zinc toothpastes |
| Unknown Effectiveness | • Artificial saliva<br><br>• Sugar-free chewing gum<br><br>• Tongue cleaning, brushing, or scraping |

Search date July 2013

**DEFINITION** Halitosis is an unpleasant odour emitted from the mouth. It may be caused by oral conditions (including poor oral hygiene and periodontal disease) or by respiratory tract conditions, such as chronic sinusitis, tonsillitis, and bronchiectasis. In this review, we deal only with physiological halitosis (i.e., confirmed persistent bad breath in the absence of systemic, oral, or periodontal disease). We have excluded halitosis caused by underlying systemic disease that would require disease-specific treatment, pseudo-halitosis (in people who believe they have bad breath but whose breath is not considered malodorous by others), and artificially induced halitosis (e.g., in studies requiring people to stop brushing their teeth). This review is only applicable, therefore, to people in whom such underlying causes have been ruled out, and in whom pseudo-halitosis has been excluded. There is no consensus regarding duration of bad breath for the diagnosis of halitosis, although the standard organoleptic test for bad breath involves smelling the breath on at least two or three different days. Professional tooth cleaning may be of value where periodontal disease or poor oral hygiene contribute to malodour.

**INCIDENCE/PREVALENCE** We found no reliable estimate of prevalence, although several studies report the population prevalence of halitosis (physiological or because of underlying disease) to be about 50%. One cross-sectional study of 491 people found that about 5% of people with halitosis have pseudo-halitosis and about 40% have physiological bad breath not caused by underlying disease. We found no reliable data about age or sex distribution of physiological halitosis.

**AETIOLOGY/RISK FACTORS** We found no reliable data about risk factors for physiological bad breath. Mass spectrometric and gas chromatographic analysis of expelled air from the mouths of people with any type of halitosis have shown that the principal malodorants are volatile sulfur compounds, including hydrogen sulfide, methyl mercaptan, and dimethyl sulfide.

**PROGNOSIS** We found no evidence on the prognosis of halitosis.

Thomas B. Dodson and Srinivas M. Susarla

## KEY POINTS

- Impacted wisdom teeth (third molars) occur because of a lack of space, obstruction, or abnormal position.

  They can cause pain, swelling, and infection, and may destroy adjacent teeth and bone.

  The incidence of impacted wisdom teeth is high, with some 72% of Swedish people aged 20 to 30 years having at least one impacted wisdom tooth.

- Non-RCT evidence indicates that about one third of asymptomatic, unerupted wisdom teeth will change position, resulting in wisdom teeth that are partially erupted but non-functional or non-hygienic.

  Between 30% and 60% of people who retain their asymptomatic wisdom teeth proceed to extraction of one or more of them between 4 and 12 years after their first visit.

- Removal of impacted wisdom teeth (symptomatic and asymptomatic) is a commonly performed procedure.

- While symptomatic or diseased impacted wisdom teeth should be recommended for removal, current evidence neither refutes nor confirms the practice of prophylactic removal of asymptomatic, disease-free wisdom teeth.

  Some non-RCT evidence indicates that extraction of the asymptomatic tooth may be beneficial when disease, such as caries, is present in the adjacent second molar, or if periodontal pockets are present distal to the second molar.

- We do not know whether active surveillance is effective for asymptomatic, disease-free wisdom teeth, as we found no RCTs or prospective cohort studies on this topic.

- We don't know which is the most effective operative (surgical) technique for extracting impacted wisdom teeth.

 **Please visit http://clinicalevidence.bmj.com for full text and references**

| Should asymptomatic, disease-free impacted wisdom teeth be removed prophylactically? | |
|---|---|
| Unknown Effectiveness | • Active surveillance<br><br>• Prophylactic extraction versus no extraction plus no active surveillance |

| What are the effects of different operative (surgical) techniques for removing impacted wisdom teeth? | |
|---|---|
| Unknown Effectiveness | • Extraction of impacted wisdom teeth: different operative (surgical) techniques (different bone removal techniques versus each other; complete extraction versus coronectomy) |

Search date October 2013

**DEFINITION** Wisdom teeth are present in most adults, and they generally become apparent between the ages of 18 and 24 years, although there is wide variation in the age of presentation. Impacted wisdom teeth are third molars that are not ordinarily expected to erupt into functional teeth. Wisdom teeth become partially or completely impacted owing to lack of space, obstruction, or abnormal position. Impacted wisdom teeth may be diagnosed because of symptoms such as pressure, pain, or swelling; by physical examination with probing or direct visualisation; or incidentally by routine dental radiography.

**INCIDENCE/PREVALENCE** Wisdom tooth (third molar) impaction is common. More than 72% of Swedish people aged 20 to 30 years have at least one impacted lower wisdom tooth. Removal of impacted wisdom teeth (symptomatic and asymptomatic) is a commonly performed operation. The incidence of wisdom tooth removal is estimated to be 4 per 1000 person-years in England and Wales, making it one of the top 10 inpatient and day-case procedures. In a report from 1994, up to 90% of people on oral and maxillofacial surgery hospital waiting lists were awaiting removal of wisdom teeth. Fewer operations are done now, possibly because of guidance.

**AETIOLOGY/RISK FACTORS** Wisdom tooth impaction may be more common now than in the past, as modern diet tends to be softer.

**PROGNOSIS** Impacted wisdom teeth can cause pain, swelling, and infection, and may destroy adjacent teeth and bone. The removal of diseased or symptomatic wisdom teeth alleviates pain and suffering, and improves oral health and function. About one third of asymptomatic, unerupted wisdom teeth have been found to change position with time, resulting in wisdom teeth that are partially erupted but non-functional or non-hygienic. Three prospective cohort studies have also demonstrated that 30% to 60% of people with previously asymptomatic impacted wisdom teeth will undergo extraction of one or more of their wisdom teeth because of symptoms or disease, between 4 and 12 years following study enrolment. In another cohort study, a surprisingly high percentage (25%) of people with asymptomatic wisdom teeth had periodontal disease, as evidenced by probing depths greater than 5 mm. Probing depths could be an indicator of future periodontal status. One prospective cohort study demonstrated that 40% of people with asymptomatic wisdom teeth with probing depths of more than 4 mm had clinically significant progression of their periodontal status (probing depth increase of >2 mm) in the subsequent 24 months. The same study also found that, for those people with wisdom teeth with a probing depth of less than 4 mm, only 3% of teeth demonstrated progression of periodontal disease as evidenced by increasing probing depths.

# Postoperative pulmonary infections

Michelle Conde and Valerie Lawrence

## KEY POINTS

- Postoperative pulmonary infections are associated with cough, phlegm, shortness of breath, chest pain, temperature above 38°C, and pulse rate above 100 bpm.

  Up to half of people may have asymptomatic chest signs after surgery, and up to a quarter develop symptomatic disease.

  The main risk factor is the type of surgery, with higher risks associated with surgery to the chest, abdomen, and head and neck compared with other operations.

  Other risk factors include age over 50 years, COPD, smoking, hypoalbuminemia, and being functionally dependent.

- Prophylactic lung expansion techniques are commonly used to reduce the risk of postoperative pulmonary infection, but we don't know whether they are of benefit in people having abdominal or cardiac surgery.

  We don't know which is the most effective lung expansion technique to use.

- Regional anaesthesia (epidural or spinal), either alone or with general anaesthesia, may reduce the risk of developing postoperative pulmonary infections compared with general anaesthesia alone, although studies have given conflicting results.

  It has been estimated that one infection would be prevented for every 50 people having regional anaesthesia.

  Regional anaesthesia is associated with a small risk (around 4/10,000 procedures in total) of seizures, cardiac arrest, respiratory depression, or neurological injury.

- Selective postoperative nasogastric decompression reduces the risk of developing postoperative pulmonary infections after abdominal surgery compared with routine use.

  Routine use does not shorten the return of bowel function and tube insertion is uncomfortable in up to a fifth of people.

- We don't know whether advice to stop smoking before surgery reduces the risk of developing postoperative pulmonary infections.

  It is possible that people need to have stopped smoking at least 2 months before surgery in order to reduce the risks of chest infection.

(i) **Please visit http://clinicalevidence.bmj.com for full text and references**

| What are the effects of interventions to prevent postoperative pulmonary infections? | |
|---|---|
| Likely To Be Beneficial | • Nasogastric decompression after abdominal surgery (selective more effective than routine postoperative use)<br><br>• Regional (epidural or spinal) anaesthesia |
| Unknown Effectiveness | • Advice to stop smoking preoperatively<br><br>• Prophylactic lung expansion techniques |

**Search date May 2007**

©BMJ Publishing Group Ltd 2015

**DEFINITION** A working diagnosis of postoperative pulmonary infection may be based on three or more new findings from: cough, phlegm, shortness of breath, chest pain, temperature above 38°C, and pulse rate above 100 bpm. In this review, we focus on postoperative pneumonia. However, as RCTs usually estimate risk for combined outcomes (atelectasis; bronchospasm; bronchitis; pneumonia; respiratory failure, or exacerbation of underlying chronic disease, or both), it has not always been feasible to separate specific pneumonia rates from combined pulmonary outcomes. We examine a selection of pre-, intra-, and postoperative techniques to reduce the risk of postoperative pulmonary complications. In this review, the diagnosis of pneumonia implies consolidation observed in a chest radiograph.

**INCIDENCE/PREVALENCE** Reported morbidity for chest complications depends on how carefully they are investigated, and on the type of surgery performed. One observational study found blood gas and chest radiograph abnormalities in about 50% of people after open cholecystectomy. However, less than 20% of these had abnormal clinical signs, and only 10% had a clinically significant chest infection. One observational study found the incidence of pneumonia to be 17.5% after thoracic and abdominal surgeries. Another observational study found the incidence of pneumonia to be 2.8% (using a more restrictive definition of pneumonia) after laparotomy.

**AETIOLOGY/RISK FACTORS** Risk factors include: increasing age (over 50 years), with the odds of developing postoperative pneumonia systematically increasing with each decile above the age of 50 years; functional dependency; COPD; weight loss of over 10% in the last 6 months; impaired sensorium (acute confusion/delirium associated with current illness); cigarette smoking; recent alcohol use; and blood urea nitrogen level greater than 7.5 mmol/L. Serum albumin level of less than 35 g/L is also a risk factor for the development of overall postoperative pulmonary complications. The strongest risk factor, however, is the type of surgery (particularly aortic aneurysm repair, thoracic surgery, abdominal surgery, neurosurgery, head and neck surgery, and vascular surgery). Obesity was not found to be an independent risk factor in a recent systematic review of preoperative pulmonary risk stratification for non-cardiothoracic surgery. Nasogastric tube placement was found to be a risk factor by multivariate analysis in the development of postoperative pulmonary complications in a systematic review of blinded studies examining risk factors for pulmonary complications after non-thoracic surgery.

**PROGNOSIS** In one large systematic review (search date 1997, 141 RCTs, 9559 people), 10% of people with postoperative pneumonia died. If systemic sepsis ensues, mortality rate is likely to be high. Pneumonia delays recovery from surgery, and poor tissue oxygenation may contribute to delayed wound healing. In a cohort of 160,805 US veterans having major non-cardiac surgery, 1.5% of people developed postoperative pneumonia, and the 30-day mortality rate was 10-fold higher in these people compared with those without postoperative pneumonia.

# Carbon monoxide poisoning (acute)

Craig Smollin and Kent Olson

## KEY POINTS

- The main symptoms of carbon monoxide poisoning are non-specific in nature and relate to effects on the brain and heart. The symptoms correlate poorly with serum carboxyhaemoglobin levels.

    People with comorbidity, elderly or very young people, and pregnant women are most susceptible.

    Carbon monoxide is produced by the incomplete combustion of carbon fuels, including inadequately ventilated heaters and car exhausts, or from chemicals such as methylene chloride paint stripper.

    Poisoning is considered to have occurred at carboxyhaemoglobin levels of over 10%, and severe poisoning is associated with levels over 20–25%, plus symptoms of severe cerebral or cardiac ischaemia. However, people living in areas of pollution may have levels of 5%, and heavy smokers can tolerate levels up to 15%.

    Severe poisoning can be fatal, and up to a third of survivors have delayed neurological sequelae.

- Immediate care requires removal of the person from the source of carbon monoxide and giving oxygen through a non-re-breather mask.

    Normobaric 100% oxygen reduces the half-life of carboxyhaemoglobin and is considered to be effective, but studies confirming benefit compared with air or lower concentrations of oxygen have not been identified, and would be unethical.

    Paramedics use 28% oxygen, which is thought to be beneficial compared with air but may be less effective than higher concentrations of oxygen.

    We don't know what is the optimum duration of oxygen treatment, but it is usually continued for at least 6 hours, or until carboxyhaemoglobin levels fall below 5%.

- We don't know whether hyperbaric oxygen is more effective than normobaric 100% oxygen at preventing neurological complications in people with mild to moderate or moderate to severe carbon monoxide poisoning.

    Clinical benefit of hyperbaric 100% oxygen may depend on the treatment regimen used.

    The possible benefits of hyperbaric oxygen for an individual need to be weighed against the hazards of a long journey by ambulance.

(i) **Please visit http://clinicalevidence.bmj.com for full text and references**

| What are the effects of oxygen treatments for acute carbon monoxide poisoning? | |
| --- | --- |
| Likely To Be Beneficial | • Oxygen 100% by non-re-breather mask (compared with air)* |
| | • Oxygen 28% (compared with air)* |
| Unknown Effectiveness | • Hyperbaric oxygen 100% (mild to moderate poisoning) |
| | • Hyperbaric oxygen 100% at 2–3 ATA (moderate to severe poisoning) |

**Search date June 2010**

*Categorisation based on consensus and physiological studies.

**DEFINITION** Carbon monoxide is an odourless, colourless gas, and poisoning causes hypoxia, cell damage, and death. **Diagnosis of carbon monoxide poisoning:** Exposure to carbon monoxide is measured either directly from blood samples and expressed as a percentage of carboxyhaemoglobin, or indirectly using the carbon monoxide in expired breath. Carboxyhaemoglobin percentage is the most frequently used biomarker of carbon monoxide exposure. Although the diagnosis of carbon monoxide poisoning can be confirmed by detecting elevated levels of carboxyhaemoglobin in the blood, the presence of clinical signs and symptoms after known exposure to carbon monoxide should not be ignored. The signs and symptoms of carbon monoxide poisoning are mainly associated with the brain and heart, which are most sensitive to hypoxia. The symptoms of carbon monoxide poisoning are non-specific and varied, and include headache, fatigue, malaise, 'trouble thinking', confusion, nausea, dizziness, visual disturbances, chest pain, shortness of breath, loss of consciousness, and seizures. In people suffering from co-morbidities, symptoms such as shortness of breath or chest pain may be more evident. The classical signs of carbon monoxide poisoning — described as cherry-red lips, peripheral cyanosis, and retinal haemorrhages — are rarely seen. **Interpretation of carboxyhaemoglobin levels:** Non-smokers living away from urban areas have carboxyhaemoglobin levels of 0.4% to 1.0%, reflecting endogenous carbon monoxide production, whereas levels of up to 5% may be considered normal in a busy urban or industrial setting. Smokers are exposed to increased levels of carbon monoxide in cigarettes, and otherwise healthy heavy smokers can tolerate levels of carboxyhaemoglobin of up to 15%. The use of carboxyhaemoglobin percentage as a measure of severity of carbon monoxide poisoning, or to predict treatment options, is limited because carboxyhaemoglobin levels are affected by removal from the source of carbon monoxide and any oxygen treatment given before measurement of percentage carboxyhaemoglobin. Additionally, people with co-morbidities that make them more sensitive to the hypoxia associated with carbon monoxide can present with symptoms of poisoning at carboxyhaemoglobin levels that are either low or within the normal range. Attempts have been made in the literature to equate symptoms and signs to different carboxyhaemoglobin levels, but it is accepted that carboxyhaemoglobin levels in an acutely poisoned person only roughly correlate with clinical signs and symptoms, especially those relating to neurological function. Earlier studies attempted to differentiate between smokers and non-smokers. Attempts have also been made in the literature to divide carbon monoxide poisoning into mild, moderate, and severe based on carboxyhaemoglobin percentage levels and clinical symptoms, but there is no clear clinical consensus or agreement on this issue. The degrees of poisoning have been described as *mild carbon monoxide poisoning:* a carboxyhaemoglobin level of over 10% without clinical signs or symptoms of carbon monoxide poisoning; *moderate carbon monoxide poisoning:* a carboxyhaemoglobin level of over 10%, but under 20–25%, with minor clinical signs and symptoms of poisoning, such as headache, lethargy, or fatigue; and *severe carbon monoxide poisoning:* a carboxyhaemoglobin level of over 20–25%, loss of consciousness, and confusion or signs of cardiac ischaemia, or both. **Population:** For the purpose of this review, we have included adults presenting to healthcare professionals with suspected carbon monoxide poisoning. Although there is no clear consensus on this issue, most studies examining carbon monoxide poisoning and its management use a carboxyhaemoglobin level of 10% or more, or the presence of clinical signs and symptoms after known exposure to carbon monoxide, to be indicative of acute carbon monoxide poisoning. Unless otherwise stated, this definition of acute carbon monoxide poisoning has been used throughout this review. Where appropriate, the terms mild, moderate, or severe have been used to reflect the descriptions of populations in individual studies.

**INCIDENCE/PREVALENCE** Carbon monoxide poisoning is considered to be one of the leading causes of death and injury worldwide, and is a major public health problem. In 2000, carbon monoxide was the recorded cause of 521 deaths (ICD 9–E986) in England and Wales compared with 1363 deaths recorded in 1985; a trend that has also been observed in the USA. Of the 521 deaths attributed to carbon monoxide poisoning, 148 were accidental and the remaining 373 the result of suicide or self-inflicted injury. Poisoning by carbon monoxide is almost certainly underdiagnosed because of the varied ways in which it can present, and it has been estimated that, in the USA, there are over 40,000 emergency department visits a year; many presenting with a flu-like illness. In 2003, 534 recorded medical episodes in English hospitals involved people suffering from the toxic effects of carbon monoxide. This

*(continued over)*

*(from previous page)*

may be a substantial underestimate if the US experience reflects the true morbidity associated with carbon monoxide poisoning. Studies in the USA have shown that the incidence of accidental carbon monoxide poisoning peaks during the winter months, and is associated with increased use of indoor heating and petrol powered generators, and reduced external ventilation. This seasonal rise in numbers coincides with the annual increase in influenza notifications, and given the similarity in symptoms, many cases of mild carbon monoxide poisoning are probably misdiagnosed.

**AETIOLOGY/RISK FACTORS People at high risk:** People who are most at risk from carbon monoxide poisoning include those with CHD, CVD, or anaemia; pregnant women and their fetus; infants; and elderly people. In people with CHD, experimentally induced blood carboxyhaemoglobin levels of 4.5% shorten the period of exercise before the onset of anginal pain, and the duration of pain is prolonged. In people with anaemia, the oxygen-carrying capacity of the blood is already compromised and therefore they will be more sensitive to carbon monoxide. Elderly people are at risk because of existing co-morbidities, such as heart disease or respiratory disease, and because of a reduced compensatory response to hypoxic situations. During pregnancy, a woman's oxygen-carrying capacity is reduced because of an increased endogenous carbon monoxide production and additional endogenous carbon monoxide from the developing fetus, leading to an increased carboxy-haemoglobin concentration. A higher ventilation rate during pregnancy will lead to increased uptake of carbon monoxide at any given carbon monoxide concentration. The fetus is also at risk, and there have been occasional fetal deaths in non-fatal maternal exposures. In the developing fetus, oxygen is released at a lower oxygen partial pressure, and fetal haemoglobin binds with carbon monoxide more quickly compared with adults. Carbon monoxide may be a teratogen where there is a significant increase in maternal carboxyhae-moglobin or where there is moderate to severe maternal toxicity. Infants may be more susceptible to the effects of carbon monoxide because of their greater oxygen consumption in relation to adults, and their response and symptoms are more variable. There are recorded instances of children travelling in the same car and having varying symptoms with similar carboxyhaemoglobin levels, or widely varying carboxyhaemoglobin levels with similar carbon monoxide exposure. **Sources of carbon monoxide:** Carbon monoxide is produced by the incomplete combustion of carbon-containing fuel, such as gas (domestic or bottled), charcoal, coke, oil, and wood. Potential sources include: gas stoves, fires, and boilers; gas-powered water heaters; car exhaust fumes; charcoal barbecues; paraffin heaters; solid fuel-powered stoves; boilers; and room heaters that are faulty or inadequately ventilated. An overlooked source of carbon monoxide is methylene chloride in some paint strippers and sprays. Methylene chloride is readily absorbed through the skin and lungs and, once in the liver, is converted to carbon monoxide. Methylene chloride is stored in body tissues and released gradually; the carbon monoxide elimination half-life in people exposed to methylene chloride is more than twice that of inhaled carbon monoxide. Natural background levels of carbon monoxide in the outdoor environment range from 0.01 to 0.23 $mg/m^3$ (0.009–0.2 ppm), but, in urban traffic in the UK, the 8 hour mean concentrations are higher at about 20 $mg/m^3$ (17.5 ppm); exposure to this level for prolonged periods could result in a carboxyhaemoglobin level of about 3%.

**PROGNOSIS** Prognosis data in carbon monoxide poisoning are inconclusive and contradic-tory. However, there is general agreement that outcome and prognosis are related to the level of carbon monoxide that a person is exposed to, the duration of exposure, and the presence of underlying risk factors. A poor outcome is predicted by lengthy carbon monoxide exposure, loss of consciousness, and advancing age. In addition, hypotension and cardiac arrest independently predict permanent disability and death. After acute carbon monoxide poisoning the organs most sensitive to hypoxia (the brain and heart) will be most affected. Pre-existing co-morbidities that affect these organs will, to an extent, influence the clinical presentation and the prognosis; an individual with pre-existing heart disease may present with myocardial ischaemia that could lead to infarction and death. The prognosis for people resuscitated after experiencing cardiac arrest with carbon monoxide poisoning is poor. In a small retrospective study, 18 people with carboxyhaemoglobin levels of 31.7 ± 11.0% given hyperbaric oxygen after resuscitation post-cardiac arrest all died. The effects on the brain are more subtle, given that different sections of the brain are more sensitive to hypoxic insults, either as a consequence of reduced oxygen delivery, or by direct effects on intracellular metabolism. Therefore, in addition to the acute neurological sequelae leading to loss of consciousness, coma, and death, neurological sequelae, such as poor concentration and memory problems, may be apparent in people recovering from carbon monoxide poisoning (persistent neurological sequelae) or develop after a period of apparent normality (delayed neurological sequelae). Delayed neurological sequelae develop between 2 and 240 days after exposure, and are reported to affect 10% to 32% of people recovering from carbon monoxide poisoning. Symptoms include cognitive changes, personality changes, incontinence, psychosis, and Parkinsonism. Fortunately, 50% to 75% of people recover within 1 year.

## 472 | **Organophosphorus poisoning (acute)**

Peter G Blain

### KEY POINTS

- Acetylcholinesterase inhibition by organophosphorus pesticides or organophosphate nerve agents can cause acute parasympathetic system dysfunction, muscle weakness, seizures, coma, and respiratory failure.

  Prognosis depends on the dose and relative toxicity of the specific compound, as well as pharmacokinetic factors.

- Initial resuscitation, then atropine and oxygen, are considered to be the mainstays of treatment, although good-quality studies to show benefit have not been found.

  The optimum dose of atropine has not been determined, but common clinical practice is to administer sufficient to keep the heart rate >80 bpm, systolic blood pressure above 80 mmHg, and the lungs clear.

  Glycopyrronium bromide may be as effective as atropine in preventing death, with fewer adverse effects, although no adequately powered studies have been done.

- Removing contaminated clothes and then washing the poisoned person is a sensible approach, but no studies have been reported that evaluate benefit.

  Healthcare workers should ensure that washing does not distract them from other intervention priorities, and should protect themselves from contamination.

- Benzodiazepines are considered to be standard treatment to control organophosphorus-induced seizures, although we found no specific studies.

- It is not known whether activated charcoal, alpha$_2$ adrenergic receptor agonists (clonidine), butyrylcholinesterase replacement therapy using fresh frozen plasma or plasmapheresis, magnesium sulphate, N-methyl-D-aspartate receptor antagonists, organophosphorus hydrolases, sodium bicarbonate, milk and other 'home remedies' taken soon after ingestion, cathartics, or extracorporeal clearance improve outcomes.

  Oximes have not been shown to improve outcomes, but most studies have been of poor quality so a definite conclusion cannot be made.

  Potential benefits from gastric lavage or ipecacuanha are likely to be outweighed by the risks of harm, such as aspiration.

(i) **Please visit http://clinicalevidence.bmj.com for full text and references**

| What are the effects of treatments for acute organophosphorus poisoning? | |
|---|---|
| **Likely To Be Beneficial** | • Atropine* |
| | • Benzodiazepines to control organophosphorus-induced seizures* |
| | • Glycopyrronium bromide (glycopyrrolate)* |
| | • Removing contaminated clothes and washing the poisoned person* |
| **Unknown Effectiveness** | • Activated charcoal (single or multiple dose) |
| | • Alpha$_2$ adrenergic receptor agonists |
| | • Butyrylcholinesterase replacement therapy |
| | • Extracorporeal clearance |
| | • Gastric lavage |

|  | |
|---|---|
|  | • Magnesium sulphate |
|  | • Milk or other home remedy immediately after ingestion |
|  | • N-methyl-D-aspartate receptor antagonists |
|  | • Organophosphorus hydrolases |
|  | • Oximes |
|  | • Sodium bicarbonate |
| **Unlikely To Be Beneficial** | • Cathartics* |
| **Likely To Be Ineffective Or Harmful** | • Ipecacuanha (ipecac)* |

**Search date April 2010**

*Based on consensus, RCTs would be considered unethical.

**DEFINITION** Acute organophosphorus poisoning occurs after dermal, respiratory, or oral exposure to either low volatility pesticides (e.g., chlorpyrifos, dimethoate) or high volatility nerve agents (e.g., sarin, tabun). Inhibition of acetylcholinesterase at synapses results in accumulation of acetylcholine and overactivation of acetylcholine receptors at the neuromuscular junction and in the autonomic and central nervous systems. Early clinical features (the acute cholinergic crisis) reflect involvement of the parasympathetic system and include bronchorrhoea, bronchospasm, miosis, salivation, defecation, urination, and hypotension. Features indicating involvement of the neuromuscular junction (muscle weakness and fasciculations) and central nervous system (seizures, coma, and respiratory failure) are common at this stage. Respiratory failure may also occur many hours later, either separated in time from the cholinergic crisis (intermediate syndrome) or merged into the acute cholinergic crisis. The pathophysiology of this late respiratory failure seems to involve downregulation of nicotinic acetylcholine receptors. Intermediate syndrome is particularly important since people who are apparently well can progress rapidly to respiratory arrest. A late motor or motor/sensory peripheral neuropathy can develop after recovery from acute poisoning with some organophosphorus pesticides. Acute poisoning may result in long-term neurological and psychiatric effects but the evidence is still unclear. There are differences between pesticides in the clinical syndrome they produce and in the frequency and timing of respiratory failure and death.

**INCIDENCE/PREVALENCE** Most cases occur in the developing world as a result of occupational or deliberate exposure to organophosphorus pesticides. Although data are sparse, organophosphorus pesticides seem to be the most important cause of death from deliberate self poisoning worldwide, causing about 200,000 deaths each year. For example, in Sri Lanka, about 10,000 to 20,000 admissions to hospital for organophosphorus poisoning occur each year. Of these, at least 10% die. In most cases, the poisoning is intentional. Case mortality across the developing world is commonly >20%. In Central America, occupational poisoning is reported to be more common than intentional poisoning, and deaths are fewer. Deaths from organophosphorus nerve agents occurred during the Iran–Iraq war and military or terrorist action with these chemical weapons remains possible. Twelve people died in a terrorist attack in Tokyo and several thousands died in Iran following military use.

**AETIOLOGY/RISK FACTORS** The widespread accessibility of pesticides in rural parts of the developing world makes them easy options for acts of self harm. Occupational exposure is usually because of insufficient or inappropriate protective equipment.

*(continued over)*

*(from previous page)*

**PROGNOSIS** There are no validated scoring systems for categorising severity or predicting outcome of acute organophosphorus poisoning. The highly variable natural history and difficulty in determining the dose and identity of the specific organophosphorus compound ingested make predicting outcome for an individual person inaccurate and potentially hazardous, because people admitted in good condition can deteriorate rapidly and require intubation and mechanical ventilation. Prognosis in acute self poisoning is likely to depend on dose and toxicity of the organophosphorus compound that has been ingested (e.g., neurotoxicity potential, half life, rate of ageing, whether activation to a toxic compound is required (e.g., parathion to paraoxon [pro-poison]), and whether it is dimethylated or diethylated. Prognosis in occupational exposure is better because the dose is normally smaller, the route is dermal, and the compound more easily identified.

Nick Buckley and Michael Eddleston

## KEY POINTS

- Paracetamol (acetaminophen) is a common means of self-poisoning in Europe and North America, often taken as an impulsive act of self-harm in young people.

  Mortality from paracetamol overdose is now about 0.4%, although without treatment severe liver damage occurs in at least half of people with blood paracetamol levels above the UK standard treatment line.

  In adults, ingestion of less than 125 mg/kg is unlikely to lead to hepatotoxicity; even higher doses may be tolerated by children without causing liver damage.

- Standard treatment of paracetamol overdose is acetylcysteine, which based on animal studies and clinical experience, is widely believed to reduce liver damage and mortality, although few studies have been done.

  Adverse effects from acetylcysteine include rash, urticaria, vomiting, and anaphylaxis which can, rarely, be fatal.

  We don't know what the optimal dose, route, and duration of acetylcysteine treatment should be. However, liver damage is less likely to occur if treatment is started within 8–10 hours of ingestion.

- It is possible that methionine reduces the risk of liver damage and mortality after paracetamol poisoning compared with supportive care, but we don't know for sure.

- We don't know whether activated charcoal, gastric lavage, or ipecacuanha reduce the risks of liver damage after paracetamol poisoning.

  The rapid absorption of paracetamol suggests that a beneficial effect from treatments that reduce gastric absorption is unlikely in many cases.

- Liver transplantation may increase survival rates in people with fulminant liver failure after paracetamol poisoning compared with waiting list controls, but long-term outcomes are unknown.

 **Please visit http://clinicalevidence.bmj.com for full text and references**

## What are the effects of treatments for acute paracetamol poisoning?

| | |
|---|---|
| **Beneficial** | ● Acetylcysteine |
| **Likely To Be Beneficial** | ● Methionine |
| **Unknown Effectiveness** | ● Activated charcoal (single or multiple dose) |
| | ● Gastric lavage |
| | ● Ipecacuanha |
| | ● Liver transplant |

Search date March 2007

---

**DEFINITION** Paracetamol poisoning occurs as a result of either accidental or intentional overdose with paracetamol (acetaminophen).

*(continued over)*

*(from previous page)*

**INCIDENCE/PREVALENCE** Paracetamol is the most common drug used for self-poisoning in the UK. It is also a common means of self-poisoning in the rest of Europe, North America, and Australasia. There has been an exponential rise in the number of hospital admissions caused by paracetamol poisoning in England and Wales from 150 in 1968 to a peak of 41,200 in 1989–1990, before falling to around 25,000 in 2001–2002. Overdoses from paracetamol alone result in an estimated 150–200 deaths and 15–20 liver transplants each year in England and Wales (data from routinely collected health and coronial statistics). Pack-size restrictions instituted in the UK in 1998 resulted in modest reductions in large overdoses, liver transplants, and deaths in England and Wales. In Scotland, the reduction in admissions and mortality from paracetamol overdose was short lived.

**AETIOLOGY/RISK FACTORS** Most cases in the UK are impulsive acts of self-harm in young people. In one cohort study of 80 people who had overdosed with paracetamol, 42 had obtained the tablets for the specific purpose of taking an overdose, and 33 had obtained them less than 1 hour before the act.

**PROGNOSIS** People with blood paracetamol concentrations above the standard treatment line (defined in the UK as a line joining 200 mg/L at 4 hours and 30 mg/L at 15 hours on a semilogarithmic plot) have a poor prognosis without treatment. In one cohort study of 57 untreated people with blood concentrations above this line, 33/57 (58%) developed severe liver damage and 3/57 (5%) died. People with a history of chronic alcohol misuse, use of enzyme inducing drugs, eating disorders, or multiple paracetamol overdoses may be at risk of liver damage with blood concentrations below this line. In the USA, a lower line is used as an indication for treatment, but we found no data relating this line to prognostic outcomes. More recently, a modified nomogram specifically designed to estimate prognosis (not need for treatment) has been developed by modelling data from a large cohort. This takes into account time to initiation of acetylcysteine treatment, and the effect of alcohol use. However, it has not yet been validated, and is not widely used. Reversible renal injury occurs in some people, most commonly (but not always) in association with hepatic injury. **Dose effect:** The dose ingested also indicates the risk of hepatotoxicity. One case series showed that people ingesting less than 125 mg/kg had no significant hepatotoxicity, with a sharp dose-dependent rise for higher doses. The threshold for toxicity after acute ingestion may be higher in children, where a single dose of less than 200 mg/kg has not been reported to lead to death and rarely causes hepatotoxicity. The higher threshold for toxicity in children may relate to different metabolic pathways or their larger relative liver size. For people who present later than 24 hours, or an unknown time after ingestion, several other prognostic indicators have been proposed, including prothrombin time, and abnormal liver function tests. These have not been validated prospectively. **Slow-release preparations:** Pharmacokinetic studies of small overdoses of slow-release paracetamol formulations in healthy volunteers showed that peak plasma concentrations usually still occur within 4 hours, and the apparent half-life is the same as or only slightly longer than that of conventional paracetamol preparations. The bioavailability was not increased. The nomogram has not specifically been validated for these formulations. However, only a small proportion of cases of slow release preparation ingestion have resulted in initial non-toxic levels and subsequent toxic levels on the usual nomograms. In just one case, with other risk factors, the use of the nomogram led to treatment being ceased, and this may have contributed to a fatal outcome. **Children and repeated supra-therapeutic doses:** There are reports of major dosing errors leading to severe hepatotoxicity in children. Of more concern are other cases of apparent toxicity with repeated doses only slightly above the current maximum recommended doses (around 75 mg/kg/day). There are possibly additional risk factors in these cases, but these have not been established.

Juan C Vazquez

## KEY POINTS

- Constipation, heartburn, and haemorrhoids are common gastrointestinal complaints during pregnancy.
- Constipation occurs in between 11% and 38% of pregnant women.

  We don't know whether stimulant, bulk-forming, or osmotic laxatives are of benefit for constipation in pregnancy.

  Stimulant laxatives may be more effective than bulk laxatives in improving constipation in pregnancy, although adverse effects, such as abdominal pain and diarrhoea, could limit their use.

  We found limited evidence that dietary fibre may improve constipation in pregnant women compared with placebo.

  We don't know whether increasing fluid intake improves constipation in pregnancy. However, because of other health benefits, increased fluid intake may be recommended as one of the first measures to relieve constipation.

- Although the exact prevalence of haemorrhoids during pregnancy is unknown, the condition is common, and the prevalence of symptomatic haemorrhoids in pregnant women is higher than in non-pregnant women.

  Rutosides improve the symptoms of haemorrhoids compared with placebo. However, further studies are needed to assess their potential adverse effects.

  We don't know whether increased fibre or fluid intake are effective in relieving the symptoms of haemorrhoids in pregnancy, although it seems reasonable to encourage pregnant women to consume a fluid- and fibre-rich diet as a preventive measure.

  We don't know whether stimulant laxatives, bulk-forming laxatives, or osmotic laxatives are effective in relieving symptomatic haemorrhoids in pregnancy, although, if constipation is associated with haemorrhoids, treating constipation with stimulant laxatives may relieve straining, and thereby provide some symptomatic relief.

  We found no good evidence assessing the effects of sitz baths, topical anaesthetics, topical corticosteroids, or compound topical corticosteroids plus anaesthetics to treat symptomatic haemorrhoids in pregnancy. However, despite this, women who have painful complicated haemorrhoids may be offered topical anaesthetic agents unless contraindicated.

- The incidence of heartburn in pregnancy is reported to be between 17% and 45%.

  Antacids may provide effective heartburn relief in pregnancy.

  We don't know whether acid-suppressing drugs, such as ranitidine, are beneficial in treating heartburn in pregnancy.

  We don't know whether dietary and lifestyle modifications are beneficial in preventing or treating heartburn in pregnancy. However, recommendations have been made that lifestyle and dietary modifications, including avoiding fatty foods and reducing the size and frequency of meals, should remain first-line treatment for heartburn in pregnant women. Other lifestyle modifications that could be considered are reducing caffeine intake and raising the head of the bed.

(i) **Please visit http://clinicalevidence.bmj.com for full text and references**

## What are the effects of interventions to prevent or treat constipation in pregnancy?

| Unknown Effectiveness | • Bulk-forming laxatives for constipation in pregnant women |
| --- | --- |

- Increased fibre intake for constipation in pregnant women

- Increased fluid intake for constipation in pregnant women

- Osmotic laxatives for constipation in pregnant women

- Stimulant laxatives for constipation in pregnant women

## What are the effects of interventions to prevent or treat haemorrhoids in pregnancy?

| | |
|---|---|
| Likely To Be Beneficial | • Rutosides (improve symptoms of haemorrhoids but insufficient evidence about adverse effects) |
| Unknown Effectiveness | • Anaesthetics (topical) for haemorrhoids in pregnant women<br><br>• Bulk-forming laxatives for haemorrhoids in pregnant women<br><br>• Compound corticosteroids plus anaesthetics (topical) for haemorrhoids in pregnant women<br><br>• Corticosteroids (topical) for haemorrhoids in pregnant women<br><br>• Increased fibre intake for haemorrhoids in pregnant women<br><br>• Increased fluid intake for haemorrhoids in pregnant women<br><br>• Osmotic laxatives for haemorrhoids in pregnant women<br><br>• Sitz baths for haemorrhoids in pregnant women<br><br>• Stimulant laxatives for haemorrhoids in pregnant women |

## What are the effects of interventions to prevent or treat heartburn in pregnancy?

| | |
|---|---|
| Likely To Be Beneficial | • Antacids with or without alginates for heartburn in pregnant women |
| Unknown Effectiveness | • Acid-suppressing drugs for heartburn in pregnant women<br><br>• Raising the head of the bed for heartburn in pregnant women<br><br>• Reducing caffeine intake for heartburn in pregnant women<br><br>• Reducing the intake of fatty foods for heartburn in pregnant women |

- Reducing the size and frequency of meals for heartburn in pregnant women

**Search date February 2010**

**DEFINITION Constipation:** Some women will have experienced chronic constipation prior to becoming pregnant, and in others constipation develops for the first time during pregnancy. For a full definition of constipation, see review on constipation in adults, p 157. The diagnosis of constipation is mainly clinical, based on a history of decreased frequency of defecation, as well as on the characteristics of the faeces. An extensive evaluation is usually unnecessary for women who present with chronic constipation, or if constipation develops for the first time during pregnancy. **Haemorrhoids:** Haemorrhoids (piles) are swollen veins at or near the anus, which are usually asymptomatic. Haemorrhoids can become symptomatic if they prolapse (the forward or downward displacement of a part of the rectal mucosae through the anus) or because of other complications such as thrombosis. Associated anal fissures (a break or slit in the anal mucosa) can also lead to symptoms. Haemorrhoids can be classified by severity: first-degree haemorrhoids bleed but do not prolapse; second-degree haemorrhoids prolapse on straining and reduce spontaneously; third-degree haemorrhoids prolapse on straining and require manual reduction; and fourth-degree haemorrhoids are prolapsed and incarcerated. Diagnosis of haemorrhoids is based on history and examination. Symptoms include bleeding, mucosal or faecal soiling, itching, and occasionally pain. Fourth-degree haemorrhoids may become 'strangulated' and present with acute severe pain. Progressive venous engorgement and incarceration of the acutely inflamed haemorrhoid leads to thrombosis and infarction. The diagnosis of haemorrhoids is confirmed by rectal examination, and by inspection of the perianal area for skin tags, fissures, fistulae, polyps, or tumours. Prolapsing haemorrhoids may appear at the anal verge on straining. It is important to exclude more serious causes of rectal bleeding. Assessment should include anoscopy to view the haemorrhoidal cushions. Haemorrhoidal size, and severity of inflammation and bleeding should be assessed. **Heartburn:** Heartburn is defined as a sensation of 'burning' in the upper part of the digestive tract, including the throat. It can be associated with oesophagitis. One study reported the results of endoscopy on 73 pregnant women with heartburn, and found endoscopic and histological evidence of oesophagitis in most women. As complications associated with heartburn during pregnancy are rare (e.g., erosive oesophagitis), upper endoscopy and other diagnostic tests are infrequently needed. Therefore, the diagnosis of heartburn is mainly clinical, based on the history.

**INCIDENCE/PREVALENCE Constipation:** Constipation is common in pregnant women, and can develop or increase in severity during pregnancy. The prevalence of constipation in pregnancy is reported to be between 11% and 38%. Parity or previous caesarean section have been associated with constipation. **Haemorrhoids:** Although the exact prevalence of haemorrhoids during pregnancy is unknown, the condition is common in pregnancy, and the prevalence of symptomatic haemorrhoids is higher in pregnant than in non-pregnant women. In a population of pregnant women in Serbia and Montenegro, haemorrhoids were present in 85% of women during the second and third pregnancy. Haemorrhoids are also a frequent complaint among women who have recently given birth, and they become more common with increased age and parity. **Heartburn:** Heartburn is one of the most common gastrointestinal symptoms in pregnant women, with an incidence in pregnancy of 17% to 45%. In some studies, the prevalence of heartburn has been found to increase from 22% in the first trimester to 39% in the second trimester to between 60% and 72% in the third trimester. However, one prospective cohort study found that, in most pregnant women, heartburn, acid regurgitation, or both began in the first trimester and disappeared during the second trimester; and another cohort study also found that gastrointestinal symptoms, such as heartburn and nausea, were more common in the first trimester. The study also found that primigravidae reported more gastrointestinal symptoms than multiparae.

**AETIOLOGY/RISK FACTORS Constipation:** Constipation in pregnancy is probably caused by rising progesterone levels. Low fluid and fibre intake may also be contributing factors. There is some evidence that pregnant women consume less fibre than is currently recommended for the non-pregnant population. Low fluid intake has been linked to constipation in pregnancy, particularly in the third trimester. Some medications taken during pregnancy,

*(continued over)*

*(from previous page)*

such as iron salts and magnesium sulphate, have been also been linked to constipation. Hypothyroidism may also be a rare cause of constipation during pregnancy. **Haemorrhoids:** Haemorrhoids result from impaired venous return in prolapsed anal cushions, with dilation of the venous plexus and venous stasis. Inflammation occurs with erosion of the anal cushion's epithelium, resulting in bleeding. Constipation with prolonged straining at stool, or raised intra-abdominal pressure as occurs in pregnancy, may result in symptomatic haemorrhoids. During pregnancy, delivery, and the puerperium, sphincteral muscles and pelvic floor structures could be modified in tone and position, leading to an alteration of the normal functioning of the haemorrhoidal cushion, which may predispose to symptoms. **Heartburn:** The cause of heartburn during pregnancy is multifactorial. Increased amounts of progesterone or its metabolites cause relaxation of smooth muscle, which results in a reduction in gastric tone and motility, and a decrease in lower oesophageal sphincter pressure. It has also been found that, during pregnancy, the lower oesophageal sphincter is displaced into the thoracic cavity (an area of negative pressure), which allows food and gastric acid to pass from the stomach into the oesophagus, leading to oesophageal inflammation and a sensation of 'burning'. Pressure of the growing uterus on gastric contents as the pregnancy progresses may worsen heartburn, although some authors believe that mechanical factors have a smaller role. Heartburn may also be caused by medications taken during pregnancy, such as antiemetics.

**PROGNOSIS Constipation:** Constipation, if mild, is often self-treated with home remedies or non-prescription preparations. Primary-care providers are usually confident managing constipation in pregnancy, unless it is severe, refractory to conventional management, or necessitates additional diagnostic studies. Referral to a gastroenterologist is therefore seldom necessary. **Haemorrhoids:** In women with haemorrhoids, symptoms are usually mild and transient and include pain and intermittent bleeding from the anus. Depending on the degree of pain, quality of life can be affected, varying from mild discomfort to difficulty in dealing with the activities of everyday life. Treatment during pregnancy is mainly directed to the relief of symptoms, especially pain control. For many women, symptoms will resolve spontaneously soon after birth. **Heartburn:** Most cases of heartburn improve with lifestyle modifications and dietary changes, but in some cases severity may increase throughout the course of pregnancy.

Mario Festin

## KEY POINTS

- More than half of pregnant women suffer from nausea and vomiting, which typically begins by the fourth week and disappears by the 16th week of pregnancy.

    The cause of nausea and vomiting in pregnancy is unknown, but may be due to the rise in human chorionic gonadotrophin concentration.

    In 1 in 200 women, the condition progresses to hyperemesis gravidarum, which is characterised by prolonged and severe nausea and vomiting, dehydration, and weight loss.

- In general, the trials we found were small and of limited quality. There is a need for other large high-quality trials in this condition with consistent outcomes.

- For nausea and vomiting in early pregnancy:

    Ginger may reduce nausea and vomiting in pregnancy compared with placebo, although studies used different preparations of ginger and reported varying outcome measures.

    Pyridoxine may be more effective than placebo at reducing nausea but we don't know about vomiting, and evidence was weak.

    Pyridoxine may be as effective as ginger in reducing nausea and vomiting, although evidence was limited.

    Acupressure may be more effective than sham acupressure at reducing nausea and vomiting. However, evidence was weak, and interventions and outcomes varied between trials.

    We don't know whether acupressure is more effective than pyridoxine at reducing nausea or vomiting as we found insufficient evidence.

    We don't know whether acupuncture is more effective than sham acupuncture at reducing nausea and vomiting.

    We don't know whether prochlorperazine, promethazine, or metoclopramide reduce nausea or vomiting compared with placebo.

- In hyperemesis gravidarum:

    We don't know whether acupressure, acupuncture, corticosteroids, ginger, metoclopramide, or ondansetron are effective in treating hyperemesis gravidarum.

    Hydrocortisone may be more effective than metoclopramide at reducing vomiting episodes and reducing readmission to the intensive care unit in women with hyperemesis gravidarum.

(i) **Please visit http://clinicalevidence.bmj.com for full text and references**

| What are the effects of treatment for nausea and vomiting in early pregnancy? | |
|---|---|
| Likely To Be Beneficial | • Acupressure for treating nausea and vomiting in early pregnancy |
| | • Ginger for treating nausea and vomiting in early pregnancy |
| | • Pyridoxine (vitamin B$_6$) for treating nausea and vomiting in early pregnancy |
| Unknown Effectiveness | • Acupuncture for treating nausea and vomiting in early pregnancy |
| | • Metoclopramide for treating nausea and vomiting in early pregnancy |

| | • Prochlorperazine for treating nausea and vomiting in early pregnancy |
| | • Promethazine for treating nausea and vomiting in early pregnancy |

## What are the effects of treatments for hyperemesis gravidarum?

| Unknown Effectiveness | • Acupressure for treating hyperemesis gravidarum |
| | • Acupuncture for treating hyperemesis gravidarum |
| | • Corticosteroids for treating hyperemesis gravidarum |
| | • Ginger for treating hyperemesis gravidarum |
| | • Ondansetron for treating hyperemesis gravidarum |
| Unlikely To Be Beneficial | • Metoclopramide for treating hyperemesis gravidarum (less effective than corticosteroids) |

**Search date September 2013**

**DEFINITION** Nausea and vomiting are common problems in early pregnancy. Although often called 'morning sickness', nausea and vomiting can occur at any time of day and may persist throughout the day. Symptoms usually begin between four weeks' and seven weeks' gestation (one study found this to be the case in 70% of affected women) and disappear by 16 weeks' gestation in about 90% of women. One study found that less than 10% of affected women suffer nausea, vomiting, or both before the first missed period. Most women do not require treatment, and complete the pregnancy without any special intervention. However, if nausea and vomiting are severe and persistent, the condition can progress to hyperemesis, especially if the woman is unable to maintain adequate hydration, fluid and electrolyte balance, and nutrition. **Hyperemesis gravidarum** is a diagnosis of exclusion, characterised by prolonged and severe nausea and vomiting, dehydration, and weight loss. Laboratory investigation may show ketosis, hyponatraemia, hypokalaemia, hypouricaemia, metabolic hypochloraemic alkalosis, and ketonuria.

**INCIDENCE/PREVALENCE** Nausea affects about 70% and vomiting about 60% of pregnant women. The true incidence of hyperemesis gravidarum is not known. It has been documented to range from 3 in 1000 to 20 in 1000 pregnancies. However, most authors report an incidence of 1 in 200.

**AETIOLOGY/RISK FACTORS** The causes of nausea and vomiting in pregnancy are unknown. One theory, that they are caused by the rise in human chorionic gonadotrophin concentration, is compatible with the natural history of the condition, its severity in pregnancies affected by hydatidiform mole, and its good prognosis (see Prognosis). The cause of hyperemesis gravidarum is also uncertain. Again, endocrine and psychological factors are suspected, but evidence is inconclusive. Female fetal sex has been found to be a clinical indicator of hyperemesis. One prospective study found that *Helicobacter pylori* infection was more common in pregnant women with hyperemesis gravidarum than in pregnant women without hyperemesis gravidarum (number of women with positive serum *Helicobacter pylori* immunoglobulin G concentrations: 95/105 [91%] with hyperemesis gravidarum v 60/129 [47%] without hyperemesis gravidarum). However, it was not clear whether this link was causal.

**PROGNOSIS** One systematic review (search date 1988) found that nausea and vomiting were associated with a reduced risk of miscarriage (six studies, 14,564 women; OR 0.36, 95% CI 0.32 to 0.42) but found no association with perinatal mortality. Hyperemesis gravidarum is thought by some to induce nutrient partitioning in favour of the fetus, which could explain the association with improved outcome in the fetus. Nausea and vomiting and hyperemesis usually improve over the course of pregnancy, but in one cross-sectional observational study 13% of women reported that nausea and vomiting persisted beyond 20 weeks' gestation. Although death from nausea and vomiting during pregnancy is rare, morbidities, including Wernicke's encephalopathy, splenic avulsion, oesophageal rupture, pneumothorax, and acute tubular necrosis, have been reported.

Julie Frolich and Chris Kettle

## KEY POINTS

- More than 85% of women having a vaginal birth suffer some perineal trauma.

  Spontaneous tears requiring suturing are estimated to occur in at least one third of women in the UK and US.

  Risk factors for severe perineal trauma include first vaginal delivery, large or malpositioned baby, older mother, abnormal collagen synthesis, and forceps delivery.

- Perineal trauma can lead to long-term physical and psychological problems such as long-term perineal pain, dyspareunia or urinary problems, and faecal incontinence.

- Non-suturing of all layers in first- and second-degree tears (perineal skin and muscles) may be associated with reduced wound healing at 6 weeks after birth. However, leaving the perineal skin alone unsutured (vagina and perineal muscles sutured) reduces dyspareunia and may reduce perineal pain at 14 days to 6 weeks after delivery.

- Perineal gaping may be more likely for up to 3 months after delivery, when the skin is left unsutured; although, further studies are required. There is no evidence about longer-term outcomes when the skin is left unsutured.

- Absorbable synthetic sutures for repair of first- and second-degree tears and episiotomies may be less likely to result in perineal pain and dyspareunia than catgut sutures. Rapidly absorbed synthetic sutures reduce the need for suture removal. Continuous sutures reduce short-term pain and analgesic use.

- We don't know how primary overlap repair for third- and fourth-degree anal sphincter tears and end-to-end approximation compare with each other at reducing perineal pain or faecal urgency or incontinence.

(i) **Please visit http://clinicalevidence.bmj.com for full text and references**

| What are the effects of different methods and materials for primary repair of first- and second-degree tears and episiotomies? | |
|---|---|
| Beneficial | • Absorbable synthetic sutures for perineal repair of first- and second-degree tears and episiotomies (reduced short-term analgesic use and pain compared with catgut sutures)<br><br>• Continuous sutures for second-degree tears and episiotomies (reduced short-term pain compared with interrupted sutures) |
| Likely To Be Beneficial | • Vagina and perineal muscle sutured but perineal skin left unsutured in first- and second-degree tears and episiotomies (reduced dyspareunia at 3 months compared with conventional suturing) |
| Likely To Be Ineffective Or Harmful | • Non-suturing of all layers in first- and second-degree perineal tears (poorer wound healing than with suturing) |

## What are the effects of different methods and materials for primary repair of obstetric anal sphincter injuries (third- and fourth-degree tears)?

| Unknown Effectiveness | • Different methods and materials for primary repair of obstetric anal sphincter injuries (third- and fourth-degree tears) |
|---|---|

**Search date November 2013**

**DEFINITION** Perineal trauma is any damage to the genitalia during childbirth that occurs spontaneously or intentionally by surgical incision (episiotomy). Anterior perineal trauma is injury to the labia, anterior vagina, urethra, or clitoris, and is usually associated with little morbidity. Posterior perineal trauma is any injury to the posterior vaginal wall, perineal muscles, or anal sphincter. Spontaneous tears are defined as **first degree** when they involve the perineal skin only; **second-degree** tears involve the perineal muscles and skin; **third-degree** tears involve the anal sphincter complex (classified as 3a where <50% of the external anal sphincter is torn; 3b where >50% of the external anal sphincter is torn; 3c where the internal and external anal sphincter is torn); **fourth-degree** tears involve the anal sphincter complex and anal epithelium.

**INCIDENCE/PREVALENCE** More than 85% of women having a vaginal birth sustain some form of perineal trauma, and 60% to 70% receive stitches. In England from 2012 to 2013, perineal tears during delivery were reported in 42% of deliveries for women aged 15 to 24 years, and 31% of deliveries for women aged 40 to 49 years. There are wide variations in rates of episiotomy: 8% in the Netherlands, 14% in England, and 50% in the US. Sutured spontaneous tears are reported in about one third of women in the US and the UK, but this is probably an underestimate because of inconsistencies in both reporting and classification of perineal trauma. The incidence of anal sphincter tears varies between 1% in Finland, 2% in the UK, and 17% in the US. The incidence of obstetric anal sphincter injuries in primiparous women in the UK is reported to have risen to 6% over the past decade.

**AETIOLOGY/RISK FACTORS** Perineal trauma occurs during spontaneous or assisted vaginal delivery, and is usually more extensive with the first vaginal delivery. Associated risk factors also include bigger baby, mode of delivery (especially forceps), and malpresentation and malposition of the fetus, position of the mother during birth (especially birthing stools), and prolonged pushing. Other maternal factors that may increase the extent and degree of trauma are ethnicity (Asian women in the UK have been shown to be at greater risk of obstetric anal sphincter injury), age older than 25 years, abnormal collagen synthesis, poor nutritional state, and higher socio-economic status. Clinicians' practices or preferences in terms of intrapartum interventions may influence the severity and rate of perineal trauma (e.g., use of ventouse *v* forceps or 'hands-on' *v* 'hands-off').

**PROGNOSIS** Perineal trauma affects women's physical, psychological, and social wellbeing in the immediate postnatal period as well as in the long term. It can also disrupt breastfeeding, family life, and sexual relations. In the UK, about 23% to 42% of women continue to have pain and discomfort for 10 to 12 days postpartum, and 7% to 10% of women continue to have long-term pain (3–18 months after delivery); 23% of women experience superficial dyspareunia at 3 months; 3% to 10% report faecal incontinence; and up to 24% have urinary problems. Complications depend on the severity of perineal trauma, and on the effectiveness of treatment.

**Postnatal depression**

Michael Craig, Louise Howard

**KEY POINTS**

- The differentiation between postnatal depression and other types of depression is often unclear, but there are treatment issues in nursing mothers that do not apply in other situations.

  Overall, the prevalence of depression in postpartum women is the same as the prevalence in women generally, at about 12–13%.

  Suicide is a major cause of maternal mortality in resource-rich countries, but rates are lower in women postpartum than in women who have not had a baby.

  Most episodes resolve spontaneously within 3–6 months, but a quarter of depressed mothers still have symptoms at 1 year. Depression can interfere with the mother–infant relationship.

- SSRIs may improve symptoms of postnatal depression, but we found few studies evaluating their effect specifically in postpartum women.

  We don't know whether other types of antidepressant are effective compared with placebo or psychological treatments.

  We don't know whether oestrogen treatment or St John's Wort improve symptoms compared with placebo.

- Psychological treatments such as individual CBT, non-directive counselling, interpersonal psychotherapy, and psychodynamic therapy are likely to improve symptoms compared with routine care, but long-term benefits are unclear.

  We don't know whether light therapy, group CBT, psychoeducation with the partner, mother–infant interaction coaching, telephone-based peer support, infant massage, or physical exercise improve symptoms of postnatal depression, as we found few studies.

(i) **Please visit http://clinicalevidence.bmj.com for full text and references**

| What are the effects of drug treatments for postnatal depression? | |
|---|---|
| Likely To Be Beneficial | • Antidepressants other than SSRIs* <br><br> • SSRI antidepressants (fluoxetine, paroxetine, and sertraline)* |
| Unknown Effectiveness | • Hormones <br><br> • St John's Wort (*Hypericum perforatum*) |

| What are the effects of non-drug treatments for postnatal depression? | |
|---|---|
| Likely To Be Beneficial | • CBT (individual) <br><br> • Interpersonal psychotherapy <br><br> • Non-directive counselling (effective in the short term, although may not have long-term beneficial effects) |
| Unknown Effectiveness | • CBT (group) <br><br> • Infant massage by mother <br><br> • Light therapy |

|  | • Physical exercise |
|  | • Psychodynamic therapy |
|  | • Psychoeducation with partner |
|  | • Telephone-based peer support (mother to mother) |
| **Unlikely To Be Beneficial** | • Mother–infant interaction coaching (improved maternal responsiveness but no significant difference in depression scores) |

**Search date May 2008**

*Antidepressants are categorised on the evidence of their effectiveness in the treatment of depression in general.

**DEFINITION** Postnatal depression (PND) has been variously defined as non-psychotic depression occurring during the first 6 months, the first 4 weeks, and the first 3 months postpartum; but recently 3 months postpartum was suggested in the UK as a useful clinical definition. Puerperal mental disorders have only recently been categorised separately in psychiatric classifications, but both the ICD-10 and the DSM-IV require certain qualifications to be met that limit their use: ICD-10 categorises mental disorders that occur postpartum as puerperal, but only if they cannot otherwise be classified, and DSM-IV allows "postpartum onset" to be specified for mood disorders starting within 4 weeks postpartum. In clinical practice and research, the broader definition above is often used, because whether or not PND is truly distinct from depression in general, depression in the postpartum period raises treatment issues for the nursing mother and has implications for the developing infant (see prognosis below). However, there is increased recognition that the depression often starts during pregnancy. The symptoms are similar to symptoms of depression at other times of life, but in addition to low mood, sleep disturbance, change in appetite, diurnal variation in mood, poor concentration, and irritability, women with PND also experience guilt about their inability to look after their new baby. In many countries, health visitors screen for PND using the Edinburgh Postnatal Depression Scale, which identifies depressive symptoms, but does not include somatic symptoms such as appetite changes, which can be difficult to assess in most women in the postnatal period.

**INCIDENCE/PREVALENCE** The prevalence of depression in women postpartum is similar to that found in women generally. However, the incidence of depression in the first month after childbirth is three times the average monthly incidence in non-childbearing women. A meta-analysis of studies mainly based in resource-rich countries found the incidence of PND to be 12–13%, with higher incidence in resource-poor countries.

**AETIOLOGY/RISK FACTORS** Four systematic reviews have identified the following risk factors for PND: history of any psychopathology (including history of previous PND), low social support, poor marital relationship, and recent life events. There is also an increased risk of PND amongst immigrant populations. Recent studies from India also suggest that spousal disappointment with the sex of the newborn child, particularly if the child is a girl, is associated with the development of PND.

**PROGNOSIS** Most episodes of PND resolve spontaneously within 3–6 months, but about one in four affected mothers are still depressed at the child's first birthday. In resource-rich countries, suicide remains a leading cause of maternal deaths in the first year postpartum, although the postpartum suicide rate is lower than the rate in age-matched, non-postpartum women. PND is also associated with negative effects in the infant, including reduced likelihood of secure attachment, deficits in maternal–infant interactions, and impaired cognitive and emotional development of the child, particularly in boys living in areas of socioeconomic deprivation. These associations remain significant even after controlling for subsequent episodes of depression in the mother. However, there is also evidence to suggest that later effects on the child are related to chronic or recurrent maternal depression, rather than postpartum depression *per se*. Women whose depression persists beyond 6 months postpartum have been found to have fewer positive interactions with their

*(continued over)*

*(from previous page)*

infants than women who were depressed but whose depressive symptoms ended before 6 months, suggesting that the timing of depression is an important factor in determining its effect on the mother–infant relationship.

David Chelmow

## KEY POINTS

- Loss of more than 500 mL of blood is usually caused by failure of the uterus to contract fully after delivery of the placenta, and occurs in over 10% of deliveries, with a 1% mortality worldwide.

  Other causes of postpartum haemorrhage include retained placental tissue, lacerations to the genital tract, and coagulation disorders.

  Uterine atony is more likely in women who have had a general anaesthetic or oxytocin, an over-distended uterus, a prolonged or precipitous labour, or who are of high parity.

- Active management of the third stage of labour, with controlled cord traction, early cord clamping plus drainage, and prophylactic oxytocic agents, reduces the risk of postpartum haemorrhage and its complications.

  Active management increases nausea, vomiting, and headache, but generally improves maternal satisfaction.

  Controlled cord traction may reduce the risk of retained placenta and need for medical treatment, and can be used in any resource setting.

  Uterine massage is often used to prevent postpartum haemorrhage, and is supported by a single RCT. It can be used in any resource setting.

- Oxytocin has been shown to effectively reduce the risk of postpartum haemorrhage compared with placebo.

  A combination of oxytocin plus ergometrine may be slightly more effective than oxytocin alone, although there are more adverse effects.

- Ergot alkaloids seem as effective as oxytocin, but are also associated with adverse effects including nausea, placenta retention, and hypertension.

- Prostaglandin treatments vary in their efficacy, but are all associated with adverse effects.

  Carboprost and prostaglandin E2 compounds may be as effective as oxytocin and ergot compounds, but have gastrointestinal adverse effects, such as diarrhoea.

  Misoprostol seems ineffective compared with placebo when administered orally, rectally, or vaginally, and is associated with adverse effects including shivering and fever. However, rectal misoprostol may be as effective as oxytocin.

  Sublingually administered misoprostol may be more effective than placebo in preventing postpartum haemorrhage (evidenced by a single RCT). Sublingual misoprostol has similar effects to injected agents, but is associated with more adverse effects.

  When available, oxytocin, ergometrine, or combinations are preferred to misoprostol, as misoprostol seems less effective and is associated with more adverse effects. Sublingual administration is the preferred route for misoprostol.

(i) **Please visit http://clinicalevidence.bmj.com for full text and references**

## What are the effects of non-drug interventions to prevent primary postpartum haemorrhage?

| | |
|---|---|
| Beneficial | • Active management of the third stage of labour |
| Likely To Be Beneficial | • Controlled cord traction<br>• Uterine massage |
| Unknown Effectiveness | • Immediate breastfeeding |

## What are the effects of drug interventions to prevent primary postpartum haemorrhage?

| Beneficial | • Oxytocin |
|---|---|
| **Trade-off Between Benefits And Harms** | • Carboprost injection<br>• Ergot compounds (ergometrine/methylergotamine)<br>• Misoprostol (sublingual)<br>• Oxytocin plus ergometrine combinations |
| **Unknown Effectiveness** | • Misoprostol (rectal)<br>• Prostaglandin E2 compounds |
| **Unlikely To Be Beneficial** | • Misoprostol (oral)<br>• Misoprostol (vaginal) |

**Search date March 2010**

**DEFINITION** Postpartum haemorrhage is characterised by an estimated blood loss greater than 500 mL. The leading cause of postpartum haemorrhage is uterine atony — the failure of the uterus to contract fully after delivery of the placenta. Postpartum haemorrhage is divided into immediate (primary) and delayed (secondary). Primary postpartum haemorrhage occurs within the first 24 hours after delivery, whereas secondary postpartum haemorrhage occurs between 24 hours and 6 weeks after delivery. This review addresses the effects of strategies for prevention of postpartum haemorrhage after vaginal delivery in low- and high-risk women, specifically looking at strategies to prevent uterine atony. Future updates will examine strategies to prevent postpartum haemorrhage due to other causes, as well as treatment strategies.

**INCIDENCE/PREVALENCE** The WHO reports that obstetric haemorrhage causes 127,000 deaths annually worldwide and is the world's leading cause of maternal mortality. Nearly all of these deaths are due to postpartum haemorrhages, which occur nearly 14 million times each year. In Africa, haemorrhage is estimated to be responsible for 30% of all maternal deaths. The imbalance between resource-rich and resource-poor areas probably stems from a combination of: increased prevalence of risk factors such as grand multiparity, lack of safe blood banking, no routine use of prophylaxis against haemorrhage, and lack of measures for drug and surgical management of atony.

**AETIOLOGY/RISK FACTORS** In addition to uterine atony, immediate postpartum haemorrhage is frequently caused by: retained placental tissue; trauma such as laceration of the perineum, vagina, or cervix; rupture of the uterus; or coagulopathy. Risk factors for uterine atony include: use of general anaesthetics; an over-distended uterus, particularly from multiple gestations, a large fetus, or polyhydramnios; prolonged labour; precipitous labour; use of oxytocin for labour induction or augmentation; high parity; chorioamnionitis; or history of atony in a previous pregnancy.

**PROGNOSIS** Most postpartum haemorrhage, particularly in Europe and the US, is well tolerated by women. However, in low-resource settings, where women may already be significantly anaemic during pregnancy, blood loss of 500 mL is significant. Although pregnancy-related death is rare in the US, postpartum haemorrhage accounts for 17% of deaths. Maternal death is 50 to 100 times more frequent in resource-poor countries, and postpartum haemorrhage is responsible for a similar proportion of deaths as in the US. Other significant morbidities associated with postpartum haemorrhage include renal failure, respiratory failure, multiple organ failure, need for transfusion, need for surgery including dilatation and curettage, and, rarely, hysterectomy. Some women with large blood loss will later develop Sheehan's syndrome.

# Pre-eclampsia, eclampsia, and hypertension | 491

Lelia Duley

## KEY POINTS

- Pre-eclampsia (raised blood pressure and proteinuria) complicates 2% to 8% of pregnancies, and increases morbidity and mortality in the mother and child.

  Pre-eclampsia is more common in women with multiple pregnancy and in people with conditions associated with microvascular disease.

- Antiplatelet drugs (primarily low-dose aspirin) reduce the risk of pre-eclampsia, death of the baby, and premature birth without increasing the risks of bleeding, in women at high risk of pre-eclampsia.

  Calcium supplementation reduces the risk of pre-eclampsia compared with placebo.

  We don't know whether fish oil, evening primrose oil, salt restriction, magnesium supplementation, or glyceryl trinitrate are beneficial in high-risk women because there are insufficient data to draw reliable conclusions. We don't know whether antioxidants reduce rates of pre-eclampsia as the data are inconsistent, although they are unlikely to reduce mortality.

- We don't know whether atenolol reduces the risk of pre-eclampsia, but it may worsen outcomes for babies.

- For women with mild to moderate hypertension during pregnancy, antihypertensive drugs reduce the risk of progression to severe hypertension, but may not improve other clinical outcomes.

  ACE inhibitors have been associated with fetal renal failure, and beta-blockers are associated with the baby being born small for its gestational age.

  We don't know whether bed rest or hospital admission are also beneficial.

- There is consensus that women who develop severe hypertension in pregnancy should receive antihypertensive treatment, but we don't know which antihypertensive agent is most effective.

  We don't know whether plasma volume expansion, antioxidants, epidural analgesia, or early delivery improve outcomes for women with severe pre-eclampsia.

- Magnesium sulphate reduces the risk of first or subsequent seizures in women with severe pre-eclampsia compared with placebo.

- Magnesium sulphate reduces the risk of subsequent seizures in women with eclampsia compared with either phenytoin or diazepam, with fewer adverse effects for the mother or baby.

(i) **Please visit http://clinicalevidence.bmj.com for full text and references**

## What are the effects of preventive interventions in women at risk of pre-eclampsia?

| Beneficial | • Antiplatelet drugs |
| --- | --- |
| | • Calcium supplementation |
| Unknown Effectiveness | • Antioxidants |
| | • Glyceryl trinitrate |
| | • Magnesium supplementation |
| | • Marine oil (fish oil) and other prostaglandin precursors (evening primrose oil) |

| | • Salt restriction |
|---|---|
| **Unlikely To Be Beneficial** | • Atenolol |

## What are the effects of interventions in women who develop mild to moderate hypertension during pregnancy?

| **Unknown Effectiveness** | • Antihypertensive drugs for mild to moderate hypertension<br>• Bed rest/admission |
|---|---|

## What are the effects of interventions in women who develop severe pre-eclampsia or very high blood pressure during pregnancy?

| **Beneficial** | • Prophylactic magnesium sulphate in severe pre-eclampsia |
|---|---|
| **Likely To Be Beneficial** | • Antihypertensive drugs for very high blood pressure* |
| **Unknown Effectiveness** | • Antioxidants in severe pre-eclampsia<br>• Choice of analgesia during labour with severe pre-eclampsia<br>• Early delivery for severe early-onset pre-eclampsia<br>• Plasma volume expansion in severe pre-eclampsia |

## What is the best choice of anticonvulsant for women with eclampsia?

| **Beneficial** | • Magnesium sulphate for eclampsia (better and safer than other anticonvulsants) |
|---|---|

**Search date February 2010**

*There is consensus that women with severe hypertension during pregnancy should have antihypertensive treatment and that women with eclampsia should have an anticonvulsant. Placebo-controlled trials would, therefore, be unethical.

**DEFINITION** Hypertension during pregnancy may be associated with one of several conditions: **Pregnancy-induced hypertension** or **gestational hypertension** is a rise in blood pressure, without proteinuria, during the second-half of pregnancy. **Pre-eclampsia** is a multisystem disorder, unique to pregnancy, that is usually associated with raised blood pressure and proteinuria. It rarely presents before 20 weeks' gestation. **Eclampsia** is one or more convulsions in association with the syndrome of pre-eclampsia. **Pre-existing hypertension** (not covered in this review) is known hypertension before pregnancy, or raised blood pressure before 20 weeks' gestation. It may be essential hypertension or, less commonly, secondary to an underlying disease.

**INCIDENCE/PREVALENCE** Pregnancy-induced hypertension affects 10% of pregnancies, and pre-eclampsia complicates 2% to 8% of pregnancies. Eclampsia occurs in about 1/2000 deliveries in resource-rich countries. In resource-poor countries, estimates of the incidence of eclampsia vary from 1/100 to 1/1700.

**AETIOLOGY/RISK FACTORS** The cause of pre-eclampsia is unknown. It is likely to be multifactorial, and may result from deficient placental implantation during the first-half of pregnancy. Pre-eclampsia is more common among women likely to have a large placenta (such as those with multiple pregnancy) and among women with medical conditions associated with microvascular disease (such as diabetes, hypertension, and collagen vascular disease). One systematic review found that the risk of pre-eclampsia is increased in women with a previous history of pre-eclampsia (RR 7.19, 95% CI 5.85 to 8.83) and in those with antiphospholipid antibodies (RR 9.72, 95% CI 4.34 to 21.75), pre-existing diabetes (RR 3.56, 95% CI 2.54 to 4.99), multiple (twin) pregnancy (RR 2.93, 95% CI 2.04 to 4.21), nulliparity (RR 2.91, 95% CI 1.28 to 6.61), family history (RR 2.90, 95% CI 1.70 to 4.93), raised blood pressure (diastolic 80 mm Hg or greater) at booking (RR 1.38, 95 % CI 1.01 to 1.87), raised body mass index before pregnancy (RR 2.47, 95% CI 1.66 to 3.67) or at booking (RR 1.55, 95% CI 1.28 to 1.88), or maternal age 40 years or older (RR 1.96, 95% CI 1.34 to 2.87, for multiparous women). The review reported that other factors which increase the risk are: an interval of 10 years or more since a previous pregnancy, autoimmune disease, renal disease, and chronic hypertension. A second systematic review of the accuracy of 27 predictive tests for pre-eclampsia found some appeared to have high specificity, but at the expense of compromised sensitivity. The review reported that tests with specificity above 90% were: body mass index >34, alpha-fetoprotein, and uterine artery Doppler (bilateral notching). The review found the only Doppler test with a sensitivity of over 60% was resistance index and combinations of indices. It also found that a few tests not commonly seen in routine practice (kallikreinuria and SDS-PAGE proteinuria) potentially have both high sensitivity and specificity, but these require further investigation. Cigarette smoking seems to be associated with a lower risk of pre-eclampsia, but this potential benefit is outweighed by an increase in adverse outcomes such as low birth weight, placental abruption, and perinatal death.

**PROGNOSIS** The outcome of pregnancy in women with pregnancy-induced hypertension alone is at least as good as that for normotensive pregnancies. However, once pre-eclampsia develops, morbidity and mortality rise for both mother and child. For example, perinatal mortality for women with severe pre-eclampsia is double that for normotensive women. Perinatal outcome is worse with early gestational hypertension. Perinatal mortality also increases in women with severe essential hypertension.

David M Haas

## KEY POINTS

- Around 5% to 10% of all births in resource-rich countries occur before 37 weeks' gestation, leading to increased risks of neonatal and infant death, and of neurological disability in surviving infants.

- Progesterone may reduce preterm birth in women with prior preterm birth and a short cervix, but are unlikely to be beneficial and may even be harmful in women with multiple gestations.

- Enhanced antenatal care programmes and bed rest have repeatedly been shown to be ineffective or harmful.

  Prophylactic cervical cerclage may reduce preterm births in women with cervical changes but is unlikely to be effective — and may increase infection — in women with no cervical changes or with twin pregnancies. We don't know how effective it is in women with protruding membranes.

- A single course of antenatal corticosteroids reduces respiratory distress syndrome, intraventricular haemorrhage, and neonatal mortality compared with placebo in babies born before 37 weeks' gestation.

  Adding TRH to corticosteroids has not been shown to improve outcomes compared with corticosteroids alone, and increases the risk of adverse effects.

- Antibiotics may prolong the pregnancy and reduce infection after premature rupture of the membranes, but are not beneficial when the membranes are intact.

- It is unclear if amnioinfusion for preterm rupture of membranes reduces preterm birth or neonatal mortality, as we found few RCTs.

- Calcium channel blockers may be effective at delaying labour compared with other tocolytics.

  Beta-mimetics and magnesium sulphate do not prevent premature birth, and may increase fetal and maternal adverse effects compared with placebo.

  Oxytocin receptor antagonists (such as atosiban) and prostaglandin inhibitors (such as indometacin) may prevent preterm delivery but we cannot be certain as we found few trials.

  Most tocolytic therapies don't prevent perinatal mortality or morbidity, although trials of these treatments are usually underpowered to detect clinically significant differences in these outcomes.

- Elective caesarean section increases maternal morbidity compared with selective caesarean section, but rates of neonatal morbidity and mortality seem equivalent.

(i) **Please visit http://clinicalevidence.bmj.com for full text and references**

| What are the effects of preventive interventions in women at high risk of preterm delivery? | |
|---|---|
| Likely To Be Beneficial | • Prophylactic cervical cerclage in women at risk of preterm labour with cervical changes |
| Trade-off Between Benefits And Harms | • Progesterone (likely to be beneficial in women with prior preterm birth and short cervix; however, |

| | |
|---|---|
| | unlikely to be beneficial and potentially harmful in women with multiple gestations) |
| **Unknown Effectiveness** | • Prophylactic cervical cerclage in women at risk of preterm labour with protruding membranes |
| **Unlikely To Be Beneficial** | • Enhanced antenatal care programmes for socially deprived population groups/high-risk groups |
| **Likely To Be Ineffective Or Harmful** | • Bed rest<br><br>• Prophylactic cervical cerclage in women at risk of preterm labour with no cervical changes |

## What are the effects of interventions to improve neonatal outcome after preterm rupture of membranes?

| | |
|---|---|
| **Likely To Be Beneficial** | • Antibiotic treatment for premature rupture of membranes (prolongs gestation and may reduce infection, but unknown effect on perinatal mortality; amoxicillin–clavulanic acid [co-amoxiclav] increases necrotising enterocolitis) |
| **Unknown Effectiveness** | • Amnioinfusion for preterm rupture of membranes |

## What are the effects of treatments to stop contractions in preterm labour?

| | |
|---|---|
| **Likely To Be Beneficial** | • Calcium channel blockers<br><br>• Prostaglandin inhibitors (more effective than other tocolytics at reducing the proportion of women delivering before 37 weeks' gestation) |
| **Unknown Effectiveness** | • Oxytocin receptor antagonists (atosiban) |
| **Unlikely To Be Beneficial** | • Beta-mimetics (compared with other tocolytic medications)<br><br>• Magnesium sulphate |

## What are the effects of elective compared with selective caesarean delivery for women in preterm labour?

| | |
|---|---|
| **Unlikely To Be Beneficial** | • Elective rather than selective caesarean delivery in preterm labour |

## What are the effects of interventions to improve neonatal outcome in preterm delivery?

| Beneficial | • Corticosteroids (antenatal) |
|---|---|
| Unlikely To Be Beneficial | • Antibiotic treatment for preterm labour with intact membranes |
| Likely To Be Ineffective Or Harmful | • TRH plus corticosteroids before preterm delivery |

**Search date June 2010**

**DEFINITION** Preterm or premature birth is defined by the WHO as delivery of an infant before 37 completed weeks of gestation. Clinically, deliveries under 34 weeks' gestation may be a more relevant definition. There is no set lower limit to this definition, but 23 to 24 weeks' gestation is widely accepted, which approximates to an average fetal weight of 500 g.

**INCIDENCE/PREVALENCE** Preterm birth occurs in about 5% to 10% of all births in resource-rich countries, but in recent years the incidence seems to have increased in some countries, particularly in the USA, where the rate reached 12.7% in 2005. We found little reliable evidence for incidence (using the definition of premature birth given above) in resource-poor countries. For example, the rate in northwestern Ethiopia has been reported to vary from 11% to 22% depending on the age group of mothers studied, and is highest in teenage mothers.

**AETIOLOGY/RISK FACTORS** About 30% of preterm births are unexplained and spontaneous. Multiple pregnancy accounts for about another 30% of cases. Other known risk factors include genital tract infection, preterm rupture of the membranes, antepartum haemorrhage, cervical incompetence, and congenital uterine abnormalities, which collectively account for about 20% to 25% of cases. The remaining cases (15–20%) are attributed to elective preterm delivery secondary to hypertensive disorders of pregnancy, intrauterine fetal growth restriction, congenital abnormalities, trauma, and medical disorders of pregnancy. About 50% of women receiving placebo therapy do not give birth within 7 days from the start of treatment. This statistic could be interpreted as indicating either that a large proportion of preterm labour resolves spontaneously, or that there are inaccuracies in the diagnosis. The two strongest risk factors for idiopathic preterm labour are low socioeconomic status and previous preterm delivery. Women with a history of preterm birth had a significantly increased risk of subsequent preterm birth (before 34 weeks' gestation) compared with women who had previously given birth after 35 weeks' gestation (OR 5.6, 95% CI 4.5 to 7.0).

**PROGNOSIS** Preterm birth is the leading cause of neonatal death and infant mortality, often as a result of respiratory distress syndrome due to immature lung development. Children who survive are also at high risk of neurological disability. Observational studies have found that one preterm birth significantly raises the risk of another in a subsequent pregnancy.

Kirsten Duckitt and Aysha Qureshi

## KEY POINTS

- Recurrent miscarriage is the spontaneous loss of three or more consecutive pregnancies with the same biological father in the first trimester; it affects 1% to 2% of women, in half of whom there is no identifiable cause.

  Overall, 75% of affected women will have a successful subsequent pregnancy, but this rate falls for older mothers and with increasing number of miscarriages.

  Antiphospholipid syndrome, with anticardiolipin or lupus anticoagulant antibodies, is present in 15% of women with recurrent first- and second-trimester miscarriage.

- We don't know whether bed rest, early scanning, lifestyle adaptation (to stop smoking, reduce alcohol consumption, and lose weight), low-dose aspirin, human chorionic gonadotrophin, trophoblastic membrane infusion, or vitamin supplementation increase the likelihood of a successful pregnancy in women with unexplained recurrent miscarriage.

- We also don't know whether oestrogen supplementation increases the live birth rate in women with unexplained recurrent miscarriage, but it may increase the miscarriage rate and cause abnormalities in the fetus.

  We don't know whether progesterone supplementation or corticosteroids reduce miscarriage rates compared with placebo in women with unexplained recurrent miscarriage.

- Paternal white cell immunisation and intravenous immunoglobulin treatment do not seem likely to improve live birth rates compared with placebo in women with unexplained recurrent miscarriage.

- We don't know whether low-dose aspirin, alone or combined with heparin, can increase the live birth rate compared with placebo in women with antiphospholipid syndrome.

  Prednisolone plus aspirin does not seem to increase live birth rates, compared with placebo or aspirin alone, in women with antiphospholipid syndrome, and it increases the risk of adverse effects including hypertension, preterm birth, low birth weight, and admission to neonatal intensive care.

 **Please visit http://clinicalevidence.bmj.com for full text and references**

| What are the effects of treatments for unexplained recurrent miscarriage? | |
|---|---|
| Unknown Effectiveness | • Aspirin (low dose) in unexplained recurrent miscarriage |
| | • Bed rest in unexplained recurrent miscarriage |
| | • Corticosteroids in unexplained recurrent miscarriage |
| | • Early scanning in subsequent pregnancies of women with unexplained recurrent miscarriage |
| | • Human chorionic gonadotrophin in unexplained recurrent miscarriage |
| | • Lifestyle adaptation (smoking cessation, reducing alcohol consumption, losing weight) in unexplained recurrent miscarriage |
| | • Progesterone in unexplained recurrent miscarriage |

| | |
|---|---|
| | • Trophoblastic membrane infusion in unexplained recurrent miscarriage<br>• Vitamin supplementation in unexplained recurrent miscarriage |
| **Unlikely To Be Beneficial** | • Intravenous immunoglobulin in unexplained recurrent miscarriage<br>• Paternal white cell immunisation in unexplained recurrent miscarriage |
| **Likely To Be Ineffective Or Harmful** | • Oestrogen in unexplained recurrent miscarriage |

### What are the effects of treatments for recurrent miscarriage caused by antiphospholipid syndrome?

| | |
|---|---|
| **Unknown Effectiveness** | • Aspirin (low dose) in antiphospholipid syndrome<br>• Aspirin (low dose) plus heparin |
| **Likely To Be Ineffective Or Harmful** | • Corticosteroids in antiphospholipid syndrome |

**Search date January 2010**

**DEFINITION** Recurrent miscarriage is usually defined as three or more consecutive, spontaneous miscarriages occurring in the first trimester, with the same biological father. They may or may not follow a successful birth. About half of recurrent miscarriages are unexplained. **Antiphospholipid syndrome (APS)** is one of the known causes of first- and second-trimester recurrent miscarriage. APS is defined as the presence of anticardiolipin antibodies or lupus anticoagulant antibodies, in association with either three or more consecutive fetal losses before week 10 of gestation, one or more unexplained intrauterine deaths beyond 10 weeks of gestation, or one or more premature births before 34 weeks due to severe pre-eclampsia or impaired fetal growth. This review covers unexplained recurrent miscarriages and both first- and second-trimester recurrent miscarriages in women with APS.

**INCIDENCE/PREVALENCE** In Western populations, recurrent miscarriage affects 1% to 2% of women of childbearing age, and about half of these are unexplained. Antiphospholipid antibodies are present in 15% of women with recurrent miscarriage.

**AETIOLOGY/RISK FACTORS** Increasing maternal age and number of previous miscarriages increase the risk of further miscarriages. No separate risk factors for APS are known.

**PROGNOSIS** On average, the live birth rate for women with unexplained recurrent miscarriage is 75% in a subsequent pregnancy, with a miscarriage rate of 20% up to 9 weeks, and a 5% miscarriage rate after this period. However, prognosis varies depending on maternal age and number of previous miscarriages. The chance of a successful subsequent pregnancy after three previous unexplained miscarriages varies from about 54% in a 45-year-old woman to about 90% in a 20-year-old woman. A 30-year-old woman with two previous unexplained miscarriages has about an 84% chance of a successful subsequent pregnancy, whereas for a woman of the same age with 5 previous unexplained miscarriages, the success rate drops to about 71%. Prospective studies of low-risk pregnancies have found that the presence of anticardiolipin antibodies carried a three to 9 times greater risk of fetal loss. Women with a history of at least three prior miscarriages and no abnormality other than the presence of antiphospholipid antibodies are highly likely to have a future miscarriage.

Rajesh Varma and Janesh Gupta

## KEY POINTS

- Approximately 1/100 pregnancies are ectopic, with the conceptus usually implanting in the fallopian tube. Some tubal ectopic pregnancies resolve spontaneously, but others continue to grow and lead to rupture of the tube.

  Risks for ectopic pregnancy are higher in women with damage to the fallopian tubes because of pelvic infections, pelvic surgery, or previous ectopic pregnancy, and in smokers.

  The IUD does not increase the absolute risk of ectopic pregnancy, but pregnancy that does occur with IUD use is more likely to be ectopic than intrauterine.

- Primary treatment success and reduced risk of future pregnancy (intrauterine and/or ectopic) are prioritised outcomes for women with ectopic pregnancy not desiring future fertility. However, treatment success and repeat intrauterine pregnancy are the prioritised outcomes for women with ectopic pregnancy desiring future fertility. Given these individualised outcome preferences, even though data from RCTs are absent, the most effective treatment for ectopic pregnancy in women not desiring future fertility is salpingectomy.

- Salpingotomy, salpingectomy, or methotrexate show similar rates of primary treatment success in women with ectopic pregnancy desiring future pregnancy; however, there is uncertainty over which treatment option is superior given the individualised outcome preference for this group of women and the absence of data from RCTs.

- Salpingotomy by laparoscopy may lead to fewer complications and shorter recovery times compared with laparotomy, but may also be less likely to remove all the trophoblast.

- Single- or multiple-dose methotrexate seems as likely as salpingotomy to eliminate trophoblast material and leave a patent fallopian tube in women with non-invasively diagnosed small ectopic pregnancies with no tubal rupture or bleeding, no sign of fetal cardiac activity, and low beta hCG levels.

  About 15% to 40% of ectopic pregnancies may be suitable for such non-surgical management.

  Adding mifepristone to systemic methotrexate seems unlikely to increase treatment success compared with methotrexate alone, other than in women with higher progesterone levels.

  Expectant management of unruptured ectopic pregnancies may lead to similar subsequent intrauterine pregnancy rates compared with surgery, but few studies have been done.

- A single prophylactic dose of methotrexate after salpingotomy is more effective at reducing persistent trophoblast compared with salpingotomy alone.

(i) **Please visit http://clinicalevidence.bmj.com for full text and references**

| What treatments improve outcomes in women with unruptured tubal ectopic pregnancy? | |
|---|---|
| Beneficial | • Salpingectomy (more effective than salpingotomy and methotrexate in women not desiring future fertility; unknown if superior to salpingotomy or methotrexate in women desiring future fertility) |
| Likely To Be Beneficial | • Methotrexate (single- or multiple-dose systemic; in women desiring future fertility; however, unknown if superior to salpingectomy or methotrexate) |

| | • Methotrexate (systemic prophylactic) following salpingotomy

• Salpingotomy* (in women desiring future fertility; however, unknown if superior to salpingectomy or methotrexate) |
|---|---|
| **Unknown Effectiveness** | • Expectant management of unruptured ectopic pregnancies |
| **Unlikely To Be Beneficial** | • Methotrexate plus mifepristone (systemic combination no better than systemic methotrexate alone) |

**Search date July 2011**

*Categorisation based on consensus.

**DEFINITION** Ectopic pregnancy is defined as a conceptus implanting outside the uterine endometrium. The most common implantation site is within the fallopian tube (95.5%), followed by ovarian (3.2%), and abdominal (1.3%) sites. The sites of tubal implantation in descending order of frequency are ampulla (73.3%), isthmus (12.5%), fimbrial (11.6%), and interstitial (2.6%). **Population:** In this systematic review, we consider haemodynamically stable women with unruptured tubal ectopic pregnancy, diagnosed by either non-invasive or invasive techniques.

**INCIDENCE/PREVALENCE** About 10,000 ectopic pregnancies are diagnosed annually in the UK. The incidence of ectopic pregnancy in the UK is 11.1/1000 pregnancies. Differing rates are reported in other countries such as Norway (14.9/1000), Australia (16.2/1000), and the US (6.4/1000). Since 1994, the overall rates of ectopic pregnancy and resulting mortality (0.35/1000 ectopic pregnancies in 2003–2005) have been static in the UK. Until recently, most epidemiological studies failed to distinguish between ectopic pregnancies occurring in women who did not use contraception (reproductive failure) and women who used contraception (contraceptive failure). A French population study undertaken from 1992 to 2002 found that, over the duration of the study, the rate of reproductive-failure ectopic pregnancies increased by 17%, whereas the rate of contraceptive-failure ectopic pregnancies decreased by 29%. Increasing rates of chlamydia infection, smoking, and assisted reproductive technology use may have contributed to the disproportionate increase in the reproductive-failure ectopic pregnancies. Widespread use of dedicated early pregnancy-assessment units and non-invasive diagnostic algorithms are likely to have contributed to increasing rates of ectopic pregnancy diagnosis.

**AETIOLOGY/RISK FACTORS** The aetiology of ectopic pregnancy is unclear. Ectopic pregnancy arising from reproductive or contraceptive failure should be considered as separate entities with differing aetiology, risk factors, and reproductive outcomes. The main risk factors for reproductive failure are: previous ectopic pregnancy, previous pelvic inflammatory disease, previous pelvic and tubal surgery, infertility, smoking, and use of assisted conception. The main risk factor for contraceptive-failure ectopic pregnancy is IUD failure. IUDs do not increase the absolute risk of ectopic pregnancy, but a pregnancy occurring with an IUD is more likely to be ectopic than intrauterine. Other risk factors for ectopic pregnancy include prior spontaneous miscarriage, endometriosis, uterotubal anomalies, and prior in utero exposure to diethylstilbestrol. However, less than half of diagnosed ectopic pregnancies are associated with risk factors.

**PROGNOSIS Ectopic pregnancies:** As the pregnancy advances, tubal pregnancies may either diminish in size and spontaneously resolve, or increase in size and eventually lead to tubal rupture, with consequent maternal morbidity and mortality. There are no reliable clinical, sonographic, or biological markers (e.g., serum beta hCG or serum progesterone) that can predict rupture of tubal ectopic pregnancy. Maternal mortality following ectopic pregnancy is an uncommon short-term outcome in resource-rich countries. The 2003–2005

UK Confidential Enquiry into Maternal Deaths cited ectopic pregnancy as a cause of 10 maternal deaths (0.47/100,000 pregnancies). Short-term maternal morbidity relates to pain, transfusion requirement, and operative complications. Primary treatment success and long-term fertility outcomes depend on the clinical characteristics of the ectopic pregnancy (e.g., whether the ectopic pregnancy occurred in a woman using contraception or not, tubal rupture or not, contralateral tubal disease) and the type of surgical or medical treatment chosen. A 10-year follow-up of ectopic pregnancies showed that the rate of repeat ectopic pregnancy was much higher in women with an IUD in place at the time of the index ectopic pregnancy, compared with women whose ectopic pregnancy was not associated with IUD use. By contrast, the rate of intrauterine pregnancy was 1.7 times higher (fecundity rate ratio [FRR] 1.7, 95% CI 1.3 to 2.3) in women who had an IUD in place at the time of the index ectopic pregnancy compared with women whose index ectopic pregnancy was not associated with IUD use. Short- and long-term consequences on health-related quality of life and psychological issues (e.g., bereavement) are also important, but are rarely quantified.
**Pregnancies of unknown location (PUL):** PUL is the absence of pregnancy localisation (either intrauterine or extrauterine) by transvaginal sonography when serum beta hCG levels are below the discriminatory zone (1000–1500 IU/L). One observational study of pregnancies of unknown location has shown that 55% spontaneously resolve, 34% are subsequently diagnosed as viable, and 11% are subsequently diagnosed as ectopic pregnancies.

# Acute respiratory distress syndrome

Sat Sharma

## KEY POINTS

- Acute respiratory distress syndrome (ARDS) is a syndrome of inflammation and increased permeability that is associated with clinical, radiological, and physiological abnormalities, which usually develops over 4 to 48 hours and persists for days or weeks. Pathologically, ARDS is associated with complex changes in the lungs, manifested by an early exudative phase and followed by proliferative and fibrotic phases.

  The main causes of ARDS are infections, aspiration of gastric contents, and trauma.

  Between one third and one half of people with ARDS die, but mortality depends on the underlying cause. Some survivors have long-term respiratory or cognitive problems.

  The treatment of ARDS is supportive care, including optimised mechanical ventilation, nutritional support, manipulation of fluid balance, source control and treatment of sepsis, and prevention of intervening medical complications.

- Low tidal-volume ventilation, at 6 mL/kg of predicted body weight, reduces mortality compared with high tidal-volume ventilation, but can lead to respiratory acidosis.

  Positive end expiratory pressure (PEEP) that maintains $PaO_2$ above 60 mmHg is considered effective in people with ARDS, but no difference in mortality has been found for high PEEP compared with lower PEEP strategies.

- People with ARDS may remain hypoxic despite mechanical ventilation. Nursing in the prone position may improve oxygenation but it has not been shown to reduce mortality, and it can increase adverse effects such as pressure ulcers.

  The prone position is contraindicated in people with spinal instability and should be used with caution in people with haemodynamic and cardiac instability, or in people who have had recent thoracic or abdominal surgery.

- We found insufficient evidence to draw reliable conclusions on the effects of corticosteroids on mortality or reversal of ARDS.

- Nitric oxide has not been shown to improve survival or duration of ventilation, or hospital stay, compared with placebo. It may modestly improve oxygenation in the short term but the improvement is not sustained.

(i) **Please visit http://clinicalevidence.bmj.com for full text and references**

## What are the effects of interventions in adults with acute respiratory distress syndrome?

| Beneficial | • Low tidal-volume mechanical ventilation |
|---|---|
| Likely To Be Beneficial | • Open lung strategy (positive end expiratory pressure, PEEP) (consensus PEEP is effective; however, optimal regimen is unclear) |
| Trade-off Between Benefits And Harms | • Prone position |
| Unknown Effectiveness | • Corticosteroids |
| Unlikely To Be Beneficial | • Nitric oxide |

**Search date December 2009**

**DEFINITION** Acute respiratory distress syndrome (ARDS) is a syndrome of inflammation and increased permeability that is associated with clinical, radiological, and physiological abnormalities, which usually develops over 4 to 48 hours and persists for days or weeks. Pathologically, ARDS is associated with complex changes in the lung, manifested by an early exudative phase and followed by proliferative and fibrotic phases. ARDS, originally described by Ashbaugh et al in 1967, is a clinical syndrome that represents the severe end of the spectrum of acute lung injury (ALI). In 1994, the American–European Consensus Conference on ARDS recommended the following definitions. Widespread acceptance of these definitions by clinicians and researchers has improved standardisation of clinical research. **Acute lung injury:** a syndrome of acute and persistent inflammatory disease of the lungs characterised by three clinical features: 1) bilateral pulmonary infiltrates on the chest radiograph; 2) a ratio of the partial pressure of arterial oxygen to the fraction of inspired oxygen ($PaO_2/FiO_2$) of <300; 3) absence of clinical evidence of left atrial hypertension (if measured, the pulmonary capillary wedge pressure is no more than 18 mmHg). **Acute respiratory distress syndrome:** The definition of ARDS is the same as that of ALI, except that the hypoxia is severe, a $PaO_2/FiO_2$ ratio of 200 mmHg or less. The distinction between ALI and ARDS is arbitrary, because the severity of hypoxia does not correlate reliably with the extent of the underlying pathology, and does not influence predictably clinical course or survival. ARDS is an acute disorder. Other sub-acute or chronic lung diseases, such as sarcoidosis and idiopathic pulmonary fibrosis, are excluded from the definition of ARDS. The early pathological features of ARDS are generally described as diffuse alveolar damage. Recognition of diffuse alveolar damage requires histological examination of the lung tissue, which is not necessary to make a clinical diagnosis. **Population:** For the purpose of this review, we have defined ARDS as including people with ALI and ARDS. It therefore includes adults with ALI and ARDS from any cause and with any level of severity. Neonates and children <12 years of age have been excluded.

**INCIDENCE/PREVALENCE** Between 10% and 15% of all people admitted to an ICU, and up to 20% of mechanically ventilated people, meet the criteria for ARDS. The incidence of ALI in the USA (17–64/100,000 person-years) seems higher than in Europe, Australia, and other developed countries (17–34/100,000 person-years). One prospective, population-based cohort study (1113 people in Washington State, aged >15 years) found the crude incidence of ALI to be 78.9/100,000 person-years, and the age-adjusted incidence to be 86.2/100,000 person-years. An annual national incidence of 15.5 cases per year or 5.9 cases/100,000 people per year was reported in one epidemiological study from Iceland. An observational cohort reported that, in Shanghai, China, of 5320 adults admitted to ICUs in 1 year, 108 (2%) had clinical features that met with ARDS criteria.

*(continued over)*

*(from previous page)*

**AETIOLOGY/RISK FACTORS** ARDS encompasses many distinct disorders that share common clinical and pathophysiological features. More than 60 causes of ARDS have been identified. Although the list of possible causes is long, most episodes of ARDS are associated with a few common causes or predisposing conditions, either individually or in combination. These include sepsis, aspiration of gastric contents, infectious pneumonia, severe trauma, surface burns, lung contusion, fat embolism syndrome, massive blood transfusion, lung and bone marrow transplantation, drugs, acute pancreatitis, near drowning, cardiopulmonary bypass, and neurogenic pulmonary oedema. Sepsis and pneumonia account for about 60% of cases. The incidence of ALI in a large cohort of people with subarachnoid haemorrhage has been reported to be 27% (170/620 people; 95% CI 24% to 31%). One or more of these predisposing conditions are often evident at the onset of ALI. When ARDS occurs in the absence of common risk factors such as trauma, pneumonia, sepsis, or aspiration, an effort should be made to identify a specific cause for lung injury. In such cases, a systematic review of the events that immediately preceded the onset of ARDS is normally undertaken to identify the predisposing factors.

**PROGNOSIS Mortality:** Survival for people with ARDS has improved remarkably in recent years, and cohort studies have found mortality to range from 34% to 58%. In an Icelandic study, hospital mortality was 40%, mean length of ICU stay was 21 days, and mean length of hospital stay was 39 days. Mortality varies with the cause; however, by far the most common cause of death is multiorgan system failure rather than acute respiratory failure. In a prospective cohort study (207 people at risk of developing ARDS, of which 47 developed ARDS during the trial), only 16% of deaths were considered to have been caused by irreversible respiratory failure. Most deaths in the first 3 days of being diagnosed with ARDS could be attributed to the underlying illness or injury. Most late deaths (after 3 days, 16/22 [72.7%]) were related to the sepsis syndrome. One prospective cohort study (902 mechanically ventilated people with ALI) found that an age of 70 years or younger significantly increased the proportion of people who survived at 28 days (74.6% aged up to 70 years *v* 50.3% aged at least 71 years or older; P <0.001). In one observational study (2004), the overall ICU mortality was 10.3%. In-hospital mortality was 68.5%, and 90-day mortality was 70.4% in people with ARDS, and accounted for 13.5% of the overall ICU mortality. **Lung function and morbidity:** One cohort study of 16 long-term survivors of severe ARDS (lung injury score at least 2.5) found that only mild abnormalities in pulmonary function (and often none) were observed. Restrictive and obstructive ventilatory defects (each noted in 4/16 [25%] people) were observed in ARDS survivors treated with low or conventional tidal volumes. One cohort study of 109 people found no significant difference between various ventilatory strategies and long-term abnormalities in pulmonary function or health-related quality of life. However, it did find an association between abnormal pulmonary function and decreased quality of life at 1-year follow-up. One retrospective cohort study (41 people with ARDS) found that duration of mechanical ventilation and severity of ARDS were important determinants of persistent symptoms 1 year after recovery. Better lung function was observed when no subsequent illness was acquired during the ICU stay, and with rapid resolution of multiple organ failure (e.g., pneumonia during ARDS: 7/41 [17.1%] people with long-term impairment *v* 2/41 [4.9%] with no long-term impairment; significance assessment not performed). Persistent disability 1 year after discharge from the ICU in survivors of ARDS is secondary to extrapulmonary conditions, most importantly muscle wasting and weakness. **Cognitive morbidity:** One cohort study (55 people 1 year after ARDS) found that 17/55 (30.1%) exhibited generalised cognitive decline and 43/55 (78.2%) had all, or at least one, of the following: impaired memory, attention, concentration, and decreased mental processing speed. These deficits may be related to hypoxaemia, drug toxicity, or complications of critical illness. To date, no association between different ventilatory strategies and long-term neurological outcomes has been found.

Gustavo Rodrigo

## KEY POINTS

- About 10% of adults have suffered an attack of asthma, and up to 5% of these have severe disease that responds poorly to treatment. These people have an increased risk of death.

- Most guidelines about the management of asthma follow stepwise protocols. This review does not endorse or follow any particular protocol, but presents the evidence about specific interventions.

- Inhaled short-acting beta$_2$ agonists are considered the mainstay of treatment for acute asthma.

- In people with an acute attack of asthma, supplementation of beta$_2$ agonists with low oxygen concentrations, systemic corticosteroids (short courses), additional beta$_2$ agonists (various routes of administration), or ipratropium bromide improves symptoms.

  Inhaled corticosteroids seem to improve lung function in people with acute asthma. However, we don't know whether inhaled corticosteroids are as effective as systemic corticosteroids at improving symptom severity, lung function, and hospital admissions.

  Inhaled plus oral corticosteroids and oral corticosteroids alone may have similar effects in preventing relapse.

  Beta$_2$ agonists delivered from a metered-dose inhaler using a spacer are as effective at improving lung function as those given by a nebuliser or given iv. Giving beta$_2$ agonists iv is more invasive than giving beta$_2$ agonists by nebuliser.

  In people with severe acute asthma, continuous nebulised short-acting beta$_2$ agonists may also improve lung function more than intermittent nebulised short-acting beta$_2$ agonists.

  The inhaled long-acting beta$_2$ agonist formoterol seems to be at least equivalent to the short-acting beta$_2$ agonists salbutamol and terbutaline in terms of pulmonary function in moderate to severe acute asthma treatment. On the basis of research undertaken in people with chronic asthma, the FDA has recommended minimising the use of long-acting beta agonists because of an increased risk of asthma exacerbations, hospital admissions, and death. The FDA acknowledges that they do have an important role in helping some patients control asthma symptoms.

  We don't know if iv magnesium sulphate, nebulised magnesium alone, or adding nebulised magnesium to inhaled beta$_2$ agonists improves lung function in people with acute asthma.

  We don't know whether helium–oxygen mixture (heliox) is more effective at improving lung function compared with usual care.

  Mechanical ventilation may be life saving in severe acute asthma, but it is associated with high levels of morbidity.

  Specialist care of acute asthma may lead to improved outcomes compared with generalist care.

  We don't know whether education to help self-manage asthma improves symptom severity, lung function, or quality of life, but it may reduce hospital admissions.

 **Please visit http://clinicalevidence.bmj.com for full text and references**

## What are the effects of treatments for acute asthma?

| Beneficial | • Controlled oxygen supplementation (28% oxygen better than 100% oxygen) |
|---|---|

|  | • Corticosteroids (inhaled)<br><br>• Corticosteroids (short courses given systemically are more effective than placebo)<br><br>• Ipratropium bromide (inhaled) plus short-acting beta$_2$ agonists (inhaled)<br><br>• Oral corticosteroids alone (as effective as combined inhaled plus oral corticosteroids)<br><br>• Short-acting beta$_2$ agonists delivered by metered-dose inhalers plus spacer devices/holding chambers (as good as delivery by nebulisation) |
| --- | --- |
| **Likely To Be Beneficial** | • Formoterol (inhaled) (may be as effective as inhaled short-acting beta$_2$ agonists in the emergency department setting)<br><br>• Mechanical ventilation for people with severe acute asthma*<br><br>• Short-acting beta$_2$ agonists (delivered by continuous nebulisation are more effective than short-acting beta$_2$ agonists delivered by intermittent nebulisation)<br><br>• Specialist care (more effective than generalist care) |
| **Unknown Effectiveness** | • Education about acute asthma<br><br>• Magnesium sulphate (iv)<br><br>• Magnesium sulphate (nebulised)<br><br>• Magnesium sulphate (nebulised) plus short-acting beta$_2$ agonists (inhaled) |
| **Unlikely To Be Beneficial** | • Helium–oxygen mixture (heliox)<br><br>• Short-acting beta$_2$ agonists (given iv, are no more effective than nebulised short-acting beta$_2$ agonists) |

**Search date April 2010**

*Categorisation based on consensus. Limited RCT evidence available.
Most guidelines about the management of asthma follow stepwise protocols. This review does not endorse or follow any particular protocol, but it presents the evidence about specific interventions.

**DEFINITION** Asthma is characterised by variable airflow obstruction and airway hyper-responsiveness. Symptoms include dyspnoea, cough, chest tightness, and wheezing. The normal diurnal variation of peak expiratory flow rate (PEFR) is increased in people with asthma. **Acute asthma** is defined here as an exacerbation of underlying asthma requiring urgent treatment. Most guidelines about the management of asthma follow stepwise protocols. This review does not endorse or follow any particular protocol, but presents the evidence about specific interventions in no particular order.

**INCIDENCE/PREVALENCE** The reported prevalence of asthma has been increasing world-wide, but may have currently reached a plateau. About 10% of people have suffered an attack of asthma, but epidemiological studies have also found marked variations in prevalence between and within countries.

**AETIOLOGY/RISK FACTORS** Most people with asthma are atopic. Exposure to certain stimuli initiates inflammation and structural changes in airways causing airway hyper-responsiveness and variable airflow obstruction, which in turn cause most asthma symptoms. There are many such stimuli; the more important include environmental allergens, occupational sensitising agents, and respiratory viral infections.

**PROGNOSIS** About 10% to 20% of people presenting to the emergency department with asthma are admitted to hospital. Of these, less than 10% receive mechanical ventilation. Those who are ventilated are at 19-fold increased risk of ventilation for a subsequent episode. It is unusual for people to die unless they have suffered respiratory arrest before they reach hospital. One prospective study of 939 people discharged from emergency care found that 106/641 (17%, 95% CI 14% to 20%) relapsed by 2 weeks.

Peter Wark

## KEY POINTS

- Acute bronchitis affects more than 40 in 1000 adults per year in the UK.

  The causes are usually considered to be infective, but only around half of people have identifiable pathogens.

  The role of smoking or environmental tobacco smoke inhalation in predisposing to acute bronchitis is unclear.

  One third of people may have longer-term symptoms or recurrence.

- We searched for evidence of effectiveness from RCTs and systematic reviews of RCTs.

- Antibiotics may have a modest effect on improving cough and other clinical signs of acute bronchitis compared with placebo, but they also increase the risks of adverse effects.

- There remain concerns that widespread use of antimicrobials will lead to resistance.

- We don't know how different antibiotic regimens compare with each another, as we found insufficient evidence from RCTs.

  One review found that azithromycin (a macrolide) may be more effective than amoxicillin or amoxicillin plus clavulanic acid (co-amoxiclav) at reducing clinical failure in people with acute bronchitis. However, this analysis included two open-label studies and evidence was weak.

  We don't know whether smokers without lung disease are more likely to benefit from antibiotics than non-smokers.

- We don't know whether antihistamines, antitussives, inhaled beta$_2$ agonists, or expectorants and mucolytics improve symptoms of acute bronchitis compared with placebo, as we found few good-quality RCTs.

 **Please visit http://clinicalevidence.bmj.com for full text and references**

| What are the effects of treatments for acute bronchitis in people without chronic respiratory disease? | |
|---|---|
| **Trade-off Between Benefits And Harms** | • Antibiotics versus placebo and other non-antibiotic treatments (modest improvement in cough, but concerns about resistance and adverse effects; insufficient evidence to compare with other treatments) |
| **Unknown Effectiveness** | • Antibiotics (amoxicillin, cephalosporins, and macrolides) versus each other<br><br>• Antihistamines<br><br>• Antitussives<br><br>• Beta$_2$ agonists (inhaled)<br><br>• Expectorants and mucolytics |

**Search date May 2015**

**DEFINITION** Acute bronchitis is a transient inflammation of the trachea and major bronchi. Clinically, it is diagnosed on the basis of cough and occasionally sputum, dyspnoea, and wheeze. This overview is limited to episodes of acute bronchitis in people (smokers and non-smokers) with no pre-existing respiratory disease (such as a pre-existing diagnosis of asthma or chronic bronchitis, evidence of fixed airflow obstruction, or both) and excluding those with clinical or radiographic evidence of pneumonia. However, the reliance on a clinical definition for acute bronchitis implies that people with conditions such as transient/mild asthma or mild COPD may have been recruited in some of the reported studies.

**INCIDENCE/PREVALENCE** Acute bronchitis affects around 44 in 1000 adults (age over 16 years) per year in the UK, with around 82% of episodes occurring in autumn or winter. One survey found that acute bronchitis was the fifth most common reason for people of any age to present to a general practitioner in Australia.

**AETIOLOGY/RISK FACTORS** Infection is believed to be the trigger for acute bronchitis. However, pathogens have been identified in less than 55% of people. Community studies that attempted to isolate pathogens from the sputum of people with acute bronchitis found viruses in 8% to 23% of people, typical bacteria (*Streptococcus pneumoniae, Haemophilus influenzae, Moraxella catarrhalis*) in 45%, and atypical bacteria (*Mycobacterium pneumoniae, Chlamydia pneumoniae, Bordetella pertussis*) in 0% to 25%, but their presence did not predict outcomes. It is unclear whether smoking affects the risk for developing acute bronchitis.

**PROGNOSIS** Acute bronchitis is regarded as a mild, self-limiting illness, but there are limited data on prognosis and rates of complications, such as chronic cough or progression to chronic bronchitis or pneumonia. One prospective longitudinal study reviewed 653 previously well adults who presented to suburban general practices over a 12-month period with symptoms of acute lower respiratory tract infection. It found that, within the first month of the illness, 20% of people re-presented to their general practitioner with persistent or recurrent symptoms, mostly persistent cough. One RCT of 212 people (in which around 16% took antibiotics outside of the study protocol) found that participants in the no-treatment control group had at least a slight problem with cough for a mean of 11.4 days, with 'moderately bad' cough lasting for a mean of 5.7 days. A large RCT of 2061 adults (aged over 18 years) who presented with acute cough (up to 28 days' duration) or were likely to have a lower respiratory tract infection (excluding clinical pneumonia), but including participants with asthma or COPD (15%), was informative as to the short-term natural history of acute bronchitis. They found that 356/2027 (18%) had a deterioration in illness, the majority with re-consultation due to worsened symptoms. Only three people were hospitalised (2 in the placebo arm, 1 in the antibiotic arm) with a cardiac or respiratory disease within the month. This demonstrates that serious complications are rare in this group, with the sample size unable to determine if comorbidities (heart disease, lung disease, or diabetes), smoking status, or the presence of green sputum would predict worsened outcomes. Another prospective study of 138 previously well adults found that 34% had symptoms consistent with either chronic bronchitis or asthma 3 years after initial presentation with acute bronchitis. It is also unclear whether acute bronchitis plays a causal role in the progression to chronic bronchitis, or is simply a marker of predisposition to chronic lung disease. Although smoking has been identified as the most important risk factor for chronic bronchitis, it is unclear whether the inflammatory effects of cigarette smoke and infection causing acute bronchitis have additive effects in leading to chronic inflammatory airway changes. In children, exposure to parental environmental tobacco smoke is associated with an increase in risk for community lower respiratory tract infection in children aged 0 to 2 years, and an increase in symptoms of cough and phlegm in those aged 5 to 16 years.

Bruce Arroll

## KEY POINTS

- Transmission of common cold infections is mostly through hand-to-hand contact rather than droplet spread. Several types of virus can cause symptoms of colds.

  Each year, children suffer up to 5 colds and adults have two to three infections, leading to time off school or work and considerable discomfort. Most symptoms resolve within 1 week, but coughs often persist for longer.

- Nasal and oral decongestants reduce nasal congestion over 3 to 10 hours, but we don't know how effective decongestants are for longer-term relief (>10 hours).

- Antibiotics don't reduce symptoms overall, and can cause adverse effects and increase antibiotic resistance.

  Antibiotics may improve symptoms after 5 days compared with placebo in people with nasopharyngeal culture-positive *Haemophilus influenzae*, *Moraxella catarrhalis*, or *Streptococcus pneumoniae*, but it is difficult to identify which people may have these infections.

- Vitamin C seems unlikely to reduce the duration or severity of cold symptoms compared with placebo.

  We don't know whether zinc gel or lozenges, echinacea, steam inhalation, or analgesics or anti-inflammatory drugs reduce the duration of symptoms of colds.

- Antihistamines may slightly reduce runny nose and sneezing, but their overall effect seems small. Some antihistamines may cause sedation or arrhythmias.

- We found insufficient evidence to assess whether decongestants plus antihistamines are effective in reducing cold symptoms.

 Please visit http://clinicalevidence.bmj.com for full text and references

| What are the effects of treatments for common cold? | |
|---|---|
| **Likely To Be Beneficial** | • Antihistamines (may improve runny nose and sneezing, no significant difference in overall symptoms) |
| | • Decongestants (norephedrine, oxymetazoline, or pseudoephedrine provide short-term [3- to 10-hour] relief of congestive symptoms) |
| **Unknown Effectiveness** | • Analgesics or anti-inflammatory drugs |
| | • Decongestants (insufficient evidence to assess longer-term [>10 hours] effects on congestive symptoms) |
| | • Decongestants plus antihistamines |
| | • Echinacea |
| | • Steam inhalation |

| | |
|---|---|
| | • Zinc (intranasal gel or lozenges) |
| **Unlikely To Be Beneficial** | • Vitamin C |
| **Likely To Be Ineffective Or Harmful** | • Antibiotics |

**Search date January 2010**

---

**DEFINITION** Common colds are defined as upper respiratory tract infections that affect the predominantly nasal part of the respiratory mucosa. Because upper respiratory tract infections can affect any part of the mucosa, it is often arbitrary whether an upper respiratory tract infection is called a 'cold' or 'sore throat' ('pharyngitis' or 'tonsillitis'), 'sinusitis', 'acute otitis media', or 'bronchitis'. Sometimes all areas (simultaneously or at different times) are affected during one illness. Symptoms include sneezing, rhinorrhoea (runny nose), headache, and general malaise. In addition to nasal symptoms, half of sufferers experience sore throat, and 40% experience cough. This review does not include treatments for people with acute sinusitis (see review on acute sinusitis, p 195), acute bronchitis (see review on acute bronchitis, p 508), or sore throat (see review on sore throat, p 514). One prospective US study (1246 children enrolled at birth) found that children who had frequent colds when aged 2 or 3 years were twice as likely to experience frequent colds at year 6 compared with children who had infrequent colds at 2 or 3 years (RR 2.8, 95% CI 2.1 to 3.9).

**INCIDENCE/PREVALENCE** Upper respiratory tract infections, nasal congestion, throat complaints, and cough are responsible for 11% of general practice consultations in Australia. Each year, children suffer about 5 such infections and adults two to three infections. One cross-sectional study in Norwegian children aged 4 to 5 years found that 48% experienced more than two common colds annually.

**AETIOLOGY/RISK FACTORS** Transmission of common cold infection is mostly through hand-to-hand contact, with subsequent passage to the nostrils or eyes — rather than, as commonly perceived, through droplets in the air. Common cold infections are mainly caused by viruses (typically rhinovirus, but also coronavirus and respiratory syncytial virus, or metapneumovirus and others). For many colds, no infecting organism can be identified.

**PROGNOSIS** Common colds are usually short lived, lasting a few days, with a few lingering symptoms lasting longer, especially cough. Symptoms peak within 1 to 3 days and generally clear by 1 week, although cough often persists. Although they cause no mortality or serious morbidity, common colds are responsible for considerable discomfort, lost work, and medical costs.

**Community-acquired pneumonia**

Mark Loeb

## KEY POINTS

- In the northern hemisphere about 12/1000 people a year (on average) contract pneumonia while living in the community, with most cases caused by *Streptococcus pneumoniae*.

  People at greatest risk include those at the extremes of age, smokers, alcohol-dependent people, and people with lung or heart disease or immunosuppression.

  Mortality ranges from about 5% to 35% depending on severity of disease, with a worse prognosis in older people, men, and people with chronic diseases.

- Deaths from influenza are usually caused by pneumonia. Influenza vaccine reduces the risk of clinical influenza, and may reduce the risk of pneumonia and mortality in older people.

  Pneumococcal vaccine is unlikely to reduce all-cause pneumonia or mortality in immunocompetent adults, but may reduce pneumococcal pneumonia in this group.

- Antibiotics lead to clinical cure in at least 80% of people with pneumonia being treated in the community or in hospital, although no one regimen has been shown to be superior to the others in either setting.

  Early mobilisation may reduce hospital stay compared with usual care in people being treated with antibiotics.

  Intravenous antibiotics have not been shown to improve clinical cure rates or survival compared with oral antibiotics in people treated in hospital for non-severe community-acquired pneumonia.

- Prompt administration of antibiotics may improve survival compared with delayed treatment in people receiving intensive care for community-acquired pneumonia, although we found few studies.

  We don't know which is the optimum antibiotic regimen to use in these people.

(i) **Please visit http://clinicalevidence.bmj.com for full text and references**

| What are the effects of interventions to prevent community-acquired pneumonia? | |
|---|---|
| Likely To Be Beneficial | ● Influenza vaccine (in older people)* |
| Unlikely To Be Beneficial | ● Pneumococcal vaccine (for all-cause pneumonia and mortality in immunocompetent adults) |

| What are the effects of treatments for community-acquired pneumonia in outpatient settings? | |
|---|---|
| Likely To Be Beneficial | ● Antibiotics in outpatient settings (compared with no antibiotics)* |

| What are the effects of treatments for community-acquired pneumonia in people admitted to hospital? | |
|---|---|
| Likely To Be Beneficial | ● Antibiotics in hospital (compared with no antibiotics)* |

| | • Early mobilisation (may reduce hospital stay compared with usual care)* |
|---|---|
| **Unlikely To Be Beneficial** | • Intravenous antibiotics in immunocompetent people in hospital without life-threatening illness (compared with oral antibiotics) |

## What are the effects of treatments in people with community-acquired pneumonia receiving intensive care?

| **Likely To Be Beneficial** | • Prompt administration of antibiotics in people admitted to intensive care with community-acquired pneumonia (improved outcomes compared with delayed antibiotic treatment)* |
|---|---|
| **Unknown Effectiveness** | • Different combinations of antibiotics in intensive care settings |

**Search date January 2010**

*Based on consensus.

**DEFINITION** Community-acquired pneumonia is pneumonia contracted in the community rather than in hospital. It is defined by clinical symptoms (such as cough, sputum production, and pleuritic chest pain) and signs (such as fever, tachypnoea, and rales), with radiological confirmation.

**INCIDENCE/PREVALENCE** In the northern hemisphere, community-acquired pneumonia affects about 12/1000 people a year, particularly during winter, and in people at the extremes of age (annual incidence in people aged <1 year old: 30–50/1000; 15–45 years old: 1–5/1000; 60–70 years old: 10–20/1000; 71–85 years old: 50/1000).

**AETIOLOGY/RISK FACTORS** More than 100 micro-organisms have been implicated in community-acquired pneumonia, but most cases are caused by *Streptococcus pneumoniae*. Case-control study data suggest that smoking is probably an important risk factor. One large cohort study conducted in Finland (4175 people aged at least 60 years) suggested that risk factors for pneumonia in older people included alcoholism (RR 9.0, 95% CI 5.1 to 16.2), bronchial asthma (RR 4.2, 95% CI 3.3 to 5.4), immunosuppression (RR 3.1, 95% CI 1.9 to 5.1), lung disease (RR 3.0, 95% CI 2.3 to 3.9), heart disease (RR 1.9, 95% CI 1.7 to 2.3), institutionalisation (RR 1.8, 95% CI 1.4 to 2.4), and increasing age (age at least 70 years *v* 60–69 years; RR 1.5, 95% CI 1.3 to 1.7).

**PROGNOSIS** Severity varies from mild to life-threatening illness within days of the onset of symptoms. A prospective cohort study (>14,000 people) found that old age was an extremely important factor in determining prognosis. One systematic review of prognosis studies for community-acquired pneumonia (search date 1995, 33,148 people) found overall mortality to be 13.7%, ranging from 5.1% for ambulant people to 36.5% for people who required intensive care. Prognostic factors significantly associated with mortality were: male sex (OR 1.3, 95% CI 1.2 to 1.4), absence of pleuritic chest pain (OR 2.00, 95% CI 1.25 to 3.30), hypothermia (OR 5.0, 95% CI 2.4 to 10.4), systolic hypotension (OR 4.8, 95% CI 2.8 to 8.3), tachypnoea (OR 2.9, 95% CI 1.7 to 4.9), diabetes mellitus (OR 1.3, 95% CI 1.1 to 1.5), neoplastic disease (OR 2.8, 95% CI 2.4 to 3.1), neurological disease (OR 4.6, 95% CI 2.3 to 8.9), bacteraemia (OR 2.8, 95% CI 2.3 to 3.6), leukopenia (OR 2.5, 95% CI 1.6 to 3.7), and multilobar radiographic pulmonary infiltrates (OR 3.1, 95% CI 1.9 to 5.1).

Tim Kenealy

## KEY POINTS

- Sore throat is an acute upper respiratory tract infection that affects the respiratory mucosa of the throat.

- About 10% of people in Australia present to primary healthcare services with sore throat each year.

  The causative organisms of sore throat may be bacteria (most commonly *Streptococcus*) or viruses (typically rhinovirus), but it is difficult to distinguish bacterial from viral infections clinically.

- Paracetamol seems to effectively reduce the pain of acute infective sore throat after regular doses over 2 days.

  There is a risk of rare but serious skin reactions with paracetamol (acetaminophen).

- Non-steroidal anti-inflammatory drugs (NSAIDs) may reduce the pain of sore throat at 2 to 5 days.

  NSAIDs are associated with gastrointestinal and renal adverse effects.

- Antibiotics can reduce the proportion of people with symptoms associated with sore throat at 3 days.

  Reduction in symptoms seems greater for people with positive throat swabs for *Streptococcus* than for people with negative swabs.

  Antibiotics are generally associated with adverse effects such as nausea, rash, vaginitis, and headache, and widespread use may lead to bacterial resistance.

- Corticosteroids added to antibiotics may reduce the severity of pain from sore throat in people compared with antibiotics alone.

  Most trials used a single dose of corticosteroid. However, data from other disorders suggest that long-term use of corticosteroids is associated with serious adverse effects.

 **Please visit http://clinicalevidence.bmj.com for full text and references**

| What are the effects of interventions to reduce symptoms of acute infective sore throat? | |
|---|---|
| Likely To Be Beneficial | • Corticosteroids (in people receiving antibiotics)<br>• Paracetamol (acetaminophen) |
| Trade-off Between Benefits And Harms | • Antibiotics<br>• NSAIDs |

**Search date September 2013**

**DEFINITION** Sore throat is an acute upper respiratory tract infection that affects the respiratory mucosa of the throat. Since infections can affect any part of the mucosa, it is often arbitrary whether an acute upper respiratory tract infection is called 'sore throat' ('pharyngitis' or 'tonsillitis'), 'common cold', 'sinusitis', 'otitis media', or 'bronchitis'. Sometimes, all areas are affected (simultaneously or at different times) in one illness. In this review, we aim to cover people whose principal presenting symptom is sore throat. This may be associated with headache, fever, and general malaise. Suppurative complications include acute otitis media (most commonly), acute sinusitis, and peritonsillar abscess (quinsy). Non-suppurative complications include acute rheumatic fever and acute glomerulo-nephritis.This review does not include people with previous rheumatic fever or previous glomerulonephritis, who are importantly different from the general population of people with sore throats. It also does not include people who are clinically seriously unwell (as these people are typically not included in the primary studies).

**INCIDENCE/PREVALENCE** There is little seasonal fluctuation in sore throat. About 10% of the Australian population present to primary healthcare services annually with an upper respiratory tract infection consisting predominantly of sore throat. This reflects about one fifth of the overall annual incidence. However, it is difficult to distinguish between the different types of upper respiratory tract infection. A Scottish mail survey found that 31% of adult respondents reported a severe sore throat in the previous year, for which 38% of these people visited a doctor.

**AETIOLOGY/RISK FACTORS** The causative organisms of sore throat may be bacteria (*Streptococcus*, most commonly group A beta-haemolytic, but sometimes *Haemophilus influenzae*, *Moraxella catarrhalis*, and others) or viruses (typically rhinovirus, but also coronavirus, respiratory syncytial virus, metapneumovirus, Epstein-Barr virus, and others). It is difficult to distinguish bacterial from viral infections clinically. Features suggestive of *Streptococcus* infection are: fever >38.5°C, exudate on the tonsils, anterior neck lymphadenopathy, and absence of cough. Sore throat can be caused by processes other than primary infections, including GORD, physical or chemical irritation (e.g., from nasogastric tubes or smoke), and occasionally hay fever. However, we consider only primary infections in this review.

**PROGNOSIS** The untreated symptoms of sore throat disappear by 3 days in about 40% of people, and untreated fevers in about 85%. By 1 week, 85% of people are symptom-free. This natural history is similar in *Streptococcus*-positive, *Streptococcus*-negative, and untested people.

# Spontaneous pneumothorax

Abel P Wakai

## KEY POINTS

- Spontaneous pneumothorax is defined as air entering the pleural space without any provoking factor, such as trauma, surgery, or diagnostic intervention.

  Incidence is 24/100,000 a year in men, and 10/100,000 a year in women in England and Wales, and the major contributing factor is smoking, which increases the likelihood by 22 times in men and by 8 times in women.

  While death from spontaneous pneumothorax is rare, rates of recurrence are high, with one study of men in the US finding a total recurrence rate of 35%.

- Overall, we found insufficient RCT evidence to determine whether any intervention is more effective than no intervention for spontaneous pneumothorax.

- Chest-tube drainage seems to be a useful treatment for spontaneous pneumothorax, although RCT evidence is somewhat sparse.

  Small (8 French gauge) chest tubes are generally easier to insert, and may reduce the risk of subcutaneous emphysema, although successful resolution may be less likely in people with large pneumothoraces (>50% lung volume). We don't know whether there is a difference in duration of drainage with small tubes.

  The trials investigating the efficacy of adding suction to chest-tube drainage are too small and underpowered to detect a clinically important difference.

  We don't know whether using one-way valves on a chest tube is more effective than using drainage bottles with underwater seals. There is a suggestion, however, that one-way valves might reduce hospital admission and the need for analgesia.

- It seems that needle aspiration might be beneficial in treating people with spontaneous pneumothorax, although it is not clear whether it is more effective than chest-tube drainage.

- Pleurodesis seems to be effective in preventing recurrent spontaneous pneumothorax, although there are some adverse effects associated with the intervention.

  Chemical pleurodesis successfully reduces recurrence of spontaneous pneumothorax, although the injection has been reported to be intensely painful.

  Thoracoscopic surgery with talc instillation also seems to reduce recurrence of spontaneous pneumothorax, but leads to a modest increase in pain during the first 3 days.

  Video-assisted thoracoscopic surgery, while less invasive than thoracotomy, may be associated with higher recurrence rates.

  We found no RCT evidence examining when pleurodesis should be given, although there is general consensus that it is warranted after the second or third episode of spontaneous pneumothorax.

(i) **Please visit http://clinicalevidence.bmj.com for full text and references**

| What are the effects of treatments in people presenting with spontaneous pneumothorax? | |
|---|---|
| Likely To Be Beneficial | • Chest-tube drainage alone<br>• Needle aspiration |
| Unknown Effectiveness | • Chest-tube drainage plus suction<br>• One-way valves on chest tubes |

> - Small- versus standard-sized chest tubes for drainage

## What are the effects of interventions to prevent recurrence in people with previous spontaneous pneumothorax?

| Trade-off Between Benefits And Harms | • Pleurodesis |
|---|---|
| Unknown Effectiveness | • Optimal timing of pleurodesis (after first, second, or subsequent episode/s) |

**Search date January 2010**

**DEFINITION** A pneumothorax is air in the pleural space. A **spontaneous pneumothorax** occurs when there is no provoking factor — such as trauma, surgery, or diagnostic intervention. It implies a leak of air from the lung parenchyma through the visceral pleura into the pleural space, which causes the lung to collapse and results in pain and shortness of breath. This review does not include people with **tension pneumothorax.**

**INCIDENCE/PREVALENCE** In a survey in Minnesota, USA, the incidence of spontaneous pneumothorax was 7/100,000 for men and 1/100,000 for women. In England and Wales, the overall rate of people consulting with pneumothorax (in both primary and secondary care combined) is 24/100,000 a year for men and 10/100,000 a year for women. The overall annual incidence of emergency hospital admissions for pneumothorax in England and Wales is 16.7/100,000 for men and 5.8/100,000 for women. Smoking increases the likelihood of spontaneous pneumothorax by 22 times for men and by 8 times for women. The incidence is directly related to the amount smoked.

**AETIOLOGY/RISK FACTORS** Primary spontaneous pneumothorax is thought to result from congenital abnormality of the visceral pleura, and is typically seen in young, otherwise fit people. Secondary spontaneous pneumothorax is caused by underlying lung disease, typically affecting older people with emphysema or pulmonary fibrosis.

**PROGNOSIS** Death from spontaneous pneumothorax is rare, with UK mortality of 1.26 per million a year for men and 0.62 per million a year for women. Published recurrence rates vary. One cohort study in Denmark found that, after a first episode of primary spontaneous pneumothorax, 23% of people had a recurrence within 5 years, most of them within 1 year. Recurrence rates had been thought to increase substantially after the first recurrence, but one retrospective case-control study (147 US military personnel) found that 28% of men with a first primary spontaneous pneumothorax had a recurrence; 23% of the 28% had a second recurrence; and 14% of that 23% had a third recurrence, resulting in a total recurrence rate of 35%.

Rodolfo J Dennis and Ivan Solarte

## KEY POINTS

- About 10% of adults have suffered an attack of asthma, and up to 5% of these have severe disease that responds poorly to treatment. These people have an increased risk of death.

- Most guidelines about the management of asthma follow stepwise protocols. This review does not endorse or follow any particular protocol, but presents the evidence about specific interventions.

- Taking short-acting beta$_2$ agonists as needed is as likely to relieve symptoms and improve lung function as a regular dosing schedule in adults with chronic asthma.

- Adding long-acting beta$_2$ agonists to inhaled corticosteroids decreases the number of exacerbations and improves symptoms, lung function, and quality of life in people with mild-to-moderate persistent asthma that is poorly controlled with corticosteroids.

- CAUTION: Long-acting beta$_2$ agonists have been associated with increased asthma-related mortality, and should always be used with inhaled corticosteroids.

- Low-dose inhaled corticosteroids improve symptoms and lung function in persistent asthma compared with placebo or regular inhaled beta$_2$ agonists.

  Leukotriene antagonists are more effective than placebo at reducing symptoms, but we don't know if adding leukotriene antagonists to low-dose inhaled corticosteroids is of benefit in people with chronic asthma.

  CAUTION: Leukotriene antagonists have been associated with a possible increased risk of neuropsychiatric events.

  Adding theophylline to inhaled corticosteroids may improve lung function in people with mild or moderate chronic asthma that is poorly controlled with inhaled corticosteroids, but we don't know if they are of benefit compared with long-acting beta$_2$ agonists or leukotriene antagonists.

  Anti-IgE treatment (omalizumab) as an adjunct to treatment with inhaled and oral corticosteroids improves symptom severity, decreases exacerbation frequency, and may decrease hospital admission rates in people with chronic moderate to severe asthma.

 **Please visit http://clinicalevidence.bmj.com for full text and references**

| What are the effects of treatments for chronic asthma? | |
|---|---|
| Beneficial | • Adding long-acting beta$_2$ agonists (inhaled) to corticosteroids (inhaled) in people with mild-to-moderate chronic asthma that is partly or poorly controlled by inhaled corticosteroids alone |
| | • Low-dose corticosteroids (inhaled) in chronic asthma |
| | • Short-acting beta$_2$ agonists (inhaled) as needed for symptom relief (as effective as regular use) in mild-to-moderate chronic asthma |
| Likely To Be Beneficial | • Adding anti-IgE treatment to corticosteroids (inhaled) plus long-acting beta$_2$ agonists, plus either leukotriene antagonists, theophylline, or corticosteroids (oral), alone or in any combination, in people with severe, chronic asthma |

| | |
|---|---|
| | • Adding theophylline to corticosteroids (inhaled) in people with mild-to-moderate chronic asthma poorly controlled by inhaled corticosteroids alone (likely to be better than adding placebo but may be less effective than increasing dose of corticosteroids) |
| | • Leukotriene antagonists in people with mild-to-moderate chronic asthma not taking inhaled corticosteroids (likely to be better than placebo, but may be less effective than inhaled corticosteroids) |
| Unknown Effectiveness | • Adding leukotriene antagonists to corticosteroids (inhaled) in people with mild-to-moderate chronic asthma |

## Search date April 2010

*Categorisation based on consensus. Limited RCT evidence available.
Most guidelines about the management of asthma follow stepwise protocols. This review does not endorse or follow any particular protocol, but it presents the evidence about specific interventions.

**DEFINITION** Asthma is characterised by variable airflow obstruction and airway hyper-responsiveness. Symptoms include dyspnoea, cough, chest tightness, and wheezing. The normal diurnal variation of PEFR is increased in people with asthma. Chronic asthma is defined here as asthma requiring maintenance treatment to achieve part or total control. In a newly diagnosed person, and when confronted with the first treatment decision, asthma should be classified by severity (intermittent, chronic mild, moderate, or severe). As further classification of disease status depends both on the severity of the disease and the response to treatment, it is now recommended that the terms 'controlled', 'partly controlled', and 'uncontrolled' are used for people receiving treatment. Most guidelines about the management of asthma follow stepwise protocols. This review does not endorse or follow any particular protocol, but presents the evidence about specific interventions in no particular order. We assume that most adults will be taking as needed or regular use of short-acting beta$_2$ agonists for symptom relief, and in some cases long-acting beta$_2$ agonists. We have not excluded papers with combinations of any type of beta$_2$ agonists; however, the type of beta$_2$ agonist therapy should be the same in all arms to be included in the review.

**INCIDENCE/PREVALENCE** The reported prevalence of asthma has been increasing world-wide, but may have currently reached a plateau. About 10% of people have suffered an attack of asthma, but epidemiological studies have also found marked variations in prevalence between and within countries.

**AETIOLOGY/RISK FACTORS** Most people with asthma are atopic. Exposure to certain stimuli initiates inflammation and structural changes in airways causing airway hyper-responsiveness and variable airflow obstruction, which in turn cause most asthma symptoms. There are many such stimuli; the more important include environmental allergens, occupational sensitising agents, and respiratory viral infections.

**PROGNOSIS** In people with mild asthma, prognosis is good and progression to severe disease is rare. However, as a group, people with asthma lose lung function faster than those without asthma, although less quickly than people without asthma who smoke. People with chronic asthma can improve with treatment. However, some people (possibly up to 5%) have severe disease that responds poorly to treatment. These people are most at risk of morbidity and death from asthma.

Cecile Magis-Escurra and Monique H.E. Reijers

## KEY POINTS

- Bronchiectasis is characterised by irreversible widening of medium- to small-sized airways, with inflammation, chronic bacterial infection, and destruction of bronchial walls.

  Bronchiectasis is usually a complication of previous lower respiratory infection and/or inflammation, and causes chronic cough, production of copious sputum (often purulent), and recurrent infections. It may cause airway obstruction bearing some similarities with that seen in COPD.

  Bronchiectasis may complicate respiratory conditions such as asthma or COPD. It can be associated with primary ciliary dyskinesia, primary immunodeficiencies, certain systemic diseases such as inflammatory bowel disease and rheumatoid arthritis, and foreign body inhalation. Bronchiectasis can be due to cystic fibrosis (CF) but this is excluded from this review.

- Exercise or inspiratory muscle training may improve quality of life and exercise endurance in people with non-CF bronchiectasis.

- Prolonged-use antibiotics may reduce exacerbation rates and severity of symptoms (physician assessment of diary cards or of overall medical condition, sputum weight or volume).

  Prolonged-use antibiotics may also reduce some measures for infection (such as sputum bacterial density) compared with placebo, although this seems to vary depending on the antibiotic regimen used.

  We don't know whether prolonged-use antibiotics decrease mortality, hospital admission for exacerbations, and number of days off work compared with placebo. Inconsistent results have led to uncertainty on the effect of prolonged-use antibiotics on quality of life scores.

  Interpretation of studies concerning prolonged-use antibiotics and translation of results to individual patient care needs to be considered carefully. There may be a different pathogenesis for the condition and unknown co-existent use of other treatments, such as airway clearance techniques.

- We don't know whether airway clearance techniques, mucolytics, or inhaled hyperosmolar agents are beneficial, as we found few studies.

- We don't know whether inhaled corticosteroids are more effective than placebo at improving symptom scores at 6 months or at reducing exacerbations.

- Surgery is often considered for people with extreme damage to one or two lobes of the lung who are at risk of recurrent infection or bleeding, but we found no good-quality trials.

(i) **Please visit http://clinicalevidence.bmj.com for full text and references**

| What are the effects of treatments in people with non-cystic fibrosis (non-CF) bronchiectasis? | |
|---|---|
| Likely To Be Beneficial | • Exercise or physical training<br>• Prolonged-use antibiotics |
| Unknown Effectiveness | • Airway clearance techniques (tappotage, chest drainage, postural drainage, bronchopulmonary hygiene vibration, mucociliary clearance)<br><br>• Corticosteroids (inhaled)<br><br>• Hyperosmolar agents (inhaled) (mannitol, normal saline, hypertonic saline, saline with hyaluronic acid) |

- Mucolytics (bromhexine or recombinant human deoxyribonuclease [rhDNase])
- Surgery

**Search date January 2014**

**DEFINITION** Bronchiectasis is defined as irreversible widening of medium- to small-sized airways (bronchi) in the lung. It is characterised by inflammation, destruction of bronchial walls, and frequent colonisation with bacteria. The condition may be limited to a single lobe or lung segment, or it may affect one or both lungs more diffusely. Clinically, the condition manifests as chronic cough and chronic over-production of sputum, which is often purulent. People with severe bronchiectasis may have life-threatening haemoptysis, and may develop features of chronic obstructive airway disease, such as wheezing, chronic respiratory failure, pulmonary hypertension, and right-sided heart failure.

**INCIDENCE/PREVALENCE** We found few reliable data. Overall, over the past 50 years, incidence has declined. However, one study, using data from 640 GP practices in the UK, found that the incidence of people given a diagnosis of bronchiectasis increased over time (18 per 100,000 person-years at risk in 2004; 32 per 100,000 person-years at risk in 2011). Over an 8-year period, 0.7% of patients (27,258 people) had been given a diagnostic code for bronchiectasis, and prevalence increased over time. Prevalence is generally low in higher-income countries, but much higher in lower-income countries, where bronchiectasis is a major cause of morbidity and mortality.

**AETIOLOGY/RISK FACTORS** Bronchiectasis is most commonly a long-term complication of previous lower respiratory infections, such as pneumonia (especially with measles, *Bordetella pertussis*, and *Mycobacterium tuberculosis* complex). Foreign-body inhalation and allergic, autoimmune (for instance, associated with rheumatoid arthritis or ulcerative colitis), and chemical lung damage also predispose to the condition. Underlying congenital disorders such as cystic fibrosis, cilial dysmotility syndromes, alpha$_1$ antitrypsin deficiency, and congenital immunodeficiencies may also predispose to bronchiectasis, and may be of greater aetiological importance in higher-income countries than respiratory infection. Cystic fibrosis is the most common congenital cause (excluded from this review).

**PROGNOSIS** Bronchiectasis is a chronic condition, with frequent relapses of varying severity. Long-term prognosis is variable. Data on morbidity and mortality are still sparse. One study reported retrospective data exploring the factors influencing survival. It found lung function characteristics and chronic *Pseudomonas* infection may be associated with mortality. The more recently published FACED score and BSI index (published later than our search for this update) confirm these findings and provide a more detailed scoring system for morbidity and mortality. Bronchiectasis frequently co-exists with other respiratory disease, making it difficult to distinguish prognosis for bronchiectasis alone.

Robert A McIvor, Marcel Tunks, and David C Todd

## KEY POINTS

- The main risk factor for the development and deterioration of chronic obstructive pulmonary disease (COPD) is smoking.

- Inhaled anticholinergics and beta$_2$ agonists improve lung function and symptoms and reduce exacerbations in stable COPD compared with placebo.

   It is unclear whether inhaled anticholinergics or inhaled beta$_2$ agonists are the more consistently effective drug class in the treatment of COPD.

   Short-acting anticholinergics seem to be associated with a small improvement in quality of life compared with beta$_2$ agonists.

   Long-acting inhaled anticholinergics may improve lung function compared with long-acting beta$_2$ agonists.

   Combined treatment with inhaled anticholinergics plus beta$_2$ agonists may improve symptoms and lung function and reduce exacerbations compared with either treatment alone, although long-term effects are unknown.

- Inhaled corticosteroids reduce exacerbations in COPD and reduce decline in FEV$_1$, but the beneficial effects are small.

   Oral corticosteroids may improve short-term lung function, but have serious adverse effects.

   Combined inhaled corticosteroids plus long-acting beta$_2$ agonists improve lung function, symptoms, and health-related quality of life, and reduce exacerbations compared with placebo, and may be more effective than either treatment alone.

- Long-term domiciliary oxygen treatment may improve survival in people with severe daytime hypoxaemia.

- Theophylline may improve lung function compared with placebo, but adverse effects limit its usefulness in stable COPD.

- We don't know whether mucolytic drugs, prophylactic antibiotics, or alpha$_1$ antitrypsin improve outcomes in people with COPD compared with placebo.

- Combined psychosocial and pharmacological interventions for smoking cessation can slow the deterioration of lung function, but have not been shown to reduce long-term mortality compared with usual care.

- Multi-modality pulmonary rehabilitation can improve exercise capacity, dyspnoea, and health-related quality of life in people with stable COPD; general physical exercises and peripheral muscle training can improve exercise capacity; inspiratory muscle training may improve lung function and exercise capacity; but nutritional supplementation has not been shown to be beneficial.

(i) **Please visit http://clinicalevidence.bmj.com for full text and references**

| What are the effects of maintenance drug treatment in stable COPD? | |
|---|---|
| **Beneficial** | • Anticholinergics (inhaled anticholinergics reduce exacerbation rate, and improve symptoms and FEV$_1$ compared with placebo) |
| | • Anticholinergics plus beta$_2$ agonists (inhaled anticholinergics plus beta$_2$ agonists improve FEV$_1$ compared with either drug alone) |
| | • Beta$_2$ agonists (inhaled beta$_2$ agonists reduce exacerbation rate compared with placebo) |

| | |
|---|---|
| | • Corticosteroids (inhaled corticosteroids reduce exacerbation rate compared with placebo) |
| | • Corticosteroids plus long-acting beta$_2$ agonists (inhaled combination reduces exacerbation rate, and improves symptoms, quality of life, and FEV$_1$ compared with placebo) |
| Likely To Be Beneficial | • Oxygen (long-term domiciliary treatment effective in people with severe hypoxaemia) |
| Trade-off Between Benefits And Harms | • Theophylline |
| Unknown Effectiveness | • Alpha$_1$ antitrypsin <br> • Antibiotics (prophylactic) <br> • Anticholinergics versus beta$_2$ agonists (both treatments effective; unclear if one consistently more effective than the other) <br> • Mucolytics |
| Unlikely To Be Beneficial | • Corticosteroids (oral; evidence of harm but no evidence of long-term benefits) |

## What are the effects of smoking cessation interventions in people with stable COPD?

| | |
|---|---|
| Beneficial | • Psychosocial plus pharmacological interventions for smoking cessation |
| Unknown Effectiveness | • Pharmacological interventions alone for smoking cessation <br> • Psychosocial interventions alone for smoking cessation |

## What are the effects of non-drug interventions in people with stable COPD?

| | |
|---|---|
| Beneficial | • Pulmonary rehabilitation |
| Likely To Be Beneficial | • General physical activity <br> • Inspiratory muscle training <br> • Peripheral muscle training |
| Unlikely To Be Beneficial | • Nutritional supplementation |

**Search date April 2010**

**DEFINITION** Chronic obstructive pulmonary disease (COPD) is a disease state characterised by airflow limitation that is not fully reversible. The airflow limitation is usually progressive

*(continued over)*

*(from previous page)*

and associated with an abnormal inflammatory response of the lungs to noxious particles or gases. Classically, it is thought to be a combination of emphysema and chronic bronchitis, although only one of these may be present in some people with COPD. Emphysema is abnormal permanent enlargement of the air spaces distal to the terminal bronchioles, accompanied by destruction of their walls, and without obvious fibrosis. Chronic bronchitis is chronic cough or mucous production for at least 3 months in at least 2 successive years when other causes of chronic cough have been excluded.

**INCIDENCE/PREVALENCE** COPD mainly affects middle-aged and older people. In 1998, the WHO estimated that COPD was the fifth most common cause of death worldwide, responsible for 4.8% of all mortality (estimated 2,745,816 deaths in 2002), and morbidity is increasing. Estimated prevalence in the USA rose by 41% between 1982 and 1994, and age-adjusted death rates rose by 71% between 1966 and 1985. All-cause age-adjusted mortality declined over the same period by 22% and mortality from cardiovascular diseases by 45%. In the UK, physician-diagnosed prevalence was 2% in men and 1% in women between 1990 and 1997.

**AETIOLOGY/RISK FACTORS** COPD is largely preventable. The main cause in developed countries is exposure to tobacco smoke. In developed countries, 85% to 90% of people with COPD have smoked at some point. The disease is rare in lifelong non-smokers (estimated prevalence 5% in 3 large representative US surveys of non-smokers from 1971–1984), in whom "passive" exposure to environmental tobacco smoke has been proposed as a cause. Other proposed causes include bronchial hyper-responsiveness, indoor and outdoor air pollution, and allergy.

**PROGNOSIS** Airway obstruction is usually progressive in those who continue to smoke, resulting in early disability and shortened survival. Smoking cessation reverts the rate of decline in lung function to that of non-smokers. Many people will need medication for the rest of their lives, with increased doses and additional drugs during exacerbations.

Alan J Neville, Mridula Sara Kuruvilla

## KEY POINTS

- Lung cancer is the leading cause of cancer deaths in both men and women, with 80% to 90% of cases caused by smoking.

  Small cell lung cancer accounts for 20% of all cases, and is usually treated with chemotherapy. Adenocarcinoma is the main non-small cell pathology, and is treated initially with surgery.

- Postoperative adjuvant chemotherapy improves survival compared with surgery alone in people with resectable non-small cell lung cancer.

  Cisplatin regimens or uracil plus tegafur regimens have been shown to improve survival when given postoperatively, but to increase toxicity.

- We don't know whether preoperative chemotherapy improves survival in people with resectable non-small cell lung cancer.

- First-line platinum-based regimens improve survival in people with unresectable non-small cell lung cancer compared with older, non-platinum agents, but we don't know whether platinum-based chemotherapy is more effective than non-platinum third-generation chemotherapeutic agents.

- Adding chemotherapy to thoracic irradiation may improve survival at 2 to 5 years in people with unresectable non-small cell lung cancer compared with thoracic irradiation alone, but increases adverse effects.

- We don't know how continuous hyperfractionated accelerated radiotherapy (CHART) compares with conventional radiotherapy in unresectable non-small cell lung cancer. Non-CHART hyperfractionated radiotherapy has not been shown to increase survival compared with standard radiotherapy.

- Targeted therapy with gefitinib or erlotinib does not increase survival when used as first-line palliative therapy in people with unresectable non-small cell lung cancer. We don't know whether it is beneficial as second-line therapy.

- Adding thoracic irradiation to chemotherapy improves survival in people with limited-stage small cell lung cancer, but may increase complications.

- We don't know whether intensifying the chemotherapy dose increases survival in small cell lung cancer, and it may increase treatment-related toxicity.

- Prophylactic cranial irradiation may improve survival in people in remission from small cell lung cancer.

(i) **Please visit http://clinicalevidence.bmj.com for full text and references**

## What are the effects of treatments for resectable non-small cell lung cancer?

| Likely To Be Beneficial | • Postoperative chemotherapy (cisplatin-based or uracil plus tegafur-based regimens) in resected stage 1 to 3 non-small cell lung cancer |
| --- | --- |
| Trade-off Between Benefits And Harms | • Preoperative chemotherapy in resectable non-small cell lung cancer |

## What are the effects of treatments for unresectable non-small cell lung cancer?

| Beneficial | • Thoracic irradiation plus chemotherapy in unresectable non-small cell lung cancer (reduces mortality compared with thoracic irradiation alone) |
|---|---|
| Trade-off Between Benefits And Harms | • First-line platinum-based chemotherapy in unresectable non-small cell lung cancer (reduces mortality compared with non-platinum-based regimens but with increased adverse effects) |
| Unknown Effectiveness | • Continuous hyperfractionated accelerated radiotherapy (CHART) in unresectable non-small cell lung cancer<br><br>• Second-line molecular-targeted therapy with gefitinib or erlotinib in unresectable non-small cell lung cancer<br><br>• Single-agent second-line chemotherapy regimens versus each other in unresectable non-small cell lung cancer |
| Unlikely To Be Beneficial | • First-line molecular-targeted therapy with gefitinib or erlotinib for unresectable advanced non-small cell lung cancer (no better at reducing mortality than chemotherapy alone and more adverse effects)<br><br>• Hyperfractionated radiotherapy excluding continuous hyperfractionated accelerated radiotherapy (CHART) in unresectable stage 3 non-small cell lung cancer (no better at reducing mortality than standard radiotherapy and more adverse effects) |

## What are the effects of treatments for small cell lung cancer?

| Beneficial | • Prophylactic cranial irradiation in people in complete remission from limited- or extensive-stage small cell lung cancer<br><br>• Thoracic irradiation plus chemotherapy in limited-stage small cell lung cancer (improves survival compared with chemotherapy alone) |
|---|---|
| Unknown Effectiveness | • Dose intensification of chemotherapy versus standard chemotherapy in limited-stage small cell lung cancer |

**Search date October 2009**

**DEFINITION** Lung cancer (bronchogenic carcinoma) is an epithelial cancer arising from the bronchial surface epithelium or bronchial mucous glands. It is broadly divided into small cell (about 20% of all lung cancers) and non-small cell lung cancer (about 80% of all lung cancers, of which adenocarcinoma is the most prevalent form).

**INCIDENCE/PREVALENCE** Lung cancer is the leading cause of cancer deaths in both men and women, annually affecting about 100,000 men and 80,000 women in the USA, and about 40,000 men and women in the UK.

**AETIOLOGY/RISK FACTORS** Smoking remains the major preventable risk factor, accounting for about 80% to 90% of all cases. Other respiratory tract carcinogens have been identified that may enhance the carcinogenic effects of tobacco smoke, either in the workplace (e.g., asbestos and polycyclic aromatic hydrocarbons) or in the home (e.g., indoor radon).

**PROGNOSIS** At the time of diagnosis, 10% to 15% of people with lung cancer have localised disease. Of these, half will die within 5 years despite potentially curative surgery. A similar number have locally advanced disease, and over half of people have metastatic disease at the time of diagnosis. Surgery is the treatment of choice in people with stages 1 and 2 non-small cell lung cancer, unless they are not well enough to have surgery. People with stage 1A disease have an excellent overall survival with surgery alone. Complete resection of the cancer with or without chemotherapy and radiotherapy may be performed in some people with locally advanced stage 3 disease, but in others the disease is inoperable, and their prognosis is poorer. People with inoperable stage 3 or metastatic disease can be offered palliative chemotherapy. Chemotherapy is the mainstay of treatment in the 20% of people with small cell lung cancer, which has a high risk of metastases. About 5% to 10% of people with small cell lung cancer present with central nervous system involvement, and half develop symptomatic brain metastases within 2 years. Of these, only half respond to palliative radiotherapy, and their median survival is less than 3 months.

# Chlamydia (uncomplicated, genital)

Megan Crofts and Paddy Horner

## KEY POINTS

- Genital chlamydia is caused by *Chlamydia trachomatis* (serotypes D-K), an obligate intracellular organism that is sexually transmitted. It infects the urethra and rectum in men and women, as well as the endocervix in women. It is defined as uncomplicated if it has not ascended to the upper genital tract or caused sexually acquired reactive arthritis.

    It is the most common bacterial sexually transmitted infection in developed countries. Over 200,000 chlamydia diagnoses were made in the UK in 2013, with almost 70% of cases detected in young adults under the age of 25 years.

    Infection is usually asymptomatic, particularly in women. Most people infected do not present for testing or treatment. Therefore, population rates based on routine surveillance data underestimate the true disease burden. The highest positivity rates are seen in sexually active 15- to 24-year-olds, with rates of 10% being observed.

    If untreated, chlamydial infection may persist or resolve spontaneously, with the average duration of infection in women being 1.36 years.

    If untreated, *Chlamydia* infection in women causes pelvic inflammatory disease (PID) in approximately 16% of women. This may result in infertility, ectopic pregnancy, or chronic pelvic pain.

    Partner notification and treatment is an important part of effective management.

    Young adults who test positive for chlamydia are at greater risk of re-testing positive within the next year. Repeated chlamydial infections have been shown to increase the risk of PID and its associated complications. Therefore, the National Chlamydia Screening Programme (NCSP) in England now recommends repeat testing at 3 months for positive individuals.

- Multiple-dose regimens of tetracyclines (doxycycline or tetracycline) achieve microbiological cure in at least 95% of men and non-pregnant women with genital chlamydia.

    Erythromycin also seems beneficial as a multiple-dose regimen, but we don't know which regimen of erythromycin is more effective.

    Ciprofloxacin may be less effective at leading to microbiological cure compared with multiple-dose doxycycline. There were also a greater number of adverse effects with multiple-dose ciprofloxacin, most commonly gastrointestinal side effects.

    We don't know whether multiple-dose regimens of other antibiotics (such as other macrolides, quinolones, and penicillins) are effective, as we found few adequate studies.

- In men and non-pregnant women with uncomplicated genital chlamydia, one single dose of azithromycin seems as beneficial as a 7-day course of doxycycline and produces similar rates of adverse effects.

    Single-dose treatments have the obvious advantage of improving adherence.

    Treatment cure rates of over 95% have been reported. However, two recent randomised controlled treatment trials in men with urethritis suggest it may not be as effective in symptomatic men.

- In pregnant women, multiple-dose regimens of erythromycin or amoxicillin seem effective in treating chlamydial infection.

    One small study has also suggested that clindamycin and multiple-dose erythromycin are equally effective at curing infection, although the size of the study makes it hard to draw definitive conclusions.

- Single-dose azithromycin may be effective in treating chlamydia in pregnant women.

- In pregnant women, no antibiotic regimen has a microbiological cure rate of over 95%, and pregnant women should be offered a test of cure no sooner than 5 weeks after treatment was initiated to ensure that the infection has cleared.

(i) Please visit http://clinicalevidence.bmj.com for full text and references

## What are the effects of antibiotic treatment for men and non-pregnant women with uncomplicated genital chlamydial infection?

| Beneficial | • Azithromycin (single dose) for men and non-pregnant women (as effective as multiple-dose antibiotics)<br><br>• Doxycycline or tetracycline (multiple-dose regimens) |
| --- | --- |
| Likely To Be Beneficial | • Erythromycin (multiple-dose regimens) for men and non-pregnant women |
| Unknown Effectiveness | • Antibiotics (multiple-dose regimens) other than tetracycline, doxycycline, ciprofloxacin, or erythromycin for men and non-pregnant women |
| Unlikely To Be Beneficial | • Ciprofloxacin (multiple-dose regimens) for men and non-pregnant women |

## What are the effects of antibiotic treatment for pregnant women with uncomplicated genital chlamydial infection?

| Likely To Be Beneficial | • Azithromycin (single dose) for pregnant women (higher microbiological cure rate than multiple-dose erythromycin, with fewer gastrointestinal adverse effects)<br><br>• Erythromycin or amoxicillin (multiple-dose regimens) for pregnant women (more effective than placebo, but less effective than single-dose azithromycin) |
| --- | --- |
| Unknown Effectiveness | • Clindamycin (multiple-dose regimens) for pregnant women |

Search date February 2014

**DEFINITION** Genital chlamydia (*Chlamydia trachomatis* serotypes D-K) is a sexually transmitted infection (STI) that infects the urethra and rectum in men and women, as well as the endocervix in women. It can also infect other mucosal surfaces, including conjunctiva and nasopharynx. It is defined as an **uncomplicated** genital infection if it has not ascended to the upper genital tract or has not caused sexually acquired reactive arthritis. Infection in women is asymptomatic in the majority of cases but may cause non-specific symptoms,

*(continued over)*

*(from previous page)*

including vaginal discharge and intermenstrual and post-coital bleeding. Infection in men causes urethral discharge and urethral irritation or dysuria, but may also be asymptomatic in up to 50% of cases. **Complicated** chlamydial infection includes spread to the upper genital tract (causing pelvic inflammatory disease [PID] in women [see review on PID, p 539] and epididymo-orchitis in men), or development of sexually acquired reactive arthritis. Lymphogranuloma venereum (LGV) caused by *C trachomatis* serovars L1-3 (predominantly serovar L2) has also emerged as an important genital tract pathogen in men who have sex with men. In most cases, men infected with LGV present with symptomatic rectal disease. Interventions for complicated chlamydial infection (including LGV) are not included in this review.

**INCIDENCE/PREVALENCE** Genital chlamydia is the most common bacterial STI in developed countries. In 2013, more than 200,000 cases of chlamydia were reported to Public Health England. Infection is most common in people under 25 years of age, with rates decreasing thereafter. In 15- to 24-year-olds, the chlamydia diagnosis rate was more than 2000 per 100,000 population in 2013, as a result of the National Chlamydia Screening Programme (NCSP). Testing coverage in the NCSP in 2013 was 25% across England.

**AETIOLOGY/RISK FACTORS** Infection is caused by the bacterium *C trachomatis* serotypes D-K. It is transmitted primarily through sexual intercourse, but also perinatally and through direct or indirect oculogenital transfer. Risk factors include age under 25 years, new partner or more than one partner in the past year, and failure to use condoms correctly.

**PROGNOSIS** In women, untreated chlamydial infection can ascend to the upper genital tract, causing PID in approximately 16% of women (see review on PID, p 539). Tubal infertility has been found to occur in about 18% of women after a single episode of PID, and the risk of ectopic pregnancy is increased six- to sevenfold. Ascending infection in men causes epididymitis, and there is mounting evidence that acute chlamydia infection is possibly associated with male infertility by direct effect on sperm production and maturation. Mother-to-infant transmission can lead to neonatal conjunctivitis and pneumonitis. Chlamydia may coexist with other genital infections, and may facilitate transmission of HIV infection. A recent modelling study, combining all the evidence on duration of infection in women, concluded that the mean duration of infection was 1.36 years, with nearly a quarter testing negative, as a result of clearance of 'passive' infection within a few weeks of testing positive, despite not being treated. There is limited evidence regarding the duration of infection in men, although it is assumed to be similar in those who are asymptomatic. Men and women who are chlamydia-positive are at high risk of retesting positive after treatment. Therefore, the NCSP in England now recommends repeat testing at 3 months for positive individuals. Although the assumption that positive tests for chlamydia after treatment are always due to re-infection, cure rates of less than 95% have been observed in prospective studies where repeat infection is unlikely, particularly with azithromycin 1 gram. A large partner-treatment RCT found an 8% (95% CI 5% to 11%) failure rate in 289 women who had been sexually inactive 3 to 20 weeks after treatment. A subset analysis of men enrolled in an RCT and who had tested positive for chlamydia found a positive-retest rate of 37% (25/68) in chlamydia-positive men with urethritis at a median of 43 days after treatment. Interestingly, the proportion of men who tested positive for chlamydia at re-screening yet denied sexual exposure was 36% (9/25). The authors of the study concluded that this higher than expected rate of positive re-screening tests could have been the result of inaccurate reporting by the index patient or treatment failure. *C trachomatis* resistance to antibiotics seems to be rare. However, due to technical difficulties, limited studies have been undertaken *in vivo*. At high multiplicities of infection (load), in-vitro persistence to antimicrobials (heterotypic resistance) can often be demonstrated. It has been proposed that people with high organism loads, which are associated with symptomatic infection and younger age, may be at increased risk of treatment failure. All antibiotics seem to have lower efficacy in pregnant women, with no antibiotic regimen having a microbiological cure rate of over 95%. In pregnant women, a repeat test is recommended no sooner than 5 weeks after treatment, to ensure that the infection has cleared. Partner notification and treatment is an important part of effective management (see our review on Partner notification, p 536). Innovative and effective partner treatment strategies have been associated with lower rates of re-infection.

# Genital herpes: oral antiviral treatments

Lisa M. Hollier and Catherine Eppes

## KEY POINTS

- Genital herpes is an infection with herpes simplex virus type 1 (HSV-1) or type 2 (HSV-2). The typical clinical features include painful, shallow anogenital ulceration.

  It is among the most common sexually transmitted diseases, with up to 23% of adults in the UK and US having antibodies to HSV-2.

- Genital herpes, like other genital ulcer diseases, is a significant risk factor for acquiring HIV for both men and women. People with HIV can have severe herpes outbreaks, and this may help facilitate transmission of both herpes and HIV infections to others.

- Oral antiviral treatment of a first episode of genital herpes can decrease symptoms in HIV-negative people.

  Data from one RCT indicated that oral valaciclovir and oral aciclovir were equally effective in treating a first episode of genital herpes in HIV-negative people.

  We found no RCTs of sufficient quality comparing either oral valaciclovir or oral aciclovir with oral famciclovir in treating a first episode of genital herpes in HIV-negative people.

- Daily oral antiviral treatment seems to be effective in preventing recurrence of genital herpes in HIV-positive people.

  Data from one RCT indicated that daily oral valaciclovir and daily oral aciclovir seemed equally effective in preventing recurrence of genital herpes in HIV-positive people.

  We found no RCTs of sufficient quality comparing either oral valaciclovir or oral aciclovir with oral famciclovir in preventing recurrence of genital herpes in HIV-positive people.

- We found no RCTs of sufficient quality to assess whether one oral antiviral is more effective than another in treating first episodes of genital herpes in HIV-positive people.

(i) **Please visit http://clinicalevidence.bmj.com for full text and references**

| What are the effects of different oral antiviral treatments versus each other for a first episode of genital herpes in HIV-negative people? | |
|---|---|
| Unknown Effectiveness | • Oral antiviral treatments (aciclovir, valaciclovir, famciclovir) versus each other for treatment of a first episode of genital herpes in HIV-negative people (oral valaciclovir and oral acyclovir are equally effective in treating a first episode of genital herpes in HIV-negative people) |

| What are the effects of different oral antiviral treatments for genital herpes in HIV-positive people? | |
|---|---|
| Beneficial | • Daily oral antiviral treatment (aciclovir, valaciclovir, famciclovir) for preventing recurrence of genital herpes in HIV-positive people |
| Unknown Effectiveness | • Oral antiviral treatments (aciclovir, famciclovir, valaciclovir) versus each other for first episodes of genital herpes in HIV-positive people |

**Search date October 2013**

**DEFINITION** Genital herpes is an infection with herpes simplex virus type 1 (HSV-1) or type 2 (HSV-2). The typical clinical features include painful, shallow anogenital ulceration. HSV infections can be confirmed on the basis of virological (e.g., polymerase chain reaction) and serological findings. Using these findings, infections can be categorised as: **primary infection**, which is defined as HSV confirmed in a person without HSV-1 or HSV-2 antibodies; **first episode non-primary infection**, which is defined as detection of one viral type in an individual with serological evidence of past infection with the other viral type; and **recurrent genital herpes**, which is characterised by reactivation of latent HSV-1 or HSV-2 in the presence of antibodies of the same serotype. HSV-1 can also cause gingivostomatitis and orolabial ulcers. HSV-2 can also cause other types of herpes infection, such as ocular herpes. Both virus types can cause infection of the central nervous system (e.g., encephalitis). Genital herpes can be diagnosed using various methods (e.g., clinical diagnosis, culture or PCR of lesions, or serological testing). Clinical diagnosis alone has been shown to be both insensitive and non-specific, therefore, guidelines recommend that evaluation for genital, anal, or perianal ulcers include syphilis serology and darkfield examination, culture for HSV or PCR testing for HSV, and serological testing for type-specific HSV antibody.

**INCIDENCE/PREVALENCE** Genital herpes infections are among the most common sexually transmitted diseases. Seroprevalence studies showed that 17% of adults in the US, 9% of adults in Poland, and 12% of adults in Australia had HSV-2 antibodies. The studies carried out in Poland and Australia also showed higher seroprevalence in women than in men (HSV-2 seroprevalence in Poland: 10% for women v 9% for men; P = 0.06; HSV-2 seroprevalence in Australia: 16% for women v 9% for men; RR 1.81, 95% CI 1.52 to 2.14). A UK study found that 23% of adults attending sexual health clinics, and 8% of blood donors in London, had antibodies to HSV-2. On the basis of seroprevalence studies, the total number of people who were newly infected with HSV-2 in 2003 has been estimated at 23.6 million, and the total number of people aged 15 to 49 years who were living with HSV-2 infection worldwide in 2003 has been estimated at 536 million.

**AETIOLOGY/RISK FACTORS** Both HSV-1 and HSV-2 can cause genital infection, but HSV-2 is associated with a higher frequency of recurrences. Most individuals with genital HSV infection have only mild symptoms and remain unaware that they have genital herpes. However, these people can still transmit the infection to sexual partners and newborns.

**PROGNOSIS** Sequelae of HSV infection include neonatal HSV infection, opportunistic infection in immunocompromised people, recurrent genital ulceration, and psychosocial morbidity. HSV-2 infection is associated with an increased risk of HIV transmission and acquisition. In a large meta-analysis of longitudinal studies in which the relative timing of HSV-2 infection and HIV infection could be established, HSV-2 seropositivity was a significant risk factor for HIV acquisition in general population studies of men (summary adjusted RR 2.7, 95% CI 1.9 to 3.9), women (RR 3.1, 95% CI 1.7 to 5.6), and men who had sex with men (RR 1.7, 95% CI 1.2 to 2.4). Aciclovir suppressive therapy did not seem to reduce the rate of HIV infection in two RCTs that assessed this question. The first RCT (821 HIV-negative, HSV-2-seropositive women) found no significant difference between aciclovir (400 mg twice-daily) and placebo in the incidence of HIV infection (incidence of HIV infection: 4.4 per 100 person-years with aciclovir v 4.1 per 100 person-years with placebo; RR 1.08, 95% CI 0.64 to 1.83). The second RCT (3172 HIV-negative, HSV-2-seropositive people) also found no significant difference between aciclovir (400 mg twice-daily) and placebo in the incidence of HIV infection (3.9 per 100 person-years with aciclovir v 3.3 per 100 person-years with placebo; HR 1.16, 95% CI 0.83 to 1.62). Among the sequelae of HSV infection, the most common neurological complications are aseptic meningitis (reported in about 25% of women during primary infection) and urinary retention (reported in up to 15% of women during primary infection). The absolute risk of neonatal infection is high (41%, 95% CI 26% to 56%) in babies born to women who acquire infection near the time of delivery, and low (<3%) in women with established infection, even in those who have a recurrence at delivery. About 15% of neonatal infections result from postnatal transmission from oral lesions of relatives or hospital personnel.

Sarah Creighton

## KEY POINTS

- Gonorrhoea is caused by infection with *Neisseria gonorrhoeae*. In men, uncomplicated urethritis is the most common manifestation; while in women, less than half of cases produce symptoms (such as vaginal discharge and dyspareunia).

    Rates of diagnosed gonorrhoea infection in the UK rose by more than 70% between 2008 and 2012. This may be, in part, explained by improved diagnostic techniques.

    In 2012, the diagnosis rates for gonorrhoea among adults aged 20 to 24 years in the UK were 249 per 100,000 for men and 140 per 100,000 for women.

    Rates are highest in adults aged 20 to 24 years.

    Resistance to single-dose antimicrobials develops frequently, and antimicrobial sensitivity of gonococcal isolates is monitored nationally to monitor and inform prescribing guidelines.

    Co-infection with *Chlamydia trachomatis* is reported in 10% to 40% of people with gonorrhoea in the US and UK.

- Single-dose antibiotic regimens have achieved cure rates of 95% and higher in men and non-pregnant women with urogenital or rectal gonorrhoea, although we don't know how different single-dose antibiotic regimens compare with each other.

    Single-dose antibiotics are also effective for curing gonorrhoea in pregnant women.

- In people with disseminated gonococcal infection, there is consensus that multiple-dose regimens using cephalosporins or fluoroquinolones (when the infecting organism is known to be susceptible) are the most effective treatments, although evidence supporting this is somewhat sparse.

- We found insufficient evidence to judge the best treatment for people with both gonorrhoea and chlamydia, although theory, expert opinion, and clinical experience suggest that a combination of antimicrobials active against both *N gonorrhoeae* and *C trachomatis* is effective.

 **Please visit http://clinicalevidence.bmj.com for full text and references**

| What are the effects of treatments for uncomplicated infections in men and non-pregnant women? | |
| --- | --- |
| Likely To Be Beneficial | • Single-dose antibiotic regimens in men and non-pregnant women† |

| What are the effects of treatments for uncomplicated infections in pregnant women? | |
| --- | --- |
| Likely To Be Beneficial | • Single-dose antibiotic regimens in pregnant women† |

| What are the effects of treatments for disseminated gonococcal infection? | |
| --- | --- |
| Likely To Be Beneficial | • Multi-dose antibiotic regimens for disseminated gonorrhoea* |

<table>
<tr><td colspan="2">What are the effects of dual treatment for gonorrhoea and chlamydia infection?</td></tr>
<tr><td>Likely To Be Beneficial</td><td>● Dual antibiotic treatment for gonorrhoea and chlamydia*</td></tr>
</table>

**Search date September 2013**

† Based on results in individual arms of RCTs and observational studies.
* Based on non-RCT evidence and consensus.

**DEFINITION** Gonorrhoea is caused by infection with *Neisseria gonorrhoeae*. In men, uncomplicated urethritis is the most common manifestation, with dysuria and urethral discharge. Less typically, signs and symptoms are mild and indistinguishable from those of chlamydial urethritis. In women, the most common site of infection is the uterine cervix, infection of which results in symptoms (such as vaginal discharge, lower abdominal discomfort, and dyspareunia) in less than half of cases. **Diagnosis:** Advances in nucleic acid amplification techniques (NAAT) allow testing on non-invasively collected specimens (urine and self-taken vaginal swabs). NAAT may have sensitivity of >90%, compared with 75% sensitivity of culture. However, NAAT cannot provide data on antimicrobial sensitivity, so culture and sensitivity testing are required before commencement of antimicrobial therapy. In addition, the specificity of NAAT ranges from 98.1% to 99.7% and caution is required when interpreting positive results. NAAT is also used off licence to test pharyngeal and genital sites. The sensitivity of NAAT in extragenital diagnosis is considerably greater than culture, but the specificity of extragenital NAAT is such that all reactive results need to be confirmed using a separate platform. **Resistance:** Resistance to single-dose antimicrobials develops frequently and antimicrobial sensitivity of gonococcal isolates is monitored nationally to monitor and inform prescribing guidelines. Clinicians need to be aware of their local resistance profile and the resistance profiles of individual isolates to make appropriate treatment choices. All infected individuals should have a test of cure 2 weeks after treatment to ensure complete eradication of the organism. All sexual partners of infected individuals should be identified and treated concurrently (see review on Partner notification, p 536). The index patient should be advised to refrain from sexual intercourse with any untreated partner. **Co-infection:** *Chlamydia trachomatis* infection co-exists in 10% to 41% of adults with gonorrhoea. Treatment for potential co-existent chlamydia is advised whenever treating gonorrhoea.

**INCIDENCE/PREVALENCE** In UK genitourinary medicine clinics, after a downward trajectory between 2002 and 2008, the number of diagnosed gonorrhoea infections rose by 70% between 2008 and 2012. This apparent rise in infection may be, in part, due to increased testing since the introduction of NAAT. In 2012, the incidence of gonorrhoea in the UK was 48 per 100,000. The highest prevalence was seen in adults age 20 to 24 years, at 249 per 100,000 in men and 141 per 100,000 in women. In the UK, infection is over-represented in specific populations (men who have sex with men [MSM] and black Caribbean people), mainly in urban areas.

**AETIOLOGY/RISK FACTORS** Most gonococcal infections result from penile-vaginal, penile-rectal, or penile-pharyngeal contact. An important minority of infections are transmitted from mother to child during birth, which can cause a sight-threatening purulent conjunctivitis (ophthalmia neonatorum).

**PROGNOSIS** The natural history of untreated gonococcal infection is spontaneous resolution and microbiological clearance after weeks or months of unpleasant symptoms. During this time, there is a substantial likelihood of transmission to others and of complications developing in the infected individual. In many women, the lack of readily discernible signs or symptoms of cervicitis means that infections go unrecognised and untreated. An unknown proportion of untreated infections causes local complications, including lymphangitis, periurethral abscess, bartholinitis, and urethral stricture; epididymitis in men; and, in women, involvement of the uterus, fallopian tubes, or ovaries causing pelvic inflammatory disease (see review on Pelvic inflammatory disease, p 539). One review found that *N gonorrhoeae* was cultured from 8% to 32% of women with acute pelvic inflammatory disease in 11 European studies and from 27% to 80% of women in eight US studies. The proportion of *N gonorrhoeae* infections in women that lead to pelvic inflammatory disease has not been well studied. However, one study of 26 women exposed to men with gonorrhoea found that 19 women were culture-positive and, of these, five women had pelvic inflammatory disease and another four had uterine adnexal tenderness. Pelvic inflammatory disease may lead to infertility (see review on Pelvic inflammatory disease, p 539). In some people, localised gonococcal infection may disseminate. A US study estimated the risk of dissemination to be 0.6% to 1.1% among women, whereas a European study estimated it to be 2.3% to 3.0%. The same European study found a lower risk in men, estimated to be 0.4% to 0.7%. When gonococci disseminate, they cause petechial or pustular skin lesions; asymmetrical arthropathies, tenosynovitis, or septic arthritis; and, rarely, meningitis or endocarditis.

# Partner notification

Catherine Mathews and Nicol Coetzee

## KEY POINTS

- Many people diagnosed with an STD do not have symptoms, and may not inform their past or current sexual partners of their diagnosis or routinely use condoms.

- Several strategies have been used to notify and treat partners of people diagnosed with STDs, but only a limited number of RCTs of their effectiveness have been undertaken.

- Patient referral is where the index patient is encouraged to inform their past and present partners.

- Provider referral is where health professionals notify the partner without disclosing the identity of the index patient, and outreach assistance is where members of an outreach team indigenous to the community notify the partner without disclosing the identity of the index patient.

- Contract referral is where the index patient is encouraged to notify their partners, but the health professional does so if they fail to attend for treatment within an allotted time.

- Various methods are used to improve patient referral, including: patient-delivered partner therapy; home sampling kits; information, education, reminders, and counselling for the index patient; and the use of different healthcare professionals.

- Contract referral may lead to more partners of people with HIV infection being notified compared with patient referral alone.

  We don't know whether provider referral or outreach assistance are beneficial in tracing partners of people with HIV.

- Contract referral may increase the proportion of partners presenting for treatment compared with patient referral in people with gonorrhoea.

  We don't know whether either provider referral or outreach assistance are effective partner notification strategies in people with gonorrhoea.

- Provider referral may increase the proportion of partners treated compared with patient referral in people with chlamydia.

  We don't know whether either contract referral or outreach assistance are effective partner notification strategies in people with chlamydia.

- Contract referral strategies seem to be as effective as provider referral in people with syphilis, with similar proportions of partners of people with syphilis being notified with each strategy.

  We don't know whether either patient referral or outreach assistance are effective partner notification strategies in people with syphilis.

- Supplementing patient referral with patient-delivered partner therapy may reduce the risk of persistent or recurrent infection in index patients with chlamydia or gonorrhoea.

  Supplementing patient referral with patient-delivered partner therapy seems to improve the proportion of partners elicited who received treatment compared with supplementation with written information for partners in people with chlamydia or gonorrhoea infections.

- In people with chlamydia, home-sampling kits for partners seem to increase the number of partners who are tested for infection compared with simple patient referral.

- We don't know whether supplementing patient referral with health education or counselling, either alone or in combination, for index patients improves the number of partners tested or treated.

- We don't know whether adding telephone reminders plus counselling, reminders for the index patient, or information pamphlets to patient referral improves partner notification rates, or whether different health professionals are more effective at improving patient referral rates.

 **Please visit http://clinicalevidence.bmj.com for full text and references**

## What are the effects of partner notification strategies in people with different STDs?

| Likely To Be Beneficial | • Contract referral in people with HIV infection (improves partner notification rates compared with patient referral)<br><br>• Contract referral in people with gonorrhoea (increases number of partners presenting for assessment compared with patient referral)<br><br>• Provider referral in people with chlamydia (increases proportion of partners treated compared with patient referral in people with non-gonococcal urethritis [mainly chlamydia]) |
|---|---|
| Unknown Effectiveness | • Contract referral in people with chlamydia<br><br>• Contract referral in people with syphilis (seems to be as effective as provider referral)<br><br>• Outreach assistance in people with HIV (insufficient evidence to assess effectiveness compared with patient referral)<br><br>• Outreach assistance in people with chlamydia<br><br>• Outreach assistance in people with gonorrhoea<br><br>• Outreach assistance in people with syphilis<br><br>• Patient referral in people with syphilis<br><br>• Provider referral in HIV<br><br>• Provider referral in people with gonorrhoea |

## What are the effects of interventions to improve the effectiveness of partner notification by patient referral in people with different STDs?

| Likely To Be Beneficial | • Patient-delivered partner therapy (reduces risk of recurrent or persistent infection in index patients compared with patient referral alone) |
|---|---|
| Unknown Effectiveness | • Adding telephone reminders to counselling<br><br>• Counselling<br><br>• Health education<br><br>• Health education plus counselling<br><br>• Home-sampling kit for partners<br><br>• Information pamphlets<br><br>• Patient referral by different types of healthcare professional |

| • Reminders (any format) alone |

**Search date August 2008**

**DEFINITION** Partner notification is a process whereby the sexual partners of people with a diagnosis of STDs are informed of their exposure to infection. The main methods are patient referral, provider referral, contract referral, and outreach assistance.

**INCIDENCE/PREVALENCE** A large proportion of people with an STD will have neither symptoms nor signs of infection. For example, 22% to 68% of men with gonorrhoea who were identified through partner notification were asymptomatic. Partner notification is one of the two strategies to reach such individuals, the other strategy being screening. Managing infection in people with more than one current sexual partner is likely to have the greatest impact on the spread of STDs.

**PROGNOSIS** We found no studies showing that partner notification results in a health benefit, either to the partner or to future partners of infected people. Obtaining such evidence would be technically and ethically difficult. One RCT in asymptomatic women compared identifying, testing, and treating women at increased risk for cervical chlamydia infection versus usual care (women saw healthcare providers as necessary). It found that this strategy reduced incidence of pelvic inflammatory disease compared with usual care (RR 0.44, 95% CI 0.20 to 0.90). This evidence suggests that partner notification, which also aims to identify and treat people who are largely unaware of infection, would provide a direct health benefit to partners who are infected.

Jonathan Ross

## KEY POINTS

- Pelvic inflammatory disease (PID) is caused by infection of the upper female genital tract, and is often asymptomatic.

  PID is the most common gynaecological reason for admission to hospital in the US, and is diagnosed in 1.1% of women aged 16 to 45 years consulting their GP in England and Wales.

  Epithelial damage from infections such as *Chlamydia trachomatis* or *Neisseria gonorrhoeae* may allow opportunistic infection from many other bacteria.

  About 20% of women with PID become infertile, 40% develop chronic pain, and 1% of women who conceive have an ectopic pregnancy.

  Spontaneous resolution of symptoms may occur in some women.

  Empirical treatment is started as soon as the diagnosis of PID is suspected to minimise the risk of sequelae such as tubal obstruction and infertility.

  The positive predictive value of clinical diagnosis is 65% to 90% compared with laparoscopy, and observational studies suggest that delaying treatment by 3 days may impair fertility.

  The absence of infection from the lower genital tract does not exclude a diagnosis of PID.

- Oral antibiotics are likely to be beneficial, and are associated with the resolution of symptoms and signs of pelvic infection, but we don't know which antibiotic regimen is best.

  Clinical and microbiological cure rates of 88% to 100% have been reported after oral antibiotic treatment.

  The risks of tubal occlusion and infertility depend on severity of infection before treatment. Clinical improvement following treatment may not necessarily translate into improved long-term fertility.

- Oral antibiotics may be as effective as parenteral antibiotics in reducing symptoms and preserving fertility in women with mild-to-moderate PID, with fewer adverse effects. However, we don't know the optimal duration of treatment.

- Women at high risk for PID include those with prior infection with *C trachomatis* or *N gonorrhoeae*, young age at onset of sexual activity, unprotected sexual intercourse with multiple partners, and prior history of PID. Risks of PID may be increased after instrumentation of the cervix, and testing for infection before such procedures is advisable. We don't know whether prophylactic antibiotics before IUD insertion reduce these risks.

(i) **Please visit http://clinicalevidence.bmj.com for full text and references**

| How do different antimicrobial regimens compare when treating women with confirmed PID? | |
|---|---|
| Likely To Be Beneficial | • Antibiotics (for symptoms and microbiological clearance in women with confirmed PID) |
| | • Different durations of antibiotic treatment (no evidence as to which duration is best) |
| | • Oral antibiotics (as effective as parenteral antibiotics for mild-to-moderate PID) |

## What are the effects of routine antibiotic prophylaxis to prevent PID before IUD insertion?

| Unknown Effectiveness | • Routine antibiotic prophylaxis before IUD insertion in women at high risk |
|---|---|
| Unlikely To Be Beneficial | • Routine antibiotic prophylaxis before IUD insertion in women at low risk |

**Search date September 2013**

**DEFINITION** Pelvic inflammatory disease (PID) is inflammation and infection of the upper genital tract in women, typically involving the uterus and adnexae. Mild-to-moderate PID is defined as the absence of a tubo-ovarian abscess. Severe disease is defined as severe systemic symptoms or the presence of tubo-ovarian abscess.

**INCIDENCE/PREVALENCE** The exact incidence of PID is unknown because the disease cannot be diagnosed reliably from clinical symptoms and signs. Direct visualisation of the fallopian tubes by laparoscopy is the best single diagnostic test, but it is invasive, lacks sensitivity, and is not used routinely in clinical practice. PID is the most common gynaecological reason for admission to hospital in the US, accounting for 18 per 10,000 recorded hospital discharges. A diagnosis of PID is made in 1.1% of women aged 16 to 45 years attending their primary-care physician in England and Wales. However, because most PID is asymptomatic, this figure under-estimates the true prevalence. A crude marker of PID in resource-poor countries can be obtained from reported hospital admission rates, where it accounts for 17% to 40% of gynaecological admissions in sub-Saharan Africa, 15% to 37% in Southeast Asia, and 3% to 10% in India.

**AETIOLOGY/RISK FACTORS** Factors associated with PID mirror those for STDs — young age, reduced socioeconomic circumstances, lower educational attainment, and recent new sexual partner. Women considered at high risk for PID include those with prior infection with chlamydia or gonorrhoea, young age at onset of sexual activity, unprotected sexual intercourse with multiple partners, and prior history of PID. Infection ascends from the cervix, and initial epithelial damage caused by bacteria (especially *Chlamydia trachomatis* and *Neisseria gonorrhoeae*) may allow the opportunistic entry of other organisms. Many different microbes, including *Mycoplasma genitalium* and anaerobes, may be isolated from the upper genital tract. The spread of infection to the upper genital tract can be increased by instrumentation of the cervix, but reduced by barrier methods of contraception, levonorg-estrel implants, and by oral contraceptives compared with other forms of contraception.

**PROGNOSIS** PID has a high morbidity; about 20% of affected women become infertile, 40% develop chronic pelvic pain, and 1% of those who conceive have an ectopic pregnancy. Uncontrolled observations suggest that clinical symptoms and signs resolve in a significant proportion of untreated women.

Henry W. Buck, Jr

## KEY POINTS
- The ultimate goal in management of disease is its prevention. For external genital warts (EGWs), there is extensive evidence that vaccination is more than 90% effective. It is important to use either the quadrivalent or new nonavalent vaccine, both containing HPVs 6 and 11. The bivalent vaccine contains neither.

- EGWs are sexually transmitted, benign epidermal growths caused by the human papillomavirus (HPV) on the anogenital areas of both women and men, as well as, occasionally, in other locations.

  In the US, about 50% to 60% of sexually active women aged 18 to 25 years have been exposed to HPV infection, but only 10% to 15% will have genital warts. Warts are more common in people with impaired immune systems but, in people with adequate immune function, about one third may resolve spontaneously.

  Some lesions, particularly those that are pigmented, should be biopsied to rule out severe dysplasia or melanoma; but EGWs rarely, if ever, progress to cancer.

- The previous version of this overview presented the evidence for single treatments in people with EGWs, and interventions for prevention of transmission. At this update, we have looked for evidence on combination therapy (ablative procedure plus imiquimod), as well as the treatment of EGWs in pregnancy.

  We searched for evidence from RCTs and systematic reviews of RCTs.

- The desirability of promoting action of the immune system creates a rationale for combining ablation and imiquimod:

  Ablation reduces the the viral load

  Imiquimod increases response of the immune system.

- We assessed the effects of combination therapy using ablation treatments (cryotherapy, laser therapy, electrosurgery, or surgical excision) plus imiquimod in people with external genital warts.

  We found no RCTs comparing ablation plus imiquimod with placebo or no treatment.

  We don't know how ablation plus imiquimod compares with ablation alone or imiquimod alone at increasing wart clearance or reducing wart recurrence, as we found insufficient evidence from one trial.

- We also assessed the effects of treatments for external genital warts in pregnancy.

  We don't know how effective podophyllotoxin, podophyllin, bi- and trichloroacetic acid, cryotherapy, electrosurgery, laser surgery, surgical excision, or imiquimod are as we found no evidence.

- Due to the immune suppression that occurs with pregnancy, the results of any treatment during pregnancy generally do not compare favourably with those for women who are not pregnant. However, improvement in immune function usually returns rapidly after delivery, with subsequent response towards clearing. Therefore, in the absence of evidence for any specific treatment, it is considered reasonable to attempt any of the treatment options considered in the question on pregnancy.

(i) **Please visit http://clinicalevidence.bmj.com for full text and references**

| What are the effects of ablative procedure (cryotherapy, laser therapy, electrosurgery, surgical excision) plus imiquimod in people with external genital warts? | |
|---|---|
| Unknown Effectiveness | • Ablative procedure (cryotherapy, laser therapy, electrosurgery, surgical excision) plus imiquimod |

| What are the effects of treatments for external genital warts in pregnancy? | |
|---|---|
| Unknown Effectiveness | • Bi- and trichloroacetic acid |
| | • Cryotherapy |
| | • Electrosurgery |
| | • Imiquimod |
| | • Laser surgery |
| | • Podophyllin |
| | • Podophyllotoxin |
| | • Surgical excision |

**Search date June 2014**

**DEFINITION** External genital warts (EGWs) are benign epidermal growths on the anogenital regions, as well as occasionally in other locations, which can occur in both women and men. There are four morphological types: condylomatous, keratotic, papular, and flat warts. EGWs are caused by the human papillomavirus (HPV). **Diagnosis:** Most EGWs are diagnosed by inspection. Some clinicians apply 5% acetic acid (white vinegar) to help visualise lesions because it produces so-called 'acetowhite' change and, more importantly, defines vascular patterns characteristic for EGWs. However, the 'acetowhite' change also occurs with conditions other than EGWs, so differential diagnoses should be considered. Some lesions, particularly those that are pigmented, should be biopsied to rule out severe dysplasia or melanoma. **Prevention:** The ultimate goal in management of disease is its prevention. Fortunately, for EGWs extensive evidence has accumulated that vaccination is more than 90% effective. It is important to use either the quadrivalent or new nonavalent vaccine, both containing HPVs 6 and 11. The bivalent vaccine contains neither. Therefore, this overview has focused on treatments where there is greater uncertainty.

**INCIDENCE/PREVALENCE** In the US in 2004, EGWs accounted for more than 310,000 initial visits to private physicians' clinics. Also, 1% of sexually active men and women aged 18 to 49 years are estimated to have EGWs. It is believed that external and cervical lesions caused by HPV constitute the most prevalent STD among people aged 18 to 25 years. In the US, 50% to 60% of women aged 18 to 25 years test positive for HPV DNA, but no more than 10% to 15% ever have genital warts. By the age of 50 years, at least 80% of women will have acquired genital HPV infection. About 6.2 million people in the US acquire a new genital HPV infection each year.

**AETIOLOGY/RISK FACTORS** EGWs are caused by HPV and are sexually transmitted. They are more common in people with impaired immune function. Although more than 100 types of HPV have been identified, about one third of which are found in the anogenital regions, most EGWs in immunocompetent people are caused by HPV types 6 and 11.

**PROGNOSIS** The ability to clear and remain free of EGWs is a function of cellular immunity. In immunocompetent people, the prognosis in terms of clearance and avoiding recurrence is good; but people with impaired cellular immunity (e.g., people with HIV and AIDS) have great difficulty in achieving and maintaining wart clearance. Without treatment, EGWs may remain unchanged, or may increase in size or number, and about one third will clear. Clinical trials found that recurrences may happen and may necessitate repeated treatment. EGWs rarely, if ever, progress to cancer. Recurrent respiratory papillomatosis (RRP), a rare and sometimes life-threatening condition, occurs in children of women with a history of genital warts. Its rarity makes it difficult to design studies that can evaluate whether treatment in pregnant women alters the risk.

# Acne vulgaris

Sarah Purdy and David de Berker

## KEY POINTS

- Acne vulgaris affects over 80% of teenagers, and persists beyond the age of 25 years in 3% of men and 12% of women.

  Typical lesions of acne include comedones, inflammatory papules, and pustules. Nodules and cysts occur in more severe acne, and can cause scarring and psychological distress.

- Topical benzoyl peroxide should be considered as first-line treatment in mild acne.

  Topical benzoyl peroxide and topical azelaic acid reduce inflammatory and non-inflammatory lesions compared with placebo, but can cause itching, burning, stinging, and redness of the skin.

- Topical antibiotics such as clindamycin and erythromycin (alone or with zinc) reduce inflammatory lesions compared with placebo, but have not been shown to reduce non-inflammatory lesions. Tetracycline may reduce overall acne severity.

  Antimicrobial resistance can develop with use of topical or oral antibiotics, and their efficacy may decrease over time.

  Tetracyclines may cause skin discoloration, and should be avoided in pregnant or breastfeeding women.

  Topical preparations of tretinoin, adapalene, and isotretinoin may reduce inflammatory and non-inflammatory lesions, but can also cause redness, burning, dryness, and soreness of the skin.

- Oral antibiotics (doxycycline, erythromycin, lymecycline, minocycline, oxytetracycline, and tetracycline) are considered useful for people with more severe acne, although we don't know for sure whether they are effective.

  Oral antibiotics can cause adverse effects such as contraceptive failure.

  Minocycline has been associated with an increased risk of systemic lupus erythematosus and liver disorders.

  Oral isotretinoin has been associated with skin problems, change in liver function, teratogenesis, and psychiatric disorders.

(i) **Please visit http://clinicalevidence.bmj.com for full text and references**

| What are the effects of topical treatments in people with acne vulgaris? | |
|---|---|
| **Beneficial** | • Benzoyl peroxide<br><br>• Clindamycin (reduced the number of inflammatory lesions)<br><br>• Erythromycin (reduced the number of inflammatory lesions)<br><br>• Tretinoin |
| **Likely To Be Beneficial** | • Adapalene<br><br>• Azelaic acid<br><br>• Erythromycin plus zinc<br><br>• Isotretinoin<br><br>• Tetracycline |

## What are the effects of oral treatments in people with acne vulgaris?

| Likely To Be Beneficial | • Erythromycin |
|---|---|
| Trade-off Between Benefits And Harms | • Doxycycline<br>• Isotretinoin<br>• Lymecycline<br>• Minocycline<br>• Oxytetracycline<br>• Tetracycline |

**Search date February 2010**

**DEFINITION** Acne vulgaris is a common inflammatory pilosebaceous disease characterised by comedones; papules; pustules; inflamed nodules; superficial pus-filled cysts; and (in extreme cases) canalising and deep, inflamed, sometimes purulent sacs. Lesions are most common on the face, but the neck, chest, upper back, and shoulders may also be affected. Acne can cause scarring and considerable psychological distress. It is classified as mild, moderate, or severe. **Mild acne** is defined as non-inflammatory lesions (comedones), a few inflammatory (papulopustular) lesions, or both. **Moderate acne** is defined as more inflammatory lesions, occasional nodules, or both, and mild scarring. **Severe acne** is defined as widespread inflammatory lesions, nodules, or both, and scarring; moderate acne that has not settled with 6 months of treatment; or acne of any 'severity' with serious psychological upset. This review does not cover acne rosacea, acne secondary to industrial occupations, and treatment of acne in people under 13 years of age.

**INCIDENCE/PREVALENCE** Acne is the most common skin disease of adolescence, affecting over 80% of teenagers (aged 13–18 years) at some point. Estimates of prevalence vary depending on study populations and the method of assessment used. Prevalence of acne in a community sample of 14- to 16-year-olds in the UK has been recorded as 50%. In a sample of adolescents from schools in New Zealand, acne was present in 91% of males and 79% of females, and in a similar population in Portugal the prevalence was 82%. It has been estimated that up to 30% of teenagers have acne of sufficient severity to require medical treatment. Acne was the presenting complaint in 3.1% of people aged 13 to 25 years attending primary care in a UK population. Overall incidence is similar in both men and women, and peaks at 17 years of age. The number of adults with acne, including people over 25 years, is increasing; the reasons for this increase are uncertain.

**AETIOLOGY/RISK FACTORS** The exact cause of acne is unknown. Four factors contribute to the development of acne: increased sebum secretion rate, abnormal follicular differentiation causing obstruction of the pilosebaceous duct, bacteriology of the pilosebaceous duct, and inflammation. The anaerobic bacterium *Propionibacterium acnes* plays an important role in the pathogenesis of acne. Androgen secretion is the major trigger for adolescent acne.

**PROGNOSIS** In 3% of men (95% CI 1.2% to 4.8%) and 12% of women (95% CI 9% to 15%), facial acne persists after the age of 25 years, and in a few people (1% of men and 5% of women) acne persists into their 40s.

Fay Crawford

### KEY POINTS

- Fungal infection of the feet can cause white and soggy skin between the toes, dry and flaky soles, or reddening and blistering of the skin all over the foot.

  Around 15% to 25% of people are likely to have athlete's foot at any one time.

  The infection can spread to other parts of the body and to other people.

- Topical allylamines (naftifine and terbinafine), topical azoles (clotrimazole, miconazole nitrate, tioconazole, sulconazole nitrate, bifonazole, and econazole nitrate) and topical ciclopirox olamine are all more likely to cure fungal skin infections compared with placebo.

  Topical allylamines seem to have fewer treatment failures compared with topical azoles.

  We don't know whether any one treatment is more effective than others.

- We don't know whether improving foot hygiene or changing footwear can help to cure athlete's foot.

 **Please visit http://clinicalevidence.bmj.com for full text and references**

| What are the effects of topical treatments for athlete's foot? | |
|---|---|
| **Beneficial** | • Azoles (topical) |
| | • Ciclopirox olamine (topical) |
| | • Naftifine, terbinafine (topical allylamines) |
| **Unknown Effectiveness** | • Improved foot hygiene, including socks and hosiery |

**Search date July 2008**

---

**DEFINITION** Athlete's foot is a cutaneous fungal infection caused by dermatophyte infection. It is characterised by itching, flaking, and fissuring of the skin. It may manifest in three ways: the skin between the toes may appear macerated (white) and soggy; the soles of the feet may become dry and scaly; and the skin all over the foot may become red, and vesicular eruptions may appear. It is conventional in dermatology to refer to fungal skin infections as superficial in order to distinguish them from systemic fungal infections.

**INCIDENCE/PREVALENCE** Epidemiological studies have produced various estimates of the prevalence of athlete's foot. Studies are usually conducted in populations of people who attend dermatology clinics, sports centres, or swimming pools, or who are in the military. UK estimates suggest that athlete's foot is present in about 15% of the general population. Studies conducted in dermatology clinics found prevalences of 25% in Italy (722 people) and 27% in China (1014 people). A population-based study conducted in 1148 children in Israel found the prevalence among children to be 30%.

**AETIOLOGY/RISK FACTORS** Swimming-pool users and industrial workers may be at increased risk of fungal foot infection. However, one survey identified fungal foot infection in only 9% of swimmers, with the highest prevalence (20%) being in men aged 16 years and older.

**PROGNOSIS** Fungal infections of the foot are not life threatening in people with normal immune status, but in some people they cause persistent itching and, ultimately, fissuring. Some people are apparently unaware of persistent infection. The infection can spread to other parts of the body and to other individuals.

Anthony Ormerod, Sanjay Rajpara, and Fiona Craig

## KEY POINTS

- Basal cell carcinoma (BCC) is the most common form of skin cancer, predominantly affecting the head and neck, and can be diagnosed clinically in most cases.

  Metastasis of BCC is rare, but localised tissue invasion and destruction can lead to morbidity.

  Risk factors for BCC include tendency to freckle, degree of sun exposure, excessive sun-bed use, and smoking.

  Incidence of BCC increases markedly after the age of 40 years, but incidence in younger people is rising, possibly as a result of increased sun exposure.

- Excisional surgery is considered likely to be effective in treating BCC.

  Similar treatment-response rates at 1 year after treatment have been reported for excisional surgery compared with curettage plus cryotherapy and photodynamic therapy.

  Excisional surgery is associated with fewer adverse effects compared with photodynamic therapy and curettage plus cryotherapy, and seems to be associated with improved cosmetic results compared with curettage plus cryotherapy 1 year after treatment.

  We can't compare the effectiveness of surgical excision with Mohs' micrographic surgery in treating recurrent BCC, but excisional surgery seems associated with more adverse effects compared with Mohs' micrographic surgery.

- Cryotherapy, with or without curettage, photodynamic therapy, and curettage and cautery/electrodesiccation may be effective treatments for BCC in the short term (up to 1 year after treatment).

  Cryotherapy alone seems as effective as photodynamic therapy for superficial and nodular BCCs, but photodynamic therapy may produce better cosmetic results compared with cryotherapy alone.

  We don't know how cryotherapy with curettage compares with photodynamic therapy or cryotherapy alone.

  Twofold treatments with photodynamic therapy performed 1 week apart with delta-aminolaevulinic acid (ALA-PDT) may be more effective than single treatments in the short term.

  There seems to be no difference in effectiveness between ALA-PDT using a broadband halogen light source and ALA-PDT using a laser light source.

- Imiquimod 5% cream may be beneficial for the treatment of superficial and nodular BCCs compared with placebo in the short term (within 6 months after starting treatment).

  It seems that more frequent application of imiquimod 5% improves response rates compared with lower-frequency regimens, but is also associated with increased frequency of adverse effects.

- We don't know whether fluorouracil is effective in the short-term treatment of BCC.

- Excisional surgery, cryotherapy alone, photodynamic therapy, and curettage and cautery/electrodesiccation are thought to be beneficial in preventing long-term recurrence of BCC.

- We don't know whether imiquimod 5% and fluorouracil are effective in preventing BCC recurrence in the longer term (at or beyond 2 years' treatment).

(i) **Please visit http://clinicalevidence.bmj.com for full text and references**

## What are the effects of interventions on treatment response/recurrence (within 1 year of therapy) in people with basal cell carcinoma?

| Likely To Be Beneficial | • Cryotherapy/cryosurgery (as effective as photodynamic therapy; in combination with curettage seems to be as effective as excisional surgery)<br><br>• Curettage and cautery/electrodesiccation (likely to be beneficial for low-risk BCC)*<br><br>• Imiquimod 5% cream (better than placebo at 6 months, insufficient evidence to compare with other treatments)<br><br>• Photodynamic therapy<br><br>• Surgery (excisional or Mohs' micrographic surgery)* |
|---|---|
| Unknown Effectiveness | • Fluorouracil |

## What are the effects of interventions on long-term recurrence (a minimum of 2 years after treatment) in people with basal cell carcinoma?

| Likely To Be Beneficial | • Cryotherapy/cryosurgery*<br><br>• Curettage and cautery/electrodesiccation*<br><br>• Photodynamic therapy*<br><br>• Surgery (conventional or Mohs' micrographic surgery)† |
|---|---|
| Unknown Effectiveness | • Fluorouracil<br><br>• Imiquimod 5% cream |

**December 2009**

*Categorisation is based on consensus and expert opinion.
†Categorisation is based on consensus and observational data.

**DEFINITION** Basal cell carcinoma (BCC) is the most common cancer found in humans. It is a slow-growing, locally invasive, malignant epidermal skin tumour which mainly affects white people. Although metastasis is rare, BCC can cause morbidity by local tissue invasion and destruction, particularly on the head and neck. The clinical appearances and morphology are diverse, including nodular, cystic, ulcerated ('rodent ulcer'), superficial, morphoeic (sclerosing), keratotic, and pigmented variants. Most BCCs (85%) develop on the head and neck. **Diagnosis:** The diagnosis of BCC is made clinically in most cases. A biopsy is performed for histological diagnosis when there is doubt about clinical diagnosis, and when people are referred for specialised forms of treatment.

**INCIDENCE/PREVALENCE** The reported incidence of BCC varies in the literature. The incidence was reported to be 788 per 100,000 population per year in 1995 in Australia, and 146 per 100,000 population per year in 1990 in the USA. A Dutch study reported an incidence of 200 per 100,000 population per year, whereas the incidence in the UK is reported to be lower, at about 100 cases per 100,000 population per year. Because of incomplete registration of cases, some of these estimates may be low. The incidence of BCC increases markedly after the age of 40 years, and the incidence in younger people is increasing, possibly as a result of increased sun exposure.

**AETIOLOGY/RISK FACTORS** The reported risk factors for developing BCC include fair skin, tendency to freckle, degree of sun exposure, excessive sun-bed use, smoking, radiotherapy, phototherapy, male gender, and a genetic predisposition. Although cumulative lifetime sunlight exposure is a major risk factor for the development of BCC, it does not accurately predict the frequency of BCC development at a particular site on its own. Other contributory factors are skin phototype (e.g., Fitzpatrick I and II), number of lifetime visits to tanning beds, number of pack years of smoking, and number of blistering sunburns. Immunosuppressed people are also at increased risk for non-melanoma skin cancer, including BCC. The risk increases with duration of immunosuppression, and about 16% of people with renal transplants develop BCC — a 10-fold increased risk compared with the general population. An autosomal-dominant condition, naevoid BCC syndrome (Gorlin's syndrome) is characterised by the occurrence of multiple BCCs and developmental abnormalities.

**PROGNOSIS** The following factors can affect prognosis: tumour size, site, type, growth pattern/histological subtype, failure of previous treatment (recurrence), and immunosuppression. BCCs in close proximity to important body structures can potentially increase morbidity as a result of local tissue invasion or recurrence, and so BCCs can be categorised based on their location as: high risk (nose, nasal-labial fold, eyelids and periorbital areas, lips, chin, and ears); medium risk (scalp, forehead, pre- and postauricular areas, and malar areas); and low risk (neck, trunk, and extremities). Histologically, micronodular, infiltrative, morphoeic, and basosquamous types of BCC are classed as high risk. Distant metastases are rare. Although some BCCs tend to infiltrate tissues in a three-dimensional manner, growth is usually localised to the area of origin. However, if left untreated, BCC can cause extensive tissue destruction with infiltration in deeper tissues, such as bone and brain. BCCs may remain small for years with little tendency to grow, grow rapidly, or proceed by successive spurts of extension of tumour and partial regression. Therefore, the clinical course of BCC is unpredictable.

## 550 | Cellulitis and erysipelas

Andrew D Morris

**KEY POINTS**

- Cellulitis is a common problem caused by spreading bacterial inflammation of the skin, with redness, pain, and lymphangitis. Up to 40% of people have systemic illness.

    Erysipelas is a form of cellulitis with marked superficial inflammation, typically affecting the lower limbs and the face.

    Risk factors include lymphoedema, leg ulcer, toe-web intertrigo, and traumatic wounds.

    The most common pathogens in adults are streptococci and *Staphylococcus aureus*.

    Cellulitis and erysipelas can result in local necrosis and abscess formation. Around a quarter of people have more than one episode of cellulitis within 3 years.

- Antibiotics cure 50–100% of infections, but we don't know which antibiotic regimen is most successful.

    We don't know whether antibiotics are as effective when given orally as when given intravenously, or whether intramuscular administration is more effective than intravenous.

    A 5-day course of antibiotics may be as effective as a 10-day course at curing the infection and preventing early recurrence.

- Although there is consensus that treatment of predisposing factors can prevent recurrence of cellulitis or erysipelas, we found no studies that assessed the benefits of this approach.

(i) **Please visit http://clinicalevidence.bmj.com for full text and references**

| What are the effects of treatments for cellulitis and erysipelas? | |
| --- | --- |
| Unknown Effectiveness | • Comparative effects of different antibiotics |
| | • Comparative effects of different routes of administration of antibiotics |
| | • Duration of antibiotics |

| What are the effects of treatments to prevent recurrence of cellulitis and erysipelas? | |
| --- | --- |
| Likely To Be Beneficial | • Antibiotics (prophylactic) to prevent recurrence of cellulitis and erysipelas |
| Unknown Effectiveness | • Treatment of predisposing factors |

**Search date May 2007**

**DEFINITION** Cellulitis is a spreading bacterial infection of the dermis and subcutaneous tissues. It causes local signs of inflammation, such as warmth, erythema, pain, lymphangitis, and frequently systemic upset with fever and raised white blood cell count. **Erysipelas** is a form of cellulitis and is characterised by pronounced superficial inflammation. The term erysipelas is commonly used when the face is affected. The lower limbs are by far the most common sites affected by cellulitis and erysipelas, but any area, such as the ears, trunk, fingers, and toes, can be affected.

**INCIDENCE/PREVALENCE** We found no validated recent data on the incidence of cellulitis or erysipelas worldwide. UK hospital incidence data reported 69,576 episodes of cellulitis and 516 episodes of erysipelas in 2004–2005. Cellulitis infections of the limb accounted for most of these infections (58,824 episodes).

**AETIOLOGY/RISK FACTORS** The most common infective organisms for cellulitis and erysipelas in adults are streptococci (particularly *Streptococcus pyogenes*) and *Staphylococcus aureus*. In children, *Haemophilus influenzae* was a frequent cause before the introduction of the *Haemophilus influenzae* type B vaccination. Several risk factors for cellulitis and erysipelas have been identified in a case-control study (167 cases and 294 controls): lymphoedema (OR 71.2, 95% CI 5.6 to 908.0), leg ulcer (OR 62.5, 95% CI 7.0 to 556.0), toe web intertrigo (OR 13.9, 95% CI 7.2 to 27.0), and traumatic wounds (OR 10.7, 95% CI 4.8 to 23.8).

**PROGNOSIS** Cellulitis can spread through the bloodstream and lymphatic system. A retrospective case study of people admitted to hospital with cellulitis found that systemic symptoms, such as fever and raised white blood cell count, were present in up to 42% of cases at presentation. Lymphatic involvement can lead to obstruction and damage of the lymphatic system that predisposes to recurrent cellulitis. Recurrence can occur rapidly, or after months or years. One prospective cohort study found that 29% of people with erysipelas had a recurrent episode within 3 years. Local necrosis and abscess formation can also occur. It is not known whether the prognosis of erysipelas differs from cellulitis. We found no evidence about factors that predict recurrence, or a better or worse outcome. We found no good evidence on the prognosis of untreated cellulitis.

# Eczema

Jochen Schmitt, Christian J Apfelbacher, and Carsten Flohr

## KEY POINTS

- Eczema, as defined by the World Allergy Organization (WAO) revised nomenclature in 2003, affects 15% to 20% of school children worldwide and 2% to 5% of adults. Only about 50% of people with eczema demonstrate allergic sensitisation.

  Remission occurs in two-thirds of children by the age of 15 years, but relapses may occur later.

- Emollients are generally considered to be effective for treating the symptoms of eczema. However, the few small short-term RCTs that have been done so far do not confirm this. Sufficiently powered long-term RCTs are needed to clarify the role of emollients in the treatment of eczema.

- Corticosteroids improve clearance of lesions and decrease relapse rates compared with placebo in adults and children with eczema, although we don't know which is the most effective corticosteroid or the most effective dosing regimen.

  Topical corticosteroids seem to have few adverse effects when used intermittently, but if they are of potent or very potent strength, they may cause burning, skin thinning, and telangiectasia, especially in children.

- The calcineurin inhibitors pimecrolimus and tacrolimus improve clearance of lesions compared with placebo and may have a role in people in whom corticosteroids are contraindicated. They also seem suitable for topical use in body areas where the skin is particularly thin, such as the face.

- CAUTION: An association has been suggested between pimecrolimus and tacrolimus and skin cancer in animal models. Although this association has not been confirmed in humans, calcineurin inhibitors should be used only when other treatments have failed.

- We don't know whether vitamin E or multivitamins reduce symptoms in adults with eczema or whether pyridoxine, zinc supplementation, exclusion diets, or elemental diets are effective in children with eczema, as there are insufficient good-quality studies.

  Probiotics do not seem to reduce symptoms in children with established eczema.

  Essential fatty acids, such as evening primrose oil, blackcurrant seed oil, or fish oil, do not seem to reduce symptoms in people with eczema.

- We don't know whether control of house dust mites or maternal dietary restriction can prevent the development of eczema in children.

  Observational data suggest that exclusive breastfeeding for at least 3 months does not reduce eczema risk and there is no evidence to suggest that exclusive breastfeeding alleviates eczema symptoms, unless a child is allergic to cow's milk protein.

  Introduction of probiotics in the last trimester of pregnancy and during breastfeeding may reduce the risk of eczema in the baby, although it remains unclear whether both antenatal and postnatal supplementation together yields the strongest protective effect. It is equally unclear which strains of probiotics are most effective.

 Please visit http://clinicalevidence.bmj.com for full text and references

## What are the effects of topical medical treatments in adults and children with established eczema?

| Beneficial | |
|---|---|
| | • Corticosteroids |
| | • Pimecrolimus |

| | |
|---|---|
| | • Tacrolimus |
| **Likely To Be Beneficial** | • Emollients* |

### What are the effects of dietary interventions in adults with established eczema?

| | |
|---|---|
| **Unknown Effectiveness** | • Vitamin E and multivitamins |

### What are the effects of dietary interventions in children with established eczema?

| | |
|---|---|
| **Unknown Effectiveness** | • Egg and cow's milk exclusion diet |
| | • Elemental diet |
| | • Few-foods diet |
| | • Pyridoxine (Vitamin B6) |
| | • Zinc supplementation |
| **Unlikely To Be Beneficial** | • Probiotics |
| **Likely To Be Ineffective Or Harmful** | • Essential fatty acids (evening primrose oil, blackcurrant seed oil, fish oil) |

### What are the primary preventive effects of breastfeeding in predisposed infants?

| | |
|---|---|
| **Unknown Effectiveness** | • Prolonged breastfeeding by mother straight after birth |

### What are the primary preventive effects of reducing allergens in predisposed infants?

| | |
|---|---|
| **Unknown Effectiveness** | • Control of house dust mite |

### What are the primary preventive effects of dietary interventions in infants?

| | |
|---|---|
| **Likely To Be Beneficial** | • Early introduction of probiotics (in last trimester and/or shortly after birth) |
| **Unknown Effectiveness** | • Maternal dietary restriction during pregnancy and lactation |

**Search date May 2009**

*Based on consensus.

**DEFINITION** As defined by the World Allergy Organization (WAO) revised nomenclature in 2003, eczema (also known as atopic dermatitis) is a chronic, relapsing, and itchy inflammatory skin condition. In the acute stage, eczematous lesions are characterised by poorly defined erythema with surface change (oedema, vesicles, and weeping). In the chronic stage, lesions are marked by skin thickening (lichenification). Although lesions can occur anywhere on the body, infants often have eczematous lesions on their cheeks and outer limbs before they develop eczema in the typical flexural areas such as behind the knees and in the folds of the elbow and neck. About 50% of people suffering from eczema also become sensitised to environmental allergens, such as house dust mite, and may then be classified as having atopic eczema under the revised WAO nomenclature. **Diagnosis:** There is no definitive diagnostic 'gold standard' for diagnosing eczema. However, a UK Working Party developed a minimum list of validated diagnostic criteria for eczema using the Hanifin and Rajka list of clinical features as building blocks. The criteria were shown to have a sensitivity of 85% and a specificity of 96% in children when compared with a dermatologist's diagnosis. Although there are a large number of eczema severity scores for eczema in the public domain, only the SCORing Atopic Dermatitis (SCORAD) index, the Eczema Area Severity Index (EASI), the Patient Oriented Eczema Measure (POEM), and the Six Area, Six Sign Atopic Dermatitis severity index (SASSAD) have been shown to have adequate validity and reliability. **Population:** For the purposes of this review, we included all adults and children defined as having established eczema. Where adults or children are considered separately, this is highlighted in the text. We also included studies assessing primary prevention of eczema using specific interventions: prolonged breastfeeding, maternal dietary restriction, house dust mite restriction, and early introduction of probiotics.

**INCIDENCE/PREVALENCE** In Europe, eczema affects 15% to 20% of school age children at some stage, and 2% to 5% of adults. Global prevalence data for the symptoms of eczema were collected as part of the International Study of Asthma and Allergies in Childhood (ISAAC). The results suggest that eczema is not only a problem in industrialised countries, but also in urban areas of developing nations. One UK-based population study showed that 2% of children under the age of 5 years have severe disease and 84% have mild disease. Affected adults more frequently have chronic and severe eczema and are also at an increased risk of developing allergic contact dermatitis.

**AETIOLOGY/RISK FACTORS** Although eczema has become increasingly common over past decades, the causes are not well understood and are probably a combination of genetic and environmental factors. Eczema risk is increased in first degree relatives, and the discovery of the filaggrin gene strongly suggests that an impaired skin barrier is fundamentally involved in eczema development. However, genetics alone cannot explain the raise in the prevalence of eczema over past decades and also cannot explain why eczema often clears spontaneously. Migrant studies have found that children acquire the background population risk of their new home country. There is also some evidence to suggest that eczema is associated with factors linked to a 'Western' lifestyle, as the disease tends to be more common in industrialised countries and urban centres of developing nations. Eczema is also more common in people of higher socioeconomic class. Several individual environmental influences have been studied. For instance, broad-spectrum antibiotics during pregnancy and in early life seem to increase eczema risk, and it has been speculated that this may be because of alterations in the infant's gut microflora. The influence of specific bacterial and viral pathogens both *in utero* and postnatally on disease development remains uncertain, but studies on day-care attendance during infancy, endotoxin exposure, consumption of unpasteurised cow's milk, and dog exposure in early life point towards a protective effect from non-pathogenic microbial exposure. There is also the suggestion that helminth parasites can partially protect against allergic sensitisation and eczema. At the same time, bacterial skin infection, for instance with *Staphylococcus aureus*, is known to worsen eczema. Allergic sensitisation, for instance to house dust mite, is also associated with higher eczema risk, but seems a secondary phenomenon rather than a primary cause. With the heightened interest in skin barrier dysfunction, one of the key future research areas is the interaction between skin barrier gene mutation carriage and environmental factors, such as house dust mite sensitisation, water hardness, and washing practices, which could all contribute to an impaired skin barrier and therefore eczema phenotype.

**PROGNOSIS** Remission occurs by the age of 15 years in 60% to 70% of cases, although a large number of people re-present with hand eczema later on in life. While no treatments are currently known to alter the natural history of eczema, several interventions can help to control symptoms and prevent flares.

Jill Ferrari

## KEY POINTS

- Fungal toenail infection (onychomycosis) is characterised as infection of part or all of the toenail unit, which includes the nail plate, the nail bed, and the nail matrix. Over time, the infection causes discoloration and distortion of part or all of the nail unit.

  Fungal infections are reported to cause 23% of foot diseases and 50% of nail conditions in people seen by dermatologists, but are less common in the general population, affecting 3% to 12% of people.

  Infection can cause discomfort in walking, pain, or limitation of activities.

- People taking oral antifungal drugs reported greater satisfaction and fewer onychomycosis-related problems, such as embarrassment, self-consciousness, and being perceived as unclean by others, compared with people using topical antifungals.

  Oral antifungals have general adverse effects, including gastrointestinal complaints (such as diarrhoea), rash, and respiratory complaints. It was rare for people to withdraw from an RCT because of adverse effects.

- Both oral itraconazole and oral terbinafine effectively increase cure rates; terbinafine seems slightly more effective.

  Adverse effects unique to terbinafine include sensory loss, such as taste, smell, or hearing disturbance. These are usually temporary/reversible.

- An alternative oral antifungal treatment is fluconazole, which seems to modestly improve cure rates but the evidence is insufficient to allow us to say for certain.

- Topical ciclopirox seems to modestly improve symptoms compared with placebo.

  We found no evidence examining the effectiveness of other topical agents such as ketoconazole, fluconazole, amorolfine, terbinafine, tioconazole, or butenafine.

 Please visit http://clinicalevidence.bmj.com for full text and references

| What are the effects of oral treatments for fungal toenail infections in adults? | |
|---|---|
| Beneficial | • Itraconazole (oral) (more effective than placebo, but probably less effective than terbinafine) <br><br> • Terbinafine (oral) |
| Likely To Be Beneficial | • Fluconazole (oral) (although benefits are modest, even after long-term treatment) |

| What are the effects of topical treatments for fungal toenail infections in adults? | |
|---|---|
| Likely To Be Beneficial | • Ciclopirox (topical) (although benefits are modest, even after long-term treatment) |
| Unknown Effectiveness | • Amorolfine (topical) <br><br> • Butenafine (topical) <br><br> • Fluconazole (topical) <br><br> • Ketoconazole (topical) |

- Terbinafine (topical)
- Tioconazole (topical)

**Search date October 2013**

**DEFINITION** Fungal toenail infection (onychomycosis) is characterised as infection of part or all of the nail unit, which includes the nail plate, the nail bed, and the nail matrix. Over time, the infection causes discoloration and distortion of part or all of the nail unit. The tissue under and around the nail may also thicken. This review deals exclusively with dermatophyte toenail infections (see Aetiology) and excludes candidal or yeast infections.

**INCIDENCE/PREVALENCE** Fungal infections are reported to cause 23% of foot diseases and 50% of nail conditions in people seen by dermatologists, but are less common in the general population, affecting 3% to 12% of people. The prevalence varies among populations, which may be due to differences in screening techniques. In one large European project (13,695 people with a range of foot conditions), 35% had a fungal infection diagnosed by microscopy/culture. One prospective study in Spain (1000 adults aged >20 years) reported a prevalence of fungal toenail infection as 2.7% (infection defined as clinically abnormal nails with positive microscopy and culture). In Denmark, one study (5755 adults aged >18 years) reported the prevalence of fungal toenail infection as 4.0% (determined by positive fungal cultures). The incidence of mycotic nail infections may have increased in the past few years, perhaps because of increasing use of systemic antibiotics, immunosuppressive treatment, more advanced surgical techniques, and the increasing incidence of HIV infection. However, this was contradicted by one study in an outpatient department in Eastern Croatia, which compared the prevalence of fungal infections between two periods (1986–1988, 47,832 people; 1997–2001, 75,691 people). It found that the prevalence of fungal infection overall had increased greatly over the 10 years, but that the percentage of fungal infections affecting the nails had decreased by 1% (fungal infections overall: 0.26% in 1986–1988 v 0.73% in 1997–2001; nail: 10.31% in 1986–1988 v 9.31% in 1997–2001).

**AETIOLOGY/RISK FACTORS** Fungal nail infections are most commonly caused by anthropophilic fungi called dermatophytes. The genera *Trichophyton*, *Epidermophyton*, and *Microsporum* are typically involved, specifically *T rubrum*, *T mentagrophytes* var *interdigitale*, and *E floccosum*. Other fungi, moulds, or yeasts may be isolated, such as *Scopulariopsis brevicaulis*, *Aspergillus*, *Fusarium*, and *Candida albicans*. *T rubrum* is now regarded as the most common cause of onychomycosis worldwide. Several factors that increase the risk of developing a fungal nail infection have been identified. One survey found that 26% of people with diabetes had onychomycosis, and that diabetes increased the risk of infection, but the type and severity of diabetes was not correlated with infection (OR 2.77, 95% CI 2.15 to 3.57). A further study also found that the condition was not correlated to the severity of diabetes, but found a lower prevalence of onychomycosis in people with diabetes (7.8%) and more typically the causative organism was yeast rather than dermatophyte. Another survey found that peripheral vascular disease (OR 1.78, 95% CI 1.68 to 1.88) and immunosuppression (OR 1.19, 95% CI 1.01 to 1.40) increased the risk of infection. These factors may explain the general increase in prevalence of onychomycosis in the older population. Environmental exposures such as occlusive footwear or warm, damp conditions and close living conditions have been cited as risk factors, as has trauma. Fungal skin infection has been proposed as a risk factor. However, one large observational study, which included 5413 people with positive mycology, found that only a small proportion (21.3%) had both skin and toenail infections.

**PROGNOSIS** Onychomycosis does not have serious consequences in otherwise healthy people. However, the Achilles project (846 people with fungal toenail infection) found that many people complain of discomfort in walking (51%), pain (33%), or limitation of their work or other activities (13%). Gross distortion and dystrophy of the nail may cause trauma to the adjacent skin, and may lead to secondary bacterial infection. In immunocompromised people, there is a risk that this infection will disseminate. Quality-of-life measures specific to onychomycosis have been developed. Studies using these indicators suggest that onychomycosis has negative physical and psychosocial effects.

Ian F. Burgess and Paul Silverston

## KEY POINTS

- Head louse infestation is diagnosed by finding live lice. Most eggs take 7 days to hatch (but a few may take longer, up to 13 days), and may appear viable for weeks after death of the egg.

  Infestation may be more likely in school children, with risks increased in children with more siblings or of lower socioeconomic group. Factors such as longer hair make diagnosis and treatment more difficult.

  Anecdotal reports suggest that prevalence during the 1990s has increased in most communities in Europe, the Americas, and Australasia. However, considerable differences are found between countries in terms of the number of products available, dosage form, and active substances used in treatment products.

- For this review, we have focused on the evidence for the efficacy of some of the physically acting topical treatments for head lice and compared these with each other and some of the insecticides. There is interest in this type of treatment as resistance to one or more insecticides that act on the insect nervous system is now common in most developed countries.

  In the US, there are no registered physically acting treatments for head lice (nearly all products being based on insecticides of one form or another), whereas in some countries in Europe (e.g., the UK) almost all treatments sold are currently based on physically acting principles.

  In other European countries, there are varying mixes of physically acting and insecticide-based products available. In Australia, the majority of products are based on plant extracts and essential oils.

  Generally the evidence for physically acting topical head lice treatments is weak. All of the RCTs we found were small and were sponsored by industry. Interpretation of the results presents challenges due, for instance, to the variations in the formulations of products containing the same active treatment (e.g., lotions v mousses v shampoos; other included constituents, such as alcohols and conditioning agents; differing application procedures), reducing the quality of the evidence. Furthermore, there is some question about what exactly constitutes 'physically acting', as different authors describe the actions of some materials in different ways.

- Dimeticone is a silicone and is a physically acting topical treatment working by occlusion. It does not act on the insect nervous system and is unlikely to be affected by resistance to older insecticides.

  Dimeticone seems to be more effective at eradicating head lice compared with malathion or permethrin.

- 1,2-octanediol is a detergent that dissolves some components of the lipid waterproofing layer of the louse cuticle, reducing the ability of the louse to prevent water loss through the cuticle, and resulting in dehydration.

  We found no direct information from RCTs meeting *BMJ Clinical Evidence* inclusion criteria on the effectiveness of any commercially available formulation of 1,2-octanediol in people with head lice infestation.

- In general, we don't know whether herbal and essential oils (we evaluated evidence on eucalyptus oil, tea tree oil, and tocopheryl acetate only) are effective at eradicating head lice compared with other treatments, as we found few RCTs. Efficacy is likely to depend upon the compound(s) or extracts used and the mode of action is unclear.

- Isopropyl myristate (a physically acting treatment that may work by occlusion or by dissolving cuticle wax) may be more effective at eradicating head lice than permethrin, pyrethrum, or malathion, although the evidence is weak from a small number of trials.

(i) **Please visit http://clinicalevidence.bmj.com for full text and references**

## What are the effects of physically acting treatments for head lice?

| Likely To Be Beneficial | • Dimeticone<br>• Isopropyl myristate |
|---|---|
| Unknown Effectiveness | • 1,2-octanediol<br>• Herbal and essential oils (eucalyptus oil, tea tree oil, and tocopheryl acetate) |

**Search date March 2014**

**DEFINITION** Head lice are obligate ectoparasites of socially active humans. They infest the scalp and attach their eggs to the hair shafts. Itching, resulting from multiple bites, is not diagnostic, but may increase the index of suspicion. Most eggs take 7 days to hatch (but a few may take longer, up to 13 days) and may appear viable for weeks after death of the egg. Therefore eggs glued to hairs, whether hatched (nits) or unhatched, are not proof of active infection. A conclusive diagnosis is made by finding live lice. One observational study compared two groups of children with lice eggs but no lice at initial assessment. Over 14 days, more children with five or more eggs within 6 mm of the scalp developed infestations compared with those with fewer than five eggs. Adequate follow-up examinations using detection combing are more likely to be productive than nit removal to detect and identify the need for treatment of any re-infestation. Infestations are not self-limiting. Various treatment options have been used that can broadly be divided into five groups as follows: topically applied insecticides; topically applied, physically acting agents; topically applied, homeo-pathic, plant formulations and other remedies; oral drugs; mechanical agents (combs, electronic devices, heating devices). This review focuses on the topically applied, physically acting agents.

**INCIDENCE/PREVALENCE** We found no studies on incidence and few recently published studies of prevalence in resource-rich countries. Anecdotal reports suggest that prevalence has increased during the early 1990s in most communities in Europe, the Americas, and Australasia. A cross-sectional study from Belgium (6169 children aged 2.5–12.0 years) found a prevalence of 8.9%. An earlier pilot study (677 children aged 3–11 years) showed that, in individual schools, the prevalence was as high as 19.5%. One cross-sectional study from Belgium found that head lice were significantly more common in children from families with lower socioeconomic status (OR 1.25, 95% CI 1.04 to 1.47), in children with more siblings (OR 1.2, 95% CI 1.1 to 1.3), and in children with longer hair (OR 1.20, 95% CI 1.02 to 1.43), although hair length may primarily influence the ability to detect infestation. The socioeconomic status of the family was also a significant influence on the ability to treat infestations successfully — the lower the socioeconomic status, the greater the risk of treatment failure (OR 1.70, 95% CI 1.05 to 2.70).

**AETIOLOGY/RISK FACTORS** Observational studies indicate that infestations occur most frequently in school children, although there is no evidence of a link with school attendance. We found no evidence that lice prefer clean hair to dirty hair.

**PROGNOSIS** The infestation is largely harmless. Sensitisation reactions to louse saliva and faeces may result in localised irritation and erythema. Secondary infection of scratches may occur. Lice have been identified as primary mechanical vectors of scalp pyoderma caused by streptococci and staphylococci usually found on the skin.

### 560 | Herpes labialis

Graham Worrall

**KEY POINTS**

- Herpes simplex virus type 1 infection usually causes a mild, self-limiting painful blistering around the mouth, with 20% to 40% of adults affected at some time.

  Primary infection usually occurs in childhood, after which the virus is thought to remain latent in the trigeminal ganglion.

  Recurrence may be triggered by factors such as exposure to bright light, stress, and fatigue.

- Oral antiviral agents such as aciclovir may reduce the duration of pain and time to healing for a first attack of herpes labialis compared with placebo. However, evidence is very limited.

  We don't know whether topical antiviral agents can reduce pain or time to healing in a first attack.

- Prophylactic oral antiviral agents may reduce the frequency and severity of attacks compared with placebo, but we don't know the best timing and duration of treatment.

  We don't know whether topical antiviral treatments are beneficial as prophylaxis against recurrent attacks.

  Ultraviolet sunscreen may reduce recurrent attacks, however, evidence is very limited.

- Oral antiviral agents may reduce the duration of symptoms and the time to heal in recurrent attacks of herpes labialis.

  Oral aciclovir, famciclovir, and valaciclovir may marginally reduce healing time if taken early in a recurrent attack, but valaciclovir may cause headache.

- We found limited evidence that topical antiviral agents may reduce pain and healing time in recurrent attacks. However, results are inconsistent and of marginal clinical importance.

- We don't know whether topical anaesthetic agents or zinc oxide cream reduce healing time. Zinc oxide cream may increase skin irritation.

 **Please visit http://clinicalevidence.bmj.com for full text and references**

| What are the effects of antiviral treatments for the first attack of herpes labialis? | |
|---|---|
| Likely To Be Beneficial | • Oral antiviral agents (aciclovir) |
| Unknown Effectiveness | • Topical antiviral agents |

| What are the effects of interventions aimed at preventing recurrent attacks of herpes labialis? | |
|---|---|
| Likely To Be Beneficial | • Oral antiviral agents (aciclovir)<br><br>• Sunscreen |
| Unknown Effectiveness | • Topical antiviral agents |

## What are the effects of treatments for recurrent attacks of herpes labialis?

| | |
|---|---|
| **Likely To Be Beneficial** | • Oral antiviral agents (aciclovir, famciclovir, and valaciclovir) |
| **Unknown Effectiveness** | • Topical anaesthetic agents<br>• Topical antiviral agents (some evidence of statistical benefit; however, benefit is of marginal clinical importance)<br>• Zinc oxide cream |

**Search date February 2009**

**DEFINITION** Herpes labialis is a mild, self-limiting infection with herpes simplex virus type 1 (HSV-1). It causes pain and blistering on the lips and perioral area (cold sores); fever and constitutional symptoms are rare. Most people have no warning of an attack, but some experience a recognisable prodrome. In this review, we have included studies in people with normal immunity and excluded studies in people who are immunocompromised (e.g., studies in people with HIV or with cancer undergoing chemotherapy).

**INCIDENCE/PREVALENCE** Herpes labialis accounts for about 1% of primary care consultations in the UK each year; 20% to 40% of people have experienced cold sores at some time.

**AETIOLOGY/RISK FACTORS** Herpes labialis is caused by HSV-1. After the primary infection, which usually occurs in childhood, the virus is thought to remain latent in the trigeminal ganglion. A variety of factors, including exposure to bright sunlight, fatigue, or psychological stress, can precipitate a recurrence.

**PROGNOSIS** In most people, herpes labialis is a mild, self-limiting illness. Recurrences are usually shorter and less severe than the initial attack. Healing is usually complete in 7 to 10 days without scarring. Rates of reactivation are unknown. Herpes labialis can cause serious illness in immunocompromised people.

# Malignant melanoma (metastatic)

Rosalie Fisher and James Larkin

## KEY POINTS

- There are 8100 new cases of malignant melanoma and 1800 deaths a year in the UK, largely as a result of metastatic disease.

  The median survival of people with metastatic melanoma is 6 to 9 months after diagnosis, with 10% of people alive at 5 years.

  Chemotherapy is given with palliative rather than curative intent for metastatic disease.

- There is consensus that it is reasonable to give chemotherapy to people with metastatic melanoma.

  Chemotherapy for metastatic melanoma has been associated with serious adverse effects. However, these tend to be manageable, and it is reasonable to give chemotherapy to people with metastatic melanoma, although there are no good-quality studies to support this view, and only a small proportion of people may benefit.

- Dacarbazine or temozolomide are the standard first-line chemotherapy.

  Both dacarbazine and temozolomide are associated with similar progression-free survival and fewer adverse effects compared with other single-agent or combination chemotherapy.

  Combination chemotherapy is no more effective than single-agent chemotherapy at increasing overall survival. Combination chemotherapy is associated with more adverse effects compared with single-agent chemotherapy.

- Immunotherapy (interferon alfa or interferon alfa plus interleukin-2) is unlikely to increase survival when added to chemotherapy, and is associated with influenza-like symptoms and myelosuppression.

(i) **Please visit http://clinicalevidence.bmj.com for full text and references**

| What are the effects of chemotherapy for metastatic melanoma? | |
| --- | --- |
| Trade-off Between Benefits And Harms | • Cytotoxic chemotherapy plus supportive palliative care versus supportive palliative care alone* <br><br> • Dacarbazine or temozolomide (both associated with similar progression-free survival and fewer adverse effects compared with other single-agent or combination chemotherapy) |
| Unlikely To Be Beneficial | • Combination cytotoxic chemotherapy (no more effective at increasing overall survival than single-agent and associated with serious adverse effects) |

| What are the effects of immunotherapy for metastatic melanoma? | |
| --- | --- |
| Unlikely To Be Beneficial | • Adding interferon alfa plus interleukin-2 to cytotoxic chemotherapy (increased adverse effects and no benefit in overall survival compared with chemotherapy alone) |

- Adding interferon alfa to cytotoxic chemotherapy (increased adverse effects and no benefit in overall survival compared with chemotherapy alone)

**Search date March 2010**

*Categorisation based on consensus.

**DEFINITION** Malignant melanoma is a tumour derived from melanocytes in the basal layer of the epidermis. The systemic treatment of malignant melanoma with distant metastases is reviewed here. For the purposes of this review, we will cover only cutaneous melanoma with distant metastases (stage IV). Non-metastatic malignant melanoma is covered in a separate review; see review on malignant melanoma (non-metastatic), p 564.

**INCIDENCE/PREVALENCE** There are 8100 new cases of malignant melanoma and 1800 deaths a year in the UK. Malignant melanoma accounts for 10% of all skin cancers and is the primary cause of death from skin cancer. It occurs more frequently on exposed skin, such as men's backs and women's lower legs.

**AETIOLOGY/RISK FACTORS** Environmental factors, such as exposure to ultraviolet light (especially episodes of severe sunburn in childhood), and genetic factors, such as a family history of the disease, are known to be risk factors for the development of melanoma. In addition, skin colour and the number of moles a person has correlate closely with the risk of developing malignant melanoma.

**PROGNOSIS** The median survival of people with metastatic melanoma is 6 to 9 months after diagnosis, with 10% of people alive at 5 years. Chemotherapy is given with palliative rather than curative intent in metastatic disease.

Philip Savage

## KEY POINTS

- The incidence of malignant melanoma has increased over the past 25 years in the UK, but death rates have remained fairly constant. Five-year survival ranges from 20–95% depending on disease stage.

  Risks are greater in white populations and in people with higher numbers of skin naevi.

  Prognosis depends on depth of tumour, ulceration, and number of lymph nodes involved. Survival may be better in women compared with men, and for lesions on the limbs compared with the trunk.

  Lesions can recur after 5–10 years, so long-term surveillance may be required.

- Sunscreens have not been shown to reduce the risk of malignant melanoma, but sunscreen use does not necessarily correlate with reduced total ultraviolet light exposure.

- Wide (3 cm) excision of lesions leads to reduced local recurrence compared with narrow (1 cm) excision in people with tumours greater than 2 mm Breslow thickness.

  Wide (3–5 cm) excision is unlikely to be more beneficial than narrow (1–2 cm) excision in people with tumours of less than 2 mm Breslow thickness, and may increase the need for skin grafts.

- Elective lymph-node dissection is unlikely to increase survival in people without clinically detectable lymph-node metastases.

  We don't know whether sentinel lymph-node biopsy is beneficial.

- We don't know whether adjuvant treatment with vaccines, high-dose interferon alfa, or surveillance for early treatment of recurrence improve survival.

  Low- and intermediate-dose interferon are unlikely to improve relapse rates or survival compared with no adjuvant treatment.

  High-dose interferon alfa may increase the time until relapse compared with no adjuvant treatment, but overall survival seems to be unchanged.

  Severe adverse effects occur in 10–75% of people receiving interferon alfa treatment.

(i) **Please visit http://clinicalevidence.bmj.com for full text and references**

| What are the effects of interventions to prevent malignant melanoma? | |
| --- | --- |
| Unknown Effectiveness | • Sunscreens |

| Is there an optimal surgical margin for the primary excision of melanoma? | |
| --- | --- |
| Likely To Be Beneficial | • Wide (3 cm) excision in tumours greater than 2 mm Breslow depth (less local recurrence than narrow 1 cm excision) |
| Unlikely To Be Beneficial | • Wide (3–5 cm) excision in tumours less than 2 mm Breslow depth (no better than narrow 1–2 cm excision) |

| What are the effects of elective lymph-node dissection in people with malignant melanoma with clinically uninvolved lymph nodes? | |
|---|---|
| Unlikely To Be Beneficial | • Elective lymph-node dissection |

| What are the effects of sentinel lymph-node biopsy in people with malignant melanoma with clinically uninvolved lymph nodes? | |
|---|---|
| Unknown Effectiveness | • Sentinel lymph-node biopsy |

| What are the effects of adjuvant treatment for malignant melanoma? | |
|---|---|
| Unknown Effectiveness | • Adjuvant vaccines in people with malignant melanoma <br><br> • High-dose adjuvant interferon alfa <br><br> • Surveillance for early treatment of recurrence |
| Unlikely To Be Beneficial | • Low- and intermediate-dose adjuvant interferon alfa |

**Search date October 2006**

**DEFINITION** Malignant melanoma is a tumour derived from melanocytes in the basal layer of the epidermis. After malignant transformation, the cancer cells become invasive and penetrate into and beyond the dermis. Malignant melanoma is described by stages (I–IV), which relate to the depth of dermal invasion and the presence of ulceration. Metastatic spread can occur to the regional lymph nodes or to distant sites, particularly the lungs, liver, and central nervous system.

**INCIDENCE/PREVALENCE** The incidence of melanoma varies widely in different populations and is about 10–20 times higher in white than non-white populations. Estimates suggest that the number of cases of melanoma in the UK has increased about fourfold over the past 25 years. Despite this rising incidence, death rates have changed more modestly, and in some populations are now beginning to fall. The increased early diagnosis of thin, good prognosis melanoma and melanoma *in situ* are the main reasons for the divergent findings on incidence and death rates.

**AETIOLOGY/RISK FACTORS** The risk factors for the development of melanoma can be divided into genetic and environmental. Alongside the genetic risk factors of skin type and hair colour, the number of naevi a person has correlates closely with the risk of developing malignant melanoma. Although the risk of developing malignant melanoma is higher in fair-skinned populations living in areas of high sun exposure, the exact relationship between sun exposure, sunscreen use, skin type, and risk is not clear. High total lifetime exposure to excessive sunlight, and episodes of severe sunburn in childhood, are both associated with an increased risk of developing malignant melanoma in adult life. However, people do not necessarily develop malignancy at the sites of maximum exposure to the sun.

**PROGNOSIS** The prognosis of early-stage malignant melanoma, which is clinically limited to the primary skin site (stages I–II), is predominantly related to the depth of dermal invasion and the presence of ulceration. In stage III disease, where disease is present in the regional lymph nodes, the prognosis becomes worse with the increasing number of nodes involved.

*(continued over)*

*(from previous page)*

For example, a person with a thin lesion (Breslow thickness below 1.0 mm) without lymph node involvement has a 95% chance of surviving 5 years. However, if the regional lymph nodes are macroscopically involved, the overall survival at 5 years is only 20–50%. In addition to tumour thickness and lymph node involvement, several studies have shown a better prognosis in women and in people with lesions on the limbs compared with those with lesions on the trunk. Lesions can recur after after 5–10 years, so long-term surveillance may be required.

Luigi Naldi and Berthold Rzany

## KEY POINTS

- Psoriasis affects 1% to 3% of the population, causing changes to the nails and joints in addition to skin lesions in some people.

- We don't know whether treatments that might affect possible triggers, such as acupuncture, balneotherapy, fish oil supplementation, or psychotherapy, improve symptoms of psoriasis, as we found few studies.

- There is consensus that topical emollients and salicylic acid are effective as initial and adjunctive treatment for people with chronic plaque psoriasis, but we don't know whether tars are effective.

  Dithranol may improve lesions compared with placebo. It may be less effective than topical vitamin D derivatives such as calcipotriol.

  Topical potent corticosteroids may improve psoriasis compared with placebo, and efficacy may be increased by adding tazarotene, oral retinoids, or vitamin D and derivatives, or by wrapping in occlusive dressings. Short-term, placebo-controlled randomised trials of topical corticosteroids and vitamin D derivatives are still currently performed in psoriasis mainly for regulatory purposes. From a clinical point of view, there is no need for further trials of this sort, but there is a need still for additional long-term or comparative trials.

  We don't know whether tars are more effective than ultraviolet light or vitamin D derivatives in people with chronic plaque psoriasis.

- CAUTION: Tazarotene, vitamin D and derivatives, and oral retinoids are potentially teratogenic and are contraindicated in women who may be pregnant.

- Heliotherapy, PUVA, and UV-B may improve lesions and reduce relapse, but they increase the risks of photoaging and skin cancer.

- There is consensus that heliotherapy and UV-B are beneficial.

- Methotrexate and ciclosporin seem to be similarly effective at clearing lesions and maintaining remission, but both can cause serious adverse effects.

- Oral retinoids may improve clearance of lesions, alone or with ultraviolet light, but may be less effective than ciclosporin.

- Cytokine inhibitors (etanercept, infliximab, and adalimumab) and T cell-targeted therapies (alefacept, efalizumab) may improve lesions, but long-term effects are unknown.

- We don't know whether leflunomide improves psoriasis.

- The Ingram regimen is considered effective, but we don't know whether Goeckerman treatment or other combined treatments are beneficial.

ⓘ **Please visit http://clinicalevidence.bmj.com for full text and references**

## What are the effects of non-drug treatments (other than ultraviolet light) for chronic plaque psoriasis?

| Unknown Effectiveness | • Acupuncture |
| --- | --- |
| | • Balneotherapy |
| | • Fish oil supplementation |
| | • Psychotherapy |

### What are the effects of topical drug treatments for chronic plaque psoriasis?

| Beneficial | • Tazarotene |
| | • Vitamin D derivatives (topical) |
| **Likely To Be Beneficial** | • Dithranol |
| | • Emollients* |
| | • Keratolytics (salicylic acid, urea) (as an adjunct to other treatments)* |
| **Trade-off Between Benefits And Harms** | • Corticosteroids (topical) |
| **Unknown Effectiveness** | • Tars |

### What are the effects of ultraviolet light treatments for chronic plaque psoriasis?

| Likely To Be Beneficial | • Heliotherapy* |
| | • PUVA* |
| | • UV-B* |
| **Unknown Effectiveness** | • Phototherapy plus balneotherapy |
| | • UV-A |

### What are the effects of systemic drug treatments for chronic plaque psoriasis?

| Trade-off Between Benefits And Harms | • Adalimumab |
| | • Alefacept |
| | • Ciclosporin |
| | • Efalizumab |
| | • Etanercept |
| | • Fumaric acid derivatives |
| | • Infliximab |
| | • Methotrexate |
| | • Retinoids (oral etretinate, acitretin) |
| **Unknown Effectiveness** | • Leflunomide |
| | • Pimecrolimus (oral) |

## What are the effects of combined treatment with drugs plus ultraviolet light on chronic plaque psoriasis?

| | |
|---|---|
| **Likely To Be Beneficial** | • Ingram regimen* |
| **Trade-off Between Benefits And Harms** | • Adding oral retinoids to PUVA<br>• UV-B plus oral retinoids (combination better than either treatment alone) |
| **Unknown Effectiveness** | • Adding calcipotriol (topical) to PUVA or UV-B<br>• Goeckerman treatment<br>• UV-B light plus emollients |

## What are the effects of combined systemic plus topical drug treatments for chronic plaque psoriasis?

| | |
|---|---|
| **Trade-off Between Benefits And Harms** | • Retinoids (oral) plus topical corticosteroids (more effective than either treatment alone) |
| **Unknown Effectiveness** | • Systemic drug treatment plus topical vitamin D derivatives |

**Search date August 2007**

*Based on consensus.

**DEFINITION** Chronic plaque psoriasis, or psoriasis vulgaris, is a chronic inflammatory skin disease characterised by well-demarcated, erythematous, scaly plaques on the extensor surfaces of the body and scalp. The lesions may occasionally itch or sting, and may bleed when injured. Dystrophic nail changes or nail pitting are found in more than a third of people with chronic plaque psoriasis, and psoriatic arthropathy occurs in 1% to more than 10%. The condition waxes and wanes, with wide variations in course and severity among individuals. Other varieties of psoriasis include guttate, inverse, pustular, and erythrodermic psoriasis. This review deals only with treatments for chronic plaque psoriasis and does not cover nail involvement or scalp psoriasis.

**INCIDENCE/PREVALENCE** Psoriasis affects 1% to 3% of the general population. It is believed to be less frequent in people from Africa and Asia, but we found no reliable epidemiological data to support this.

**AETIOLOGY/RISK FACTORS** About a third of people with psoriasis have a family history of the disease, but physical trauma, acute infection, and some medications (e.g., lithium and beta-blockers) are believed to trigger the condition. A few observational studies have linked the onset or relapse of psoriasis with stressful life events, and with personal habits including cigarette smoking and, less consistently, alcohol consumption. Others have found an association between psoriasis and BMI, and with a diet low in fruit and vegetables.

**PROGNOSIS** We found no long-term prognostic studies. With the exceptions of erythrodermic and acute generalised pustular psoriasis (severe conditions that affect less than 1% of people with psoriasis, and require intensive hospital care), psoriasis is not known to affect mortality. Psoriasis may substantially affect quality of life, by influencing a negative body image and self-image, and by limiting daily activities, social contacts, and work. One systematic review (search date 2000; 17 cohort studies) suggested that severe psoriasis may be associated with lower levels of quality of life than mild psoriasis. At present, there is no cure for psoriasis. However, in many people it can be well controlled with treatment, at least in the short term.

### 570 | Scabies

Paul Johnstone and Mark Strong

**KEY POINTS**

- Scabies is an infestation of the skin by the mite *Sarcoptes scabiei*. In adults, the most common sites of infestation are the fingers and the wrists, although infection may manifest in older people as a diffuse truncal eruption.

  It is a very common public health problem. In many resource-poor settings, scabies is an endemic problem; whereas in industrialised countries, it is most common in institutionalised communities.

- Topical permethrin seems highly effective at increasing clinical cure of scabies within 28 days.

  Topical permethrin use has been associated with isolated reports of serious adverse effects, including death.

- Topical crotamiton seems effective at increasing clinical cure of scabies at 28 days, although it is less effective than topical permethrin.

- We found insufficient evidence to judge the effectiveness of topical benzyl benzoate, topical malathion, or topical sulfur compounds for treating scabies.

- Oral ivermectin seems more effective at increasing clinical cure of scabies compared with placebo. It may be more effective at increasing clinical cure compared with topical benzyl benzoate. However, it may be less effective than topical permethrin in the short term.

  There have been isolated reports of severe adverse effects with oral ivermectin, including death and convulsion, but these are rare.

  Observational data suggest that oral ivermectin may be effective in certain circumstances, such as when included in the treatment of hyperkeratotic crusted scabies, in people with concomitant HIV, and in treating outbreaks in residential facilities.

  Although tested in RCTs, oral ivermectin is not presently licensed for the treatment of scabies in most countries. It is only available on a named patient basis in the UK.

- Topical lindane use has either been restricted or is not available in many parts of the world owing to the mounting evidence for serious adverse effects. We have not included it in this review. However, it may be the most effective treatment that is locally available in some countries. Harms must be carefully weighed against benefits before it is used.

(i) **Please visit http://clinicalevidence.bmj.com for full text and references**

| What are the effects of topical treatments for scabies? | |
|---|---|
| Beneficial | • Permethrin (topical) |
| Likely To Be Beneficial | • Crotamiton (topical; less effective than topical permethrin) |
| Unknown Effectiveness | • Benzyl benzoate (topical)<br>• Malathion (topical)<br>• Sulfur compounds (topical) |

| What are the effects of systemic treatments for scabies? | |
|---|---|
| Likely To Be Beneficial | • Ivermectin (oral; although tested in RCTs, it is not presently licensed for the treatment of scabies in most countries) |

**Search date July 2013**

**DEFINITION** Scabies is an infestation of the skin by the mite *Sarcoptes scabiei*. Typical sites of infestation are skin folds and flexor surfaces. In adults, the most common sites are between the fingers and on the wrists, although infection may manifest in older people as a diffuse truncal eruption. In infants and children, the face, scalp, palms, and soles are also often affected. Infection with the scabies mite causes discomfort and intense itching, particularly at night, with irritating papular or vesicular eruptions. The discomfort and itching can be especially debilitating in immunocompromised people, such as those with HIV/AIDS.

**INCIDENCE/PREVALENCE** Scabies is a common public health problem. In many resource-poor settings, scabies is an endemic problem; whereas in industrialised countries, it is most common in institutionalised communities. Case studies suggest that epidemic cycles occur every 7 to 15 years, and that these partly reflect the population's immune status.

**AETIOLOGY/RISK FACTORS** Scabies is particularly common where there is social disruption, overcrowding with close body contact, and limited access to water. Young children, immobilised older people, people with HIV/AIDS, and other medically and immunologically compromised people are predisposed to infestation and have particularly high mite counts. Although not based on RCT evidence, treating family members and other close contacts at the same time as treating the index case is advisable to minimise reinfection and further spread. Clothing and bed linen belonging to the index case should also be washed.

**PROGNOSIS** Scabies is not life-threatening but the severe, persistent itch and secondary infections may be debilitating. Occasionally, crusted scabies develops. This form of the disease is resistant to routine treatment and can be a source of continued reinfestation and of spread to others.

# 572 | Seborrhoeic dermatitis of the scalp

Luigi Naldi and Janouk Diphoorn

## KEY POINTS
- Seborrhoeic dermatitis affects at least 3% to 10% of the population and causes red patches with greasy scales on the face, chest, skin flexures, and scalp.

  The cause of seborrhoeic dermatitis is unknown. *Malassezia* yeast species are thought to have an important role.

  The inflammatory process may be mediated in susceptible people by fungal metabolites, namely free fatty acids, released from sebaceous triglycerides. The lipid layer of *Malassezia* can also modulate pro-inflammatory cytokine production by keratinocytes.

  Known risk factors include immunodeficiency, neurological or cardiac disease, and alcoholic pancreatitis. In this review, however, we deal with treatment in immunocompetent adults who have no known predisposing conditions.

  Seborrhoeic dermatitis tends to relapse after treatment.

- In adults with seborrhoeic dermatitis of the scalp, topical antifungal preparations containing ketoconazole seem to improve symptoms compared with placebo and are also useful as treatment in the maintenance phase.

  Ciclopirox seems to improve symptoms compared with placebo and may reduce relapse up to 12 weeks after initial treatment phase.

  Bifonazole and selenium sulfide are also likely to be effective, but we don't know whether terbinafine is beneficial as we found no RCTs.

  We found insufficient RCT evidence to fully assess the effectiveness of short courses of topical corticosteroids; however, there is consensus that topical corticosteroids are effective in treating seborrhoeic dermatitis of the scalp in adults. We found limited evidence that clobetasol propionate 0.05% may improve some symptoms of seborrhoeic dermatitis.

  Tar shampoo may reduce scalp dandruff and redness compared with placebo; however, nowadays it is rarely used.

  Pyrithione zinc may be more effective than vehicle shampoo at reducing dandruff severity; however, the evidence is too weak and limited to draw conclusions about the effectiveness.

- Ketoconazole and ciclopirox have both been shown to be beneficial compared to placebo. In the next update of this review we will look for head-to-head comparisons of these.

ⓘ **Please visit http://clinicalevidence.bmj.com for full text and references**

## What are the effects of topical treatments for seborrhoeic dermatitis of the scalp in adults?

| Beneficial | • Ciclopirox/ciclopirox olamine scalp preparations |
|---|---|
|  | • Ketoconazole |
| Likely To Be Beneficial | • Bifonazole |
|  | • Corticosteroids (topical) (hydrocortisone, betamethasone valerate, clobetasone butyrate, mometasone furoate, clobetasol propionate)* |
|  | • Selenium sulfide |

| | • Tar shampoo |
|---|---|
| **Unknown Effectiveness** | • Pyrithione zinc scalp preparations<br>• Terbinafine |

**Search date November 2013**

*Based on consensus.

**DEFINITION** Seborrhoeic dermatitis is one of the most common skin conditions. It occurs in areas of the skin with a rich supply of sebaceous glands and manifests as red, sharply marginated lesions with greasy-looking scales. The scalp is almost inevitably affected. Other areas commonly involved are the face and the chest; however, this review focuses on seborrhoeic dermatitis of the scalp. On the scalp it manifests as dry, flaking desquamation (dandruff) or yellow, greasy scaling with erythema. Dandruff is a lay term commonly used in the context of mild seborrhoeic dermatitis of the scalp. However, any scalp condition that produces scales could be labelled as dandruff. There is also an infantile variant, commonly affecting the scalp, flexures, and genital area, but this infantile variant seems to have a different pathogenesis from adult seborrhoeic dermatitis. Common differential diagnoses for seborrhoeic dermatitis of the scalp are psoriasis, eczema (see review on Atopic eczema, p 552), and tinea capitis.

**INCIDENCE/PREVALENCE** Seborrhoeic dermatitis is estimated to affect from 3% to 10% of the general population. The broad range in the prevalence depends on the age composition of the sample and the country analysed. The disease occurs more frequently in men than in women.

**AETIOLOGY/RISK FACTORS** The cause of seborrhoeic dermatitis is unknown and the disease seems to be multifactorial. *Malassezia* yeasts, a genus classified in 10 species, are considered to play an important role, especially *M globosa* and *M restricta*. They cause an inflammatory reaction that seems to be mediated by free fatty acids, released from sebaceous triglycerides by fungal enzymes such as lipases. The lipid layer of *Malassezia* can also modulate pro-inflammatory cytokine production by keratinocytes. Conditions that have been reported to predispose to seborrhoeic dermatitis include HIV, neurological conditions such as Parkinson's disease, neuronal damage such as facial nerve palsy, spinal injury, ischaemic heart disease, and alcoholic pancreatitis. In this review, we deal with treatment in immunocompetent adults who have no known predisposing conditions.

**PROGNOSIS** Seborrhoeic dermatitis is a chronic condition that tends to flare and remit spontaneously, and is prone to recurrence after treatment.

# 574 | Squamous cell carcinoma of the skin (non-metastatic)

Adèle Green and Penelope McBride

## KEY POINTS

- Cutaneous squamous cell carcinoma is a malignant tumour of keratinocytes arising in the epidermis, with histological evidence of dermal invasion.

  Incidence varies by country, skin colour, and outdoor behaviour, and is as high as 400 per 100,000 in Australia.

  People with fair skin colour who have high sun exposure and sunburn easily with little or no tanning, people with xeroderma pigmentosum, and people who are immunosuppressed are most susceptible to squamous cell carcinoma.

- Regular sunscreen application to the head, neck, arms, and hands seems to reduce the incidence of squamous cell carcinoma more than discretionary use or no use.

  The evidence regarding regular use of sunscreen to reduce squamous cell carcinoma is from an RCT of adults in a subtropical community in Queensland, Australia, half of whom had previous actinic keratoses. The generalisability of these findings will be influenced by climate and seasonality, among other factors.

  Regular sunscreen application to the head, neck, arms, and hands also seems to reduce the rate of acquisition of actinic (solar) keratoses more than discretionary or no use. Daily sunscreen application seems to reduce the incidence of new actinic keratoses in people who had previous actinic keratoses.

- With regard to surgery, we found no RCTs to assess the optimal primary excision margin required to prevent recurrence of squamous cell carcinoma.

  As with all kinds of surgery, there is a potential for tissue destruction and scarring, particularly of vital structures such as eyelids, lip margins, and motor and sensory nerves.

- We do not know whether radiotherapy after surgery reduces local recurrence compared with surgery alone.

  Although not measured, there is potential for long-term scar deterioration with post-radiation depigmentation and gradual development of chronic radiodermatitis, including telangiectasiae, thinning of the skin, and hyperkeratosis.

(i) **Please visit http://clinicalevidence.bmj.com for full text and references**

| Does the use of sunscreen help prevent cutaneous squamous cell carcinoma and actinic (solar) keratosis? | |
|---|---|
| Likely To Be Beneficial | • Daily or regular use of sunscreens for preventing development of new actinic (solar) keratosis |
| | • Regular use of sunscreens for prevention of squamous cell carcinoma |

| What is the optimal margin for primary excision of cutaneous squamous cell carcinoma (non-metastatic)? | |
|---|---|
| Unknown Effectiveness | • Optimal primary excision margin |

## Does radiotherapy after surgery affect local recurrence of cutaneous squamous cell carcinoma in people with squamous cell carcinoma of the skin (non-metastatic)?

| Unknown Effectiveness | • Radiotherapy after surgery (compared with surgery alone) |
|---|---|

**Search date August 2013**

**DEFINITION** Cutaneous squamous cell carcinoma is a malignant tumour of keratinocytes arising in the epidermis, showing histological evidence of dermal invasion.

**INCIDENCE/PREVALENCE** Incidence rates on exposed skin vary markedly around the world according to latitude, skin colour, and outdoor behaviour. Reported incidence thus ranges from negligible in black populations, to rates of around 23 per 100,000 in England (though 33 per 100,000 in the South West) and 37 per 100,000 in Scotland in 2003, to 60 per 100,000 in Canada in 2006, to 290 per 100,000 in Arizona in 1991 and up to around 400 per 100,000 in Australia in 2002.

**AETIOLOGY/RISK FACTORS** People with fair skin colour who have high sun exposure and sunburn easily with little or no tanning, people with xeroderma pigmentosum, and those who are immunosuppressed are susceptible to squamous cell carcinoma. The strongest environmental risk factor for squamous cell carcinoma is chronic sun exposure, such that those who work outdoors are at higher risk than those who work indoors. Clinical signs of chronic skin damage, especially actinic (solar) keratoses, are also predictive factors for cutaneous squamous cell carcinoma. In people with multiple actinic keratoses (>15), the risk of squamous cell carcinoma is 10 to 15 times greater than in people with no actinic keratoses.

**PROGNOSIS** Prognosis is related to the location and size of tumour, histological pattern, depth of invasion, perineural involvement, and immunosuppression. The most common site of squamous cell carcinoma is the head and neck. Follow-up of 315 consecutive patients with primary cutaneous squamous cell carcinoma of the head and neck for an average of 4 years in Thessaloniki, Greece, showed grade of differentiation, perineural involvement, the presence of inflammation, and T-stage were independent predictors for overall survival. Stage, inflammation, and perineural involvement predicted recurrence-free survival. Factors associated with poor outcomes for squamous cell carcinoma with perineural invasion were studied in a hospital series of 114 adults in Boston, MA (US). Tumours with large nerve invasion (at least 0.1 mm in calibre) rather than small (unspecified) nerve invasion were more likely to have other risk factors, including tumour diameter of 2 cm or greater, invasion beyond the subcutaneous fat, multiple nerve involvement, infiltrative growth, or lymphovascular invasion. Tumour diameter of 2 cm or greater predicted local recurrence; having multiple (of the above) risk factors predicted nodal metastasis; and lymphovascular invasion predicted death from disease.

# Vitiligo in adults and children: surgical interventions

Rubeta Matin

## KEY POINTS

- Vitiligo is an acquired skin disorder characterised by white (depigmented) patches in the skin, caused by the loss of functioning melanocytes.

  Vitiligo patches can appear anywhere on the skin, but common sites are usually around the orifices, the genitals, or sun-exposed areas such as the face and hands.

  The extent and distribution of vitiligo often changes during the course of a person's lifetime, and its progression is unpredictable.

- Vitiligo patches in certain body areas such as the acral sites, palms and soles, lips, mucosa, and nipples, and segmental forms in any area are relatively resistant to all conventional medical treatment modalities. This is thought to be related to the lack of melanocyte reservoir in non-hair bearing sites.

  In these cases, counselling and cosmetic camouflage become a priority, and often in these sites re-pigmentation is unlikely to be achieved unless surgical methods are used.

- There are a variety of medical treatments used for vitiligo, but this review has focused on surgical therapeutic options as this is an expanding field worldwide. Surgery is considered in people with stable vitiligo unresponsive to standard medical therapies.

  We do not know whether surgical treatments of vitiligo in adults and children (blister grafts, cultured cellular transplantation, non-cultured cellular transplantation, punch/mini grafts, split-thickness skin grafts) are effective, as we found limited evidence from RCTs and systematic reviews. The evidence found was of low or very low quality.

  We searched for RCTs comparing blister grafts, cultured cellular transplantation, non-cultured cellular transplantation, punch/mini grafts, and split-thickness grafts with no active treatment or with each other.

  There are significant challenges undertaking robust RCTs assessing surgical treatments, as it is difficult to offer suitable control treatments and the high cost of surgical studies can be limiting.

 **Please visit http://clinicalevidence.bmj.com for full text and references**

| What are the effects of surgical treatments for vitiligo in adults and children? | |
|---|---|
| Unknown Effectiveness | • Blister grafts |
| | • Cultured cellular transplantation |
| | • Non-cultured cellular transplantation |
| | • Punch/mini grafts |
| | • Split-thickness skin grafts |

**Search date April 2014**

---

**DEFINITION** Vitiligo is an acquired skin disorder characterised by white (depigmented) patches in the skin, caused by the loss of functioning melanocytes. The hair, and rarely the eyes, may also lose colour. Vitiligo patches can appear anywhere on the skin but common sites are usually around the orifices, the genitals, or sun-exposed areas such as the face and hands. The disease is classified according to its extent and distribution, and can be subdivided into generalised or localised. In practice, there is considerable overlap between these types, and people often have vitiligo that cannot be categorised or that will change during the course of their lifetime. Therefore, for the purposes of this review, we have included all people diagnosed with vitiligo of any type. Children were defined as people aged 15 years and under. In developing guidelines for the management of vitiligo, a consensus was agreed among clinicians that topical corticosteroid therapy would be chosen as first-line treatment for localised vitiligo (11/14 respondents [79%]), generalised vitiligo (11/14 respondents [79%]), and stable vitiligo (12/14 respondents [86%]). Other treatment options include topical tacrolimus for localised vitiligo and narrowband ultraviolet light B (UVB) or oral psoralen plus ultraviolet light A (PUVA) for moderate to severe generalised vitiligo. Surgery is considered in people with stable vitiligo unresponsive to conservative medical therapies. Stable disease is generally defined as no new lesions, no change in existing lesions, absence of koebnerisation, and spontaneous re-pigmentation. The time period for this is undefined but can range from 6 months to 3 years. The approach taken by surgical therapies is to add melanocytes into the depigmented patches of skin, taken from other pigmented areas. Currently, two types of surgery are considered, tissue grafting or cellular grafting procedures. In this review we have included split-thickness skin grafts, blister grafts, and punch/mini-grafts, which are types of tissue grafting, and cultured and non-cultured cellular transplantation, as types of cellular grafting.

**INCIDENCE/PREVALENCE** Vitiligo is estimated to affect 1% of the world's population, regardless of age, sex, and skin colour. Anyone of any age can develop vitiligo, but it is very rarely reported present at birth. In a Dutch study, 50% of people reported that the disease appeared before the age of 20 years. It is difficult to assess the true prevalence of vitiligo as the estimate of prevalence worldwide varies between 0.5% and 1.0% according to cultural and social differences. In countries where more stigma is attached to the disease for cultural or social reasons, or because it is more visible due to dark skin colour, more people with the disease are likely to consult a doctor than in other countries where this is not the case, thus reported estimates of prevalence may be high. Figures as high as 9% have been reported in India where stigma associated with the disease is high.

**AETIOLOGY/RISK FACTORS** The aetiology of vitiligo is uncertain, although genetic, immunological, biochemical (including oxidative stress), and neurogenic factors may interact to contribute to its development. Although there are few epidemiological studies of vitiligo, it is believed that one third of people with vitiligo report close family members affected by the disorder, suggesting that genetic factors have an important role in the development of the disease. This is supported by several genetic susceptibility studies. In particular, NALP-1 predisposes people to vitiligo as well as to various autoimmune diseases. However, certain triggers (e.g., trauma to the skin, hormonal changes, and stress) may be necessary for the disease to become apparent. Autoimmune mechanisms are thought to be responsible in the pathogenesis of vitiligo (especially in generalised or focal non-dermatomal vitiligo). This is supported by an increased incidence of antibodies found in people with vitiligo. Furthermore, vitiligo is often associated with autoimmune diseases, such as thyroid diseases, pernicious anaemia, and diabetes mellitus. Another indication that vitiligo may be caused by an autoimmune mechanism is that melanocyte antibodies have been found in people with vitiligo, and their incidence correlates with disease activity. Involvement of cellular immunity has been considered because T lymphocytes and macrophages in peri-lesional skin have also been frequently reported. Regarding segmental vitiligo, the neural hypothesis suggests that it is caused by an accumulation of a neurochemical substance, which decreases melanin production.

**PROGNOSIS** Vitiligo is not life threatening and is mostly asymptomatic, although it does increase the risk of sunburn of the affected areas due to the absence of melanocytic photo-protection. The association of vitiligo and skin cancer remains an area of controversy. The occurrence of skin cancer in long-lasting vitiligo is rare, although studies have demonstrated increased PUVA-associated skin cancers. A Swedish study that followed up people treated with PUVA over 21 years for a range of benign skin conditions demonstrated an increased risk of squamous cell carcinomas. Furthermore, the risk of malignant melanoma increases among people treated with PUVA by approximately 15 years after the first treatment. The effects of vitiligo can be both cosmetically and psychologically devastating, resulting in low self-esteem and poor body image. The anxieties regarding the disease exist against a background of a lack of understanding of the aetiology and unpredictability of the course. **Progression:** The course of generalised vitiligo is unpredictable; lesions may remain stable for years or (more commonly) may progress alternating with

*(continued over)*

*(from previous page)*

phases of stabilisation, or (less commonly) may slowly progress for several years to cover the entire body surface. In some instances, people may undergo rapid, complete depigmentation within 1 or 2 years. In segmental vitiligo, lesions tend to spread rapidly at onset and show a more stable course thereafter. **Predicting treatment responsiveness:** Certain disease characteristics help predict the outcome of treatment. Besides age, duration of disease, localisation, and extent of depigmentation, current disease activity should also be considered during clinical decision making. This is essential in people with vitiligo vulgaris, when the disease activity may fluctuate at a given time. Medical therapies and ultraviolet light treatments may be equally effective in active and stable disease. Surgical therapies can be effective interventions for vitiligo, but are limited by the fact that they are invasive and require significant training and expertise to be performed successfully. Surgical treatments are contraindicated in patients who have a history of hypertrophic or keloid scars. An associated skin manifestation is the phenomenon of koebnerisation, where pressure or friction on the skin can cause new lesions or worsen existing ones. Koebnerisation occurs in most people with vitiligo, but elimination of frictional trauma, in the form of occlusive garments and jewellery, prevents occurrence of new lesions in the cosmetically important areas in cases of progressive vitiligo. Also, it has been reported that the presence of positive experimentally induced Koebner phenomenon is associated with active disease, but not necessarily more severe disease (that is, in terms of the extent of depigmentation). The presence of Koebner phenomenon may be a valuable clinical factor for assessing disease activity, and may predict responsiveness to certain treatments. A case series reported that people who were Koebner phenomenon-positive (induced experimentally) were significantly more responsive to topical fluticasone propionate combined with UVA therapy; but, for narrowband UVB treatment, there was no difference in response, suggesting that people in active and stable stages of the disease may respond equally well to UVB.

Steven King-fan Loo and William Yuk-ming Tang

## KEY POINTS

- Warts are caused by the human papillomavirus (HPV), of which there are over 100 types. HPV probably infects the skin via areas of minimal trauma.

    Risk factors include use of communal showers, occupational handling of meat, and immunosuppression.

    In immunocompetent people, warts are harmless and resolve as a result of natural immunity within months or years.

    For what is such a common condition, there are few large, high-quality RCTs available to inform clinical practice.

- Topical salicylic acid increases the cure rate of warts compared with placebo.

- Cryotherapy may be as effective at increasing the cure rate of warts as topical salicylic acid, but we don't know about wart recurrence. We found insufficient evidence on the effects of cryotherapy versus placebo.

- Contact immunotherapy with dinitrochlorobenzene may increase wart clearance compared with placebo, but it can cause inflammation.

- We don't know whether intralesional bleomycin speeds up clearance of warts compared with placebo, as studies have given conflicting results.

- We found no systematic reviews or RCTs about the effects of intralesional candida antigens.

- We don't know whether duct tape occlusion, pulsed dye laser, photodynamic treatment, or surgery increase cure rates compared with placebo, as few high-quality studies have been found.

- We found limited evidence from one small RCT that photodynamic treatment plus topical salicylic acid may increase the proportion of warts cured compared with placebo plus topical salicylic acid; however, it may increase pain or discomfort compared with placebo.

(i) **Please visit http://clinicalevidence.bmj.com for full text and references**

| What are the effects of treatments for warts (non-genital)? | |
|---|---|
| **Beneficial** | • Salicylic acid (topical) |
| **Likely To Be Beneficial** | • Contact immunotherapy (dinitrochlorobenzene) <br> • Cryotherapy (limited evidence that may be as effective as topical salicylic acid) |
| **Unknown Effectiveness** | • Bleomycin (intralesional) <br> • Candida antigen (intralesional) <br> • Duct tape occlusion <br> • Photodynamic treatment <br> • Pulsed dye laser <br> • Surgical procedures |

**Search date October 2013**

---

**DEFINITION** Non-genital warts (verrucas) are an extremely common, benign, and usually a self-limited skin disease. Infection of epidermal cells with the human papillomavirus (HPV)

*(continued over)*

*(from previous page)*

results in cell proliferation and a thickened, warty papule on the skin. There are over 100 different types of HPV. The appearance of warts is determined by the type of virus and the location of the infection. Any area of skin can be infected, but the most common sites are the hands and feet. Genital warts are not covered in this review (see review on Genital warts, p 541). We have also excluded RCTs in people with immunosuppression in this review. **Common warts** are most often seen on the hands and present as skin-coloured papules with a rough 'verrucous' surface. **Flat warts** are most often seen on the backs of the hands and on the legs. They appear as slightly elevated, small plaques that are skin-coloured or light brown. **Plantar warts** occur on the soles of the feet and look like very thick callouses.

**INCIDENCE/PREVALENCE** There are few reliable, population-based data on the incidence and prevalence of non-genital warts. Prevalence probably varies widely between different age groups, populations, and periods of time. Two large population-based studies found prevalence rates of 0.84% in the US and 12.9% in Russia. Prevalence is highest in children and young adults, and two studies in school populations have shown prevalence rates of 12% in 4- to 6-year-olds in the UK and 24% in 16- to 18-year-olds in Australia.

**AETIOLOGY/RISK FACTORS** Warts are caused by HPV, of which there are over 100 different types. They are most common at sites of trauma, such as the hands and feet, and probably result from inoculation of virus into minimally damaged areas of epithelium. Warts on the feet can be acquired from walking barefoot in areas where other people walk barefoot. One observational study (146 adolescents) found that the prevalence of warts on the feet was 27% in those that used a communal shower room and 1.3% in those that used the locker (changing) room. Warts on the hand are also an occupational risk for butchers and meat handlers. One cross-sectional survey (1086 people) found that the prevalence of warts on the hand was 33% in abattoir workers, 34% in retail butchers, 20% in engineering fitters, and 15% in office workers. Immunosuppression is another important risk factor. One observational study in immunosuppressed renal transplant recipients found that, at 5 years or longer after transplantation, 90% had warts.

**PROGNOSIS** Non-genital warts in immunocompetent people are harmless and usually resolve spontaneously as a result of natural immunity within months or years. The rate of resolution is highly variable and probably depends on several factors, including host immunity, age, HPV type, and site of infection. One cohort study (1000 children in long-stay accommodation) found that two-thirds of warts resolved without treatment within a 2-year period.

Juan Jorge Manríquez, Karina Cataldo, Cristián Vera-Kellet, and Isidora Harz-Fresno

## KEY POINTS

- Skin disorders associated with damage by ultraviolet light include wrinkles, hyperpigmentation, tactile roughness, and telangiectasia, and are more common in people with white skin compared with those with other skin types.

  Wrinkles are also associated with ageing, hormonal status, smoking, and intercurrent disease.

- Exposure to ultraviolet light may be associated with photodamage to the skin. Guidelines suggest that avoiding direct sunlight, either by staying indoors or in the shade, or by wearing protective clothing, is the most effective measure for reducing exposure to ultraviolet light.

- Botulinum toxin injection (given in a single session) seems to be more effective than placebo at improving wrinkles at up to 120 days.

  We found no RCTs comparing repeated injections of botulinum toxin versus placebo over a long period of time.

- Topical tretinoin may improve fine wrinkles when applied daily, compared with vehicle cream, in people with mild to severe photodamage, but its effect on coarse wrinkles is unclear.

  Topical tretinoin may cause itching, burning, erythema, and skin peeling.

  Isotretinoin cream applied daily may improve fine and coarse wrinkles compared with vehicle cream in people with mild to severe photodamage, but may cause severe irritation of the face.

- Tazarotene applied daily may improve the appearance of fine wrinkles compared with placebo/vehicle cream. However, it can cause burning of the skin.

  We don't know whether tazarotene is more effective than tretinoin at improving fine and coarse wrinkles in people with moderate photodamage, as studies have given inconclusive results.

- We don't know whether chemical peel (including alpha and beta hydroxyl acids) is beneficial.

- We don't know whether dermabrasion is more effective at improving wrinkles compared with carbon dioxide laser treatment, as studies have given inconclusive results, but adverse effects are common with both treatments, especially erythema.

  We don't know whether variable pulse erbium:YAG laser treatment improves wrinkles, as few studies were found.

(i) **Please visit http://clinicalevidence.bmj.com for full text and references**

| What are the effects of treatments for skin wrinkles? | |
|---|---|
| **Beneficial** | • Botulinum toxin injection (e.g., botulinum toxin type A and type B) |
| **Trade-off Between Benefits And Harms** | • Isotretinoin<br>• Tazarotene (improved fine wrinkles)<br>• Tretinoin (improved fine wrinkles) |
| **Unknown Effectiveness** | • Carbon dioxide laser<br>• Chemical peel (including alpha and beta hydroxyl acids) |

- Dermabrasion

- Variable pulse erbium:YAG laser

**Search date February 2014**

**DEFINITION** Wrinkles are visible creases or folds in the skin. Wrinkles less than 1 mm in width and depth are defined as fine wrinkles. Wrinkles that are 1 mm or more in width and depth are defined as coarse wrinkles. Most RCTs have studied wrinkles on the face, forearms, and hands.

**INCIDENCE/PREVALENCE** We found no information on the incidence of wrinkles alone, only on the incidence of skin photodamage, which includes a spectrum of features such as wrinkles, hyperpigmentation, tactile roughness, and telangiectasia. The incidence of skin disorders associated with ultraviolet light increases with age and develops over several decades. One Australian study (1539 people, aged 20–55 years, living in Queensland) found moderate to severe photodamage in 72% of men and 47% of women under 30 years of age. Severity of photodamage was significantly greater with increasing age, and was independently associated with solar keratoses and skin cancer. Wrinkling was more common in people with white skin (especially skin phototypes I and II). We found few reports of photodamage in black skin (phototypes V and VI). One study reported that the incidence of photodamage in European and North American populations with Fitzpatrick skin types I, II, and III is about 80% to 90%. As Asian skin is more pigmented (Fitzpatrick skin types III–V), wrinkling is not readily apparent until approximately the age of 50 years, with wrinkles being less severe than in white skin of similar age. A prospective study (85 white women living in North America and 70 Japanese women living in Tokyo, aged 20–69 years) comparing age-related changes in wrinkles in eight areas of the facial skin (forehead, glabella, upper eyelid, corner of the eye, lower eyelid, nasolabial groove, cheek, and corner of the mouth) and sagging in the subzygomatic area found more wrinkle formation in all areas of the face in younger age groups of white women than in Japanese women (aged 20–29 years). Another prospective study (160 Chinese women and 160 French women, aged 20–60 years) found that wrinkle onset was delayed by about 10 years in Chinese women compared with French women.

**AETIOLOGY/RISK FACTORS** Wrinkles may be caused by intrinsic factors (e.g., ageing, hormonal status, and intercurrent diseases) and by extrinsic factors (e.g., exposure to ultraviolet radiation and cigarette smoke). These factors contribute to epidermal thinning, loss of elasticity, skin fragility, and creases and lines in the skin. The severity of photodamage varies with skin type, which includes skin colour and the capacity to tan. It is becoming increasingly clear that brief incidental sun exposures, which occur during the activities of daily living, add significantly to the average individual's daily exposure to ultraviolet light. One review of five observational studies found that facial wrinkles in men and women were more common in smokers than in non-smokers. It also found that the risk of moderate to severe wrinkles in lifelong smokers was more than twice that in current smokers who had been smoking for a shorter period (RR 2.57, 95% CI 1.83 to 3.06). A twin study (67 pairs of Japanese monozygotic twins) found that facial texture or wrinkle scores were significantly higher in twins who smoked or did not use skin protection compared with twins not exposed to cigarettes or using skin protection (P = 0.04 and P = 0.03, respectively). Another study (400 German women, aged 70–80 years) found a significant correlation between exposure to air pollutants and signs of extrinsic skin ageing, including wrinkles. The effects of pregnancy and menopause on facial wrinkling have also been investigated by some researchers. In postmenopausal women, oestrogen deficiency is thought to be an important contributory factor for development of wrinkles. One observational study (186 Korean women, aged 20–89 years) found that facial wrinkling increased significantly with an increase in the number of full-term pregnancies (OR 1.84, 95% CI 1.02 to 3.31) and the number of years since menopause (OR 3.91, 95% CI 1.07 to 14.28). However, postmenopausal women who had HRT had significantly less facial wrinkling compared with postmenopausal women who had no history of HRT (OR 0.22, 95% CI 0.05 to 0.95). The effects of sleep positioning and facial wrinkles have also been studied. One cross-sectional study (100 US women, aged 23–71 years) found no significant correlation between sleep side preference and the appearance of wrinkles.

**PROGNOSIS** Wrinkles cannot be considered a medical illness requiring intervention, but concerns about changes in physical appearance brought on by ageing can have a detrimental effect on quality of life. In some cases, concerns about physical appearance can affect personal interactions, occupational functioning, and self-esteem. Geographical differences, culture, and personal values potentially influence a person's anxieties about ageing. In societies in which the maintenance of a youthful appearance is valued, the demand for interventions that ameliorate visible signs of ageing grows as ageing populations expand.

Cathy Alessi and Michael V. Vitiello

## KEY POINTS

- Up to 40% of older adults have insomnia, with difficulty getting to sleep, early waking, or feeling unrefreshed on waking.

    The prevalence of insomnia increases with age. Other risk factors include medical and psychiatric illnesses, psychological factors, stress, daytime napping, and hyperarousal.

    Primary insomnia is a chronic and relapsing condition that may increase the risks of accidents. It is chronic insomnia without specific underlying medical, psychiatric, or other sleep disorders.

    This review only covers primary insomnia in older people (aged 60 years and older). It examines evidence solely from RCTs and systematic reviews of RCTs.

- Cognitive behavioural therapy for insomnia (CBT-I) improves sleep compared with no treatment.

- Exercise may improve symptoms compared with no treatment, but evidence is weak.

- We don't know whether timed exposure to bright light improves sleep quality compared with no treatment, as we found insufficient evidence.

(i) **Please visit http://clinicalevidence.bmj.com for full text and references**

| What are the effects of non-drug treatments for primary insomnia in older people (aged 60 years and older)? | |
| --- | --- |
| Beneficial | • Cognitive behavioural therapy for insomnia (CBT-I) |
| Unknown Effectiveness | • Exercise programmes <br> • Timed exposure to bright light |

**Search date May 2014**

**DEFINITION** Insomnia is defined in the latest update of the International Classification of Sleep Disorders, third edition (ICSD-3) as repeated difficulty initiating sleep, maintaining sleep, or waking up earlier than desired, which is associated with daytime symptoms and which is not explained purely by inadequate opportunity or circumstances for sleep. Additional types of sleep disturbance and daytime symptoms are included that occur primarily in children. This update of the ICSD also indicates that the sleep disturbance and associated daytime symptoms must occur at least three times per week. The latest update of the Diagnostic and Statistical Manual, fifth edition (DSM-5), defines insomnia disorder as dissatisfaction with sleep quantity or quality associated with difficulty initiating sleep, maintaining sleep, or early-morning awakening, which causes clinically significant distress or impaired functioning, despite adequate opportunity for sleep, and occurs at least 3 nights per week, with some additional criteria. Both ICSD-3 and DSM-5 require a duration of (chronic) insomnia for at least 3 months. Since the ICSD-3 was published in 2014 and the DSM-5 was published in 2013, the studies included in this review generally used earlier versions of these or other definitions for insomnia. **Primary insomnia** has been defined as chronic insomnia without specific underlying medical, psychiatric, or other sleep disorders, such as sleep apnoea, depression, dementia, periodic limb movement disorder, or circadian rhythm sleep disorder. This review only covers primary insomnia in older people. For this review we define older people as aged 60 years and older (we included studies where at least 80% of participants were recorded as aged 60 years or older).

**INCIDENCE/PREVALENCE** One population survey in Sweden found that, across all adult age groups, up to 40% of people have insomnia. A US survey in people aged 18 to 79 years found that insomnia affected 35% of all adults during the course of 1 year, and that prevalence increased with age, with estimates ranging from 31% to 38% in people aged 18 to 64 years, to 45% in people aged 65 to 79 years. One US prospective cohort study in people aged over 65 years found that between 23% and 34% had insomnia, and between 7% and 15% had chronic insomnia. It also reported a higher incidence of insomnia in women than in men.

**AETIOLOGY/RISK FACTORS** The cause of insomnia is uncertain. The risk of primary insomnia increases with age and may be related to changes in circadian rhythms associated with age or the onset of chronic conditions and poorer health as a result of ageing. Psychological factors and lifestyle changes may exacerbate perceived effects of changes in sleep patterns associated with age, leading to reduced satisfaction with sleep. Other possible risk factors in all age groups include hyperarousal, chronic stress, and daytime napping.

**PROGNOSIS** We found few reliable data on long-term morbidity and mortality in people with primary insomnia. Primary insomnia is a chronic and relapsing condition. Likely consequences include reduced quality of life and increased risk of accidents owing to daytime sleepiness. People with primary insomnia may be at greater risk of dependence on hypnotic medication, depression, dementia, and falls, and may be more likely to require residential care.

Andrew Herxheimer

### KEY POINTS

- Jet lag is a syndrome associated with long-haul flights across several time zones, characterised by sleep disturbances, daytime fatigue, reduced performance, gastrointestinal problems, and generalised malaise.

  It is caused by a disruption of the 'body clock', which gradually adapts under the influence of light and dark, mediated by melatonin secreted by the pineal gland: darkness switches on melatonin secretion; exposure to strong light switches it off.

  The incidence and severity of jet lag increase with the number of time zones crossed; it is worse on eastward than on westward flights.

- Melatonin reduces subjective ratings of jet lag on eastward and on westward flights compared with placebo.

  The adverse effects of melatonin have not been systematically studied, but people with epilepsy and people taking an oral anticoagulant should not use it without medical supervision.

  There may be a risk of fixed drug eruption, an allergic manifestation, with melatonin.

  Routine pharmaceutical quality control of melatonin products is necessary.

- Hypnotics (zopiclone or zolpidem), taken before bedtime on the first few nights after flying, may reduce the effects of jet lag by improving sleep quality and duration but not other components of jet lag.

  Hypnotics are associated with various adverse effects, including headache, dizziness, nausea, confusion, and amnesia, which can outweigh any short-term benefits.

- We found no studies that examined the effectiveness of lifestyle or environmental adaptations (such as eating, avoiding alcohol or caffeine, sleeping, daylight exposure, or arousal).

  After a westward flight, it is worth staying awake while it is daylight at the destination and trying to sleep when it gets dark. After an eastward flight, one should stay awake but avoid bright light in the morning, and be outdoors as much as possible in the afternoon. This will help to adjust the body clock and turn on the body's own melatonin secretion at the right time.

 Please visit http://clinicalevidence.bmj.com for full text and references

| What are the effects of interventions to prevent or minimise jet lag? | |
|---|---|
| **Likely To Be Beneficial** | • Melatonin* |
| **Trade-off Between Benefits And Harms** | • Hypnotics |
| **Unknown Effectiveness** | • Lifestyle and environmental adaptations (eating, avoiding alcohol or caffeine, sleeping, daylight exposure, or arousal) |

**Search date January 2014**

*The adverse effects of melatonin have not yet been adequately investigated.

**DEFINITION** Jet lag is a syndrome associated with long-haul flights across several time zones, characterised by sleep disturbances, daytime fatigue, reduced performance, gastro-intestinal problems, and generalised malaise. As with most syndromes, not all of the components must be present in any one case. It is caused by the 'body clock' continuing to function in the day–night rhythm of the place of departure. The rhythm adapts gradually under the influence of light and dark, mediated by melatonin secreted by the pineal gland: darkness switches on melatonin secretion; exposure to strong light switches it off.

**INCIDENCE/PREVALENCE** Jet lag affects most air travellers crossing five or more time zones. The incidence and severity of jet lag increase with the number of time zones crossed.

**AETIOLOGY/RISK FACTORS** Someone who has previously experienced jet lag is liable to do so again. Jet lag worsens with the more time zones crossed in one flight, or series of flights, within a few days. Westward travel causes less disruption than eastward travel as it is easier to lengthen, rather than to shorten, the natural circadian cycle.

**PROGNOSIS** Jet lag is worst immediately after travel and gradually resolves over 4 to 6 days as the person adjusts to the new local time. The more time zones crossed, the longer it takes to wear off.

# Sleep apnoea

Michael Hensley and Cheryl Ray

## KEY POINTS

- Sleep apnoea is the popular term for OSAHS. OSAHS is abnormal breathing during sleep that causes recurrent arousals, sleep fragmentation, daytime sleepiness, and nocturnal hypoxaemia.

  Apnoea may be 'central', in which there is cessation of inspiratory effort, or 'obstructive', in which inspiratory efforts continue but are ineffective because of upper airway obstruction.

  OSAHS affects up to 4% of men and 2% of women in the US, with obesity being a major determinant.

- In people with severe OSAHS, nasal CPAP has been shown to reduce daytime sleepiness compared with control treatments.

  Although effective, it can be difficult getting people to comply with the prescribed CPAP regimen. Compliance seems no better with variations of CPAP, such as automatically titrated CPAP, bi-level positive airway pressure, patient-titrated CPAP, or CPAP plus humidification. We don't know whether educational or psychological interventions may improve compliance with CPAP.

- Oral appliances that produce anterior advancement of the mandible seem to be effective in improving sleep-disordered breathing in people with OSAHS (either severe or non-severe).

  Oral appliances are probably not as effective as CPAP, and we don't know how well they work in the long term.

- We found no sufficient evidence judging the effectiveness of weight loss on OSAHS (either severe or non-severe), although there is consensus that advice about weight reduction is an important component of management of OSAHS.

- Nasal CPAP also seems beneficial to people suffering from non-severe OSAHS.

  Nasal CPAP is less acceptable in people with non-severe OSAHS, and we don't know whether measures aimed at improving compliance effectively increase usage.

(i) **Please visit http://clinicalevidence.bmj.com for full text and references**

| What are the effects of treatment for severe OSAHS? | |
|---|---|
| **Beneficial** | • Nasal CPAP (severe OSAHS) |
| **Likely To Be Beneficial** | • Oral appliances (severe OSAHS) |
| **Unknown Effectiveness** | • Measures aimed at improving compliance with nasal CPAP (severe OSAHS) <br><br> • Weight loss (severe OSAHS) |

| What are the effects of treatment for non-severe OSAHS? | |
|---|---|
| **Likely To Be Beneficial** | • Nasal CPAP (non-severe OSAHS) <br><br> • Oral appliances (non-severe OSAHS; more effective than no treatment, control appliance, or |

| | placebo, but less effective than nasal CPAP at improving symptoms including sleep-disordered breathing) |
|---|---|
| **Unknown Effectiveness** | • Measures aimed at improving compliance with nasal CPAP (non-severe OSAHS) <br> • Weight loss (non-severe OSAHS) |

**Search date May 2008**

**DEFINITION** Sleep apnoea is the popular term for OSAHS. OSAHS is abnormal breathing during sleep that causes recurrent arousals, sleep fragmentation, and nocturnal hypoxaemia. The syndrome includes daytime sleepiness, impaired vigilance and cognitive functioning, and reduced quality of life. Apnoea is the absence of airflow at the nose and mouth for at least 10 seconds, and hypopnoea is a major reduction (greater than 50%) in airflow also for at least 10 seconds. Apnoeas may be 'central', in which there is cessation of inspiratory effort, or 'obstructive', in which inspiratory efforts continue, but are ineffective because of upper airway obstruction. The diagnosis of OSAHS is made when a person with daytime symptoms has significant obstructive sleep-disordered breathing revealed by polysomnography (study of sleep state, breathing, and oxygenation) or by more limited studies (e.g., measurement of oxygen saturation overnight). Criteria for the diagnosis of significant sleep-disordered breathing have not been rigorously assessed, but they have been set by consensus and convention. Diagnostic criteria have variable sensitivity and specificity. For example, an apnoea/hypopnoea index (AHI) of fewer than five episodes of apnoea or hypopnoea per hour of sleep is considered normal. However, people with upper airway resistance syndrome have an index below five episodes an hour, and many healthy elderly people have an index greater than five episodes an hour. In an effort to achieve international consensus, new criteria have been proposed and are becoming more widely used. The severity of OSAHS can be classified by the severity of two factors: daytime sleepiness and AHI. Severe OSAHS is defined as severe sleep-disordered breathing (AHI >30 episodes per hour) plus symptoms of excessive daytime sleepiness (such as Epworth Sleepiness Scale >10 or Multiple Sleep Latency Test <5 minutes). Central sleep apnoea and sleep-associated hypoventilation syndromes are not covered in this review.

**INCIDENCE/PREVALENCE** The Wisconsin Sleep Cohort Study (>1000 people; mean age 47 years) in North America found prevalence rates for an AHI of more than five episodes an hour of 24% in men and 9% in women, and for OSAHS with an index greater than five episodes an hour plus excessive sleepiness of 4% in men and 2% in women. There are international differences in the occurrence of OSAHS, of which obesity is considered to be an important determinant. Ethnic differences in prevalence have also been found after adjustment for other risk factors. Little is known about the incidence in resource-poor countries.

**AETIOLOGY/RISK FACTORS** The site of upper airway obstruction in OSAHS is around the level of the tongue, soft palate, or epiglottis. Disorders that predispose to either narrowing of the upper airway or reduction in its stability (e.g., obesity, certain craniofacial abnormalities, vocal cord abnormalities, enlarged tonsils, and enlarged tongue) have been associated with an increased risk of OSAHS. It has been estimated that a 1 kg/$m^2$ increase in BMI (3.2 kg for a person 1.8 m tall) leads to a 30% increase (95% CI 13% to 50%) in the relative risk of developing abnormal sleep-disordered breathing (AHI 5 or more episodes/hour) over a period of 4 years. Other strong associated risk factors include increasing age, and sex (male to female ratio is 2:1). Weaker associations include menopause, family history, smoking, and night-time nasal congestion.

**PROGNOSIS** The long-term prognosis of people with untreated severe OSAHS is poor quality of life, likelihood of motor vehicle accidents, hypertension, and possibly CVD and premature mortality. Unfortunately, the prognosis of treated OSAHS is unclear. The limitations in the evidence include bias in the selection of participants, short duration of follow-up, and variation in the measurement of confounders (e.g., smoking, alcohol use, and other cardiovascular risk factors). Treatment is widespread, making it difficult to find evidence on

*(continued over)*

*(from previous page)*

prognosis for untreated OSAHS. Observational studies support a causal association between OSAHS and systemic hypertension, which increases with the severity of OSAHS (OR 1.21 for non-severe OSAHS to 3.07 for severe OSAHS). OSAHS increases the risk of motor vehicle accidents three- to sevenfold. It is associated with increased risk of premature mortality, CVD, and impaired neurocognitive functioning.

# Constipation in people prescribed opioids

Sam H Ahmedzai and Jason Boland

## KEY POINTS

- Constipation is reported in 52% of people with advanced malignancy. This figure rises to 87% in people who are terminally ill and taking opioids. Constipation may be the most common adverse effect of opioids. There is no reason to believe that people with chronic non-malignant disease who take opioids will be any less troubled by this adverse effect.

- There is some RCT evidence, supported by consensus, that the oral laxatives lactulose, macrogol/electrolyte solutions, and senna are probably of similar efficacy in people with opioid-induced constipation.

  Macrogol/electrolyte solutions may have a better adverse-effect profile than the other oral laxatives.

  We found no good-quality studies on other oral laxatives such as ispaghula husk and liquid paraffin. Liquid paraffin is associated with severe adverse effects and is not recommended for long-term use.

  Sodium phosphate enemas have a high incidence of adverse effects. We found no RCT evidence assessing other rectally applied agents (arachis oil enema, glycerol suppository, sodium citrate micro-enema).

- We found no RCT evidence assessing rectally applied agents (arachis oil enema, glycerol suppository, phosphate enema, sodium citrate micro-enema).

- There is consensus that the opioid antagonists alvimopan, methylnaltrexone, and naloxone can reverse not only the constipation but potentially the other gastrointestinal symptoms induced by opioids.

  Naloxone may provoke reversal of opioid analgesia, but this is less likely with alvimopan or methylnaltrexone. Naloxone may also cause mild degrees of opioid withdrawal, but this has not been reported with methylnaltrexone or alvimopan.

- Further RCTs assessing all the currently available treatments are needed.

(i) Please visit http://clinicalevidence.bmj.com for full text and references

| What are the effects of oral laxatives for constipation in people prescribed opioids? | |
|---|---|
| **Beneficial** | • Lactulose* |
| | • Macrogols (polyethylene glycols) plus electrolyte solutions* |
| | • Senna* |
| **Unknown Effectiveness** | • Bisacodyl |
| | • Co-danthrusate/co-danthramer |
| | • Docusate |
| | • Ispaghula husk |
| | • Liquid paraffin |
| | • Magnesium salts |
| | • Methylcellulose |
| | • Sodium picosulfate |

| What are the effects of rectally applied medications in people for constipation in people prescribed opioids? | |
| --- | --- |
| Unknown Effectiveness | • Arachis oil enema |
| | • Glycerol suppository |
| | • Phosphate enema |
| | • Sodium citrate micro-enema |

| What are the effects of opioid antagonists for constipation in people prescribed opioids? | |
| --- | --- |
| Beneficial | • Opioid antagonists (alvimopan, methylnaltrexone, naloxone) |

**Search date July 2009**

**DEFINITION** Constipation is infrequent defecation with increased difficulty or discomfort and with reduced number of bowel movements, which may or may not be abnormally hard. It can have many causes, one of which is opioid use. Opioid-induced bowel dysfunction (OBD) encompasses a wide range of associated symptoms including abdominal distension and pain, gastric fullness, nausea, vomiting, anorexia, confusion, and overflow diarrhoea. These symptoms may also be associated with constipation from other causes. This review focuses only on constipation in people prescribed opioids. For the purposes of this review, we have used the UK National Institute for Health and Clinical Excellence definition of supportive care as follows: supportive care 'helps the patient and their family to cope with cancer and treatment of it — from pre-diagnosis, through the process of diagnosis and treatment, to cure, continuing illness or death and into bereavement. It helps the patient to maximise the benefits of treatment and to live as well as possible with the effects of the disease. It is given equal priority alongside diagnosis and treatment'. This definition was written in relation to people with cancer but is applicable to all people with chronic or terminal illness; for example, heart failure or lung disease. We have used the WHO definition of palliative care as follows: 'Palliative care is an approach that improves the quality of life of patients and their families facing the problems associated with life-threatening illness, through the prevention and relief of suffering by means of early identification and impeccable assessment and treatment of pain and other problems, physical, psychosocial and spiritual'. Although this definition of palliative care does not specify incurable or terminal illness, there is consensus that palliative care applies to people approaching the end of life; that is, people with a prognosis of less than 1 year. Thus, both supportive and palliative care embrace the same priorities of maximising quality of life; but supportive care aims to do this in people who may live longer, become cured, or who are living in remission from their disease.

**INCIDENCE/PREVALENCE** In one prospective cohort study (1000 people with advanced cancer), constipation was reported to occur in 52% of people. In another prospective cohort study (498 people in hospice with advanced cancer) this figure rose to 87% in people who were terminally ill and taking opioids. A survey (76 people) carried out by the American Pain Society found that, in people with chronic pain of non-cancer origin treated with opioids, the incidence of constipation was five times higher than in another US survey of 10,018 US controls (health status of controls not defined). Fifty-eight percent of people who took opioids regularly required more than two types of treatment for constipation. A British cohort study (274 people with cancer attending a tertiary referral cancer hospital) found that 72% of people taking oral morphine for pain had mild to severe grades of constipation. The prevalence of constipation is not the same with all opioids. One RCT (212 people with cancer), assessing people who were taking opioids for 14 days or less, found that significantly more people taking modified-release oral morphine than taking transdermal fentanyl had constipation (27% with transdermal fentanyl v 45% with modified-release oral morphine; P <0.001). One systematic review (search date 2004, 6 RCTs, 1220 people, 657 with cancer, 563 with chronic painful diseases taking opioids for 28 days or more) found that significantly more people had constipation when taking modified-release oral morphine than taking transdermal fentanyl (16% with transdermal fentanyl $v$ 37% with modified-release oral morphine; P <0.001). A more recent systematic review (search date 2007, 4 RCTs, 425 people with moderate to severe cancer pain) comparing oral morphine versus transdermal opioids (fentanyl and buprenorphine) found that both transdermal drugs were associated with a significantly reduced incidence of constipation (31/214 [14%] with transdermal opioids $v$ 62 /211[29%] with oral morphine).

**AETIOLOGY/RISK FACTORS** The constipating effect of opioids is through their action on mu opioid receptors in the submucosal plexus of the gastrointestinal tract. This decreases gastrointestinal motility by decreasing propulsive peristalsis (at the same time increasing circular contractions), decreases secretions (pancreatic and biliary), and increases intestinal fluid absorption. There is also a central descending opioid-mediated effect so that even spinally administered opioids cause decreased gastric emptying and prolonged oral–caecal transit time. The opioid-induced increase in circular muscle contractions causes colicky pain. There is good evidence from RCTs and animal studies that, compared with water-soluble opioids such as morphine and oxycodone, the more lipid-soluble opioids such as fentanyl and buprenorphine are less likely to cause constipation while maintaining the same degree of analgesic effect. This is probably caused by their much reduced time in the systemic circulation. Other risk factors for constipation and bowel dysfunction in people taking opioids for advanced cancer include hypercalcaemia, reduced mobility, reduced fluid and food intake, dehydration, anal fissures, and mechanical obstruction. Lack of privacy for defecation may also play a part for people in hospital. Drugs that can cause or exacerbate constipation include anticholinergics. In the treatment of cancer, thalidomide, vinca alkaloids, and $5HT_3$ antagonists can all cause constipation. Additionally there is an increased risk of constipation in people with autonomic neuropathy caused by diabetes mellitus, for example, and in people with neuromuscular problems such as spinal cord compression.

**PROGNOSIS** One single-centre observational study (50 people) found a correlation between persistent constipation and poorer performance status (94% of people with Eastern Cooperative Oncology Group [ECOG] score 3 or 4 were constipated). This study found no relationship between total opioid dose and degree of constipation. However, a more recent single-centre observational study (50 people with advanced cancer) found increased constipation in people taking opioids, but found no relationship between constipation and a more sophisticated measure of physical functioning such as the Barthel Index.

Paul Keeley

## KEY POINTS

- Delirium is common in the last weeks of life, occurring in 26% to 44% of people with advanced cancer in hospital, and in up to 88% of people with terminal illness in the last days of life.

  Delirium is part of a wide range of organic mental disorders, which includes dementia, organic mood disorder, and organic anxiety disorder. Delirium, like dementia, is marked by a general cognitive impairment whereas, in other organic mental disorders, impairment is more selective. Delirium is distinguished from dementia in that it is deemed to be, at least potentially, reversible.

- This systematic review focuses on people with delirium secondary to underlying terminal illness, who are being treated in the supportive and palliative care setting.

- We found little RCT evidence in people with delirium caused by underlying terminal illness. It would be unethical to perform a placebo-controlled trial, and it should be acknowledged that undertaking any form of clinical trial in this particularly vulnerable group of people is difficult.

  There is consensus based on observational evidence and experience that haloperidol and other butyrophenones, such as droperidol, are effective for the management of delirium, and they are widely used. However, few RCTs assessing their effects have been undertaken.

  Although benzodiazepines (especially midazolam) are used extensively in people with delirium who are terminally ill, we found no evidence from well-conducted trials that they are beneficial.

  We also don't know whether haloperidol, barbiturates, phenothiazines, or propofol are effective in people with delirium caused by underlying disease. All of these drugs are associated with serious adverse effects and some, such as barbiturates, may in fact cause confusion and agitation. We also don't know whether artificial hydration is effective in people with delirium.

- We don't know whether switching opioids is helpful in people who have developed opioid-induced delirium.

(i) **Please visit http://clinicalevidence.bmj.com for full text and references**

| What are the effects of interventions at the end of life in people with delirium caused by underlying terminal illness? | |
|---|---|
| **Likely To Be Beneficial** | • Haloperidol* |
| **Unknown Effectiveness** | • Artificial hydration |
| | • Barbiturates |
| | • Benzodiazepines |
| | • Opioid switching |
| | • Phenothiazines |
| | • Propofol |

**Search date February 2009**

* Based on consensus.

**DEFINITION** Delirium is defined as a non-specific, global cerebral dysfunction with concurrent disturbances of consciousness, attention, thinking, perception, memory, psychomotor behaviour, emotion, and the sleep–wake cycle. In assessing clinical research, there is some difficulty in that the terms delirium and cognitive failure are at times used interchangeably. Cognitive failure encompasses both delirium (which is common in people with advanced disease in the last weeks of life) and dementia, and amnesic disorders (which are relatively rare in this population). This systematic review covers only people with delirium secondary to underlying terminal illness, who are being treated in the palliative care setting. For the purposes of this review, we have used the NICE definition of supportive care as follows: supportive care "helps the patient and their family to cope with cancer and treatment of it — from prediagnosis, through the process of diagnosis and treatment, to cure, continuing illness or death and into bereavement. It helps the patient to maximise the benefits of treatment and to live as well as possible with the effects of the disease. It is given equal priority alongside diagnosis and treatment." This definition was written in relation to people with cancer, but it is applicable to all people with terminal illness. We have used the WHO definition of palliative care as follows: "Palliative care is an approach that improves the quality of life of patients and their families facing the problems associated with life-threatening illness, through the prevention and relief of suffering by means of early identification and impeccable assessment and treatment of pain and other problems, physical, psychosocial and spiritual." Although this definition of palliative care does not specify incurable or terminal illness, there is consensus that palliative care applies to people approaching the end of life: that is, people with prognosis of less than 1 year. Thus, both supportive and palliative care embrace the same priorities of maximising quality of life; but supportive care aims to do this in people who may live longer, become cured, or who are in remission from their disease.

**INCIDENCE/PREVALENCE** Delirium is common in the last weeks of life, occurring in 26% to 44% of people with advanced cancer in hospital, and in up to 88% of people with a terminal illness in the last days of life. A key difficulty in assessing the prevalence and incidence of delirium in a population with advanced disease relates to the variety of screening instruments, scales, and terminology used (cognitive failure, delirium, agitation, and restlessness).

**AETIOLOGY/RISK FACTORS** Delirium is part of a wide range of organic mental disorders that includes dementia, organic mood disorder, and organic anxiety disorder. Delirium, like dementia, is marked by a general cognitive impairment whereas, in other organic mental disorders, impairment is more selective. Delirium is distinguished from dementia in that delirium is deemed to be, at least potentially, reversible. In a palliative care population (47 people with terminal cancer who died in hospital in which there were 66 episodes of cognitive failure over 3 days), it was possible to attribute a cause for the delirium in less than 50% of people. These causes included drugs, sepsis, brain metastasis, organ failure, hypercalcaemia, and hyponatraemia. The list of potential causes of delirium is extensive, but in end-stage disease can be subdivided as follows: **Central nervous system causes:** primary brain tumours; metastatic spread to the central nervous system; **Metabolic causes:** organ failure (e.g., hyperbilirubinaemia and uraemia); electrolyte disturbance (e.g., hyponatraemia and hypercalcaemia); hypoxia; **Treatment effects:** cytotoxic chemotherapy; radiotherapy (especially cranial irradiation); **Other drug effects:** commonly: corticosteroids; opioids; and anticholinergics; **Other causes:** anaemia; nutritional deficiencies (e.g., vitamin $B_{12}$ deficiency); and paraneoplastic syndromes.

**PROGNOSIS** The prognosis of terminal illness is worsened by delirium. In one systematic review, six of seven prospective studies found a significant association with decreased survival in people with delirium and end-stage cancer.

Paul W Keeley

## KEY POINTS

- Nausea and vomiting occur in 40–70% of people with cancer, and are also common in other chronic conditions such as hepatitis C and inflammatory bowel disease. Nausea and vomiting become more common as disease progresses.

- Nausea and vomiting may occur as a result of the disease, or its treatment.

- The evidence base for treatment-related causes of nausea and vomiting (chemotherapy and radiotherapy) is much greater and more robust than for disease-related causes.

- Metoclopramide is likely to be effective for reducing episodes of vomiting in people having chemotherapy.

   Dexamethasone, in combination with other antiemetics, reduces acute and delayed emesis compared with placebo in people receiving emetogenic chemotherapy, and it may be more effective than metoclopramide in this population.

   $5HT_3$ antagonists also reduce acute vomiting in people having chemotherapy compared with metoclopramide-based regimens, and this benefit is enhanced by the addition of dexamethasone.

   There is consensus that haloperidol, phenothiazines, and venting gastrostomy are effective for controlling nausea and vomiting in people with cancer.

- Cannabinoids are effective for nausea and vomiting in people receiving chemotherapy, but may be associated with a high and often unacceptable burden of adverse effects.

- We don't know whether antihistamines, antimuscarinics, antipsychotics, benzodiazepines, or NK1 antagonists are effective in people with cancer-related nausea and vomiting.

- We don't know whether $5HT_3$ antagonists alone reduce nausea and vomiting in people having radiotherapy. However, adding dexamethasone to $5HT_3$ antagonists seems more effective than $5HT_3$ antagonists alone.

- Despite the lack of robust RCT evidence, there is a consensus based on clinical experience that antihistamines have a place in the management of nausea and vomiting, especially that related to motion sickness, mechanical bowel obstruction, and raised intracranial pressure.

   We don't know whether any other interventions are effective for controlling nausea and vomiting in people with chronic conditions other than cancer.

(i) **Please visit http://clinicalevidence.bmj.com for full text and references**

| What are the effects of treatments for nausea and vomiting occurring either as a result of the disease or its treatment in adults with cancer? | |
|---|---|
| Beneficial | • $5HT_3$ antagonists for the control of chemotherapy-related nausea and vomiting<br><br>• Dexamethasone for the control of chemotherapy-related nausea and vomiting |
| Likely To Be Beneficial | • $5HT_3$ antagonists plus corticosteroids for the control of radiotherapy-related nausea and vomiting |

|  | • Aprepitant for the control of nausea and vomiting in people with cancer (enhances effects of a conventional antiemetic regimen)<br><br>• Haloperidol for the control of nausea and vomiting in people with cancer*<br><br>• Metoclopramide for the control of chemotherapy-related nausea and vomiting<br><br>• Phenothiazines for the control of nausea and vomiting in people with cancer*<br><br>• Venting gastrostomy for the control of nausea and vomiting in people with cancer* |
|---|---|
| **Trade-off Between Benefits And Harms** | • Cannabinoids for the control of chemotherapy-related nausea and vomiting |
| **Unknown Effectiveness** | • 5HT$_3$ antagonists for the control of radiotherapy-related nausea and vomiting<br><br>• Antihistamines for the control of nausea and vomiting in people with cancer<br><br>• Antimuscarinics for the control of nausea and vomiting in people with cancer<br><br>• Antipsychotics (atypical) for the control of nausea and vomiting in people with cancer<br><br>• Benzodiazepines for the control of chemotherapy-related nausea and vomiting |

## What are the effects of treatments for nausea and vomiting occurring either as a result of the disease or its treatment in adults with chronic diseases other than cancer?

| **Likely To Be Beneficial** | • Antihistamines for the control of nausea and vomiting in chronic diseases other than cancer* |
|---|---|
| **Unknown Effectiveness** | • 5HT$_3$ antagonists for the control of nausea and vomiting in chronic diseases other than cancer<br><br>• Antimuscarinics for the control of nausea and vomiting in chronic diseases other than cancer<br><br>• Antipsychotics (atypical) for the control of nausea and vomiting in chronic diseases other than cancer<br><br>• Benzodiazepines for the control of nausea and vomiting in chronic diseases other than cancer<br><br>• Butyrophenones for the control of nausea and vomiting in chronic diseases other than cancer<br><br>• Cannabinoids for the control of nausea and vomiting in chronic diseases other than cancer<br><br>• Corticosteroids for the control of nausea and vomiting in chronic diseases other than cancer<br><br>• NK1 antagonists for the control of nausea and vomiting in chronic diseases other than cancer |

- Phenothiazines for the control of nausea and vomiting in chronic diseases other than cancer
- Prokinetics for the control of nausea and vomiting in chronic diseases other than cancer
- Venting gastrostomy for the control of nausea and vomiting in chronic diseases other than cancer

**Search date April 2008**

*Based on consensus; RCTs unlikely to be conducted.

**DEFINITION** Nausea and vomiting (emesis) are common in people with cancer and other chronic diseases. They may occur because of several factors, most easily categorised as disease-related and treatment-related. The evidence base for treatment-related causes of nausea and vomiting (chemotherapy and radiotherapy) is much greater and more robust than for disease-related causes. This review focuses on the management of nausea and vomiting in people with cancer or other chronic conditions, and does not include people with postoperative nausea and vomiting. For the purposes of this review, we have used the NICE definition of supportive care as follows: supportive care 'helps the patient and their family to cope with cancer and treatment of it — from pre-diagnosis, through the process of diagnosis and treatment, to cure, continuing illness or death and into bereavement. It helps the patient to maximise the benefits of treatment and to live as well as possible with the effects of the disease. It is given equal priority alongside diagnosis and treatment.' This definition was written in relation to people with cancer but is applicable to all people with chronic or terminal illness: for example, heart failure or lung disease. We have used the WHO definition of palliative care as follows: 'Palliative care is an approach that improves the quality of life of patients and their families facing the problem associated with life-threatening illness, through the prevention and relief of suffering by means of early identification and impeccable assessment and treatment of pain and other problems, physical, psychosocial and spiritual.' Although this definition of palliative care does not specify incurable or terminal illness, there is consensus that palliative care applies to people approaching the end of life: that is, people with a prognosis of less than a year. Thus both supportive and palliative care embrace the same priorities of maximising quality of life; but supportive care aims to do this in people who may live longer, become cured, or who are living in remission from their disease.

**INCIDENCE/PREVALENCE** Nausea and vomiting occur in 40–70% of people with cancer and are also common in other chronic conditions, such as hepatitis C and inflammatory bowel disease. Nausea and vomiting become more common as disease progresses.

**AETIOLOGY/RISK FACTORS** Nausea and vomiting are complex neurological and physical phenomena involving a range of areas of the central nervous system and gastrointestinal tract. In palliative and supportive care, nausea may be due to chemotherapy, especially platinum-based chemotherapy, other drugs (opiates, antibiotics), or radiotherapy. It may also have disease-related causes: for example, metabolic (hypercalcaemia, uraemia), cranial (raised intracranial pressure, VIIIth nerve tumours), gastrointestinal (gastric outflow obstruction, hepatomegaly constipation, bowel obstruction, or ileus), or psychogenic (anticipatory nausea and vomiting, anxiety, or fear).

**PROGNOSIS** In many cases, nausea will respond to treatment of the underlying cause: for example, nausea resulting from metabolic disturbance such as hypercalcaemia. Nausea resulting from emetogenic drugs such as opioids may resolve if the opioid is switched.

Columba Quigley

## KEY POINTS

- Up to 80% of people with cancer experience pain at some time during their illness, and most will need opioid analgesics. This review focuses on assessing how different opioid analgesics compare, in terms of both pain control and adverse effects, in people with cancer.

- Oral morphine is the standard treatment for the management of moderate to severe cancer-related pain. Despite lack of large, robust clinical trials, morphine is, to date, the most tried-and-tested opioid for this indication.

- There is an increasing number of opioids now available that are also effective for the same clinical indication. However, we found insufficient evidence to assess the equivalence, in terms of analgesic benefit and adverse effects, of morphine compared with codeine, dihydrocodeine, fentanyl, hydromorphone, methadone, oxycodone, or tramadol.

 Please visit http://clinicalevidence.bmj.com for full text and references

| What are the effects of opioids in treating cancer-related pain? | |
|---|---|
| Trade-off Between Benefits And Harms | • Fentanyl (transdermal) |
| | • Hydromorphone |
| | • Methadone |
| | • Morphine |
| | • Oxycodone |
| | • Tramadol |
| Unknown Effectiveness | • Codeine |
| | • Dihydrocodeine |

Search date July 2007

---

**DEFINITION** Up to 80% of people with cancer experience pain at some time during their illness, and most will need opioid analgesics. This review focuses on assessing how different opioid analgesics compare, in terms of both pain control and adverse effects, in people with cancer. For the purposes of this review, we have used the NICE definition of supportive care as follows: supportive care "helps the patient and their family to cope with cancer and treatment of it — from pre-diagnosis, through the process of diagnosis and treatment, to cure, continuing illness or death and into bereavement. It helps the patient to maximise the benefits of treatment and to live as well as possible with the effects of the disease. It is given equal priority alongside diagnosis and treatment". This definition was written in relation to people with cancer, but is applicable to all people with chronic or terminal illness: for example, heart failure or lung disease. We have used the WHO definition of palliative care as follows: "Palliative care is an approach that improves the quality of life of patients and their families facing the problem associated with life-threatening illness, through the prevention and relief of suffering by means of early identification and impeccable assessment and treatment of pain and other problems, physical, psychosocial and spiritual". Although this definition of palliative care does not specify incurable or terminal illness, there is consensus that palliative care applies to people approaching the end of life: that is, in the last year or less. Thus, both supportive and palliative care embrace the same priorities of maximising quality of life, although supportive care aims to do this in people who may live longer, become cured, or who are living in remission from their disease.

*(continued over)*

*(from previous page)*

**INCIDENCE/PREVALENCE** One population-based survey of 3030 people with cancer from 143 palliative-care centres in 21 European countries found that most (97%) people received analgesics: 32% were assessed as having moderate or severe pain. Morphine was the most frequently used opioid for moderate to severe pain (oral normal-release morphine: 21%; oral sustained-release morphine: 19%; intravenous or subcutaneous morphine: 10%). Other opioids used for moderate to severe pain were transdermal fentanyl (14%), oxycodone (4%), methadone (2%), diamorphine (2%), and hydromorphone (1%). Opioids administered for mild to moderate pain were codeine (8%), tramadol (8%), dextropropoxyphene (5%), and dihydrocodeine (2%). The survey observed large variations in the use of opioids across countries.

Justin Stebbing and Sarah Ngan

## KEY POINTS

- Median survival from metastatic breast cancer is 12 months without treatment, but young people can survive up to 20 years with the disease, whereas in other metastatic cancers this would be considered very unusual.
- Anti-oestrogens (tamoxifen) result in tumour responses in about one third of women with oestrogen receptor-positive metastatic breast cancer when used as first-line treatment, but most women eventually develop resistant disease.

  Progestins and ovarian ablation may be as effective as tamoxifen as first-line treatment but are associated with more adverse effects, while adding tamoxifen to gonadorelin analogues increases survival and response rates.

  Selective aromatase inhibitors may be as effective in delaying disease progression as tamoxifen for first-line treatment, and as effective as tamoxifen or progestins as second-line treatment in postmenopausal women, with similar overall survival. The benefit may be greatest in oestrogen receptor-positive women.

- Hormonal treatment using tamoxifen or progestins may be preferable to chemotherapy as first-line treatment in women with oestrogen receptor-positive disease.
- First-line chemotherapy is associated with an objective tumour response in 40% to 60% of women, of median duration of 6 to 12 months. Complete remission may occur in some women, whereas others show little or no response.

  First-line classical non-taxane combination chemotherapy, especially those containing anthracyclines, may be more effective than modified regimens and as effective as hormonal treatments in prolonging survival.

  The optimum duration of chemotherapy is unknown. Increasing the dose may increase serious adverse effects without prolonging survival.

- Adding trastuzumab to standard first-line chemotherapy increases response rates and overall survival in women with *HER2/neu* overexpression, but risks of cardiac function are increased in women also receiving anthracyclines.

  Adding bevacizumab or lapatinib to standard first-line chemotherapy may also be more effective than standard chemotherapy alone but we cannot be certain as high-quality evidence is still emerging.

- Taxane-based chemotherapy may increase tumour response and survival compared with some non-taxane regimens as second-line treatment. No clear benefit has been found in first-line treatment.
- We don't know how capecitabine or semisynthetic vinca alkaloids perform as second-line treatment for anthracycline-resistant disease.

  Adding bevacizumab or lapatinib to capecitabine may also be more effective at increasing response rates and improving quality of life than second-line capecitabine alone, and adding lapatinib may also increase survival, but we cannot be certain as high-quality evidence is still emerging.

- Bisphosphonates reduce skeletal complications from bone metastases, while radiotherapy may reduce pain and complications from bone metastases, cranial nerve or spinal cord compression, and in brain or choroidal metastases.

(i) **Please visit http://clinicalevidence.bmj.com for full text and references**

## What are the effects of first-line hormonal treatment?

| Beneficial | • Anti-oestrogens (tamoxifen) or progestins as first-line treatment (no significant difference in |
|---|---|

| | survival compared with non-taxane combination chemotherapy, so may be preferable in women with oestrogen receptor-positive disease)<br><br>• Selective aromatase inhibitors as first-line treatment in postmenopausal women (at least as effective as tamoxifen in delaying disease progression)<br><br>• Tamoxifen as first-line treatment in oestrogen receptor-positive women |
|---|---|
| **Likely To Be Beneficial** | • Combined gonadorelin analogues plus tamoxifen as first-line treatment in premenopausal women (better than gonadorelin analogues alone) |
| **Trade-off Between Benefits And Harms** | • Ovarian ablation as first-line treatment in premenopausal women (no significant difference in response rates or survival compared with tamoxifen but associated with substantial adverse effects)<br><br>• Progestins as first-line treatment (beneficial in women with bone metastases or anorexia compared with tamoxifen; higher doses associated with adverse effects) |

## What are the effects of second-line hormonal treatment in women who have not responded to tamoxifen?

| **Beneficial** | • Selective aromatase inhibitors as second-line treatment in postmenopausal women (no significant difference in time to progression compared with anti-oestrogens) |
|---|---|
| **Likely To Be Ineffective Or Harmful** | • Progestins as second-line treatment (less effective in prolonging survival than selective aromatase inhibitors and have more adverse effects) |

## What are the effects of first-line chemotherapy?

| **Beneficial** | • Classical non-taxane combination chemotherapy (CMF) increases response rates and survival compared with modified CMF; anthracycline-based non-taxane combination chemotherapy regimens (CAF) containing doxorubicin delay progression, increase response rates and survival compared with non-anthracycline-based regimens |
|---|---|
| **Trade-off Between Benefits And Harms** | • Taxane-based combination chemotherapy for first-line treatment (may increase response rates compared with non-taxane combination chemotherapy but with increased adverse effects) |
| **Likely To Be Ineffective Or Harmful** | • High-dose chemotherapy for first-line treatment (no significant difference in overall survival |

| | compared with standard chemotherapy and increased adverse effects) |
|---|---|

## What are the effects of first-line chemotherapy in combination with a monoclonal antibody?

| Beneficial | • Chemotherapy plus trastuzumab for first-line treatment in women with overexpressed *HER2/neu* oncogene |
|---|---|
| Unknown Effectiveness | • Chemotherapy plus bevacizumab for first-line treatment |

## What are the effects of first-line chemotherapy in combination with a tyrosine kinase inhibitor?

| Unknown Effectiveness | • Chemotherapy plus tyrosine kinase inhibitor for first-line treatment in women with overexpressed *HER2/neu* oncogene |
|---|---|

## What are the effects of second-line chemotherapy?

| Likely To Be Beneficial | • Taxane-based combination chemotherapy for second-line treatment (increases response rate in women with anthracycline-resistant disease compared with non-taxane combination chemotherapy) |
|---|---|
| Unknown Effectiveness | • Capecitabine for second-line treatment of anthracycline-resistant disease<br><br>• Semisynthetic vinca alkaloids for second-line treatment of anthracycline-resistant disease |

## What are the effects of second-line chemotherapy in combination with a monoclonal antibody?

| Unknown Effectiveness | • Chemotherapy plus bevacizumab for second-line treatment |
|---|---|

## What are the effects of second-line chemotherapy in combination with a tyrosine kinase inhibitor?

| Unknown Effectiveness | • Chemotherapy plus tyrosine kinase inhibitor for second-line treatment in women with overexpressed *HER2/neu* oncogene |
|---|---|

## What are the effects of treatments for bone metastases?

| Beneficial | • Radiotherapy plus appropriate analgesia* |
|---|---|
| Likely To Be Beneficial | • Bisphosphonates |

## What are the effects of treatments for spinal cord metastases?

| Beneficial | • Radiotherapy plus high-dose corticosteroids in women with spinal cord compression |
| | • Radiotherapy* |

## What are the effects of treatments for cerebral metastases?

| Likely To Be Beneficial | • Radiotherapy* |
| Unknown Effectiveness | • Intrathecal chemotherapy |
| | • Radiation sensitisers |
| | • Surgical resection |

## What are the effects of treatments for choroidal metastases?

| Likely To Be Beneficial | • Radiotherapy* |

**Search date June 2009**

*Not based on RCT evidence.

**DEFINITION** Metastatic or advanced breast cancer is the presence of disease at distant sites such as the bone, liver, or lung. Symptoms may include pain from bone metastases, breathlessness from spread to the lungs, and nausea or abdominal discomfort from liver involvement.

**INCIDENCE/PREVALENCE** Breast cancer is the second most frequent cancer in the world, and is by far the most common malignant disease in women (22% of all new cancer cases). Worldwide, the ratio of mortality to incidence is about 36%. It ranks fifth as a cause of death from cancer overall (although it is the leading cause of cancer mortality in women — the 370,000 annual deaths represent 13.9% of cancer deaths in women). Metastatic breast cancer causes 46,000 deaths annually in the US, and 15,000 deaths annually in the UK. It is the most prevalent cancer in the world today and there are an estimated 3.9 million women alive who have had breast cancer diagnosed in the past 5 years (compared, for example, with lung cancer, where there are 1.4 million alive). The true prevalence of metastatic disease is high because some women live with the disease for many years. Since 1990, there has been an overall increase in incidence rates of about 1.5% annually.

**AETIOLOGY/RISK FACTORS** The risk of metastatic disease relates to known adverse prognostic factors in the original primary tumour. These factors include oestrogen receptor-negative disease, primary tumours of 3 cm or more in diameter, and axillary node involvement — recurrence occurred within 10 years of adjuvant chemotherapy for early breast cancer in 60% to 70% of node-positive women and 25% to 30% of node-negative women in one large systematic review.

**PROGNOSIS** Metastatic breast cancer is not treatable by primary surgery and is currently considered incurable. Prognosis depends on age, extent of disease, and oestrogen receptor status. There is also evidence that overexpression of the product of the *HER2/neu* oncogene, which occurs in about one third of women with metastatic breast cancer, is associated with a worse prognosis. A short disease-free interval (e.g., <1 year) between surgery for early breast cancer and developing metastases suggests that the recurrent disease is likely to be resistant to adjuvant treatment. In women who receive no treatment for metastatic disease, the median survival from diagnosis of metastases is 12 months. However, young people with good performance status may survive for 15 to 20 years (whereas in other metastatic cancers, this would be considered very unusual). The choice of first-line treatment (hormonal or chemotherapy) is based on a variety of clinical factors. In many countries, such as the US, Canada, and some countries in Europe, there is evidence of a decrease in death rates in recent years. This probably reflects improvements in treatment (and therefore improved survival) as well as earlier diagnosis.

Geoff Delaney, Justin Stebbing, and Alastair Thompson

## KEY POINTS

- Breast cancer affects at least 1 in 10 women in the UK, but most present with primary operable disease, which has an 80% 5-year survival rate overall.
- In women with ductal carcinoma in situ (DCIS), radiotherapy reduces local recurrence and invasive carcinoma after breast-conserving surgery. The role of tamoxifen added to radiotherapy for DCIS remains unclear because of conflicting results.
- In women with primary operable breast cancer, survival may be increased by full surgical excision, tamoxifen, chemotherapy, radiotherapy, ovarian ablation, or trastuzumab (in women who over-express *HER2/neu* oncogene).

   Incomplete excision may increase the risk of local recurrence, but less-extensive mastectomy that excises all local disease is as effective as radical mastectomy at prolonging survival, with better cosmetic results.

   Axillary clearance (removal of all axillary lymph nodes) achieves local disease control, but has not been shown to increase survival, and can cause arm lymphoedema.

   Sentinel lymph node biopsy or four-node sampling may adequately stage the axilla with less morbidity compared with axillary clearance.

   Adjuvant tamoxifen reduces the risk of recurrence and death in women with oestrogen-positive tumours.

   Primary chemotherapy may facilitate successful breast-conserving surgery instead of mastectomy. Adjuvant combination chemotherapy improves survival compared with no chemotherapy, with greatest benefit likely with anthracycline-based regimens at standard doses for 4 to 6 months.

   Radiotherapy decreases recurrence and mortality after breast-conserving surgery. Post-mastectomy radiotherapy for women who are node-positive or at high risk of recurrence decreases recurrence and mortality.

   Adjuvant aromatase inhibitors improve disease-free survival compared with tamoxifen, but their effect on overall survival is unclear. Adjuvant taxane-based regimens may improve disease-free survival over standard anthracycline-based therapy.

- In women with locally advanced breast cancer, radiotherapy may be as effective as surgery or tamoxifen at increasing survival and local disease control.

   Adding tamoxifen or ovarian ablation to radiotherapy increases survival compared with radiotherapy alone, but adding chemotherapy may not reduce recurrence or mortality compared with radiotherapy alone.

   We don't know if chemotherapy alone improves survival in women with locally advanced breast cancer as we found few trials.

 **Please visit http://clinicalevidence.bmj.com for full text and references**

| What are the effects of interventions after breast-conserving surgery for ductal carcinoma in situ? | |
|---|---|
| Beneficial | • Radiotherapy after breast-conserving surgery for ductal carcinoma in situ (reduced recurrence) |
| Unknown Effectiveness | • Tamoxifen plus radiotherapy |

| What are the effects of treatments for primary operable breast cancer? | |
|---|---|
| Beneficial | • Adjuvant aromatase inhibitors |

| | |
|---|---|
| | • Adjuvant combination chemotherapy (better than no chemotherapy)<br><br>• Adjuvant tamoxifen (in women with oestrogen receptor-positive tumours)<br><br>• Adjuvant taxanes (better than standard adjuvant anthracycline regimens)<br><br>• Anthracycline regimens as adjuvant chemotherapy (better than standard CMF [cyclophosphamide, methotrexate, fluorouracil] regimens)<br><br>• Chemotherapy plus monoclonal antibody (trastuzumab) in women with overexpressed *HER2/neu* oncogene<br><br>• Less extensive mastectomy (similar survival to more extensive surgery, and better cosmetic outcome)<br><br>• Ovarian ablation in premenopausal women<br><br>• Radiotherapy after breast-conserving surgery for primary operable breast cancer (reduced local recurrence and breast cancer mortality compared with breast-conserving surgery alone)<br><br>• Radiotherapy after mastectomy for primary operable breast cancer<br><br>• Radiotherapy with or without endocrine therapy after breast-conserving surgery |
| **Likely To Be Beneficial** | • Primary chemotherapy (reduced mastectomy rates and had similar survival rates to adjuvant chemotherapy)<br><br>• Sentinel node biopsy (reduces surgical adverse effects compared with axillary dissection plus sentinel node dissection; unknown effects on breast cancer events and overall survival)<br><br>• Total nodal radiotherapy |
| **Trade-off Between Benefits And Harms** | • Axillary management |
| **Unknown Effectiveness** | • Different primary chemotherapy regimens versus each other (insufficient evidence regarding which regimen is most effective)<br><br>• Less than whole-breast radiotherapy plus breast-conserving surgery<br><br>• Radiotherapy to the internal mammary chain<br><br>• Radiotherapy to the ipsilateral supraclavicular fossa |
| **Unlikely To Be Beneficial** | • Enhanced-dose regimens of adjuvant combination chemotherapy |

| | • Prolonged adjuvant combination chemotherapy (8–12 months _v_ 4–6 months) |
|---|---|
| **Likely To Be Ineffective Or Harmful** | • High-dose chemotherapy plus autologous stem cell transplantation |

| **What are the effects of interventions in locally advanced breast cancer (stage 3B)?** | |
|---|---|
| **Beneficial** | • Postoperative radiotherapy (in women also receiving postoperative systemic treatment) |
| **Likely To Be Beneficial** | • Radiotherapy (similar effectiveness to surgery) |
| | • Surgery (similar effectiveness to radiotherapy) |
| | • Systemic treatment plus radiotherapy (adding hormonal treatment to radiotherapy improves survival compared with radiotherapy alone) |
| **Unknown Effectiveness** | • Adding chemotherapy (cyclophosphamide/methotrexate/fluorouracil or anthracycline-based regimens) to radiotherapy |
| | • Hypofractionated radiotherapy |
| **Unlikely To Be Beneficial** | • Multimodal treatment versus hormonal treatment |

**Search date April 2009**

**DEFINITION** This review examines the effects of treatment for non-metastatic, primary breast cancer. **Ductal carcinoma in situ** is a non-invasive tumour characterised by the presence of malignant cells in the breast ducts, but with no evidence that they breach the basement membrane and invade into periductal connective tissues. **Invasive breast cancer** occurs when cancer cells spread beyond the basement membrane, which covers the underlying connective tissue in the breast. This tissue is rich in blood vessels and lymphatic channels capable of carrying cancer cells beyond the breast. Invasive breast cancer can be separated into three main groups: early invasive breast cancer, locally advanced breast cancer, and metastatic breast cancer (see review on Breast cancer [metastatic], p 601). **Operable breast cancer** is disease apparently restricted to the breast and/or local lymph nodes in the absence of metastatic disease, and can be removed surgically. Although women do not have overt metastases at the time of staging, they remain at risk of local recurrence, and of metastatic spread. They can be divided into those with tumours greater than 4 to 5 cm, or multifocal cancers, or widespread malignant micro-calcifications that are usually treated by mastectomy, and those with tumours less than 4 to 5 cm that can be treated by breast-conserving surgery. **Locally advanced breast cancer** is defined according to the TNM staging system of the UICC as stage 3B (includes T4 a–d; N2 disease, but absence of metastases). It is a disease presentation with clinical and/or histopathological evidence of skin and/or chest-wall involvement, and/or axillary nodes matted together by tumour extension. **Metastatic breast cancer** is presented in a separate review (see review on Breast cancer [metastatic], p 601).

**INCIDENCE/PREVALENCE** Breast cancer affects 1 in 10 to 1 in 11 women in the UK and causes about 21,000 deaths a year. Prevalence is about five times higher, with over

100,000 women in the UK living with breast cancer at any one time. Of the 36,000 new cases of breast cancer each year in England and Wales, most will present with primary operable disease.

**AETIOLOGY/RISK FACTORS** The risk of breast cancer increases with age. Risk factors include an early age at menarche, nulliparity, older age at menopause, older age at birth of first child, family history, atypical hyperplasia, excess alcohol intake, radiation exposure to developing breast tissue, oral contraceptive use, postmenopausal HRT, and postmenopausal obesity. Risk in different countries varies fivefold. The cause of breast cancer in most women is unknown. About 5% of breast cancers can be attributed to mutations in the genes *BRCA1* and *BRCA2*, but the contribution to inherited breast cancer of other genes, including *Chk2*, *ATM*, *p53*, and *PTEN* and other lower risk alleles, is currently less well established.

**PROGNOSIS Non-metastatic carcinoma** of the breast is potentially curable. The risk of relapse depends on various clinicopathological features, including axillary node involvement, tumour grade, and tumour size, with biological markers including oestrogen receptor and *HER2* receptor status prognostically important in the first 5 years following diagnosis. For women with operable disease, survival is stage and treatment dependent with 80% alive 5 years after diagnosis and treatment (adjuvant treatment is given to most women after surgery). The risk of recurrence is highest during the first 3 years, but the risk remains even 15 to 20 years after surgery. Recurrence at 10 years, according to one large systematic review, is 60% to 70% in node-positive women, and 25% to 30% in node-negative women. The prognosis for disease-free survival at 5 years is worse for stage 3B (33%) than that for stage 3A (71%). Overall survival at 5 years is 44% for stage 3B and 84% for stage 3A. Poor survival and high rates of local recurrence characterise locally advanced breast cancer.

Amit Goyal

## KEY POINTS

- Breast pain (mastalgia) may be cyclical (worse before a period) or non-cyclical, originating from the breast or the chest wall, and occurs at some time in 70% of women.

  Cyclical breast pain resolves spontaneously in 20% to 30% of women, but tends to recur in up to 60% of women.

  Non-cyclical pain responds poorly to treatment but tends to resolve spontaneously in about half of women.

  An accurate diagnosis of true breast pain should be made and other non-breast pathology should be excluded. Other differential diagnoses include pain arising from the chest wall.

- Overall, the trials we found were small and of limited quality. There is a need for large, good-quality trials in this area.

- We found limited evidence that topical diclofenac may be effective at relieving symptoms of cyclical and non-cyclical breast pain but has been associated with adverse effects.

  There is consensus that topical non-steroidal anti-inflammatory drugs (NSAIDs) are effective in relieving breast pain and should be considered as a first-line treatment, as the benefits are thought to outweigh the risk of adverse effects.

- We found insufficient evidence to assess the effects of oral NSAIDs on breast pain.

- We don't know whether topical NSAIDs are more effective than oral NSAIDs at reducing breast pain.

- Danazol, tamoxifen, and gonadorelin analogues (goserelin) may reduce breast pain, but all can cause adverse effects. These agents would usually only be prescribed by a specialist.

  Danazol can cause weight gain, deepening of the voice, menorrhagia, and muscle cramps, and has androgenic effects on the fetus.

  There is consensus to limit the use of tamoxifen to no more than 6 months at a time under expert supervision, and with appropriate non-hormonal contraception, because of the high incidence of adverse effects including teratogenicity and venous thromboembolism.

  Goserelin injection is associated with vaginal dryness, hot flushes, decreased libido, oily skin or hair, decreased breast size, and irritability. There is consensus that goserelin injections should be reserved for severe refractory mastalgia and that treatment should be limited to 6 months.

  Danazol may be less effective than tamoxifen at reducing breast pain and has a less favourable adverse-effects profile compared with tamoxifen (10 mg daily).

  Tamoxifen (10 mg daily) under expert supervision, or danazol, may be considered when first-line treatments are ineffective.

  Tamoxifen (20 mg daily) may increase the risk of venous thromboembolism.

- There is consensus that progestogens do not have a role in treating mastalgia.

- We don't know whether the combined oral contraceptive pill or wearing a bra reduce breast pain, as we found no RCTs.

(i) **Please visit http://clinicalevidence.bmj.com for full text and references**

## What are the effects of treatments for breast pain?

| | |
|---|---|
| **Trade-off Between Benefits And Harms** | • Danazol<br><br>• Gonadorelin analogues (goserelin; luteinising hormone-releasing hormone analogues)<br><br>• NSAIDs (topical) (diclofenac may be effective at relieving symptoms but is associated with adverse effects)<br><br>• Tamoxifen |
| **Unknown Effectiveness** | • Bra-wearing<br>• Contraceptive pill (combined oral)<br>• NSAIDs (oral) |
| **Unlikely To Be Beneficial** | • Danazol compared with tamoxifen (pain relief may be greater with tamoxifen but adverse effects are common with both interventions)<br><br>• Progestogens* |

**Search date February 2014**

*Categorisation based on consensus or expert opinion.

**DEFINITION** Breast pain can be differentiated into cyclical mastalgia (worse before a menstrual period) or non-cyclical mastalgia (unrelated to the menstrual cycle). Cyclical pain is often bilateral, usually most severe in the upper outer quadrants of the breast, and may be referred to the medial aspect of the upper arm. Non-cyclical pain may be caused by true breast pain or chest wall pain, located over the costal cartilages. Specific breast pathology and referred pain unrelated to the breasts are not included in this review.

**INCIDENCE/PREVALENCE** Up to 70% of women develop breast pain in their lifetime. Of 1171 US women attending a gynaecology clinic for any reason, 69% suffered regular discomfort, which was judged as severe in 11% of women, and 36% had consulted a doctor about breast pain.

**AETIOLOGY/RISK FACTORS** Breast pain is most common in women aged 30 to 50 years.

**PROGNOSIS** Cyclical breast pain resolves spontaneously within 3 months of onset in 20% to 30% of women. The pain tends to relapse and remit, and up to 60% of women develop recurrent symptoms 2 years after treatment. Non-cyclical pain responds poorly to treatment but may resolve spontaneously in about 50% of women.

Juliana Ester Martin Lopez

## KEY POINTS

- Vulvovaginal candidiasis is characterised by vulval itching and may also present with abnormal 'cheese-like' or watery vaginal discharge.

  Vulvovaginal candidiasis is estimated to be the second most common cause of vaginitis after bacterial vaginosis. *Candida albicans* accounts for 85% to 90% of cases.

  Risk factors include pregnancy (and other situations where oestrogen levels are increased), diabetes mellitus, immunosuppression, and systemic antibiotics. Incidence increases with the onset of sexual activity, but associations with different types of contraceptives are unclear.

- Intravaginal imidazoles seem to reduce symptoms of acute vulvovaginal candidiasis in non-pregnant symptomatic women.

  Intravaginal imidazoles (butoconazole, clotrimazole, miconazole) may reduce symptoms compared with placebo, and all seem to have similar efficacy compared with each other.

  Intravaginal imidazoles (clotrimazole, miconazole, and econazole) and oral imidazoles (fluconazole or itraconazole) may be equally effective at achieving clinical cure.

- Oral itraconazole seems to reduce persistent symptoms at 1 week compared with placebo, but we don't know whether it is more effective compared with oral fluconazole.

- Intravaginal nystatin seems to reduce symptoms compared with placebo, but we don't know how it compares with intravaginal imidazoles, oral fluconazole, or oral itraconazole.

- The benefits of other intravaginal treatments to treat acute attacks remain unclear, and some may be associated with serious adverse effects.

  We found no RCT evidence comparing intravaginal tea tree oil with other interventions listed in the review.

  We found no RCT evidence comparing garlic or yoghurt, used vaginally or orally, with other interventions listed in the review.

  We found no RCT evidence comparing douching with other interventions listed in the review, but observational studies suggest it is associated with serious adverse effects such as PID and infections, endometritis, and ectopic pregnancy.

- We found no RCT evidence comparing the effects of alternative or complementary treatments with other interventions listed in the review in asymptomatic non-pregnant women with a positive swab for candidiasis.

- We found no RCT evidence on the effects of drug treatments in asymptomatic non-pregnant women with a positive swab for candidiasis.

(i) **Please visit http://clinicalevidence.bmj.com for full text and references**

| What are the effects of drug treatments for acute vulvovaginal candidiasis in non-pregnant symptomatic women? | |
|---|---|
| Beneficial | • Fluconazole (oral) |
| | • Imidazoles (intravaginal) |
| | • Itraconazole (oral) |
| Likely To Be Beneficial | • Nystatin (intravaginal) |

## What are the effects of alternative or complementary treatments for acute vulvovaginal candidiasis in non-pregnant symptomatic women?

| Unknown Effectiveness | • Douching versus other interventions listed in the review |
| --- | --- |
| | • Garlic (oral or intravaginal) versus other interventions listed in the review |
| | • Tea tree oil (intravaginal) versus other interventions listed in the review |
| | • Yoghurt containing *Lactobacillus acidophilus* (oral or intravaginal) versus other interventions listed in the review |

## What are the effects of treating asymptomatic non-pregnant women with a positive swab for candidiasis?

| Unknown Effectiveness | • Alternative or complementary treatments versus other interventions listed in the review |
| --- | --- |
| | • Drug treatments |

**Search date October 2013**

**DEFINITION** Vulvovaginal candidiasis is defined as symptomatic vaginitis (inflammation of the vagina), which often involves the vulva (erythema and swelling), caused by infection with a *Candida* yeast. The predominant symptom is vulvar itching. Abnormal vaginal discharge (which may be minimal — a 'cheese-like' material or a watery secretion) may also be present. Vulvar burning, soreness, and irritation are also common symptoms, and these may be accompanied by dysuria or dyspareunia, which worsen during the week prior to menses. Differentiation from other forms of vaginitis requires the presence of yeast on microscopy of vaginal fluid.

**INCIDENCE/PREVALENCE** Vulvovaginal candidiasis is estimated to be the second most common cause of vaginitis after bacterial vaginosis. Estimates of its incidence are limited and often derived from women who attend hospital clinics. Asymptomatic prevalence has been reported in 10% of women, so identification of vulvovaginal *Candida* is not necessarily indicative of candidal disease. Self-reported history of at least one episode of vulvovaginal candidiasis has been as high as 72%.

**AETIOLOGY/RISK FACTORS** *Candida albicans* accounts for 85% to 90% of cases of vulvovaginal candidiasis. *Candida glabrata* accounts for almost all of the remaining cases, and treatment failure with azoles is common (around 50%) in patients with *C glabrata* vaginitis. Development of symptomatic vulvovaginal candidiasis probably represents increased growth of yeast that previously colonised the vagina without causing symptoms. Risk factors for vulvovaginal candidiasis include pregnancy and other situations that increase oestrogen levels (e.g., contraceptive use and oestrogen therapy), diabetes mellitus, immunosuppression, and systemic antibiotics. The evidence that different types of contraceptives are associated with risk factors is contradictory. The incidence of vulvovaginal candidiasis rises with initiation of sexual activity, but we found no direct evidence that vulvovaginal candidiasis is sexually transmitted.

**PROGNOSIS** We found few descriptions of the natural history of untreated vulvovaginal candidiasis. Discomfort is the main complication and can include pain while passing urine or during sexual intercourse.

# Cervical cancer

Pierre L Martin-Hirsch and Nicholas J Wood

## KEY POINTS

- Worldwide, cervical cancer is the third most common cancer in women.

  In the UK, incidence fell after the introduction of the cervical screening programme to the current level of approximately 2334 women in 2008, with a mortality to incidence ratio of 0.33.

  About 80% of tumours are squamous type, and staging is based on the FIGO classification.

  Survival ranges from almost 100% 5-year disease-free survival for treated stage Ia disease to 5–15% in stage IV disease. Survival is also influenced by tumour bulk, age, and comorbid conditions.

  Development of cervical cancer is strongly associated with HPV infection, acquired mainly by sexual intercourse.

  The peak prevalence of HPV infection is 20–40% in women aged 20 to 30 years, but in 80% of cases the infection resolves within 12 to 18 months.

  Other risk factors for cervical cancer include early onset of sexual activity, multiple sexual partners, long-term use of oral contraceptives, tobacco smoking, low socioeconomic status, and immunosuppressive therapy.

- Vaccination against HPV is effective in preventing certain types of oncogenic HPV infection, and at reducing rates of cervical intraepithelial neoplasia, but there has been insufficient long-term follow-up to assess effects on cervical cancer rates.

- Conisation with adequate excision margins is considered effective for micro-invasive carcinoma (stage Ia1), and can preserve fertility, unlike simple hysterectomy; however, it has been associated with an increased risk of preterm delivery and low birth weight.

  Conisation is often performed for stage Ia1 disease, but evidence for its benefit is from observational studies only.

- We don't know how conisation of the cervix with pelvic lymphadenectomy and simple or radical hysterectomy compare with each other for stage Ia2 and low volume stage 1b cervical cancer, as we found no RCTs.

- We don't know how simple hysterectomy plus lymphadenectomy and radical hysterectomy plus lymphadenectomy compare with each other, in early cervical cancer, as we found no RCT evidence.

- Limited observational evidence shows that radical trachelectomy plus lymphadenectomy results in similar disease-free survival as radical hysterectomy in women with early-stage cervical cancer; however, we found no RCTs.

  Radical trachelectomy plus lymphadenectomy can preserve fertility.

- Limited RCT evidence shows that radiotherapy is as effective as surgery in early-stage disease.

  Overall and disease-free survival are similar after radiotherapy or radical hysterectomy plus lymphadenectomy, but radiotherapy is less likely to cause severe adverse effects.

- Chemoradiotherapy improves survival compared with radiotherapy in women with bulky early-stage cervical cancer.

  Combined chemoradiotherapy improves overall and progression-free survival when used either before or after hysterectomy, but is associated with more haematological and gastrointestinal toxicity compared with radiotherapy alone.

- The benefits of neoadjuvant chemotherapy plus surgery compared with radiotherapy alone are unknown.

(i) **Please visit http://clinicalevidence.bmj.com for full text and references**

## What are the effects of interventions to prevent cervical cancer?

| | |
|---|---|
| Unknown Effectiveness | • HPV vaccine (versus no vaccination) |

## What are the effects of interventions to manage early-stage cervical cancer?

| | |
|---|---|
| Likely To Be Beneficial | • Conisation of the cervix for microinvasive carcinoma (stage Ia1)* (consensus that as effective as simple hysterectomy for this stage and preserves fertility)<br><br>• Radiotherapy versus surgery (consensus that both are likely to be beneficial but unclear how they compare)* |
| Unknown Effectiveness | • Conisation plus lymphadenectomy versus hysterectomy for stage Ia2 and low-volume stage Ib<br><br>• Radical trachelectomy plus lymphadenectomy (can preserve fertility compared with radical hysterectomy)<br><br>• Simple hysterectomy plus lymphadenectomy versus radical hysterectomy plus lymphadenectomy |

## What are the effects of additional interventions to manage bulky early-stage cervical cancer?

| | |
|---|---|
| Beneficial | • Chemoradiotherapy (increased survival compared with radiotherapy) |
| Unknown Effectiveness | • Neoadjuvant chemotherapy |

**Search date October 2009**

*Based on consensus.

**DEFINITION** Cervical cancer is a malignant neoplasm arising from the uterine cervix. About 80% of cervical cancers are of the squamous type; the remainder are adenocarcinomas, adenosquamous carcinomas, and other rare types. Staging of cervical cancer is based on clinical evaluation (FIGO classification). Management is determined by tumour bulk and stage. **Population:** This review deals with treatments for early-stage cancer (defined as FIGO stage Ia1, Ia2, Ib1, and small IIa tumours) and bulky early-stage disease (defined as FIGO stage Ib2 and larger IIa tumours).

**INCIDENCE/PREVALENCE** Cervical cancer is the third most common cancer in women, with about 529,000 new cases diagnosed worldwide in 2008. Most (85%) cases occur in resource-poor countries that have no effective screening programmes. The incidence of cervical cancer in the UK and Europe has greatly reduced since the introduction of a screening programme for detecting precancerous cervical intraepithelial neoplasia. Cervical cancer incidence fell by 42% between 1988 and 1997 in England and Wales. This fall has been reported to be related to the cervical screening programme. In England, cervical cancer had an annual incidence of 2334 women in 2008, with a mortality to incidence ratio of 0.33.

*(continued over)*

*(from previous page)*

**AETIOLOGY/RISK FACTORS** Risk factors for cervical cancer include sexual intercourse at an early age, multiple sexual partners, tobacco smoking, long-term oral contraceptive use, low socioeconomic status, immunosuppressive therapy, and micronutrient deficiency. Persistent infection by oncogenic, high-risk strains of HPV is strongly associated with the development of cervical cancer. HPV strains 16 and 18 cause about 70% of cervical cancer and high-grade cervical intraepithelial neoplasia. The virus is acquired mainly by sexual intercourse, and has a peak prevalence of 20% to 40% in women aged 20 to 30 years, although in 80% of cases the infection is transient and resolves within 12 to 18 months. Women with persistent oncogenic HPV are at risk of developing high-grade pre-cancer and ultimately cervical cancer.

**PROGNOSIS** Overall, 5-year disease-free survival is 50% to 70% for stages Ib2 and IIb, 30% to 50% for stage III, and 5% to 15% for stage IV. In women who receive treatment, 5-year survival in stage Ia approaches 100%, falling to 70% to 85% for stage Ib1 and smaller IIa tumours. Survival in women with more locally advanced tumours is influenced by tumour bulk, the person's age, and coexistent medical conditions. Mortality in untreated locally advanced disease is high.

Pallavi M. Latthe and Rita Champaneria

## KEY POINTS

- Dysmenorrhoea may begin soon after the menarche, where it often improves with age; or it may originate later in life, after the onset of an underlying causative condition.

- Dysmenorrhoea is very common, and in up to 20% of women it may be severe enough to interfere with daily activities.

- This review has searched for evidence on pharmacological interventions for primary dysmenorrhoea.

- Non-steroidal anti-inflammatory drugs (NSAIDs) reduce moderate to severe pain in women with primary dysmenorrhoea compared with placebo, but we don't know whether any one NSAID is superior to the others.

- For simple analgesics, aspirin may reduce pain in women with primary dysmenorrhoea in the short term compared with placebo, although few studies have been of good quality.

  We don't know whether paracetamol is more effective than placebo at reducing pain in women with primary dysmenorrhoea as we found insufficient evidence.

- Combined oral contraceptives may be more effective at reducing pain in women with primary dysmenorrhoea compared with placebo; however, few trials have been of good quality.

- We found insufficient evidence on whether intrauterine progestogens reduce dysmenorrhoea.

 **Please visit http://clinicalevidence.bmj.com for full text and references**

| What are the effects of pharmacological treatments for primary dysmenorrhoea? | |
| --- | --- |
| Beneficial | • NSAIDs (other than aspirin) |
| Likely To Be Beneficial | • Contraceptives (combined oral)<br><br>• Simple analgesics (aspirin, paracetamol; aspirin may be effective short-term, insufficient evidence for paracetamol) |
| Unknown Effectiveness | • Progestogens (intrauterine) |

**Search date December 2013**

**DEFINITION** Dysmenorrhoea is painful menstrual cramps of uterine origin. It is commonly divided into primary dysmenorrhoea (pain without organic pathology) and secondary dysmenorrhoea (pelvic pain associated with an identifiable pathological condition, such as endometriosis [see review on Endometriosis, p 619]). The initial onset of primary dysmenorrhoea is usually shortly after menarche (6–12 months), when ovulatory cycles are established. Pain duration is commonly 8 to 72 hours and is usually associated with the onset of menstrual flow. Secondary dysmenorrhoea can also occur at any time after menarche, but may arise as a new symptom in a woman's 40s or 50s, after the onset of an underlying causative condition. In this review we only consider trials in women with primary dysmenorrhoea. However, the results may also be generalisable to women with secondary dysmenorrhoea. Studies in women with endometriosis, adenomyosis, pelvic congestion, and

*(continued over)*

*(from previous page)*

fibroids may also examine dysmenorrhoea/pain as an outcome. (For more information on these conditions and studies, see reviews on Endometriosis, p 619, Menorrhagia, p 632, Pelvic inflammatory disease, p 539, and Fibroids, p 621.)

**INCIDENCE/PREVALENCE** Variations in the definition of dysmenorrhoea make it difficult to determine prevalence precisely. Studies tend to report on prevalence in adolescent girls, and the type of dysmenorrhoea is not always specified. Adolescent girls tend to have a higher prevalence of primary dysmenorrhoea than older women (see Prognosis). Secondary dysmenorrhoea rates may be lower in adolescents, as onset of causative conditions may not yet have occurred. Therefore, the results from prevalence studies of adolescents may not always be extrapolated to older women, or be accurate estimates of the prevalence of secondary dysmenorrhoea. However, various types of studies have found a consistently high prevalence in women of different ages and nationalities. One systematic review (search date 1996) of the prevalence of chronic pelvic pain, summarising both community and hospital surveys from developed countries, estimated prevalence to be 45% to 95%. A second systematic review of studies in developing countries (search date 2002) found that 25% to 50% of adult women and about 75% of adolescents experienced pain with menstruation, with 5% to 20% reporting severe dysmenorrhoea or pain that prevents them from participating in their usual activities. A third systematic review and meta-analysis of prevalence rates among high-quality studies with samples representative of the general worldwide population (search date 2004) found that prevalence of dysmenorrhoea was 59% (95% CI 49% to 71%). Prevalence rates reported in the UK were between 45% and 97% for any dysmenorrhoea in community-based studies and between 41% and 62% in hospital-based studies. A further review of longitudinal, case-control, or cross-sectional studies with large community-based samples included 15 primary studies, published between 2002 and 2011. It found the prevalence of dysmenorrhoea to vary between 16% and 91% in women of reproductive age, with severe pain in 2% to 29% of women studied.

**AETIOLOGY/RISK FACTORS** A systematic review (search date 2004) of cohort and case-control studies concluded that age under 30 years, low BMI, smoking, earlier menarche (<12 years), longer cycles, heavy menstrual flow, nulliparity, premenstrual syndrome, sterilisation, clinically suspected pelvic inflammatory disease, sexual abuse, and psychological symptoms were associated with increased risk of dysmenorrhoea. Presence of an intrauterine contraceptive device may also be associated with dysmenorrhoea. A further review reported that age, parity, and use of oral contraceptives were inversely associated with dysmenorrhoea, and high stress increased the risk of dysmenorrhoea. The effect sizes were generally modest to moderate, with odds ratios varying between 1 and 4. There was inconclusive evidence for modifiable factors such as cigarette smoking, diet, obesity, depression, and abuse. Family history of dysmenorrhoea strongly increased its risk, with odds ratios between 3.8 and 20.7.

**PROGNOSIS** Primary dysmenorrhoea is a chronic recurring condition that affects most young women. Studies of the natural history of this condition are sparse. One longitudinal study in Scandinavia found that primary dysmenorrhoea often improves in the third decade of a woman's reproductive life, and is also reduced after childbirth. We found no studies that reliably examined the relationship between the prognosis of secondary dysmenorrhoea and the severity of the underlying pathology, such as endometriosis.

# Endometriosis: the effects of dienogest

Simone Ferrero, Valentino Remorgida, Pier Luigi Venturini, and Nicolò Bizzarri

## KEY POINTS

- Ectopic endometrial tissue is found in 2% to 6% of women of reproductive age, in up to 60% of those with dysmenorrhoea, and up to 30% of women with subfertility, with a peak incidence at around 40 years of age. However, symptoms may not correlate with laparoscopic findings.

    Without treatment, endometrial deposits may resolve spontaneously in up to one third of women, deteriorate in nearly half, and remain unchanged in the remainder.

    Oral contraceptives reduce the risk of endometriosis, whereas an early menarche and late menopause increase the risk.

- There are several recognised treatments for endometriosis that have been covered in a previous version of this review. At this update, we have focused on dienogest (a progestin), a new therapy for endometriosis which is licensed in a number of countries (but not all).

- We found limited evidence from one RCT that dienogest, compared with placebo, may reduce pain at 12 weeks in women with endometriosis and pelvic pain.

- However, we don't know if dienogest is more effective than placebo at improving quality of life scores.

    We also found no RCTs of longer than 12 weeks' duration.

- Dienogest and intranasal buserelin seem equally effective at improving subjective symptoms such as lower abdominal pain and lumbago at 24 weeks in women with symptomatic endometriosis.

    Dienogest and intranasal buserelin also seem equally effective at improving quality of life scores.

    However, dienogest may be associated with an increase in genital bleeding compared with buserelin, whilst buserelin may be associated with an increase in hot flushes compared with dienogest.

- We don't know how dienogest compares with gonadorelin analogues other than buserelin in treating endometriosis, as we found no RCTs that met our inclusion criteria.

- We found no RCTs assessing the effectiveness of dienogest compared with combined oral contraceptives, or dienogest compared with other progestogens in treating endometriosis.

(i) Please visit http://clinicalevidence.bmj.com for full text and references

| What are the effects of dienogest for the treatment of endometriosis? | |
|---|---|
| Beneficial | • Dienogest versus placebo (in the short-term) |
| Trade-off Between Benefits And Harms | • Dienogest versus gonadorelin analogues (evidence on intranasal buserelin only) |
| Unknown Effectiveness | • Dienogest versus combined oral contraceptives |
| | • Dienogest versus other progestogens |

Search date June 2014

**DEFINITION** Endometriosis is characterised by ectopic endometrial tissue, which can cause dysmenorrhoea, dyspareunia, non-cyclical pelvic pain, and subfertility. Diagnosis is made by laparoscopy. Most endometrial deposits are found in the pelvis (ovaries, peritoneum, uterosacral ligaments, pouch of Douglas, and rectovaginal septum). Extrapelvic deposits, including those in the umbilicus and diaphragm, are rare. Severity of endometriosis is defined by the American Society for Reproductive Medicine; this review uses the terms minimal (stage I), mild (stage II), moderate (stage III), and severe (stage IV). Endometriomas are cysts of endometriosis within the ovary. This review assesses dysmenorrhoea, dyspareunia (painful sexual intercourse), dyschezia (painful defecation), and non-cyclical pelvic pain associated with endometriosis.

**INCIDENCE/PREVALENCE** The diagnosis of endometriosis is based on surgical visualisation of the disease; therefore, the true prevalence of the disease in the general population is unknown. Variations in estimates of prevalence are thought to be mostly because of differences in diagnostic thresholds and criteria between studies, and in variations in childbearing age between populations, rather than underlying genetic differences. The estimated prevalence of endometriosis in the general population is 1.5% to 6.2%. In women with dysmenorrhoea, the incidence of endometriosis is 40% to 60%, and in women with subfertility it is 20% to 30%. The severity of symptoms and the probability of diagnosis increase with age. Incidence peaks at about 40 years of age. Symptoms and laparoscopic appearance do not always correlate.

**AETIOLOGY/RISK FACTORS** The cause of endometriosis is unknown. Risk factors include early menarche and late menopause. Embryonic cells may give rise to deposits in the umbilicus, whereas retrograde menstruation may deposit endometrial cells in the diaphragm. Use of oral contraceptives reduces the risk of endometriosis, and this protective effect persists for up to 1 year after their discontinuation.

**PROGNOSIS** We found two RCTs in which laparoscopy was repeated after treatment in women given placebo. Over 6 to 12 months, endometrial deposits resolved spontaneously in up to one third of women, deteriorated in nearly half, and were unchanged in the remainder.

Anne Lethaby and Beverley Vollenhoven

## KEY POINTS

- Between 50% and 77% of women may have fibroids, depending on the method of diagnosis used. Fibroids may be asymptomatic, or may present with menorrhagia, pain, mass and pressure effects, infertility, or recurrent pregnancy loss.

  Risk factors for fibroids include obesity, having no children, and no long-term use of the oral contraceptive pill. Fibroids tend to shrink or fibrose after the menopause.

- Myomectomy maintains fertility.

- We searched for RCT evidence. Overall, we found a limited number of trials with relatively small numbers of participants in the assessment of some outcomes. There is a need for further high-quality RCTs in this field.

- We don't know whether magnetic resonance-guided focused ultrasound surgery is beneficial in women with fibroids compared with no treatment/ sham treatment, or other procedures (uterine artery embolisation, hysteroscopic resection, rollerball endometrial ablation, myomectomy, hysterectomy, thermal balloon ablation, or thermal myolysis with laser) as we found no studies.

- We found no RCT evidence on uterine artery embolisation (UAE) compared with no treatment/sham treatment.

- UAE may reduce procedure time, hospital stay, and recovery time compared with hysterectomy, and may reduce the need for blood transfusion.

  Satisfaction rates may be similar between the two procedures at up to 5 years.

  However, UAE seems to be associated with an increased need for future treatment compared with hysterectomy.

- UAE may reduce procedure time, hospital stay, and recovery time compared with myomectomy.

  Satisfaction rates may be similar between the two procedures at up to 2 years.

  However, UAE may be associated with an increased need for future treatment compared with myomectomy.

  Myomectomy may increase pregnancy rates compared with UAE in women with fibroids who wish to retain fertility, but evidence was limited, and came from a small sample of women in one RCT.

- We don't know how UAE compares with magnetic resonance-guided focused ultrasound surgery, hysteroscopic resection, rollerball endometrial ablation, thermal balloon ablation, or thermal myolysis with laser, as we found no studies.

ⓘ **Please visit http://clinicalevidence.bmj.com for full text and references**

## What are the effects of surgical/interventional radiological treatments in women with fibroids?

| | |
|---|---|
| Trade-off Between Benefits And Harms | • Uterine artery embolisation versus hysterectomy (may reduce hospital stay, time to resume normal activities, and need for blood transfusion compared with hysterectomy, but may result in higher rates of future intervention) |
| | • Uterine artery embolisation versus myomectomy (may reduce recovery time and hospital stay |

| | |
|---|---|
| | compared with myomectomy, but may result in higher rates of future intervention) |
| **Unknown Effectiveness** | • Magnetic resonance-guided focused ultrasound surgery versus no treatment/sham treatment |
| | • Magnetic resonance-guided focused ultrasound surgery versus other interventions (hysterectomy, myomectomy, hysteroscopic resection, rollerball endometrial ablation, thermal balloon ablation, thermal myolysis with laser) |
| | • Uterine artery embolisation versus no treatment/sham treatment |
| | • Uterine artery embolisation versus other interventions (magnetic resonance-guided focused ultrasound surgery, hysteroscopic resection, rollerball endometrial ablation, thermal balloon ablation, thermal myolysis with laser) |

**Search date May 2014**

**DEFINITION** Fibroids (uterine leiomyomas) are benign tumours of the smooth muscle cells of the uterus. Women with fibroids can be asymptomatic, or may present with menorrhagia (30%), pelvic pain with or without dysmenorrhoea or pressure symptoms (34%), infertility (27%), and recurrent pregnancy loss (3%). Much of the data describing the relationship between the presence of fibroids and symptoms are based on uncontrolled studies that have assessed the effect of myomectomy on the presenting symptoms. One observational study (142 women) undertaken in the USA suggested that the prevalence of fibroids in infertile women can be as high as 13%, but no direct causal relationship between fibroids and infertility has been established.

**INCIDENCE/PREVALENCE** The reported incidence of fibroids varies from 5.4% to 77.0%, depending on the method of diagnosis used (the gold standard is histological evidence). It is not possible to state the actual incidence of fibroids, because some women with fibroids will not have symptoms, and will therefore not be tested for fibroids. Observational evidence suggests that, in premenopausal women, the incidence of fibroids increases with age, reducing during menopause. On the basis of postmortem examination, 50% of women were found to have these tumours. Gross serial sectioning at 2 mm intervals of 100 consecutive hysterectomy specimens revealed the presence of fibroids in 50/68 (73%) premenopausal women and 27/32 (84%) postmenopausal women. These women were having hysterectomies for reasons other than fibroids. The incidence of fibroids in black women is three times greater than that in white women, based on ultrasound or hysterectomy diagnosis. Submucosal fibroids have been diagnosed in 6% to 34% of women having a hysteroscopy for abnormal bleeding, and in 2% to 7% of women having infertility investigations.

**AETIOLOGY/RISK FACTORS** The cause of fibroids is unknown. Each fibroid is of monoclonal origin and arises independently. Factors thought to be involved include the sex steroid hormones oestrogen and progesterone, as well as the insulin-like growth factors, epidermal growth factor, and transforming growth factor. There may also be genetic factors associated with development; certain genes may be switched on or off making an individual more likely to develop these tumours. Risk factors for fibroid growth include nulliparity and obesity. Risk also reduces consistently with increasing number of term pregnancies; women with five term pregnancies have one quarter of the risk of nulliparous women (P <0.001). Obesity increases the risk of fibroid development by 21% with each 10-kg weight gain (P = 0.008). The combined oral contraceptive pill also reduces the risk of fibroids with increasing duration of use (women who have taken oral contraceptives for 4 to 6 years compared with women who have never taken oral contraceptives: OR 0.8, 95% CI 0.5 to 1.2; women who have taken oral contraceptives for at least 7 years compared with women who have never taken oral contraceptives: OR 0.5, 95% CI 0.3 to 0.9). Women who have had injections containing 150 mg depot medroxyprogesterone acetate also have a reduced incidence compared with women who have never had injections of this drug (OR 0.44, 95% CI 0.36 to 0.55). It is not known if other hormonal contraception, such as the hormone-releasing intrauterine device (IUD), decreases risk.

**PROGNOSIS** There are few data on the long-term untreated prognosis of these tumours, particularly in women asymptomatic at diagnosis. One small case control study reported that, in a group of 106 women treated with observation alone over 1 year, there was no significant change in symptoms and quality of life over that time. Fibroids tend to shrink or fibrose after the menopause.

Joseph Loze Onwude

## KEY POINTS

- Prolapse of the uterus or vagina is usually the result of loss of pelvic support, and causes mainly non-specific symptoms. It may affect over half of women aged 50 to 59 years, but spontaneous regression may occur.

  Risks of genital prolapse increase with advancing parity and age, increasing weight of the largest baby delivered, and hysterectomy.

- We don't know whether pelvic floor muscle exercises or vaginal oestrogen improve symptoms in women with genital prolapse, as we found few studies of adequate quality.

  The consensus is that vaginal pessaries are effective for relief of symptoms in women waiting for surgery, or in whom surgery is contraindicated, but we don't know this for sure.

- In women with anterior vaginal wall prolapse, anterior vaginal wall repair may be more effective than Burch colposuspension at reducing recurrence, and adding mesh reinforcement to anterior colporrhaphy can reduce recurrence.

  Burch colposuspension may be more effective than anterior vaginal wall repair at reducing stress incontinence.

- In women with posterior vaginal wall prolapse, posterior colporrhaphy is more likely to prevent recurrence compared with transanal repair of rectocoele or enterocoele.

  We don't know whether adding mesh reinforcement improves success rates in women having posterior colporrhaphy.

- In women with upper vaginal wall prolapse, abdominal sacral colpopexy reduces the risk of recurrent prolapse, and of postoperative dyspareunia and stress incontinence compared with sacrospinous colpopexy.

  Posterior intravaginal slingplasty may be as effective as vaginal sacrospinous colpopexy at preventing recurrent prolapse.

  Vaginal hysterectomy and repair may reduce the need for re-operation and may be more effective at reducing symptoms, compared with abdominal sacrohysteropexy.

- We don't know how surgical treatment compares with non-surgical treatment in women with prolapse of the upper, anterior, or posterior vaginal wall.

(i) **Please visit http://clinicalevidence.bmj.com for full text and references**

| What are the effects of non-surgical treatments in women with genital prolapse? | |
|---|---|
| Likely To Be Beneficial | • Vaginal pessaries* |
| Unknown Effectiveness | • Pelvic floor muscle exercises<br><br>• Vaginal oestrogen |

| What are the effects of surgical treatments in women with anterior vaginal wall prolapse? | |
|---|---|
| Beneficial | • Anterior colporrhaphy with mesh reinforcement versus traditional anterior colporrhaphy in women with anterior vaginal wall prolapse |

| | • Traditional anterior colporrhaphy versus abdominal Burch colposuspension in women with anterior vaginal wall prolapse |
|---|---|
| **Likely To Be Beneficial** | • Ultralateral anterior colporrhaphy versus traditional anterior colporrhaphy (both are likely to be beneficial but unclear how they compare with each other) |
| **Unknown Effectiveness** | • Surgical versus non-surgical treatment in women with anterior vaginal wall prolapse |

### What are the effects of surgical treatments in women with posterior vaginal wall prolapse?

| **Beneficial** | • Posterior colporrhaphy versus transanal repair in women with posterior vaginal wall prolapse |
|---|---|
| **Unknown Effectiveness** | • Posterior colporrhaphy with mesh versus posterior colporrhaphy without mesh reinforcement in women with posterior vaginal wall prolapse<br><br>• Surgical versus non-surgical treatment in women with posterior vaginal wall prolapse |

### What are the effects of surgical treatments in women with upper vaginal wall prolapse?

| **Beneficial** | • Abdominal sacral colpopexy versus sacrospinous colpopexy (vaginal sacral colpopexy) for upper vaginal wall vault prolapse |
|---|---|
| **Likely To Be Beneficial** | • Posterior intravaginal slingplasty (infracoccygeal sacropexy) versus vaginal sacrospinous colpopexy for upper vaginal wall prolapse (both are likely to be beneficial but unclear how they compare with each other)<br><br>• Vaginal hysterectomy and repair versus abdominal sacrohysteropexy for upper vaginal wall prolapse |
| **Unknown Effectiveness** | • Open abdominal surgery versus laparoscopic surgery<br><br>• Surgical versus non-surgical treatment in women with upper vaginal wall prolapse |

### What are the effects of using different surgical materials in women with genital prolapse?

| **Unknown Effectiveness** | • Different types of suture versus each other<br><br>• Mesh or synthetic grafts versus native (autologous) tissue |
|---|---|

**Search date August 2011**

*Consensus regards vaginal pessaries as effective.

**DEFINITION** Genital prolapse (also known as pelvic organ prolapse) refers to uterine, uterovaginal, or vaginal prolapse. Genital prolapse has several causes but occurs primarily from loss of support in the pelvic region. For ease of understanding, in this review we have attempted to use the most common and descriptive terminology. In uterine prolapse the uterus descends into the vaginal canal with the cervix at its leading edge; this may, in turn, pull down the vagina, in which case it may be referred to as uterovaginal prolapse. In the case of vaginal prolapse, one or more regions of the vaginal wall protrude into the vaginal canal. Vaginal prolapse is classified according to the region of the vaginal wall that is affected: a cystocoele involves the upper anterior vaginal wall; urethrocoele the lower anterior vaginal wall; rectocoele the lower posterior vaginal wall; and enterocoele the upper posterior vaginal wall. After hysterectomy, the apex of the vagina may prolapse as a vault prolapse. This usually pulls down the anterior and posterior vaginal walls as well. Mild genital prolapse may be asymptomatic. Symptoms of genital prolapse are mainly non-specific. Common symptoms include pelvic heaviness, genital bulge, and difficulties during sexual intercourse, such as loss of vaginal sensation. Symptoms that may be more commonly associated with specific forms of prolapse include: urinary incontinence, which is associated with cystocoele; incomplete urinary emptying, which is associated with cystocoele or uterine prolapse, or both; and the need to apply digital pressure to the perineum or posterior vaginal wall for defecation, which is associated with rectocoele.

**INCIDENCE/PREVALENCE** Prevalence estimates vary widely, depending on the population and the way in which women were recruited into studies. One study conducted in the US (497 women aged 18–82 years attending a routine general gynaecology clinic) found that 93.6% had some degree of genital prolapse (43.3% POPQ stage 1, 47.7% POPQ stage 2, 2.6% POPQ stage 3, and 0% POPQ stage 4). The incidence of clinically relevant prolapse (POPQ stage 2 or higher) was found to increase with advancing parity: non-parous, 14.6%; one to three births, 48.0%; and more than three births, 71.2%. One Swedish study (487 women) found that 30.8% of women between the ages of 20 and 59 years had some degree of genital prolapse on clinical assessment. The prevalence of genital prolapse increased with age, from 6.6% in women aged 20 to 29 years to 55.6% in women aged 50 to 59 years. A cross-sectional study (241 perimenopausal women aged 45–55 years seeking to enter a trial of HRT) found that 23% had POPQ stage 1 genital prolapse, 4% had POPQ stage 2 prolapse, and no women had POPQ stage 3 or 4 prolapse. One cross-sectional study conducted in the UK (285 perimenopausal and postmenopausal women attending a menopause clinic with climacteric symptoms) found that 20% had some degree of uterovaginal or vault prolapse, 51% some degree of anterior wall vaginal prolapse, and 27% some degree of posterior wall vaginal prolapse. Severe prolapse (equivalent to POPQ stage 3 or 4) was found in 6% of women. One prospective study (412 postmenopausal women aged 50–79 years) found that the baseline prevalence of cystocoele was 24.6% (prevalence was 14% for grade 1 [in vagina], 10% for grade 2 [to introitus], and 1% for grade 3 [outside vagina]), the baseline prevalence of rectocoele was 12.9% (prevalence was 7.8% for grade 1 and 5.1% for grade 2), and the baseline prevalence of uterine prolapse was 3.8% (prevalence was 3.3% for grade 1 and 0.6% for grade 2). Among women who entered the study, the annual incidence of cystocoele was 9%, rectocoele was 6%, and uterine prolapse was 2%.

**AETIOLOGY/RISK FACTORS** The strongest risk factor for pelvic organ prolapse is parity, because childbirth can cause damage to the pudendal nerves, fascia, and supporting structures, as well as muscle. A Swedish population-based study found that the prevalence of genital prolapse was higher in parous women (44%) than in non-parous women (5.8%). In addition, it found an association with pelvic floor muscle tone and genital prolapse. One case-control study found that other strong risk factors for severe (POPQ stages 3 or 4) genital prolapse are increasing age (OR 1.12 for each additional year, 95% CI 1.09 to 1.15), increasing weight of largest baby delivered vaginally (OR 1.24 for each additional 1 lb [450 g], 95% CI 1.06 to 1.44), previous hysterectomy (OR 2.37, 95% CI 1.16 to 4.86), and previous surgery for genital prolapse (OR 5.09, 95% CI 1.49 to 17.26). The study found no significant association between severe genital prolapse and chronic medical conditions such as obesity, hypertension, or COPD.

**PROGNOSIS** We found no reliable information about the natural history of untreated mild genital prolapse (POPQ stages 1 and 2, Baden–Walker grades 1 and 2). We found one prospective study on the progression of genital prolapse in women who were treated or untreated with HRT (oestrogen plus progesterone). However, the results were not reported separately by treatment group and therefore they may not apply to untreated women. In addition, the investigators used an examination technique of which the reliability, reproducibility, and ability to discriminate between absence of prolapse and mild prolapse was not known. It found that, over 1 year, cystocoeles progressed from grade 1 to grades 2 or 3 in 9% of cases, regressed from grades 2 or 3 to grade 0 in 9%, and regressed from grade 1 to grade 0 in 23%. Rectocoeles progressed from grade 1 to grades 2 or 3 in 1%, but regressed from grades 2 or 3 to grade 0 in 3%, and from grade 1 to grade 0 in 2%. Uterine prolapse regressed from grade 1 to grade 0 in 48%. The incidence of morbidity associated with genital prolapse is also difficult to estimate. The annual incidence of hospital admission for prolapse in the UK has been estimated at 2.04 per 1000 women under the age of 60 years. Genital prolapse is also a major cause of gynaecological surgery.

Carri Casteel and Laura Sadowski

## KEY POINTS

- Between 10% and 70% of women may have been physically or sexually assaulted by a partner at some stage, with reported assault rates against men about one quarter of the rate against women. In at least half of people studied, the problem lasts for 5 years or more.

  Intimate partner violence (IPV) has been associated with socioeconomic and personality factors, marital discord, exposure to violence in family of origin, and partner's drug or alcohol abuse.

  Women reporting IPV are more likely than other women to complain of poor physical or mental health, and of disability.

- Advocacy may reduce revictimisation rates compared with no treatment, but it may have low levels of acceptability.

- Cognitive trauma therapy may reduce post-traumatic stress disorder and depression compared with no treatment.

- Cognitive behavioural counselling may reduce minor physical or sexual IPV, both minor and severe psychological IPV and depression compared with no counselling.

- Career counselling plus critical consciousness awareness may increase a woman's confidence and awareness of the impact of IPV on her life compared with career counselling alone.

- We don't know whether other types of counselling are effective compared with no counselling. Although empowerment counselling seems to reduce trait anxiety, it does not seem to reduce current anxiety or depression or to improve self-esteem.

- We don't know how different types of counselling compare with each other.

- Peer support groups may improve psychological distress and decrease use of healthcare services compared with no intervention.

- Nurse support and guidance is probably unlikely to be beneficial in IPV

- Safety planning may reduce the rate of subsequent abuse in the short term, but longer-term benefit is unknown.

- We don't know whether the use of shelters reduces revictimisation, as we found little research.

(i) **Please visit http://clinicalevidence.bmj.com for full text and references**

| What are the effects of interventions initiated by healthcare professionals aimed at women victims of intimate partner violence? | |
|---|---|
| **Likely To Be Beneficial** | • Advocacy |
| | • Career counselling plus critical consciousness awareness (more effective than career counselling alone) |
| | • Cognitive behavioural counselling versus no counselling |
| | • Cognitive trauma therapy versus no treatment |
| | • Peer support groups |

| | |
|---|---|
| | • Safety planning |
| **Unknown Effectiveness** | • Counselling (various types) versus no counselling<br>• Different types of counselling versus each other (relative benefits unclear)<br>• Shelters |
| **Unlikely To Be Beneficial** | • Nurse support and guidance |

**Search date September 2009**

**DEFINITION** Intimate partner violence (IPV) is actual or threatened physical or sexual violence, or emotional or psychological abuse (including coercive tactics), by a current or former spouse or dating partner (including same-sex partners). Other terms commonly used to describe IPV include domestic violence, domestic abuse, spouse abuse, marital violence, and battering. This review only covers interventions in women currently experiencing IPV.

**INCIDENCE/PREVALENCE** Between 10% and 70% of women participating in population-based surveys in 48 countries reported being physically assaulted by a partner during their lifetime. Rates of reported assault by a partner are 4.3 times higher among women than men. Nearly 25% of surveyed women in the USA reported being physically or sexually assaulted, or both, by a current or former partner at some time, and 2% reported having been victimised during the previous 12 months. Rates of violence against pregnant women range from 1% to 20%. Between 12% and 25% of women in antenatal clinics and 6% to 17% of women in primary or ambulatory care reported having been abused by a partner in the past year.

**AETIOLOGY/RISK FACTORS** Two systematic reviews found that physical IPV towards women is associated with: unemployment and lower levels of education; low family income; marital discord; partner's lower level of occupation; childhood experiences of abuse; witnessing interparental violence; higher levels of anger, depression, or stress; heavy or problem drinking; drug use; jealousy; and lack of assertiveness with spouse.A similar review of research on psychological aggression found that the few demographic and psychological variables assessed were either inconsistently associated with psychological IPV or were found to be associated with psychological IPV in studies with serious methodological limitations.

**PROGNOSIS** A large longitudinal study of couples suggests that IPV tends to disappear over time within most relationships. However, couples reporting frequent or severe IPV are more likely to remain violent. For all ethnic groups, half of those reporting moderate IPV did not report occurrences of IPV at 5-year follow-up; although, for people of black or Hispanic origin reporting severe IPV, only one third did not report occurrences of domestic violence at 5-year follow-up. A case control study conducted in middle-class working women found that, compared with non-abused women, women abused by their partners during the previous 9 years were significantly more likely to have or report headaches (48% of abused women *v* 35% of non-abused women), back pain (40% of abused women *v* 25% of non-abused women), STDs (6% of abused women *v* 2% of non-abused women), vaginal bleeding (17% of abused women *v* 6% of non-abused women), vaginal infections (30% of abused women *v* 21% of non-abused women), pelvic pain (17% of abused women *v* 9% of non-abused women), painful intercourse (13% of abused women *v* 7% of non-abused women), UTIs (22% of abused women *v* 12% of non-abused women), appetite loss (9% of abused women *v* 3% of non-abused women), digestive problems (35% of abused women *v* 19% of non-abused women), abdominal pain (22% of abused women *v* 11% of non-abused women), and facial injuries (8% of abused women *v* 1% of non-abused women). After adjusting for age, race, insurance status, and cigarette smoking, a cross-sectional survey found that women experiencing psychological abuse are also more likely to report poor physical and mental health, disability preventing work, arthritis, chronic pain, migraine and other frequent headaches, STDs, chronic pelvic pain, stomach ulcers, spastic colon, frequent indigestion, diarrhoea, and constipation.

Nikolaos Burbos and Edward P Morris

### KEY POINTS

- In the UK, the median age for onset of menopausal symptoms is 45.5 to 47.5 years.

    Symptoms associated with the menopause include vasomotor symptoms, sleeplessness, mood changes, reduced energy levels, loss of libido, vaginal dryness, and urinary symptoms.

    Many symptoms, such as hot flushes, are temporary, but those resulting from reduced hormone levels, such as genital atrophy, may be permanent.

- Progestogens reduce menopausal vasomotor symptoms compared with placebo. However, the clinical usefulness of progestogens given alone for menopausal symptoms is limited by the unwanted adverse effects of the relatively high doses needed to achieve relief of menopausal symptoms.

- Oestrogens reduce vasomotor and sexual symptoms but, like progestogens, they increase the risk of serious adverse effects.

    Oestrogens, used alone or with progestogens, reduce vasomotor and urogenital symptoms, and improve quality of life compared with placebo over 3 to 6 months.

    However, oestrogens increase the risk of breast cancer, endometrial cancer, stroke, and venous thromboembolism.

    We don't know whether phyto-oestrogens, such as those in soy flour, reduce menopausal symptoms. Phyto-oestrogens have not been shown consistently to improve symptoms, and they may increase the risk of endometrial hyperplasia in perimenopausal women.

- CAUTION: Women with an intact uterus who are prescribed oestrogen replacement therapy should also take continuous or cyclical progestogens.

- Tibolone reduces vasomotor symptoms in postmenopausal women compared with placebo.

    Tibolone may improve sexual function compared with placebo or compared with combined oestrogens plus progestogens.

    We don't know if tibolone is more effective than oestrogen and progestogen combined treatment in reducing vasomotor symptoms.

    Tibolone may be associated with an increased risk of breast cancer recurrence in women previously treated surgically for breast cancer.

- We don't know whether testosterone alone reduces menopausal symptoms, as we found no RCTs. Testosterone plus oestrogen-based HRT reduces sexual symptoms in postmenopausal women but does not seem to reduce vasomotor symptoms, compared with oestrogen HRT alone.

- Antidepressants may be more effective than placebo at relieving vasomotor symptoms in postmenopausal women in the short term. However, we don't know whether they are effective in the long term.

- We don't know whether clonidine, black cohosh, or agnus castus reduce menopausal symptoms.

(i) **Please visit http://clinicalevidence.bmj.com for full text and references**

| What are the effects of medical treatments for menopausal symptoms? | |
|---|---|
| **Trade-off Between Benefits And Harms** | • Oestrogens alone (improved menopausal symptoms but increased risk of breast cancer, endometrial cancer, stroke severity, and venous thromboembolism after long-term use) |

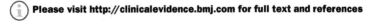

©BMJ Publishing Group Ltd 2015

| | • Oestrogens plus progestogens (improved menopausal symptoms but increased risk of breast cancer, stroke severity, and venous thromboembolism after long-term use)<br>• Progestogens alone<br>• Tibolone |
|---|---|
| **Unknown Effectiveness** | • Antidepressants<br>• Clonidine<br>• Testosterone |

## What are the effects of non-prescribed treatments for menopausal symptoms?

| **Unknown Effectiveness** | • Agnus castus<br>• Black cohosh<br>• Phyto-oestrogens |
|---|---|

**Search date June 2010**

**DEFINITION** Menopause is defined as the end of the last menstrual period. A woman is deemed to be postmenopausal 1 year after her last period. For practical purposes, most women are diagnosed as menopausal after 1 year of amenorrhoea. Menopausal symptoms often begin in the perimenopausal years. The complex of menopausal symptomatology includes vasomotor symptoms (hot flushes), sleeplessness, mood changes, reduction in energy levels, loss of libido, vaginal dryness, and urinary symptoms.

**INCIDENCE/PREVALENCE** In the UK, the mean age for the start of the menopause is 50 years and 9 months. The median onset of the perimenopause is 45.5 to 47.5 years. One Scottish survey (6096 women aged 45–54 years) found that 84% of the women had experienced at least one of the classic menopausal symptoms, with 45% finding one or more symptoms to be a problem.

**AETIOLOGY/RISK FACTORS** Urogenital symptoms of menopause are caused by decreased oestrogen concentrations, but the cause of vasomotor symptoms and psychological effects is complex and remains unclear.

**PROGNOSIS** Menopause is a physiological event. Timing of the natural menopause in healthy women may be determined genetically. Although endocrine changes are permanent, menopausal symptoms such as hot flushes, which are experienced by about 70% of women, usually resolve with time, although in some women they can persist for decades. However, some symptoms, such as genital atrophy, may remain the same or worsen.

# 632 | Menorrhagia

Kirsten Duckitt and Sally Collins

## KEY POINTS

- Menorrhagia limits normal activities, and causes anaemia in two-thirds of women with objective menorrhagia (blood loss of 80 mL or more per cycle).

  Prostaglandin disorders may be associated with idiopathic menorrhagia, and with heavy bleeding caused by fibroids, adenomyosis, or use of IUDs.

  Fibroids have been found in 10% of women with menorrhagia overall, and in 40% of women with severe menorrhagia; but half of women having a hysterectomy for menorrhagia are found to have a normal uterus.

- NSAIDs, tranexamic acid, and danazol all reduce blood loss compared with placebo.

  Tranexamic acid and danazol may be more effective than NSAIDs, etamsylate, and oral progestogens at reducing blood loss, but any benefits of danazol must be weighed against the high risk of adverse effects.

  NSAIDs reduce dysmenorrhoea, and may be as effective at reducing menstrual blood loss as oral progestogens given in the luteal phase, but we don't know how they compare with etamsylate, combined oral contraceptives, intrauterine progestogens, or gonadorelin analogues.

  We don't know whether combined oral contraceptives, levonorgestrel-releasing intrauterine devices, or gonadorelin analogues are effective at reducing menorrhagia, as we found few trials.

- Hysterectomy reduces blood loss and the need for further surgery compared with medical treatments or endometrial destruction, but can lead to complications in up to a third of women. Fewer women reported overall treatment dissatisfaction with hysterectomy.

  Endometrial destruction is more effective at reducing menorrhagia compared with medical treatment, but complications can include infection, haemorrhage, and uterine perforation.

  We don't know whether any one type of endometrial destruction is superior, or whether dilatation and curettage has any effect on menstrual blood loss.

- Preoperative gonadorelin analogues reduce long-term postoperative moderate or heavy blood loss, and increase amenorrhoea compared with placebo, but we don't know whether oral progestogens or danazol are also beneficial when used preoperatively.

(i) **Please visit http://clinicalevidence.bmj.com for full text and references**

| What are the effects of medical treatments for menorrhagia? | |
|---|---|
| Beneficial | • NSAIDs |
| | • Tranexamic acid |
| Trade-off Between Benefits And Harms | • Danazol |
| Unknown Effectiveness | • Contraceptives (combined oral) |
| | • Etamsylate |
| | • Gonadorelin analogues |
| | • Progestogens (intrauterine) |
| | • Progestogens (oral) for longer cycle |
| | • Progestogens (oral) in luteal phase only |

## What are the effects of surgical treatments for menorrhagia?

| Beneficial | • Hysterectomy (reduces menstrual blood loss compared with intrauterine progestogens or endometrial destruction; also reduces need for further surgery compared with endometrial destruction) |
|---|---|
| Likely To Be Beneficial | • Endometrial destruction (reduces menstrual blood loss compared with medical treatment) |
| Unknown Effectiveness | • Dilatation and curettage |

## What are the effects of endometrial thinning before endometrial destruction in treating menorrhagia?

| Beneficial | • Gonadorelin analogues |
|---|---|
| Unknown Effectiveness | • Danazol<br>• Progestogens (oral) |

**Search date June 2011**

**DEFINITION** Menorrhagia is defined as heavy, but regular, menstrual bleeding. **Idiopathic ovulatory menorrhagia** is regular heavy bleeding in the absence of recognisable pelvic pathology, or a general bleeding disorder. **Objective menorrhagia** is taken to be a total menstrual blood loss of 80 mL or more in each menstruation. Subjectively, menorrhagia may be defined as a complaint of regular excessive menstrual blood loss occurring over several consecutive cycles in a woman of reproductive age.

**INCIDENCE/PREVALENCE** In the UK, 5% of women aged 30 to 49 years consult their general practitioners each year with menorrhagia. In New Zealand, 2% to 4% of primary-care consultations by premenopausal women are for menstrual problems.

**AETIOLOGY/RISK FACTORS** Idiopathic ovulatory menorrhagia is thought to be caused by disordered prostaglandin production within the endometrium. Prostaglandins may also be implicated in menorrhagia associated with uterine fibroids, adenomyosis, or the presence of an IUD. Fibroids have been reported in 10% of women with menorrhagia (80–100 mL/cycle), and in 40% of women with severe menorrhagia (at least 200 mL/cycle).

**PROGNOSIS** Menorrhagia limits normal activities and causes iron-deficiency anaemia in two-thirds of women shown to have objective menorrhagia. One in five women in the UK, and one in three in the US, have a hysterectomy before the age of 60 years; menorrhagia is the main presenting problem in at least half of these women. About half of women who have a hysterectomy for menorrhagia are found to have an anatomically normal uterus.

Sean Kehoe and Jo Morrison

## KEY POINTS

- Ovarian cancer is the fourth most common cause of cancer deaths in the UK.

  Incidence rises with age, and peaks in the seventh and eighth decades of life.

  Risk factors include family history of ovarian cancer, increasing age, and low parity. Risks are reduced by using the oral contraceptive pill for more than 5 years, tubal ligation, hysterectomy, breastfeeding, increased age at menarche, decreased age at menopause, and use of NSAIDs.

  In the UK, the 5-year relative survival rate at diagnosis for women aged 15–39 years is nearly 70%. In comparison, it is only 12% for women diagnosed over 80 years of age.

- Standard treatment for advanced ovarian cancer is primary surgical debulking, followed by chemotherapy.

  We found no direct evidence on the effects of primary surgery versus no surgery, or primary surgery plus chemotherapy versus surgery or chemotherapy alone.

  Although we found no direct evidence, subgroup analysis comparing groups by the degree to which maximal surgical debulking was acheived or not, suggests that maximal surgical cytoreduction at primary surgery is strongly associated with improved survival in advanced ovarian cancer.

  Subsequent debulking and second-look surgery seem unlikely to improve survival, especially if initial surgery achieved optimal cytoreduction.

- Platinum-based regimens are now standard first-line chemotherapy and have been shown to be beneficial in prolonging survival compared with non-platinum-based regimens.

  Platinum compounds seem to be the main beneficial agent, with little additional survival benefit from adding non-platinum (excluding taxanes) chemotherapeutic agents to platinum.

  Carboplatin is as effective as cisplatin in prolonging survival, but with less-severe adverse effects.

- Taxanes may increase survival if added to platinum chemotherapy compared with platinum-based regimens alone, but studies have given conflicting results.

  One RCT suggests paclitaxel is as effective at prolonging survival as docetaxel when combined with a platinum drug.

- Platinum-based chemotherapy can also be delivered directly into the intraperitoneal cavity, as well as by the intravenous route.

- We found limited evidence that intraperitoneal platinum-based chemotherapy may increase survival compared with intravenous administration, but at the cost of increased adverse effects, both those associated with the use of an intraperitoneal catheter and from increased doses of chemotherapy.

  Any benefit seen with intraperitoneal rather than intravenous administration may be due to different chemotherapy doses, rather than the route of administration.

- Limited evidence suggests that consolidation treatment given intraperitoneally does not confer any survival benefit compared with no further treatment in women who have undergone primary surgery and chemotherapy and who have no disease at second-look laparotomy.

  However, consolidation treatment may be associated with increased adverse effects.

 **Please visit http://clinicalevidence.bmj.com for full text and references**

## What are the effects of surgical treatments for ovarian cancer that is advanced at first presentation?

| Unknown Effectiveness | • Primary surgery |
|---|---|
| Unlikely To Be Beneficial | • Interval debulking in women who have residual tumours after primary surgery<br><br>• Second-look surgery versus watchful waiting |

## What are the effects of platinum-based chemotherapy for ovarian cancer that is advanced at first presentation?

| Likely To Be Beneficial | • Carboplatin plus taxane versus cisplatin plus taxane (both may be equally effective at improving survival, but may be less severe adverse effects with carboplatin) |
|---|---|
| Unlikely To Be Beneficial | • Combination platinum-based chemotherapy versus single-agent platinum chemotherapy (cisplatin or carboplatin alone may be as effective as platinum plus non-platinum [excluding taxanes] combination regimens) |

## What are the effects of taxane-based chemotherapy for ovarian cancer that is advanced at first presentation?

| Unknown Effectiveness | • Adding a taxane to a platinum-based compound<br><br>• Paclitaxel versus docetaxel |
|---|---|

## What are the effects of intraperitoneal chemotherapy for ovarian cancer that is advanced at first presentation?

| Unknown Effectiveness | • Intraperitoneal consolidation treatment versus no further treatment in women following primary surgery and intravenous platinum-based chemotherapy<br><br>• Intraperitoneal platinum-based chemotherapy versus intravenous platinum-based chemotherapy following primary cytoreductive surgery |
|---|---|

**Search date September 2007**

**DEFINITION** Ovarian tumours are classified according to the assumed cell type of origin (surface epithelium, stroma, or germ cells). Epithelial tumours account for over 90% of ovarian cancers. These can be further grouped into histological types (serous, mucinous, endometroid, and clear cell). Epithelial ovarian cancer is staged using the FIGO classification. This review is limited to first-line treatment in women with advanced (FIGO stage 2–4) invasive epithelial ovarian cancer at first presentation.

**INCIDENCE/PREVALENCE** The worldwide incidence of ovarian cancer according to the GLOBOCAN database was 204,499 cases in 2002. There is a worldwide variation: the highest rates are in Lithuania, Denmark, and Estonia, and the lowest rates are in Egypt,

*(continued over)*

*(from previous page)*

Malawi, and Mali. This variation may be due to differences in reproductive practice, use of the oral contraceptive pill, breastfeeding habits, and age of menarche and menopause. The incidence of ovarian cancer rises steadily with increasing age and peaks in the seventh and eighth decades of life. In the UK, it is the fourth most common cause of cancer deaths, with about 6900 new cases diagnosed annually, and 4600 deaths from the disease each year. The incidence of ovarian cancer seems to be stabilising in some other countries, and declining in some resource-rich countries (Finland, Denmark, New Zealand, and the USA).

**AETIOLOGY/RISK FACTORS** Risk factors include family history of ovarian cancer, increasing age, and low parity. More controversial risk factors are subfertility and use of fertility drugs. Use of the oral contraceptive pill for more than 5 years reduces the risk by 30–40%. Other factors associated with risk reduction are tubal ligation, hysterectomy, breastfeeding, increasing age of menarche, decreasing age of menopause, and use of NSAIDs.

**PROGNOSIS** Survival rates vary according to age, disease stage, and residual tumour after surgery. The most important determination of survival seems to be disease stage at diagnosis. Early disease stage has a 5-year survival rate of greater than 70%, but for those diagnosed with advanced disease stage, it is about 15%. Younger women survive longer than older women, even after adjustments for general life expectancy. In the UK, the 5-year relative survival rate at diagnosis for women aged 15–39 years is nearly 70%. It is only 12% for women diagnosed over 80 years of age.

David J. Cahill and Katherine O'Brien

## KEY POINTS

- Polycystic ovary syndrome (PCOS) is a syndrome of ovarian dysfunction together with established features of hyperandrogenism and morphological polycystic changes in the ovary. It is a condition for which there are disputed diagnostic criterion to confirm clinical diagnosis. However, since the publication of the Rotterdam criteria, there is acceptance that menstrual cycle and endocrine dysfunction with hyperandrogenism are more important in reaching the diagnosis than ultrasound findings.

  Prevalence in the population as a whole varies from 10% to 20%, depending on which diagnostic criteria are used.

  Clinical manifestations of PCOS include infrequent or absent menses and signs of androgen excess, including acne or seborrhoea.

  PCOS has been associated with hirsutism, infertility, insulin resistance, elevated serum luteinising hormone levels, weight gain, type 2 diabetes, CVD, and endometrial hyperplasia.

- In this review, we have reported on the effects of metformin on hirsutism and menstrual frequency in people with PCOS compared with placebo/no treatment, weight loss intervention, or cyproterone acetate-ethinylestradiol.

  We have reported on clinical outcomes, such as hirsutism scores, rather than laboratory-based outcomes (such as effects on hormone levels).

- In general, we found evidence mainly from small RCTs of limited methodological quality.

- Many RCTs reported effects on infertility as their primary outcome, and any data on hirsutism and menstrual effects were more sparingly reported.

- We found limited evidence that metformin may improve menstrual frequency compared with placebo.

  Many of the trials also included a diet or a diet plus exercise intervention in both groups.

- We found insufficient evidence on the effects of metformin on hirsutism compared with placebo.

- Metformin may be associated with an increase of gastrointestinal adverse effects compared with placebo.

- We don't know whether metformin is more effective than a weight loss intervention (diet or diet plus exercise) at improving hirsutism or menstrual frequency.

  We found insufficient evidence from two small RCTs to draw reliable conclusions.

- We don't know how metformin amd cyproterone acetate-ethinylestradiol compare at improving hirsutism and menstrual frequency, as we found little high-quality evidence.

  Metformin may increase gastrointestinal effects (including nausea and diarrhoea) compared with cyproterone acetate-ethinylestradiol, resulting in the need to stop medication.

  However, cyproterone acetate-ethinylestradiol may increase other adverse effects (such as weight gain, high blood pressure, chest pain, and headache) compared with metformin, also resulting in the need to stop medication.

 **Please visit http://clinicalevidence.bmj.com for full text and references**

## What are the effects of metformin on hirsutism and menstrual frequency in women with PCOS?

| Likely To Be Beneficial | • Metformin versus placebo or no treatment (improved menstrual pattern compared with placebo; unclear effects on hirsutism compared with placebo) |
|---|---|
| Unknown Effectiveness | • Metformin versus cyproterone acetate-ethinylestradiol (unclear evidence on hirsutism and menstrual frequency from small trials)<br><br>• Metformin versus weight loss intervention (unclear effects compared with diet or diet plus exercise) |

Search date May 2014

**DEFINITION** Polycystic ovary syndrome (PCOS; Stein-Leventhal syndrome; sclerocystic ovarian disease) is, by definition, a condition for which there are disputed diagnostic criteria to confirm clinical diagnosis. It is a syndrome of ovarian dysfunction together with established features of hyperandrogenism and morphological polycystic changes in the ovary. The nomenclature of the condition is somewhat misleading, as the ultrasound findings are not a key part of the diagnostic criteria. Clinical manifestations include infrequent or absent menses and signs of androgen excess, which include acne or seborrhoea. Women with PCOS commonly have insulin resistance and elevated serum luteinising hormone (LH) levels, and are at an increased risk of type 2 diabetes and cardiovascular events. In this review, we have included studies in women aged 18 to 45 years, or where the majority of participants are aged 18 to 45 years.

**INCIDENCE/PREVALENCE** PCOS is diagnosed in 4% to 10% of women attending gynaecology clinics in resource-rich countries, but this figure may not reflect the true prevalence as the criteria used for diagnosis vary. Depending on the diagnostic criteria used, prevalence in the population as a whole varies from 10% to 20%. An international consensus definition of PCOS defined a set of agreed criteria used for diagnosis. Studies since then suggest a greater than 20% incidence and prevalence of PCOS in overweight and obese women.

**AETIOLOGY/RISK FACTORS** The aetiology is unknown. Genetic factors play a part, but the exact mechanisms are unclear. Two studies found some evidence of familial aggregation of hyperandrogenaemia (with or without oligomenorrhoea) in first-degree relatives of women with PCOS. In the first study, 22% of sisters of women with PCOS fulfilled diagnostic criteria for PCOS. In the second study, of the 78 mothers and 50 sisters evaluated clinically, 19 (24%) mothers and 16 (32%) sisters had PCOS. In a study of Dutch women, there was a doubling of the incidence of PCOS in monozygotic twins (though the prevalence was no different to dizygotic twins and the PCOS definition was non-standard). **Diagnosis:** The diagnosis excludes secondary causes, such as androgen-producing neoplasm, hyperprolactinaemia, and adult-onset congenital adrenal hyperplasia. It is characterised by irregular menstrual cycles, scanty or absent menses, multiple small follicles on the ovaries (polycystic ovaries), mild hirsutism, and infertility. Many women also have insulin resistance, acne, and weight gain. Until recently, there was no overall consensus on the criteria for diagnosing PCOS. In some studies, it has been diagnosed based on the ultrasound findings of polycystic ovaries rather than on clinical criteria. An international consensus definition of PCOS has now been published, which defines PCOS as at least two of the following criteria: reduced or no ovulation; clinical and/or biochemical signs of excessive secretion of androgens; and/or polycystic ovaries (the presence of at least 12 follicles measuring 2–9 mm in diameter, an ovarian volume in excess of 10 mL, or both).

**PROGNOSIS** There is some evidence that women with PCOS are at increased risk of developing type 2 diabetes and cardiovascular disorders secondary to hyperlipidaemia, compared with women who do not have PCOS. A meta-analysis found a two-fold increase in the risk of coronary heart disease and stroke in women with PCOS. However, although there is a higher risk of cardiovascular disorders, there is no apparent increase in risk of mortality. There is some evidence that oligomenorrhoeic and amenorrhoeic women are at increased risk of developing endometrial hyperplasia and, later, endometrial carcinoma.

Irene Kwan and Joseph Loze Onwude

## KEY POINTS

- A woman has premenstrual syndrome (PMS) if she complains of recurrent psychological and/or physical symptoms occurring during the luteal phase of the menstrual cycle, and often resolving by the end of menstruation. Symptom severity can vary between women.

  Psychological symptoms of PMS include irritability, depression, crying/tearfulness, and anxiety. Physical symptoms of PMS include abdominal bloating, breast tenderness, and headaches.

  Premenstrual symptoms occur in 95% of all women of reproductive age. Severe, debilitating symptoms occur in about 5% of those women.

  The cyclical nature of PMS makes it difficult to conduct RCTs. Furthermore, the lack of consensus on how premenstrual symptom severity should be assessed has meant that RCTs use different symptom scores and scales, which makes it difficult to synthesise data.

  There is little good quality evidence for any of the wide range of treatments available for PMS, and the selection of treatment is mainly governed by personal choice. The clinician plays a key role in facilitating this choice, and in reassuring women with PMS without coexisting gynaecological problems that there is nothing seriously wrong.

- We don't know whether continuous daily oral levonorgestrel plus ethinylestradiol is more effective than placebo at improving premenstrual symptoms because we only found one trial and this specifically studied women with premenstrual dysphoric disorder.

  We found no evidence in women with PMS who did not have premenstrual dysphoric disorder.

  Adverse effects that may occur with continuous daily oral levonorgestrel plus ethinylestradiol include vaginal haemorrhage, metrorrhagia, and flu-like symptoms. There is also a concern that the combined contraceptive pill is associated with more serious adverse events, such as deep vein thrombosis (DVT), breast cancer, pulmonary embolism, and stroke.

- We found insufficient evidence (only one RCT with small numbers) to judge the effectiveness of continuous transdermal estradiol plus cyclical oral norethisterone for treating PMS in women with an intact uterus.

- Continuous subcutaneous estradiol implant plus cyclical norethisterone may be more effective than placebo at improving premenstrual symptoms in women with an intact uterus, but this is based on one RCT.

- We found no RCTs on the effectiveness of continuous transdermal estradiol or continuous subcutaneous estradiol implant for treating PMS in women who had had a hysterectomy without bilateral salpingo-oophorectomy.

 Please visit http://clinicalevidence.bmj.com for full text and references

| What are the effects of continuous hormonal treatments in women with premenstrual syndrome? | |
|---|---|
| Unknown Effectiveness | • Continuous combined oral contraceptives (with no break in treatment) |
| | • Continuous subcutaneous estradiol implant (with no break in treatment) in women with a hysterectomy but no bilateral salpingo-oophorectomy |
| | • Continuous subcutaneous estradiol implant (with no break in treatment) in women with an intact uterus |

- Continuous transdermal estradiol (with no break in treatment) in women with an intact uterus

- Continuous transdermal estradiol (with no break in treatment) in women with hysterectomy but no bilateral salpingo-oophorectomy

**Search date April 2014**

**DEFINITION** A woman has premenstrual syndrome (PMS) if she complains of recurrent psychological and/or physical symptoms occurring specifically during the luteal phase of the menstrual cycle, and often resolving by the end of menstruation. The symptoms can also persist during the bleeding phase. **Severe premenstrual syndrome:** The definition of severe PMS varies among RCTs, but in recent studies standardised criteria have been used to diagnose one variant of severe PMS — premenstrual dysphoric disorder (PMDD). The criteria are based on at least five symptoms, including one of four core psychological symptoms (from a list of 17 physical and psychological symptoms) and being severe before menstruation starts and mild or absent after menstruation. The 17 symptoms are depression, feeling hopeless or guilty, anxiety/tension, mood swings, irritability/persistent anger, decreased interest, poor concentration, fatigue, food craving or increased appetite, sleep disturbance, feeling out of control or overwhelmed, poor coordination, headache, aches, swelling/bloating/weight gain, cramps, and breast tenderness.

**INCIDENCE/PREVALENCE** Premenstrual symptoms occur in 95% of all women of reproductive age; severe, debilitating symptoms occur in about 5% of those women.

**AETIOLOGY/RISK FACTORS** The cause is unknown but hormonal and other factors (possibly neuroendocrine) probably contribute.

**PROGNOSIS** Symptoms of PMS can recur after treatment is stopped, except after oophorectomy and menopause.

Ignacio Neumann and Philippa Moore

### KEY POINTS

- Pyelonephritis is usually caused by ascent of bacteria from the bladder, most often *Escherichia coli*, and is more likely in people with structural or functional urinary tract abnormalities.

  The prognosis of acute uncomplicated pyelonephritis is good if pyelonephritis is treated appropriately, but complications include renal abscess, renal impairment, and septic shock.

- We found no direct information from RCTs about whether oral or intravenous antibiotics are better than no active treatment. However, consensus holds that these drugs are effective.

  We don't know which is the most effective oral antibiotic regimen, or the optimum duration of treatment, although it may be sensible to continue treatment for at least 10 days.

  We don't know how switch regimens (intravenous antibiotics followed by oral antibiotics) compare with oral antibiotic regimens.

  We don't know which is the most effective intravenous antibiotic regimen, or the optimum duration of intravenous treatment.

 **Please visit http://clinicalevidence.bmj.com for full text and references**

| What are the effects of antibiotic treatments for acute pyelonephritis in non-pregnant women with uncomplicated infection? | |
|---|---|
| Likely To Be Beneficial | • Antibiotics (oral or intravenous) versus placebo* |
| Unknown Effectiveness | • Antibiotics (intravenous) versus each other<br><br>• Antibiotics (oral) versus each other<br><br>• Oral antibiotics versus switch therapy (intravenous antibiotics followed by oral antibiotics) |

Search date November 2013

---

*Categorisation is based on consensus.

---

**DEFINITION** Acute pyelonephritis, or upper urinary tract infection, is an infection of the kidney characterised by pain when passing urine, fever, chills, flank pain, nausea, and vomiting. White blood cells are almost always present in the urine. White blood cell casts are occasionally seen on urine microscopy. There is no consensus on the definitions for grades of severity. However, in practice, people with acute pyelonephritis may be divided into people who are able to take oral antibiotics and those who require intravenous antibiotics. Management may be ambulatory or in hospital. Some consider the absolute indications for hospital admission to be persistent vomiting, progression of uncomplicated urinary tract infection, suspected sepsis, or urinary tract obstruction. Pyelonephritis is considered uncomplicated if caused by a typical pathogen in an immunocompetent person who has normal renal anatomy and renal function. There is little difference in the treatment of men and non-pregnant women. **Diagnosis:** People presenting with fever and back pain suggest a possible diagnosis of acute pyelonephritis. Urinalysis and urine culture should be performed to confirm the diagnosis. Significant pyuria (defined as >20 WBCs per high-power field [hpf] on a specimen spun at 2000 rpm for 5 minutes) is present in almost all patients and can be detected rapidly with leukocyte esterase test (sensitivity: 74%–96% and specificity: 94%–98%) or the nitrite test (sensitivity: 35%–85% and specificity: 92%–100%). Bacterial growth of $10^4$ to $10^5$ colony-forming units on urine culture of a mid-stream specimen will confirm bacteriological diagnosis.

**INCIDENCE/PREVALENCE** The estimated annual incidence per 10,000 people is 27.6 cases in the US and 35.7 cases in South Korea. Worldwide prevalence and incidence are unknown. The highest incidence of pyelonephritis occurs during the summer months. Women are approximately five times more likely than men to be hospitalised with acute pyelonephritis.

**AETIOLOGY/RISK FACTORS** Pyelonephritis is most commonly caused when bacteria in the bladder ascend the ureters and invade the kidneys. In some cases, this may result in bacteria entering and multiplying in the bloodstream. The most frequently isolated organism is *Escherichia coli* (56%–85%); others include *Enterococcus faecalis, Klebsiella pneumoniae,* and *Proteus mirabilis.* In older people, *E coli* is less common (60%), whereas people with diabetes mellitus may also have infections caused by *Klebsiella, Enterobacter, Clostridium,* or *Candida.* People with structural or functional urinary tract abnormalities are more prone to pyelonephritis that is refractory to oral therapy or complicated by bacteraemia. Risk factors associated with pyelonephritis in healthy women are sexual intercourse, use of spermicide, urinary tract infection in the previous 12 months, a mother with a history of urinary tract infection, diabetes, and urinary incontinence. The most important risk factor for complicated urinary tract infection is obstruction of the urinary tract. The incidence of drug-resistant microorganisms varies in different geographical areas. Recent hospital admission, recent use of antibiotics, immunosuppression, recurrent pyelonephritis, and nephrolithiasis increase the risk of drug resistance.

**PROGNOSIS** Prognosis is good if uncomplicated pyelonephritis is treated appropriately. Complications include renal abscess, septic shock, and renal impairment, including acute renal failure. Short-term independent risk factors for mortality include age above 65 years, septic shock, being bedridden, and immunosuppression. Conditions such as underlying renal disease, diabetes mellitus, and immunosuppression may worsen prognosis, but we found no good long-term evidence about rates of sepsis or death among people with such conditions.

# Recurrent cystitis in non-pregnant women

Ayan Sen

## KEY POINTS

- Cystitis is a bacterial infection of the lower urinary tract which causes pain when passing urine, and causes frequency, urgency, haematuria, and suprapubic pain not associated with passing urine.

    Recurrent cystitis is usually defined as three episodes of UTI in the previous 12 months, or two episodes in the previous 6 months.

    It is common in young, healthy women, with one study finding 27% of women developing a second infection within 6 months of the first, and 2.7% having a second recurrence during this period.

- Continuous antibiotic prophylaxis lasting 6–12 months reduces the rate of recurrence, although there is no consensus about when to start the treatment, or about how long it should last.

    Trimethoprim, trimethoprim–sulfamethoxazole (co-trimoxazole), nitrofurantoin, cefaclor, or quinolones all seem equally effective at reducing recurrence rates.

- Postcoital antibiotics (taken within 2 hours of intercourse) reduce the rate of clinical recurrence of cystitis as effectively as continuous treatment.

- We don't know whether single-dose self-administered trimethoprim–sulfamethoxazole or continuous prophylaxis with methenamine hippurate are effective in preventing recurrence of cystitis, as the studies were too small to show any clinically relevant differences.

- Cranberry products (either juice or capsules) seem to significantly reduce the recurrence of symptomatic cystitis.

    There is no clear evidence about the amount and concentration of cranberry juice that needs to be consumed, or about the length of time needed for the treatment to be most effective.

- There is no evidence examining whether passing urine after intercourse is effective at preventing UTI.

- We found insufficient evidence on the effects of topical oestrogen in postmenopausal women in the prophylaxis of recurrent cystitis.

(i) **Please visit http://clinicalevidence.bmj.com for full text and references**

| Which interventions prevent further recurrence of cystitis in women experiencing at least two infections per year? | |
| --- | --- |
| Beneficial | • Continuous antibiotic prophylaxis (trimethoprim, trimethoprim–sulfamethoxazole, nitrofurantoin, cefaclor, or a quinolone) <br><br> • Postcoital antibiotic prophylaxis (trimethoprim–sulfamethoxazole, nitrofurantoin, or a quinolone) |
| Likely To Be Beneficial | • Cranberry juice and cranberry products |
| Unknown Effectiveness | • Continuous prophylaxis with methenamine hippurate <br><br> • Oestrogen (topical) in postmenopausal women <br><br> • Passing urine after intercourse |

- Single-dose self-administered trimethoprim–sulfamethoxazole

**Search date April 2007**

**DEFINITION** In most cases, cystitis is a bacterial infection of the lower urinary tract which causes pain when passing urine, and causes frequency, urgency, haematuria, and suprapubic pain not associated with passing urine. White blood cells and bacteria are almost always present in the urine. A recurrent UTI is a symptomatic UTI that follows clinical resolution of an earlier infection generally, but not necessarily, after treatment. Recurrent cystitis is usually defined in the literature as three episodes of UTI in the previous 12 months or two episodes in the previous 6 months. Recurrent UTIs cause serious discomfort to women, and have a high impact on ambulatory healthcare costs, through outpatient visits, diagnostic tests, and prescriptions.

**INCIDENCE/PREVALENCE** Recurrent cystitis is common among young, healthy women, even though they generally have anatomically and physiologically normal urinary tracts. One study found that nearly half of the women whose uncomplicated UTIs resolved spontaneously developed a recurrent UTI within a year. In a study of college women with their first UTI, 27% experienced at least one culture-confirmed recurrence within 6 months of the initial infection, and 2.7% had a second recurrence during this period. In a Finnish study of women aged 17–82 years who had *Escherichia Coli* cystitis, 44% had a recurrence within 1 year (53% in women older than 55 years, 36% in younger women). No large population-based studies have been done to determine proportionately how many women with UTI develop a pattern of high-frequency recurrence. Occasionally, recurrences are due to a persistent focus of infection, but the vast majority is thought to represent reinfection. A recurrence is defined clinically as a relapse if it is caused by the same species as caused the original UTI, and if it occurs within 2 weeks after treatment. It is considered reinfection if it occurs more than 2 weeks after treatment of the original infection. Most women are able to diagnose their own episodes of recurrent cystitis from symptoms (positive predictive value in one RCT 92%).

**AETIOLOGY/RISK FACTORS** Cystitis is caused by uropathogenic bacteria in the faecal flora, that colonise the vaginal and periurethral openings and ascend the urethra into the bladder. Sexual intercourse, diaphragm–spermicide use, and a history of recurrent UTI have been shown to be strong and independent risk factors for cystitis. Use of spermicide-coated condoms may also increase the risk of UTI. Antimicrobial use has been shown to adversely affect the vaginal flora in animals and humans, and recent use of antibiotics is strongly associated with risk of cystitis. However, risk factors specific to women with recurrent cystitis have received little study. In a large, case controlled study of women with and without a history of recurrent UTI, comprising 229 cases and 253 controls, the strongest risk factor for recurrence in a multivariate analysis was the frequency of sexual intercourse. Other risk factors included spermicide use in the past year, new sex partner during the past year, having a first UTI at or before 15 years of age, and having a mother with history of UTI. Urine-voiding disorders, such as those associated with prolapse, multiple sclerosis, bladder cancer, or bladder stones, are also associated with increased risk. An association has been found with pre- and postcoital voiding, frequency of urination, delayed voiding habits, douching, and BMI. A possible association between smoking (which is strongly associated with bladder cancer) and recurrent cystitis has not been assessed. These behavioural patterns have never been evaluated in prospective, randomised trials. Data suggest that pelvic anatomical differences may have a role in predisposing some young women to recurrent UTI, especially those without other risk factors. In postmenopausal women, reduced oestrogen levels seem to contribute to recurrent cystitis in healthy women. The vagina, bladder, and urethra respond to oestrogen, and when the hormonal level in the body is reduced, the tissues of these organs become thinner, weaker, and dry. The changes in the tissues of the bladder and urethra, and the associated loss of protection against infection-causing germs, may increase the risk of UTI in postmenopausal women. Cystitis is also more common during pregnancy because of changes in the urinary tract. As the uterus grows, its increased weight can block the drainage of urine from the bladder, causing an infection. Women are at increased risk for recurrent cystitis from weeks 6–24 of pregnancy.

*(continued over)*

*(from previous page)*

**PROGNOSIS** We found little evidence on the long-term effects of untreated cystitis. One study found that progression to pyelonephritis was infrequent, and that most cases of cystitis regressed spontaneously, although symptoms sometimes persisted for several months. However, bacteriuria in pregnant women carries a much greater risk of progressing to pyelonephritis than in non-pregnant women (28% *v* 1%), and is associated with serious risks.

Joseph L Onwude

## KEY POINTS

- Stress incontinence, involving involuntary leaking of urine on effort, exertion, sneezing, or coughing, affects 17% to 45% of adult women.

  Risk factors include pregnancy (especially with vaginal delivery), smoking, and obesity.

- Pelvic floor muscle exercises improve incontinence symptoms compared with no treatment. Pelvic floor electrical stimulation and vaginal cones are also effective compared with no treatment.

  Pelvic floor electrical stimulation can cause tenderness and vaginal bleeding, whereas vaginal cones can cause vaginitis and abdominal pain. Pelvic floor muscle exercises can cause discomfort.

- Oestrogen supplements increase cure rates compared with placebo, but there are risks associated with their long-term use. They can be less effective at reducing incontinence compared with pelvic floor muscle exercises.

- Serotonin reuptake inhibitors (duloxetine 80 mg/day) reduce incontinence frequency at 4 to 12 weeks compared with placebo, or compared with pelvic floor muscle exercises, but increase adverse effects, such as headache and gastric problems.

- We don't know whether adrenoceptor agonists improve incontinence compared with placebo or with other treatments, but they can cause insomnia, restlessness, and vasomotor stimulation. Phenylpropanolamine has been withdrawn from the US market because of an increased risk of haemorrhagic stroke.

- Open retropubic colposuspension may be more likely to cure stress incontinence than non-surgical treatments, anterior vaginal repair, or needle suspension at up to 5 years. Complication rates are similar to those with other surgical procedures.

- Suburethral slings and open retropubic colposuspension are equally effective in curing stress incontinence at up to 5 years.

- Tension-free vaginal tape may be as effective as open retropubic colposuspension in curing stress incontinence. Complications of tension-free vaginal tape include bladder perforation.

- Transobturator foramen procedures may be as effective as open retropubic colposuspension and tension-free vaginal tape.

- Laparoscopic colposuspension and open retropubic colposuspension seem equally effective.

(i) **Please visit http://clinicalevidence.bmj.com for full text and references**

## What are the effects of non-surgical treatments for women with stress incontinence?

| Likely To Be Beneficial | • Pelvic floor electrical stimulation |
| | • Pelvic floor muscle exercises |
| | • Serotonin reuptake inhibitors (duloxetine) |
| | • Vaginal cones |
| Trade-off Between Benefits And Harms | • Oestrogen supplements |
| Unknown Effectiveness | • Adrenoceptor agonists |

## What are the effects of surgical treatments for women with stress incontinence?

| | |
|---|---|
| **Beneficial** | • Laparoscopic colposuspension (similar cure rates to open retropubic colposuspension and tension-free vaginal tape)<br><br>• Open retropubic colposuspension (higher cure rates than non-surgical treatment, anterior vaginal repair, or needle suspension, and similar cure rates to laparoscopic colposuspension, traditional suburethral slings, TOT, and TVT)<br><br>• Suburethral slings other than tension-free vaginal tape (similar cure rates to open retropubic colposuspension, TVT, and needle suspension, but more perioperative complications than needle suspension) |
| **Likely To Be Beneficial** | • Transobturator foramen procedures (similar cure rates to tension-free vaginal tape and open retropubic colposuspension) |
| **Trade-off Between Benefits And Harms** | • Tension-free vaginal tape (similar cure rates to laparoscopic colposuspension, non-TVT suburethral slings, TOT, and open retropubic colposuspension, but associated with more bladder and vaginal perforations) |
| **Unlikely To Be Beneficial** | • Anterior vaginal repair (lower cure rates than open retropubic colposuspension but similar cure rates to needle suspension)<br><br>• Needle suspension (lower cure rates and more surgical complications than open retropubic colposuspension) |

**Search date June 2008**

**DEFINITION** Stress incontinence is involuntary leakage of urine on effort or exertion, or on sneezing or coughing. Stress incontinence predominantly affects women, and can cause social and hygiene problems. Typically, there is no anticipatory feeling of needing to pass urine. Under urodynamic testing, urodynamic stress incontinence is confirmed by demonstrating loss of urine when intravesical pressure exceeds maximum urethral pressure, in the absence of a detrusor contraction. A confirmed diagnosis of urodynamic stress incontinence is particularly important before surgical treatment, given that the symptoms of stress incontinence can occur in people with detrusor overactivity, which is confirmed by the demonstration of uninhibited bladder contractions. This review deals with stress incontinence in general.

**INCIDENCE/PREVALENCE** Stress incontinence is a common problem. Prevalence has been estimated at 17% to 45% of adult women in resource-rich countries. One cross-sectional study (15,308 women in Norway, aged <65 years) found that the prevalence of stress incontinence was 4.7% in women who had not borne a child, 6.9% in women who had had caesarean deliveries only, and 12.2% in women who had had vaginal deliveries only.

**AETIOLOGY/RISK FACTORS** Aetiological factors include pregnancy, vaginal or caesarean delivery, cigarette smoking, and obesity. One cross-sectional study (15,308 women in

Norway) found that, when compared with women who had not borne a child, the risk of stress incontinence was increased in women who had delivered by caesarean section (age-adjusted OR 1.4, 95% CI 1.0 to 2.0) or by vaginal delivery (age-adjusted OR 3.0, 95% CI 2.5 to 3.5). The risk of stress incontinence was also increased in women who had a vaginal delivery compared with women who had a caesarean section (age-adjusted OR 2.4, 95% CI 1.7 to 3.2). One case control study (606 women) found that the risk of "genuine", now called "urodynamic", stress incontinence was increased in former smokers (adjusted OR 2.20, 95% CI 1.18 to 4.11) and in current smokers (adjusted OR 2.48, 95% CI 1.60 to 3.84). The risks associated with obesity are unclear.

**PROGNOSIS** The natural history of stress incontinence is unclear. Untreated stress incontinence is believed to be a persistent, lifelong condition.

# Bites (mammalian)

David Looke and Claire Dendle

## KEY POINTS

- Mammalian bites are usually caused by dogs, cats, or humans, and are more prevalent in children (especially boys) than in adults.

  Animal bites are usually caused by the person's pet and, in children, frequently involve the face.

  Human bites tend to occur in children as a result of playing or fighting, while in adults they are usually the result of physical or sexual abuse.

  Physical and psychological trauma are the most common sequelae of a bite wound.

  Up to 18% of wounds may develop a bacterial infection with a mixture of aerobic and anaerobic organisms. *Pasteurella* species are pathogens of particular note.

  Methicillin-resistant *Staphylococcus aureus* (MRSA) is being increasingly reported in infections associated with domestic animal contact.

- There is consensus that tetanus immunisation should be given routinely as part of wound care of mammalian bites, but we found no studies assessing the benefit of this strategy.

  Immunisation does not need to be performed if there is a record of tetanus immunisation having been given in the previous 5 years.

- Antibiotics may prevent infection in high-risk bites to the hand, but we don't know if it is worth giving prophylactic antibiotics after other types of mammalian bites.

  High-risk bites are those with deep puncture or crushing, with much devitalised tissue, or those that are dirty.

  Bites that occurred less than 24 hours previously, or those with only simple epidermal stripping, scratches, and abrasions, are unlikely to benefit from antibiotic treatment.

- There is consensus that wound debridement, irrigation, decontamination, and primary wound closure are beneficial in reducing infection, but we don't know this for sure.

- There is consensus that antibiotics help cure infected bite wounds, although we found few studies.

  Selection of appropriate antibiotics depends on the likely mouth flora of the biting animal and the skin flora of the recipient, and can be based on samples of infected material examined by microscopy and culture.

  Antibiotics with activity against *Pasteurella multocida* should be selected for empirical treatment of infected bite wounds.

  There is consensus that rabies prophylaxis should be given after all animal bites in areas where rabies is known to exist, and after bat bites in all areas of the world.

ⓘ **Please visit http://clinicalevidence.bmj.com for full text and references**

## What are the effects of measures to prevent complications from mammalian bites?

| Likely To Be Beneficial | • Antibiotic prophylaxis for human bites |
| --- | --- |
| | • Debridement, irrigation, and decontamination for mammalian bites* |
| | • Primary wound closure for mammalian bites |

| | |
|---|---|
| | • Tetanus immunisation after mammalian bites* |
| Unknown Effectiveness | • Antibiotic prophylaxis for non-human bites |

## What are the effects of treatments for infected mammalian bites?

| | |
|---|---|
| Likely To Be Beneficial | • Antibiotics for treating infected mammalian bites |
| Unknown Effectiveness | • Comparative effectiveness of different antibiotics for mammalian bites |

**Search date October 2009**

*No RCT evidence, but there is consensus that treatment is likely to be beneficial.

**DEFINITION** Bite wounds are mainly caused by humans, dogs, or cats. They include superficial abrasions (30–43%), lacerations (31–45%), and puncture wounds (13–34%).

**INCIDENCE/PREVALENCE** It is estimated that up to 2% of the population of western countries are victims of a dog attack every year. Up to 3 in 1000 people present to emergency departments in western countries with dog-bite injuries annually. In the USA, an estimated 3.5 to 4.7 million dog bites occur each year, and bite wounds account for about 1% to 2% of all emergency department visits annually in the USA, costing over US $100 million annually. These figures are likely be even higher in developing countries where dog-control laws are seldom enacted or enforced. About one in five people bitten by a dog seek medical attention, and 1% of those require admission to hospital. Between one third and one half of all mammalian bites occur in children.

**AETIOLOGY/RISK FACTORS** In more than 70% of cases, people are bitten by their own pets or by an animal known to them. Males are more likely to be bitten than females, and are more likely to be bitten by dogs, whereas females are more likely to be bitten by cats. One study found that children under 5 years old were significantly more likely than older children to provoke animals before being bitten. Human bites are the most prevalent mammalian bites after those of dogs and cats, accounting for up to 2% to 3% of mammalian bites. Human bites commonly occur in children as a result of fighting or playing. In adults, bites commonly occur during physical or sexual abuse. Tooth abrasions to the knuckles (or 'clenched fist injuries') can occur during fist fighting.

**PROGNOSIS** In the USA, dog bites cause about 20 deaths a year, with similar rates estimated in other developed countries. Bite wounds not only cause significant scarring, but may involve injury to underlying structures such as joints, tendons, nerves, or blood vessels. In children, dog bites frequently involve the face, potentially resulting in severe lacerations and scarring, as well as significant psychological trauma. Up to 18% of animal bite wounds may become secondarily infected. One study of infected dog and cat bites found that the most commonly isolated species was *Pasteurella multocida*, followed by *Streptococcus*, *Staphylococcus*, *Moraxella*, *Corynebacterium*, and *Neisseria*. Mixtures of aerobic and anaerobic bacteria were the norm. Other significant pathogens of note are *Eikenella corrodens* in human-bite wound infections and *Capnocytophaga canimorsus* after dog bites, which can cause severe systemic infection in immunocompromised people. Rodent bites may transmit *Streptobacillus moniliformis*, the cause of rat-bite fever. Methicillin-resistant *Staphylococcus aureus* (MRSA) is being increasingly reported and may become an emerging pathogen in domestic-animal bite injuries. Human bites, particularly those to the hand, are often complicated by infection. One study reported infection in 48% of untreated bites to the hand.*Eikonella corrodens* may be associated with subsequent infection of tendon sheaths and joints. Transmission of blood-borne viruses such as HIV, hepatitis B, and hepatitis C have rarely been reported in association with human-bite injuries; screening and counselling

*(continued over)*

*(from previous page)*

appropriate to the circumstance of the injury is recommended. Rabies, a life-threatening viral encephalitis, may be contracted as a consequence of being bitten or scratched by a rabid animal. More than 99% of human rabies occurs in developing countries where canine rabies is endemic. Transmission of rabies from domestic animals such as dogs and cats to humans is extremely rare in the USA, Europe, and Canada. The incidence of rabies transmission in dog bites sustained in Africa, Southeast Asia, and India is significantly higher. Bats are now implicated more commonly in transmission of rabies or the similar lyssa virus infection. Monkey bites from old-world macaques may transmit *Herpes simiae* (B virus) which can cause a fatal encephalitis in humans.

Jason Wasiak and Heather Cleland

## KEY POINTS

- Superficial partial-thickness and mid-dermal partial-thickness burns can be expected, or have the potential, to heal spontaneously. Injuries which involve the deeper part of the dermis (deep partial-thickness and full-thickness burns) generally require surgical treatments to achieve healing and are not the focus of this overview.

  Most minor burns occur in the home.

  Cooling the burn for 20 minutes with cold tap water within 3 hours of the injury reduces pain and wound oedema, but prolonged cooling or use of iced water may worsen tissue damage or cause hypothermia.

- This overview focuses on the effect of selected commonly used and some more recently developed types of dressings for partial-thickness burns. Although we have searched for trials comparing the individual interventions with placebo or no treatment, there is a lack of evidence for these comparisons. The basic principles of burn wound management preclude the option of no dressing treatment for all but the most minor of burns.

  We excluded sunburn, residual wounds post injury, large surface area burns, and burns to sensitive areas (i.e., specific areas that are likely to result in either functional or cosmetic impairment; e.g., face, hands, perineum).

- We found insufficient evidence to draw any conclusions on the efficacy of alginate dressing, biosynthetic dressing, chlorhexidine-impregnated paraffin gauze dressing, hydrocolloid dressing, hydrogel dressing, paraffin gauze dressing, polyurethane film, silver-impregnated dressing, or silicone-coated nylon dressing in treating partial-thickness burns.

  Topical antibacterial substances, such as chlorhexidine, may be toxic to regenerating epithelial cells, and their use may delay healing in wounds that are not infected.

- Silver sulfadiazine cream may prolong healing times and increase pain compared with other treatments, although the evidence is limited by small sample sizes and the heterogeneity of the patient population.

- Because there is a lack of evidence to inform treatment choices, decisions on appropriate treatment in clinical practice are determined by logistical, as well as clinical, considerations. In the majority of these injuries, healing will occur in a timely fashion if infection is prevented.

ⓘ Please visit http://clinicalevidence.bmj.com for full text and references

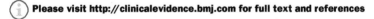

| What are the effects of treatments for partial-thickness burns? | |
|---|---|
| Unknown Effectiveness | • Alginate dressing |
| | • Biosynthetic dressing |
| | • Chlorhexidine-impregnated paraffin gauze dressing |
| | • Hydrocolloid dressing |
| | • Hydrogel dressing |
| | • Paraffin gauze dressing |
| | • Polyurethane film |
| | • Silicone-coated nylon dressing |

| | ● Silver-impregnated dressing |
|---|---|
| **Unlikely To Be Beneficial** | ● Silver sulfadiazine cream (may be associated with slower healing times compared with some other dressings; e.g., hydrocolloid, biosynthetic, silver-impregnated dressings, silicone-coated nylon gauze) |

**Search date January 2014**

**DEFINITION** Burns are classified by depth into superficial (involving epidermis only); partial-thickness (superficial, mid and deep partial-thickness), involving part of the dermis; and full-thickness burns, in which all of the dermis is destroyed, and which may extend to involve subcutaneous tissue, muscular, neurovascular, or skeletal structures. However, the depth of burn is not always static because of the various factors (e.g., inadequate tissue perfusion resulting from the injury), which may release a cascade of vaso-active and inflammatory mediators and, in turn, deepen the burn wound. Superficial partial-thickness burns are caused by exposure to heat sufficient to cause damage to the epidermis and papillary dermis of the skin. Due to the exposure of sensory nerve endings in the superficial dermis, these wounds are often painful and tender. The skin is moist, pink or red, and is perfused, as demonstrated by blanching on pressure. This type of injury can result in an immediate blister response and heal within 3 weeks with minimal scarring if no infection is present. Burn depth is an assessment tool undertaken by burns experts using clinical judgement; however, measuring blood flow, or its disruption, using laser Doppler imaging can also achieve the same task. The severity of a superficial partial-thickness burn is usually judged by the percentage of total body surface area (%TBSA) involved, with the vast majority involving less than 10% TBSA. The population studied for this overview includes adults and children with partial-thickness burns. Our search of the literature was for adults and children with minor thermal burns, including superficial and partial-thickness burns. We found that sometimes the term 'superficial' appeared to be used to describe what we suspected to be 'superficial partial-thickness'. We excluded sunburn, residual wounds post injury, large surface area burns, and burns to sensitive areas (i.e., specific areas that are likely to result in either functional or cosmetic impairment; e.g., face, hands, perineum).

**INCIDENCE/PREVALENCE** The incidence of superficial and partial-thickness burns is difficult to estimate. Generally, less than 5% of all burn injuries requiring treatment will necessitate admission to hospital. Worldwide estimates surrounding all thermal burn injuries suggest that about 2 million people are burned, up to 80,000 are hospitalised, and 6500 die of burn wounds every year.

**AETIOLOGY/RISK FACTORS** The pattern of injury varies among different age groups. Men aged 18 to 25 years seem more susceptible to injury owing to a variety of causes — mainly flame, electrical, and, to a lesser extent, chemicals. Many burn injuries in this age group are due to the inappropriate use of flammable agents, such as petrol. However, most burns occur in the home. Thermal burns, in particular scalds, are common among children as well as older adults. The kitchen is reported to be the most common place of injury for children, as is the bathroom for older people. Those with concomitant conditions or complicating factors such as motor or neurological impairment are at greater risk.

**PROGNOSIS** Superficial partial-thickness burns will heal spontaneously, with minimal hypertrophic scarring, within 2 to 3 weeks if the wound remains free of infection. The capacity to heal is also dependent on the health and age of the individual, with older people and those with concomitant medical conditions prone to delayed healing. Cooling the burn, as part of the initial emergency treatment, significantly reduces pain and wound oedema if started within 3 hours of injury. The optimal time to cool a wound may vary from 20 to 30 minutes, using tap water (at a temperature of 5–25°C). Use of iced water or prolonged periods of cooling can deepen tissue injury and induce hypothermia, and are best avoided. Cleaning solutions and dressings aim to prevent wound infection. The ideal dressing will establish an optimum micro-environment for wound healing. It will maintain the wound temperature and moisture level, permit respiration, allow epithelial migration, and exclude environmental bacteria.

## KEY POINTS

- Unrelieved pressure or friction of the skin, particularly over bony prominences, can lead to pressure ulcers, which affect up to one third of people in hospitals or community care, and one fifth of nursing home residents.

  Pressure ulcers are more likely in people with reduced mobility and poor skin condition, such as older people or those with vascular disease.

- Alternative foam mattresses (such as viscoelastic foam) reduce the incidence of pressure ulcers in people at risk compared with standard hospital foam mattresses, although we don't know which is the best alternative to use.

  Low-air-loss beds may reduce the risk of pressure ulcers compared with standard intensive-care beds, and pressure-relieving overlays on operating tables may reduce the risk of pressure ulcer development.

  Medical sheepskin overlays may reduce the risk of pressure ulcers compared with standard care.

- Hydrocellular heel supports may decrease the risk of pressure ulcers compared with orthopaedic wool padding, but air-filled vinyl boots with foot cradles and low-air-loss hydrotherapy beds may increase the risk of ulcers compared with other pressure-relieving surfaces.

  We don't know if other physical interventions, such as alternating-pressure surfaces, seat cushions, electric profiling beds, low-tech constant-low-pressure supports, repositioning, or topical lotions and dressings are effective for preventing pressure ulcers. We also don't know whether pressure ulcers can be prevented by use of nutritional interventions.

- In people with pressure ulcers, air-fluidised supports may improve healing compared with standard care, although they can make it harder for people to get in and out of bed independently.

- We don't know whether healing is improved in people with pressure ulcers by use of other treatments such as one specific specialised support surface (including alternating-pressure surfaces, low-tech constant-low-pressure supports, low-air-loss beds, and specific seat cushions) over any other specific specialised support surface, one specific wound dressing over any other specific wound dressing, or with surgery, electrotherapy, ultrasound, low-level laser therapy, topical negative pressure, topical phenytoin, or nutritional interventions.

 Please visit http://clinicalevidence.bmj.com for full text and references

| What are the effects of preventive interventions in people at risk of developing pressure ulcers? | |
|---|---|
| Beneficial | • Foam alternatives (compared with standard foam mattresses) |
| Likely To Be Beneficial | • Low-air-loss beds in intensive care (more effective than standard beds; effects relative to alternating-pressure mattresses unclear)<br>• Medical sheepskin overlays (compared with standard care)<br>• Pressure-relieving overlays on operating tables (compared with standard tables) |
| Unknown Effectiveness | • Alternating-pressure surfaces<br>• Electric profiling beds |

- Hydrocellular heel supports (compared with orthopaedic wool padding)

- Low-air-loss hydrotherapy beds (compared with other pressure-relieving surfaces)

- Low-tech constant-low-pressure supports

- Nutritional supplements

- Repositioning (including regular "turning")

- Seat cushions

- Topical lotions and dressings

| | |
|---|---|
| **Unlikely To Be Beneficial** | • Air-filled vinyl boots |

## What are the effects of treatments in people with pressure ulcers?

| | |
|---|---|
| **Likely To Be Beneficial** | • Air-fluidised supports (compared with standard care) |
| **Unknown Effectiveness** | • Alternating-pressure surfaces (compared with other specialised support surfaces)<br><br>• Debridement<br><br>• Dressings (one type versus any another type)<br><br>• Electrotherapy<br><br>• Low-air-loss beds<br><br>• Low-level laser treatment<br><br>• Low-tech constant-low-pressure supports (compared with other specialised support surfaces)<br><br>• Nutritional supplements<br><br>• Seat cushions<br><br>• Surgery<br><br>• Therapeutic ultrasound<br><br>• Topical negative pressure<br><br>• Topical phenytoin |

**Search date June 2010**

**DEFINITION** Pressure ulcers (also known as pressure sores, bed sores, and decubitus ulcers) may present as persistently hyperaemic, blistered, broken, or necrotic skin, and may extend to underlying structures, including muscle and bone. Pressure ulcers are usually graded on a scale of 1 to 4, with a higher grade indicating greater ulcer severity.

**INCIDENCE/PREVALENCE** Reported prevalence rates range from 4.7% to 32.1% for hospital populations, 4.4% to 33.0% for community-care populations, and 4.6% to 20.7% for nursing-home populations.

**AETIOLOGY/RISK FACTORS** Pressure ulcers are caused by unrelieved pressure, shear, or friction. They are most common below the waist and at bony prominences, such as the sacrum, heels, and hips. They occur in all healthcare settings. Increased age, reduced mobility, impaired nutrition, vascular disease, faecal incontinence, and skin condition at baseline consistently emerge as risk factors. However, the relative importance of these and other factors is uncertain.

**PROGNOSIS** There are few data on prognosis of untreated pressure ulcers. The presence of pressure ulcers has been associated with a two- to four-fold increased risk of death in elderly people and people in intensive care. However, pressure ulcers are a marker for underlying disease severity and other comorbidities, rather than an independent predictor of mortality.

E Andrea Nelson

### KEY POINTS

- Leg ulcers are usually secondary to venous reflux or obstruction, but 20% of people with leg ulcers have arterial disease, with or without venous disorders.

- Compression bandages and stockings heal more ulcers compared with no compression, but we don't know which bandaging technique is most effective.

  Compression is used for people with ulcers caused by venous disease who have an adequate arterial supply to the foot, and who don't have diabetes or rheumatoid arthritis.

  The effectiveness of compression bandages depends on the skill of the person applying them.

  We don't know whether intermittent pneumatic compression is beneficial compared with compression bandages or stockings.

- Occlusive (hydrocolloid) dressings are no more effective than simple low-adherent dressings in people treated with compression, but we don't know whether semi-occlusive dressings are beneficial.

- Peri-ulcer injections of granulocyte-macrophage colony-stimulating factor may increase healing, but we don't know whether other locally applied agents are beneficial, as we found few trials.

- Oral pentoxifylline increases ulcer healing in people receiving compression, and oral flavonoids, sulodexide, and mesoglycan may also be effective.

  We don't know whether therapeutic ultrasound, oral aspirin, rutosides, thromboxane alpha$_2$ antagonists, zinc, debriding agents, intravenous prostaglandin E1, superficial vein surgery, skin grafting, topical antimicrobial agents, leg ulcer clinics, laser treatment, or advice to elevate legs, increase activity, lose weight, change diet, or give up smoking increase healing of ulcers in people treated with compression.

  Larval therapy is not likely to be beneficial as it has no impact on healing and is painful.

- Compression bandages and stockings reduce recurrence of ulcers compared with no compression, and should ideally be worn for life.

  Superficial vein surgery may also reduce recurrence, but we don't know whether systemic drug treatment is effective.

 **Please visit http://clinicalevidence.bmj.com for full text and references**

| What are the effects of standard treatments for venous leg ulcers? | |
|---|---|
| Beneficial | • Compression bandages and stockings (more effective than no compression) |
| | • Different types of multilayer elastomeric high-compression regimens (equally effective at increasing healing rates) |
| | • Multilayer elastomeric high-compression bandages (more effective at increasing healing rates than single-layer bandages) |
| | • Multilayer elastomeric high-compression bandages versus short-stretch bandages or Unna's boot (both beneficial at increasing healing rates, but unclear how they compare with each other) |

| | |
|---|---|
| | • Single-layer non-elastic system versus multilayer elastic system (both beneficial, but insufficient evidence to compare treatments)<br><br>• Single-layer non-elastic system versus multilayer non-elastic system (both beneficial, but insufficient evidence to compare treatments) |
| **Likely To Be Beneficial** | • Compression stockings versus compression bandages (both likely to be beneficial, but insufficient evidence to compare treatments)<br><br>• Peri-ulcer injection of granulocyte-macrophage colony-stimulating factor |
| **Unknown Effectiveness** | • Antimicrobial agents (topical)<br><br>• Calcitonin gene-related peptide (topical)<br><br>• Compression bandages or stockings versus intermittent pneumatic compression (insufficient evidence to compare treatments)<br><br>• Debriding agents<br><br>• Foam, film, hyaluronic acid-derived dressings, collagen, cellulose, or alginate (semi-occlusive) dressings<br><br>• Intermittent pneumatic compression<br><br>• Mesoglycan (topical)<br><br>• Platelet-derived growth factor (topically applied)<br><br>• Recombinant keratinocyte growth factor 2 (topical)<br><br>• Topical negative pressure |
| **Unlikely To Be Beneficial** | • Autologous platelet lysate (topically applied)<br><br>• Freeze-dried keratinocyte lysate (topically applied)<br><br>• Hydrocolloid (occlusive) dressings in the presence of compression |

## What are the effects of adjuvant treatments for venous leg ulcers?

| | |
|---|---|
| **Beneficial** | • Pentoxifylline (oral) |
| **Likely To Be Beneficial** | • Cultured allogenic bilayer skin replacement<br><br>• Flavonoids (oral)<br><br>• Mesoglycan (systemic)<br><br>• Sulodexide (oral) |
| **Unknown Effectiveness** | • Aspirin (oral)<br><br>• Cultured allogenic single-layer dermal replacement<br><br>• Laser treatment (low-level)<br><br>• Prostaglandin E1 (intravenous) |

|  | • Rutosides (oral) |
|---|---|
|  | • Skin grafting |
|  | • Superficial vein surgery to treat venous leg ulcers |
|  | • Therapeutic ultrasound |
|  | • Thromboxane alpha$_2$ antagonists (oral) |
|  | • Zinc (oral) |
| **Unlikely To Be Beneficial** | • Larval therapy |

## What are the effects of organisational interventions for venous leg ulcers?

| **Unknown Effectiveness** | • Leg ulcer clinics |
|---|---|

## What are the effects of advice about self-help interventions in people receiving usual care for venous leg ulcers?

| **Unknown Effectiveness** | • Advice to elevate leg |
|---|---|
|  | • Advice to keep leg active |
|  | • Advice to modify diet |
|  | • Advice to reduce weight |
|  | • Advice to stop smoking |

## What are the effects of interventions to prevent recurrence of venous leg ulcers?

| **Beneficial** | • Compression stockings |
|---|---|
| **Likely To Be Beneficial** | • Superficial vein surgery to prevent recurrence |
| **Unknown Effectiveness** | • Rutoside (oral) |
|  | • Stanozolol (oral) |

**Search date June 2011**

**DEFINITION** Definitions of leg ulcers vary, but the following is widely used: loss of skin on the leg or foot that takes >6 weeks to heal. Some definitions exclude ulcers confined to the foot, whereas others include ulcers on the whole of the lower limb. This review deals with ulcers of venous origin in people without concurrent diabetes mellitus, arterial insufficiency, or rheumatoid arthritis.

**INCIDENCE/PREVALENCE** Between 1.5 and 3.0/1000 people have active leg ulcers. Prevalence increases with age to about 20/1000 in people aged over 80 years. Most leg ulcers are secondary to venous disease; other causes include arterial insufficiency, diabetes, and rheumatoid arthritis. The annual cost to the NHS in the UK has been estimated at £300 million. This does not include the loss of productivity due to illness.

**AETIOLOGY/RISK FACTORS** Leg ulceration is strongly associated with venous disease. However, about a fifth of people with leg ulceration have arterial disease, either alone or in combination with venous problems, which may require specialist referral. Venous ulcers (also known as varicose or stasis ulcers) are caused by venous reflux or obstruction, both of which lead to poor venous return and venous hypertension.

**PROGNOSIS** People with leg ulcers have a poorer quality of life than age-matched controls because of pain, odour, and reduced mobility. In the UK, audits have found wide variation in the types of care (hospital inpatient care, hospital clinics, outpatient clinics, home visits), in the treatments used (topical agents, dressings, bandages, stockings), and in healing rates and recurrence rates (26–69% in 1 year).

**NOTE**

When looking up a class of drug, the reader is advised to also look up specific examples of that class of drug where additional entries may be found. The reverse situation also applies.

# Index

# Personal Notes

# Personal Notes

# Personal Notes

# Personal Notes

# Personal Notes

# Personal Notes

# Personal Notes

# Personal Notes

# Personal Notes

# Personal Notes